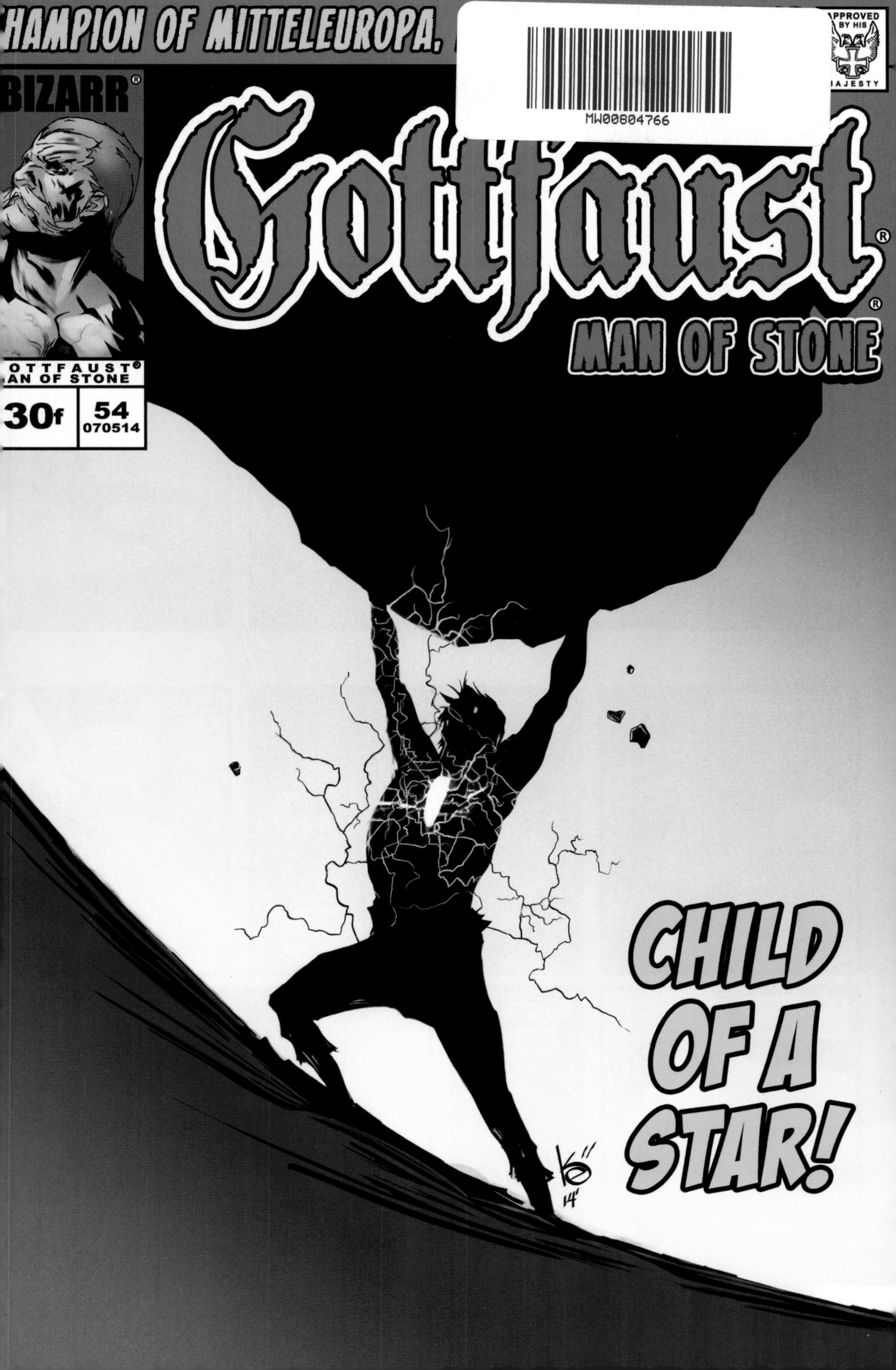
HAMPION OF MITTELEUROPA,
APPROVED BY HIS
AJESTY
BIZARR®
Gottfaust®
MAN OF STONE®
OTTFAUST®
AN OF STONE
30f
54
070514
CHILD OF A STAR!

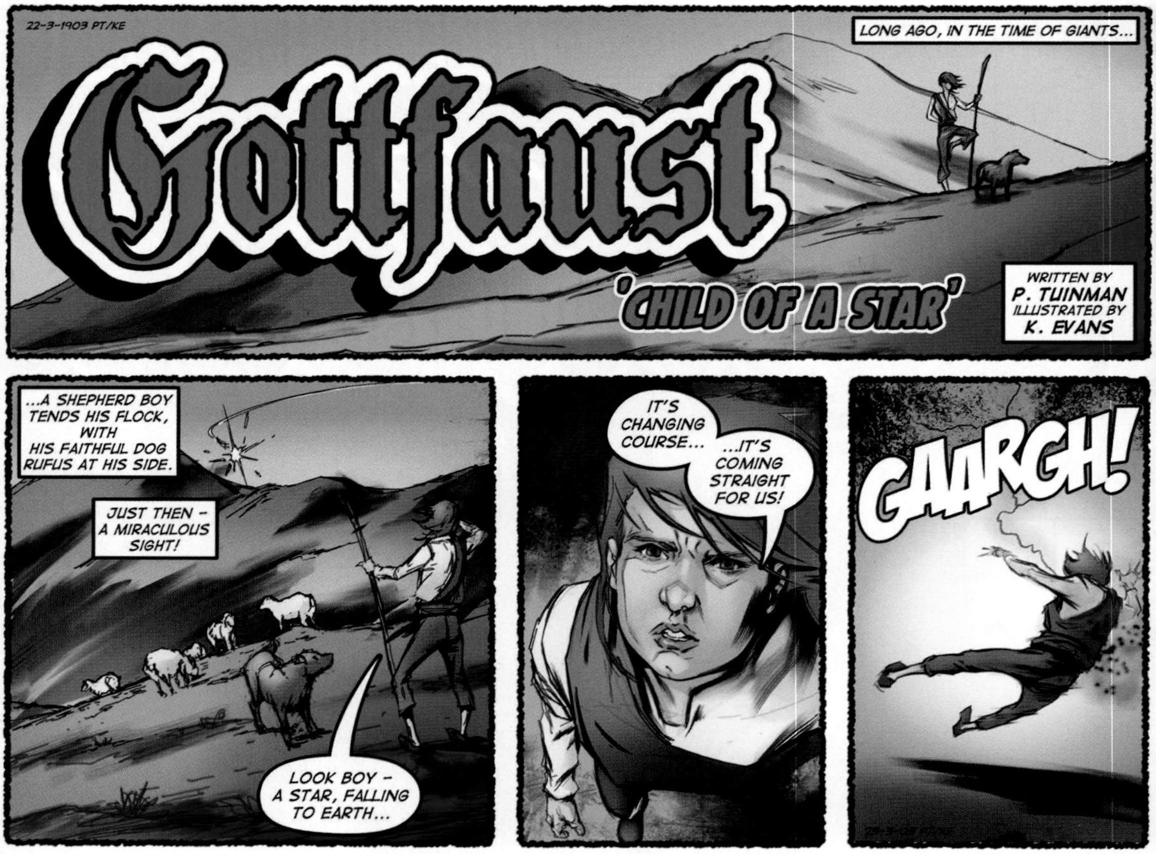
22-3-1903 PT/KE
Gottfaust
LONG AGO, IN THE TIME OF GIANTS...
'CHILD OF A STAR'
WRITTEN BY
P. TUINMAN
ILLUSTRATED BY
K. EVANS
...A SHEPHERD BOY TENDS HIS FLOCK, WITH HIS FAITHFUL DOG RUFUS AT HIS SIDE.
JUST THEN - A MIRACULOUS SIGHT!
LOOK BOY - A STAR, FALLING TO EARTH...
IT'S CHANGING COURSE...
...IT'S COMING STRAIGHT FOR US!
GAARGH!

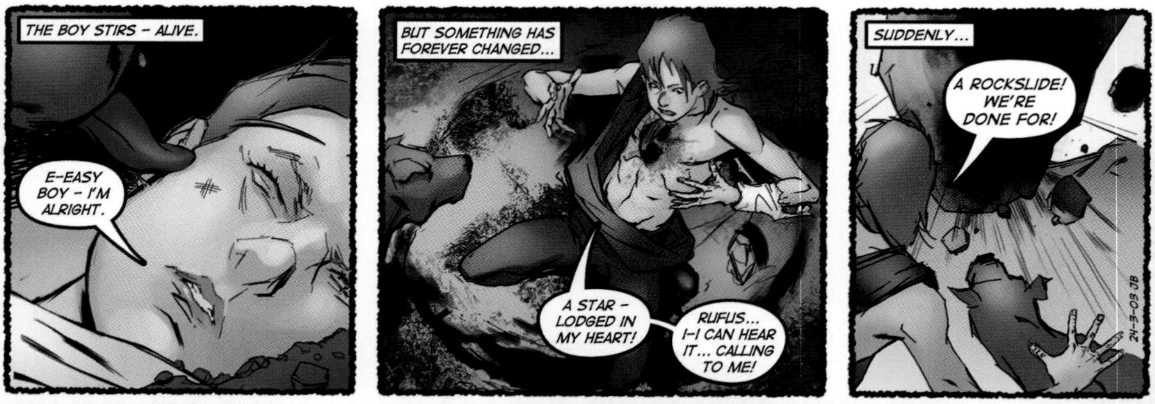
THE BOY STIRS - ALIVE.
E-EASY BOY - I'M ALRIGHT.
BUT SOMETHING HAS FOREVER CHANGED...
A STAR - LODGED IN MY HEART!
RUFUS... I-I CAN HEAR IT... CALLING TO ME!
SUDDENLY...
A ROCKSLIDE! WE'RE DONE FOR!
24-3-03 JB

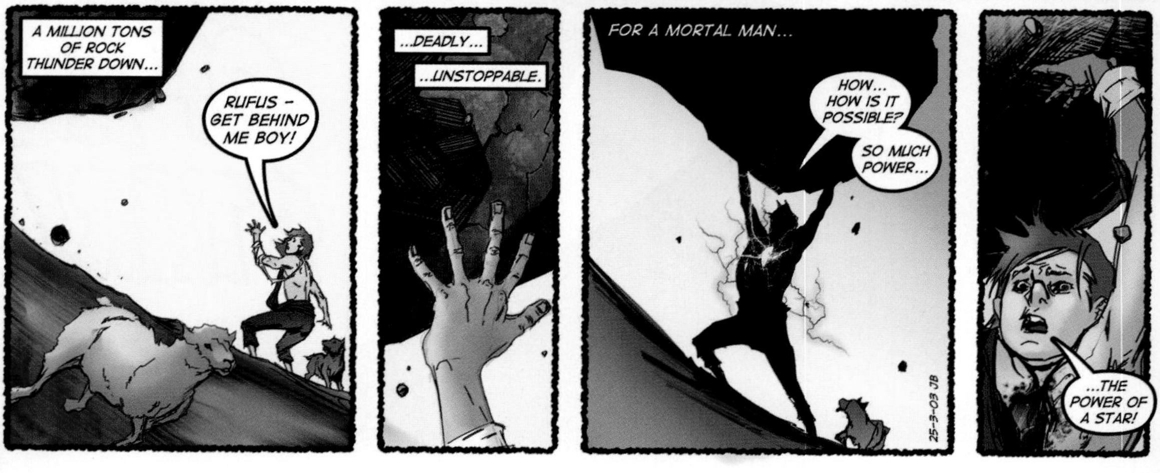
A MILLION TONS OF ROCK THUNDER DOWN...
RUFUS - GET BEHIND ME BOY!
...DEADLY...
...UNSTOPPABLE.
FOR A MORTAL MAN...
HOW... HOW IS IT POSSIBLE?
SO MUCH POWER...
25-3-03 JB
...THE POWER OF A STAR!

ACROSS THE FOOTHILLS OF THURMBERG A HUNTING PARTY RIDES.
AT THEIR LEAD THE FIRST KAISER OF MITTELEUROPA...
11-10-05 KE/JB
FATHER IN HEAVEN...
...MAGNIFICENT ASTRIDE A PUREBRED STALLION...
...REALIZES TOO LATE...
WOLVES!
...THAT HE IS THE PREY!
AS THE WOLVES ADVANCE...
...DEATH CASTS ITS SHADOW.
12-10-05 KE/JB
SALVATION ARRIVES...
...FROM THE HEAVENS!
BOOOM!
SUDDENLY -
SIRE - LOOK OUT!
STILL CRAVING HER PRIZE...
...THE SHE-WOLF LEAPS!
BUT -
O-HO!
SORRY WOLFIE!
...BUT YOU'LL NOT GO HUNGRY TONIGHT!
13-10-05 KE/JB
...HERE'S SOMETHING TO CHEW ON!
A SINGLE BLOW SKINS THE BEAST ALIVE...
...THE SHE-WOLF'S PRIZE IS DEATH!
14-10-05 KE/JB
THE KAISER IS SAVED!
SUCH STRENGH! WHAT IS YOUR NAME, BOY?
I HAVE NONE, SIRE...
THEN I SHALL CALL YOU GOTTFAUST...
...AND YOU SHALL BE MY CHAMPION.

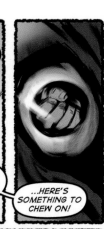

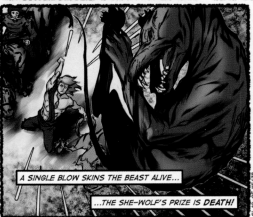

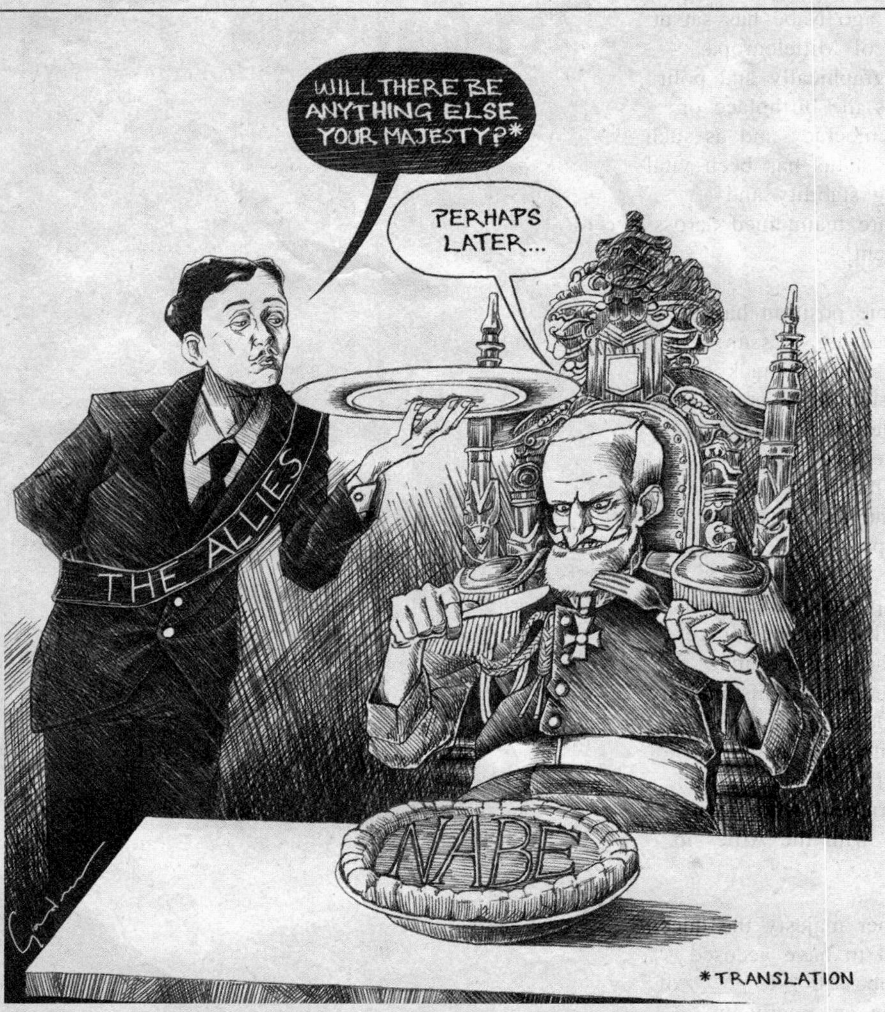
WILL THERE BE ANYTHING ELSE YOUR MAJESTY?*
PERHAPS LATER...
THE ALLIES
NABE
*TRANSLATION

A HUNGER FOR POWER

Editorial

SERVED UP ON A PLATE

Nabe sits at the center of Mitteleuropa – both geographically and politically. It is the birthplace of modern democracy and as such its neutral status has been vital to maintaining stability and harmony across the continent for the past century.

This noble position has become considerably weakened since last week's devastating bomb attack on the Axis summit, hosted here in Nabe, left leaders from six of the eight states of Mitteleuropa dead and His Majesty the Kaiser with emergency control over most of the subcontinent.

No group has yet claimed responsibility for the massacre, though sources close to the Kaiser have implied that His Majesty believes the culprits to be aligned with (and perhaps funded by) those members of Nabe's own government who favor closer ties with the New Alliance in the west. Indeed Ambassador Vasilyeva, advisor to His Majesty, is reported to have accused Nabe's Prime Minister of as much during an emergency cabinet session held yesterday.

Perhaps we should forgive Ambassador Vasilyeva's bluntness; exiled from Ursa during the revolution she seems to have refreshingly little time for the niceties of international relations. Indeed, the Ambassador has consistently demonstrated the kind of straight-talking that has to date been absent from this crisis, and may represent our best hope for reaching a diplomatic solution.

Nevertheless His Majesty has in the past openly expressed his desire to consolidate the military and industrial might of the Axis states under the flag of a single nation. His supporters assert that the Kaiser is merely responding to the potential threat posed by a growing power base in the west. Yet there is a difference; the allies' strength has been forged through consensus and cooperation, not autocracy and bullying.

Since the Kaiser centralized control of the Axis states Nabe has come under increasing pressure to fall in line with the rest of Mitteleuropa, accept His Majesty's policy of unification, and effectively surrender its autonomy – and its neutrality.

There are cynics amongst us who might find these deaths more than a little suspicious, since they have primarily served to accelerate the Kaiser's unification efforts, and have effectively silenced any criticism from within the Axis itself. Indeed it could be argued that His Majesty has been the sole beneficiary (and lone survivor) of the massacre. Furthermore, that the bombing took place here within Nabe should not be ignored. This fact has given the Kaiser the pretext needed to close Nabe's borders and blockade our trade routes, all to weed out a terrorist threat that many believe is a work of fiction.

To date the Allies have remained frustratingly diffident, tolerating (if not endorsing) His Majesty's saber-rattling – despite its member states all having ratified the Baal treaty protecting Nabe's neutral status, if necessary with military action.

Though no sane person would welcome confrontation between the world's two great powers, the danger in hesitating to act is all too apparent. Presently the forces of the Axis coalition are weak, dispersed across its vast territory, and even the threat of military action would likely be enough to drive the Kaiser from Nabe's borders. Unless the opponents of the Kaiser act now - and decisively - the opportunity for reaching a swift resolution to this crisis will have passed.

If His Majesty's plans are allowed to gather momentum the two sides will soon be more equally matched, and the prospect of all-out war almost inevitable.

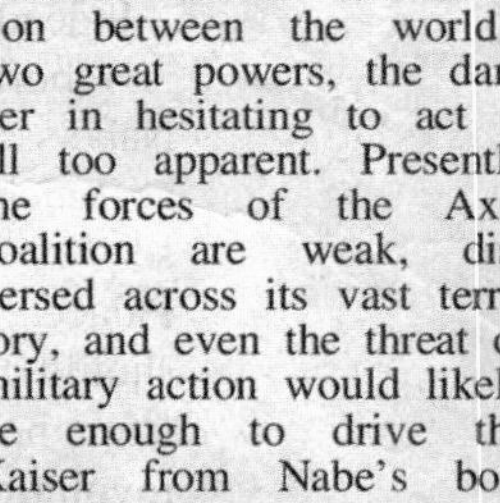

As the crow flies...

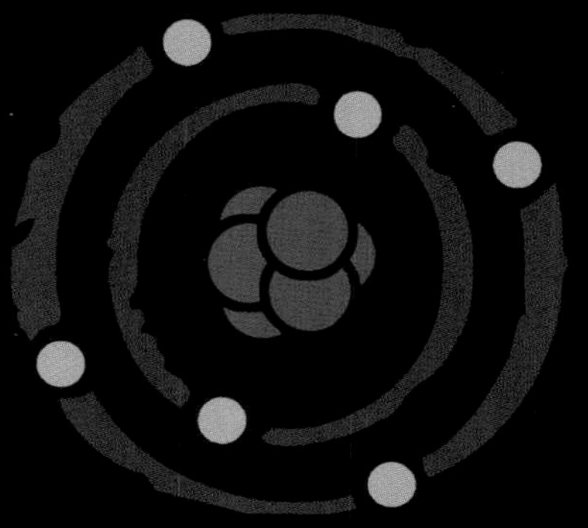

O

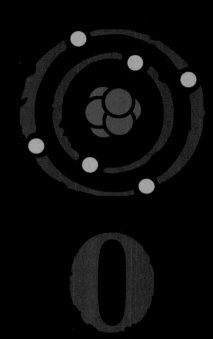

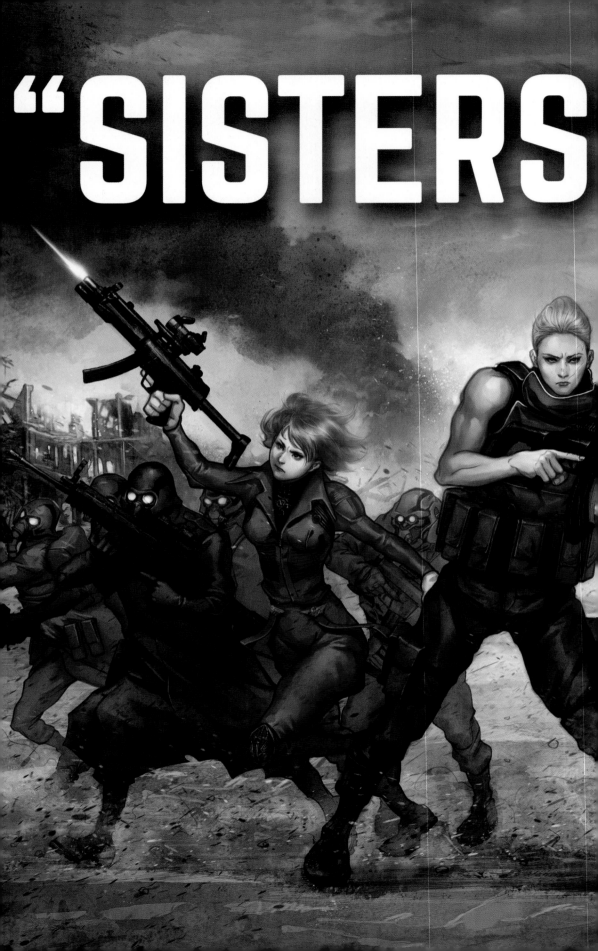

"SISTERS

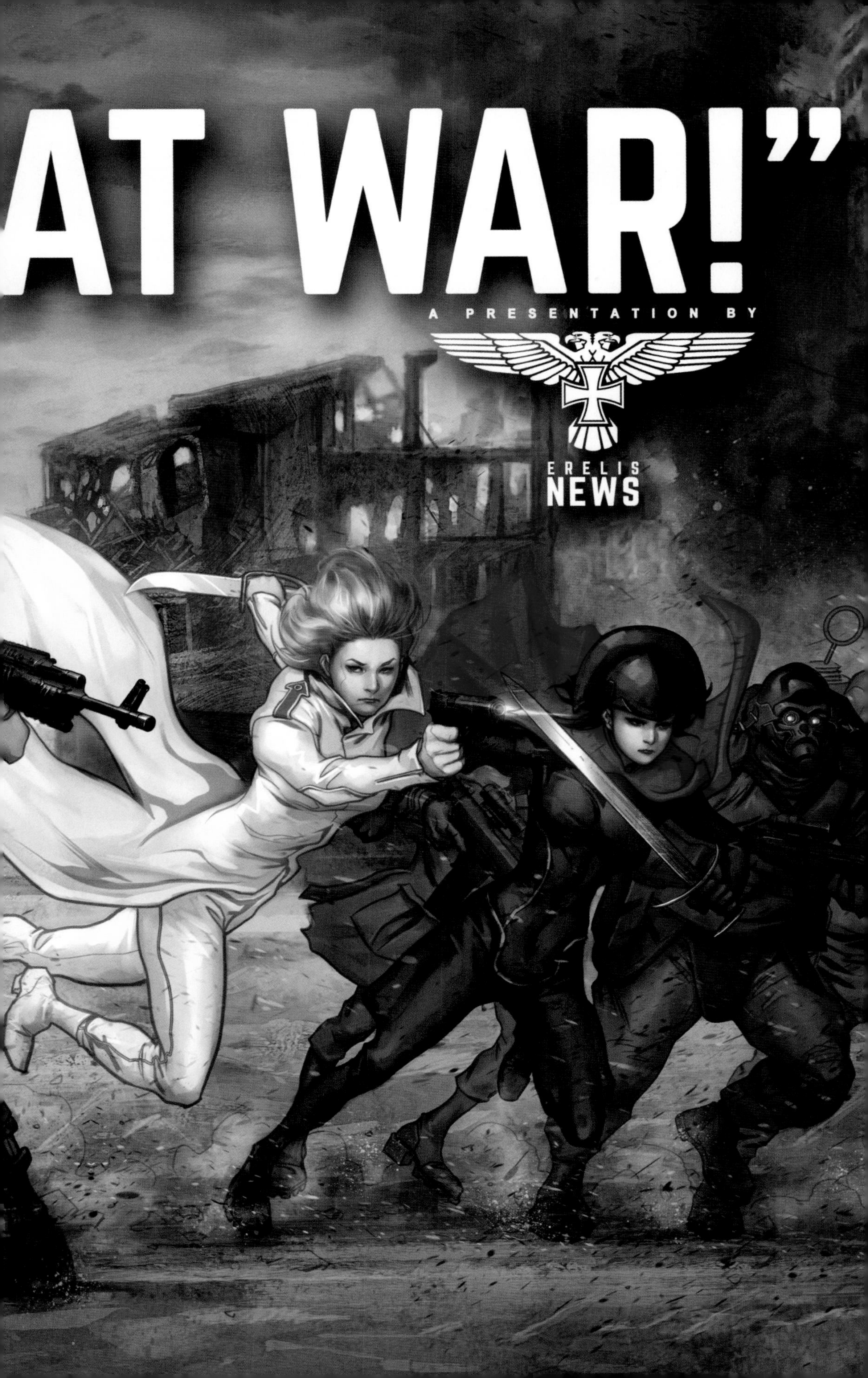
AT WAR!"
A PRESENTATION BY
ERELIS
NEWS

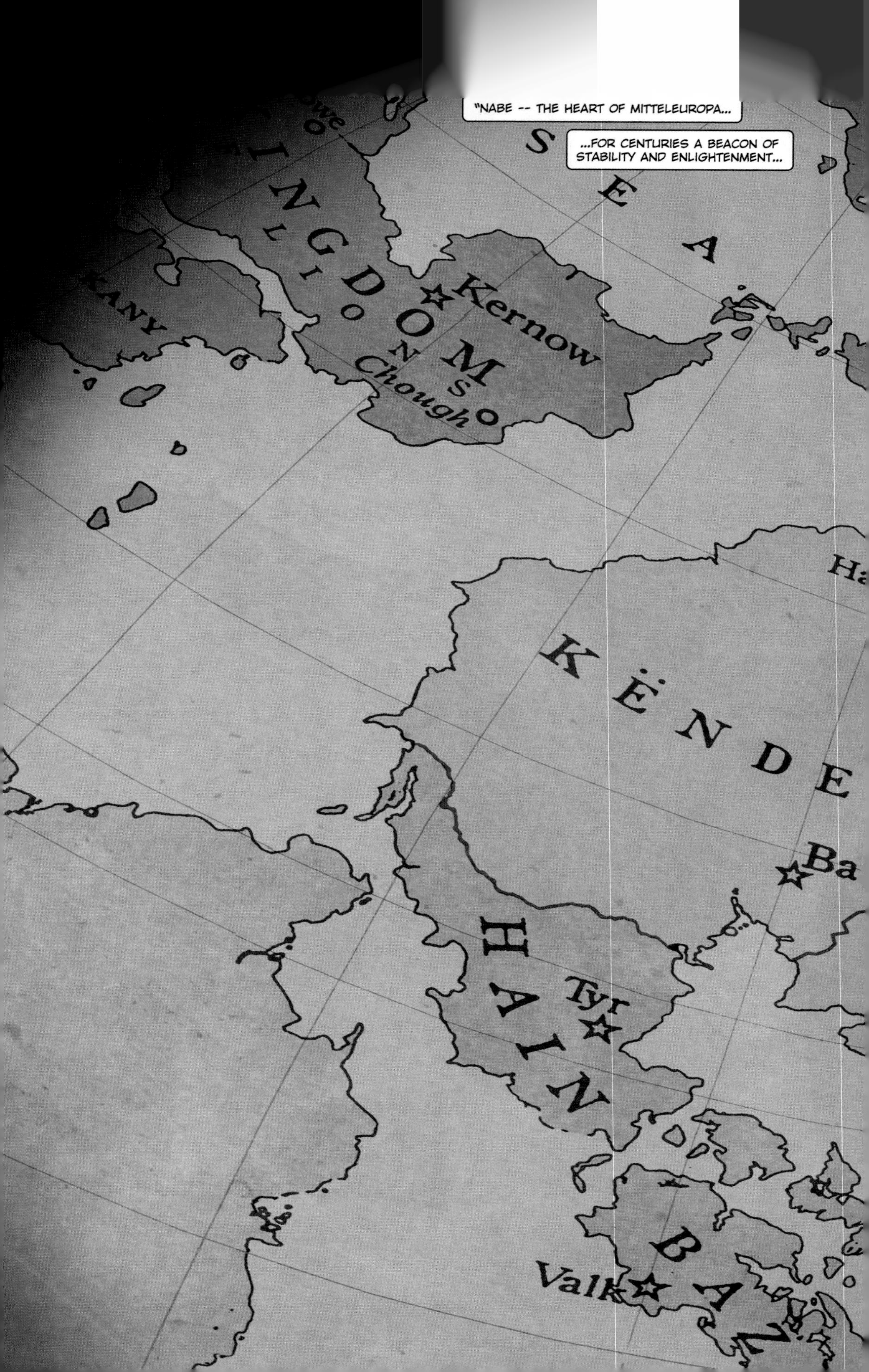
"NABE -- THE HEART OF MITTELEUROPA...
...FOR CENTURIES A BEACON OF STABILITY AND ENLIGHTENMENT...
SEA
Kernow
Chough
HAIN
Tyr
Valk

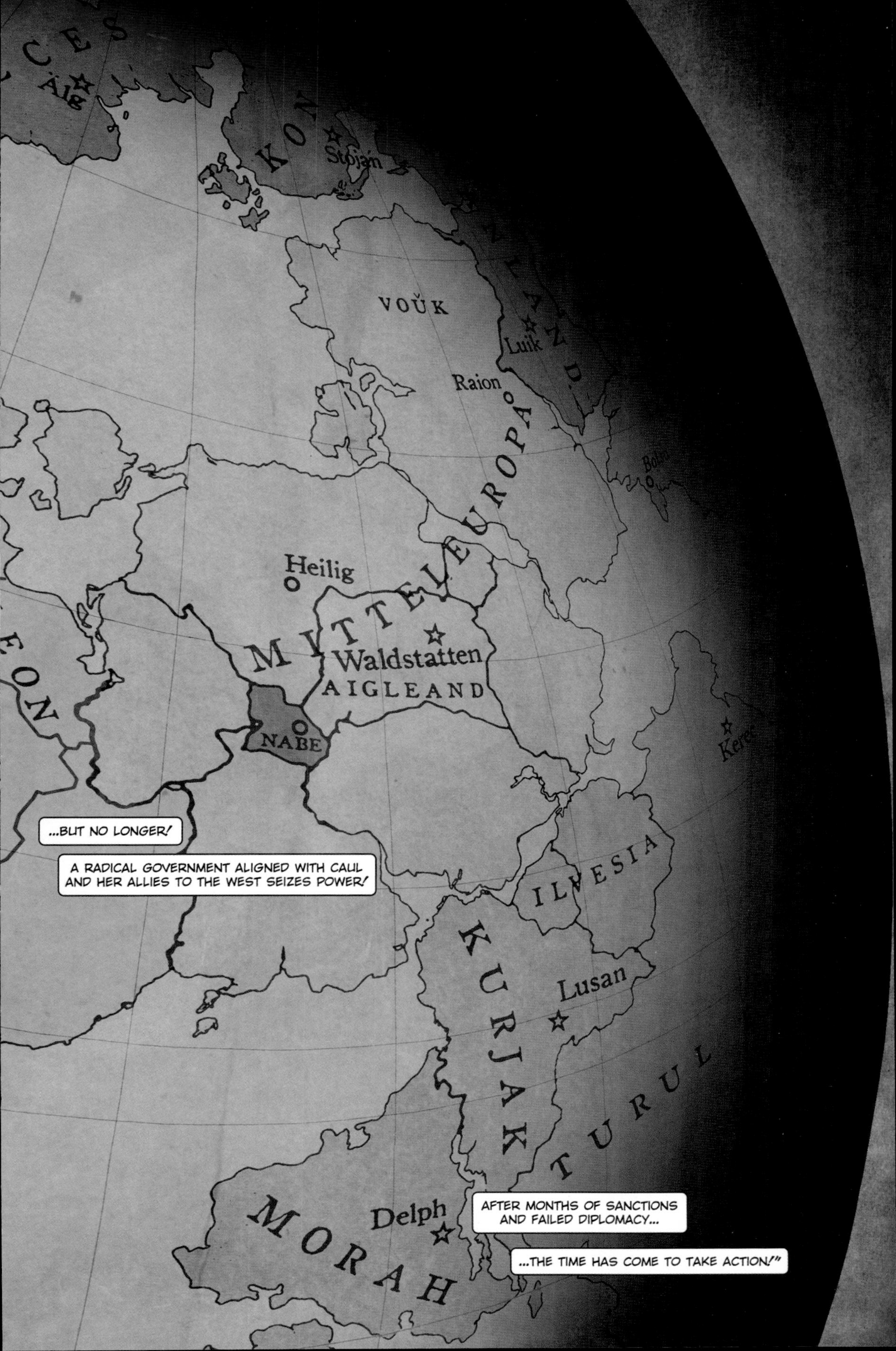

Älg
Stojan
VOŬK
Luik
Raion
MITTELEUROPA
Heilig
Waldstatten
AIGLEAND
NABE
ILVESIA
KURJAK
Lusan
TURUL
MORAH
Delph
...BUT NO LONGER!
A RADICAL GOVERNMENT ALIGNED WITH CAUL AND HER ALLIES TO THE WEST SEIZES POWER!
AFTER MONTHS OF SANCTIONS AND FAILED DIPLOMACY...
...THE TIME HAS COME TO TAKE ACTION!"

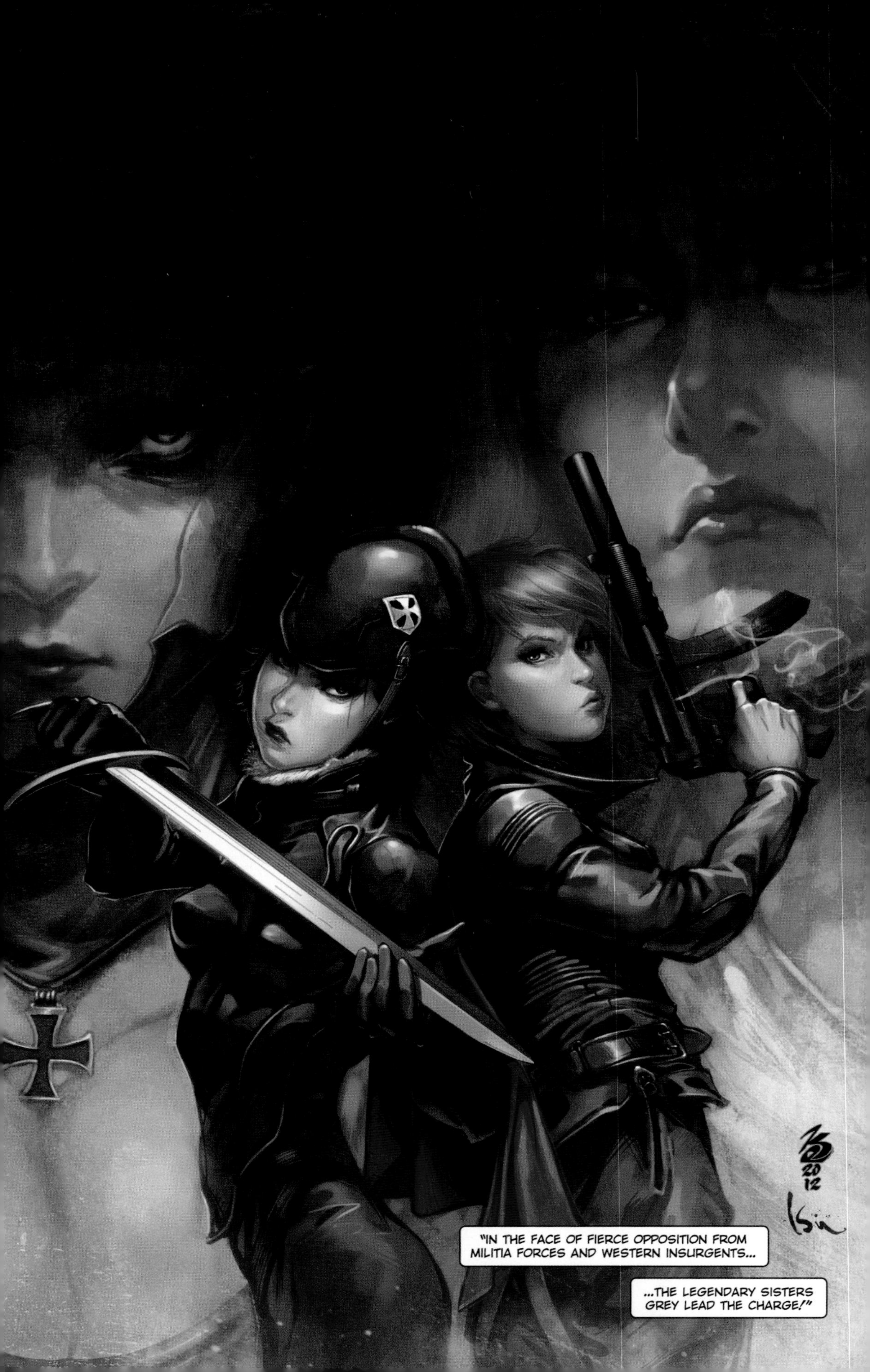

"IN THE FACE OF FIERCE OPPOSITION FROM MILITIA FORCES AND WESTERN INSURGENTS...
...THE LEGENDARY SISTERS GREY LEAD THE CHARGE!"

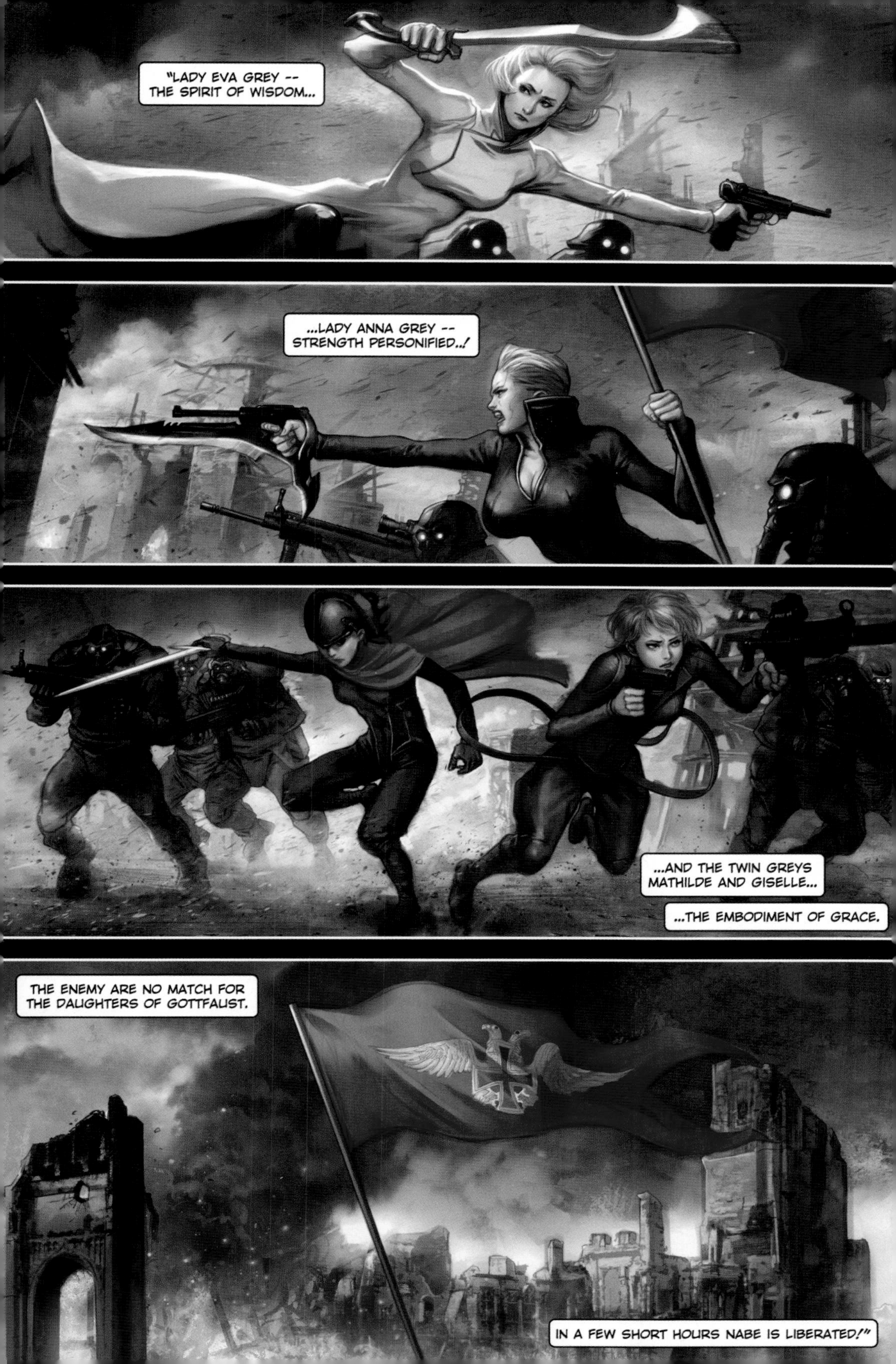
"LADY EVA GREY -- THE SPIRIT OF WISDOM...
...LADY ANNA GREY -- STRENGTH PERSONIFIED..!
...AND THE TWIN GREYS MATHILDE AND GISELLE...
...THE EMBODIMENT OF GRACE.
THE ENEMY ARE NO MATCH FOR THE DAUGHTERS OF GOTTFAUST.
IN A FEW SHORT HOURS NABE IS LIBERATED!"

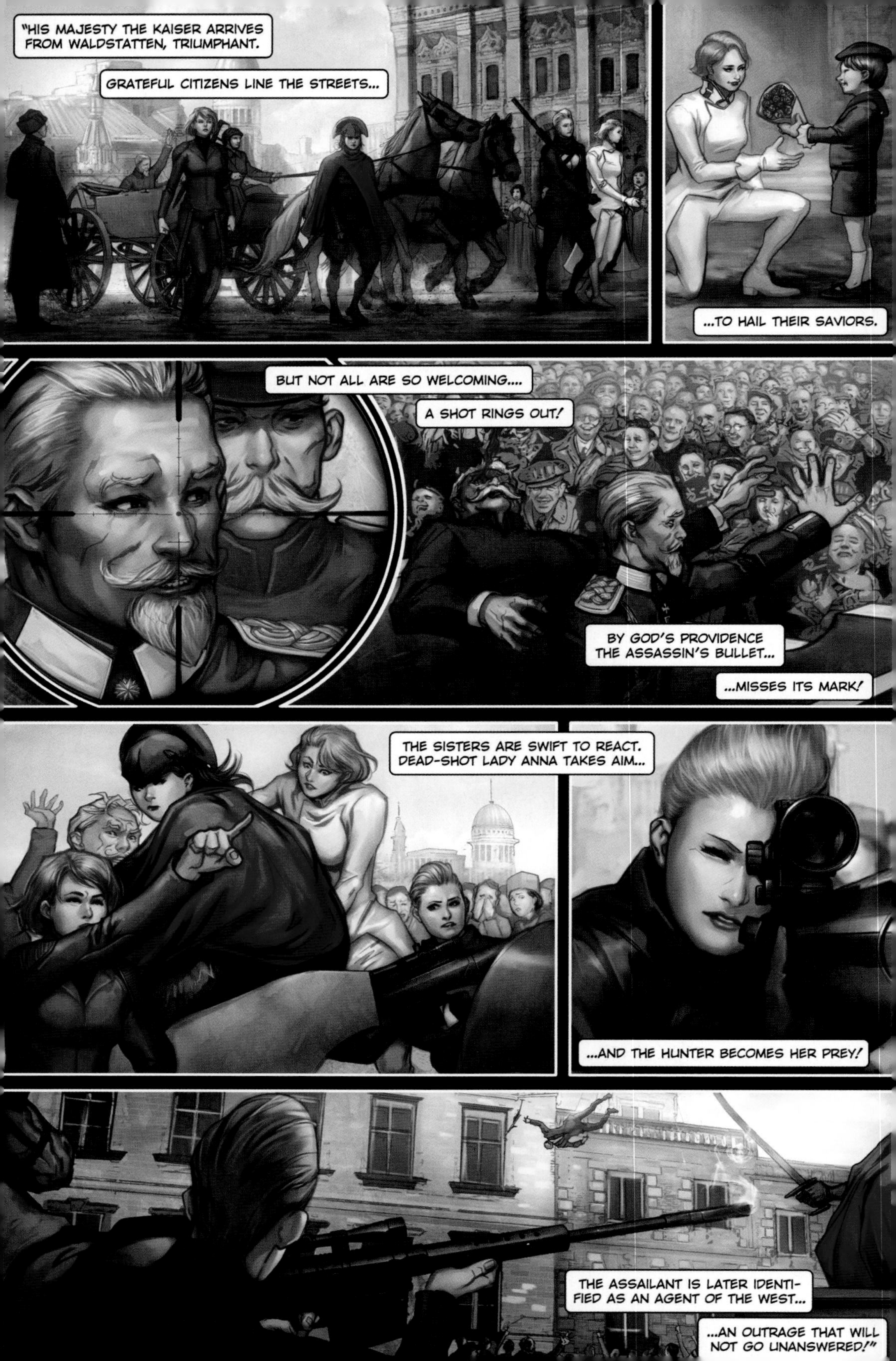
"HIS MAJESTY THE KAISER ARRIVES FROM WALDSTATTEN, TRIUMPHANT.
GRATEFUL CITIZENS LINE THE STREETS...
...TO HAIL THEIR SAVIORS.
BUT NOT ALL ARE SO WELCOMING....
A SHOT RINGS OUT!
BY GOD'S PROVIDENCE THE ASSASSIN'S BULLET...
...MISSES ITS MARK!
THE SISTERS ARE SWIFT TO REACT. DEAD-SHOT LADY ANNA TAKES AIM...
...AND THE HUNTER BECOMES HER PREY!
THE ASSAILANT IS LATER IDENTI-FIED AS AN AGENT OF THE WEST...
...AN OUTRAGE THAT WILL NOT GO UNANSWERED!"

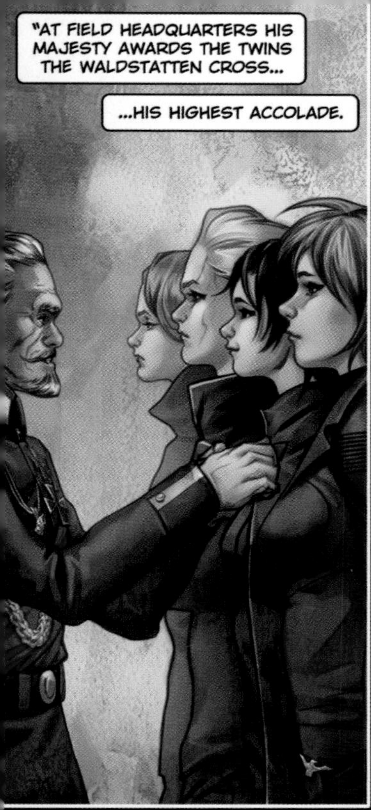
"AT FIELD HEADQUARTERS HIS MAJESTY AWARDS THE TWINS THE WALDSTATTEN CROSS...
...HIS HIGHEST ACCOLADE.
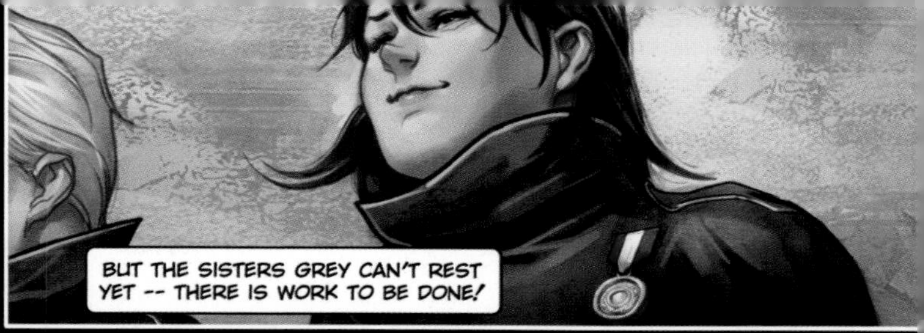
BUT THE SISTERS GREY CAN'T REST YET -- THERE IS WORK TO BE DONE!
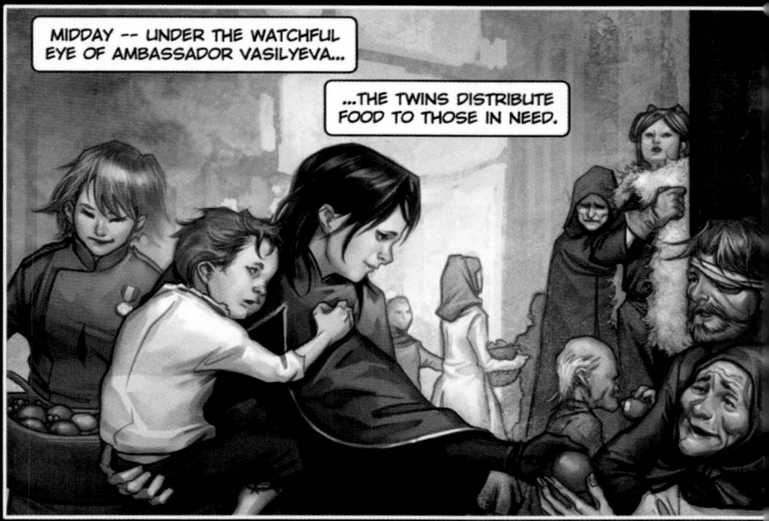
MIDDAY -- UNDER THE WATCHFUL EYE OF AMBASSADOR VASILYEVA...
...THE TWINS DISTRIBUTE FOOD TO THOSE IN NEED.
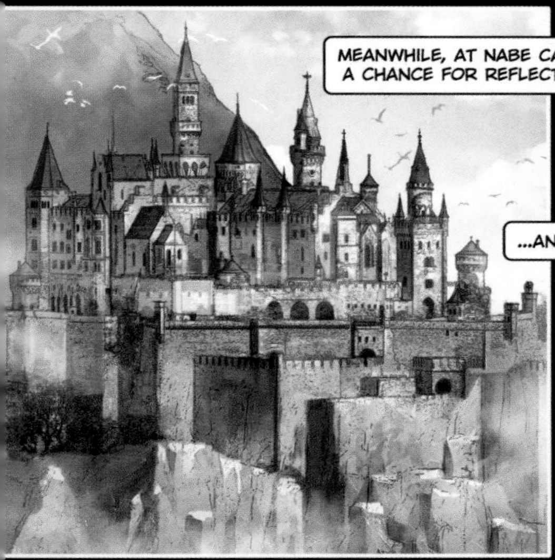
MEANWHILE, AT NABE CASTLE, A CHANCE FOR REFLECTION...
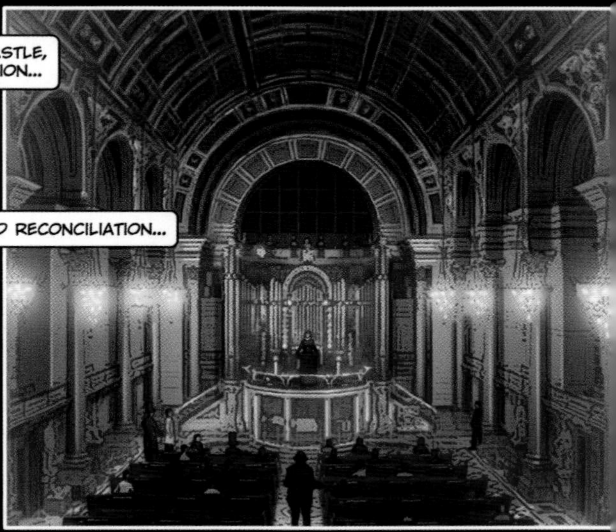
...AND RECONCILIATION...
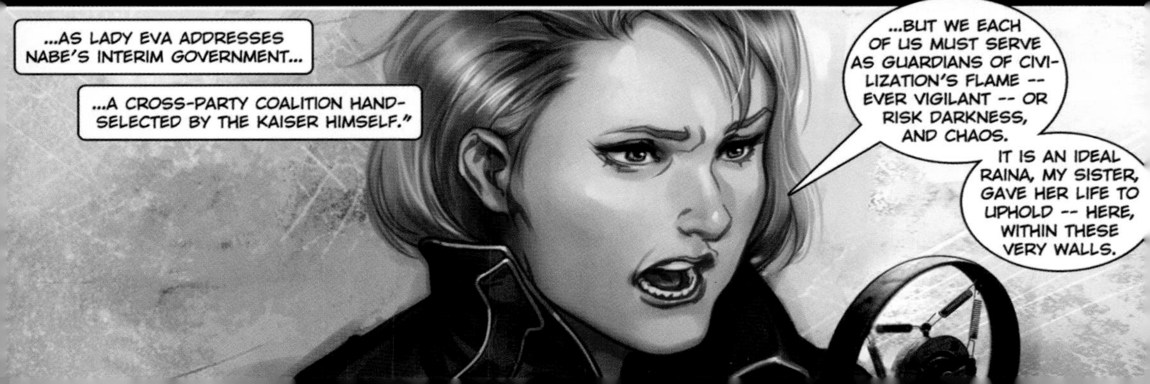
...AS LADY EVA ADDRESSES NABE'S INTERIM GOVERNMENT...
...A CROSS-PARTY COALITION HAND-SELECTED BY THE KAISER HIMSELF."
...BUT WE EACH OF US MUST SERVE AS GUARDIANS OF CIVILIZATION'S FLAME -- EVER VIGILANT -- OR RISK DARKNESS, AND CHAOS.
IT IS AN IDEAL RAINA, MY SISTER, GAVE HER LIFE TO UPHOLD -- HERE, WITHIN THESE VERY WALLS.

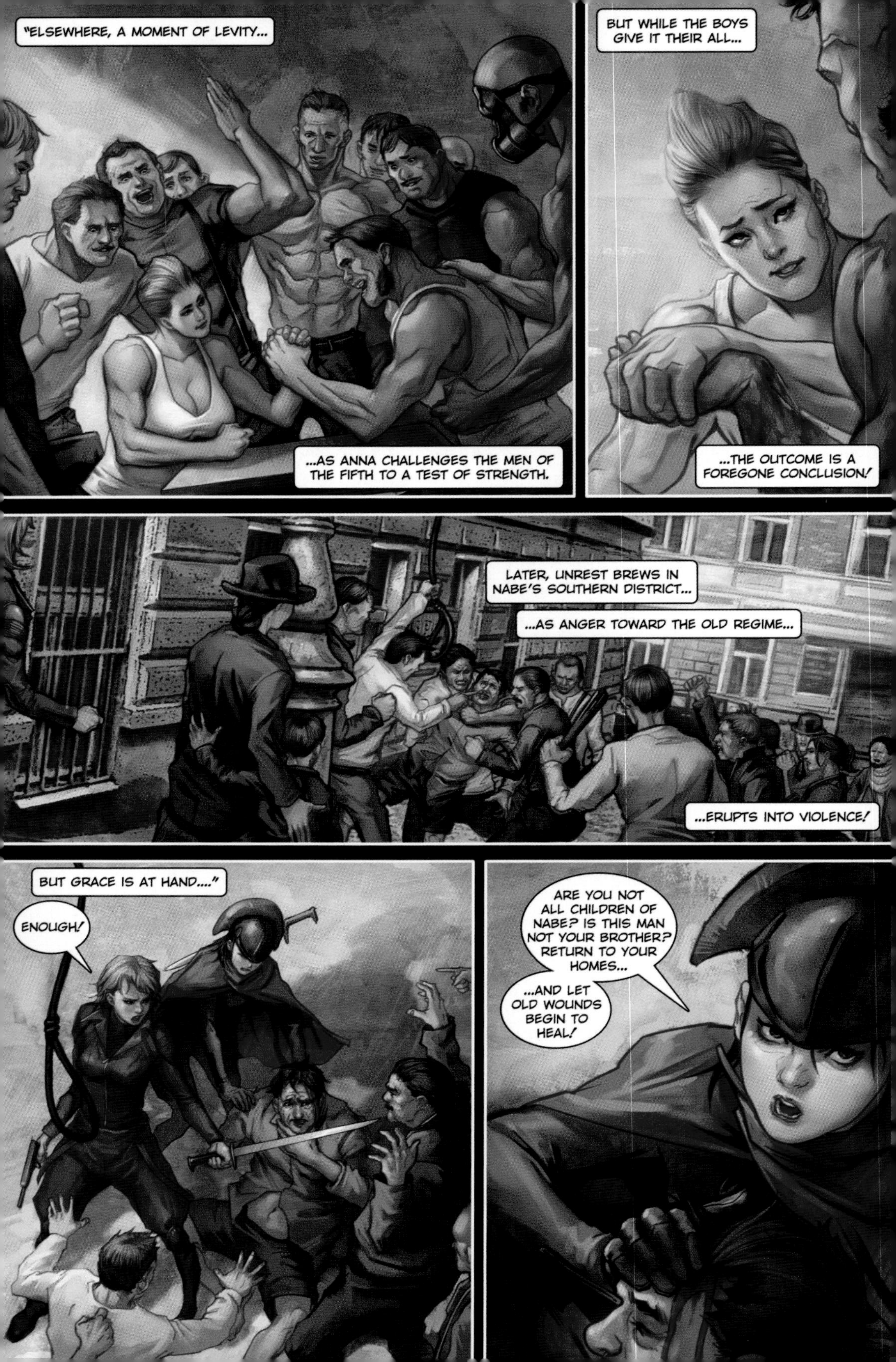
"ELSEWHERE, A MOMENT OF LEVITY...
...AS ANNA CHALLENGES THE MEN OF THE FIFTH TO A TEST OF STRENGTH.
BUT WHILE THE BOYS GIVE IT THEIR ALL...
...THE OUTCOME IS A FOREGONE CONCLUSION!
LATER, UNREST BREWS IN NABE'S SOUTHERN DISTRICT...
...AS ANGER TOWARD THE OLD REGIME...
...ERUPTS INTO VIOLENCE!
BUT GRACE IS AT HAND...."
ENOUGH!
ARE YOU NOT ALL CHILDREN OF NABE? IS THIS MAN NOT YOUR BROTHER? RETURN TO YOUR HOMES...
...AND LET OLD WOUNDS BEGIN TO HEAL!

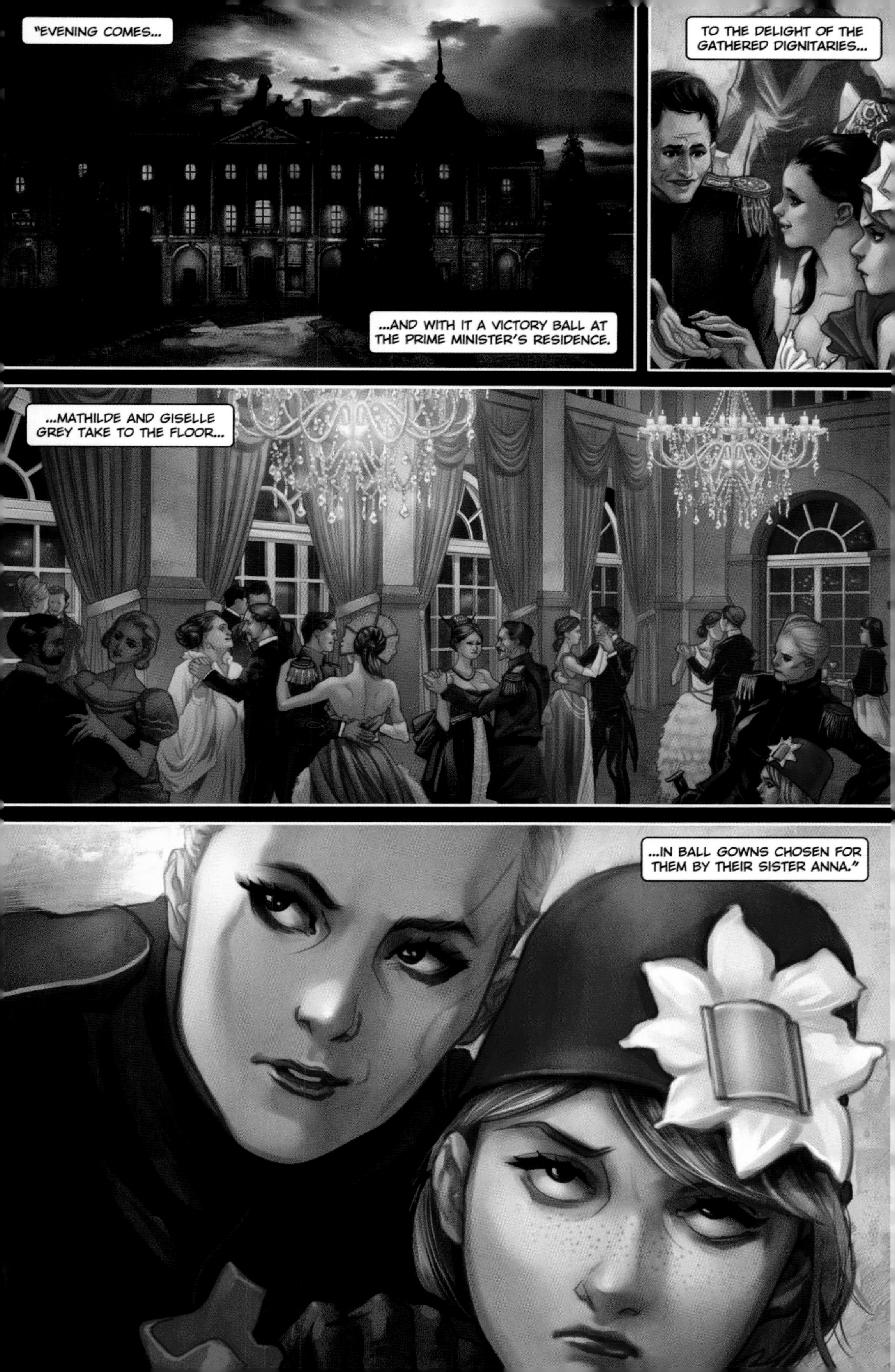
"EVENING COMES...
...AND WITH IT A VICTORY BALL AT THE PRIME MINISTER'S RESIDENCE.
TO THE DELIGHT OF THE GATHERED DIGNITARIES...
...MATHILDE AND GISELLE GREY TAKE TO THE FLOOR...
...IN BALL GOWNS CHOSEN FOR THEM BY THEIR SISTER ANNA."

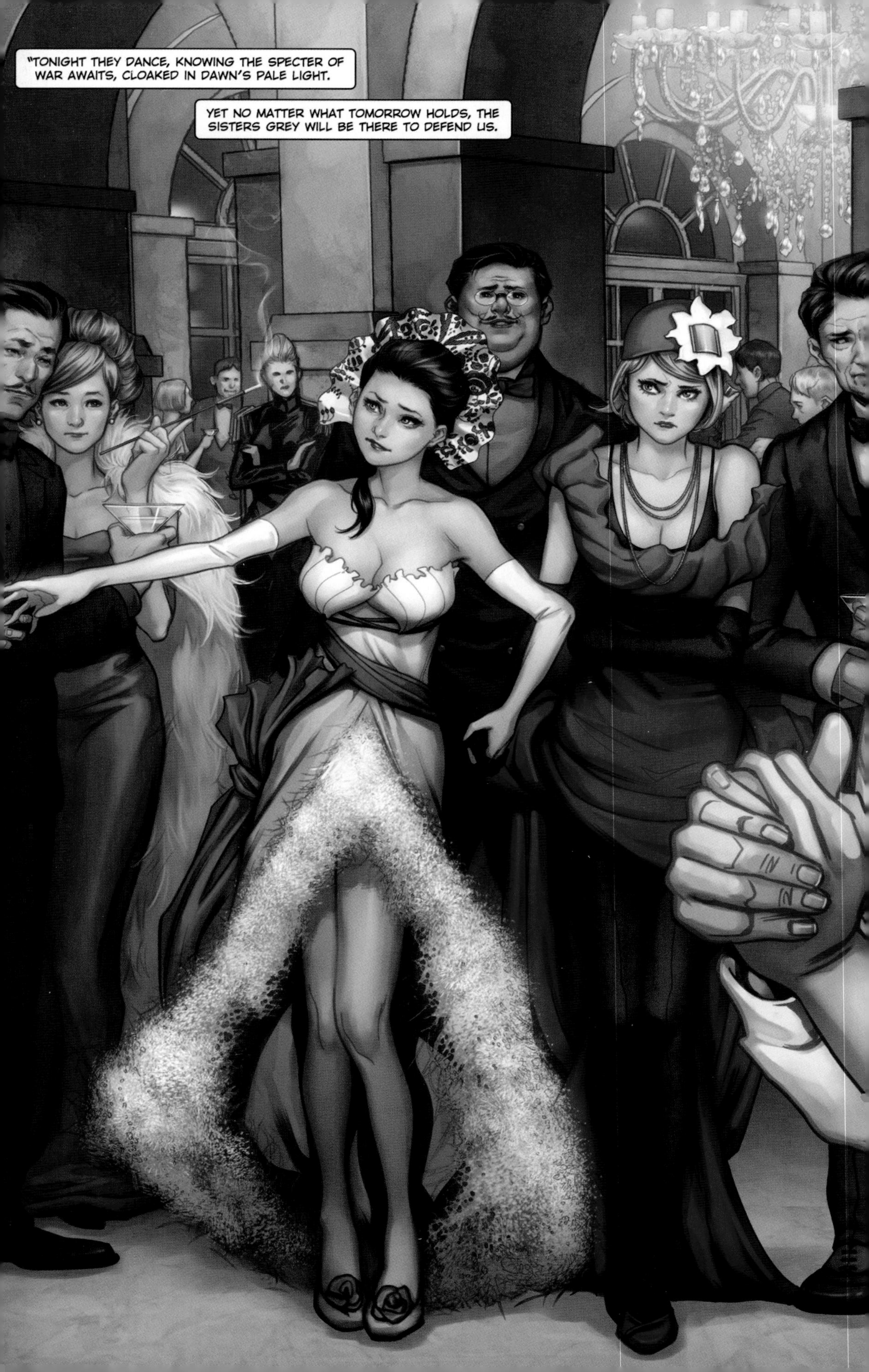
"TONIGHT THEY DANCE, KNOWING THE SPECTER OF WAR AWAITS, CLOAKED IN DAWN'S PALE LIGHT.
YET NO MATTER WHAT TOMORROW HOLDS, THE SISTERS GREY WILL BE THERE TO DEFEND US.

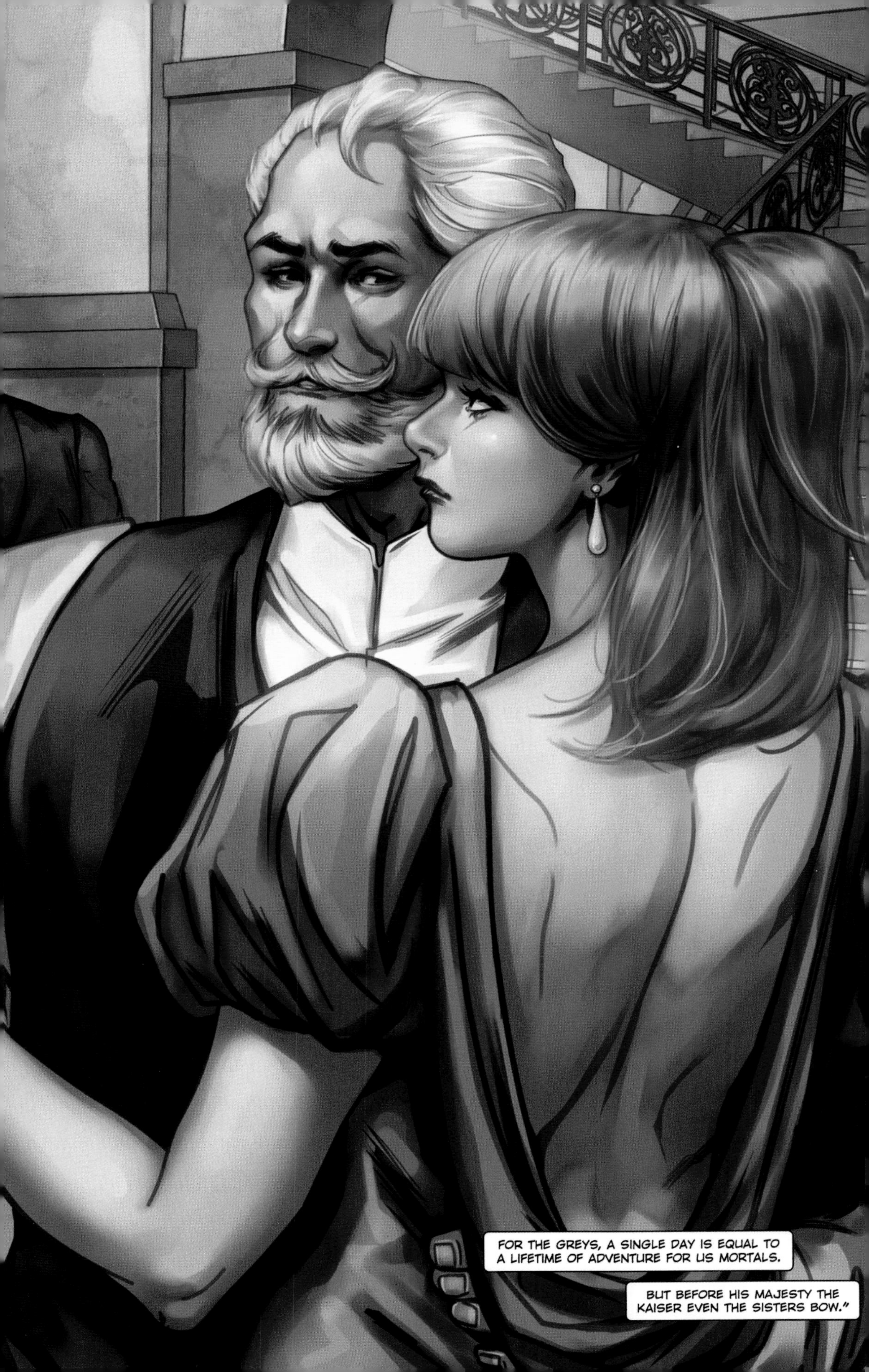
FOR THE GREYS, A SINGLE DAY IS EQUAL TO A LIFETIME OF ADVENTURE FOR US MORTALS.
BUT BEFORE HIS MAJESTY THE KAISER EVEN THE SISTERS BOW."

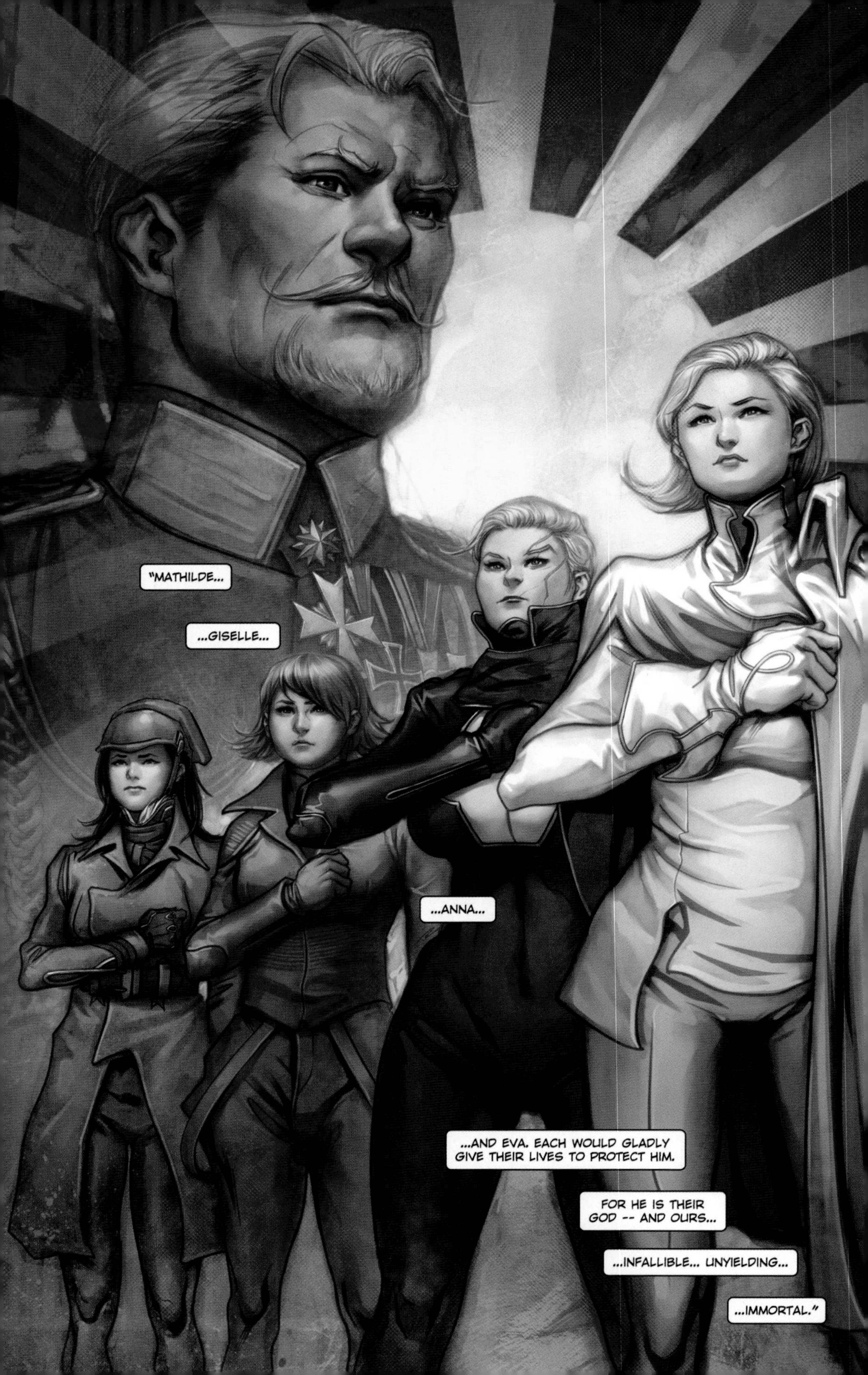
"MATHILDE...
...GISELLE...
...ANNA...
...AND EVA. EACH WOULD GLADLY GIVE THEIR LIVES TO PROTECT HIM.
FOR HE IS THEIR GOD -- AND OURS...
...INFALLIBLE... UNYIELDING...
...IMMORTAL."

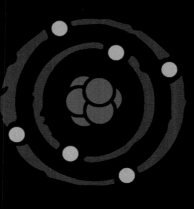

I

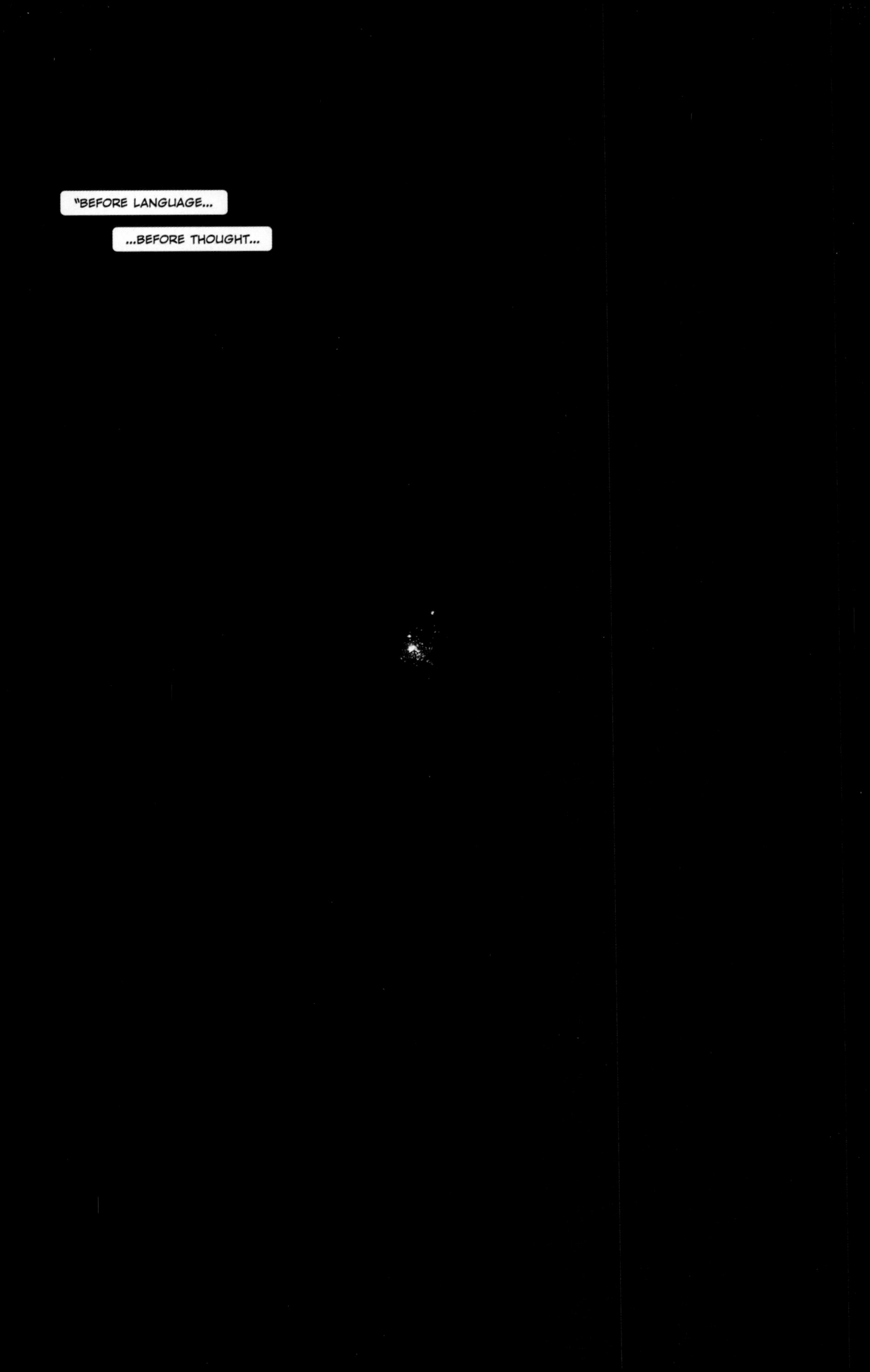
"BEFORE LANGUAGE...
...BEFORE THOUGHT...

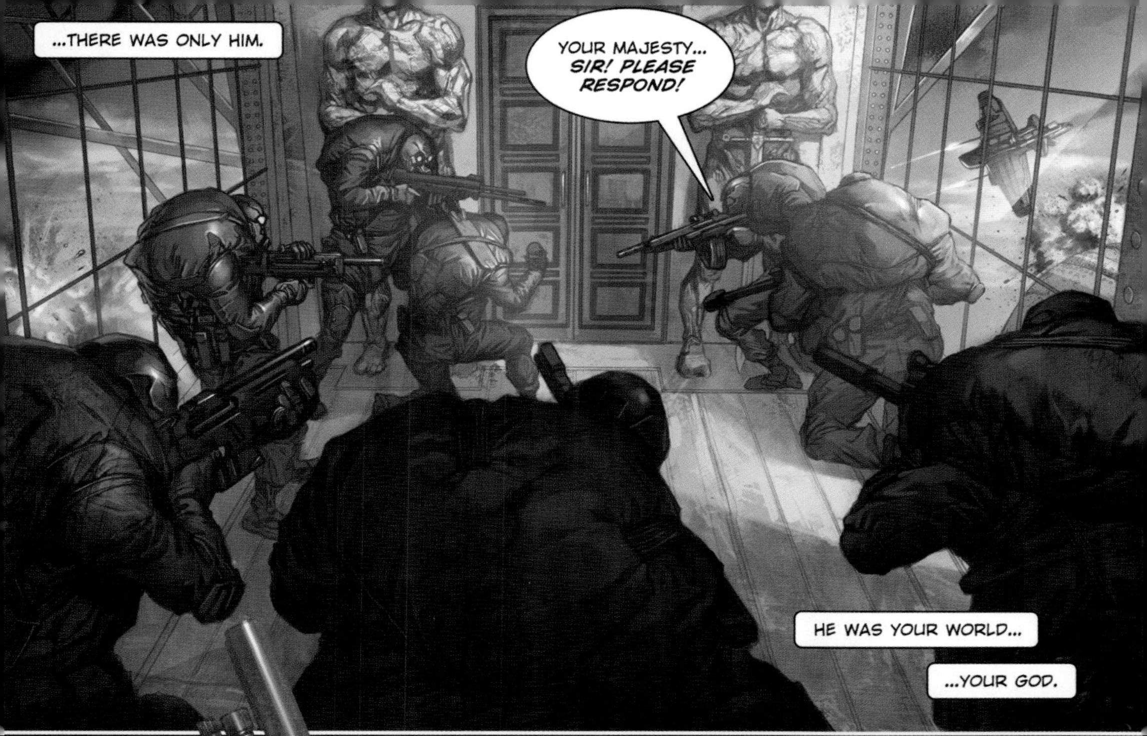
...THERE WAS ONLY HIM.
YOUR MAJESTY... SIR! PLEASE RESPOND!
HE WAS YOUR WORLD...
...YOUR GOD.
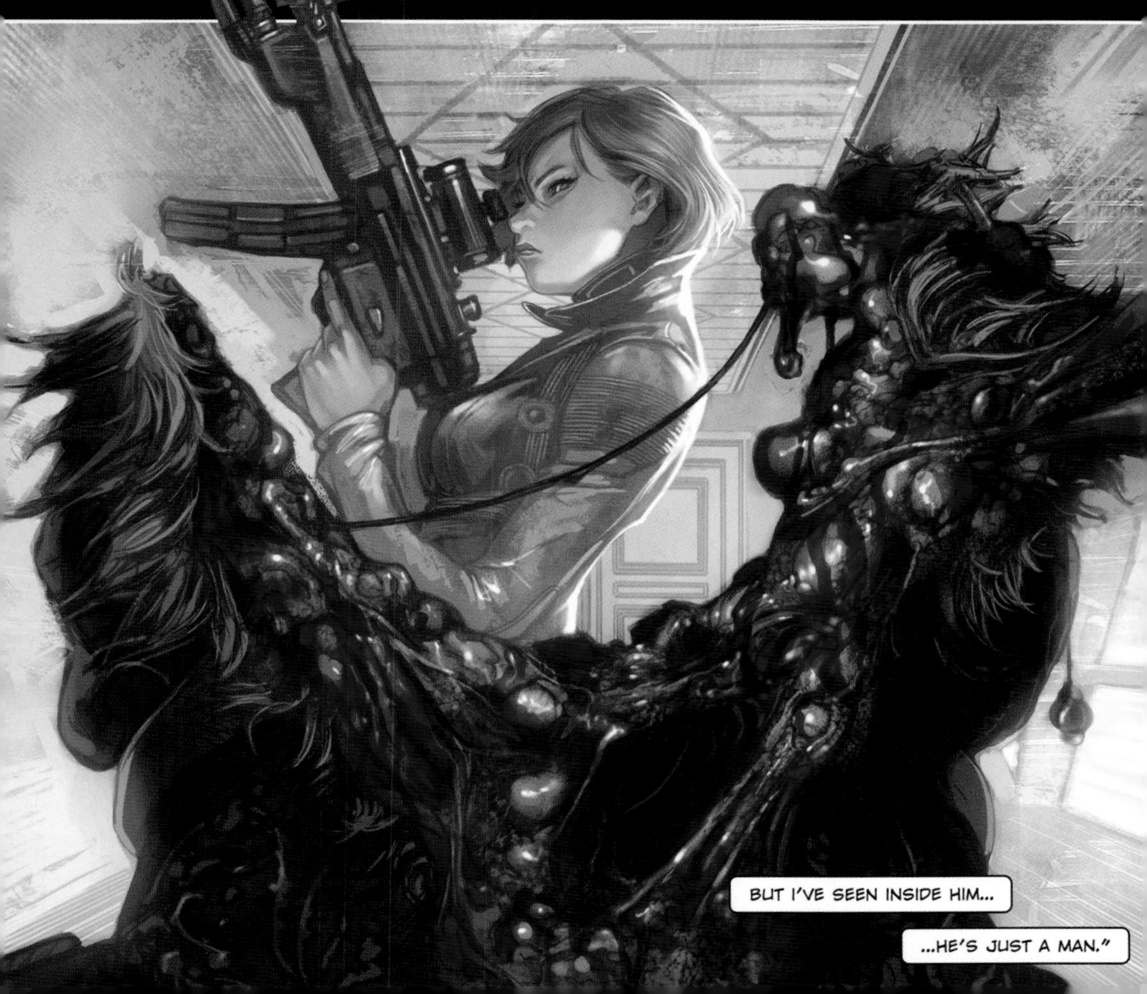
BUT I'VE SEEN INSIDE HIM...
...HE'S JUST A MAN."

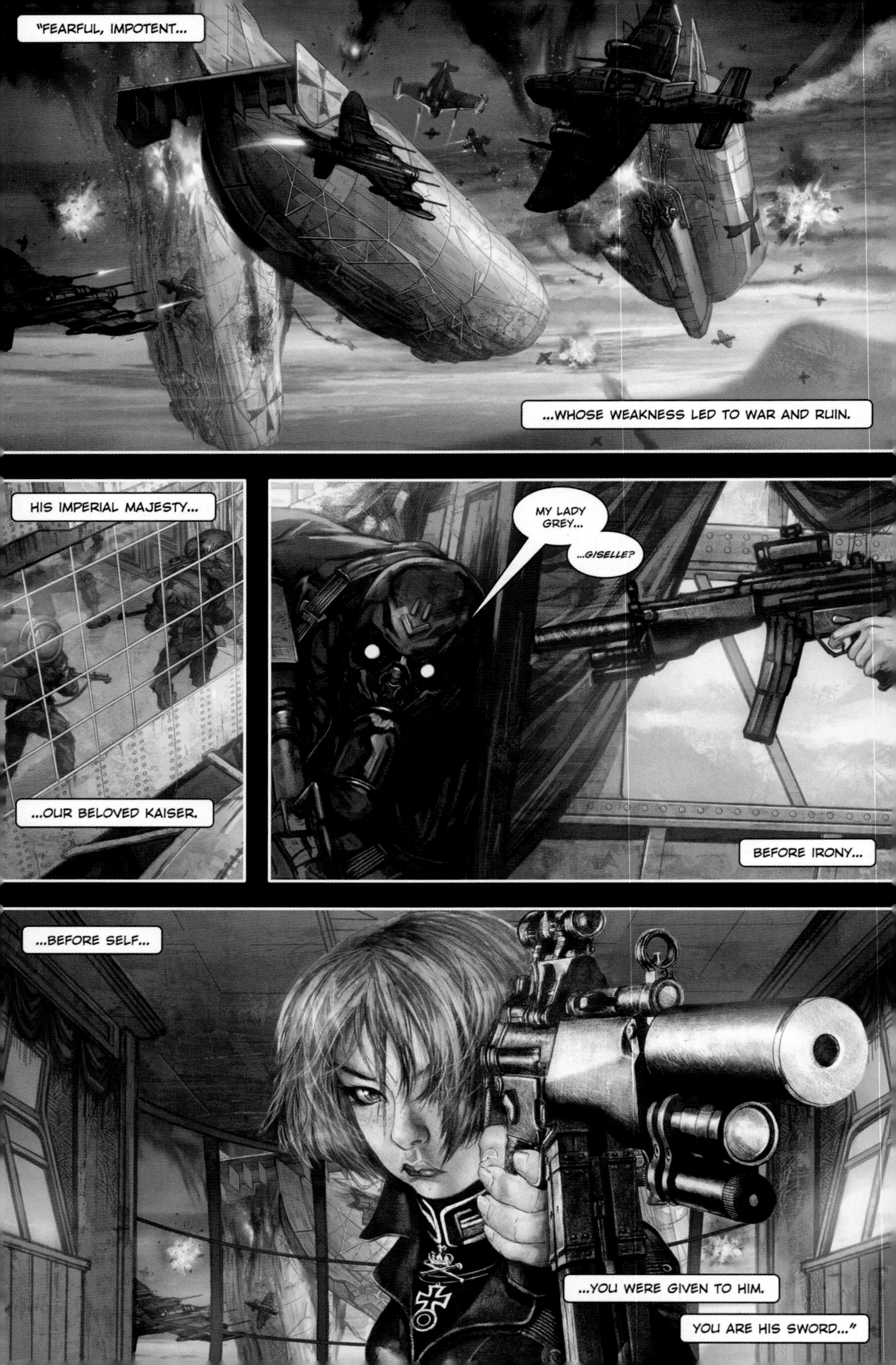
"FEARFUL, IMPOTENT...
...WHOSE WEAKNESS LED TO WAR AND RUIN.
HIS IMPERIAL MAJESTY...
...OUR BELOVED KAISER.
MY LADY GREY...
...GISELLE?
BEFORE IRONY...
...BEFORE SELF...
...YOU WERE GIVEN TO HIM.
YOU ARE HIS SWORD..."

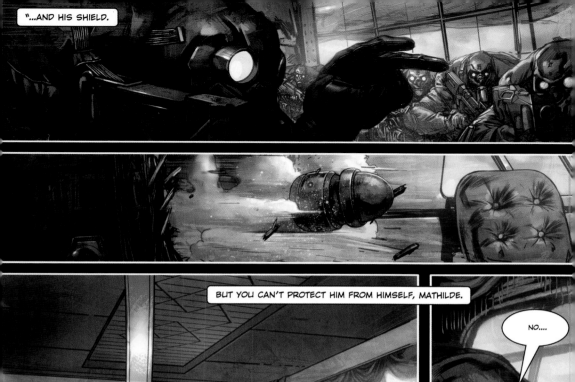

"...AND HIS SHIELD.

BUT YOU CAN'T PROTECT HIM FROM HIMSELF, MATHILDE.

NO....

HIS REIGN IS ALMOST AT AN END."

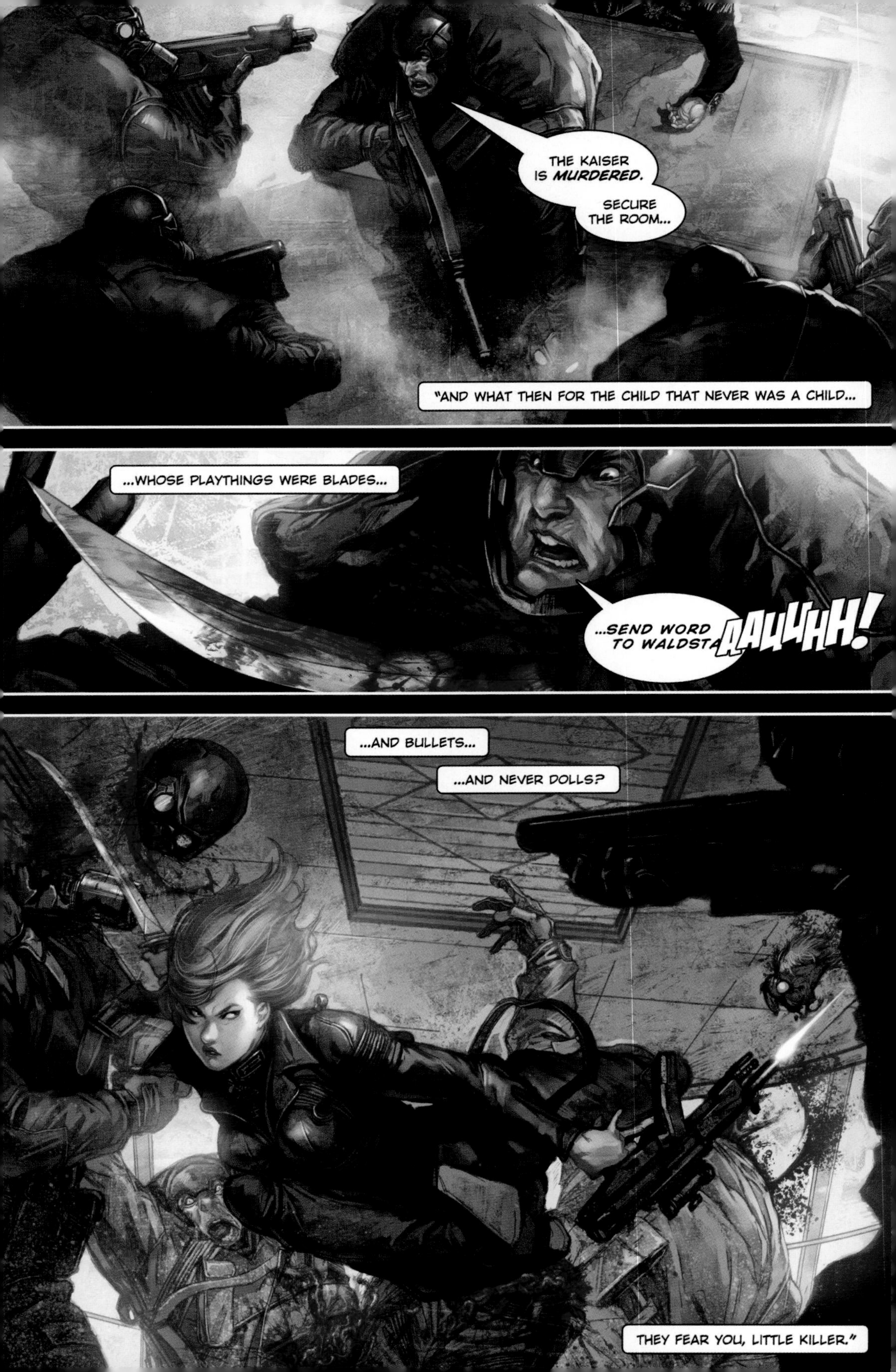
THE KAISER IS *MURDERED.*
SECURE THE ROOM...
"AND WHAT THEN FOR THE CHILD THAT NEVER WAS A CHILD...
...WHOSE PLAYTHINGS WERE BLADES...
...SEND WORD TO WALDSTA
AAUUHH!
...AND BULLETS...
...AND NEVER DOLLS?
THEY FEAR YOU, LITTLE KILLER."

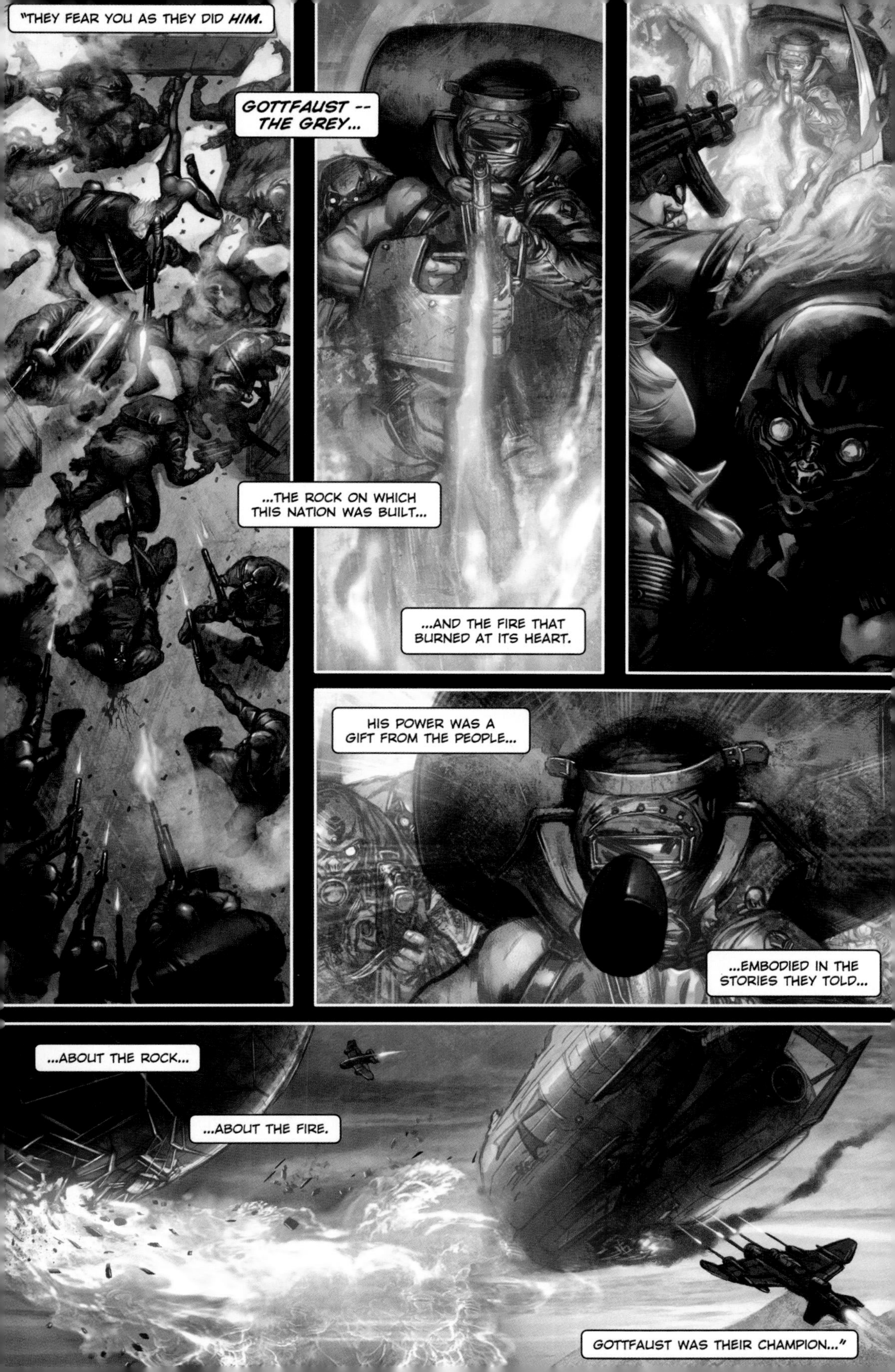
"THEY FEAR YOU AS THEY DID *HIM*.
GOTTFAUST -- THE GREY...
...THE ROCK ON WHICH THIS NATION WAS BUILT...
...AND THE FIRE THAT BURNED AT ITS HEART.
HIS POWER WAS A GIFT FROM THE PEOPLE...
...EMBODIED IN THE STORIES THEY TOLD...
...ABOUT THE ROCK...
...ABOUT THE FIRE.
GOTTFAUST WAS THEIR CHAMPION..."

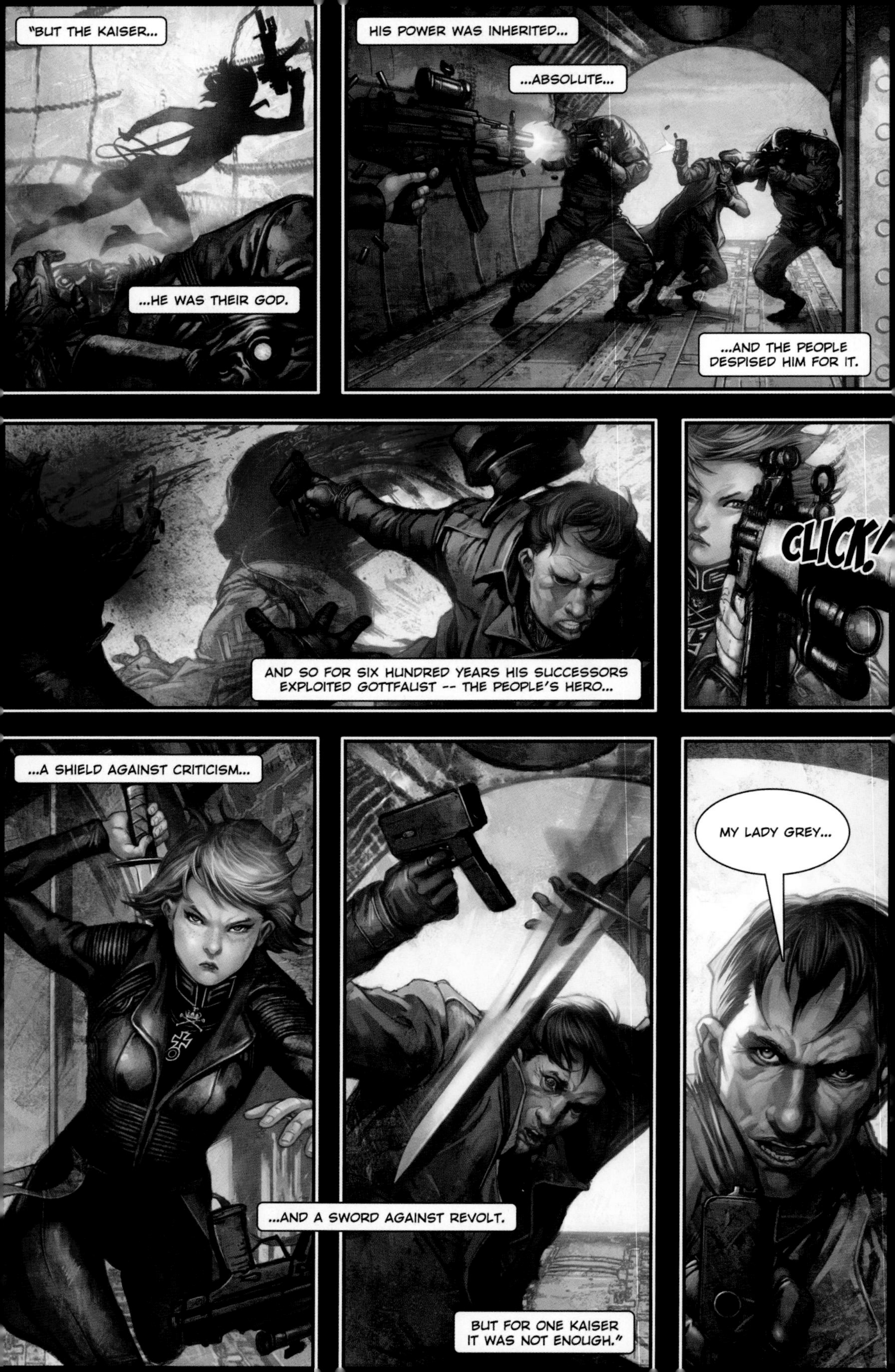
"BUT THE KAISER...
...HE WAS THEIR GOD.
HIS POWER WAS INHERITED...
...ABSOLUTE...
...AND THE PEOPLE DESPISED HIM FOR IT.
AND SO FOR SIX HUNDRED YEARS HIS SUCCESSORS EXPLOITED GOTTFAUST -- THE PEOPLE'S HERO...
CLICK!
...A SHIELD AGAINST CRITICISM...
...AND A SWORD AGAINST REVOLT.
BUT FOR ONE KAISER IT WAS NOT ENOUGH."
MY LADY GREY...

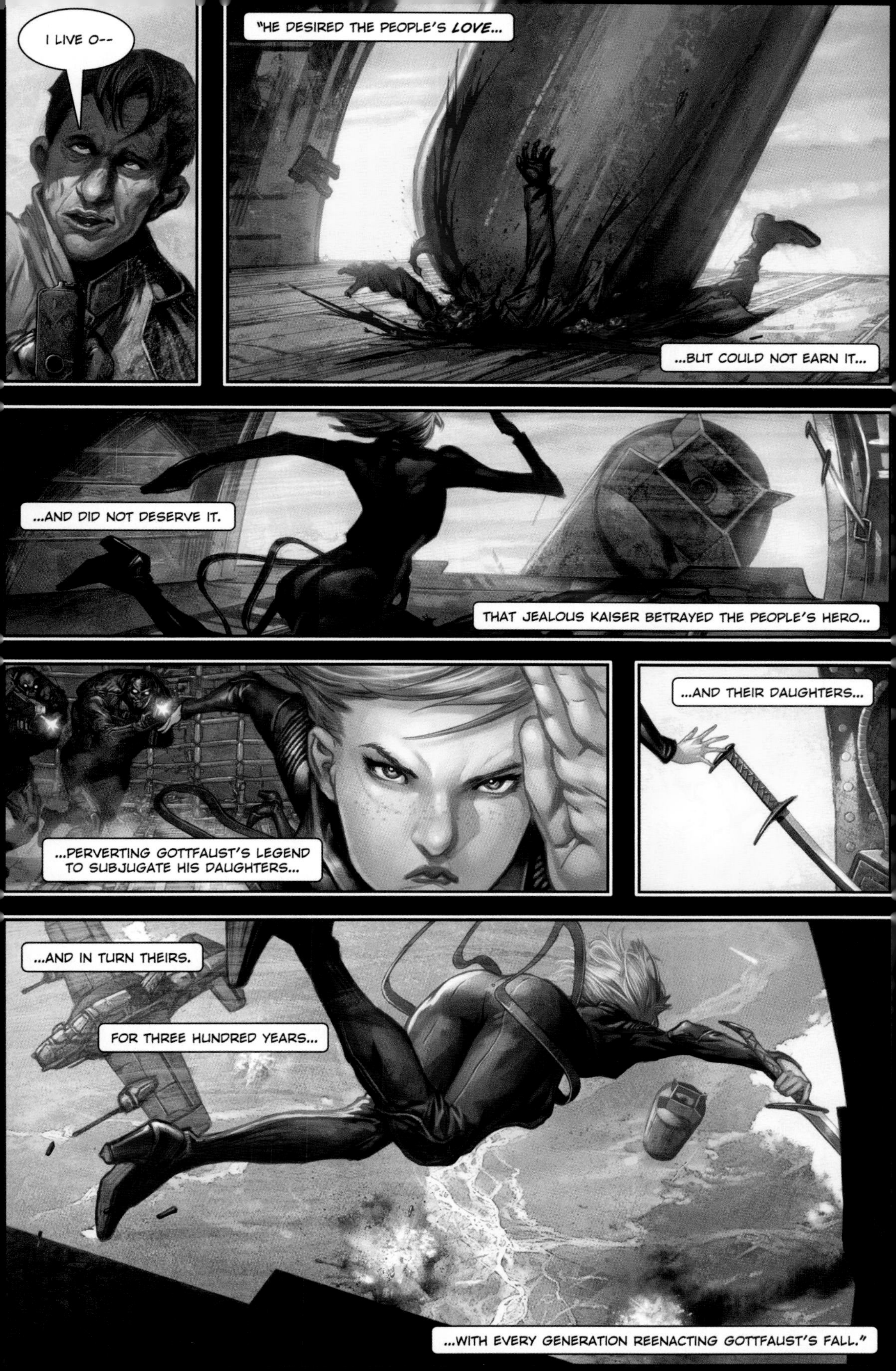
I LIVE O--
"HE DESIRED THE PEOPLE'S *LOVE*...
...BUT COULD NOT EARN IT...
...AND DID NOT DESERVE IT.
THAT JEALOUS KAISER BETRAYED THE PEOPLE'S HERO...
...PERVERTING GOTTFAUST'S LEGEND TO SUBJUGATE HIS DAUGHTERS...
...AND THEIR DAUGHTERS...
...AND IN TURN THEIRS.
FOR THREE HUNDRED YEARS...
...WITH EVERY GENERATION REENACTING GOTTFAUST'S FALL."

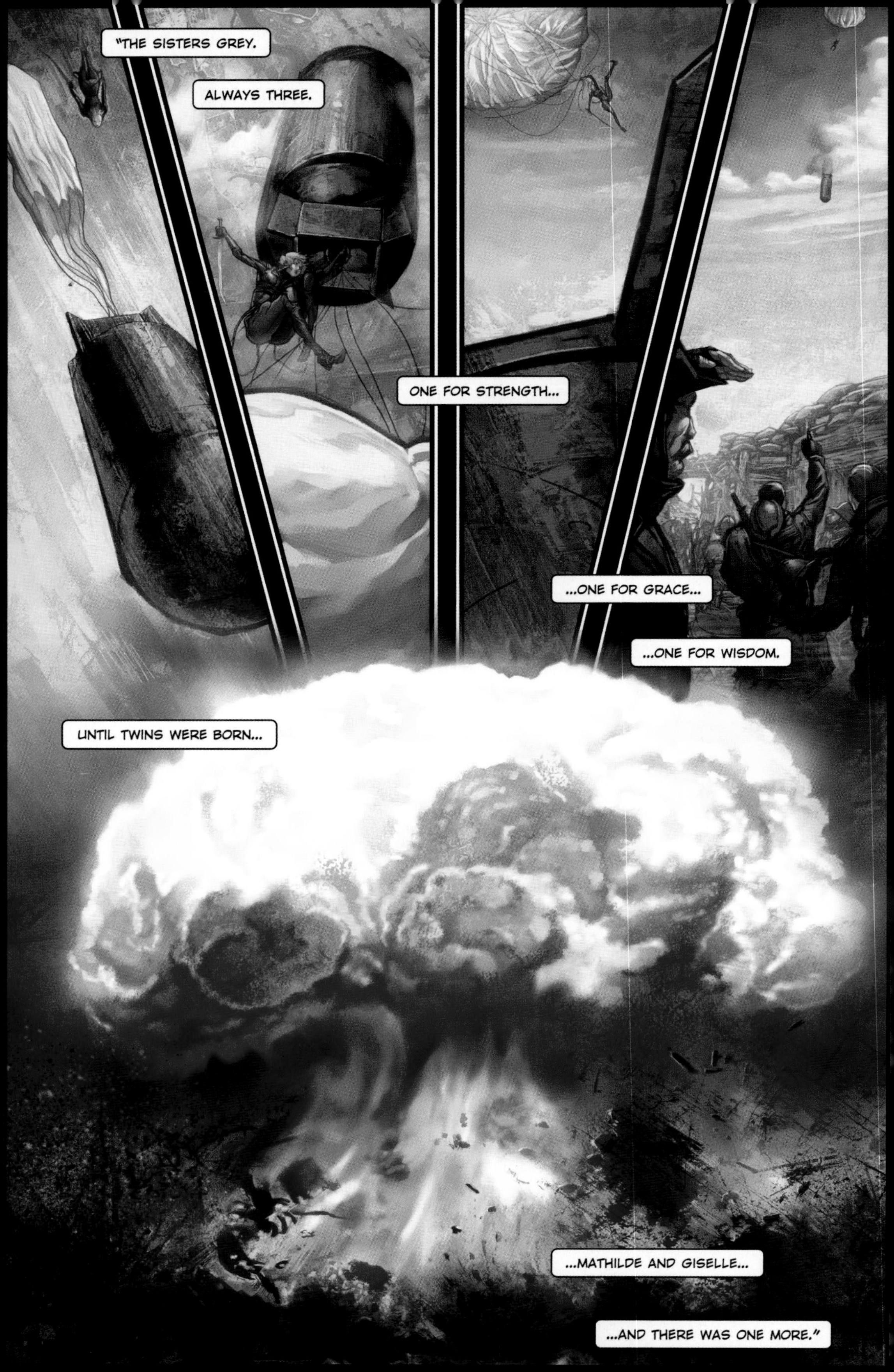
"THE SISTERS GREY.
ALWAYS THREE.
ONE FOR STRENGTH...
...ONE FOR GRACE...
...ONE FOR WISDOM.
UNTIL TWINS WERE BORN...
...MATHILDE AND GISELLE...
...AND THERE WAS ONE MORE."

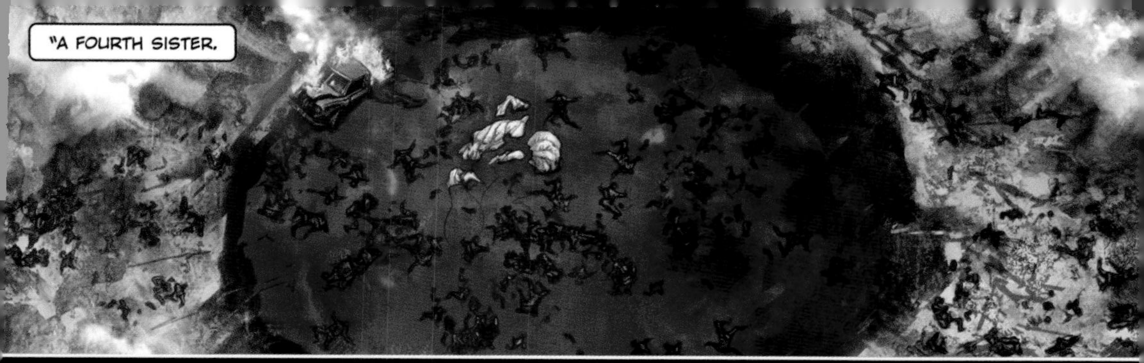
"A FOURTH SISTER.
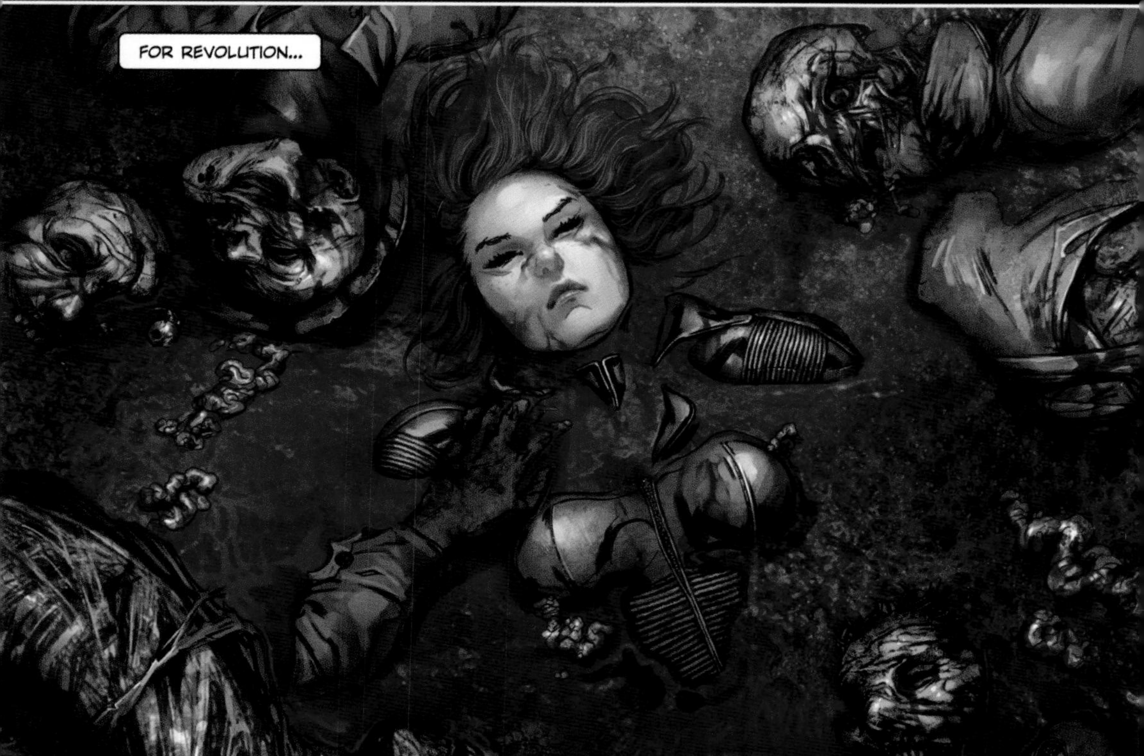
FOR REVOLUTION...
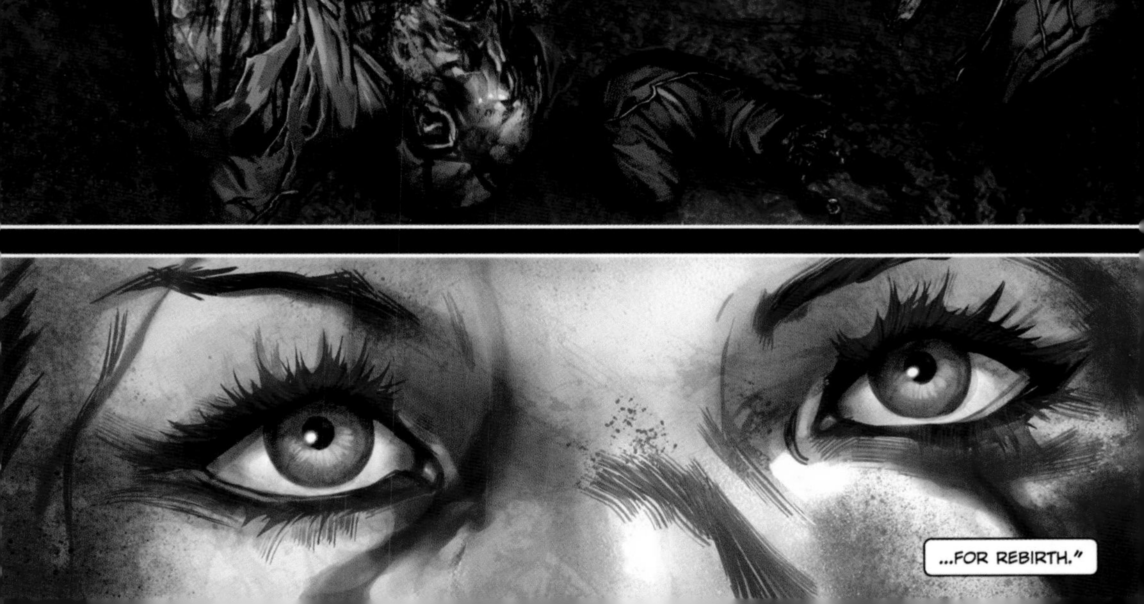
...FOR REBIRTH."

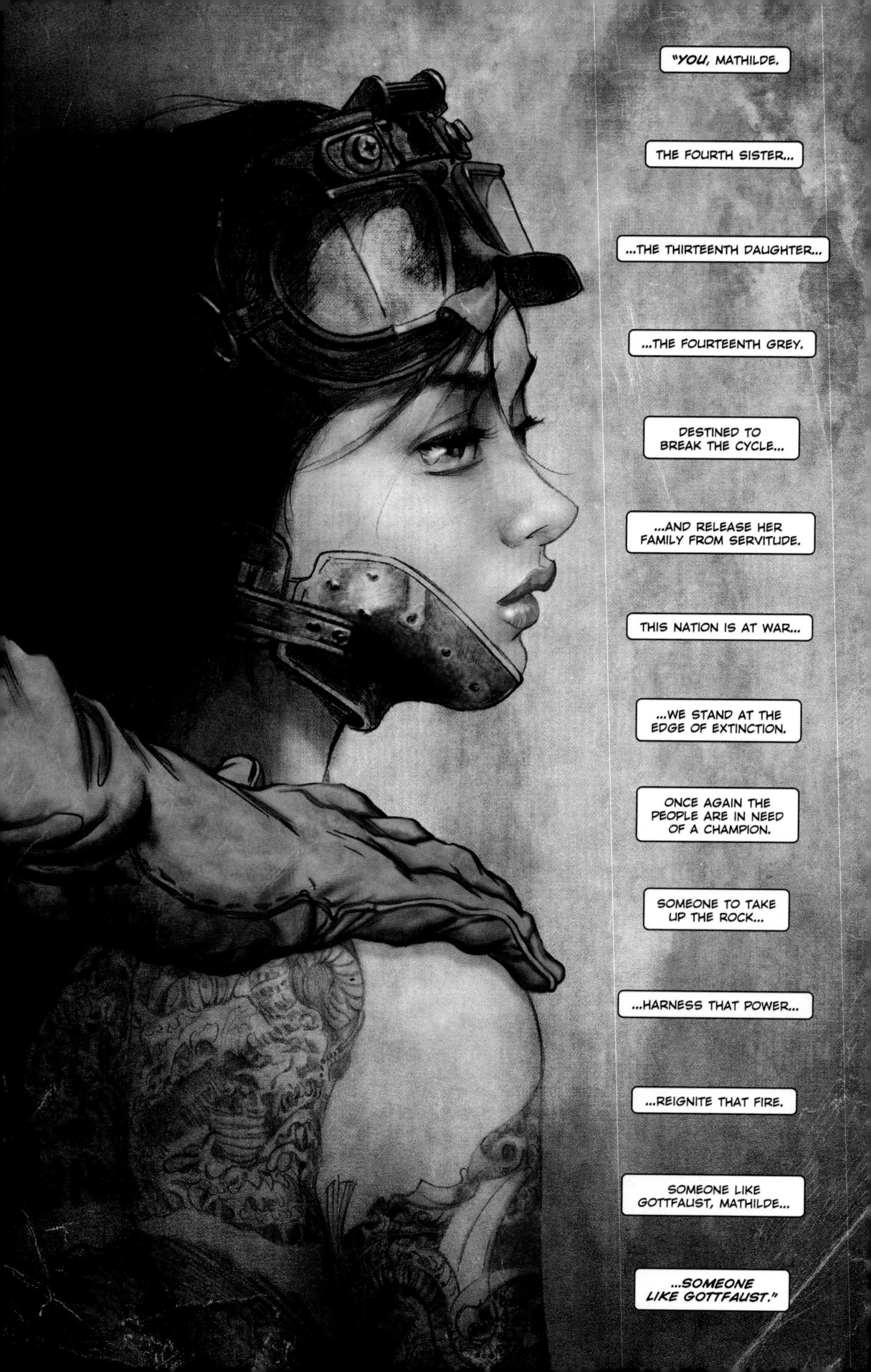
"YOU, MATHILDE.
THE FOURTH SISTER...
...THE THIRTEENTH DAUGHTER...
...THE FOURTEENTH GREY.
DESTINED TO BREAK THE CYCLE...
...AND RELEASE HER FAMILY FROM SERVITUDE.
THIS NATION IS AT WAR...
...WE STAND AT THE EDGE OF EXTINCTION.
ONCE AGAIN THE PEOPLE ARE IN NEED OF A CHAMPION.
SOMEONE TO TAKE UP THE ROCK...
...HARNESS THAT POWER...
...REIGNITE THAT FIRE.
SOMEONE LIKE GOTTFAUST, MATHILDE...
...SOMEONE LIKE GOTTFAUST."

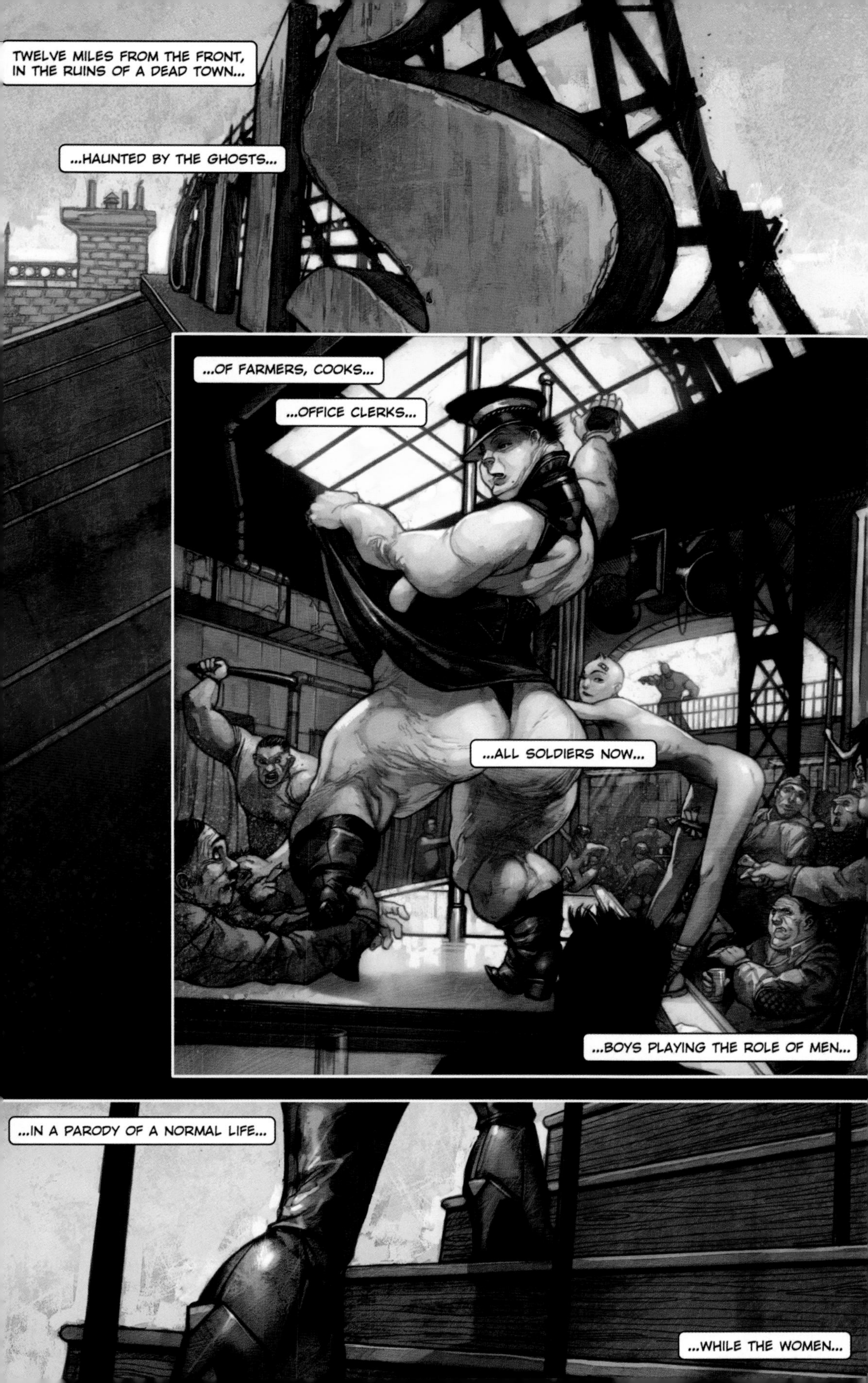
TWELVE MILES FROM THE FRONT, IN THE RUINS OF A DEAD TOWN...
...HAUNTED BY THE GHOSTS...
...OF FARMERS, COOKS...
...OFFICE CLERKS...
...ALL SOLDIERS NOW...
...BOYS PLAYING THE ROLE OF MEN...
...IN A PARODY OF A NORMAL LIFE...
...WHILE THE WOMEN...

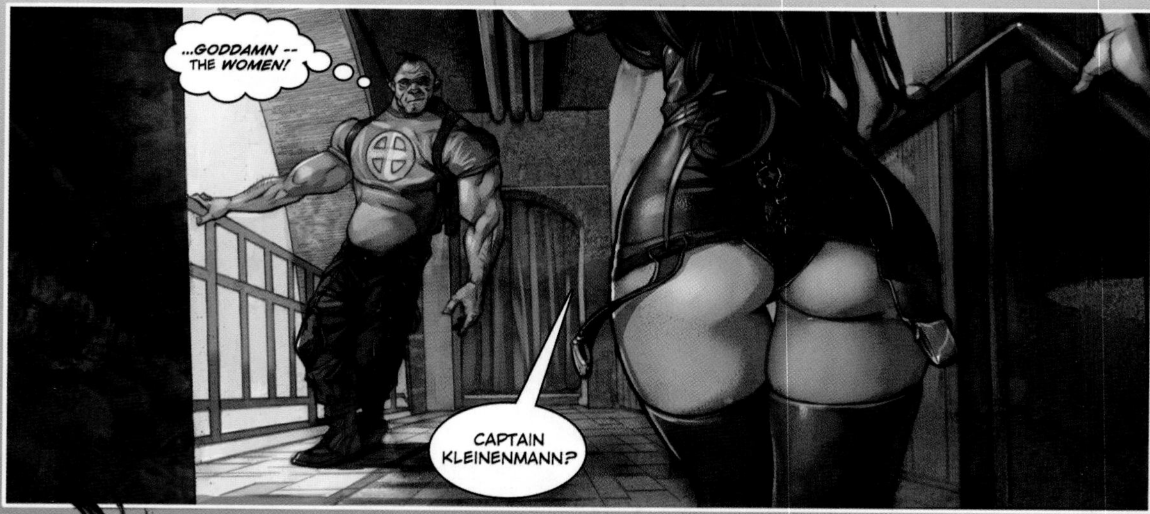
...GODDAMN -- THE WOMEN!
CAPTAIN KLEINENMANN?

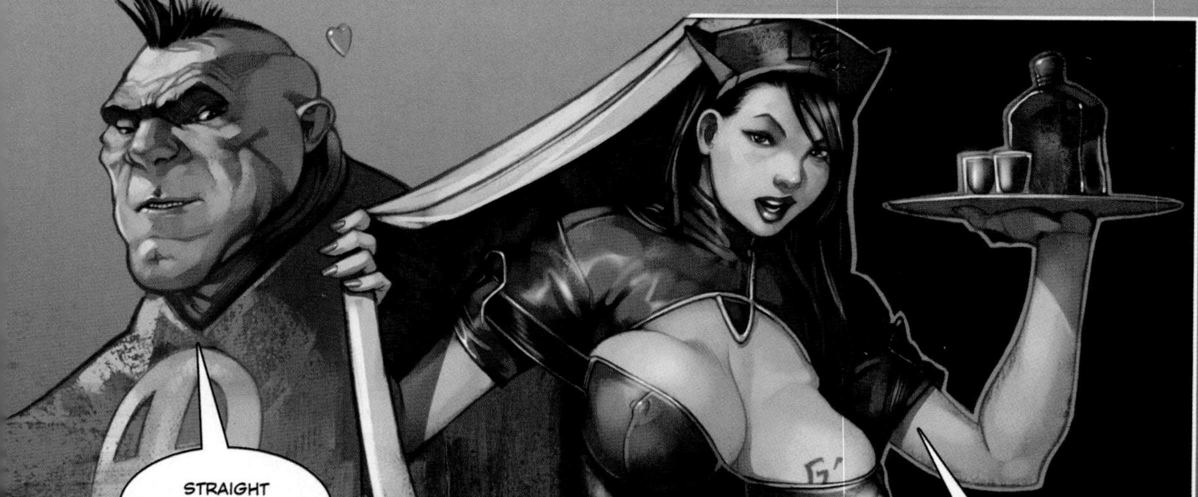
STRAIGHT THROUGH -- CURTAIN THREE.
CAPTAIN...
...YOU CALLED?

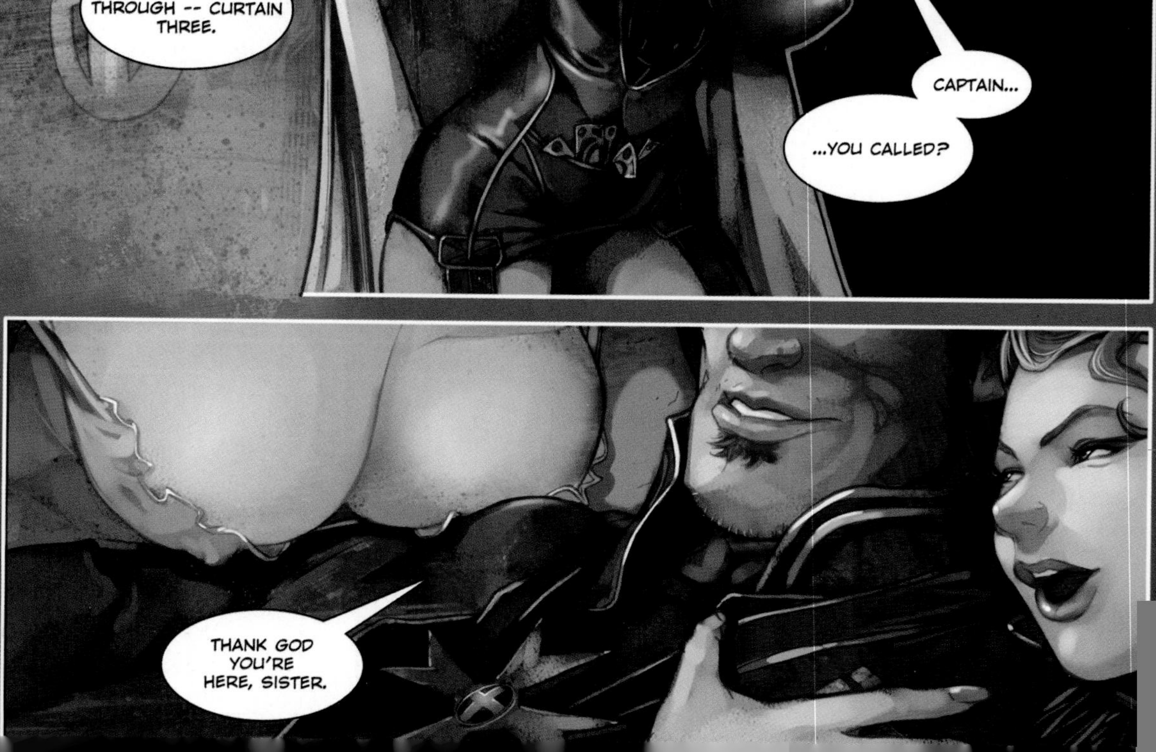
THANK GOD YOU'RE HERE, SISTER.

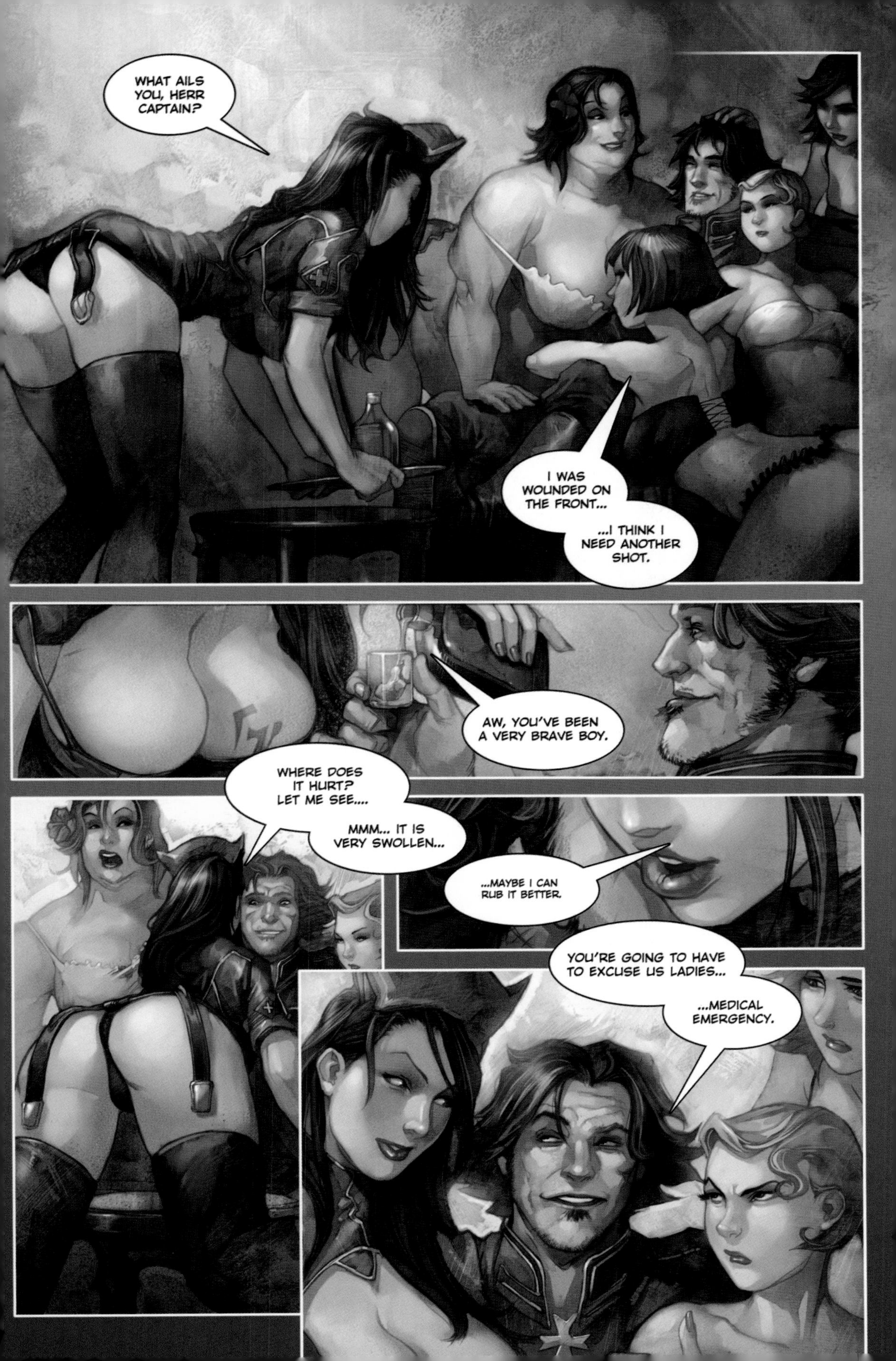
WHAT AILS YOU, HERR CAPTAIN?
I WAS WOUNDED ON THE FRONT...
...I THINK I NEED ANOTHER SHOT.
AW, YOU'VE BEEN A VERY BRAVE BOY.
WHERE DOES IT HURT? LET ME SEE....
MMM... IT IS VERY SWOLLEN...
...MAYBE I CAN RUB IT BETTER.
YOU'RE GOING TO HAVE TO EXCUSE US LADIES...
...MEDICAL EMERGENCY.

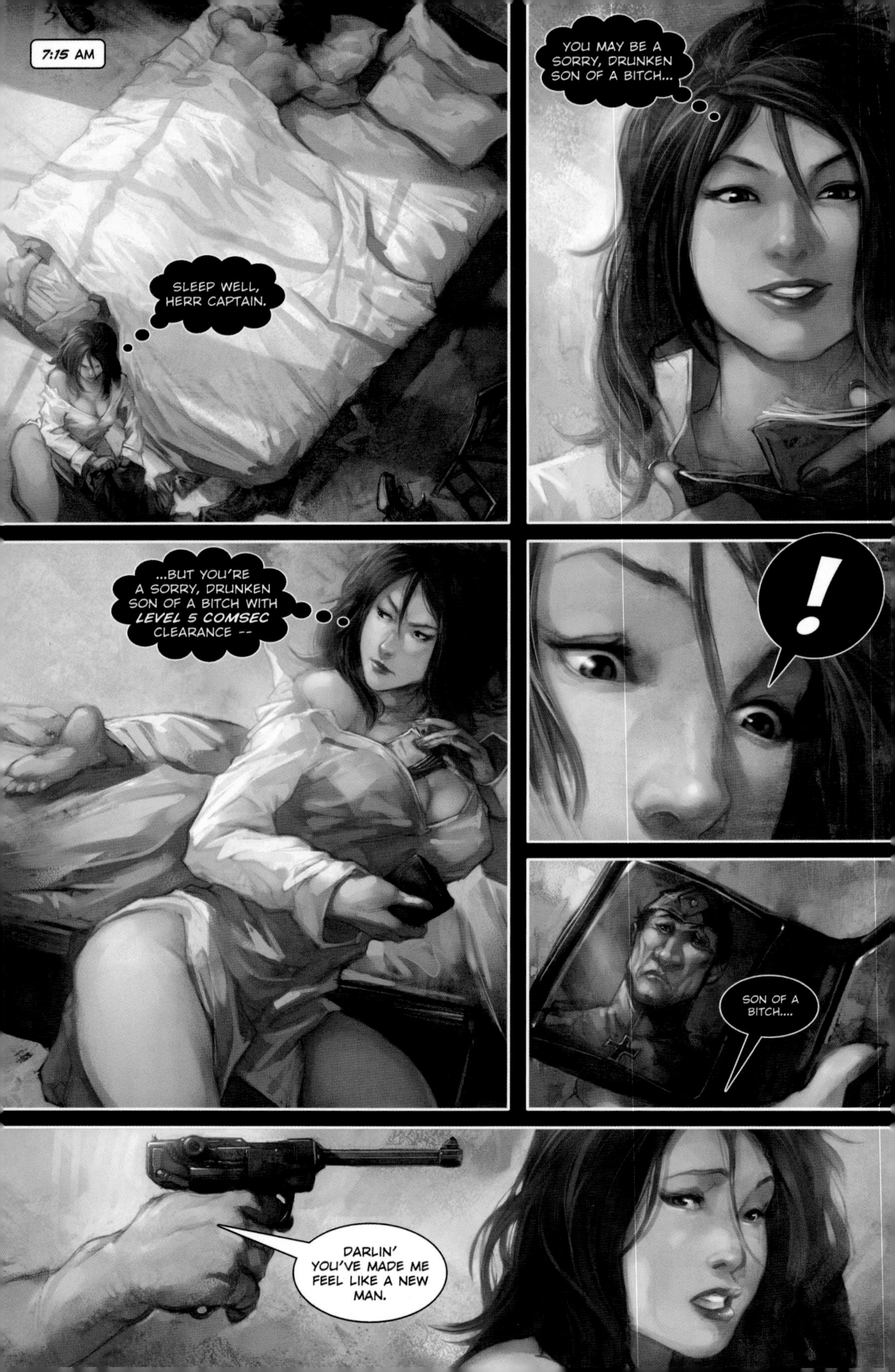
7:15 AM
SLEEP WELL, HERR CAPTAIN.
YOU MAY BE A SORRY, DRUNKEN SON OF A BITCH...
...BUT YOU'RE A SORRY, DRUNKEN SON OF A BITCH WITH *LEVEL 5 COMSEC* CLEARANCE --
!
SON OF A BITCH....
DARLIN' YOU'VE MADE ME FEEL LIKE A NEW MAN.

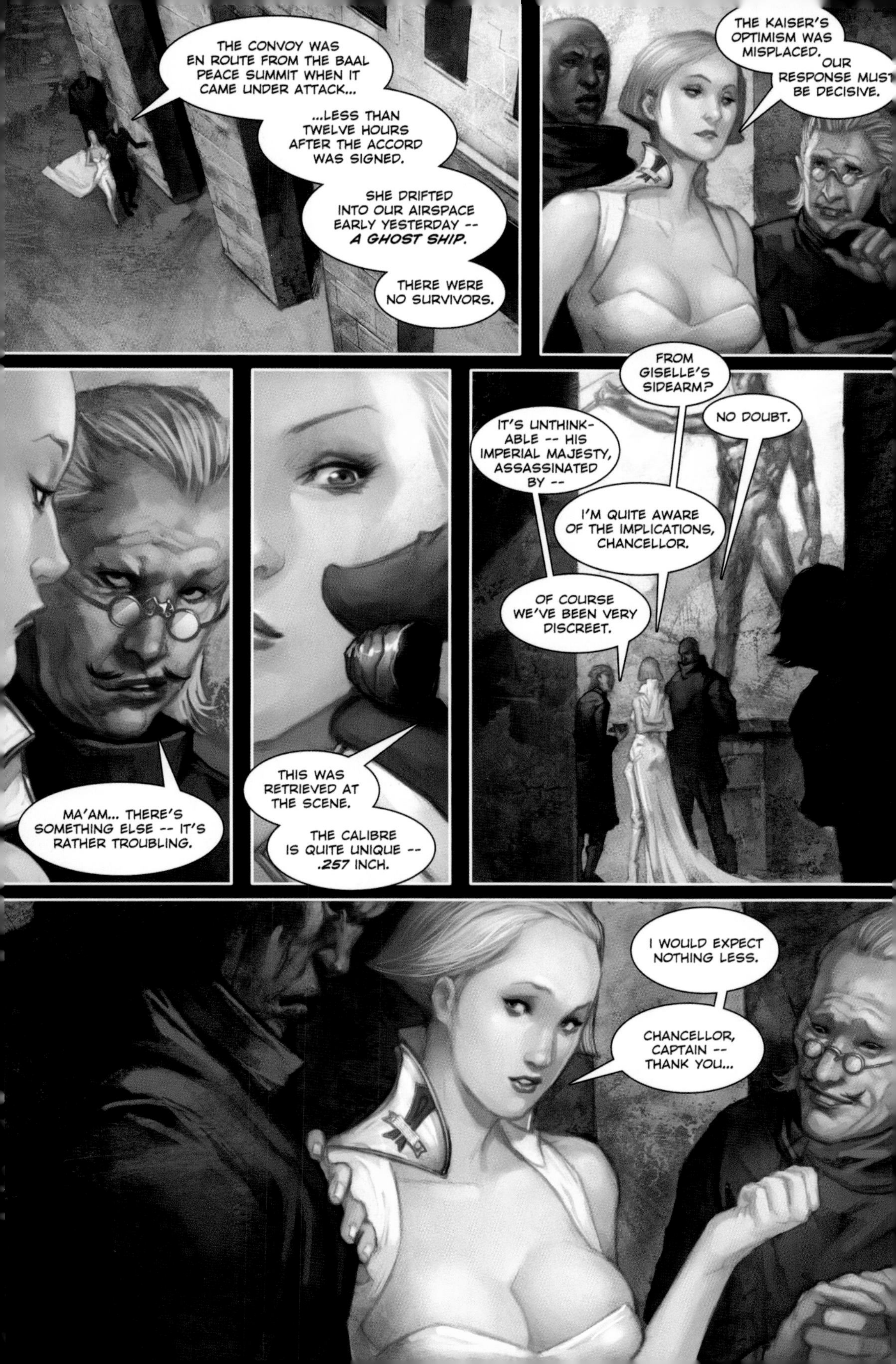
THE CONVOY WAS EN ROUTE FROM THE BAAL PEACE SUMMIT WHEN IT CAME UNDER ATTACK...
...LESS THAN TWELVE HOURS AFTER THE ACCORD WAS SIGNED.
SHE DRIFTED INTO OUR AIRSPACE EARLY YESTERDAY -- *A GHOST SHIP.*
THERE WERE NO SURVIVORS.
THE KAISER'S OPTIMISM WAS MISPLACED.
OUR RESPONSE MUST BE DECISIVE.
MA'AM... THERE'S SOMETHING ELSE -- IT'S RATHER TROUBLING.
THIS WAS RETRIEVED AT THE SCENE.
THE CALIBRE IS QUITE UNIQUE -- *.257* INCH.
FROM GISELLE'S SIDEARM?
IT'S UNTHINK-ABLE -- HIS IMPERIAL MAJESTY, ASSASSINATED BY --
NO DOUBT.
I'M QUITE AWARE OF THE IMPLICATIONS, CHANCELLOR.
OF COURSE WE'VE BEEN VERY DISCREET.
I WOULD EXPECT NOTHING LESS.
CHANCELLOR, CAPTAIN -- THANK YOU...

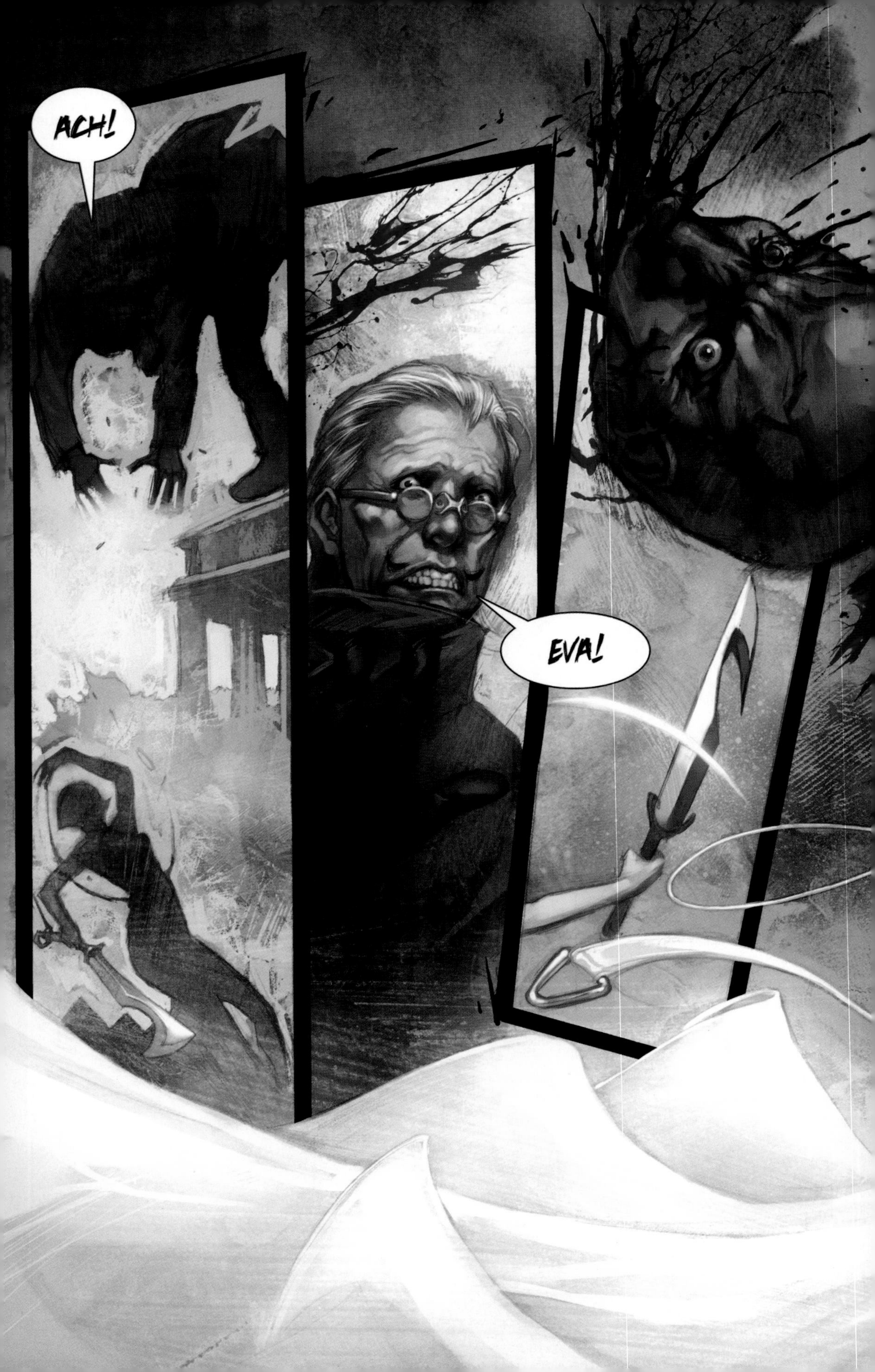
ACH!
EVA!

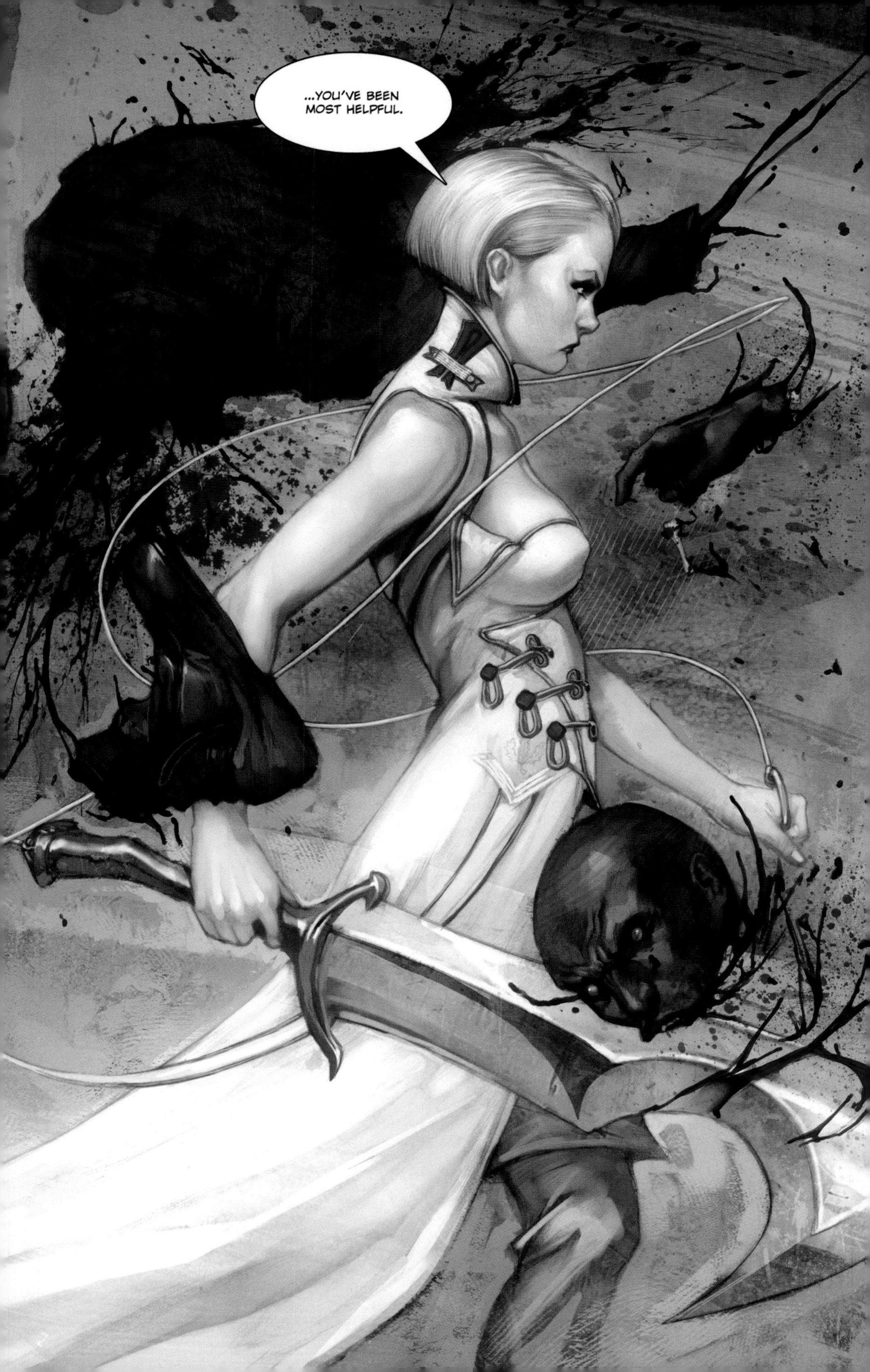
...YOU'VE BEEN MOST HELPFUL.

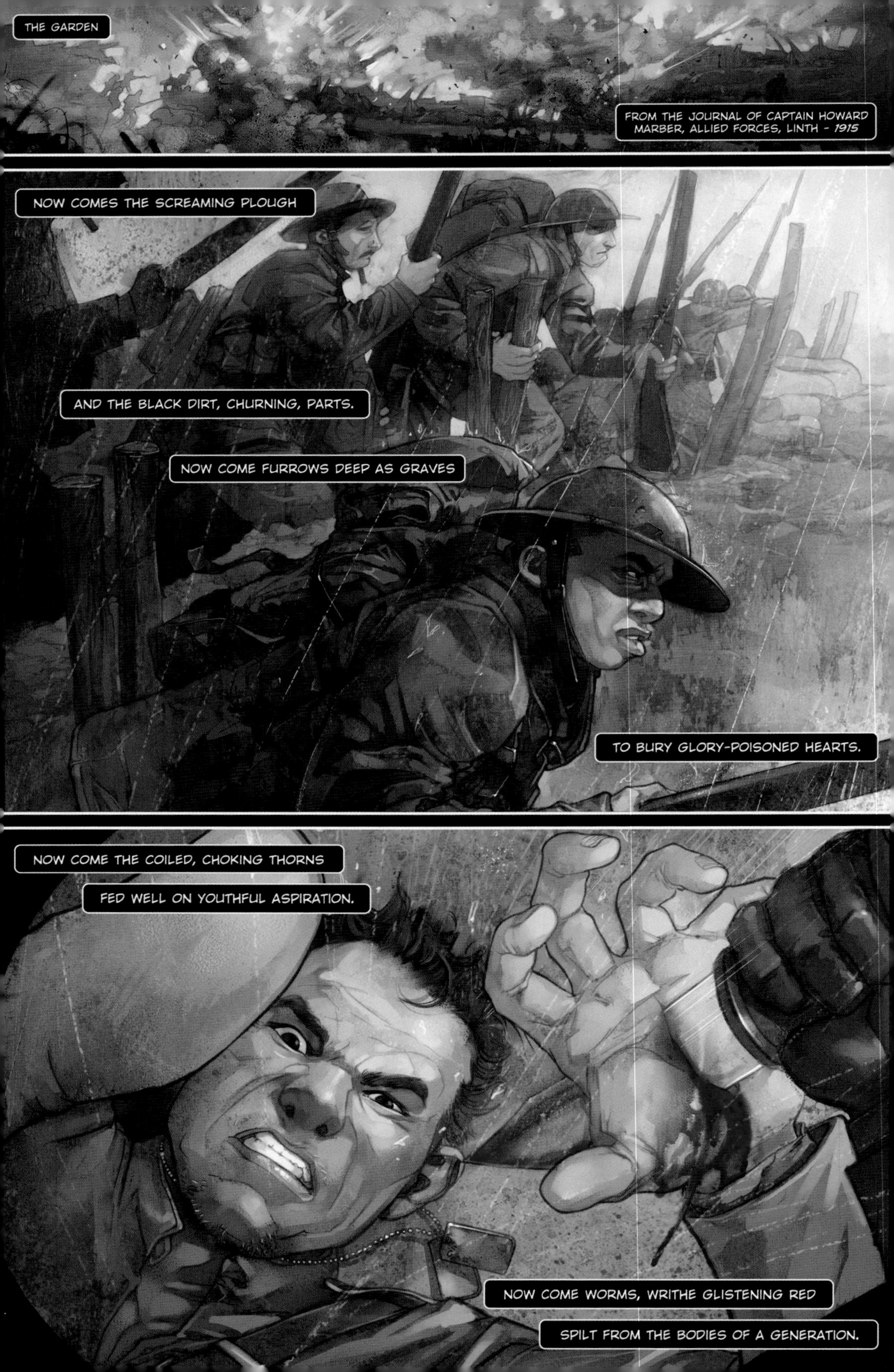
THE GARDEN
FROM THE JOURNAL OF CAPTAIN HOWARD MARBER, ALLIED FORCES, LINTH - *1915*
NOW COMES THE SCREAMING PLOUGH
AND THE BLACK DIRT, CHURNING, PARTS.
NOW COME FURROWS DEEP AS GRAVES
TO BURY GLORY-POISONED HEARTS.
NOW COME THE COILED, CHOKING THORNS
FED WELL ON YOUTHFUL ASPIRATION.
NOW COME WORMS, WRITHE GLISTENING RED
SPILT FROM THE BODIES OF A GENERATION.

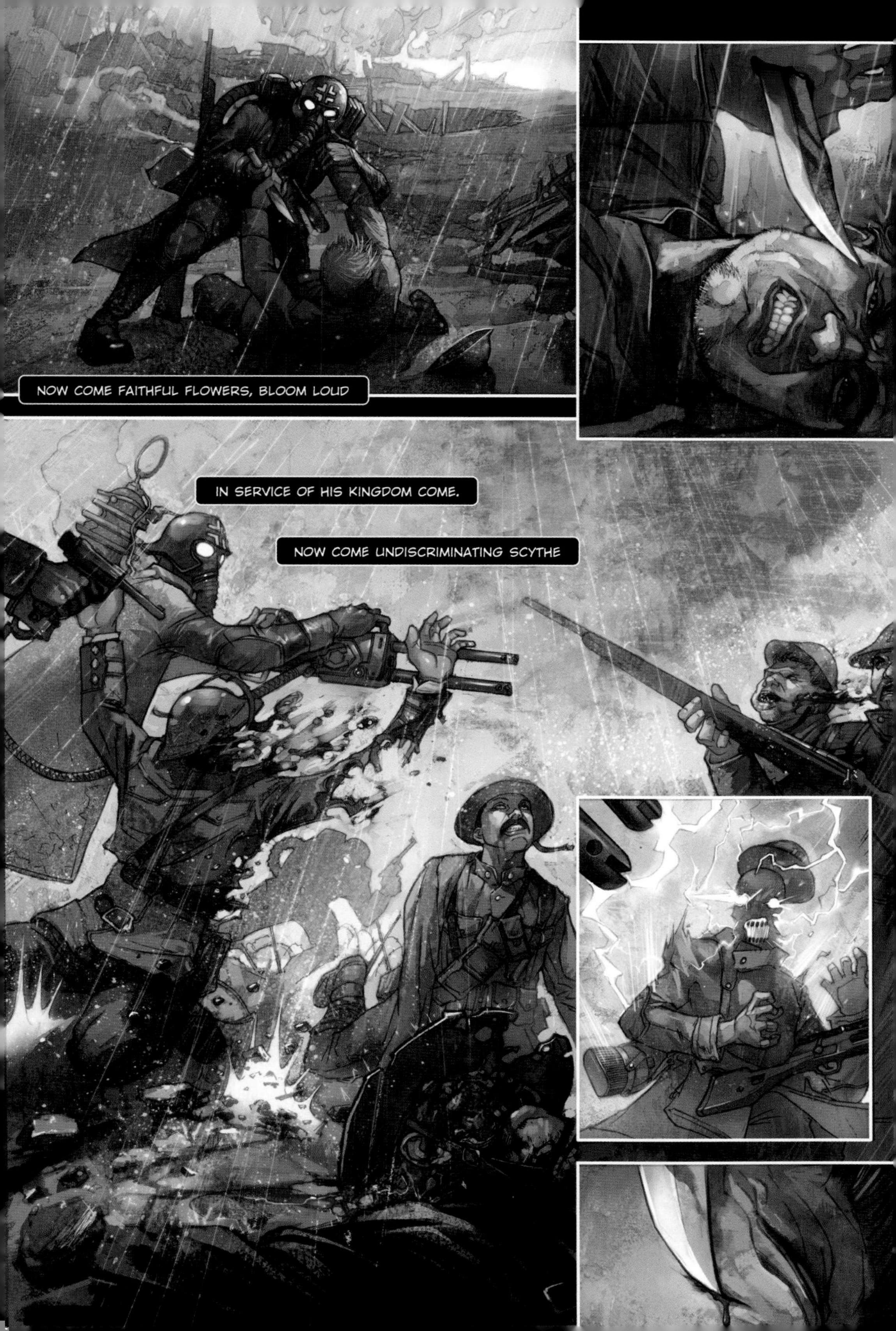
NOW COME FAITHFUL FLOWERS, BLOOM LOUD
IN SERVICE OF HIS KINGDOM COME.
NOW COME UNDISCRIMINATING SCYTHE

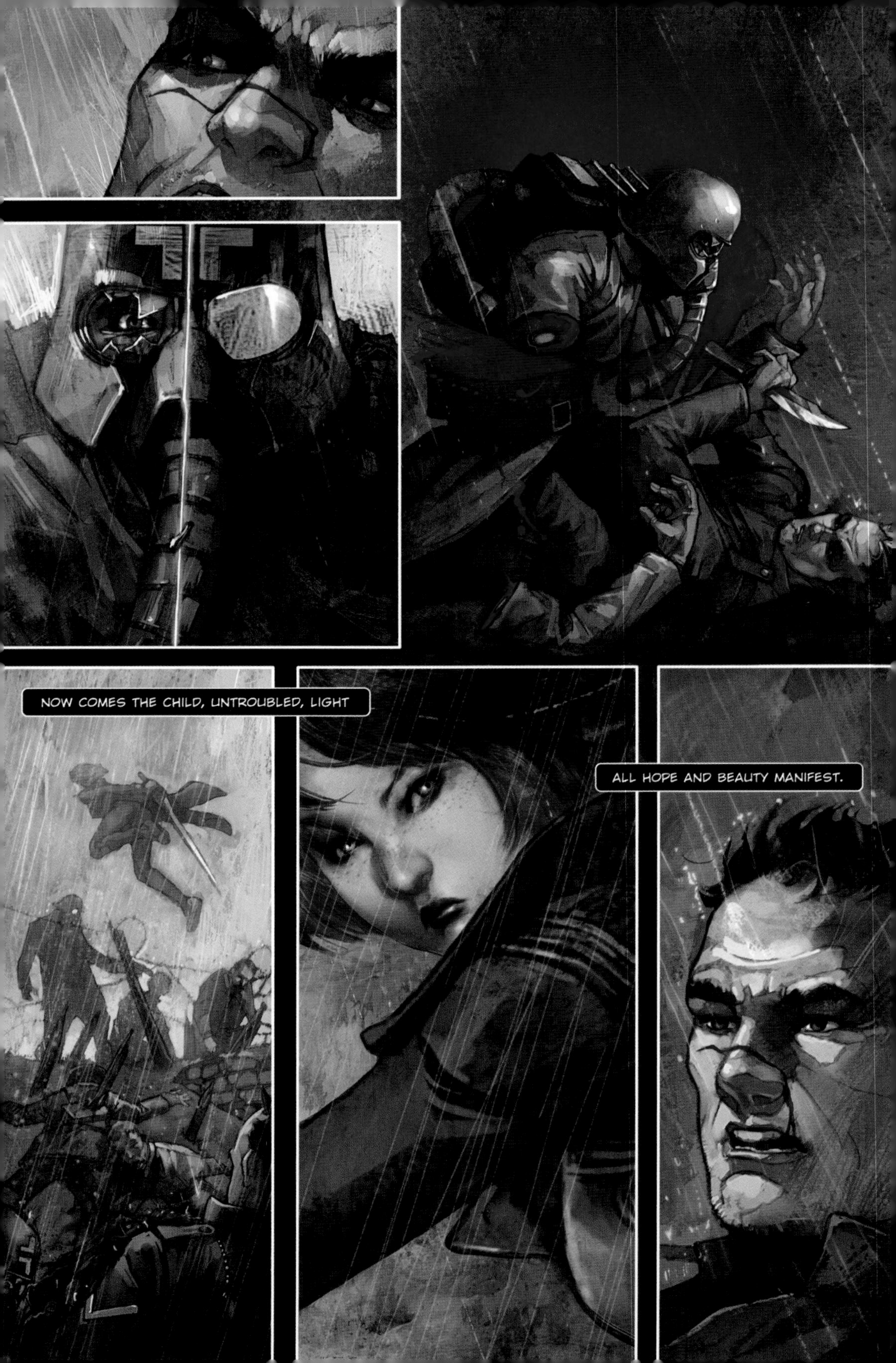
NOW COMES THE CHILD, UNTROUBLED, LIGHT
ALL HOPE AND BEAUTY MANIFEST.

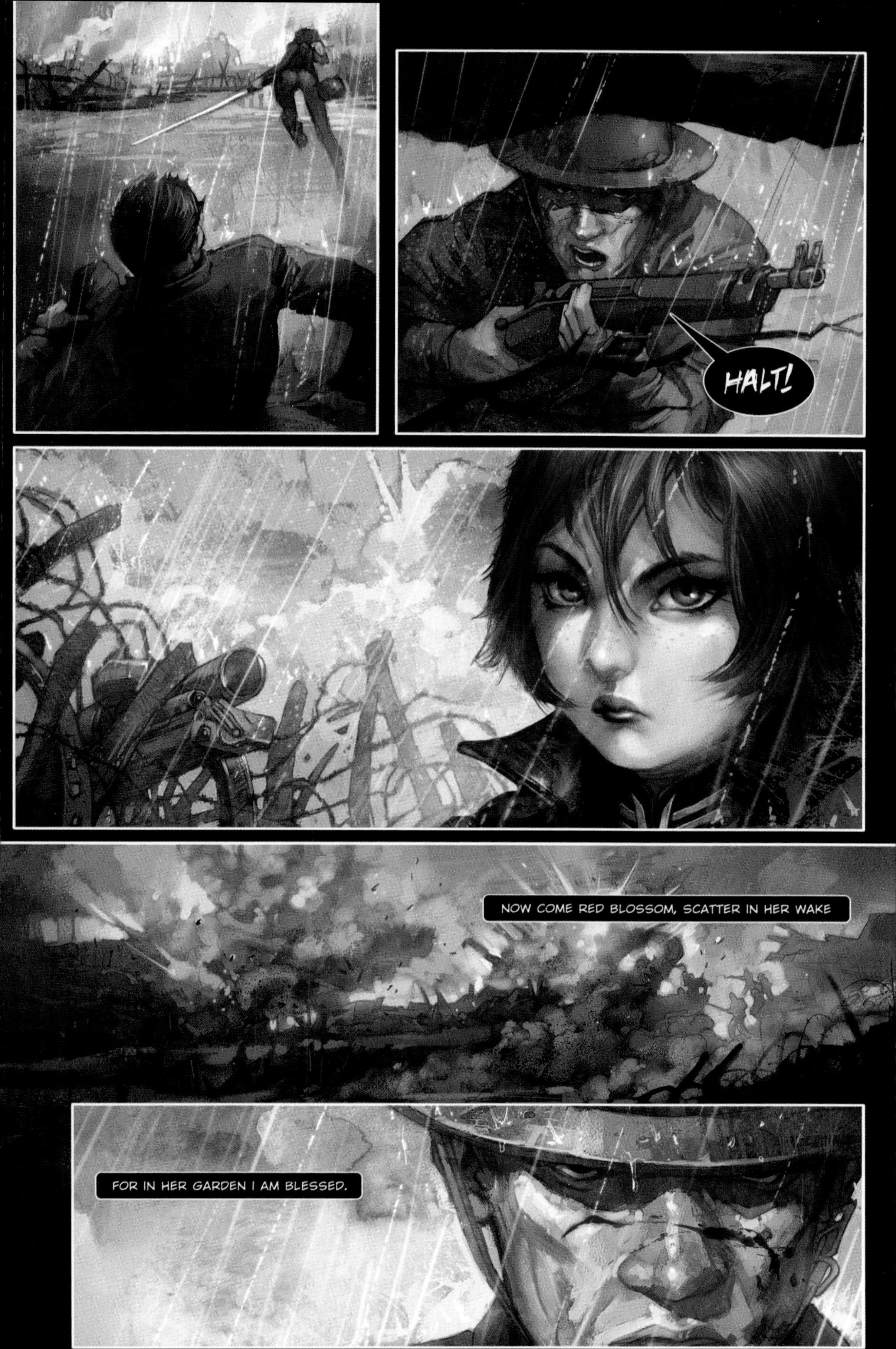
HALT!
NOW COME RED BLOSSOM, SCATTER IN HER WAKE
FOR IN HER GARDEN I AM BLESSED.

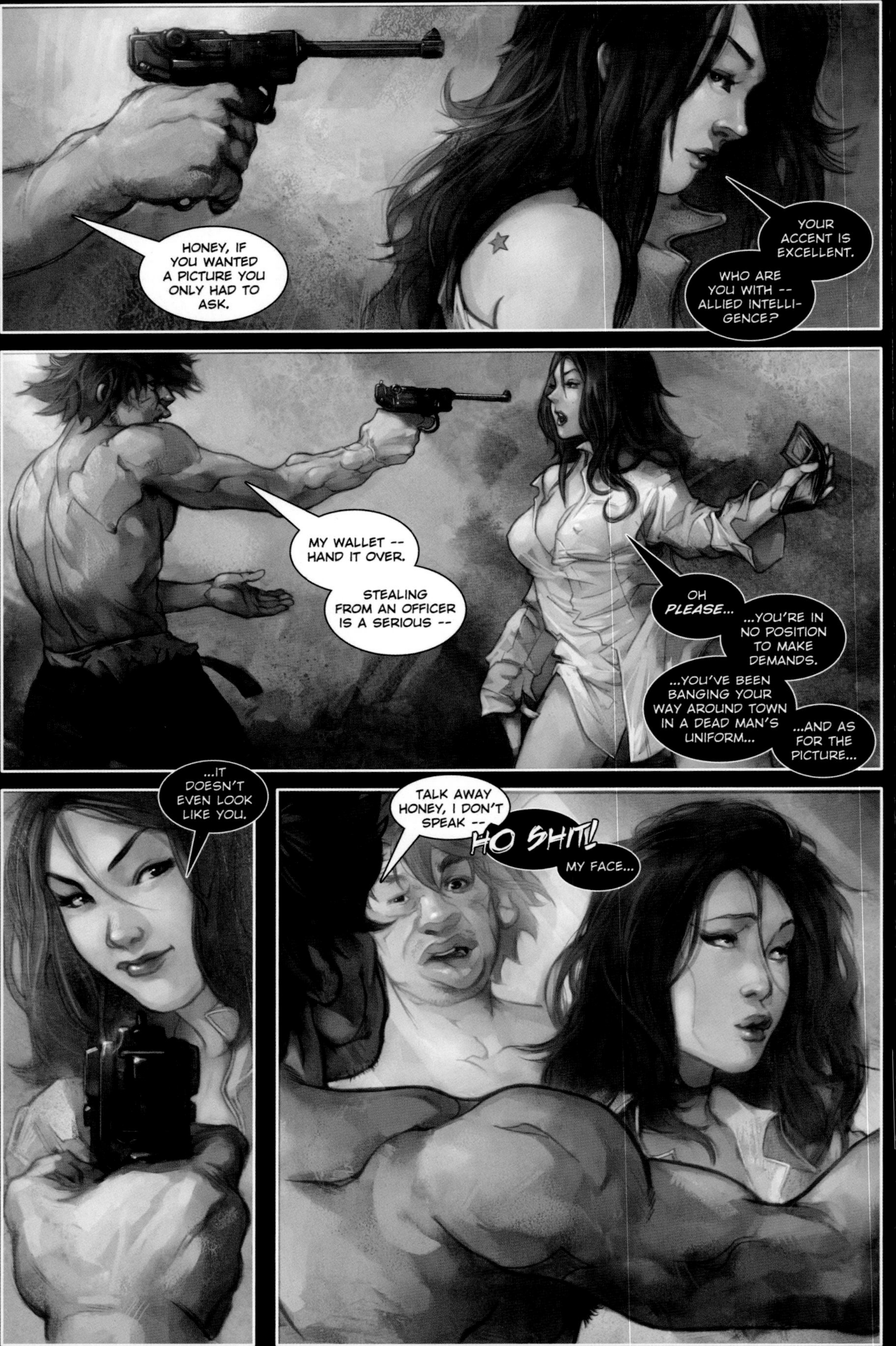
HONEY, IF YOU WANTED A PICTURE YOU ONLY HAD TO ASK.
YOUR ACCENT IS EXCELLENT.
WHO ARE YOU WITH -- ALLIED INTELLI-GENCE?
MY WALLET -- HAND IT OVER.
STEALING FROM AN OFFICER IS A SERIOUS --
OH *PLEASE*...
...YOU'RE IN NO POSITION TO MAKE DEMANDS.
...YOU'VE BEEN BANGING YOUR WAY AROUND TOWN IN A DEAD MAN'S UNIFORM...
...AND AS FOR THE PICTURE...
...IT DOESN'T EVEN LOOK LIKE YOU.
TALK AWAY HONEY, I DON'T SPEAK --
HO SHIT!
MY FACE...

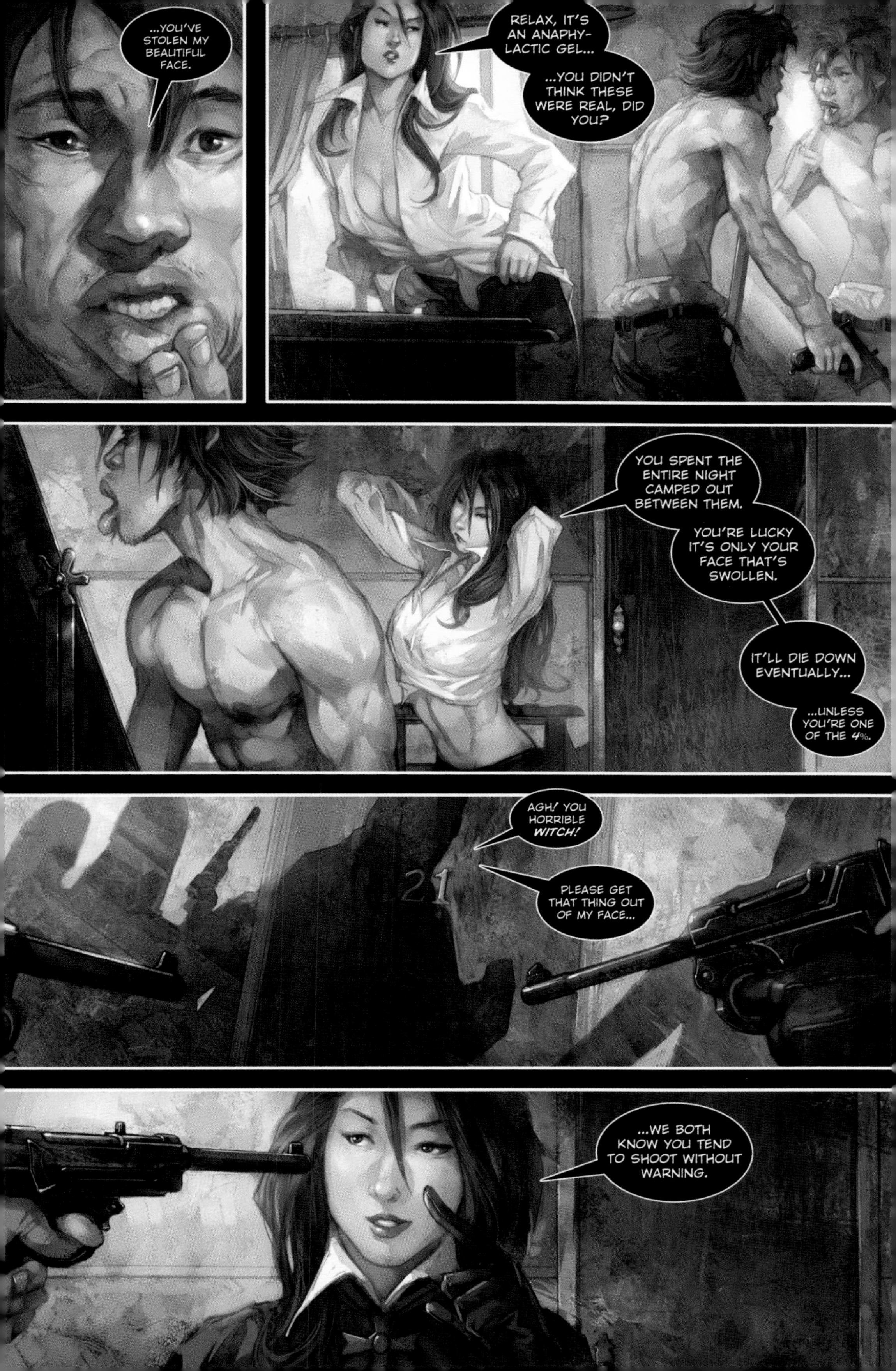
...YOU'VE STOLEN MY BEAUTIFUL FACE.
RELAX, IT'S AN ANAPHY-LACTIC GEL...
...YOU DIDN'T THINK THESE WERE REAL, DID YOU?
YOU SPENT THE ENTIRE NIGHT CAMPED OUT BETWEEN THEM.
YOU'RE LUCKY IT'S ONLY YOUR FACE THAT'S SWOLLEN.
IT'LL DIE DOWN EVENTUALLY...
...UNLESS YOU'RE ONE OF THE 4%.
AGH! YOU HORRIBLE *WITCH!*
21
PLEASE GET THAT THING OUT OF MY FACE...
...WE BOTH KNOW YOU TEND TO SHOOT WITHOUT WARNING.

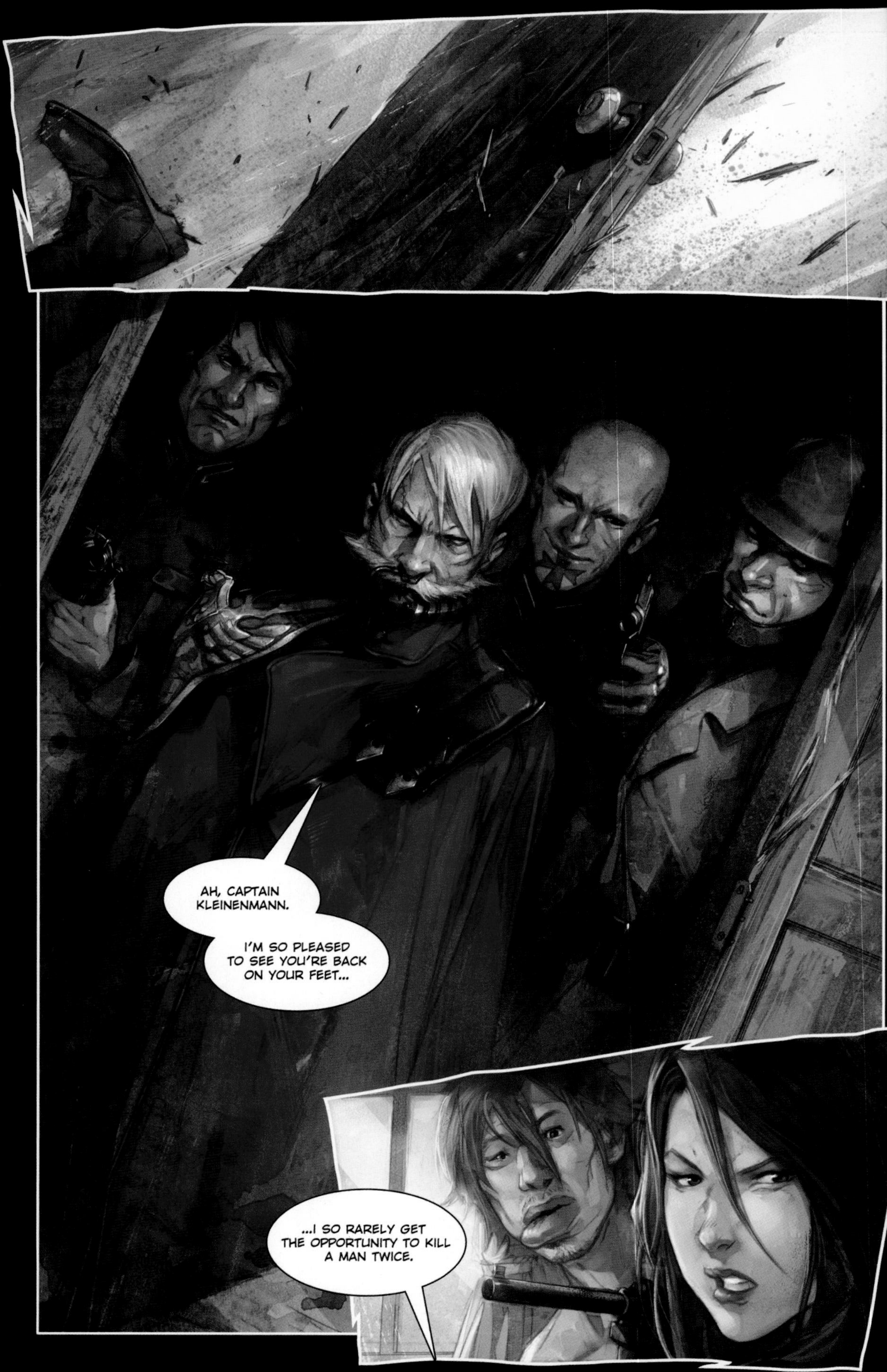
AH, CAPTAIN KLEINENMANN.
I'M SO PLEASED TO SEE YOU'RE BACK ON YOUR FEET...
...I SO RARELY GET THE OPPORTUNITY TO KILL A MAN TWICE.

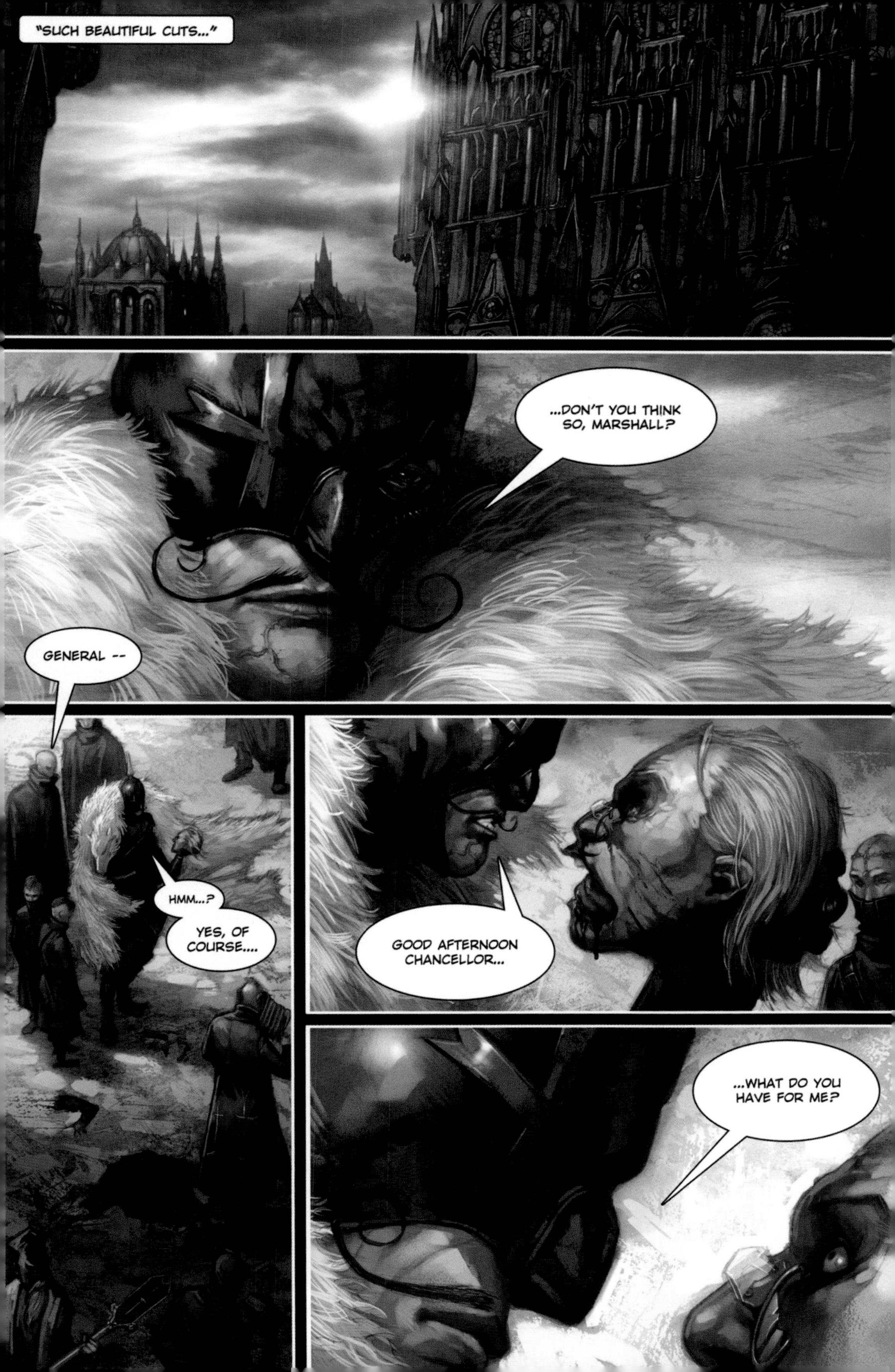
"SUCH BEAUTIFUL CUTS..."
...DON'T YOU THINK SO, MARSHALL?
GENERAL --
HMM...?
YES, OF COURSE....
GOOD AFTERNOON CHANCELLOR...
...WHAT DO YOU HAVE FOR ME?

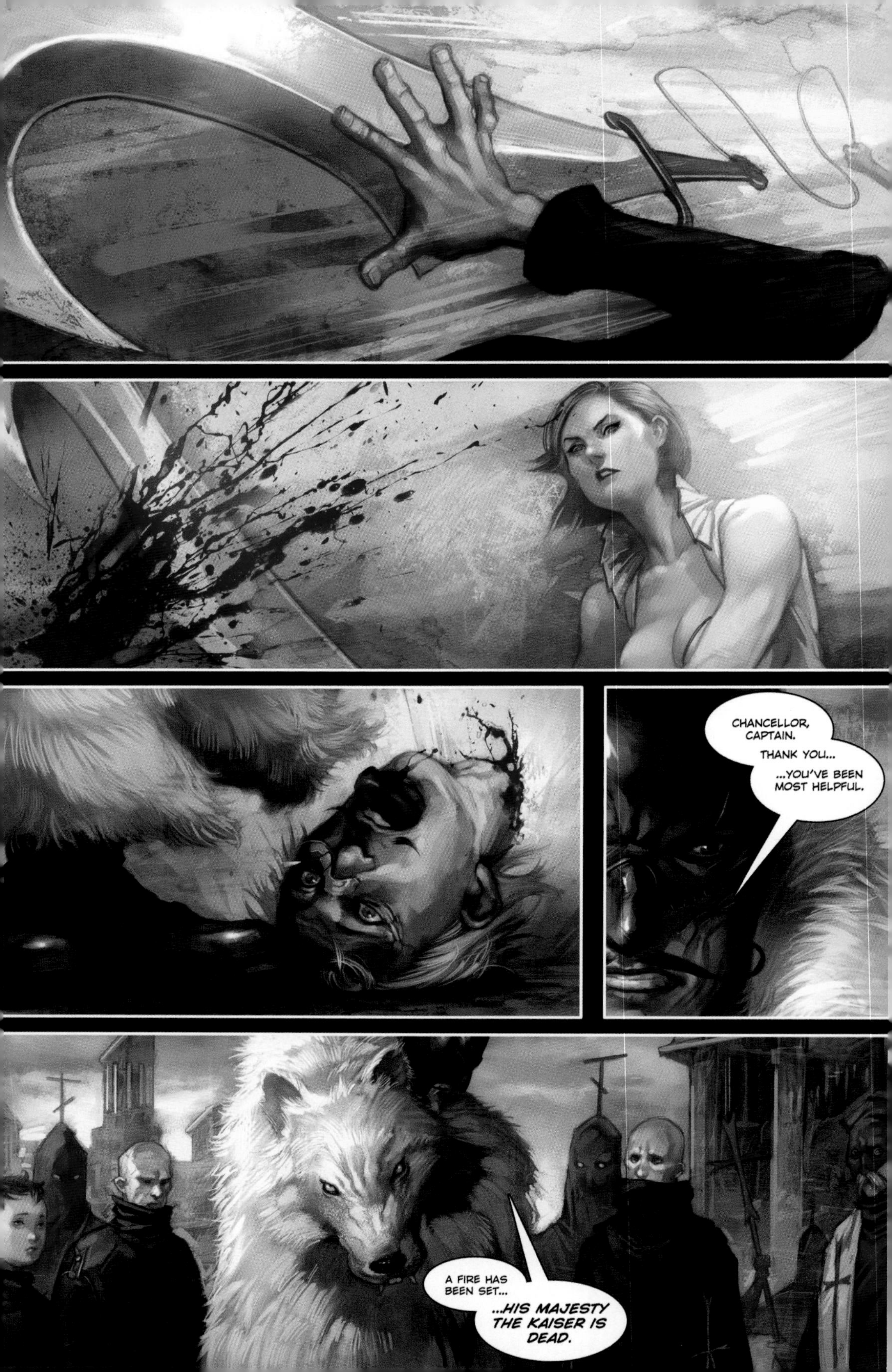
CHANCELLOR, CAPTAIN.
THANK YOU...
...YOU'VE BEEN MOST HELPFUL.
A FIRE HAS BEEN SET...
...HIS MAJESTY THE KAISER IS DEAD.

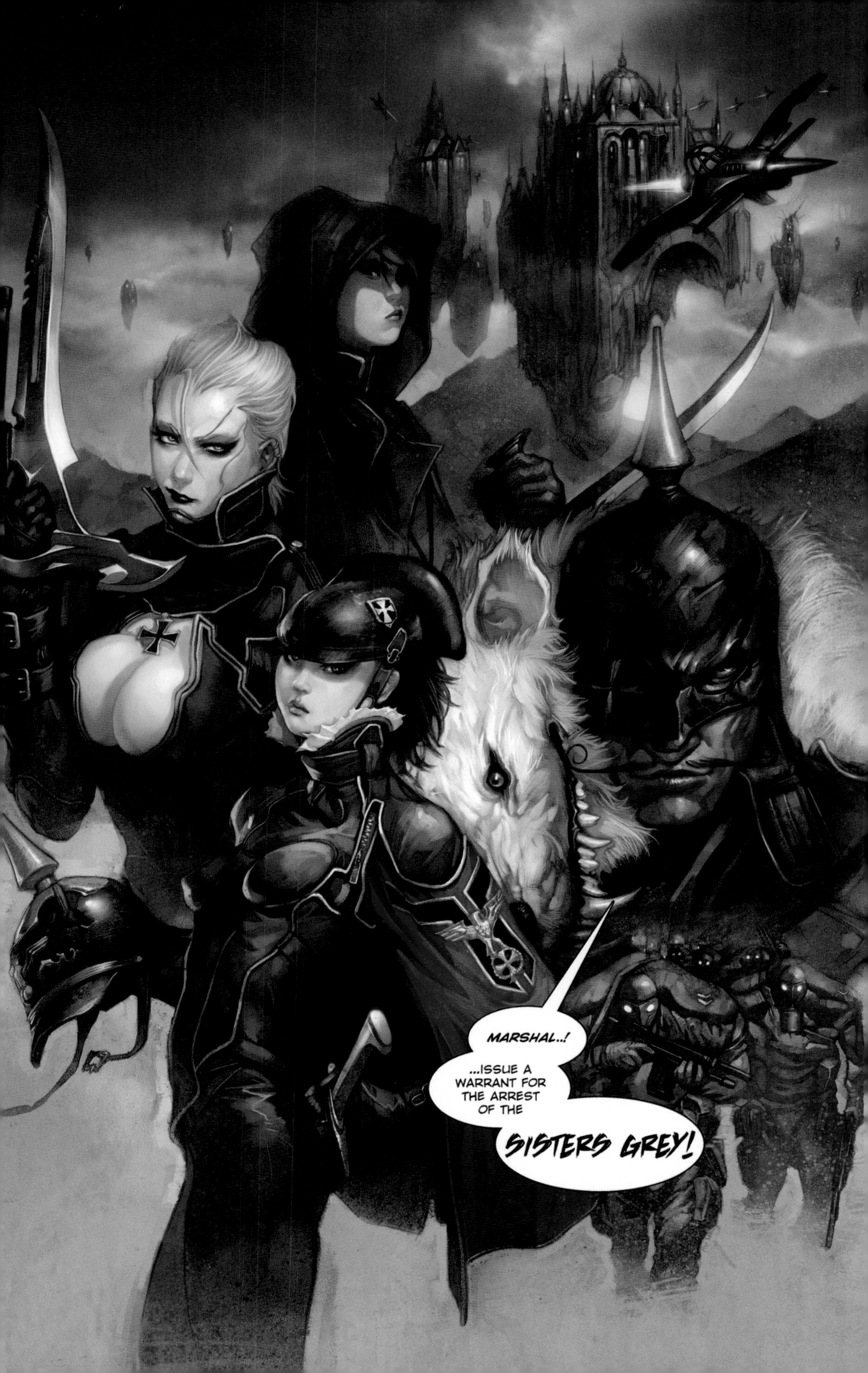
MARSHAL..!
...ISSUE A WARRANT FOR THE ARREST OF THE
SISTERS GREY!

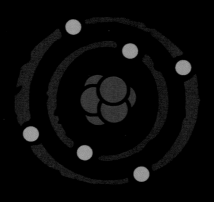

II

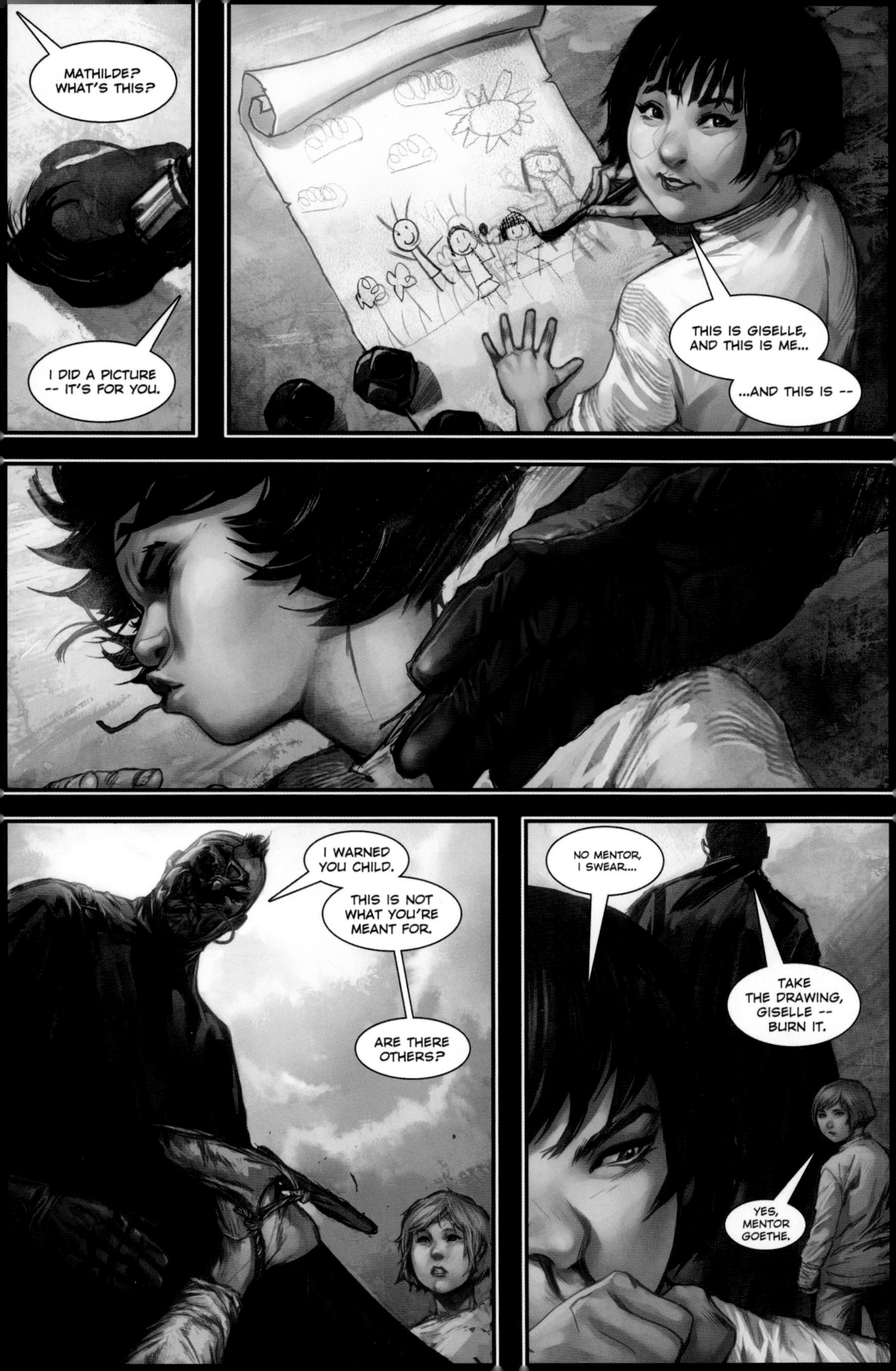
MATHILDE? WHAT'S THIS?
I DID A PICTURE -- IT'S FOR YOU.
THIS IS GISELLE, AND THIS IS ME...
...AND THIS IS --
I WARNED YOU CHILD.
THIS IS NOT WHAT YOU'RE MEANT FOR.
ARE THERE OTHERS?
NO MENTOR, I SWEAR...
TAKE THE DRAWING, GISELLE -- BURN IT.
YES, MENTOR GOETHE.

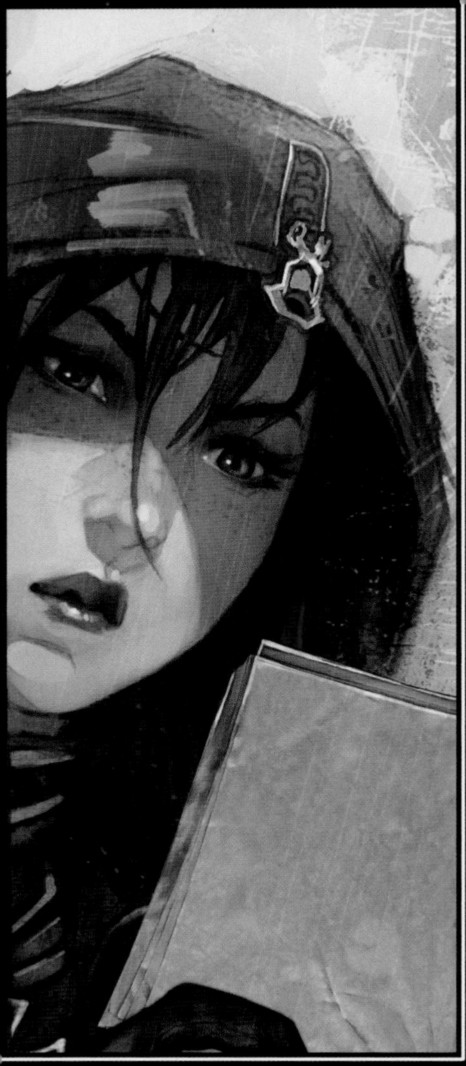
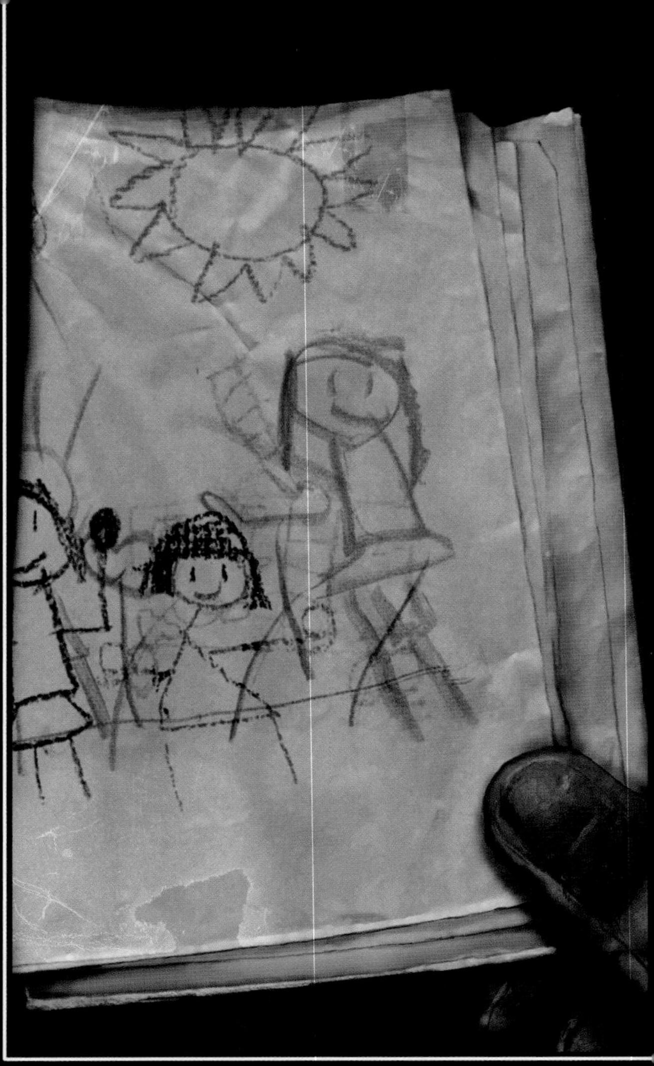
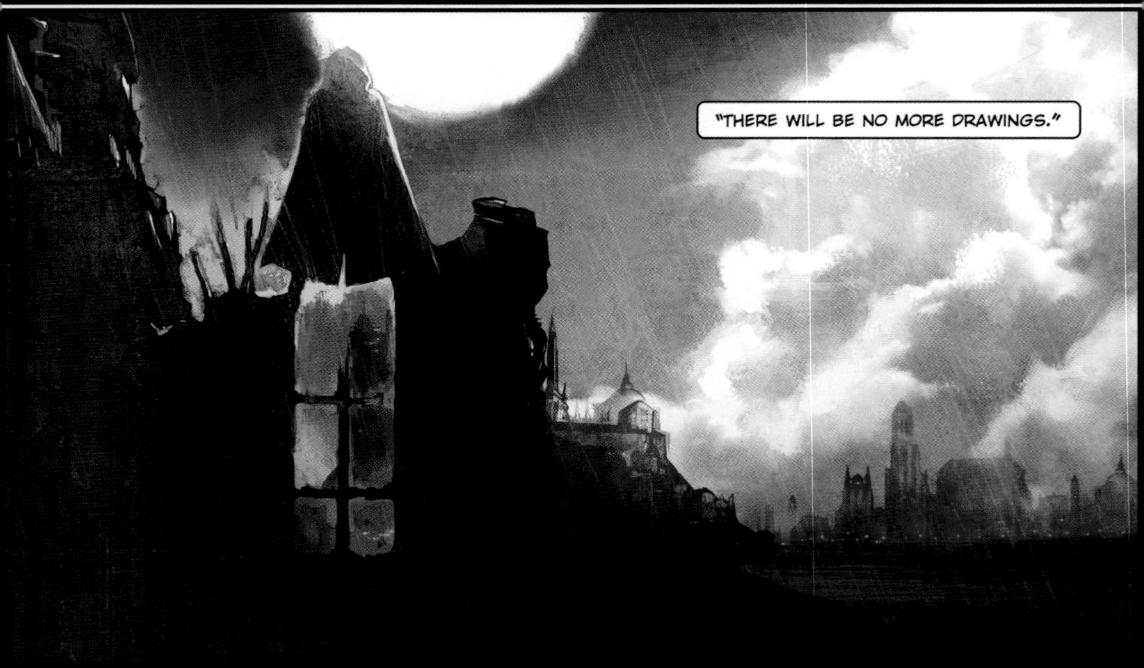
"THERE WILL BE NO MORE DRAWINGS."

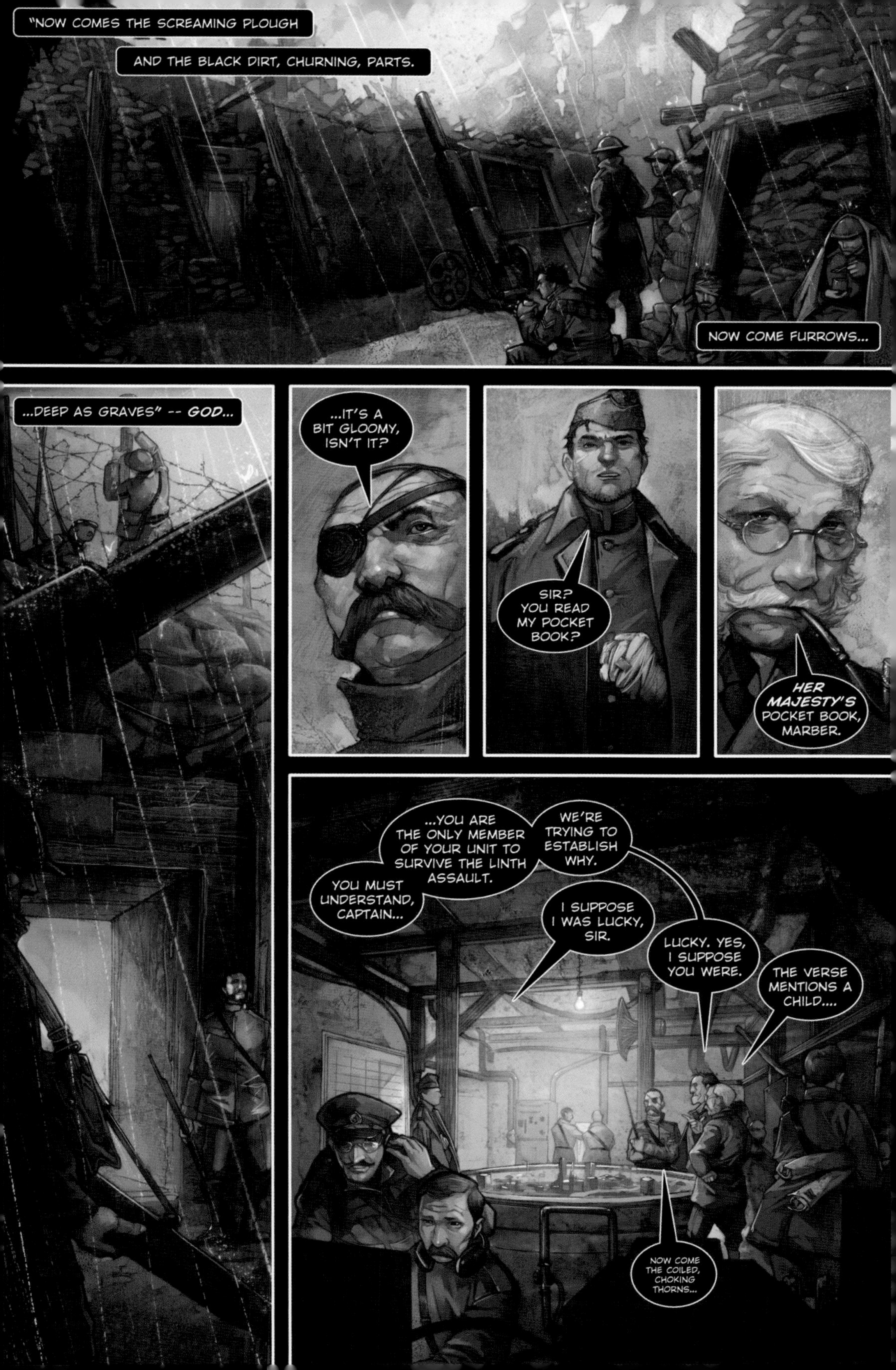
"NOW COMES THE SCREAMING PLOUGH
AND THE BLACK DIRT, CHURNING, PARTS.
NOW COME FURROWS...
...DEEP AS GRAVES" -- GOD...
...IT'S A BIT GLOOMY, ISN'T IT?
SIR? YOU READ MY POCKET BOOK?
HER MAJESTY'S POCKET BOOK, MARBER.
YOU MUST UNDERSTAND, CAPTAIN...
...YOU ARE THE ONLY MEMBER OF YOUR UNIT TO SURVIVE THE LINTH ASSAULT.
WE'RE TRYING TO ESTABLISH WHY.
I SUPPOSE I WAS LUCKY, SIR.
LUCKY. YES, I SUPPOSE YOU WERE.
THE VERSE MENTIONS A CHILD....
NOW COME THE COILED, CHOKING THORNS...

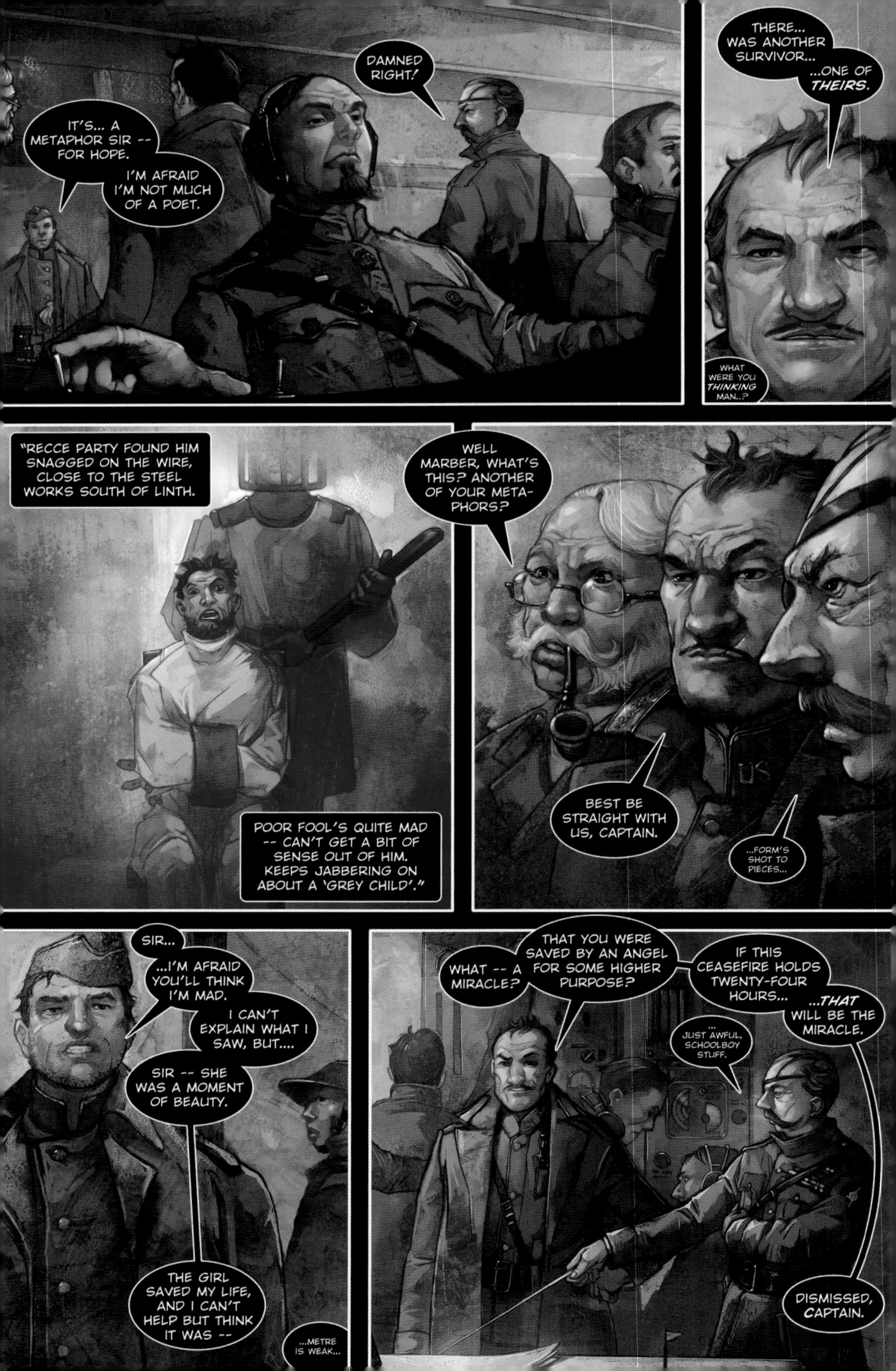

IT'S... A METAPHOR SIR -- FOR HOPE.
I'M AFRAID I'M NOT MUCH OF A POET.
DAMNED RIGHT!
THERE... WAS ANOTHER SURVIVOR...
...ONE OF *THEIRS*.
WHAT WERE YOU *THINKING* MAN..?
"RECCE PARTY FOUND HIM SNAGGED ON THE WIRE, CLOSE TO THE STEEL WORKS SOUTH OF LINTH.
POOR FOOL'S QUITE MAD -- CAN'T GET A BIT OF SENSE OUT OF HIM. KEEPS JABBERING ON ABOUT A 'GREY CHILD'."
WELL MARBER, WHAT'S THIS? ANOTHER OF YOUR META-PHORS?
BEST BE STRAIGHT WITH US, CAPTAIN.
...FORM'S SHOT TO PIECES...
SIR...
...I'M AFRAID YOU'LL THINK I'M MAD.
I CAN'T EXPLAIN WHAT I SAW, BUT....
SIR -- SHE WAS A MOMENT OF BEAUTY.
THE GIRL SAVED MY LIFE, AND I CAN'T HELP BUT THINK IT WAS --
...METRE IS WEAK...
WHAT -- A MIRACLE?
THAT YOU WERE SAVED BY AN ANGEL FOR SOME HIGHER PURPOSE?
IF THIS CEASEFIRE HOLDS TWENTY-FOUR HOURS...
...*THAT* WILL BE THE MIRACLE.
...JUST AWFUL, SCHOOLBOY STUFF.
DISMISSED, CAPTAIN.

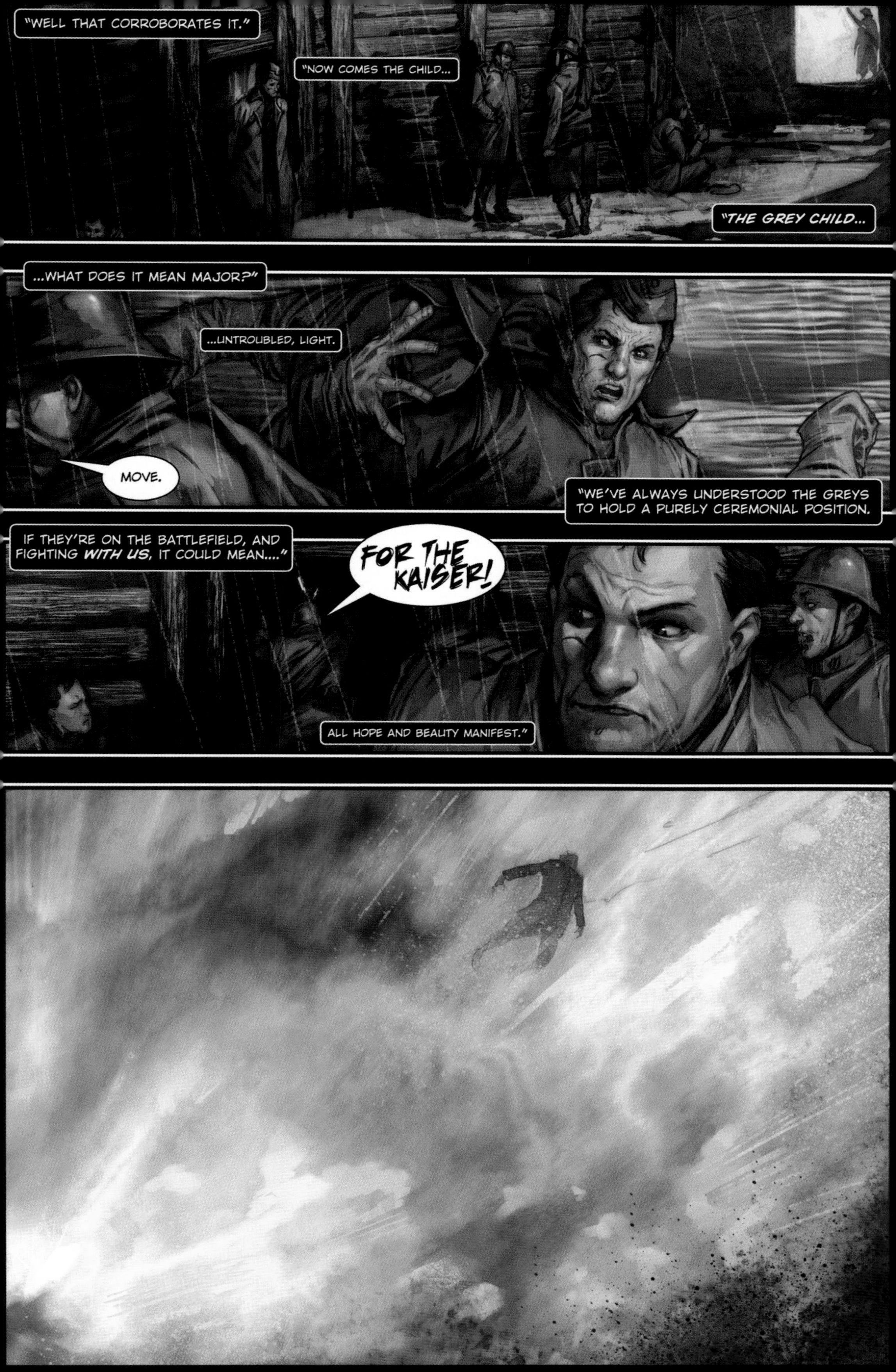
"WELL THAT CORROBORATES IT."
"NOW COMES THE CHILD...
"THE GREY CHILD...
...WHAT DOES IT MEAN MAJOR?"
...UNTROUBLED, LIGHT.
MOVE.
"WE'VE ALWAYS UNDERSTOOD THE GREYS TO HOLD A PURELY CEREMONIAL POSITION.
IF THEY'RE ON THE BATTLEFIELD, AND FIGHTING ***WITH US***, IT COULD MEAN...."
FOR THE KAISER!
ALL HOPE AND BEAUTY MANIFEST."

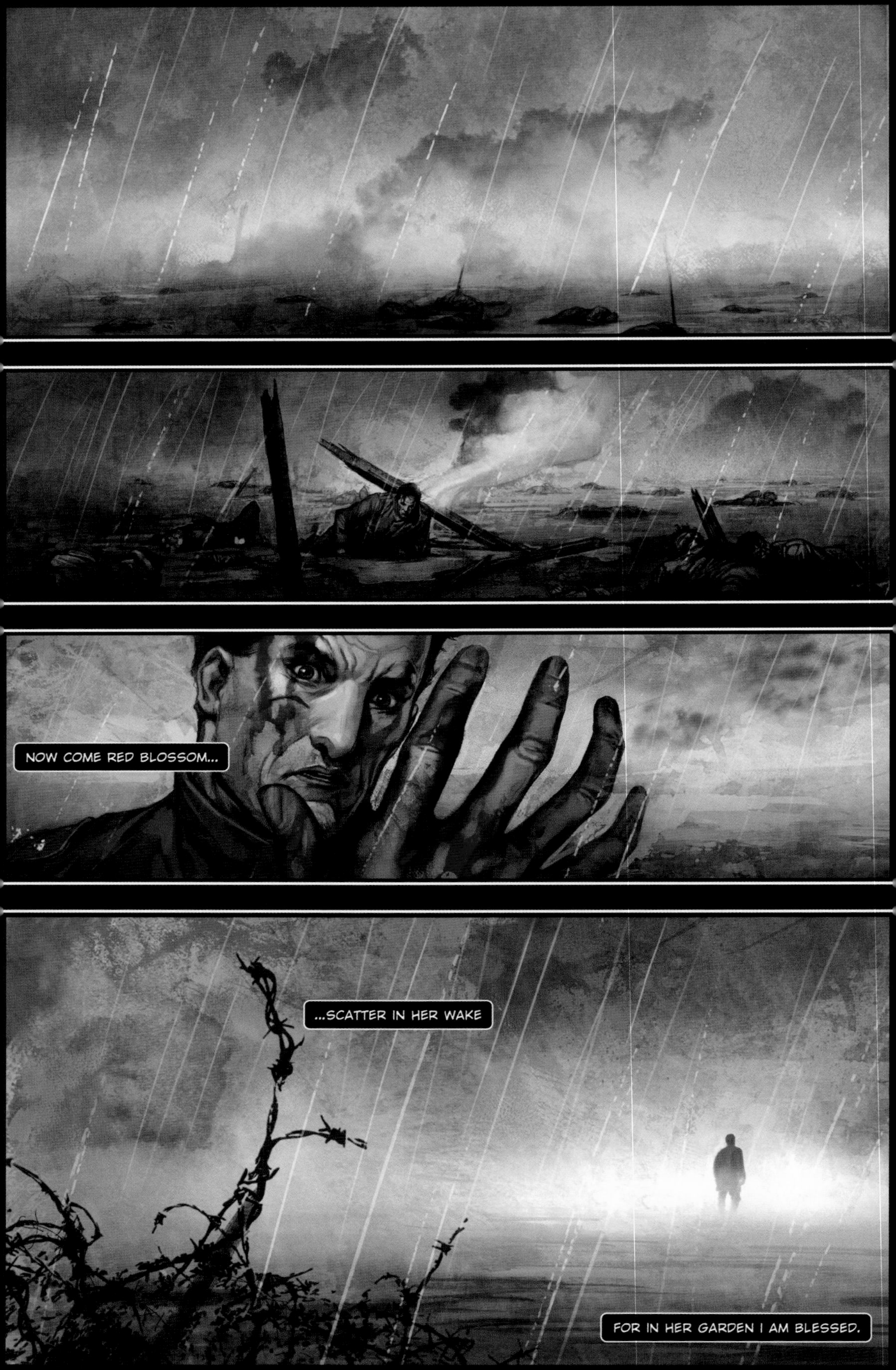
NOW COME RED BLOSSOM...
...SCATTER IN HER WAKE
FOR IN HER GARDEN I AM BLESSED.

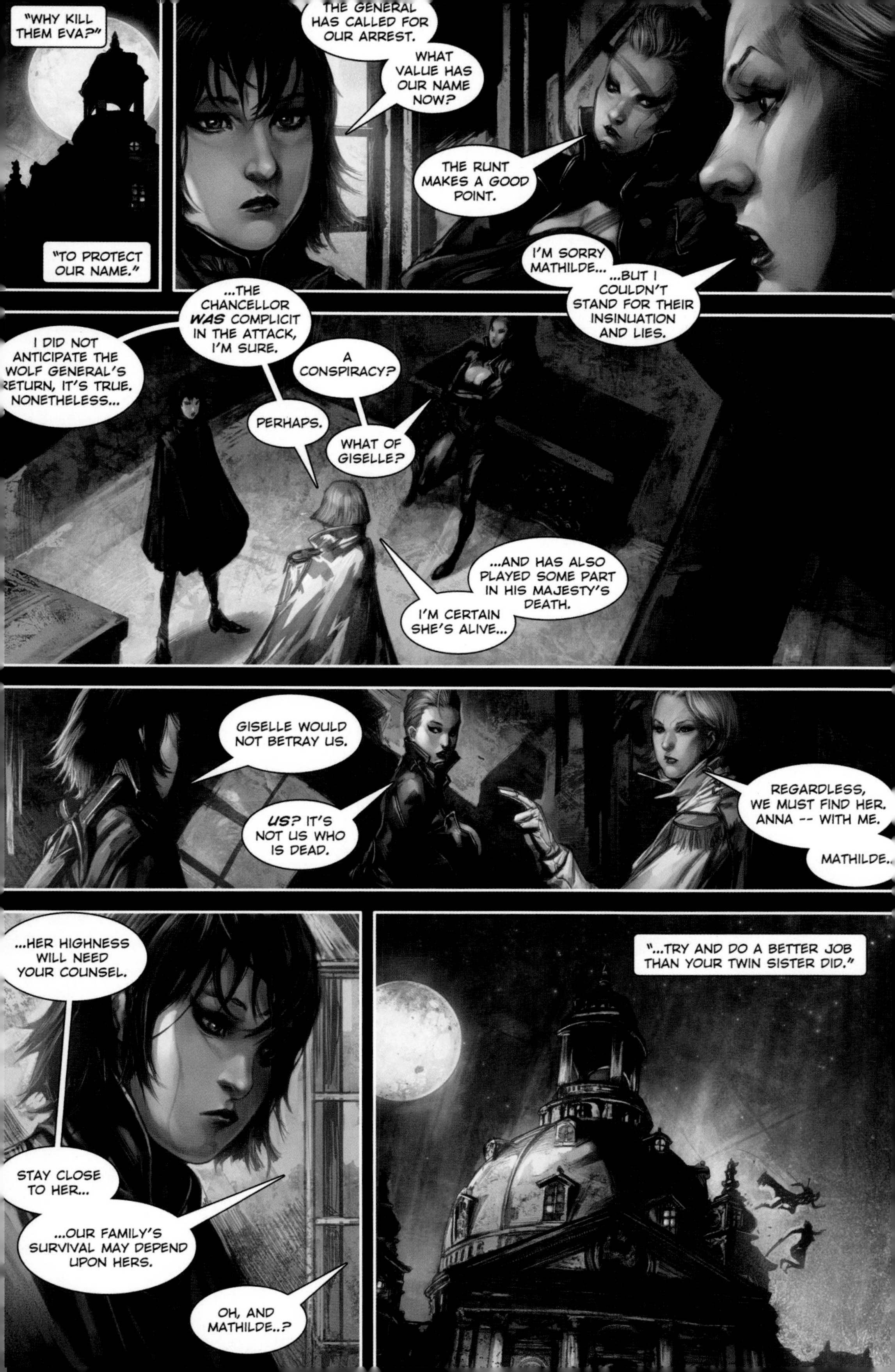

"WHY KILL THEM EVA?"
"TO PROTECT OUR NAME."
THE GENERAL HAS CALLED FOR OUR ARREST.
WHAT VALUE HAS OUR NAME NOW?
THE RUNT MAKES A GOOD POINT.
I'M SORRY MATHILDE...
...BUT I COULDN'T STAND FOR THEIR INSINUATION AND LIES.
I DID NOT ANTICIPATE THE WOLF GENERAL'S RETURN, IT'S TRUE. NONETHELESS...
...THE CHANCELLOR WAS COMPLICIT IN THE ATTACK, I'M SURE.
A CONSPIRACY?
PERHAPS.
WHAT OF GISELLE?
I'M CERTAIN SHE'S ALIVE...
...AND HAS ALSO PLAYED SOME PART IN HIS MAJESTY'S DEATH.
GISELLE WOULD NOT BETRAY US.
US? IT'S NOT US WHO IS DEAD.
REGARDLESS, WE MUST FIND HER. ANNA -- WITH ME.
MATHILDE..
...HER HIGHNESS WILL NEED YOUR COUNSEL.
STAY CLOSE TO HER...
...OUR FAMILY'S SURVIVAL MAY DEPEND UPON HERS.
OH, AND MATHILDE..?
"...TRY AND DO A BETTER JOB THAN YOUR TWIN SISTER DID."

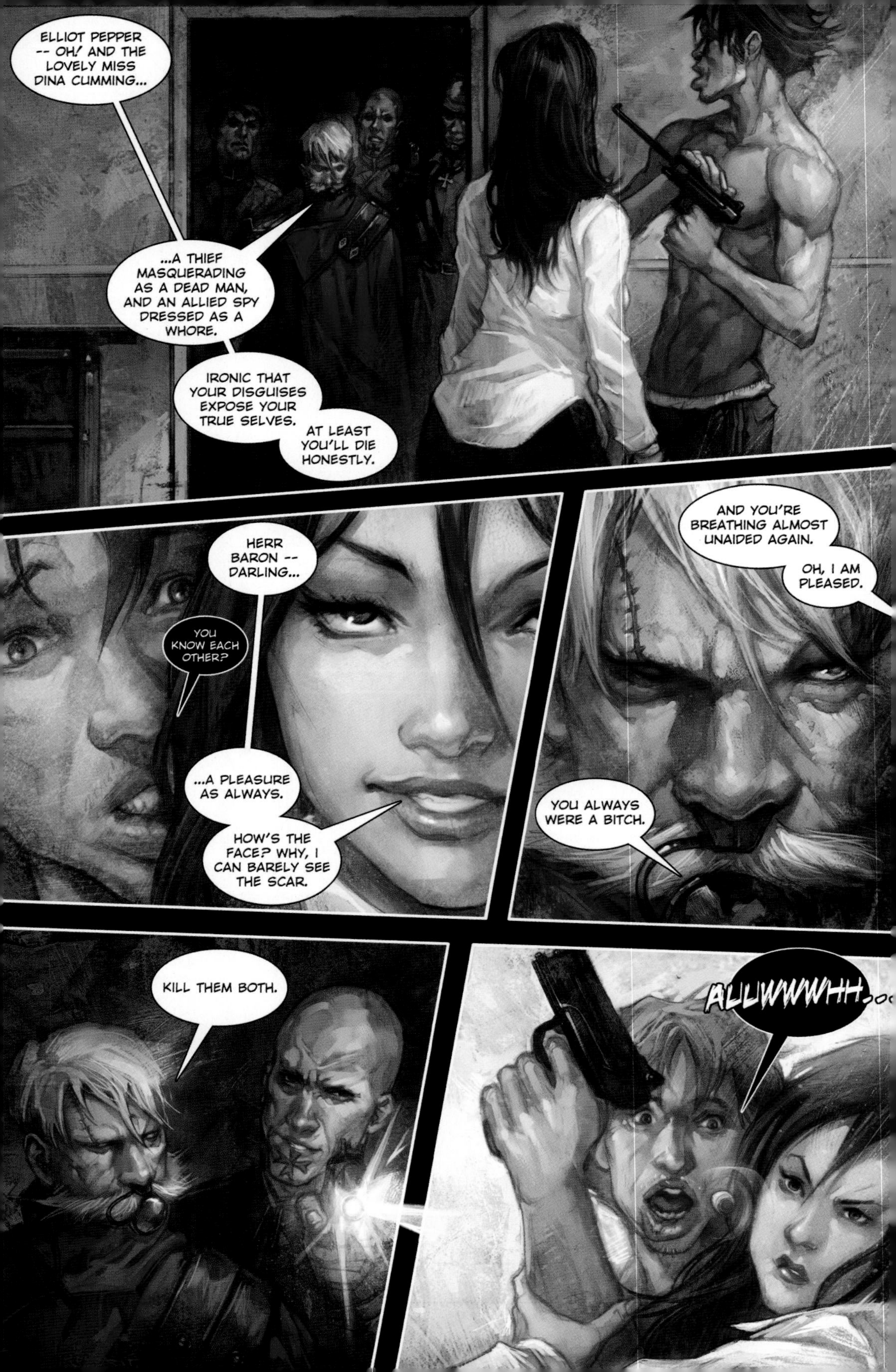
ELLIOT PEPPER -- OH! AND THE LOVELY MISS DINA CUMMING...
...A THIEF MASQUERADING AS A DEAD MAN, AND AN ALLIED SPY DRESSED AS A WHORE.
IRONIC THAT YOUR DISGUISES EXPOSE YOUR TRUE SELVES.
AT LEAST YOU'LL DIE HONESTLY.
HERR BARON -- DARLING...
YOU KNOW EACH OTHER?
...A PLEASURE AS ALWAYS.
HOW'S THE FACE? WHY, I CAN BARELY SEE THE SCAR.
AND YOU'RE BREATHING ALMOST UNAIDED AGAIN.
OH, I AM PLEASED.
YOU ALWAYS WERE A BITCH.
KILL THEM BOTH.
AUUWWWHH...

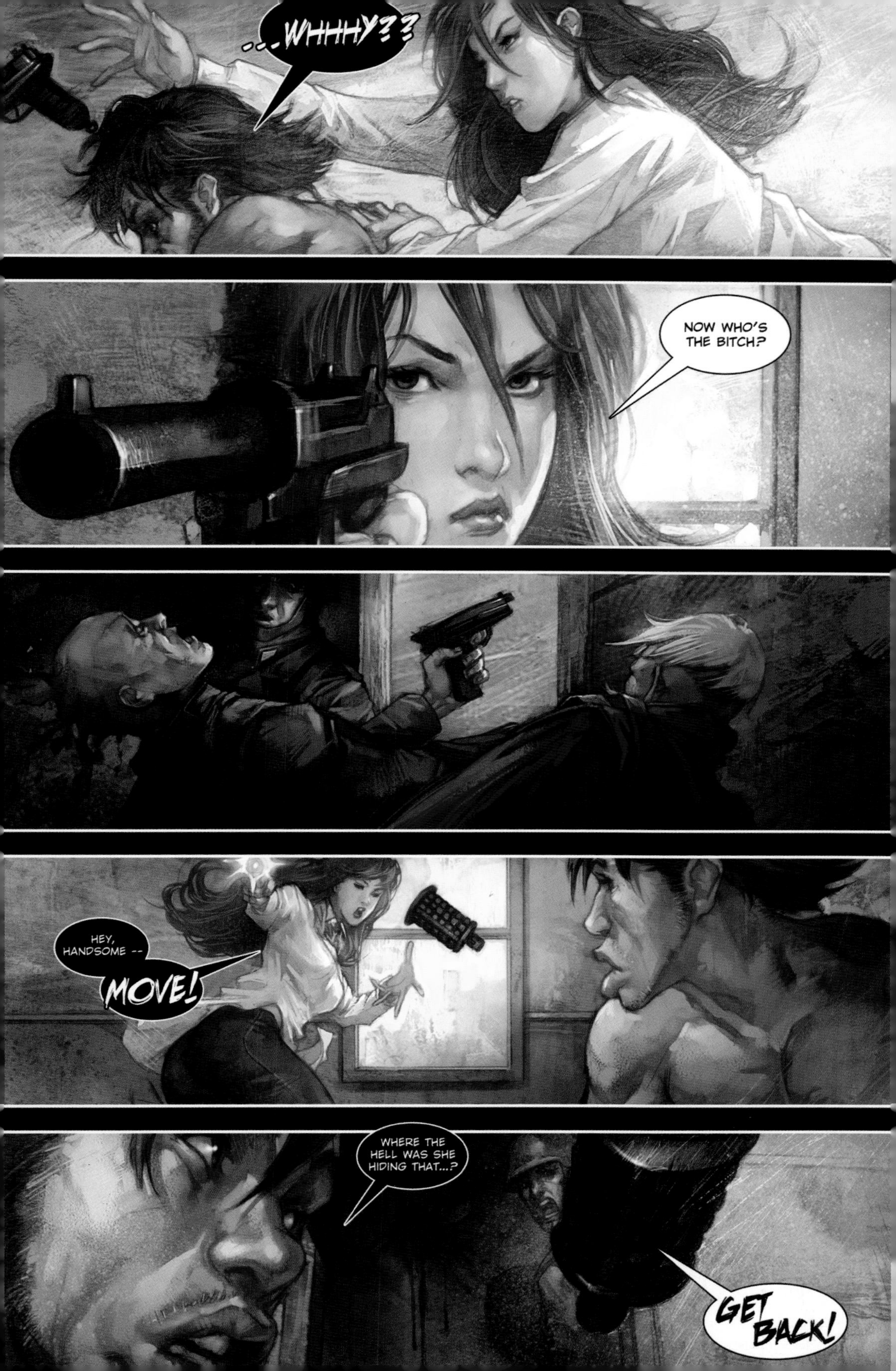
...WHHHY???
NOW WHO'S THE BITCH?
HEY, HANDSOME --
MOVE!
WHERE THE HELL WAS SHE HIDING THAT...?
GET BACK!

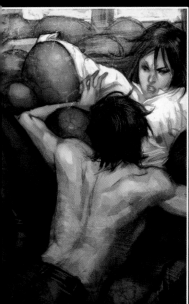

DON'T SAY IT.

GAH!

CLINGY, AIN'T HE?

FORMER CLIENT?

HUSBAND.

BUH?

LATER.

CAN'T WAIT.

C'MON GIRL, MOVE YOUR...

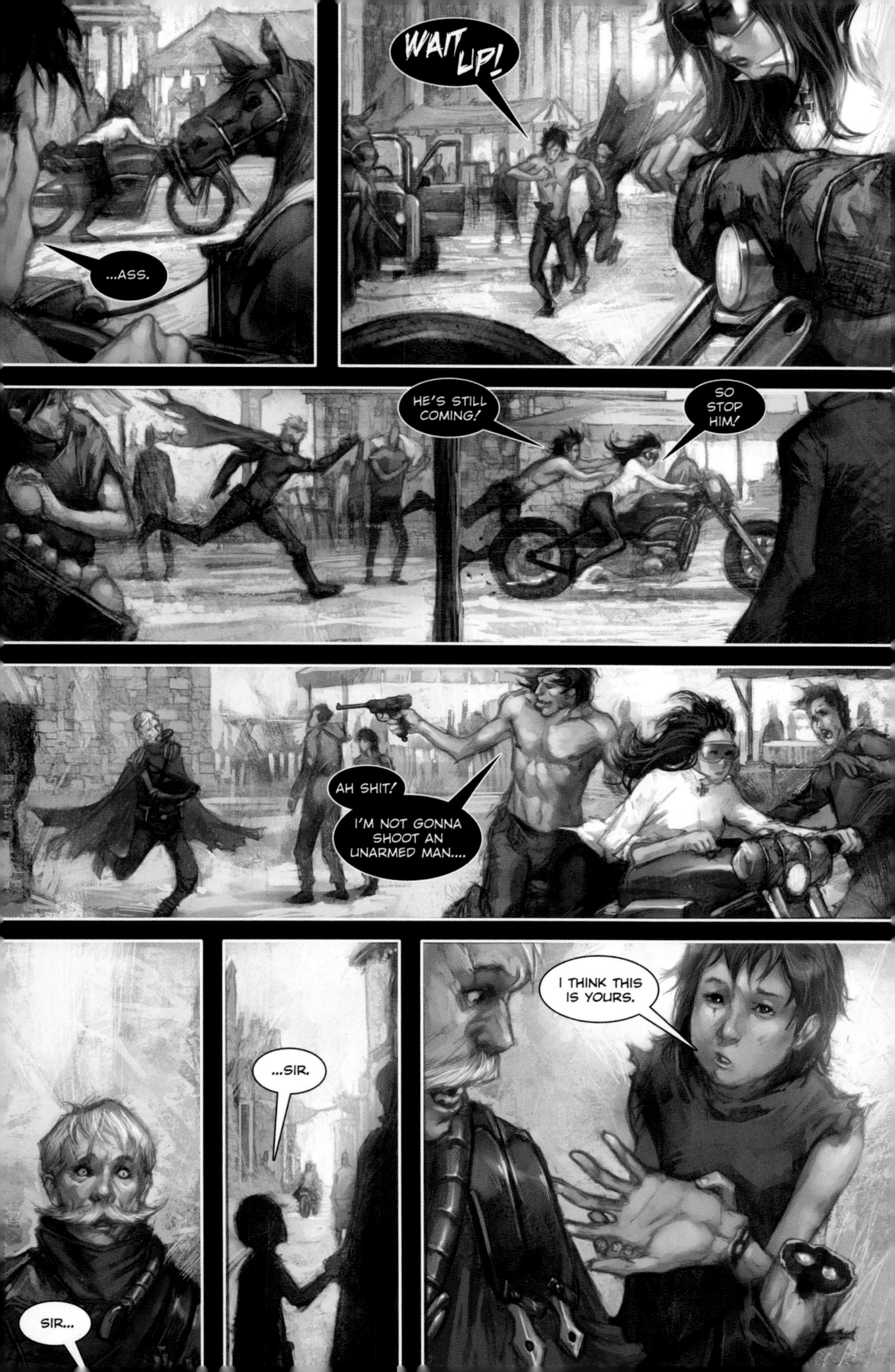
...ASS.
WAIT UP!
HE'S STILL COMING!
SO STOP HIM!
AH SHIT!
I'M NOT GONNA SHOOT AN UNARMED MAN....
SIR...
...SIR.
I THINK THIS IS YOURS.

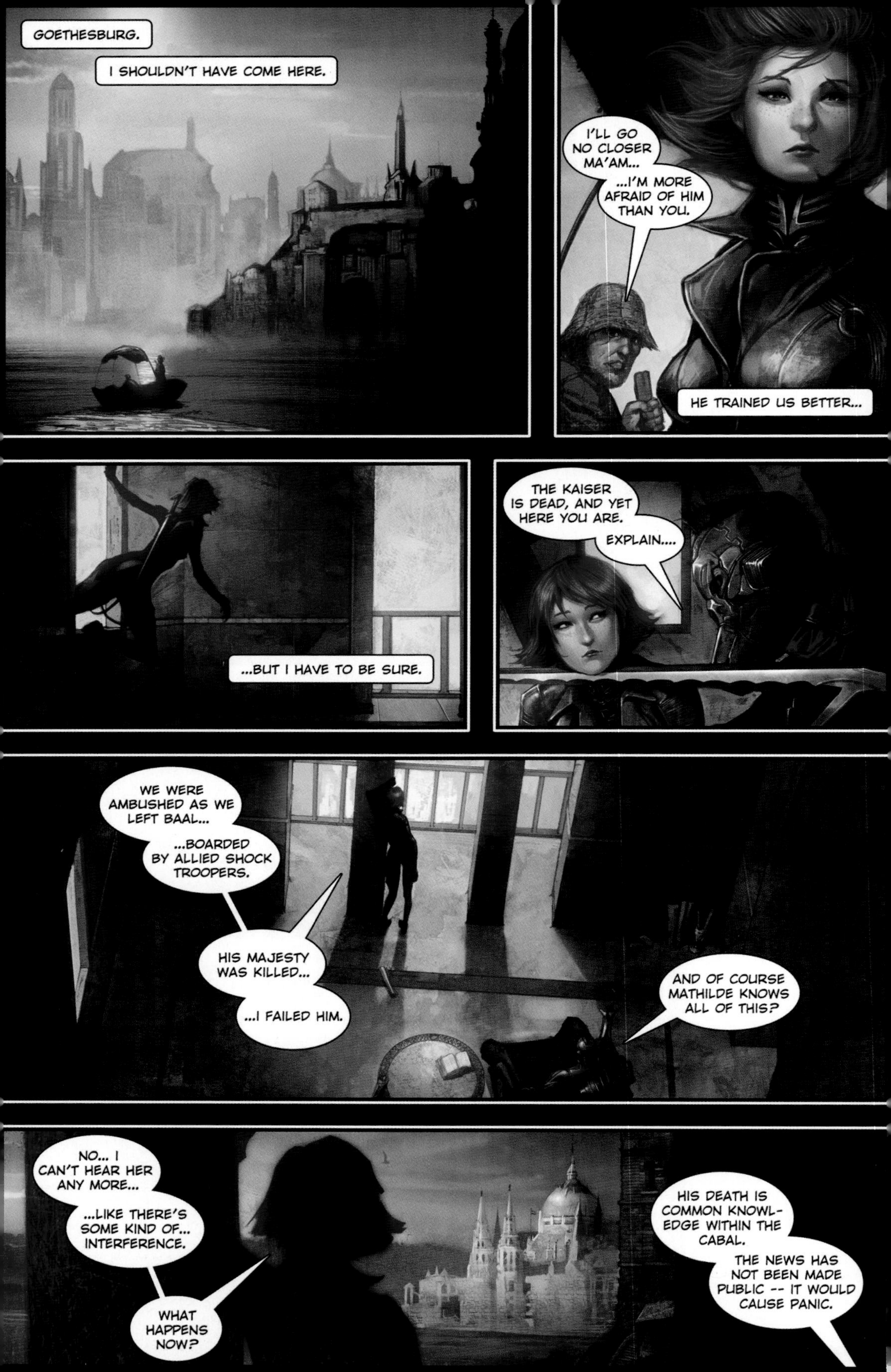
GOETHESBURG.
I SHOULDN'T HAVE COME HERE.
I'LL GO NO CLOSER MA'AM...
...I'M MORE AFRAID OF HIM THAN YOU.
HE TRAINED US BETTER...
...BUT I HAVE TO BE SURE.
THE KAISER IS DEAD, AND YET HERE YOU ARE.
EXPLAIN....
WE WERE AMBUSHED AS WE LEFT BAAL...
...BOARDED BY ALLIED SHOCK TROOPERS.
HIS MAJESTY WAS KILLED...
...I FAILED HIM.
AND OF COURSE MATHILDE KNOWS ALL OF THIS?
NO... I CAN'T HEAR HER ANY MORE...
...LIKE THERE'S SOME KIND OF... INTERFERENCE.
WHAT HAPPENS NOW?
HIS DEATH IS COMMON KNOWL-EDGE WITHIN THE CABAL.
THE NEWS HAS NOT BEEN MADE PUBLIC -- IT WOULD CAUSE PANIC.

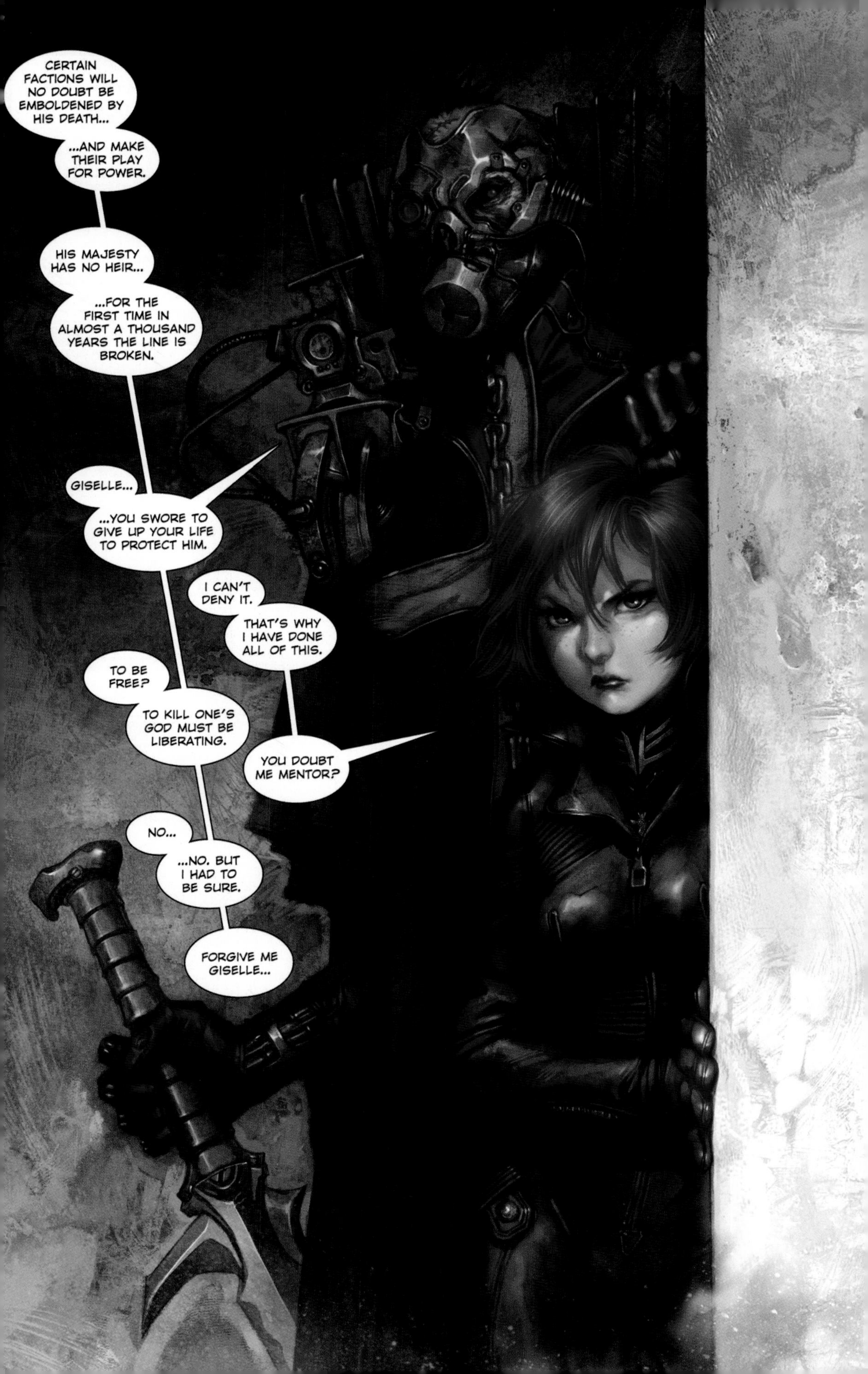
CERTAIN FACTIONS WILL NO DOUBT BE EMBOLDENED BY HIS DEATH...
...AND MAKE THEIR PLAY FOR POWER.
HIS MAJESTY HAS NO HEIR...
...FOR THE FIRST TIME IN ALMOST A THOUSAND YEARS THE LINE IS BROKEN.
GISELLE...
...YOU SWORE TO GIVE UP YOUR LIFE TO PROTECT HIM.
I CAN'T DENY IT.
THAT'S WHY I HAVE DONE ALL OF THIS.
TO BE FREE?
TO KILL ONE'S GOD MUST BE LIBERATING.
YOU DOUBT ME MENTOR?
NO...
...NO. BUT I HAD TO BE SURE.
FORGIVE ME GISELLE...

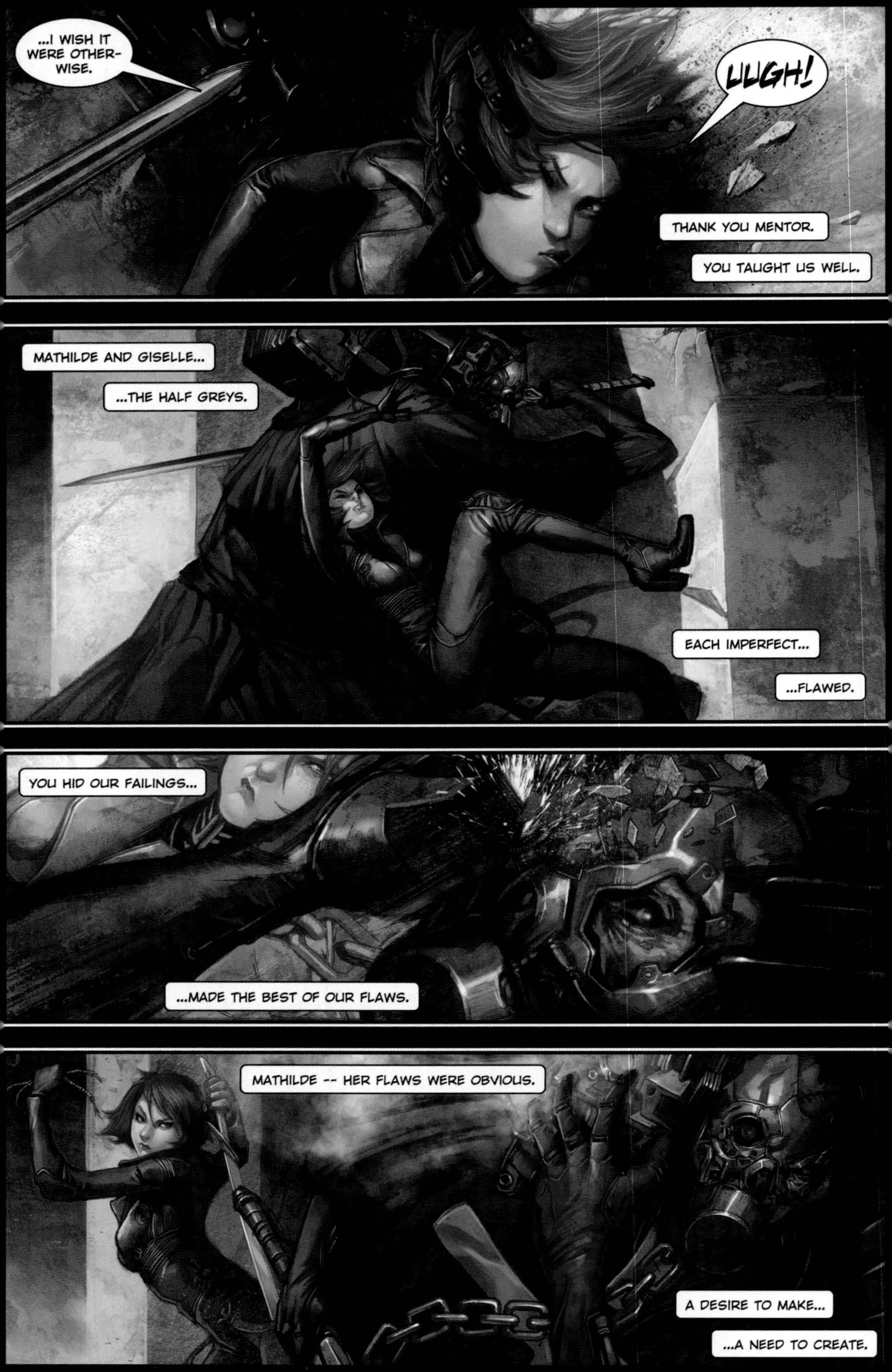
...I WISH IT WERE OTHER-WISE.
UUGH!
THANK YOU MENTOR.
YOU TAUGHT US WELL.
MATHILDE AND GISELLE...
...THE HALF GREYS.
EACH IMPERFECT...
...FLAWED.
YOU HID OUR FAILINGS...
...MADE THE BEST OF OUR FLAWS.
MATHILDE -- HER FLAWS WERE OBVIOUS.
A DESIRE TO MAKE...
...A NEED TO CREATE.

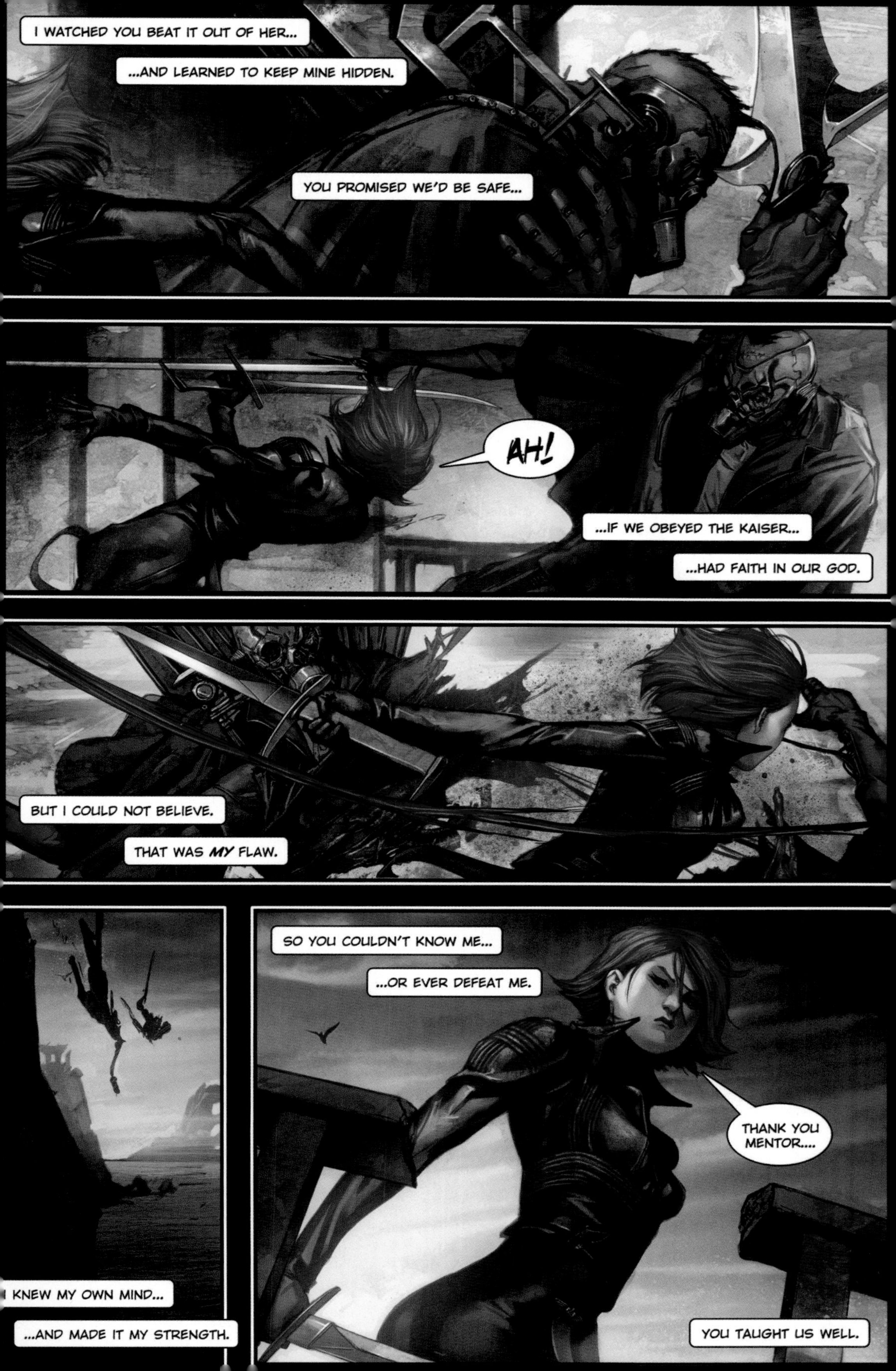
I WATCHED YOU BEAT IT OUT OF HER...
...AND LEARNED TO KEEP MINE HIDDEN.
YOU PROMISED WE'D BE SAFE...
AH!
...IF WE OBEYED THE KAISER...
...HAD FAITH IN OUR GOD.
BUT I COULD NOT BELIEVE.
THAT WAS *MY* FLAW.
I KNEW MY OWN MIND...
...AND MADE IT MY STRENGTH.
SO YOU COULDN'T KNOW ME...
...OR EVER DEFEAT ME.
THANK YOU MENTOR....
YOU TAUGHT US WELL.

WEST TOWARD LINTH?

SHE'LL BE LOOKING TO CROSS OVER...

...THE FRONT IS FURTHEST WEST THERE.

YOU STILL THINK SHE'S INNOCENT.

I DO. THE KAISER IS HER GOD...

...HIS WORD IS OUR WORLD.

SHE WOULD NOT DESTROY THAT.

AND YET IT'S US THAT GIVE HIS WORDS THEIR POWER.

ARE WE NOT THE TRUE GODS?

PERHAPS GISELLE HAS ONLY DONE WHAT WE WERE NOT BOLD ENOUGH TO DO.

MIND YOUR WORDS, ANNA -- YOU MAY HAVE TO ACCOUNT FOR THEM.

THERE ARE OTHERS WHO BELIEVE IT SO -- PERHAPS EVEN THE KAISER HIMSELF.

THE KAISER IS DEAD, ANNA.

... I SPEAK OF THE KAISER TO COME....

WAIT HERE ANNA, LET ME TALK WITH THEM...

...I'VE SEEN HOW YOUR EFFORTS AT DIPLOMACY END.

HOY, MY LADY GREY.

EVA, PLEASE.

IT'S MATHIEU, ISN'T IT?

MA'AM? HOW --?

YOU CARRIED THE STANDARD AT MY DEBUT...

...HOW COULD I FORGET?

I WAS A CHILD THEN.

WE BOTH OF US WERE, MATHIEU.

EVA...

...WE HAVE A WARRANT...

...THEY SAY YOU KILLED THE CHANCELLOR.

EXECUTED, YES -- AND IN TIME I WILL ANSWER FOR MY ACTIONS.

BUT RIGHT NOW THERE ARE EVENTS LARGER THAN US PLAYING OUT...

...EVENTS THAT MAY DESTROY ALL WE HAVE WORKED TO UPHOLD.

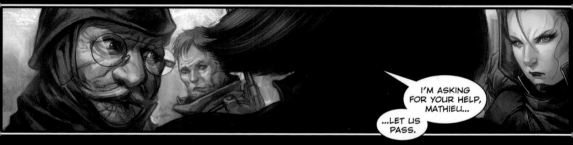

I'M ASKING FOR YOUR HELP, MATHIEU...

...LET US PASS.

ENOUGH CHIT-CHAT!

ANNA!

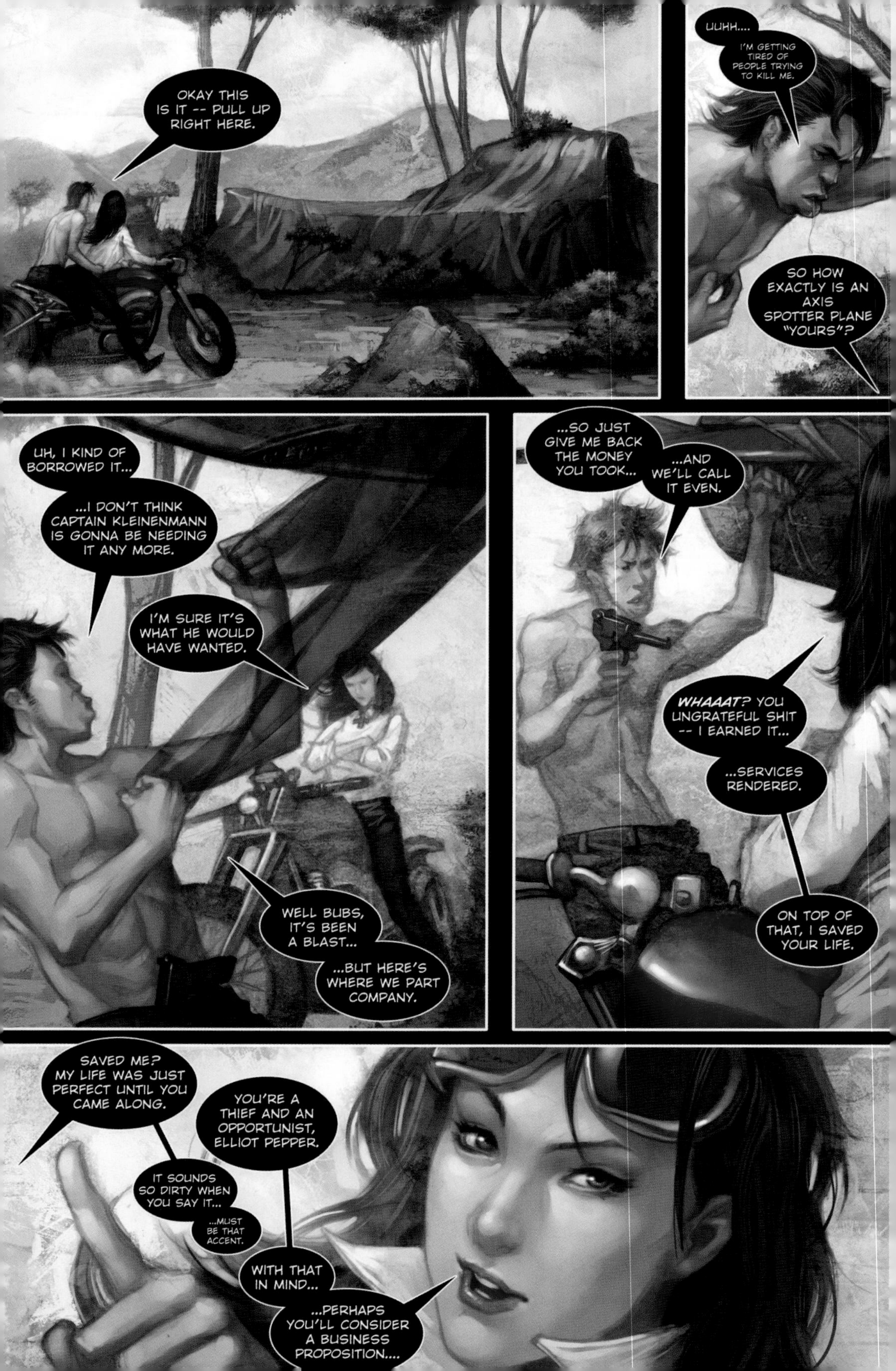
OKAY THIS IS IT -- PULL UP RIGHT HERE.
UUHH....
I'M GETTING TIRED OF PEOPLE TRYING TO KILL ME.
SO HOW EXACTLY IS AN AXIS SPOTTER PLANE "YOURS"?
UH, I KIND OF BORROWED IT...
...I DON'T THINK CAPTAIN KLEINENMANN IS GONNA BE NEEDING IT ANY MORE.
I'M SURE IT'S WHAT HE WOULD HAVE WANTED.
WELL BUBS, IT'S BEEN A BLAST...
...BUT HERE'S WHERE WE PART COMPANY.
...SO JUST GIVE ME BACK THE MONEY YOU TOOK...
...AND WE'LL CALL IT EVEN.
WHAAAT? YOU UNGRATEFUL SHIT -- I EARNED IT...
...SERVICES RENDERED.
ON TOP OF THAT, I SAVED YOUR LIFE.
SAVED ME? MY LIFE WAS JUST PERFECT UNTIL YOU CAME ALONG.
YOU'RE A THIEF AND AN OPPORTUNIST, ELLIOT PEPPER.
IT SOUNDS SO DIRTY WHEN YOU SAY IT...
...MUST BE THAT ACCENT.
WITH THAT IN MIND...
...PERHAPS YOU'LL CONSIDER A BUSINESS PROPOSITION....

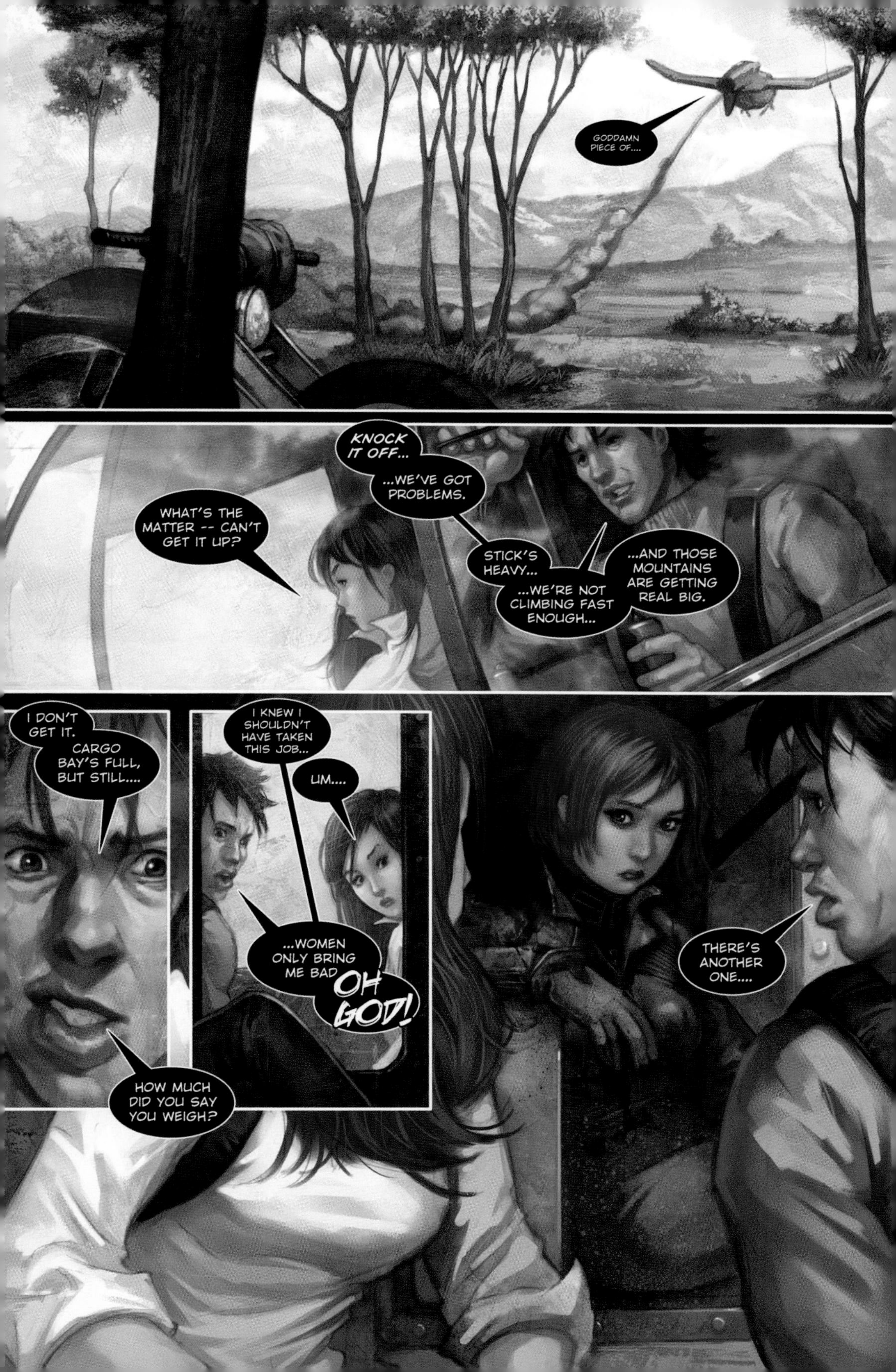

GODDAMN PIECE OF....
WHAT'S THE MATTER -- CAN'T GET IT UP?
KNOCK IT OFF...
...WE'VE GOT PROBLEMS.
STICK'S HEAVY...
...WE'RE NOT CLIMBING FAST ENOUGH...
...AND THOSE MOUNTAINS ARE GETTING REAL BIG.
I DON'T GET IT.
CARGO BAY'S FULL, BUT STILL....
HOW MUCH DID YOU SAY YOU WEIGH?
I KNEW I SHOULDN'T HAVE TAKEN THIS JOB...
UM....
...WOMEN ONLY BRING ME BAD
OH GOD!
THERE'S ANOTHER ONE....

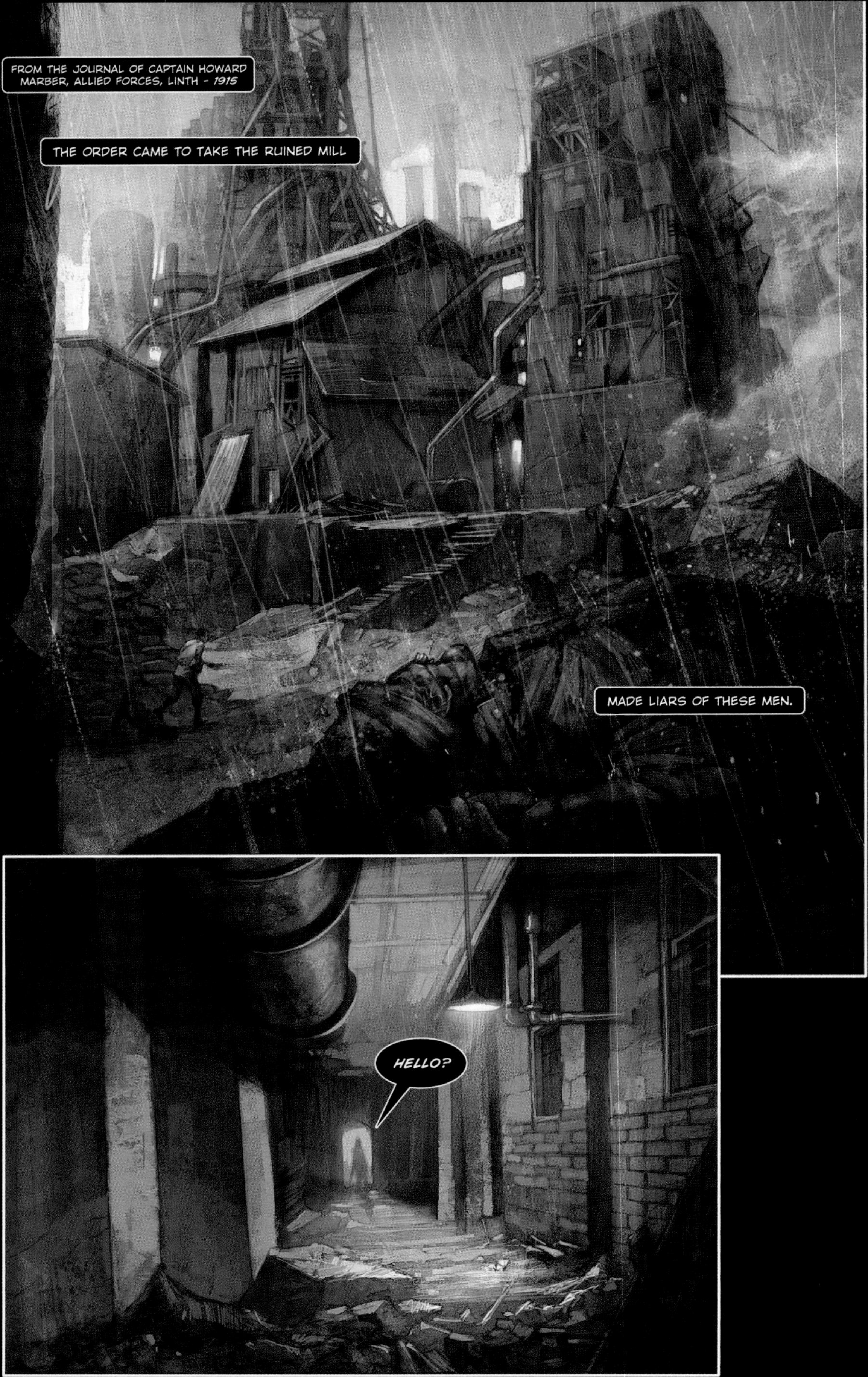
FROM THE JOURNAL OF CAPTAIN HOWARD MARBER, ALLIED FORCES, LINTH - 1915
THE ORDER CAME TO TAKE THE RUINED MILL
MADE LIARS OF THESE MEN.
HELLO?

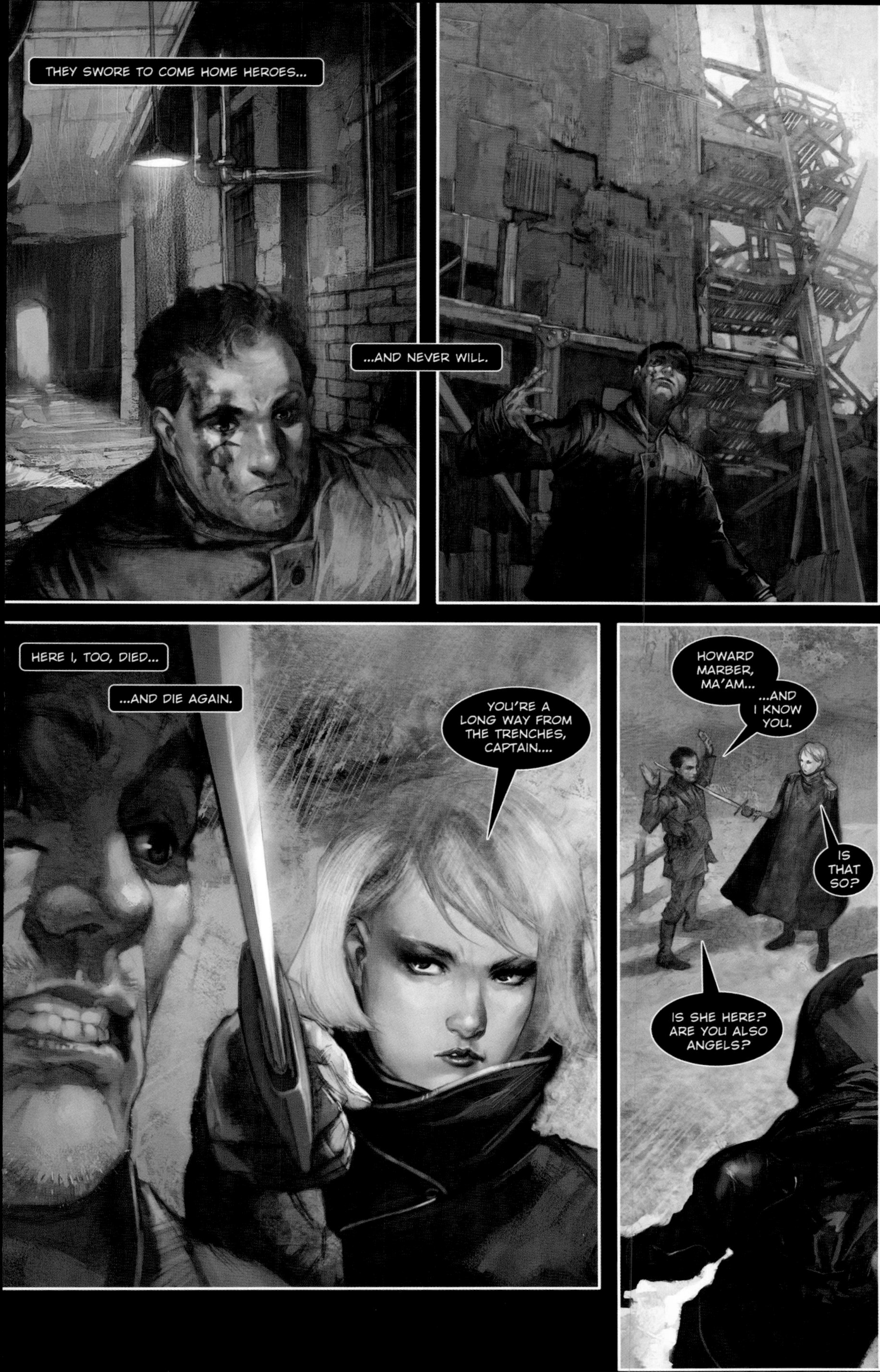
THEY SWORE TO COME HOME HEROES...
...AND NEVER WILL.
HERE I, TOO, DIED...
...AND DIE AGAIN.
YOU'RE A LONG WAY FROM THE TRENCHES, CAPTAIN....
HOWARD MARBER, MA'AM...
...AND I KNOW YOU.
IS THAT SO?
IS SHE HERE? ARE YOU ALSO ANGELS?

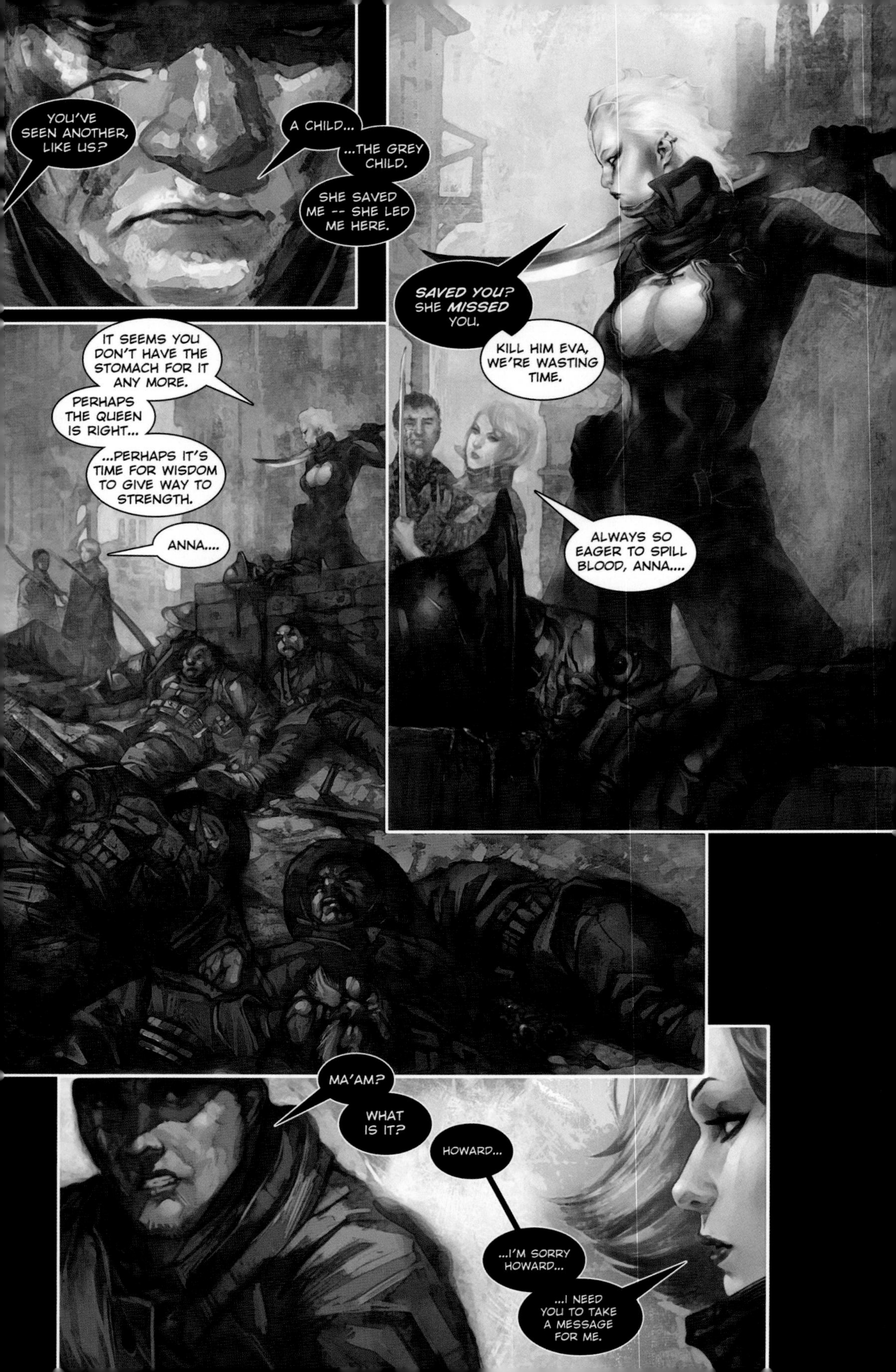
YOU'VE SEEN ANOTHER, LIKE US?
A CHILD...
...THE GREY CHILD.
SHE SAVED ME -- SHE LED ME HERE.
SAVED YOU? SHE *MISSED* YOU.
KILL HIM EVA, WE'RE WASTING TIME.
ALWAYS SO EAGER TO SPILL BLOOD, ANNA....
IT SEEMS YOU DON'T HAVE THE STOMACH FOR IT ANY MORE.
PERHAPS THE QUEEN IS RIGHT...
...PERHAPS IT'S TIME FOR WISDOM TO GIVE WAY TO STRENGTH.
ANNA....
MA'AM?
WHAT IS IT?
HOWARD...
...I'M SORRY HOWARD...
...I NEED YOU TO TAKE A MESSAGE FOR ME.

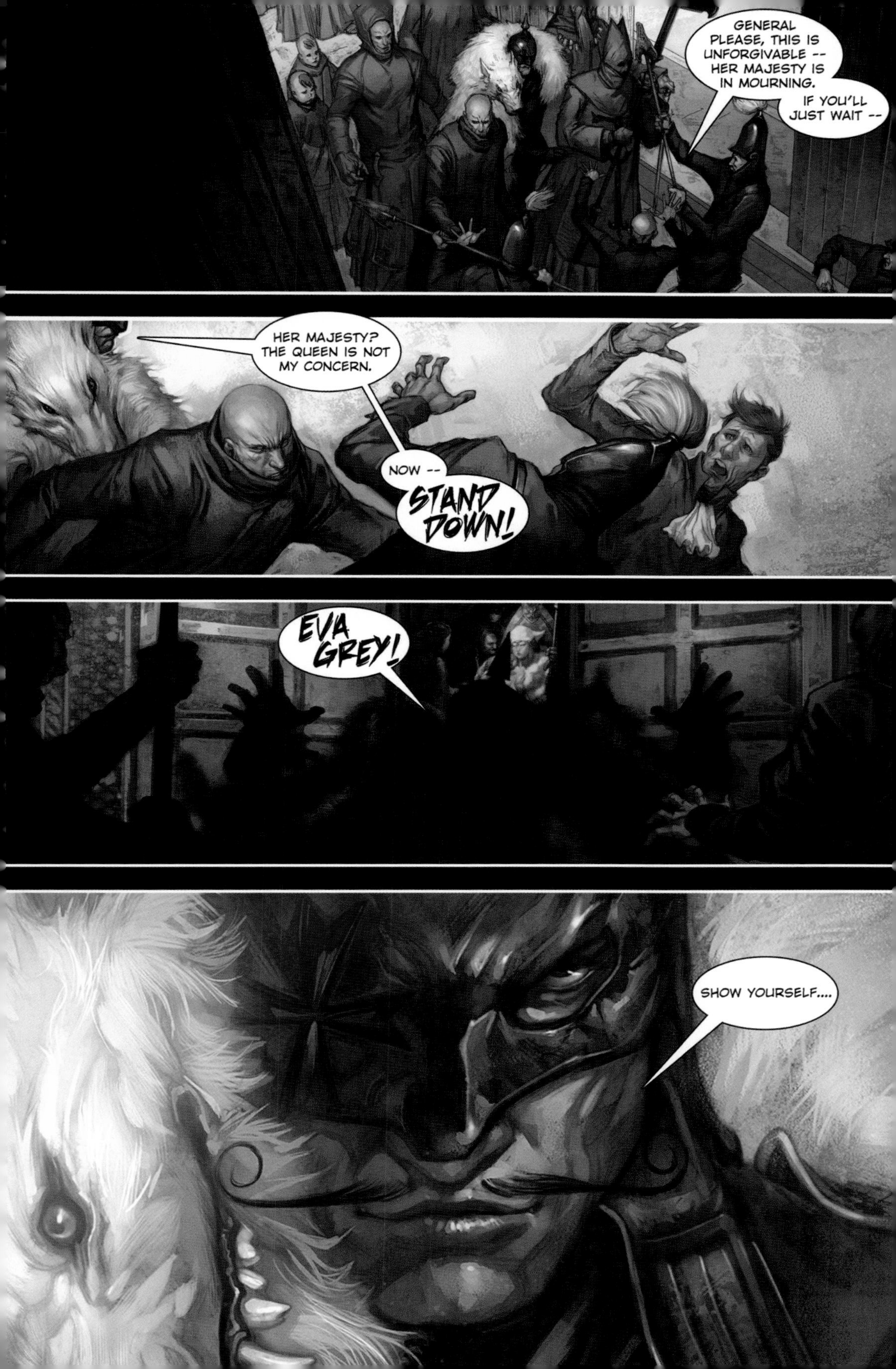
GENERAL PLEASE, THIS IS UNFORGIVABLE -- HER MAJESTY IS IN MOURNING.
IF YOU'LL JUST WAIT --
HER MAJESTY? THE QUEEN IS NOT MY CONCERN.
NOW --
STAND DOWN!
EVA GREY!
SHOW YOURSELF....

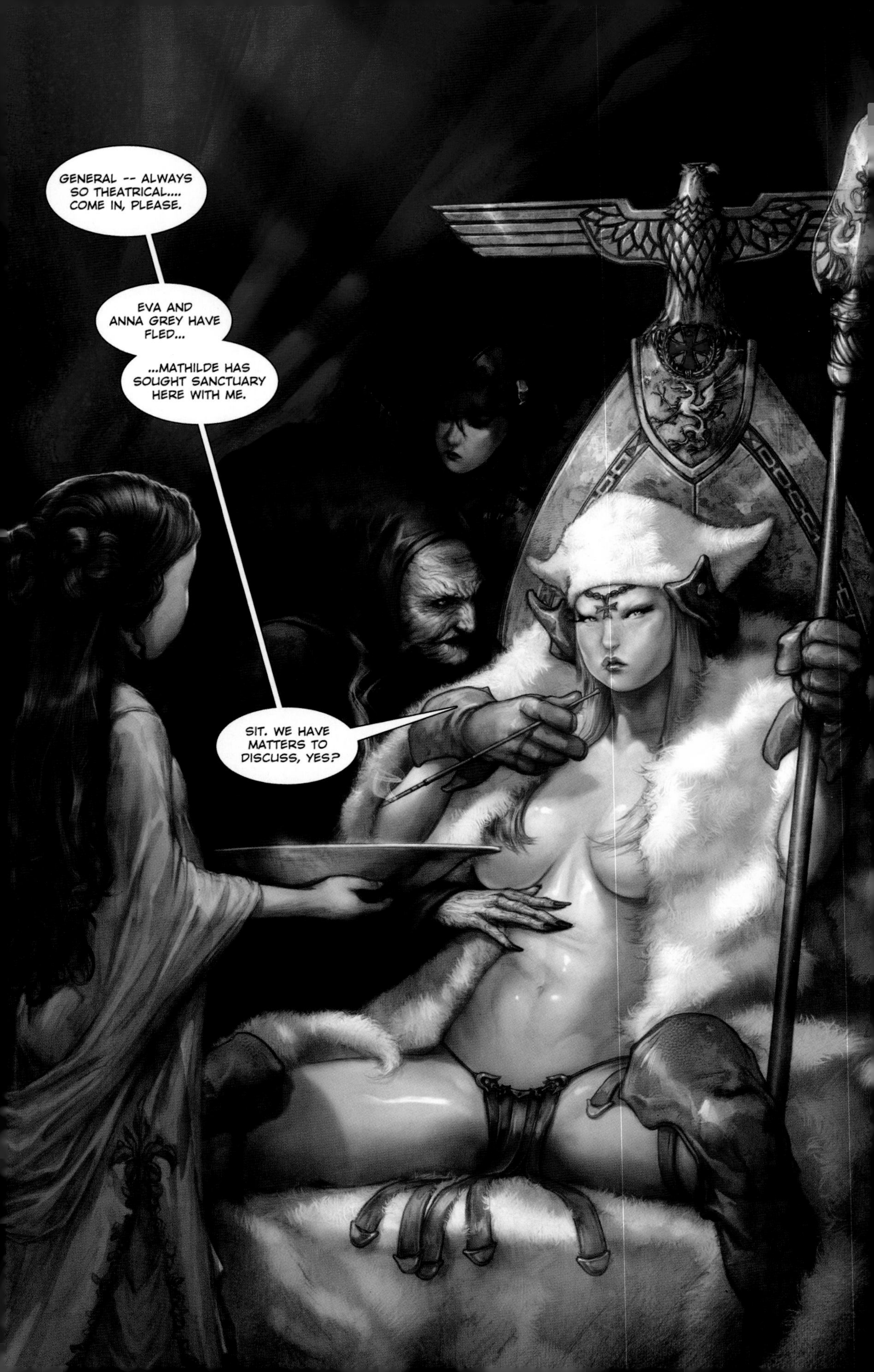
GENERAL -- ALWAYS SO THEATRICAL.... COME IN, PLEASE.
EVA AND ANNA GREY HAVE FLED...
...MATHILDE HAS SOUGHT SANCTUARY HERE WITH ME.
SIT. WE HAVE MATTERS TO DISCUSS, YES?

III

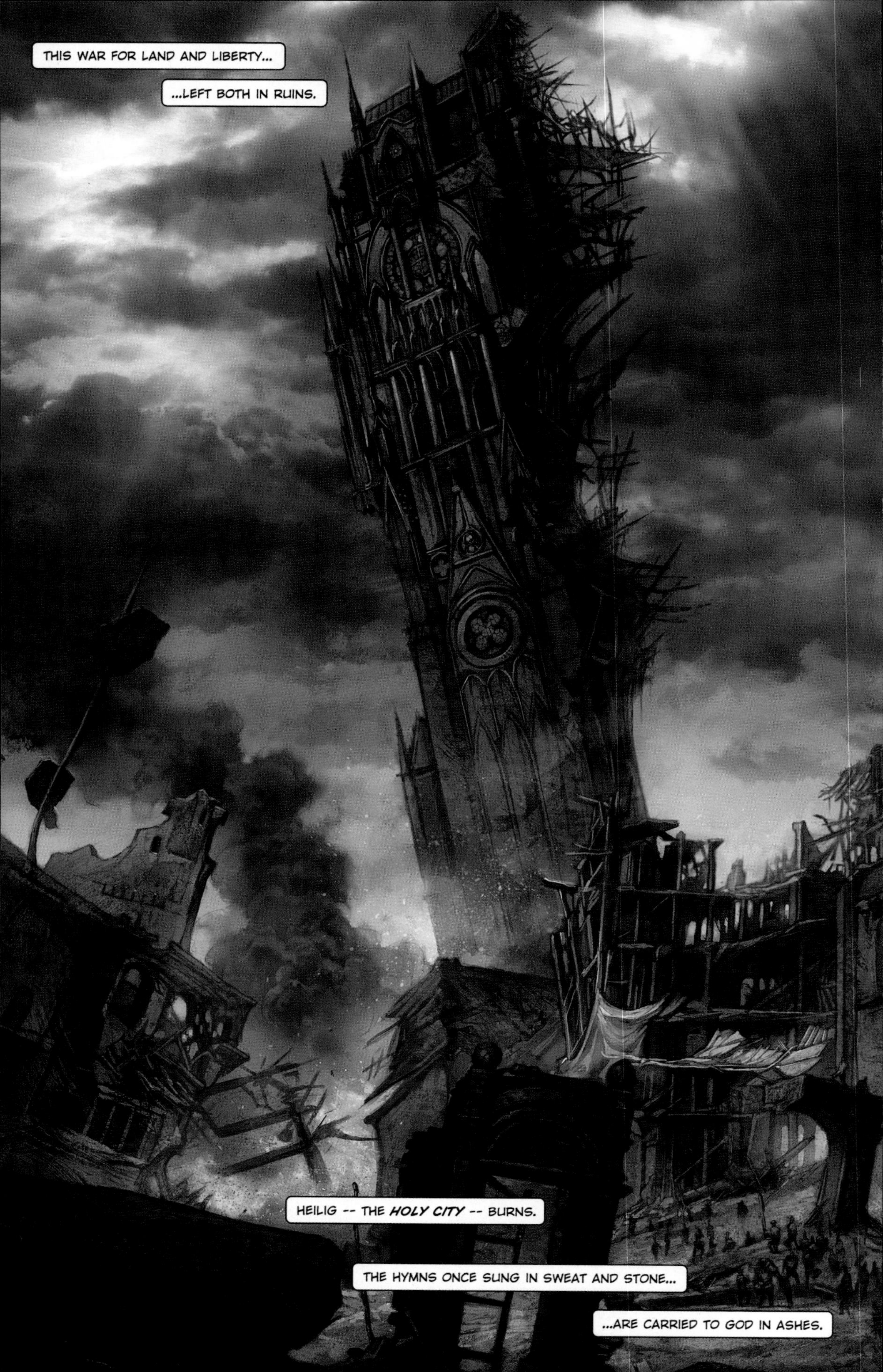
THIS WAR FOR LAND AND LIBERTY...
...LEFT BOTH IN RUINS.
HEILIG -- THE *HOLY CITY* -- BURNS.
THE HYMNS ONCE SUNG IN SWEAT AND STONE...
...ARE CARRIED TO GOD IN ASHES.

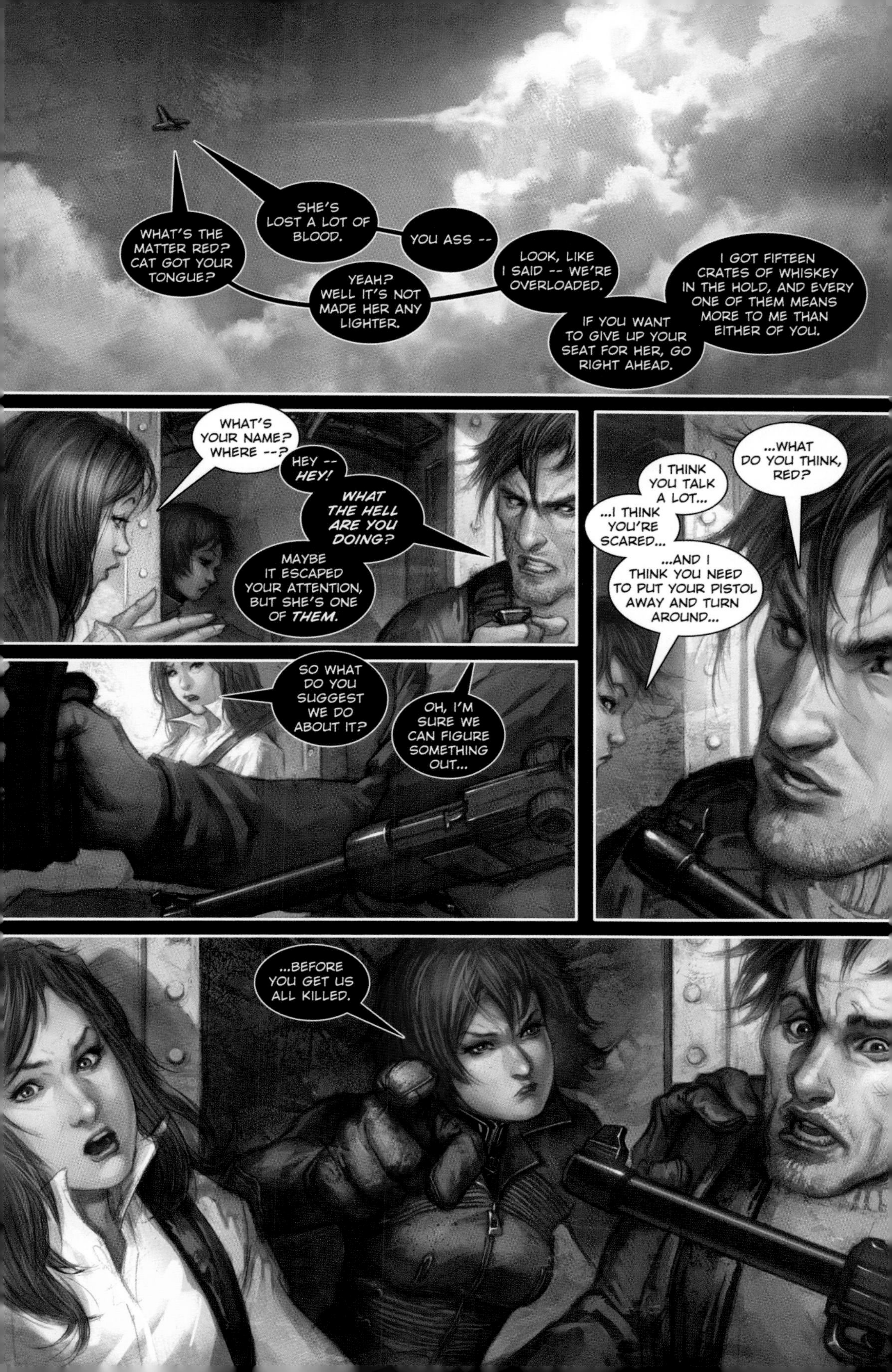
WHAT'S THE MATTER RED? CAT GOT YOUR TONGUE?
SHE'S LOST A LOT OF BLOOD.
YEAH? WELL IT'S NOT MADE HER ANY LIGHTER.
YOU ASS --
LOOK, LIKE I SAID -- WE'RE OVERLOADED.
I GOT FIFTEEN CRATES OF WHISKEY IN THE HOLD, AND EVERY ONE OF THEM MEANS MORE TO ME THAN EITHER OF YOU.
IF YOU WANT TO GIVE UP YOUR SEAT FOR HER, GO RIGHT AHEAD.
WHAT'S YOUR NAME? WHERE --?
HEY -- *HEY!*
WHAT THE HELL ARE YOU DOING?
MAYBE IT ESCAPED YOUR ATTENTION, BUT SHE'S ONE OF *THEM.*
SO WHAT DO YOU SUGGEST WE DO ABOUT IT?
OH, I'M SURE WE CAN FIGURE SOMETHING OUT...
...WHAT DO YOU THINK, RED?
I THINK YOU TALK A LOT...
...I THINK YOU'RE SCARED...
...AND I THINK YOU NEED TO PUT YOUR PISTOL AWAY AND TURN AROUND...
...BEFORE YOU GET US ALL KILLED.

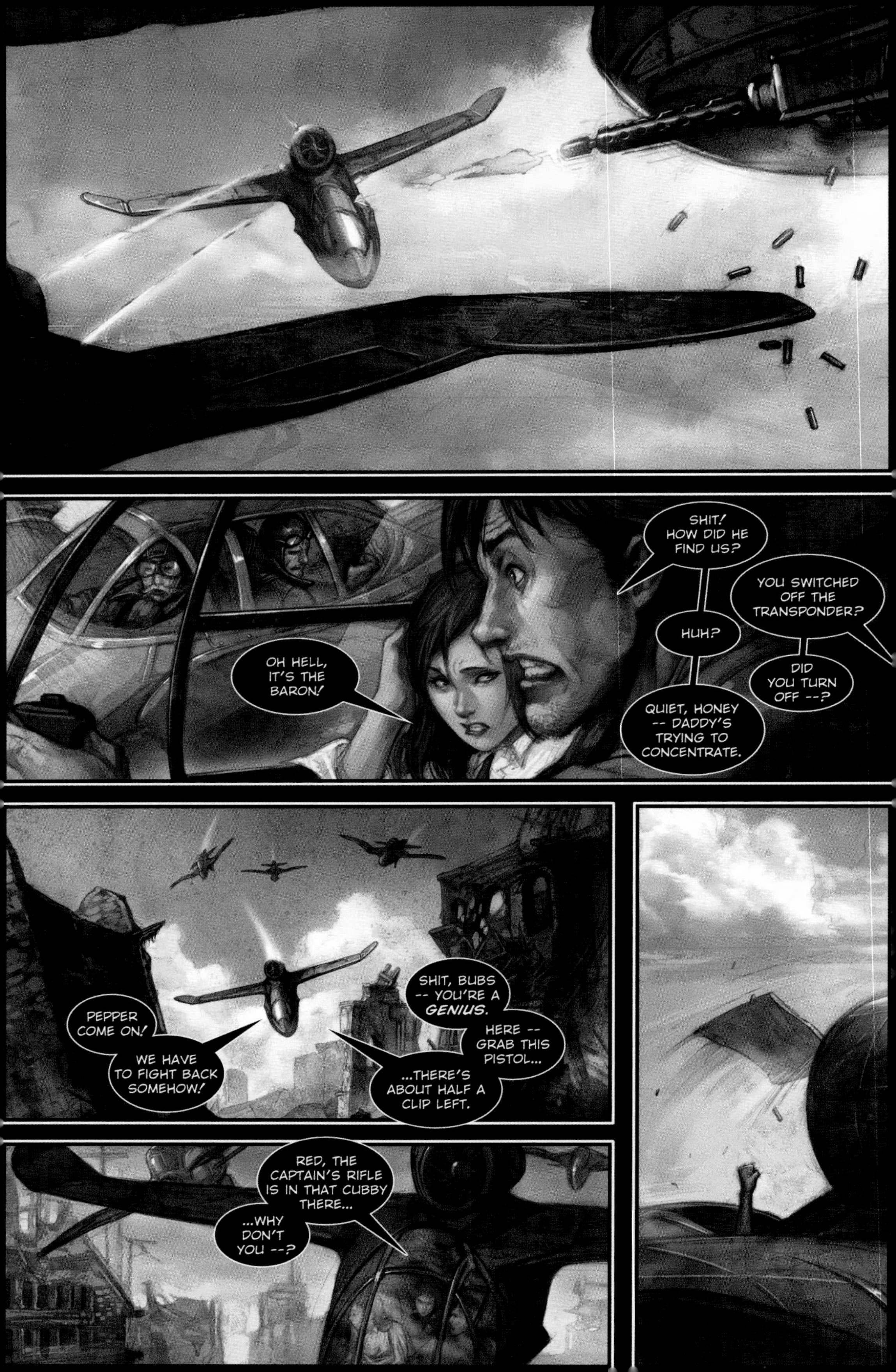
OH HELL, IT'S THE BARON!
SHIT! HOW DID HE FIND US?
YOU SWITCHED OFF THE TRANSPONDER?
HUH?
DID YOU TURN OFF --?
QUIET, HONEY -- DADDY'S TRYING TO CONCENTRATE.
PEPPER COME ON!
WE HAVE TO FIGHT BACK SOMEHOW!
SHIT, BUBS -- YOU'RE A *GENIUS*.
HERE -- GRAB THIS PISTOL...
...THERE'S ABOUT HALF A CLIP LEFT.
RED, THE CAPTAIN'S RIFLE IS IN THAT CUBBY THERE...
...WHY DON'T YOU --?

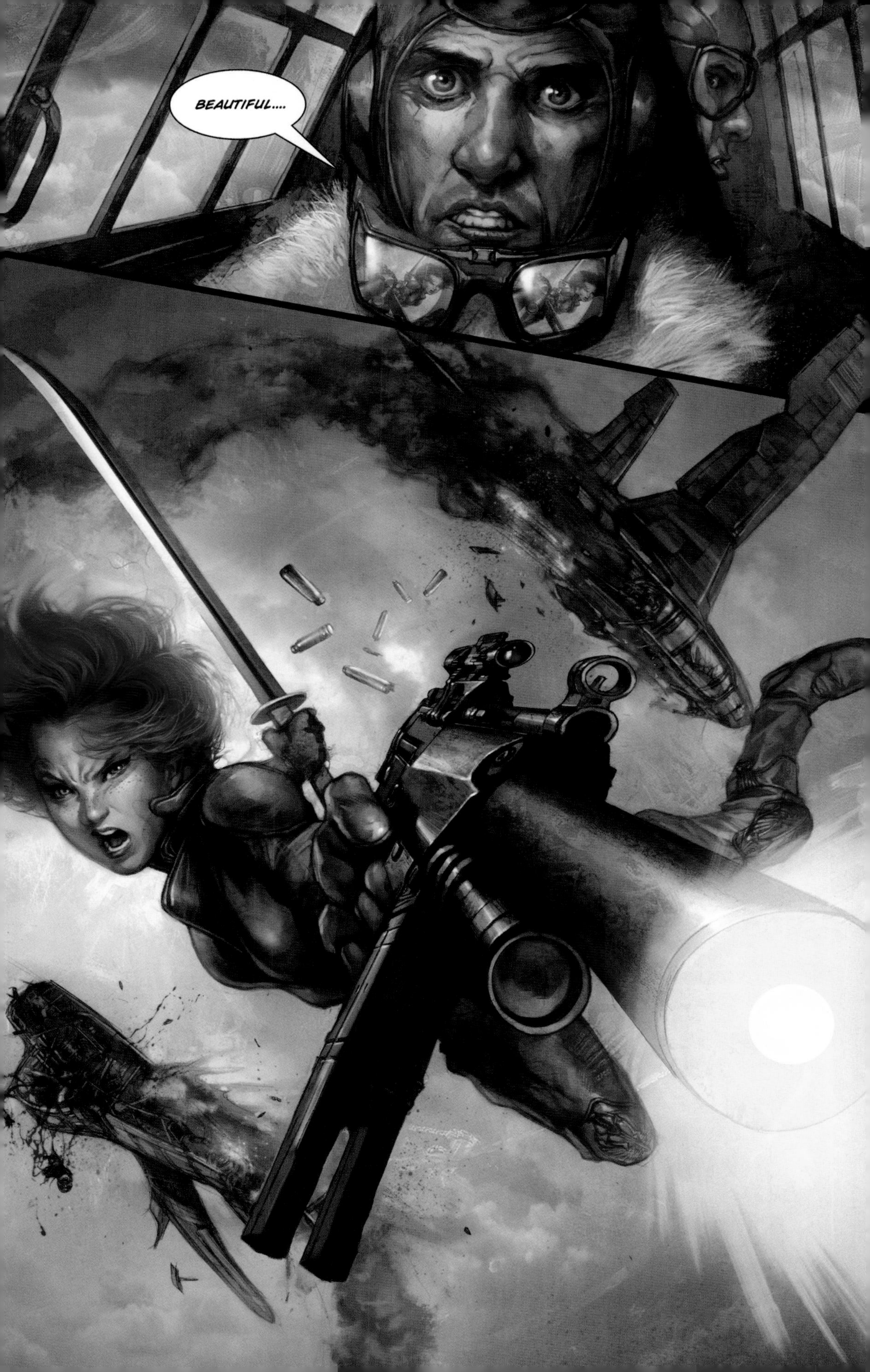
BEAUTIFUL....

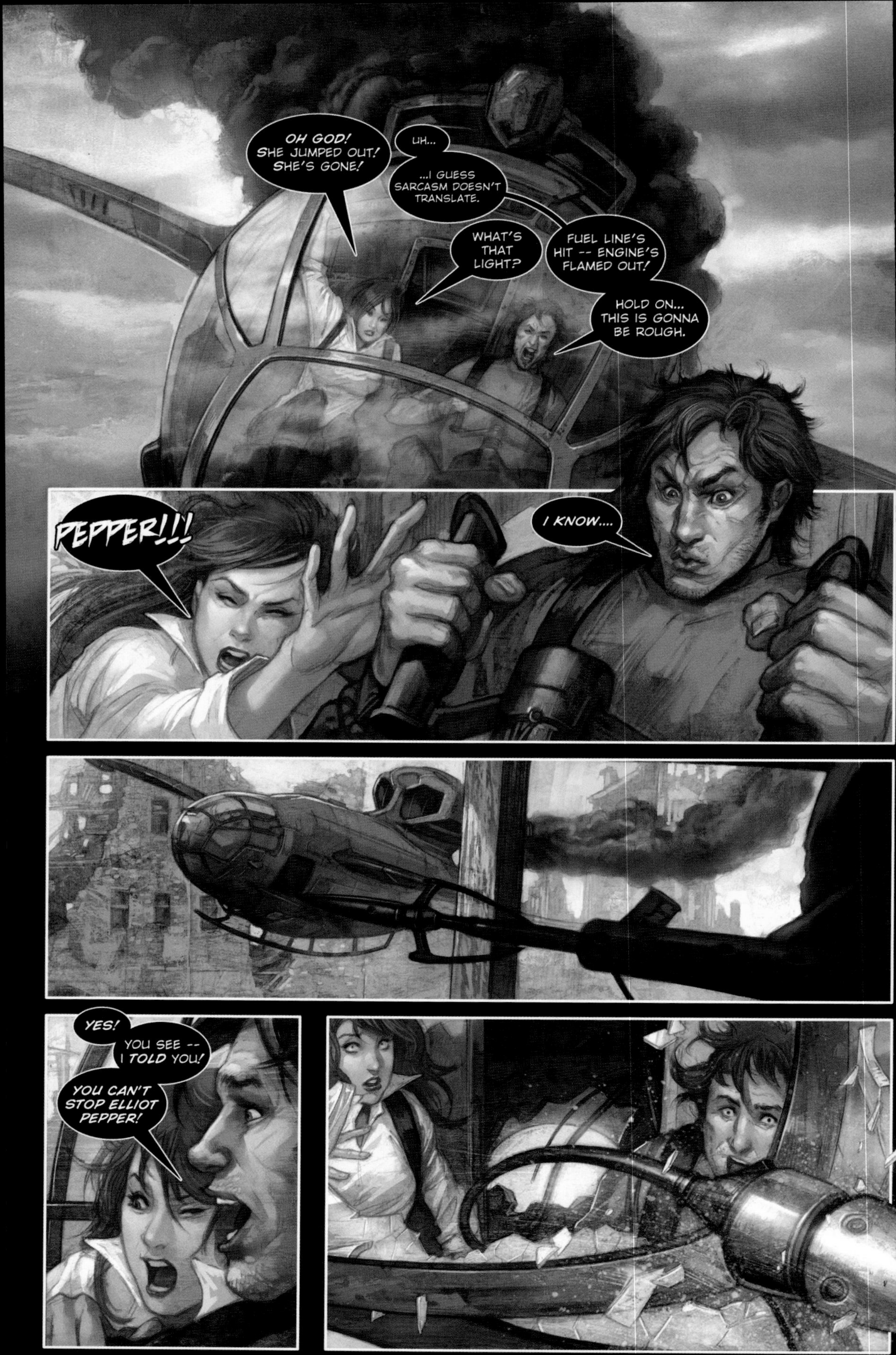
OH GOD! SHE JUMPED OUT! SHE'S GONE!
UH...
...I GUESS SARCASM DOESN'T TRANSLATE.
WHAT'S THAT LIGHT?
FUEL LINE'S HIT -- ENGINE'S FLAMED OUT!
HOLD ON... THIS IS GONNA BE ROUGH.
PEPPER!!!
I KNOW....
YES!
YOU SEE -- I TOLD YOU!
YOU CAN'T STOP ELLIOT PEPPER!

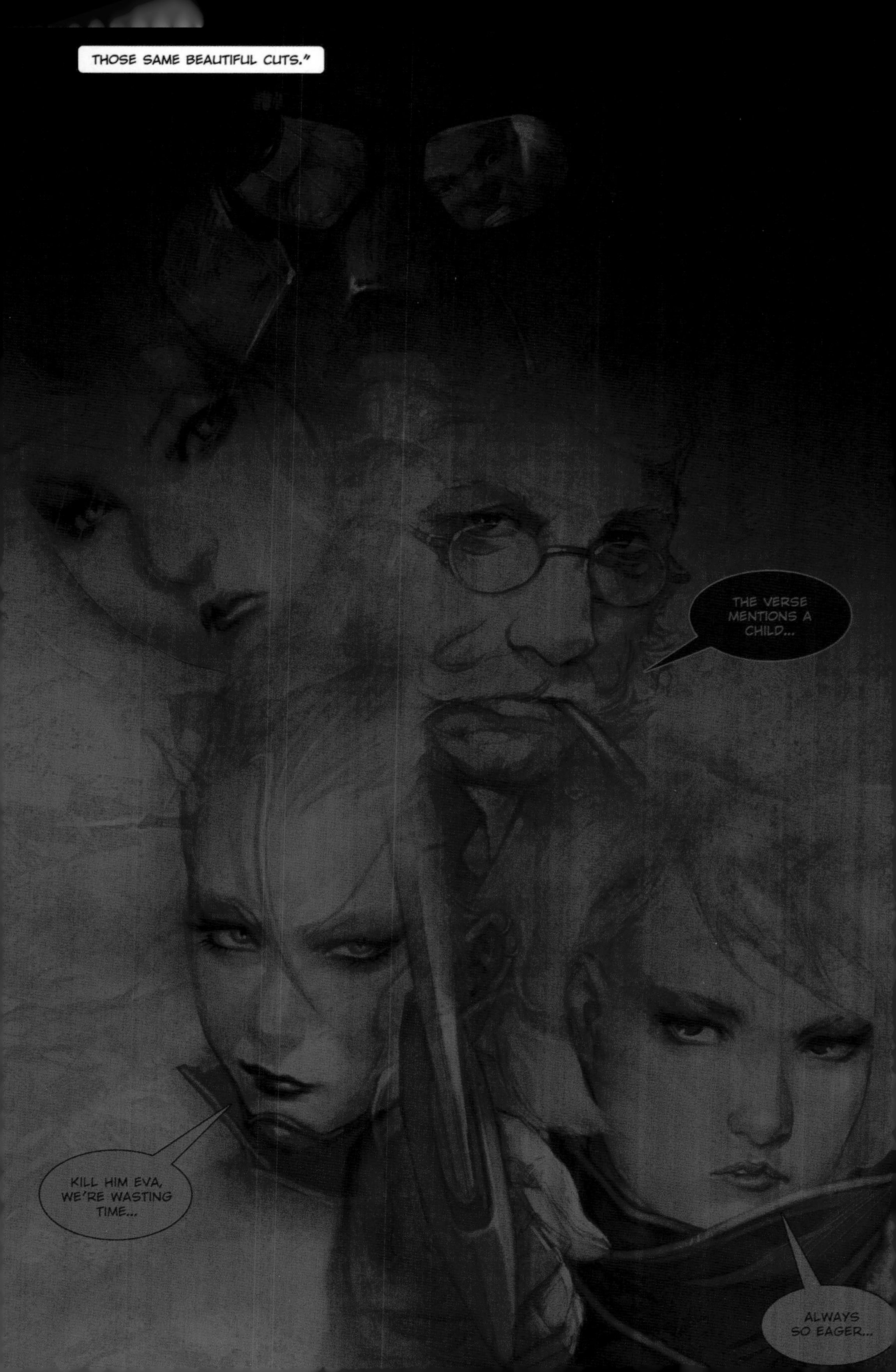
THOSE SAME BEAUTIFUL CUTS."
THE VERSE MENTIONS A CHILD...
KILL HIM EVA, WE'RE WASTING TIME...
ALWAYS SO EAGER...

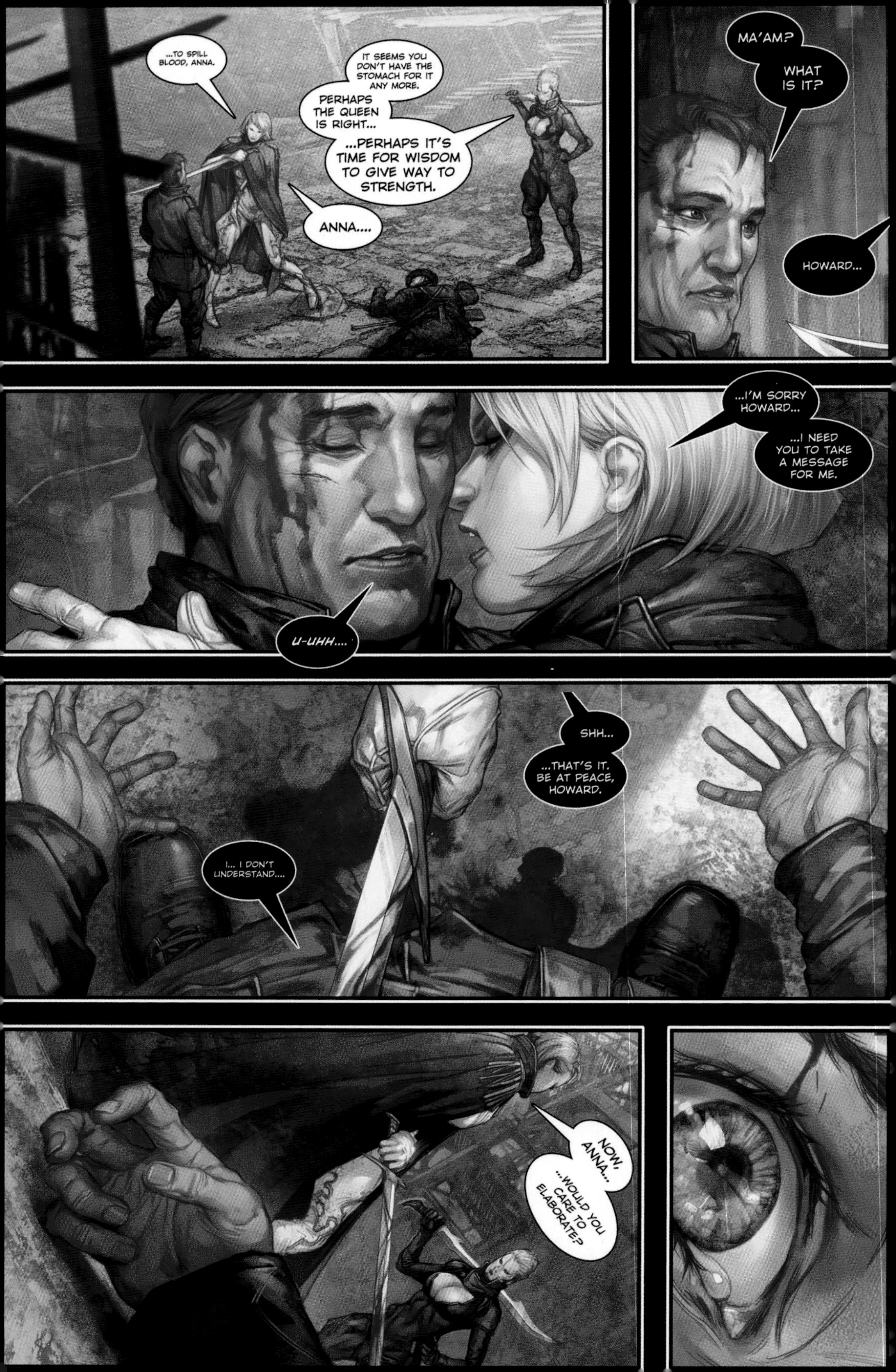

...TO SPILL BLOOD, ANNA.
IT SEEMS YOU DON'T HAVE THE STOMACH FOR IT ANY MORE.
PERHAPS THE QUEEN IS RIGHT...
...PERHAPS IT'S TIME FOR WISDOM TO GIVE WAY TO STRENGTH.
ANNA....
MA'AM?
WHAT IS IT?
HOWARD...
...I'M SORRY HOWARD...
...I NEED YOU TO TAKE A MESSAGE FOR ME.
U-UHH....
I... I DON'T UNDERSTAND....
SHH...
...THAT'S IT. BE AT PEACE, HOWARD.
NOW, ANNA...
...WOULD YOU CARE TO ELABORATE?

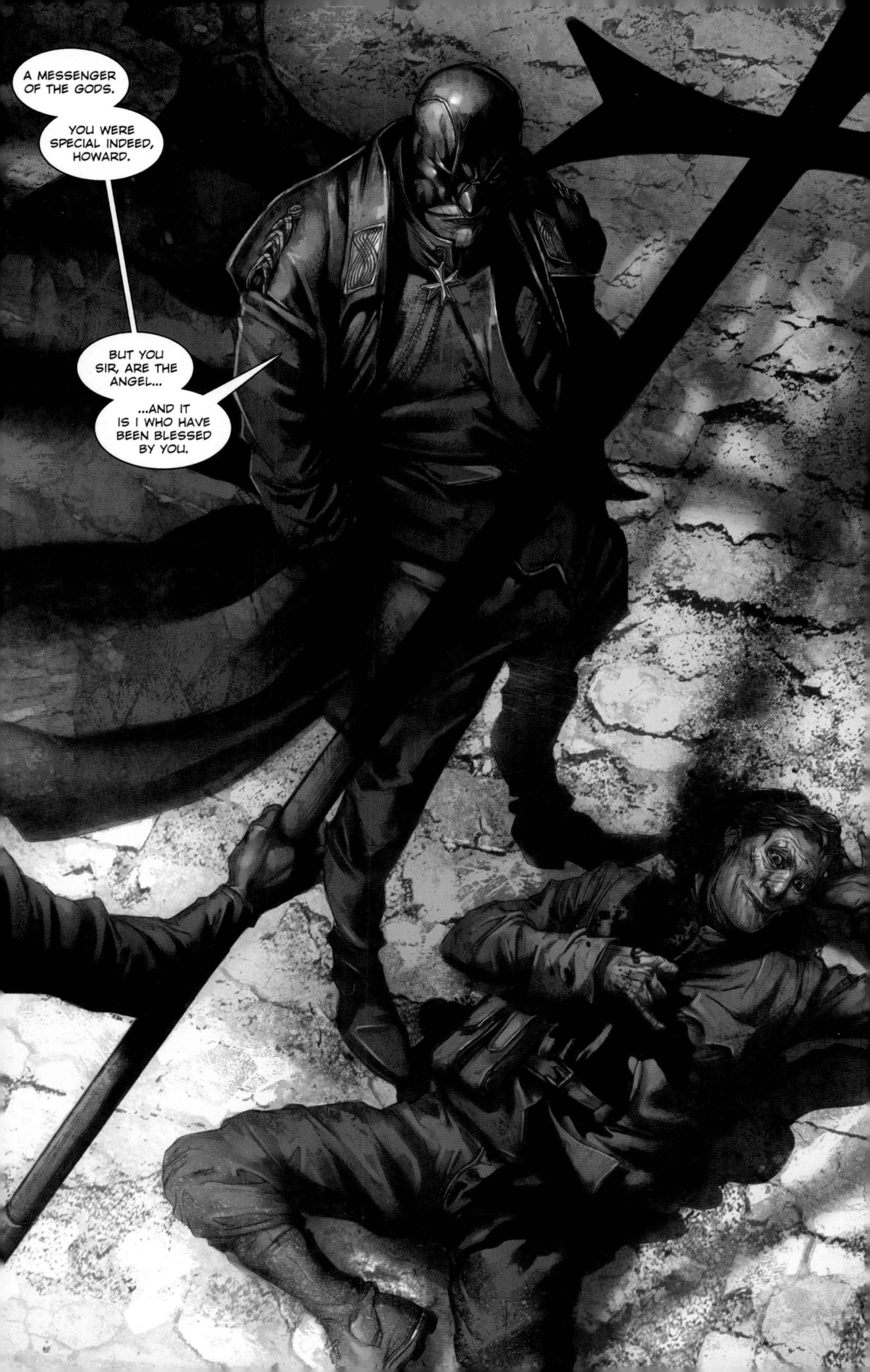
A MESSENGER OF THE GODS.
YOU WERE SPECIAL INDEED, HOWARD.
BUT YOU SIR, ARE THE ANGEL...
...AND IT IS I WHO HAVE BEEN BLESSED BY YOU.

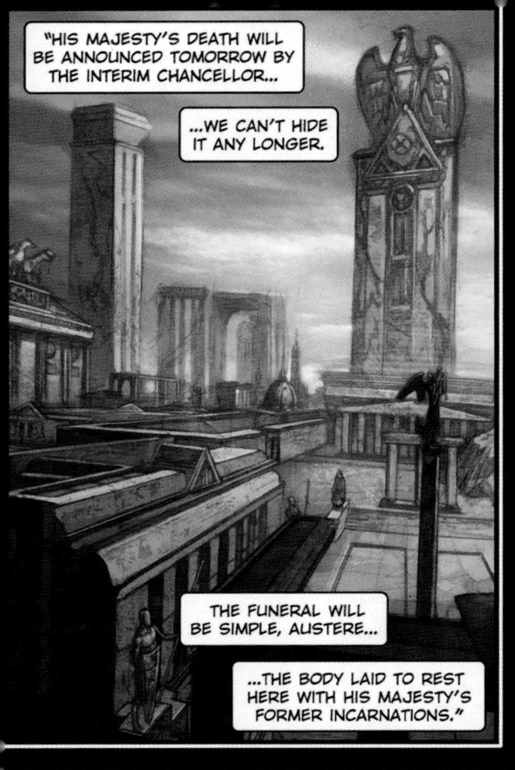
"HIS MAJESTY'S DEATH WILL BE ANNOUNCED TOMORROW BY THE INTERIM CHANCELLOR...
...WE CAN'T HIDE IT ANY LONGER.
THE FUNERAL WILL BE SIMPLE, AUSTERE...
...THE BODY LAID TO REST HERE WITH HIS MAJESTY'S FORMER INCARNATIONS."

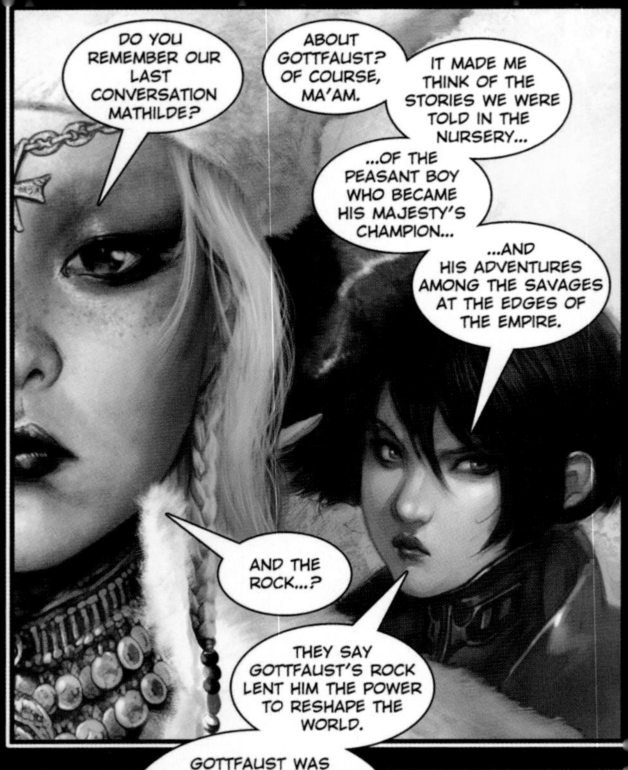
DO YOU REMEMBER OUR LAST CONVERSATION MATHILDE?
ABOUT GOTTFAUST? OF COURSE, MA'AM.
IT MADE ME THINK OF THE STORIES WE WERE TOLD IN THE NURSERY...
...OF THE PEASANT BOY WHO BECAME HIS MAJESTY'S CHAMPION...
...AND HIS ADVENTURES AMONG THE SAVAGES AT THE EDGES OF THE EMPIRE.
AND THE ROCK...?
THEY SAY GOTTFAUST'S ROCK LENT HIM THE POWER TO RESHAPE THE WORLD.

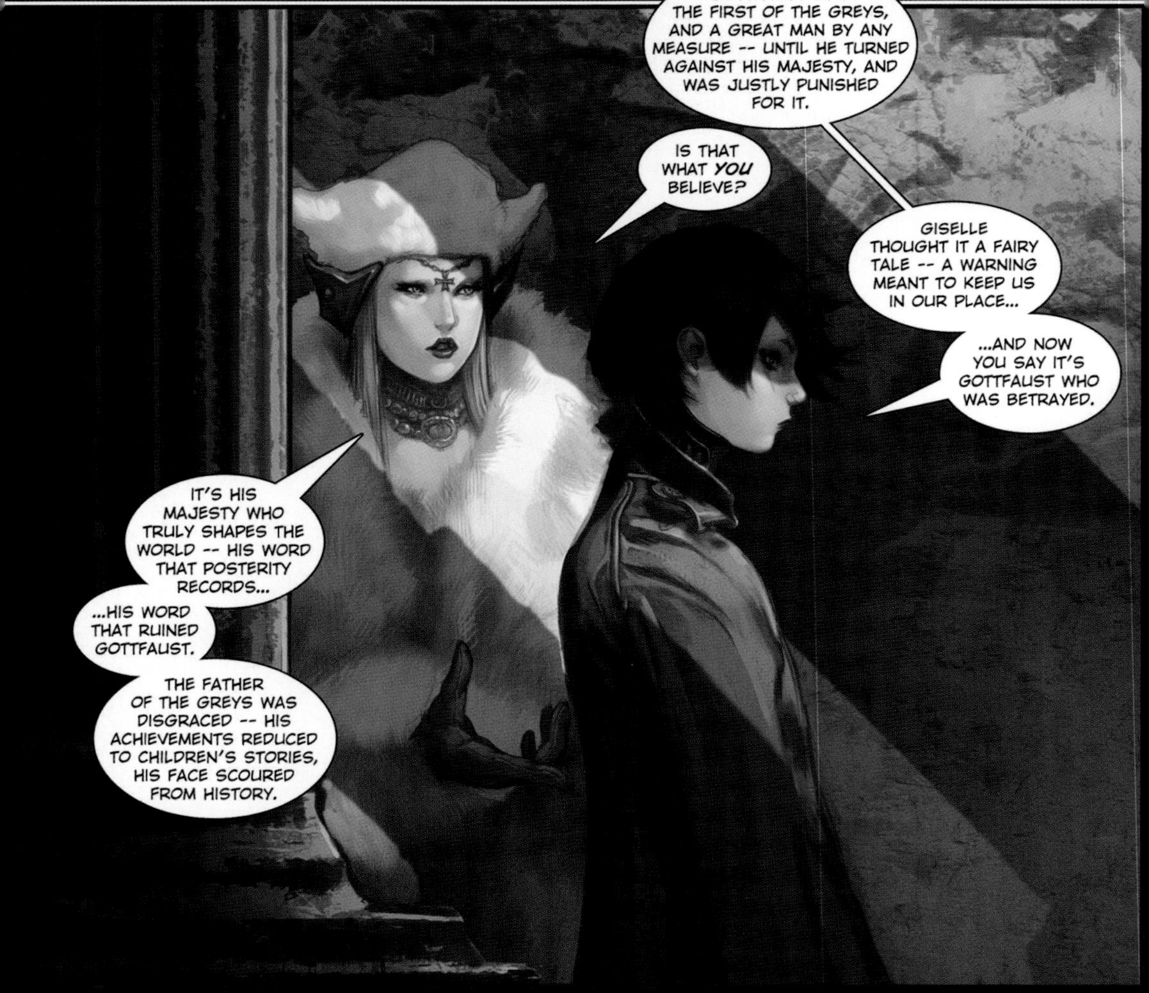
GOTTFAUST WAS THE FIRST OF THE GREYS, AND A GREAT MAN BY ANY MEASURE -- UNTIL HE TURNED AGAINST HIS MAJESTY, AND WAS JUSTLY PUNISHED FOR IT.
IS THAT WHAT *YOU* BELIEVE?
GISELLE THOUGHT IT A FAIRY TALE -- A WARNING MEANT TO KEEP US IN OUR PLACE...
...AND NOW YOU SAY IT'S GOTTFAUST WHO WAS BETRAYED.
IT'S HIS MAJESTY WHO TRULY SHAPES THE WORLD -- HIS WORD THAT POSTERITY RECORDS...
...HIS WORD THAT RUINED GOTTFAUST.
THE FATHER OF THE GREYS WAS DISGRACED -- HIS ACHIEVEMENTS REDUCED TO CHILDREN'S STORIES, HIS FACE SCOURED FROM HISTORY.

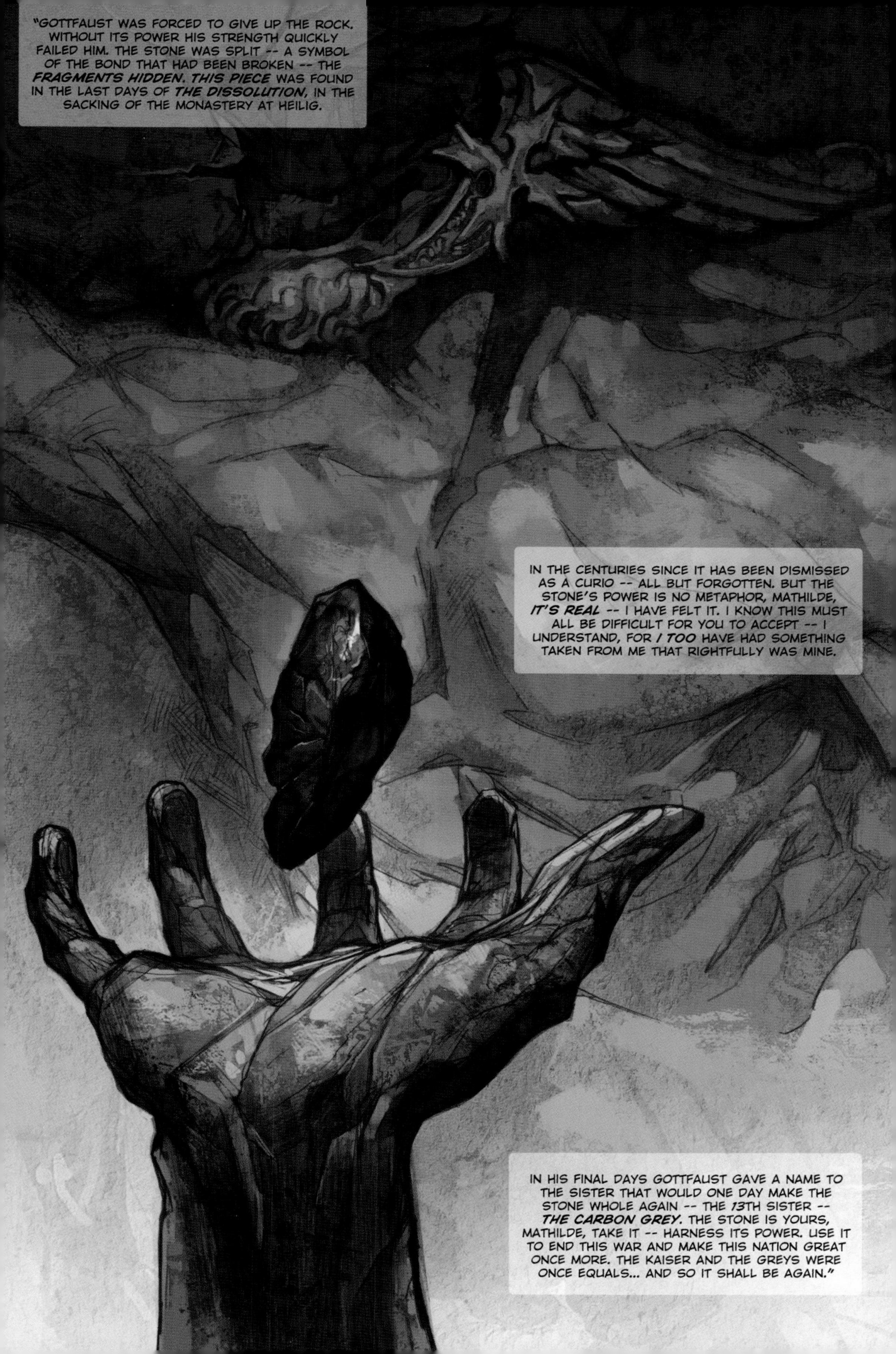
"GOTTFAUST WAS FORCED TO GIVE UP THE ROCK. WITHOUT ITS POWER HIS STRENGTH QUICKLY FAILED HIM. THE STONE WAS SPLIT -- A SYMBOL OF THE BOND THAT HAD BEEN BROKEN -- THE *FRAGMENTS HIDDEN. THIS PIECE* WAS FOUND IN THE LAST DAYS OF *THE DISSOLUTION,* IN THE SACKING OF THE MONASTERY AT HEILIG.
IN THE CENTURIES SINCE IT HAS BEEN DISMISSED AS A CURIO -- ALL BUT FORGOTTEN. BUT THE STONE'S POWER IS NO METAPHOR, MATHILDE, *IT'S REAL* -- I HAVE FELT IT. I KNOW THIS MUST ALL BE DIFFICULT FOR YOU TO ACCEPT -- I UNDERSTAND, FOR *I TOO* HAVE HAD SOMETHING TAKEN FROM ME THAT RIGHTFULLY WAS MINE.
IN HIS FINAL DAYS GOTTFAUST GAVE A NAME TO THE SISTER THAT WOULD ONE DAY MAKE THE STONE WHOLE AGAIN -- THE *13TH SISTER* -- *THE CARBON GREY.* THE STONE IS YOURS, MATHILDE, TAKE IT -- HARNESS ITS POWER. USE IT TO END THIS WAR AND MAKE THIS NATION GREAT ONCE MORE. THE KAISER AND THE GREYS WERE ONCE EQUALS... AND SO IT SHALL BE AGAIN."

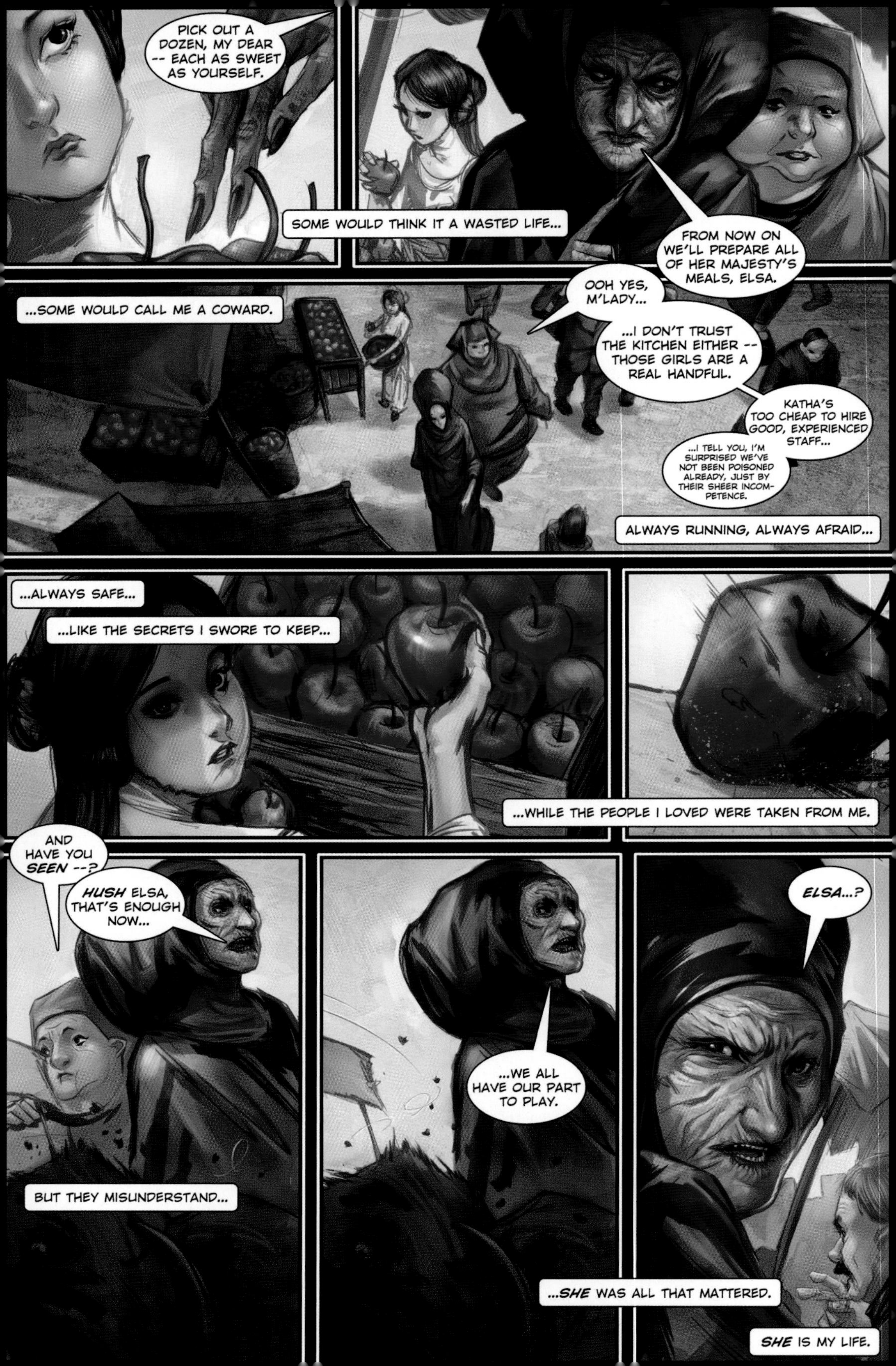
PICK OUT A DOZEN, MY DEAR -- EACH AS SWEET AS YOURSELF.
SOME WOULD THINK IT A WASTED LIFE...
FROM NOW ON WE'LL PREPARE ALL OF HER MAJESTY'S MEALS, ELSA.
...SOME WOULD CALL ME A COWARD.
OOH YES, M'LADY...
...I DON'T TRUST THE KITCHEN EITHER -- THOSE GIRLS ARE A REAL HANDFUL.
KATHA'S TOO CHEAP TO HIRE GOOD, EXPERIENCED STAFF...
...I TELL YOU, I'M SURPRISED WE'VE NOT BEEN POISONED ALREADY, JUST BY THEIR SHEER INCOMPETENCE.
ALWAYS RUNNING, ALWAYS AFRAID...
...ALWAYS SAFE...
...LIKE THE SECRETS I SWORE TO KEEP...
...WHILE THE PEOPLE I LOVED WERE TAKEN FROM ME.
AND HAVE YOU SEEN --?
HUSH ELSA, THAT'S ENOUGH NOW...
BUT THEY MISUNDERSTAND...
...WE ALL HAVE OUR PART TO PLAY.
ELSA...?
...SHE WAS ALL THAT MATTERED.
SHE IS MY LIFE.

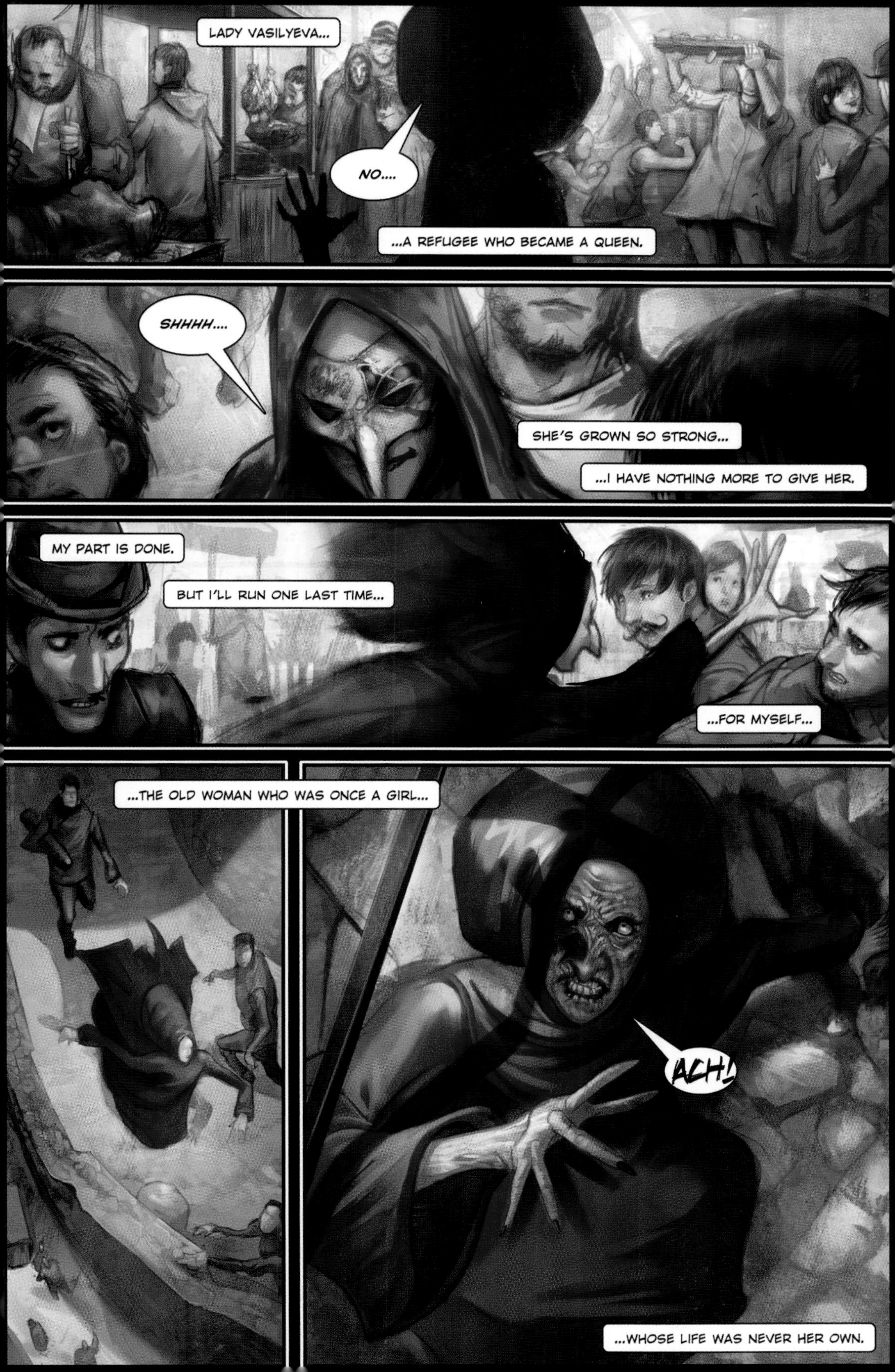

LADY VASILYEVA...
NO....
...A REFUGEE WHO BECAME A QUEEN.
SHHHH....
SHE'S GROWN SO STRONG...
...I HAVE NOTHING MORE TO GIVE HER.
MY PART IS DONE.
BUT I'LL RUN ONE LAST TIME...
...FOR MYSELF...
...THE OLD WOMAN WHO WAS ONCE A GIRL...
ACH!
...WHOSE LIFE WAS NEVER HER OWN.

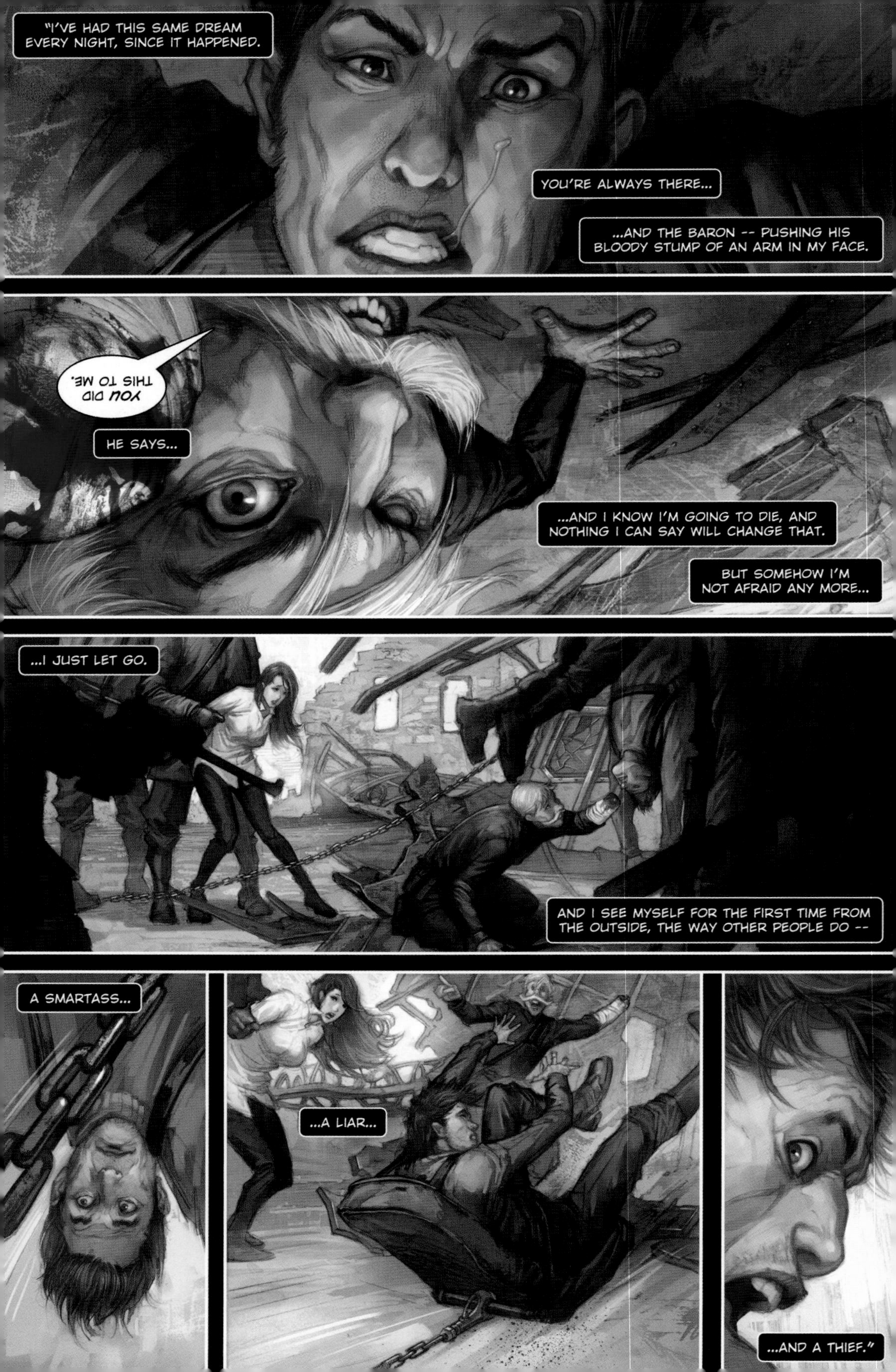
"I'VE HAD THIS SAME DREAM EVERY NIGHT, SINCE IT HAPPENED.
YOU'RE ALWAYS THERE...
...AND THE BARON -- PUSHING HIS BLOODY STUMP OF AN ARM IN MY FACE.
YOU DID THIS TO ME.
HE SAYS...
...AND I KNOW I'M GOING TO DIE, AND NOTHING I CAN SAY WILL CHANGE THAT.
BUT SOMEHOW I'M NOT AFRAID ANY MORE...
...I JUST LET GO.
AND I SEE MYSELF FOR THE FIRST TIME FROM THE OUTSIDE, THE WAY OTHER PEOPLE DO --
A SMARTASS...
...A LIAR...
...AND A THIEF."

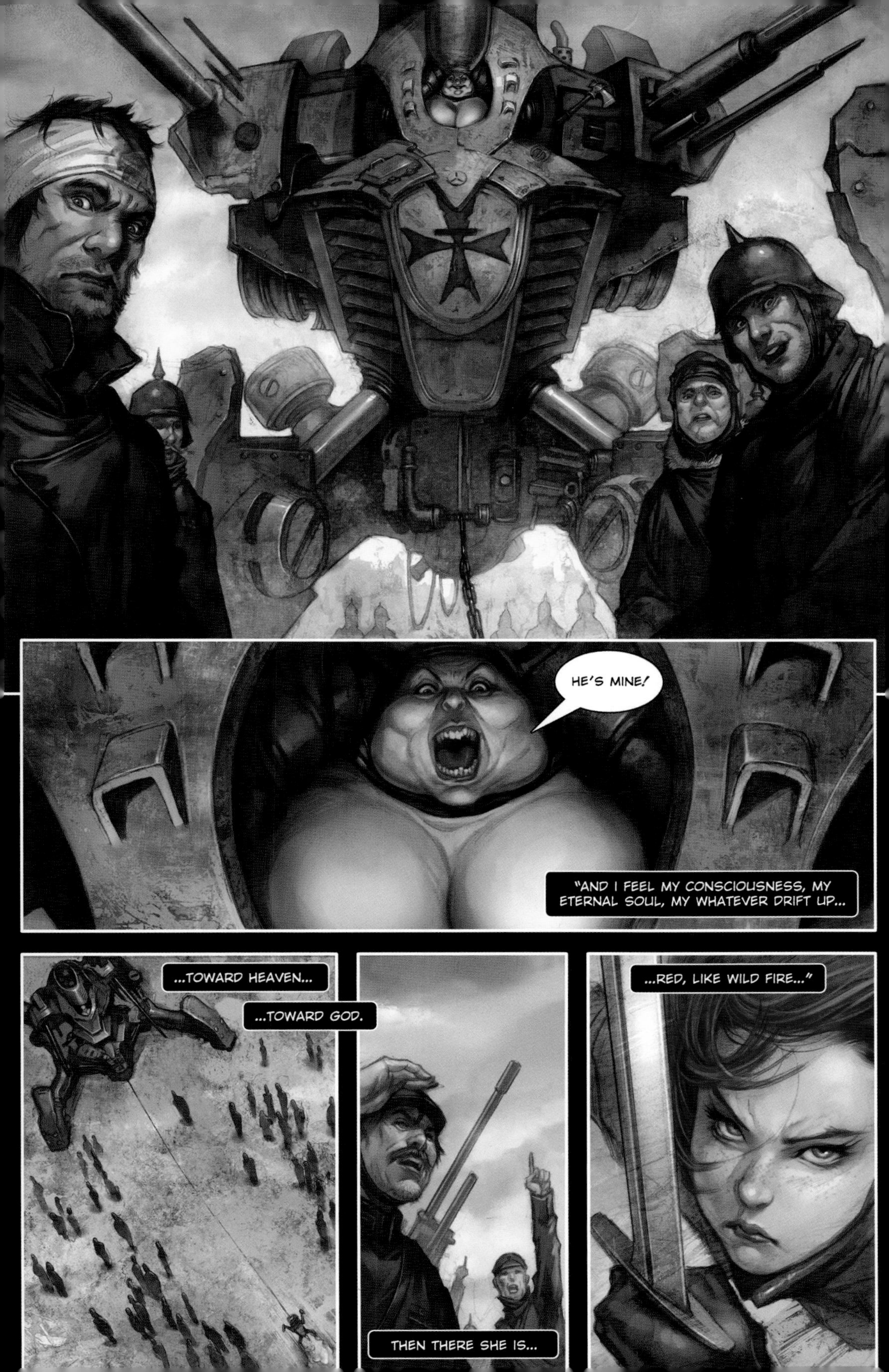
HE'S MINE!
"AND I FEEL MY CONSCIOUSNESS, MY ETERNAL SOUL, MY WHATEVER DRIFT UP...
...TOWARD HEAVEN...
...TOWARD GOD.
THEN THERE SHE IS...
...RED, LIKE WILD FIRE..."

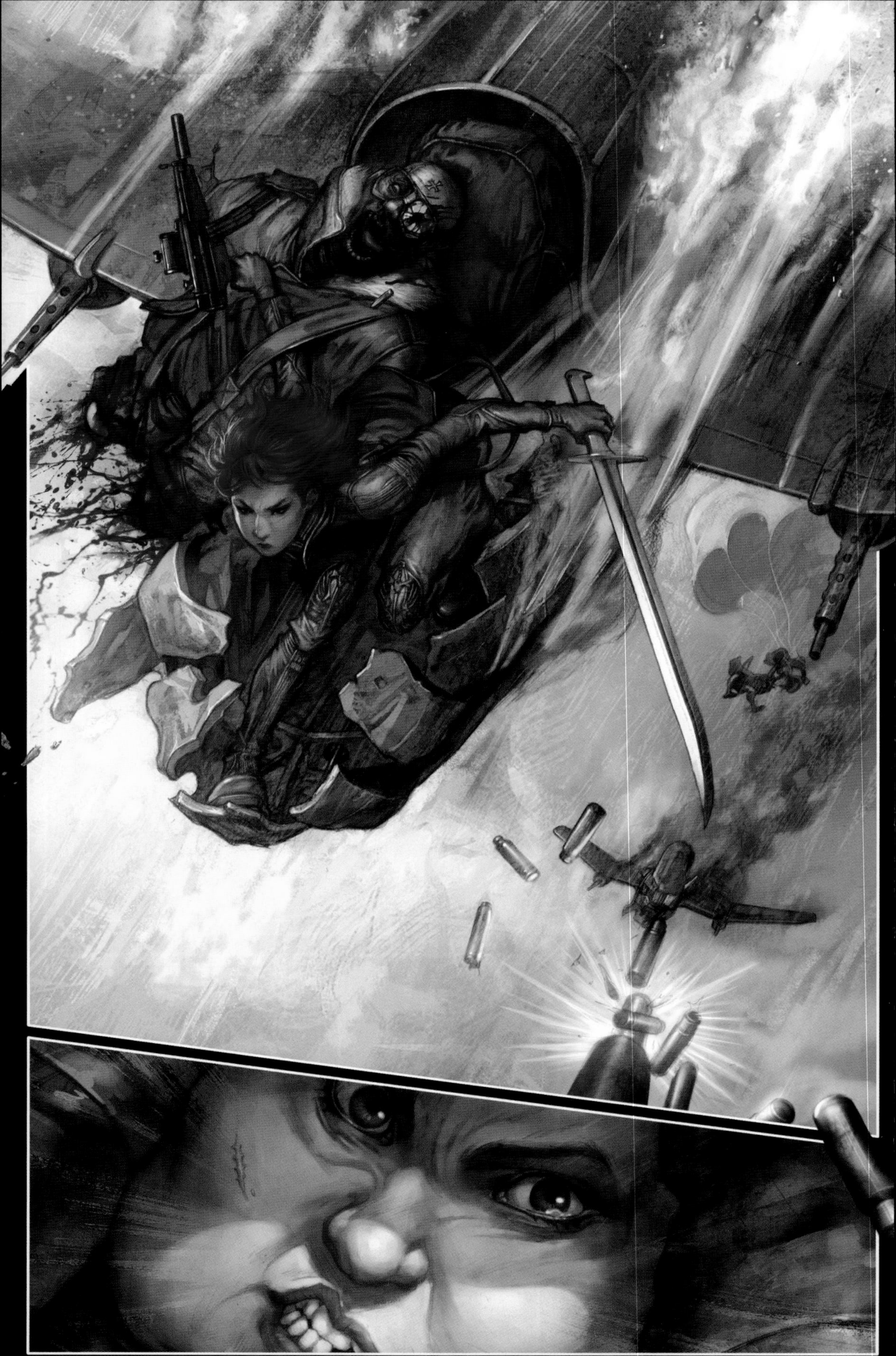

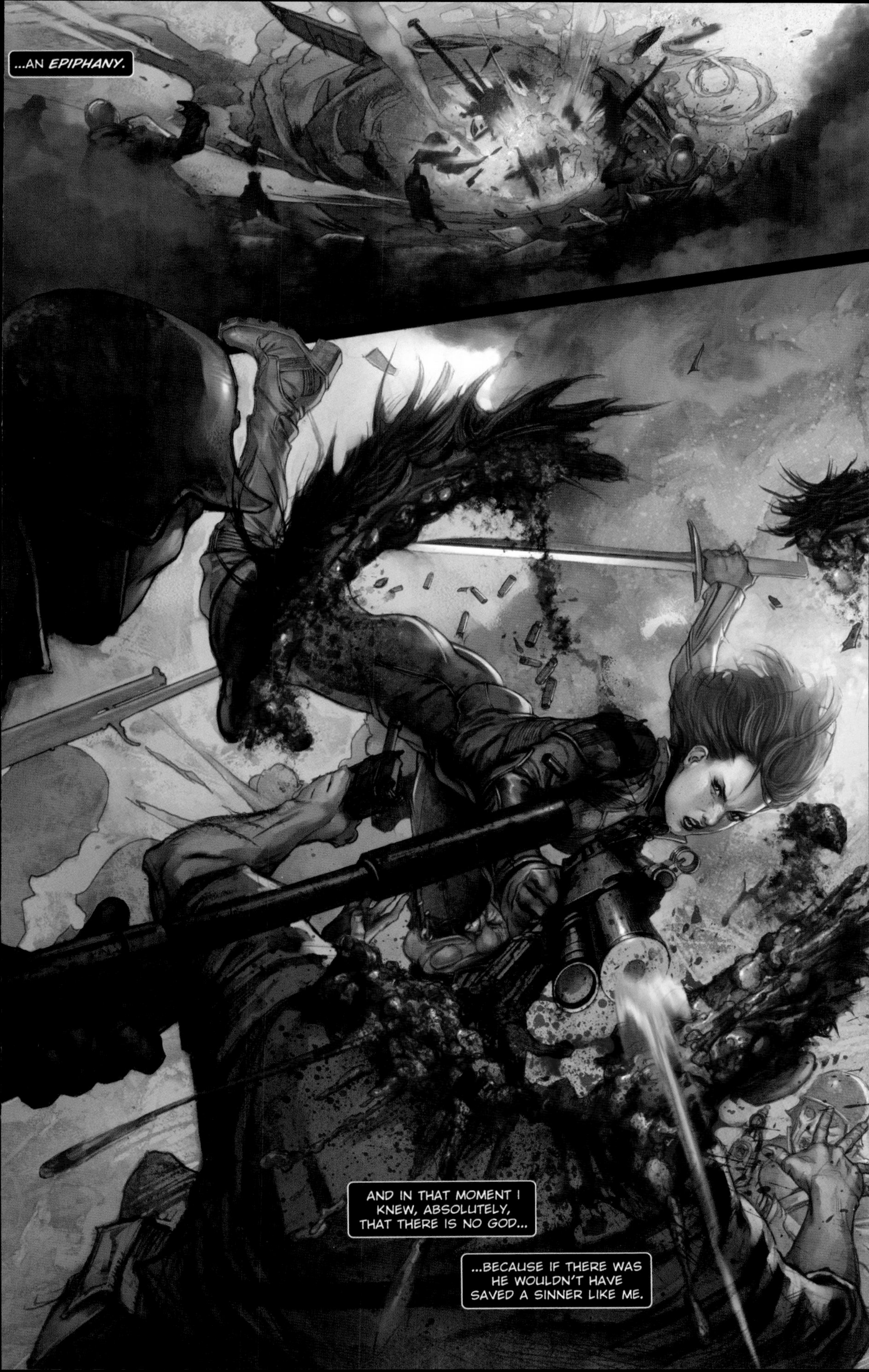
...AN *EPIPHANY*.
AND IN THAT MOMENT I KNEW, ABSOLUTELY, THAT THERE IS NO GOD...
...BECAUSE IF THERE WAS HE WOULDN'T HAVE SAVED A SINNER LIKE ME.

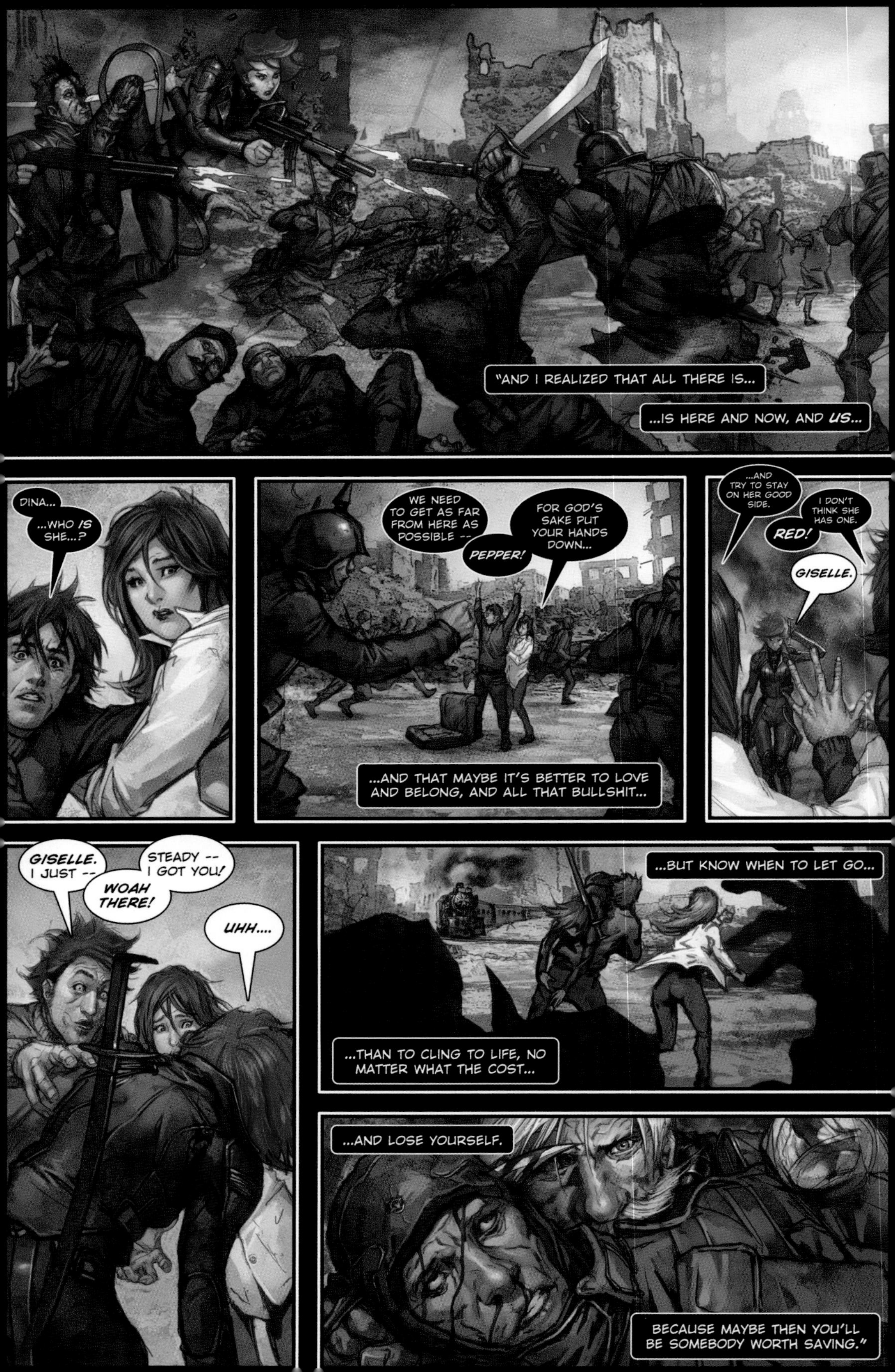
"AND I REALIZED THAT ALL THERE IS...
...IS HERE AND NOW, AND *US*...
DINA...
...WHO *IS* SHE...?
WE NEED TO GET AS FAR FROM HERE AS POSSIBLE --
PEPPER!
FOR GOD'S SAKE PUT YOUR HANDS DOWN...
...AND THAT MAYBE IT'S BETTER TO LOVE AND BELONG, AND ALL THAT BULLSHIT...
...AND TRY TO STAY ON HER GOOD SIDE.
I DON'T THINK SHE HAS ONE.
RED!
GISELLE.
GISELLE. I JUST --
WOAH THERE!
STEADY -- I GOT YOU!
UHH....
...BUT KNOW WHEN TO LET GO...
...THAN TO CLING TO LIFE, NO MATTER WHAT THE COST...
...AND LOSE YOURSELF.
BECAUSE MAYBE THEN YOU'LL BE SOMEBODY WORTH SAVING."

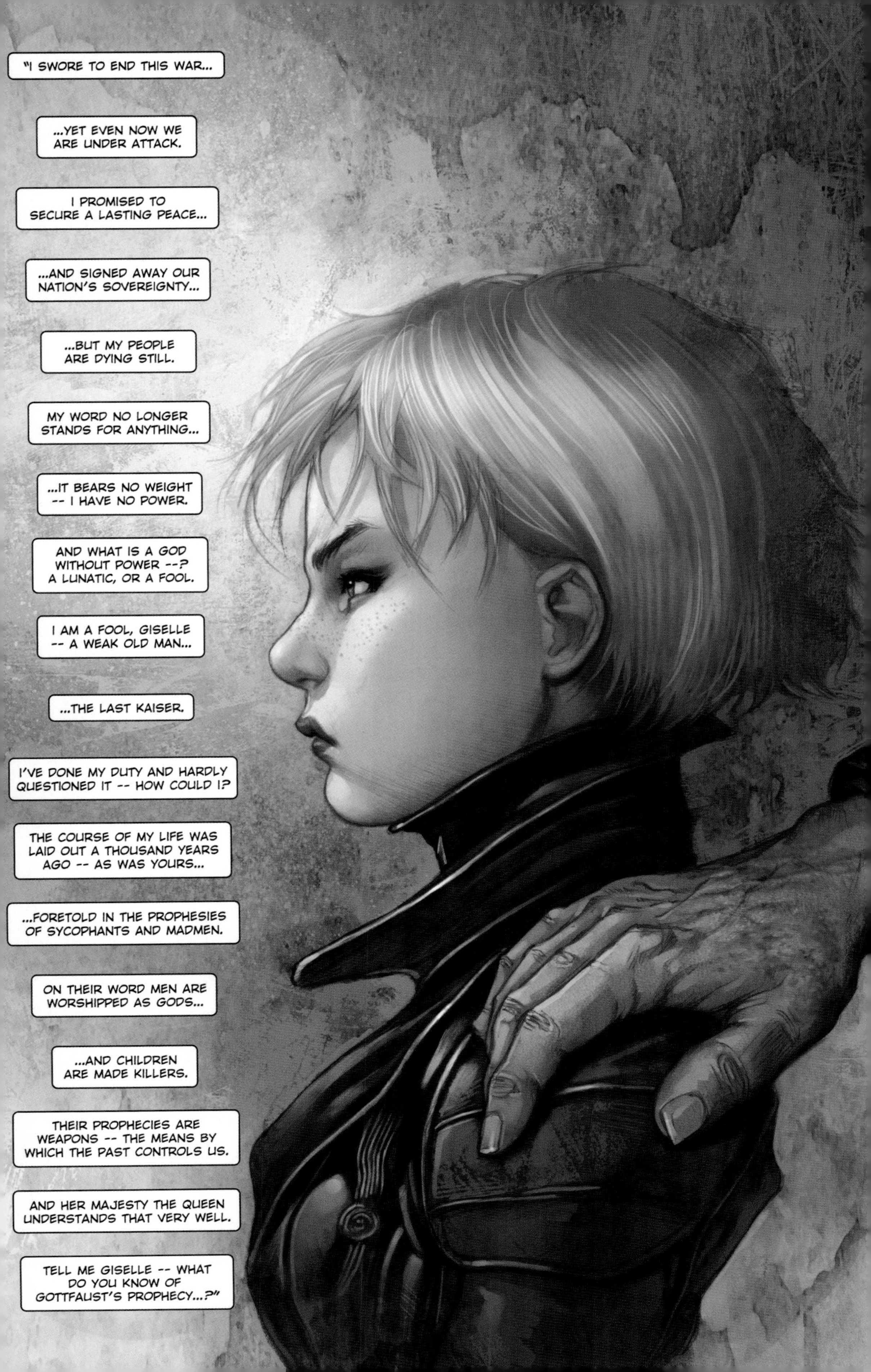
"I SWORE TO END THIS WAR...
...YET EVEN NOW WE ARE UNDER ATTACK.
I PROMISED TO SECURE A LASTING PEACE...
...AND SIGNED AWAY OUR NATION'S SOVEREIGNTY...
...BUT MY PEOPLE ARE DYING STILL.
MY WORD NO LONGER STANDS FOR ANYTHING...
...IT BEARS NO WEIGHT -- I HAVE NO POWER.
AND WHAT IS A GOD WITHOUT POWER --? A LUNATIC, OR A FOOL.
I AM A FOOL, GISELLE -- A WEAK OLD MAN...
...THE LAST KAISER.
I'VE DONE MY DUTY AND HARDLY QUESTIONED IT -- HOW COULD I?
THE COURSE OF MY LIFE WAS LAID OUT A THOUSAND YEARS AGO -- AS WAS YOURS...
...FORETOLD IN THE PROPHESIES OF SYCOPHANTS AND MADMEN.
ON THEIR WORD MEN ARE WORSHIPPED AS GODS...
...AND CHILDREN ARE MADE KILLERS.
THEIR PROPHECIES ARE WEAPONS -- THE MEANS BY WHICH THE PAST CONTROLS US.
AND HER MAJESTY THE QUEEN UNDERSTANDS THAT VERY WELL.
TELL ME GISELLE -- WHAT DO YOU KNOW OF GOTTFAUST'S PROPHECY...?"

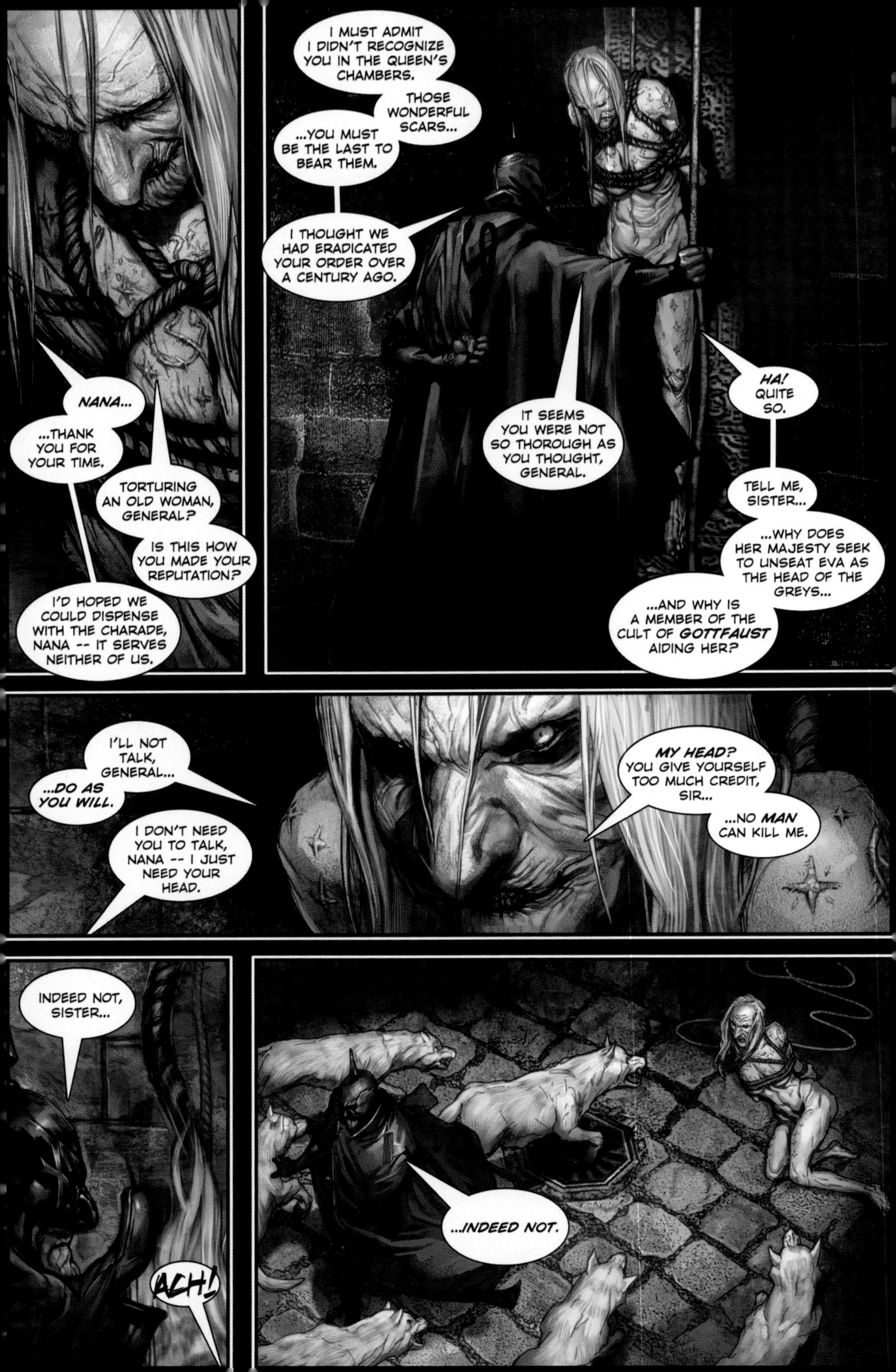

NANA...
...THANK YOU FOR YOUR TIME.
TORTURING AN OLD WOMAN, GENERAL?
IS THIS HOW YOU MADE YOUR REPUTATION?
I'D HOPED WE COULD DISPENSE WITH THE CHARADE, NANA -- IT SERVES NEITHER OF US.
I MUST ADMIT I DIDN'T RECOGNIZE YOU IN THE QUEEN'S CHAMBERS.
THOSE WONDERFUL SCARS...
...YOU MUST BE THE LAST TO BEAR THEM.
I THOUGHT WE HAD ERADICATED YOUR ORDER OVER A CENTURY AGO.
IT SEEMS YOU WERE NOT SO THOROUGH AS YOU THOUGHT, GENERAL.
HA! QUITE SO.
TELL ME, SISTER...
...WHY DOES HER MAJESTY SEEK TO UNSEAT EVA AS THE HEAD OF THE GREYS...
...AND WHY IS A MEMBER OF THE CULT OF ***GOTTFAUST*** AIDING HER?
I'LL NOT TALK, GENERAL... *...DO AS YOU WILL.*
I DON'T NEED YOU TO TALK, NANA -- I JUST NEED YOUR HEAD.
MY HEAD? YOU GIVE YOURSELF TOO MUCH CREDIT, SIR...
...NO ***MAN*** CAN KILL ME.
INDEED NOT, SISTER...
ACH!
...INDEED NOT.

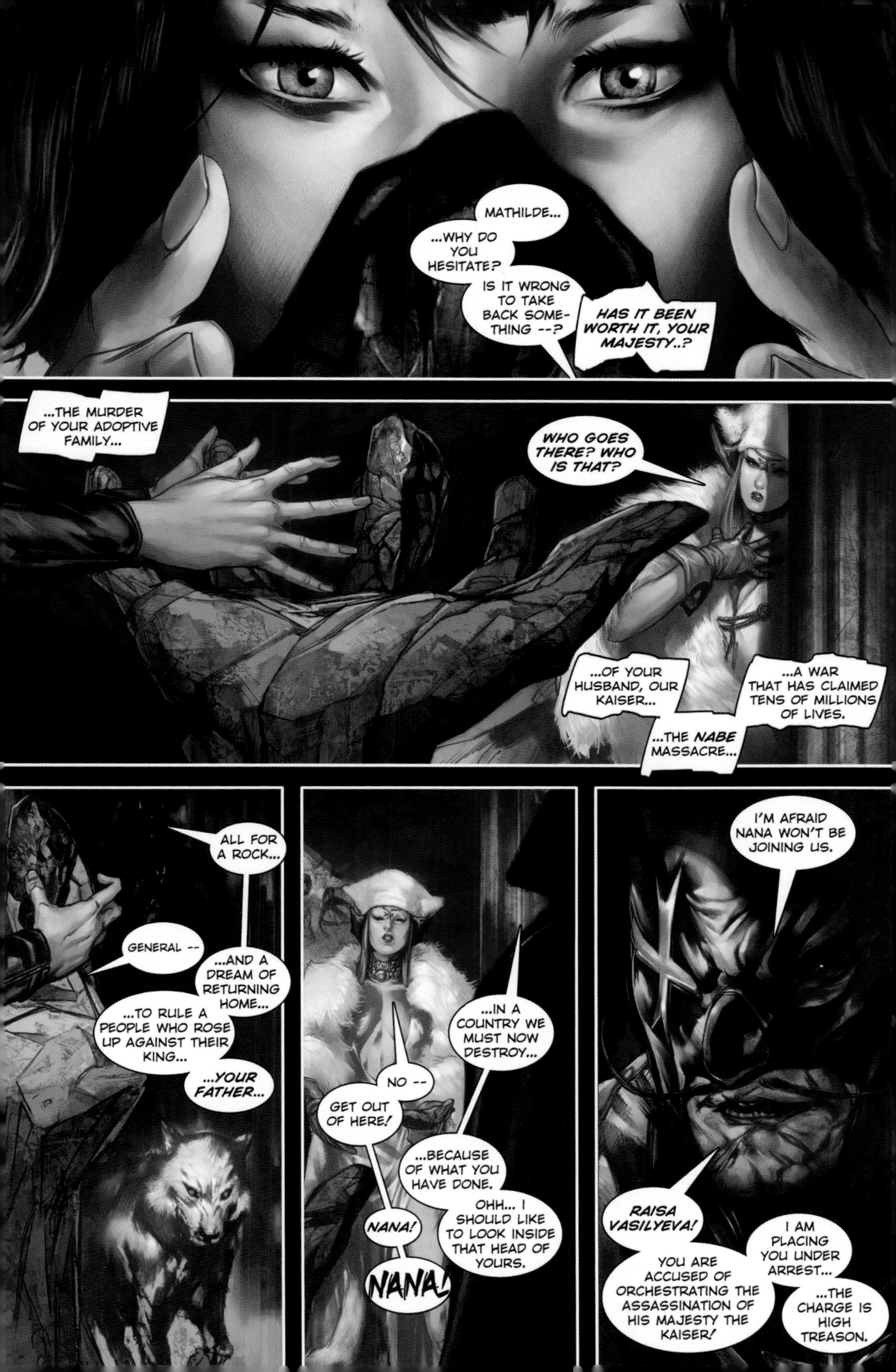
MATHILDE...
...WHY DO YOU HESITATE?
IS IT WRONG TO TAKE BACK SOME-THING --?
HAS IT BEEN WORTH IT, YOUR MAJESTY..?
...THE MURDER OF YOUR ADOPTIVE FAMILY...
WHO GOES THERE? WHO IS THAT?
...OF YOUR HUSBAND, OUR KAISER...
...THE NABE MASSACRE...
...A WAR THAT HAS CLAIMED TENS OF MILLIONS OF LIVES.
ALL FOR A ROCK...
GENERAL --
...AND A DREAM OF RETURNING HOME...
...TO RULE A PEOPLE WHO ROSE UP AGAINST THEIR KING...
...YOUR FATHER...
...IN A COUNTRY WE MUST NOW DESTROY...
NO --
GET OUT OF HERE!
...BECAUSE OF WHAT YOU HAVE DONE.
OHH... I SHOULD LIKE TO LOOK INSIDE THAT HEAD OF YOURS.
NANA!
NANA!
I'M AFRAID NANA WON'T BE JOINING US.
RAISA VASILYEVA!
YOU ARE ACCUSED OF ORCHESTRATING THE ASSASSINATION OF HIS MAJESTY THE KAISER!
I AM PLACING YOU UNDER ARREST...
...THE CHARGE IS HIGH TREASON.

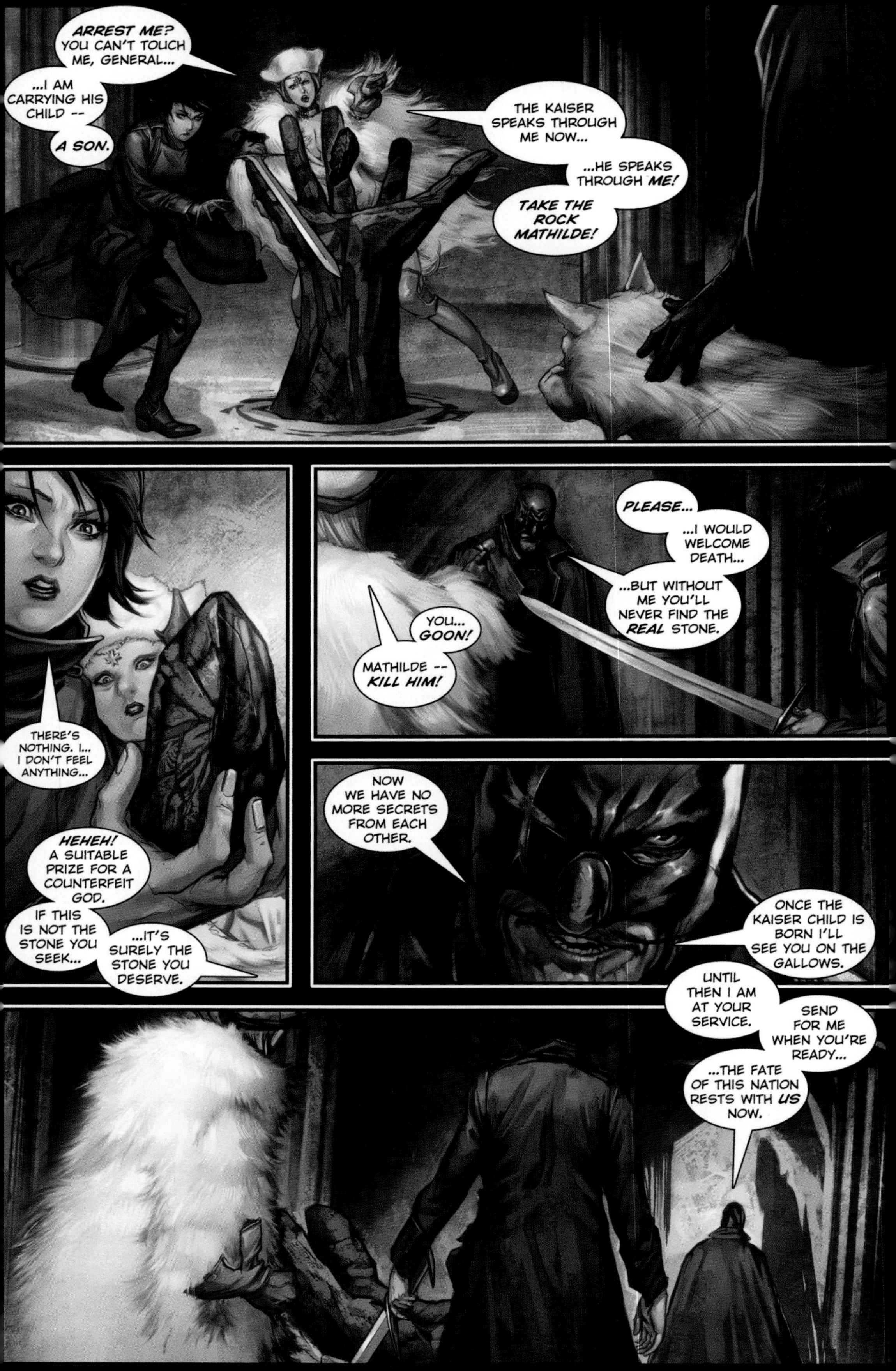
ARREST ME? YOU CAN'T TOUCH ME, GENERAL...
...I AM CARRYING HIS CHILD --
A SON.
THE KAISER SPEAKS THROUGH ME NOW...
...HE SPEAKS THROUGH ME!
TAKE THE ROCK MATHILDE!
THERE'S NOTHING. I... I DON'T FEEL ANYTHING...
HEHEH! A SUITABLE PRIZE FOR A COUNTERFEIT GOD.
IF THIS IS NOT THE STONE YOU SEEK...
...IT'S SURELY THE STONE YOU DESERVE.
PLEASE...
...I WOULD WELCOME DEATH...
...BUT WITHOUT ME YOU'LL NEVER FIND THE REAL STONE.
YOU... GOON!
MATHILDE -- KILL HIM!
NOW WE HAVE NO MORE SECRETS FROM EACH OTHER.
ONCE THE KAISER CHILD IS BORN I'LL SEE YOU ON THE GALLOWS.
UNTIL THEN I AM AT YOUR SERVICE.
SEND FOR ME WHEN YOU'RE READY...
...THE FATE OF THIS NATION RESTS WITH US NOW.

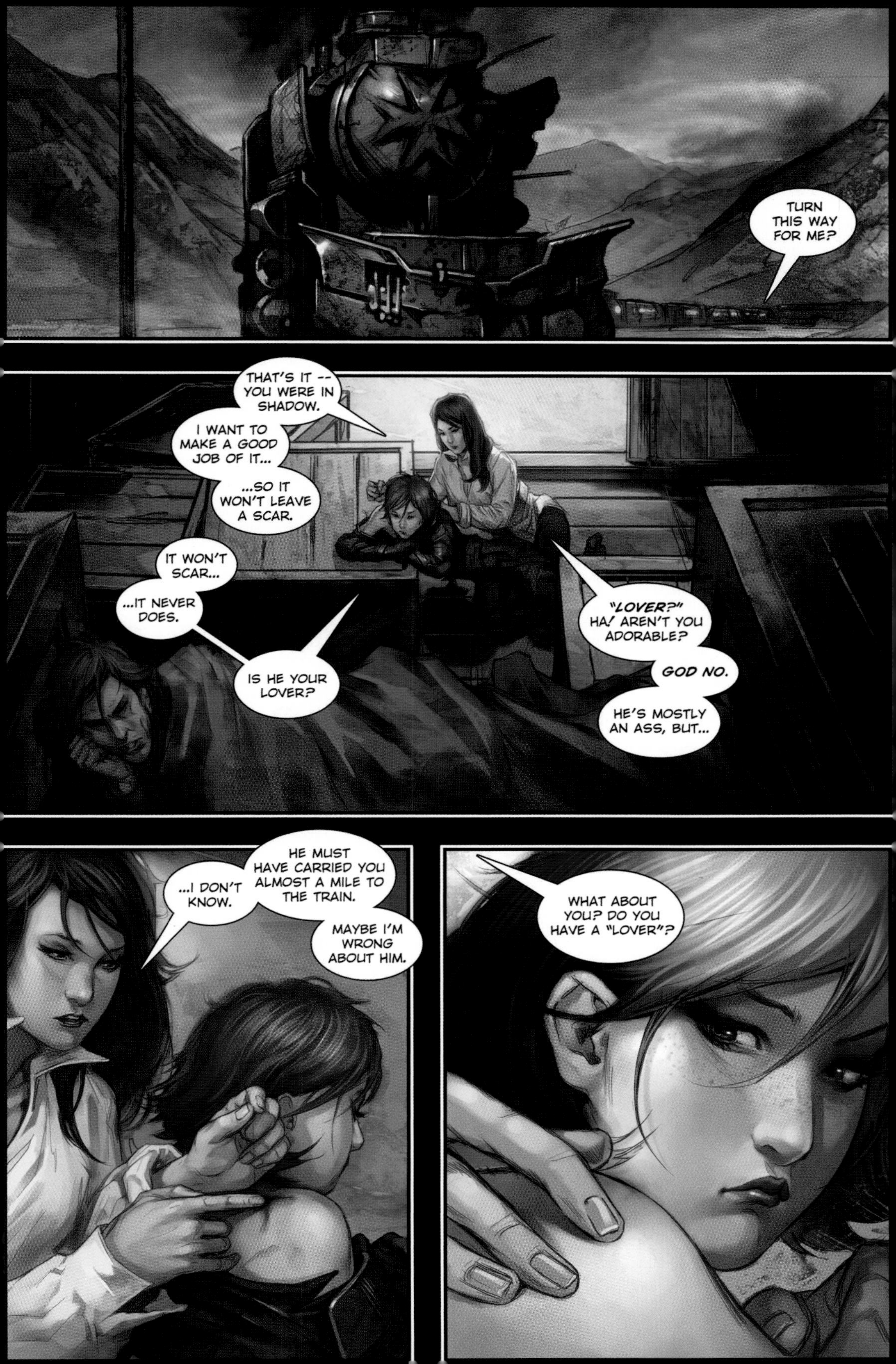
TURN THIS WAY FOR ME?
THAT'S IT -- YOU WERE IN SHADOW.
I WANT TO MAKE A GOOD JOB OF IT...
...SO IT WON'T LEAVE A SCAR.
IT WON'T SCAR...
...IT NEVER DOES.
IS HE YOUR LOVER?
"LOVER?" HA! AREN'T YOU ADORABLE?
GOD NO.
HE'S MOSTLY AN ASS, BUT...
...I DON'T KNOW.
HE MUST HAVE CARRIED YOU ALMOST A MILE TO THE TRAIN.
MAYBE I'M WRONG ABOUT HIM.
WHAT ABOUT YOU? DO YOU HAVE A "LOVER"?

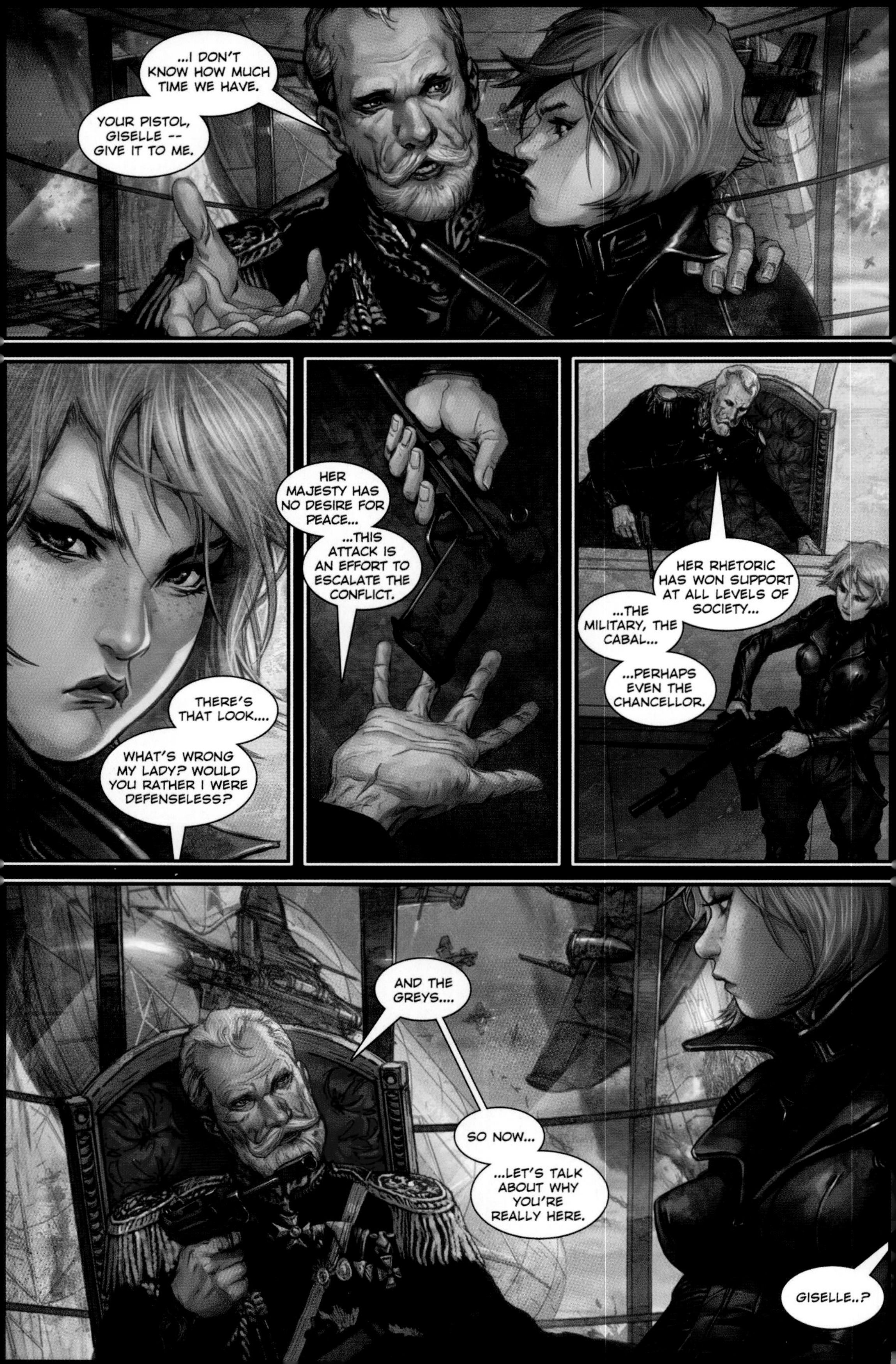
...I DON'T KNOW HOW MUCH TIME WE HAVE.
YOUR PISTOL, GISELLE -- GIVE IT TO ME.
THERE'S THAT LOOK....
WHAT'S WRONG MY LADY? WOULD YOU RATHER I WERE DEFENSELESS?
HER MAJESTY HAS NO DESIRE FOR PEACE...
...THIS ATTACK IS AN EFFORT TO ESCALATE THE CONFLICT.
HER RHETORIC HAS WON SUPPORT AT ALL LEVELS OF SOCIETY...
...THE MILITARY, THE CABAL...
...PERHAPS EVEN THE CHANCELLOR.
AND THE GREYS....
SO NOW...
...LET'S TALK ABOUT WHY YOU'RE REALLY HERE.
GISELLE..?

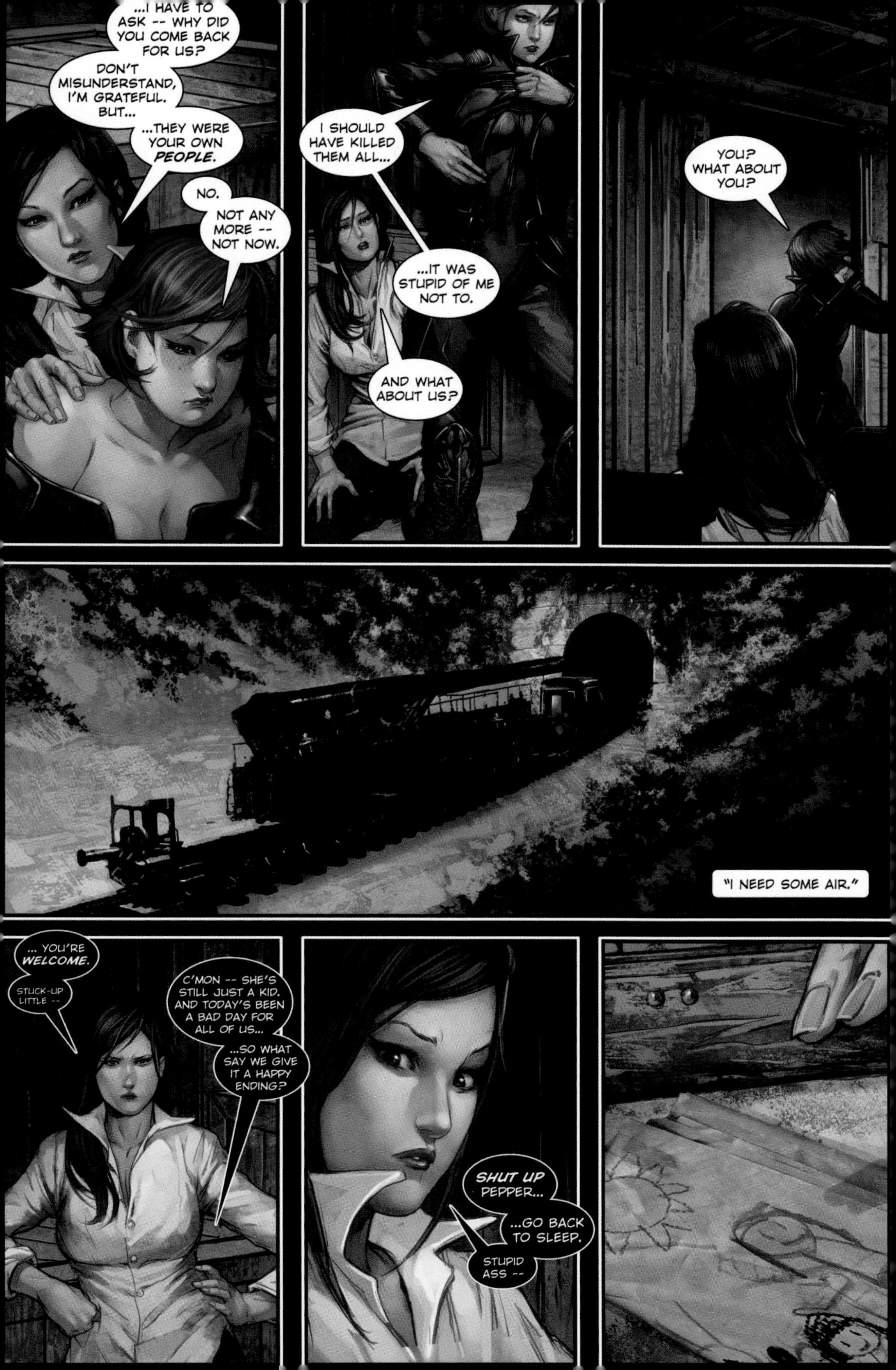
...I HAVE TO ASK -- WHY DID YOU COME BACK FOR US?
DON'T MISUNDERSTAND, I'M GRATEFUL. BUT...
...THEY WERE YOUR OWN *PEOPLE.*
NO.
NOT ANY MORE -- NOT NOW.
I SHOULD HAVE KILLED THEM ALL...
...IT WAS STUPID OF ME NOT TO.
AND WHAT ABOUT US?
YOU? WHAT ABOUT YOU?
"I NEED SOME AIR."
... YOU'RE *WELCOME.*
STUCK-UP LITTLE --
C'MON -- SHE'S STILL JUST A KID. AND TODAY'S BEEN A BAD DAY FOR ALL OF US...
...SO WHAT SAY WE GIVE IT A HAPPY ENDING?
SHUT UP PEPPER...
...GO BACK TO SLEEP.
STUPID ASS --

WHAT HAPPENED TO YOUR HAIR? YOU NEVER COULD TAKE CARE OF YOURSELF.

ANNA -- HOW...?

RADIO CHATTER. YOU KNOW BETTER THAN TO LEAVE SURVIVORS.

YOU'RE ALONE?

EVA AND I HAVE HAD A... A FALLING OUT.

RELAX, GISELLE...

...I'M HERE TO BRING YOU HOME.

YOU HAVE NOTHING TO RUN FROM ANY MORE.

THERE IS A NEW KAISER AND WE....

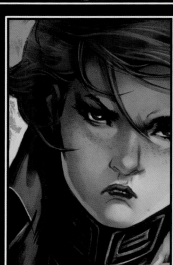

IT WASN'T YOU -- WAS IT...?

NO.

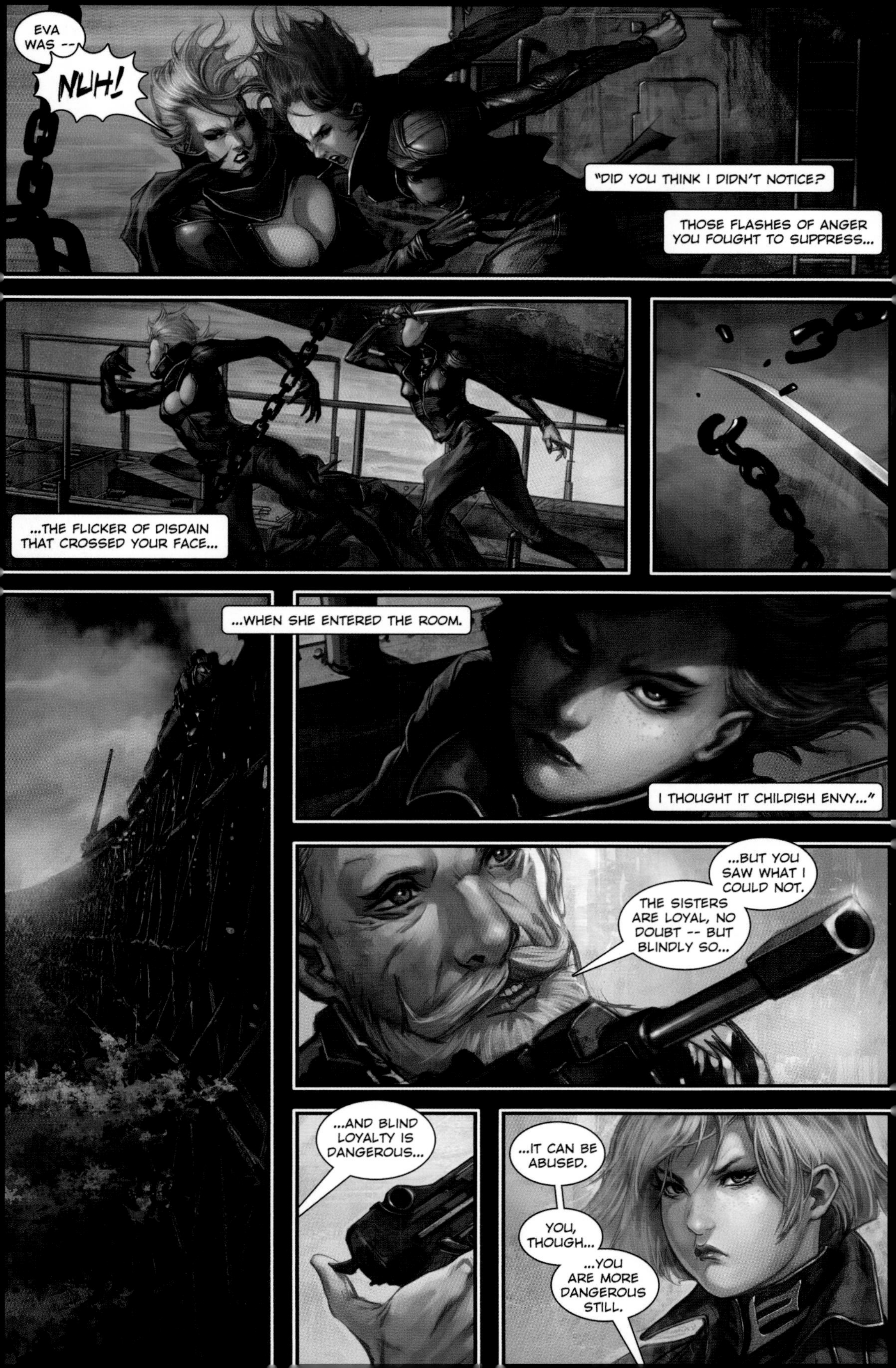
EVA WAS --
NUH!
"DID YOU THINK I DIDN'T NOTICE?
THOSE FLASHES OF ANGER YOU FOUGHT TO SUPPRESS...
...THE FLICKER OF DISDAIN THAT CROSSED YOUR FACE...
...WHEN SHE ENTERED THE ROOM.
I THOUGHT IT CHILDISH ENVY..."
...BUT YOU SAW WHAT I COULD NOT.
THE SISTERS ARE LOYAL, NO DOUBT -- BUT BLINDLY SO...
...AND BLIND LOYALTY IS DANGEROUS...
...IT CAN BE ABUSED.
YOU, THOUGH...
...YOU ARE MORE DANGEROUS STILL.

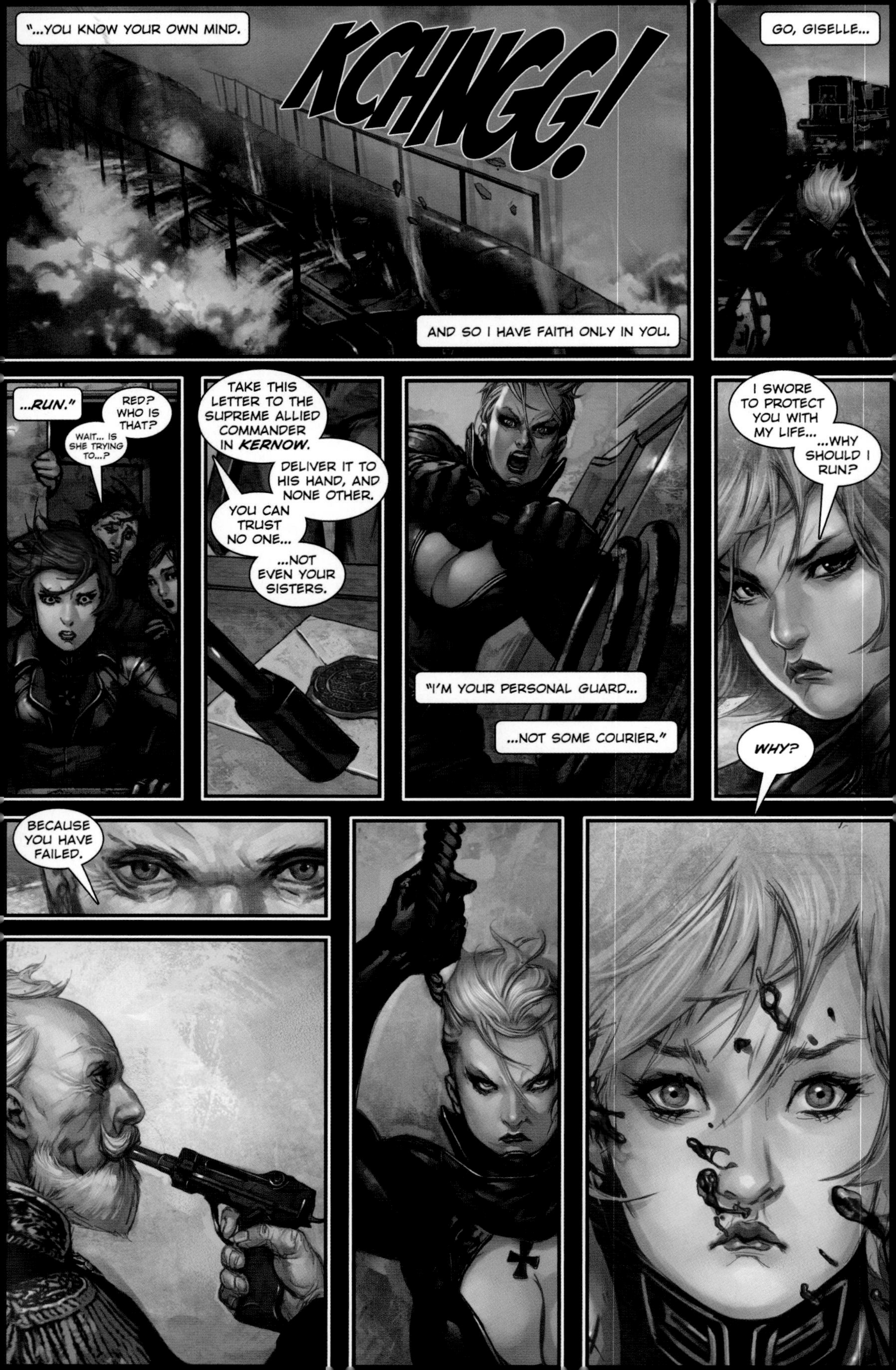
"...YOU KNOW YOUR OWN MIND.
KCHNGG!
AND SO I HAVE FAITH ONLY IN YOU.
GO, GISELLE...
...RUN."
RED? WHO IS THAT?
WAIT... IS SHE TRYING TO...?
TAKE THIS LETTER TO THE SUPREME ALLIED COMMANDER IN KERNOW.
DELIVER IT TO HIS HAND, AND NONE OTHER.
YOU CAN TRUST NO ONE...
...NOT EVEN YOUR SISTERS.
"I'M YOUR PERSONAL GUARD...
...NOT SOME COURIER."
I SWORE TO PROTECT YOU WITH MY LIFE...
...WHY SHOULD I RUN?
WHY?
BECAUSE YOU HAVE FAILED.

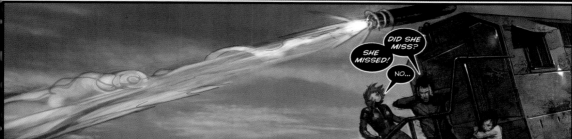

DID SHE MISS?

SHE MISSED!

NO...

...WE NEVER MISS.

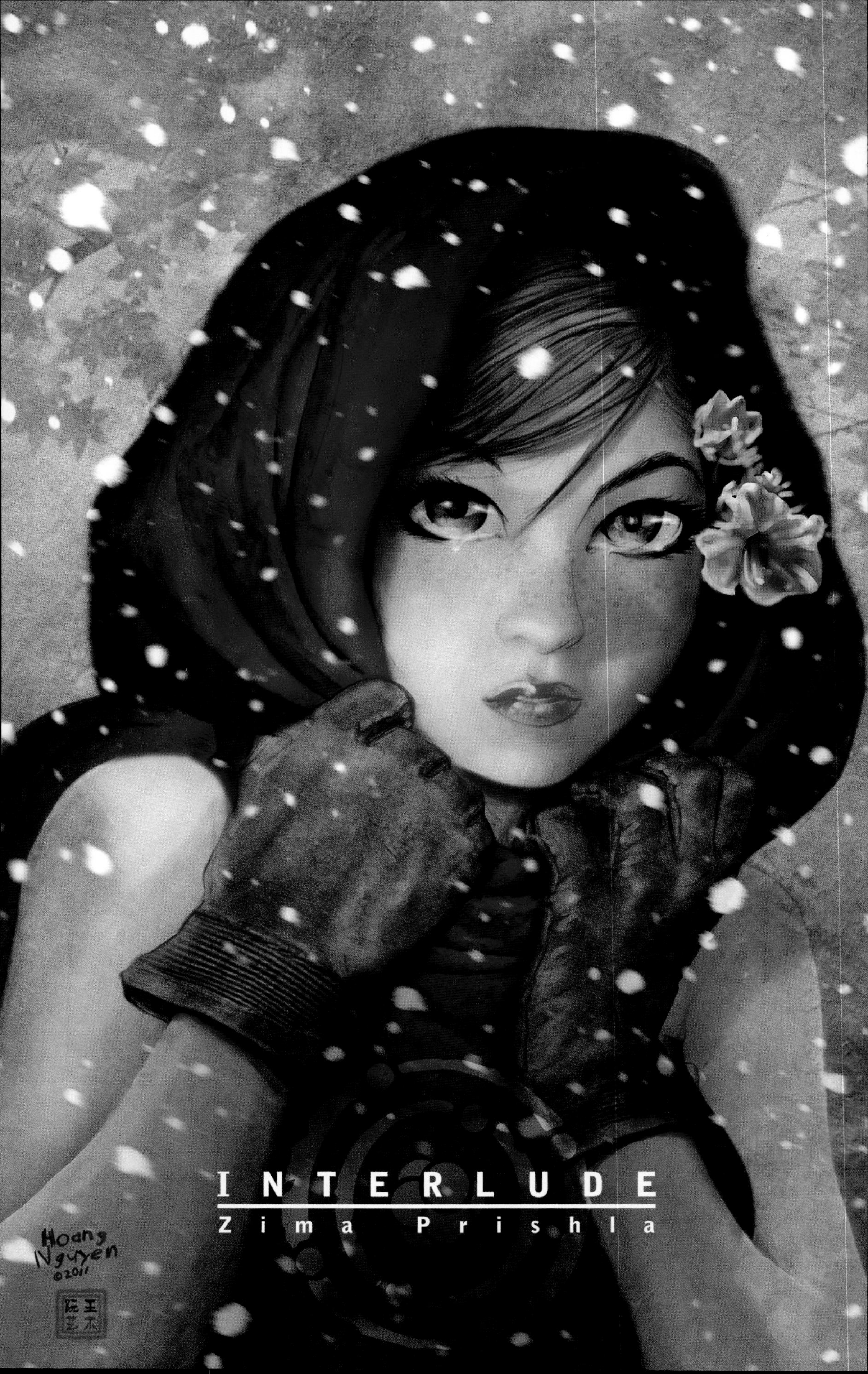
INTERLUDE
Zima Prishla
Hoang Nguyen
©2011

For countless generations the kingdom of Ursa was ruled by the noble family Zakharin. There had always been a Czar, or so it seemed, and the ancient city of Meska drew comfort from the thought that there always would be.

Then, one winter not long before this war began, there came a storm fiercer than any in the great nation's time, and for seven unbroken weeks the snow came in sheets and the wind in screams, and the cold was enough to freeze a man's prayers in his throat.

Story & Script
Tanya Landsberger · Paul Gardner
Artwork
Hoang Nguyen · Khari Evans · Kinsun Loh

Only one newborn survived the winter -- a baby girl, daughter to a palace servant and pale as the sky that had buried the city in its white grave. The servants whispered that the child carried the cold inside her, and she was not seen as a miracle but rather an omen of the storm, of hardship, and of death and disgrace.

The Czar held her just once to name her, as tradition demanded. He called her 'Raisa', perhaps hoping it would somehow bring a blush to her cheeks, but the child remained a pale winter bloom.

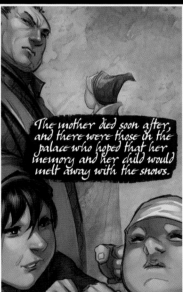

The mother died soon after, and there were those in the palace who hoped that her memory and her child would melt away with the snows.

And it would have been so, if not for dear Alena, the Czar's young daughter and only heir.

The Princess could have anything she wanted, and she wanted only Raisa, her porcelain doll. All they needed was each other -- it was enough.

But that great storm had never truly passed, for a dull sense of anger still lingered in the city. Those the winter had made widows, or left childless could only dwell on the bitterness of life, while the firelight shone from the windows of the royal palace.

The whispers of discontent that had begun those five winters before grew to a deafening roar, and this storm the palace walls could not hold back.

The palace was already in flames when the Governess slipped into the nursery and shook the girls awake.

They fled through the sewers no longer a princess and a servant's daughter but equals; both fugitives, both victims of something they did not understand.

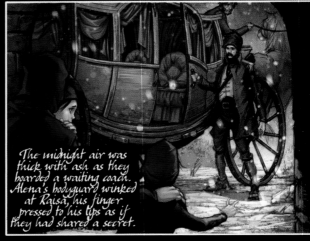

The midnight air was thick with ash as they boarded a waiting coach. Alena's bodyguard winked at Raisa, his finger pressed to his lips as if they had shared a secret.

They felt safe now, moving away from the city with their Governess and the Guardsman. Kasimir, the only man the girls had ever truly trusted. So when he told them --

CLOSE YOUR EYES, GIRLS....

of course they did.

His first shot burned itself into the Governess's belly, and the horses spooked. His second missed its mark as the carriage rolled on an icy bend and thrashed itself against the road like the Governess in her death throes.

The girls had not yet known betrayal, and it took a third shot to break the spell and make them run.

But run they did, not sure where they were going, just knowing they had to get away.

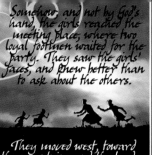

Somehow, and not by God's hand, the girls reached the meeting place, where two loyal footmen waited for the party. They saw the girls' faces, and knew better than to ask about the others.
They moved west, toward the mountains and the border beyond. Each night they made camp, their stomachs as empty as the brothers' whispered assurances.
On the fifth night they took shelter in a ruined farmhouse.
Raisa dreamt of her Mother, her face indistinct, shrouded in some suffocating fog.
She woke to a low, rasping moan, unsure at first if it came from her dreams or the timbers above her. Untangling herself from Alena's arms she slipped away from the dying embers of the fire and out into the night.
The stable was damp, and so cold, its broken belly lit by a shaft of moonlight sharp enough to pierce the walls. There was that noise again, and in the corner where even the moonlight would not go sat the ragged figure of a man.
Raisa's heart beat a Morse-coded message in her chest -- 'go to him', and she couldn't stop herself, her fascination greater than her fear. Her world was that rasping sound, and all she could see were her hands as she reached out to touch him.
Something that had once been fingers darted out and snatched up the girl's hands, his touch a searing cold, and Raisa screamed, lost to the blinding pain, the spell broken.

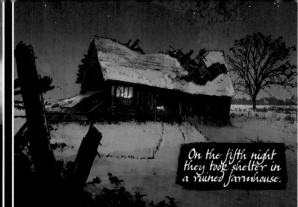

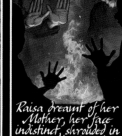

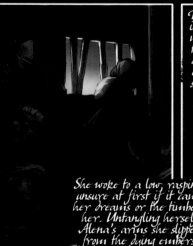

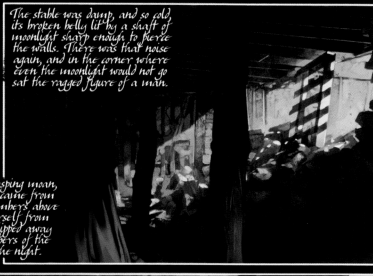

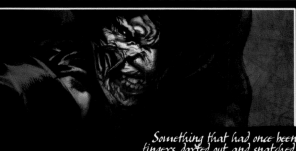

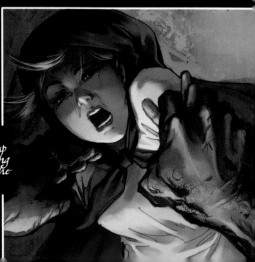

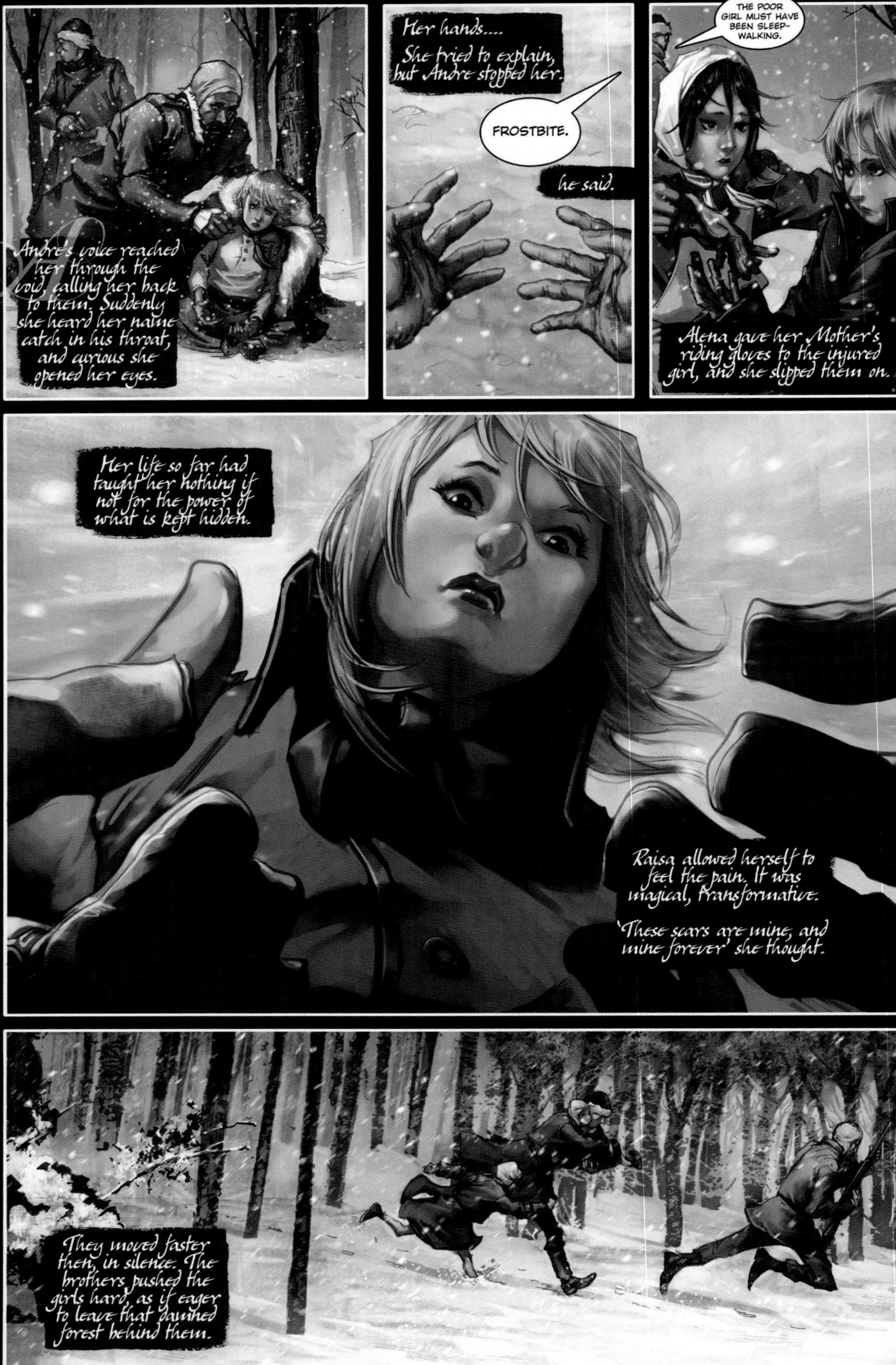
Andre's voice reached her through the void, calling her back to them. Suddenly she heard her name catch in his throat, and curious she opened her eyes.
Her hands....
She tried to explain, but Andre stopped her.
FROSTBITE.
he said.
THE POOR GIRL MUST HAVE BEEN SLEEP-WALKING.
Alena gave her Mother's riding gloves to the injured girl, and she slipped them on.
Her life so far had taught her nothing if not for the power of what is kept hidden.
Raisa allowed herself to feel the pain. It was magical, transformative.
'These scars are mine, and mine forever' she thought.
They moved faster then, in silence. The brothers pushed the girls hard, as if eager to leave that damned forest behind them.

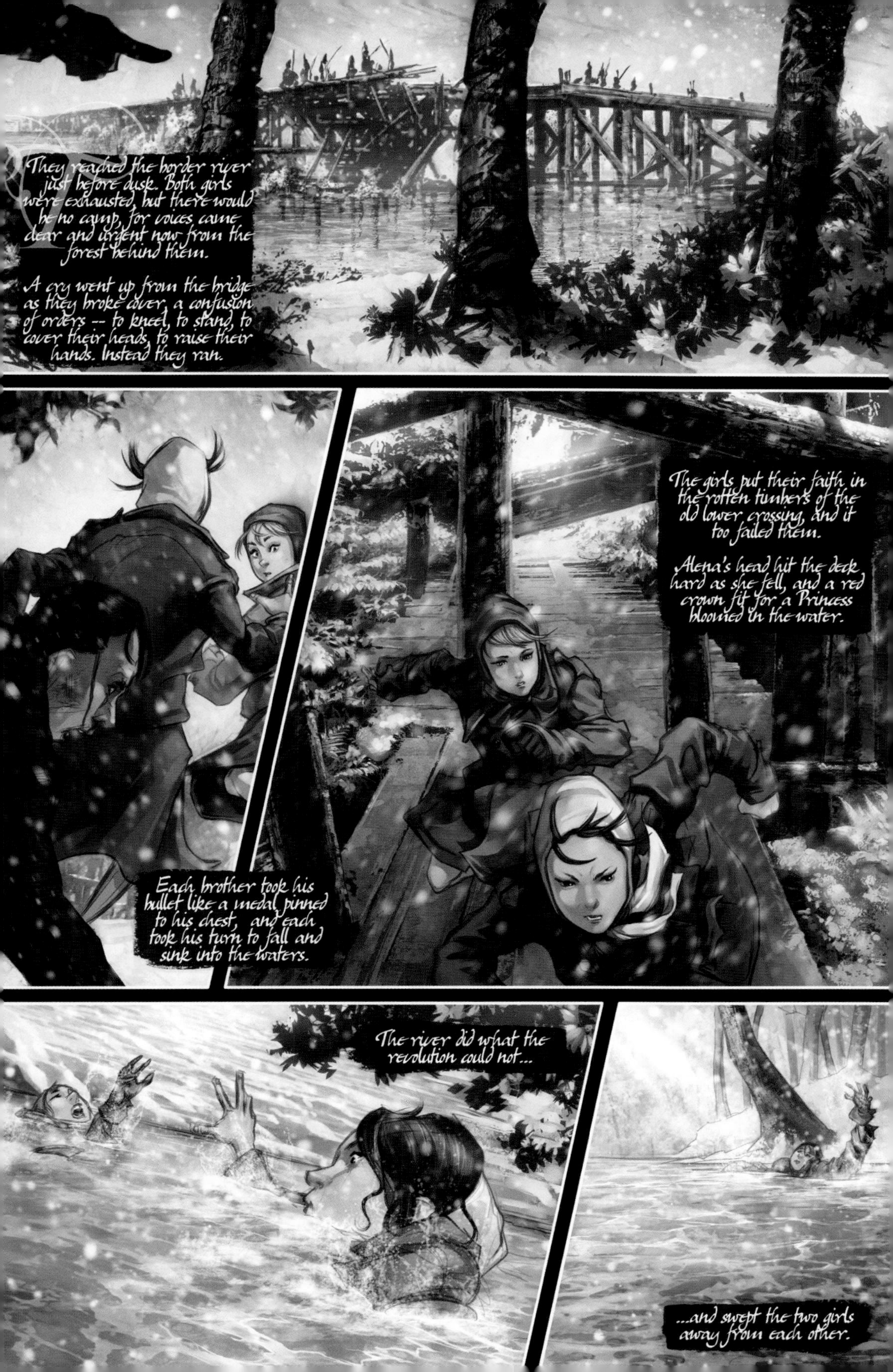
They reached the border river just before dusk. Both girls were exhausted, but there would be no camp, for voices came clear and urgent now from the forest behind them.
A cry went up from the bridge as they broke cover, a confusion of orders -- to kneel, to stand, to cover their heads, to raise their hands. Instead they ran.
Each brother took his bullet like a medal pinned to his chest, and each took his turn to fall and sink into the waters.
The girls put their faith in the rotten timbers of the old lower crossing, and it too failed them.
Alena's head hit the deck hard as she fell, and a red crown fit for a Princess bloomed in the water.
The river did what the revolution could not...
...and swept the two girls away from each other.

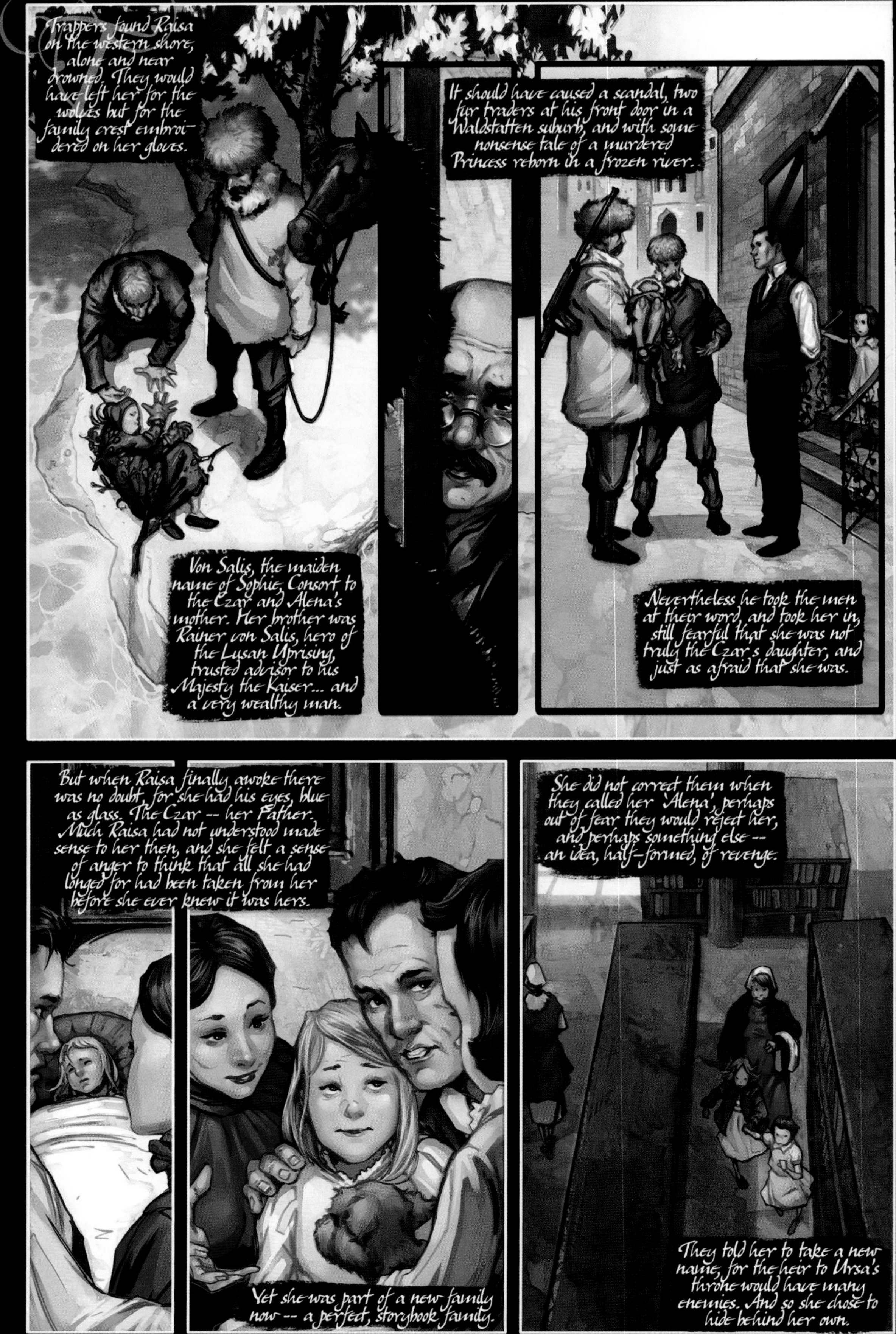
Trappers found Raisa on the western shore, alone and near drowned. They would have left her for the wolves but for the family crest embroidered on her gloves.
Von Salis, the maiden name of Sophie, Consort to the Czar and Alena's mother. Her brother was Rainer von Salis, hero of the Lusan Uprising, trusted advisor to his Majesty the Kaiser... and a very wealthy man.
It should have caused a scandal, two fur traders at his front door in a Waldstatten suburb, and with some nonsense tale of a murdered Princess reborn in a frozen river.
Nevertheless he took the men at their word, and took her in, still fearful that she was not truly the Czar's daughter, and just as afraid that she was.
But when Raisa finally awoke there was no doubt, for she had his eyes, blue as glass. The Czar -- her Father. Much Raisa had not understood made sense to her then, and she felt a sense of anger to think that all she had longed for had been taken from her before she ever knew it was hers.
Yet she was part of a new family now -- a perfect, storybook family.
She did not correct them when they called her 'Alena', perhaps out of fear they would reject her, and perhaps something else -- an idea, half-formed, of revenge.
They told her to take a new name, for the heir to Ursa's throne would have many enemies. And so she chose to hide behind her own.

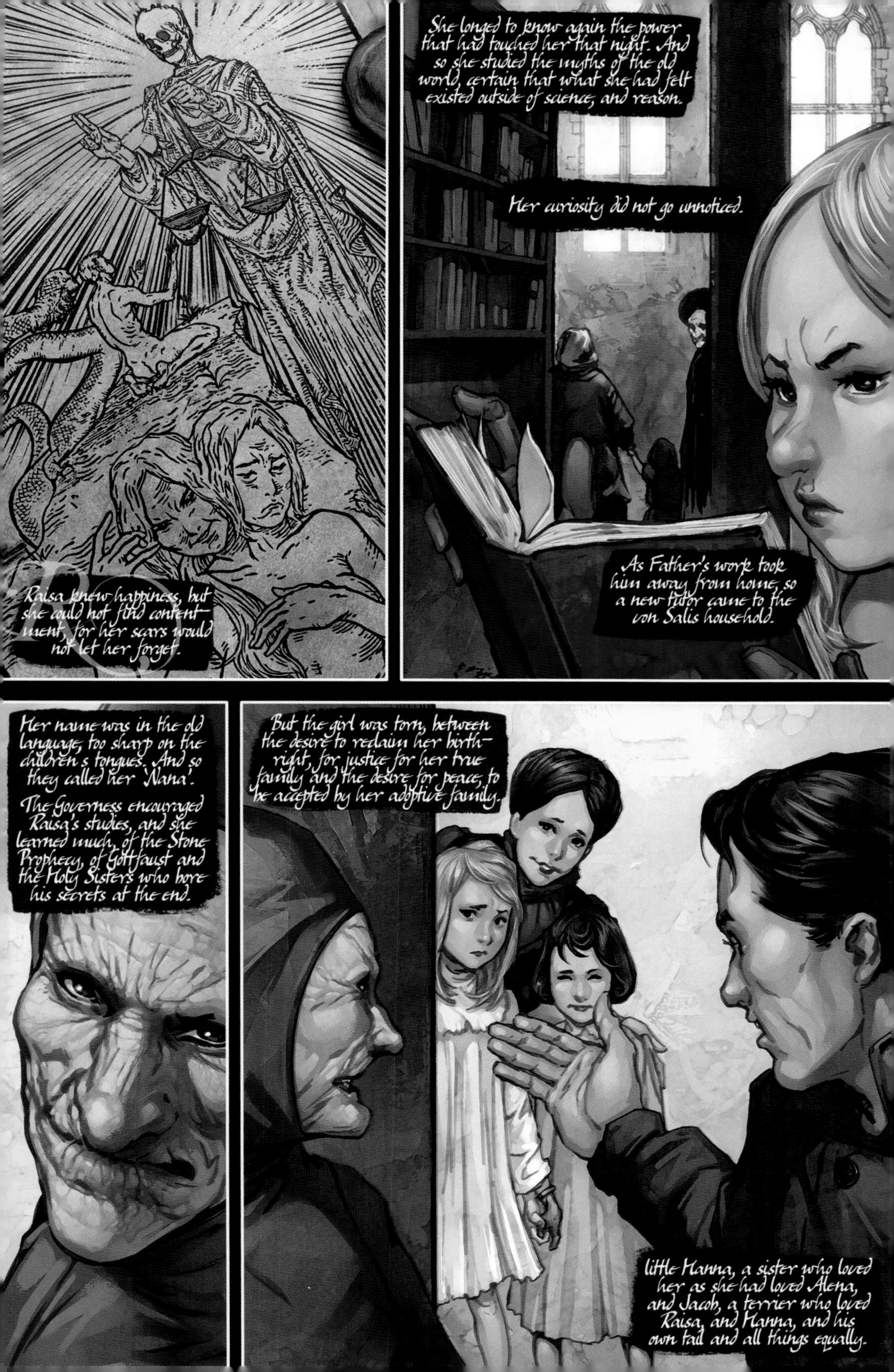
Raisa knew happiness, but she could not find content-ment, for her scars would not let her forget.
She longed to know again the power that had touched her that night. And so she studied the myths of the old world, certain that what she had felt existed outside of science, and reason.
Her curiosity did not go unnoticed.
As Father's work took him away from home, so a new tutor came to the von Salis household.
Her name was in the old language, too sharp on the children's tongues. And so they called her 'Nana'.
The Governess encouraged Raisa's studies, and she learned much, of the Stone Prophecy, of Gottfaust and the Holy Sisters who bore his secrets at the end.
But the girl was torn, between the desire to reclaim her birth-right, for justice for her true family and the desire for peace, to be accepted by her adoptive family.
little Hanna, a sister who loved her as she had loved Alena, and Jacob, a terrier who loved Raisa, and Hanna, and his own tail and all things equally.

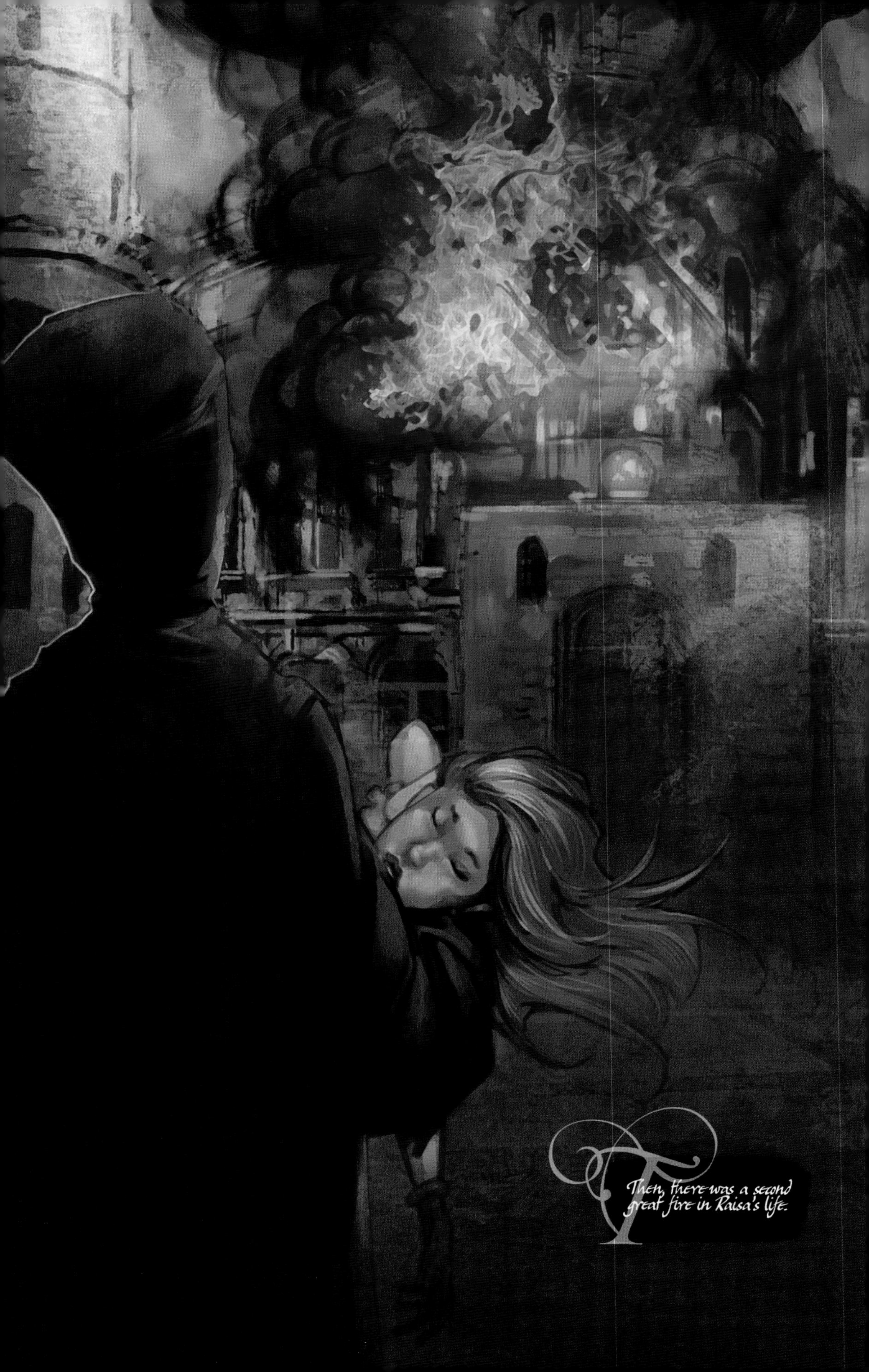
Then, there was a second great fire in Raisa's life.

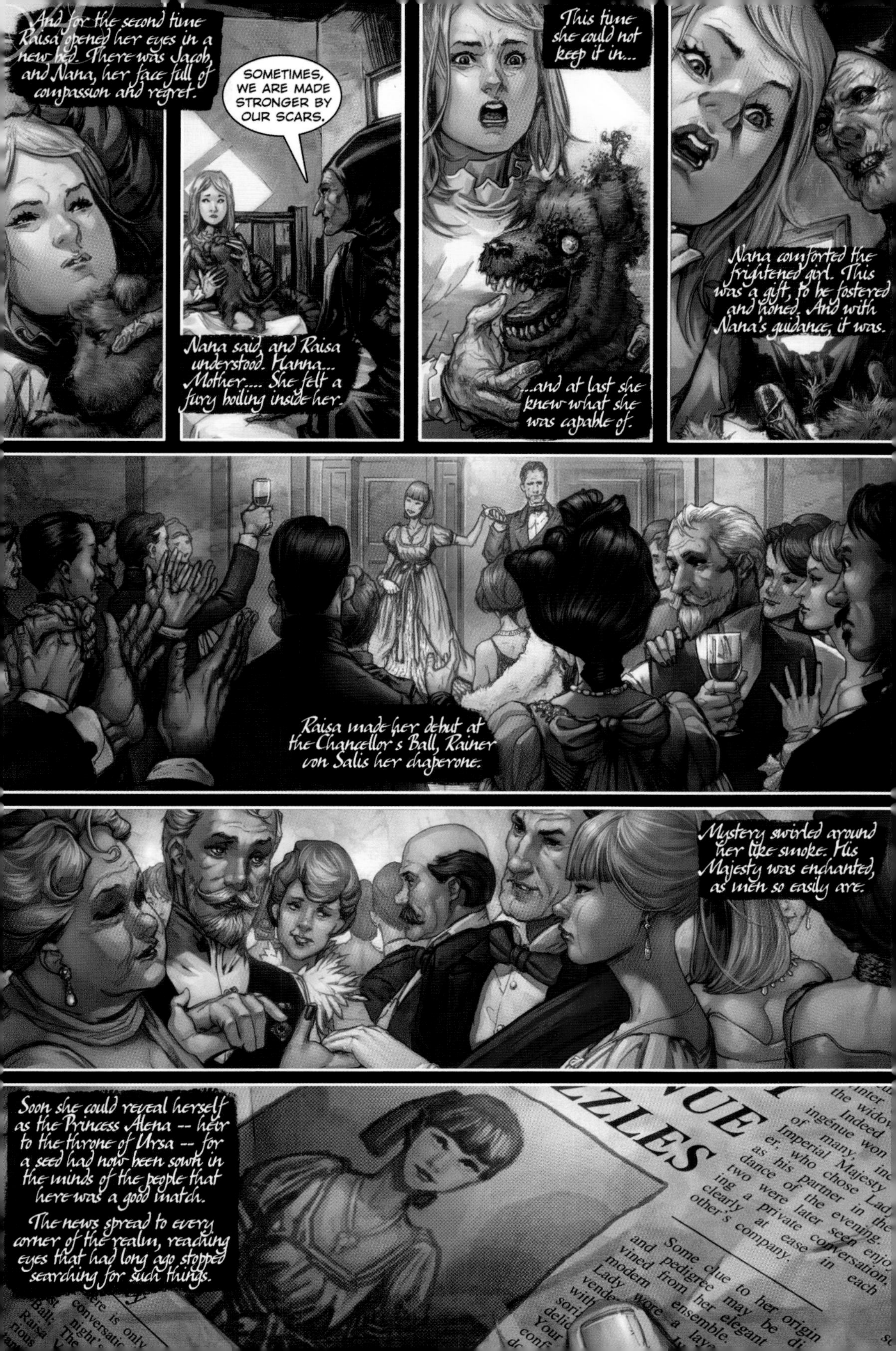
And for the second time Raisa opened her eyes in a new bed. There was Jacob, and Nana, her face full of compassion and regret.
SOMETIMES, WE ARE MADE STRONGER BY OUR SCARS.
Nana said, and Raisa understood. Hanna... Mother.... She felt a fury boiling inside her.
This time she could not keep it in...
...and at last she knew what she was capable of.
Nana comforted the frightened girl. This was a gift, to be fostered and honed. And with Nana's guidance, it was.
Raisa made her debut at the Chancellor's Ball, Rainer von Salis her chaperone.
Mystery swirled around her like smoke. His Majesty was enchanted, as men so easily are.
Soon she could reveal herself as the Princess Alena -- heir to the throne of Ursa -- for a seed had now been sown in the minds of the people that here was a good match.
The news spread to every corner of the realm, reaching eyes that had long ago stopped searching for such things.

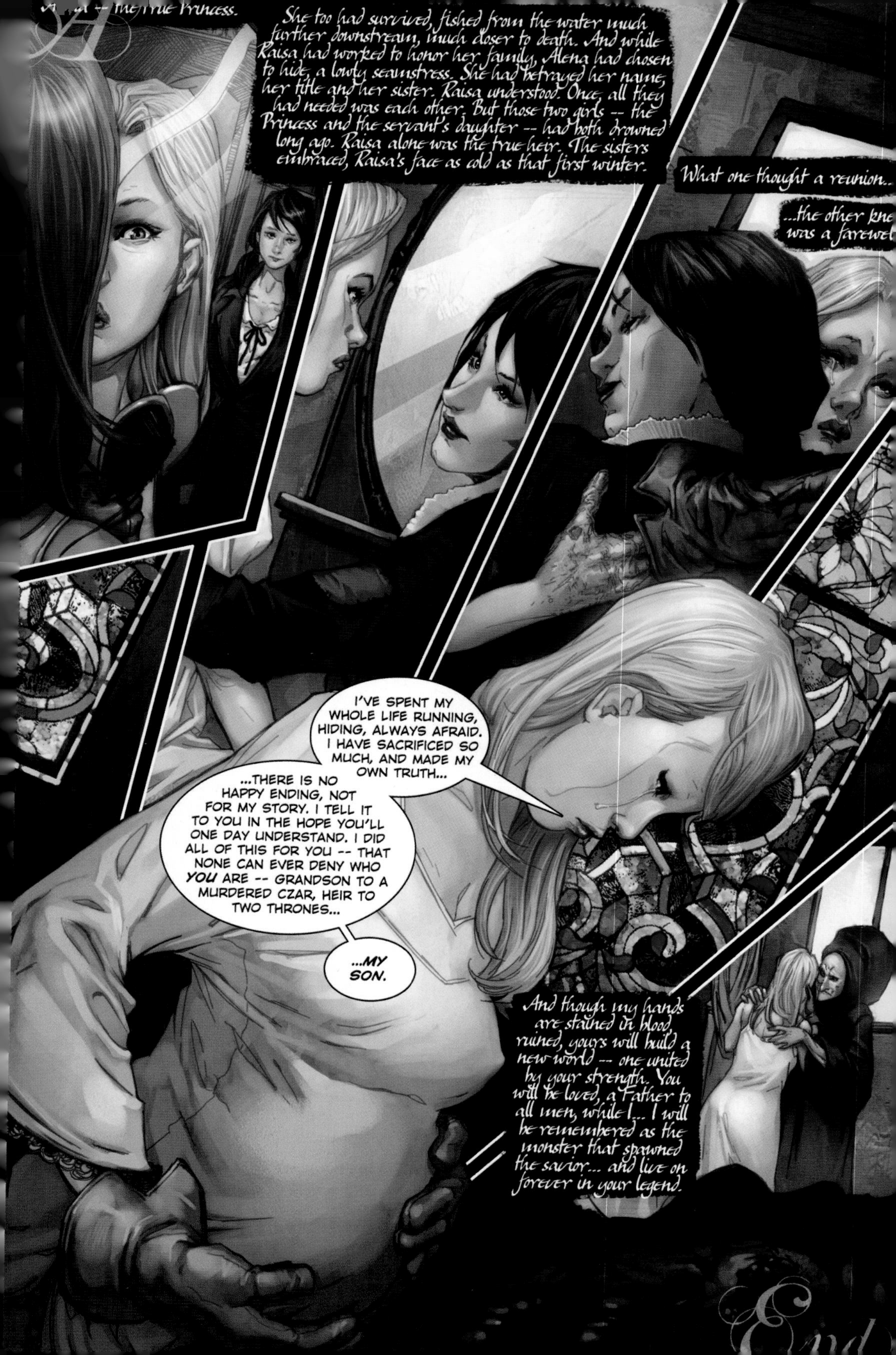
-- the True Princess.
She too had survived, fished from the water much further downstream, much closer to death. And while Raisa had worked to honor her family, Alena had chosen to hide, a lowly seamstress. She had betrayed her name, her title and her sister. Raisa understood. Once, all they had needed was each other. But those two girls -- the Princess and the servant's daughter -- had both drowned long ago. Raisa alone was the true heir. The sisters embraced, Raisa's face as cold as that first winter.
What one thought a reunion...
...the other kne
was a farewel
I'VE SPENT MY WHOLE LIFE RUNNING, HIDING, ALWAYS AFRAID. I HAVE SACRIFICED SO MUCH, AND MADE MY OWN TRUTH...
...THERE IS NO HAPPY ENDING, NOT FOR MY STORY. I TELL IT TO YOU IN THE HOPE YOU'LL ONE DAY UNDERSTAND. I DID ALL OF THIS FOR YOU -- THAT NONE CAN EVER DENY WHO *YOU* ARE -- GRANDSON TO A MURDERED CZAR, HEIR TO TWO THRONES...
...MY SON.
And though my hands are stained in blood, ruined, yours will build a new world -- one united by your strength. You will be loved, a Father to all men, while I... I will be remembered as the monster that spawned the savior... and live on forever in your legend.
End

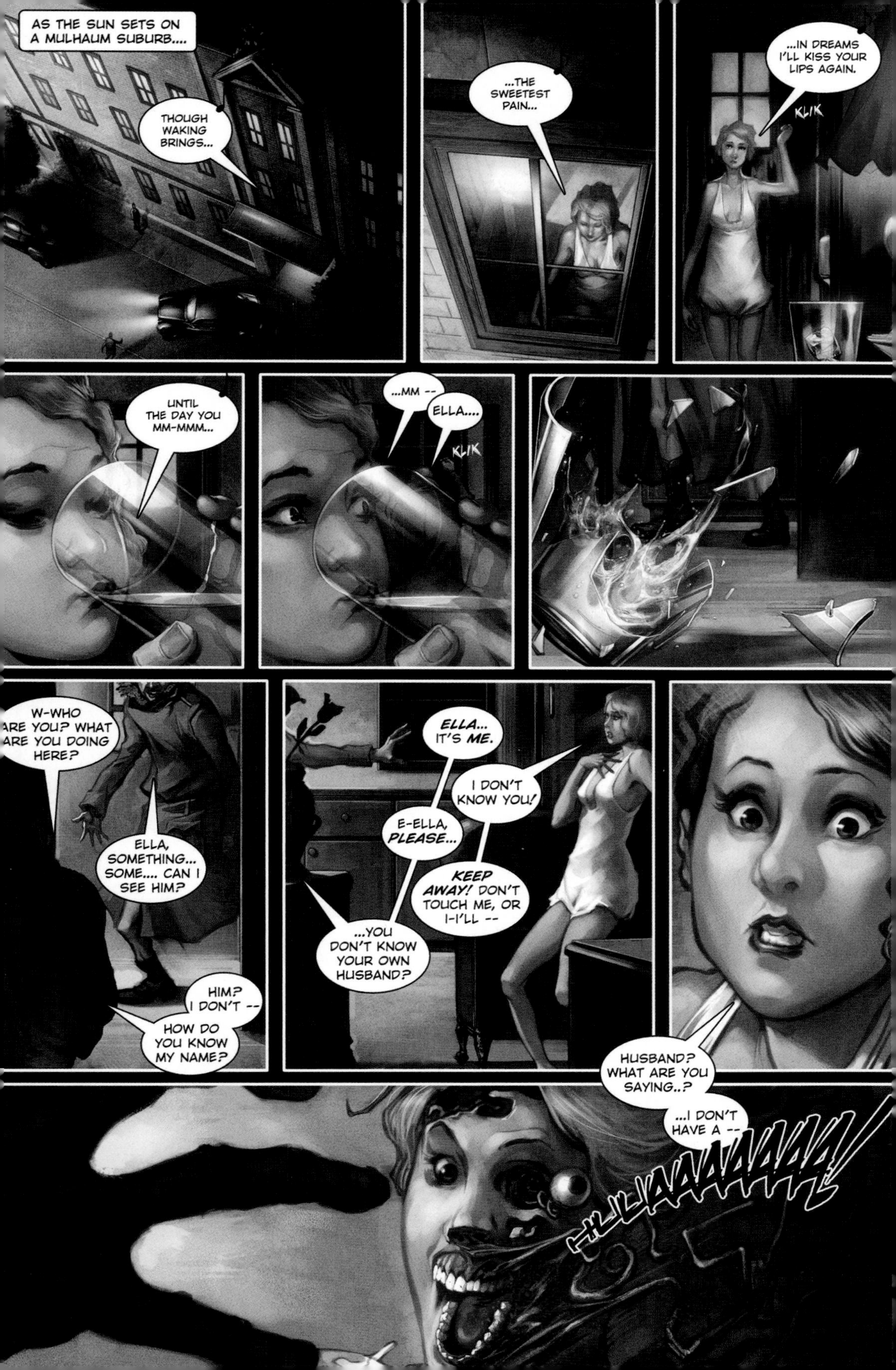
AS THE SUN SETS ON A MULHAUM SUBURB....
THOUGH WAKING BRINGS...
...THE SWEETEST PAIN...
...IN DREAMS I'LL KISS YOUR LIPS AGAIN.
KLIK
UNTIL THE DAY YOU MM-MMM...
...MM --
ELLA....
KLIK
W-WHO ARE YOU? WHAT ARE YOU DOING HERE?
ELLA, SOMETHING... SOME.... CAN I SEE HIM?
HIM? I DON'T --
HOW DO YOU KNOW MY NAME?
ELLA... IT'S ME.
I DON'T KNOW YOU!
E-ELLA, PLEASE...
KEEP AWAY! DON'T TOUCH ME, OR I-I'LL --
...YOU DON'T KNOW YOUR OWN HUSBAND?
HUSBAND? WHAT ARE YOU SAYING..?
...I DON'T HAVE A --
HLLIAAAAAAA!

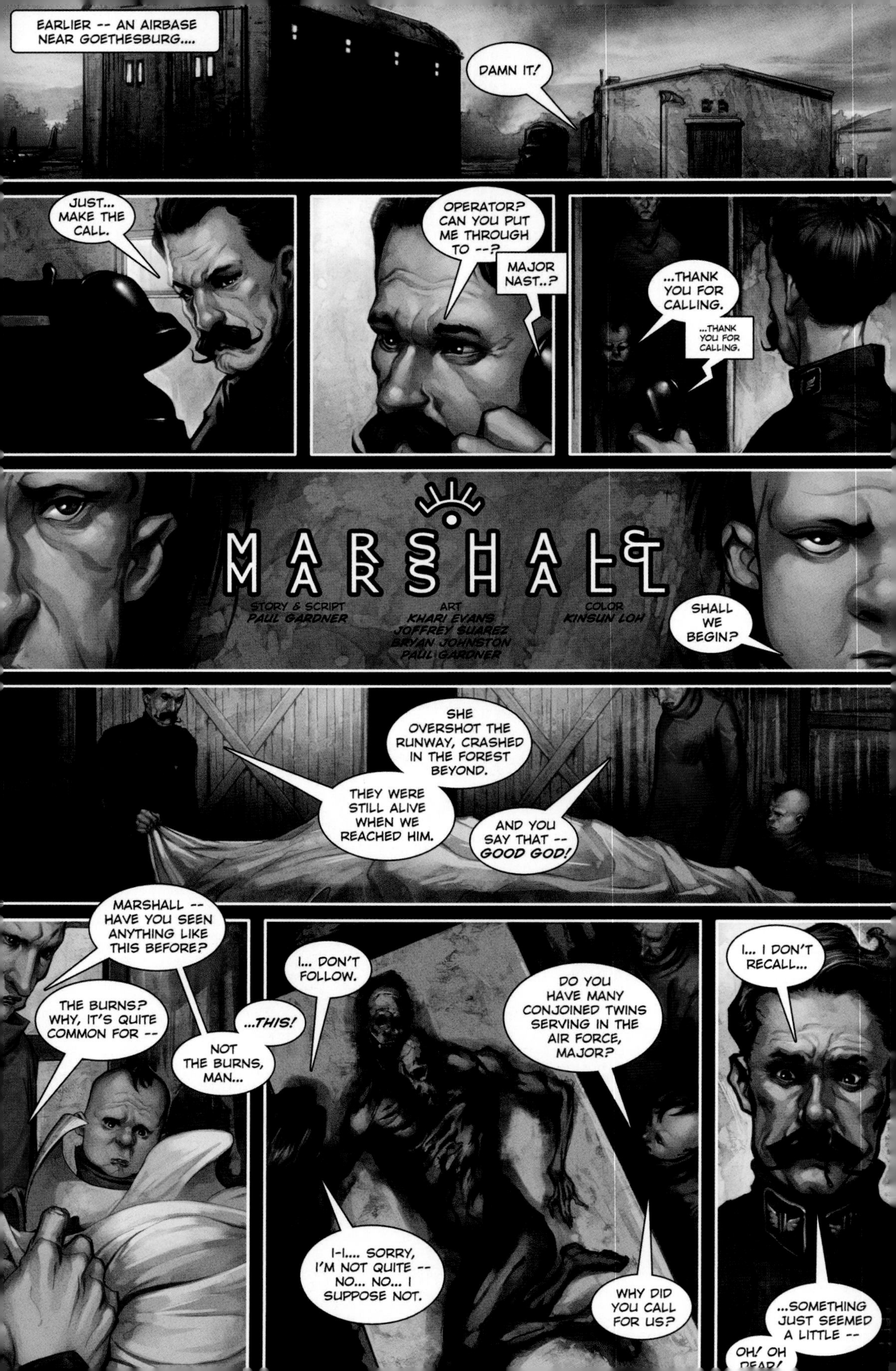
EARLIER -- AN AIRBASE NEAR GOETHESBURG....
DAMN IT!
JUST... MAKE THE CALL.
OPERATOR? CAN YOU PUT ME THROUGH TO --?
MAJOR NAST..?
...THANK YOU FOR CALLING.
...THANK YOU FOR CALLING.
MARSHALL & MARSHALL
STORY & SCRIPT PAUL GARDNER
ART KHARI EVANS JOFFREY SUAREZ BRYAN JOHNSTON PAUL GARDNER
COLOR KINSUN LOH
SHALL WE BEGIN?
SHE OVERSHOT THE RUNWAY, CRASHED IN THE FOREST BEYOND.
THEY WERE STILL ALIVE WHEN WE REACHED HIM.
AND YOU SAY THAT -- GOOD GOD!
MARSHALL -- HAVE YOU SEEN ANYTHING LIKE THIS BEFORE?
THE BURNS? WHY, IT'S QUITE COMMON FOR --
NOT THE BURNS, MAN...
...THIS!
I... DON'T FOLLOW.
DO YOU HAVE MANY CONJOINED TWINS SERVING IN THE AIR FORCE, MAJOR?
I-I.... SORRY, I'M NOT QUITE -- NO... NO... I SUPPOSE NOT.
WHY DID YOU CALL FOR US?
I... I DON'T RECALL...
...SOMETHING JUST SEEMED A LITTLE --
OH! OH DEAR!

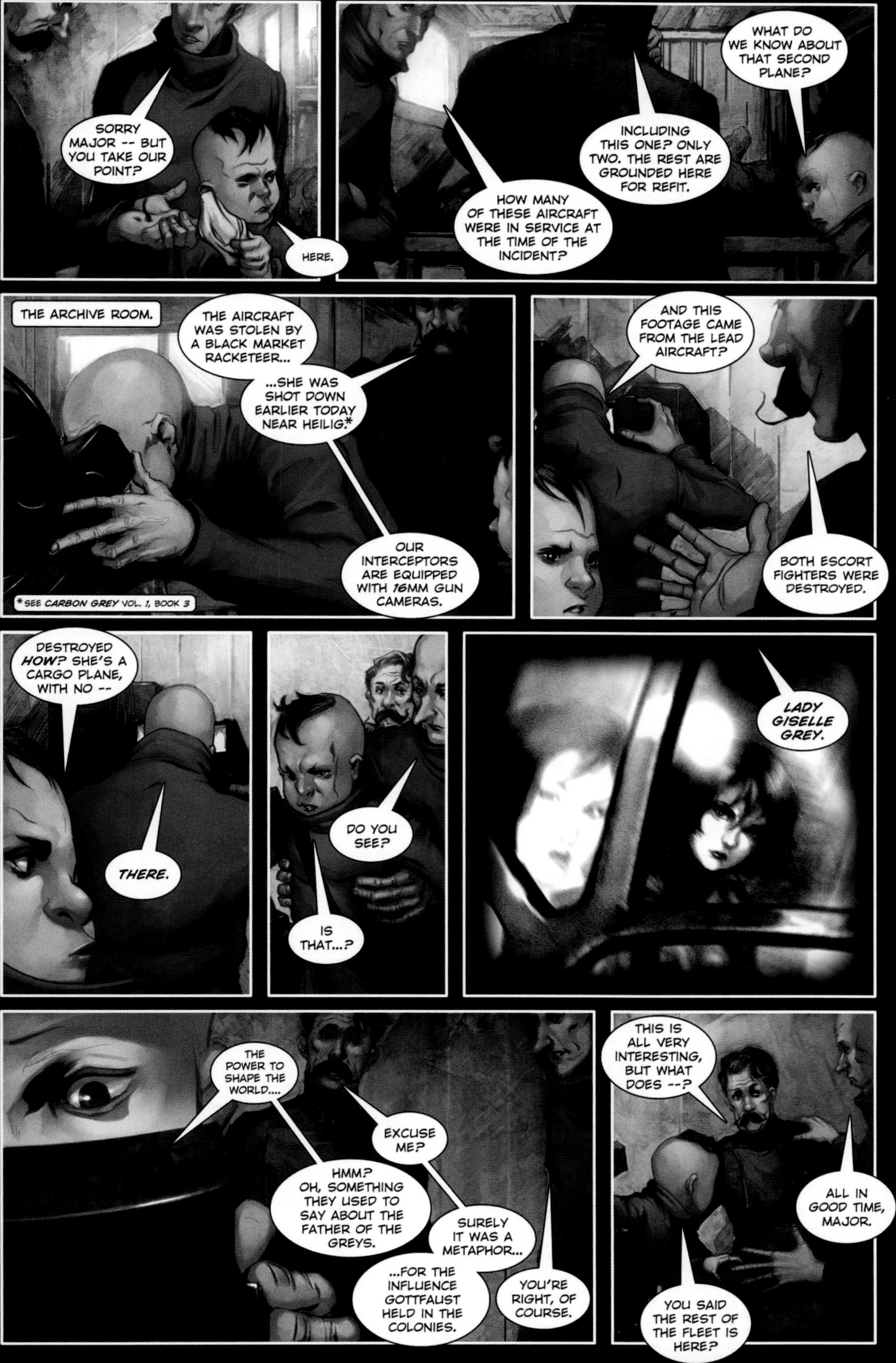
SORRY MAJOR -- BUT YOU TAKE OUR POINT?
HERE.
HOW MANY OF THESE AIRCRAFT WERE IN SERVICE AT THE TIME OF THE INCIDENT?
INCLUDING THIS ONE? ONLY TWO. THE REST ARE GROUNDED HERE FOR REFIT.
WHAT DO WE KNOW ABOUT THAT SECOND PLANE?
THE ARCHIVE ROOM.
THE AIRCRAFT WAS STOLEN BY A BLACK MARKET RACKETEER...
...SHE WAS SHOT DOWN EARLIER TODAY NEAR HEILIG.*
OUR INTERCEPTORS ARE EQUIPPED WITH 16MM GUN CAMERAS.
*SEE CARBON GREY VOL. 1, BOOK 3
AND THIS FOOTAGE CAME FROM THE LEAD AIRCRAFT?
BOTH ESCORT FIGHTERS WERE DESTROYED.
DESTROYED HOW? SHE'S A CARGO PLANE, WITH NO --
THERE.
DO YOU SEE?
IS THAT...?
LADY GISELLE GREY.
THE POWER TO SHAPE THE WORLD....
EXCUSE ME?
HMM? OH, SOMETHING THEY USED TO SAY ABOUT THE FATHER OF THE GREYS.
SURELY IT WAS A METAPHOR...
...FOR THE INFLUENCE GOTTFAUST HELD IN THE COLONIES.
YOU'RE RIGHT, OF COURSE.
THIS IS ALL VERY INTERESTING, BUT WHAT DOES --?
ALL IN GOOD TIME, MAJOR.
YOU SAID THE REST OF THE FLEET IS HERE?

...AND THIS IS THE SAME MODEL AS THE PLANE THAT CRASHED?

IDENTICAL. THEY'RE SIS--

WOULD YOU EXCUSE ME MAJOR?

YOUNG MARSHALL NEEDS TO EXAMINE THE AIRCRAFT.

WITH A CHILD'S TOY?

IT'S NOT A TOY, IT'S A THAUMATROPE -- I MADE IT.

THE DISC CREATES A MOMENT OF SACCADIC UNCERTAINTY AS IT SPINS.

IN THAT MOMENT ONE CAN SEE BOTH WHAT IS...

...AND WHAT MIGHT HAVE BEEN.

I DON'T FOLLOW.

IT'S A MAGIC EYE, MAJOR...

...A REAL LIVE MAGIC EYE.

WHAT DO YOU SEE?

IT'S AS I FEARED -- A MAJOR CONTINUITY ERROR... ...MAYBE THE WORST YET.

THE DESIGN OF THE AIRFRAME HAS ADVANCED TWO, EVEN THREE GENERATIONS, AND...

...OH NO.

WHAT IS IT?

AN OBSERVATION POD -- BELOW THE COCKPIT.

CONTINUITY ERROR...?

WHAT ARE YOU SAYING, MARSHALL?

BEFORE THE ERROR SHE WOULD HAVE BEEN A RECONNAISSANCE PLANE...

...THERE WAS THIRD CREW MEMBER.

THE MANIFEST LISTS A PHOTOGRAPHER -- CORPORAL EHREN KNUTH.

WHO?

REALLY, MARSHAL, I KNOW EVERY MAN ON THIS --

WE'LL NEED HIS FILE, MAJOR.

THE MAN DOESN'T EXIST! HOW CAN I GIVE YOU HIS FILE?

HE'S NOT AS CLEVER AS HE THINKS HE IS, IS HE MARSHALL?

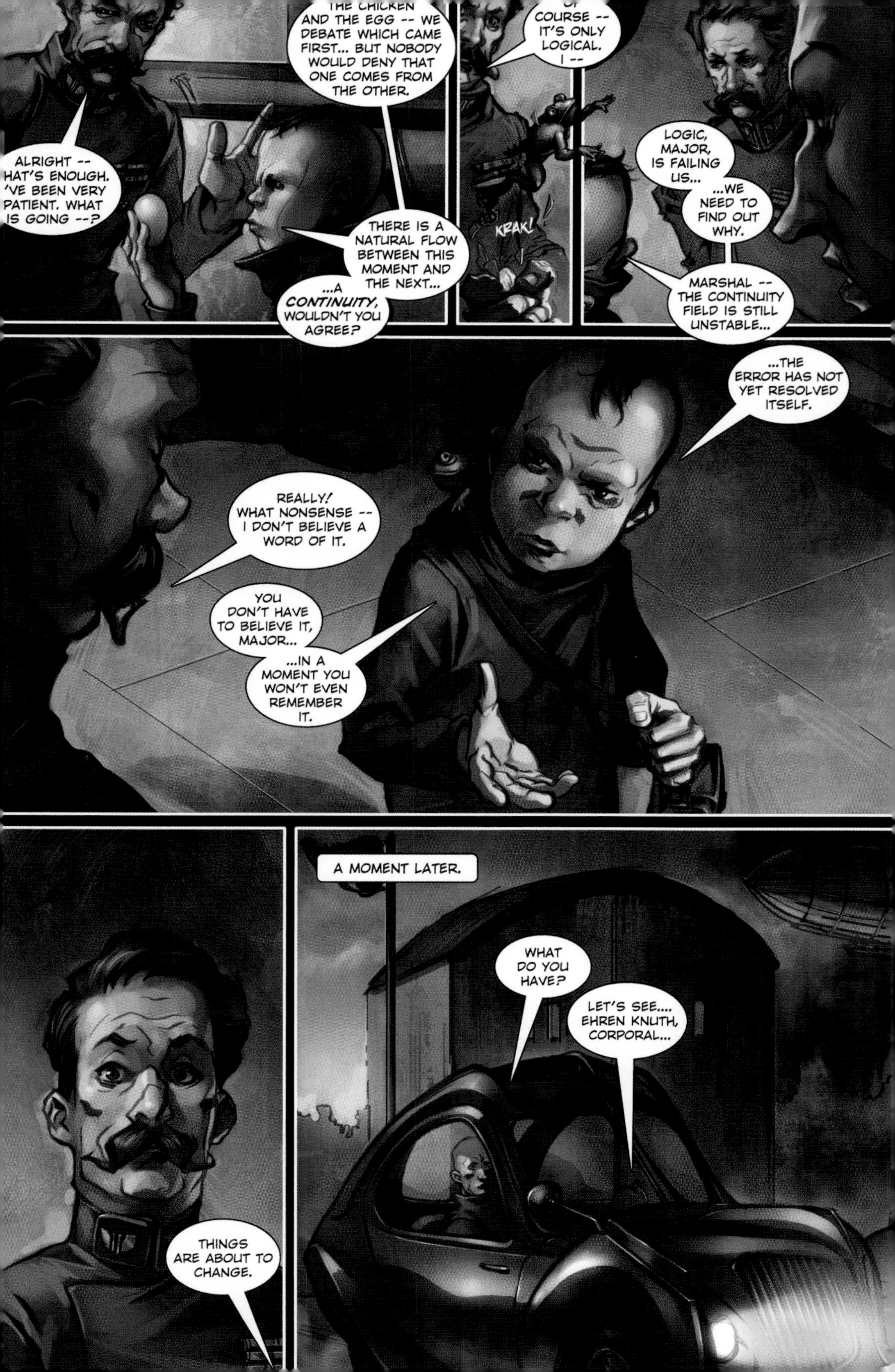
THE CHICKEN AND THE EGG -- WE DEBATE WHICH CAME FIRST... BUT NOBODY WOULD DENY THAT ONE COMES FROM THE OTHER.
ALRIGHT -- HAT'S ENOUGH. 'VE BEEN VERY PATIENT. WHAT IS GOING --?
THERE IS A NATURAL FLOW BETWEEN THIS MOMENT AND THE NEXT...
...A *CONTINUITY,* WOULDN'T YOU AGREE?
COURSE -- IT'S ONLY LOGICAL. I --
KRAK!
LOGIC, MAJOR, IS FAILING US...
...WE NEED TO FIND OUT WHY.
MARSHAL -- THE CONTINUITY FIELD IS STILL UNSTABLE...
...THE ERROR HAS NOT YET RESOLVED ITSELF.
REALLY! WHAT NONSENSE -- I DON'T BELIEVE A WORD OF IT.
YOU DON'T HAVE TO BELIEVE IT, MAJOR...
...IN A MOMENT YOU WON'T EVEN REMEMBER IT.
THINGS ARE ABOUT TO CHANGE.
A MOMENT LATER.
WHAT DO YOU HAVE?
LET'S SEE.... EHREN KNUTH, CORPORAL...

...26 YEARS OLD, MARRIED, WITH A CHILD -- A BOY OF SIX MONTHS.

HE WOULD HAVE BEEN ON ACTIVE DUTY FOR ALMOST A FULL YEAR.

IS THERE AN ADDRESS?

THERE IS, IN *MULHAUM.*

GIVE IT TO ME.

BUT WHY --?

MARSHALL, THE MAN BELIEVES HE HAS A *CHILD* HE'S NEVER SEEN...

...HE'LL BE HEADING *HOME.*

THE NEIGHBORS THOUGHT IT WAS A LOVERS' QUARREL -- THEY DIDN'T CALL US UNTIL THEY HEARD HER SCREAMS...

ELLA BAUM, 24. SHE LIVES ALONE.

...WE THINK THE MAN IS STILL INSIDE.

I'M SURE THE CAPTAIN AN TELL YOU MORE.

THANK YOU, OFFICER.

GOOD EVENING CAPTAIN, I'M --

I KNOW WHO YOU ARE, MARSHAL...

...*BOTH* OF YOU.

THEN YOU'LL ALSO KNOW WE'RE NOT HERE BECAUSE OF SOME DOMESTIC DISPUTE.

TWO MEN HAVE ALREADY LOST HIS LIFE. LET US --

THE *GENERAL* MAY INDULGE YOUR FANTASIES, MARSHAL -- I'M ONLY GRATEFUL THE GENERAL ISN'T HERE.

YOU'LL EXCUSE ME.

THAT MAN WAS RUDE.

HE WAS.

WHA NOW

LIFT ME UP!

I WANT TO SEE.

TEAM ONE...

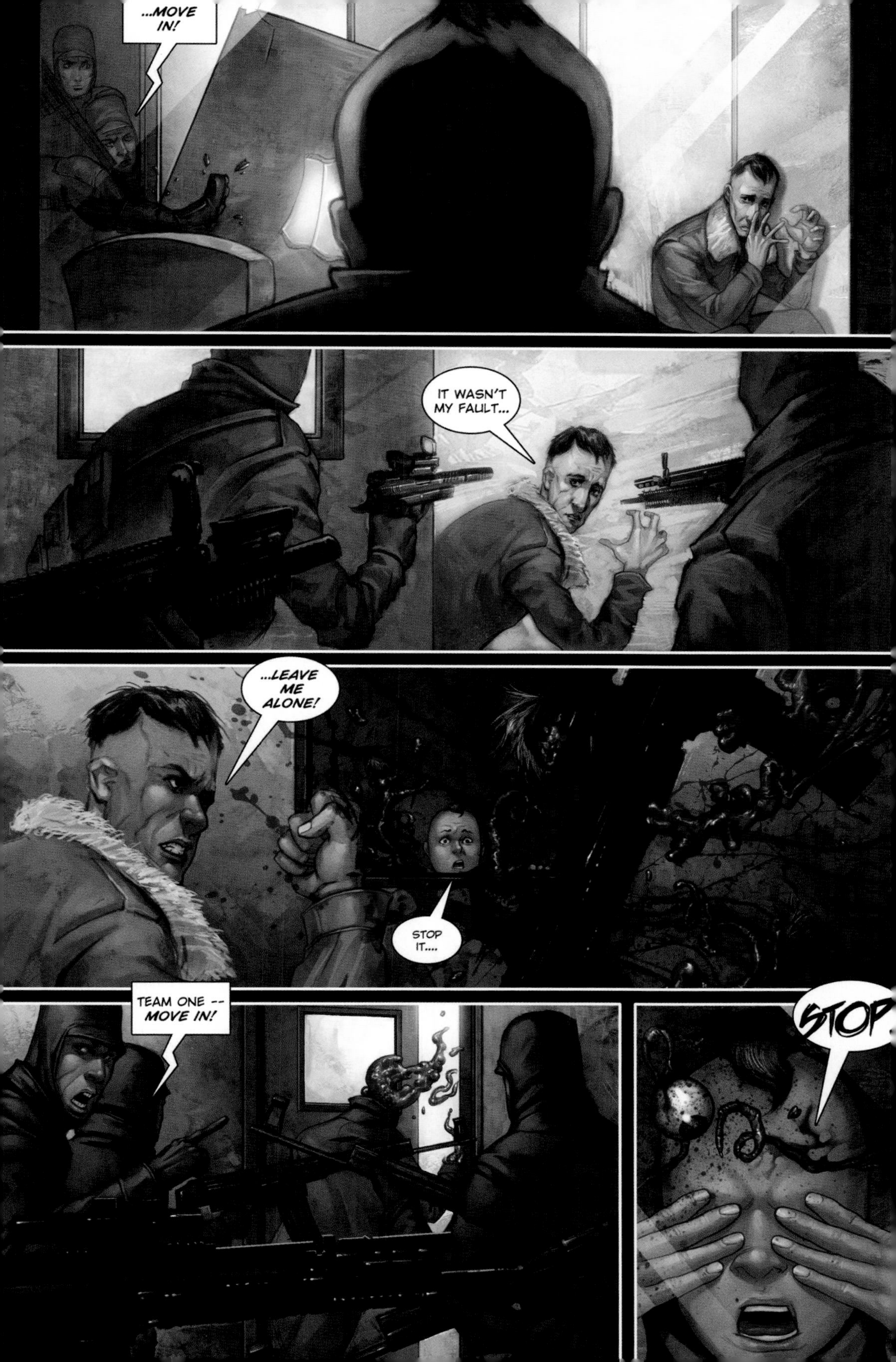
...MOVE IN!
IT WASN'T MY FAULT...
...LEAVE ME ALONE!
STOP IT....
TEAM ONE -- MOVE IN!
STOP

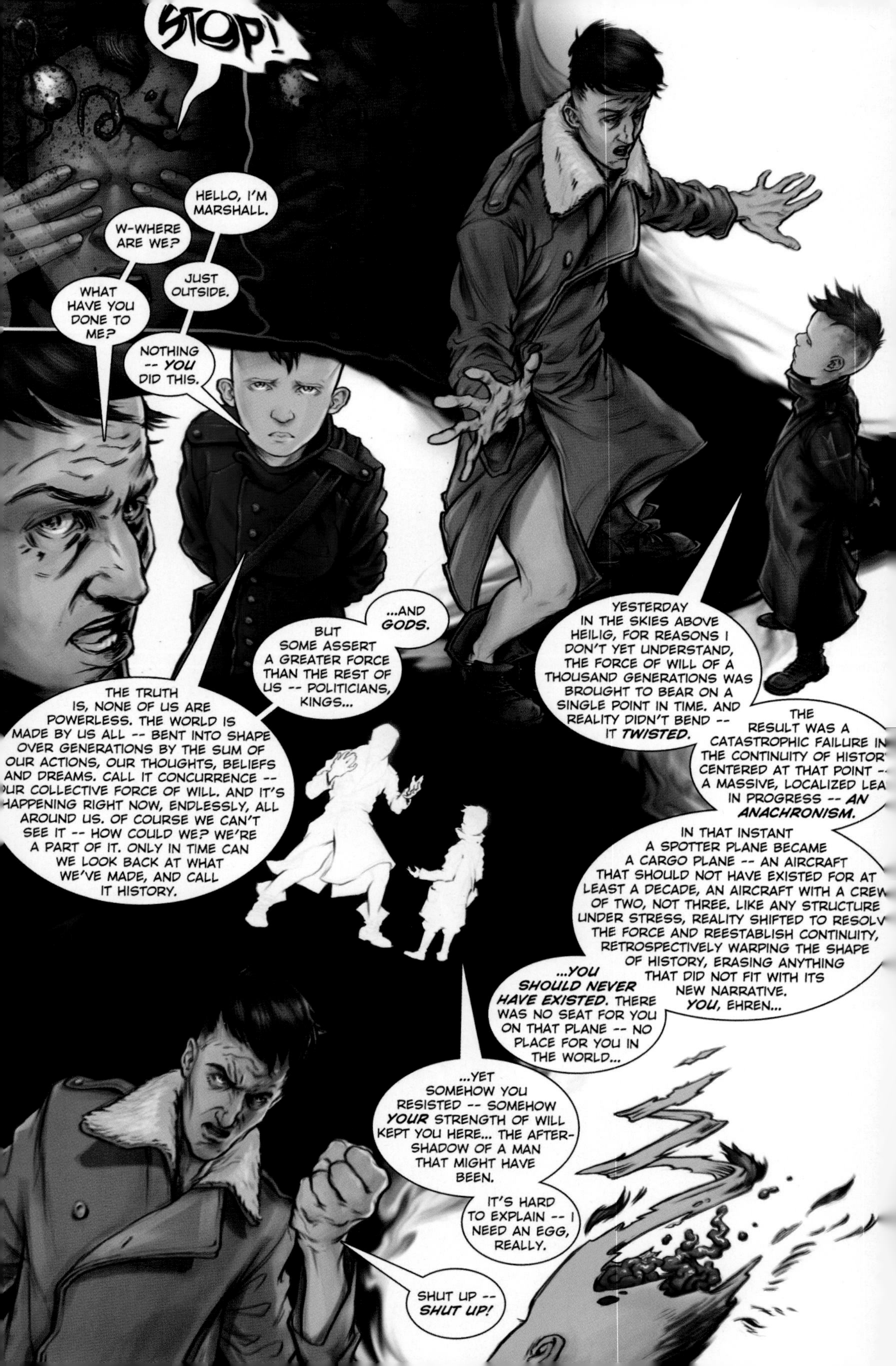
STOP!
HELLO, I'M MARSHALL.
W-WHERE ARE WE?
JUST OUTSIDE.
WHAT HAVE YOU DONE TO ME?
NOTHING -- YOU DID THIS.
THE TRUTH IS, NONE OF US ARE POWERLESS. THE WORLD IS MADE BY US ALL -- BENT INTO SHAPE OVER GENERATIONS BY THE SUM OF OUR ACTIONS, OUR THOUGHTS, BELIEFS AND DREAMS. CALL IT CONCURRENCE -- OUR COLLECTIVE FORCE OF WILL. AND IT'S HAPPENING RIGHT NOW, ENDLESSLY, ALL AROUND US. OF COURSE WE CAN'T SEE IT -- HOW COULD WE? WE'RE A PART OF IT. ONLY IN TIME CAN WE LOOK BACK AT WHAT WE'VE MADE, AND CALL IT HISTORY.
BUT SOME ASSERT A GREATER FORCE THAN THE REST OF US -- POLITICIANS, KINGS...
...AND GODS.
YESTERDAY IN THE SKIES ABOVE HEILIG, FOR REASONS I DON'T YET UNDERSTAND, THE FORCE OF WILL OF A THOUSAND GENERATIONS WAS BROUGHT TO BEAR ON A SINGLE POINT IN TIME. AND REALITY DIDN'T BEND -- IT TWISTED.
THE RESULT WAS A CATASTROPHIC FAILURE IN THE CONTINUITY OF HISTORY CENTERED AT THAT POINT -- A MASSIVE, LOCALIZED LEAP IN PROGRESS -- AN ANACHRONISM.
IN THAT INSTANT A SPOTTER PLANE BECAME A CARGO PLANE -- AN AIRCRAFT THAT SHOULD NOT HAVE EXISTED FOR AT LEAST A DECADE, AN AIRCRAFT WITH A CREW OF TWO, NOT THREE. LIKE ANY STRUCTURE UNDER STRESS, REALITY SHIFTED TO RESOLVE THE FORCE AND REESTABLISH CONTINUITY, RETROSPECTIVELY WARPING THE SHAPE OF HISTORY, ERASING ANYTHING THAT DID NOT FIT WITH ITS NEW NARRATIVE. YOU, EHREN...
...YOU SHOULD NEVER HAVE EXISTED. THERE WAS NO SEAT FOR YOU ON THAT PLANE -- NO PLACE FOR YOU IN THE WORLD...
...YET SOMEHOW YOU RESISTED -- SOMEHOW YOUR STRENGTH OF WILL KEPT YOU HERE... THE AFTER-SHADOW OF A MAN THAT MIGHT HAVE BEEN.
IT'S HARD TO EXPLAIN -- I NEED AN EGG, REALLY.
SHUT UP -- SHUT UP!

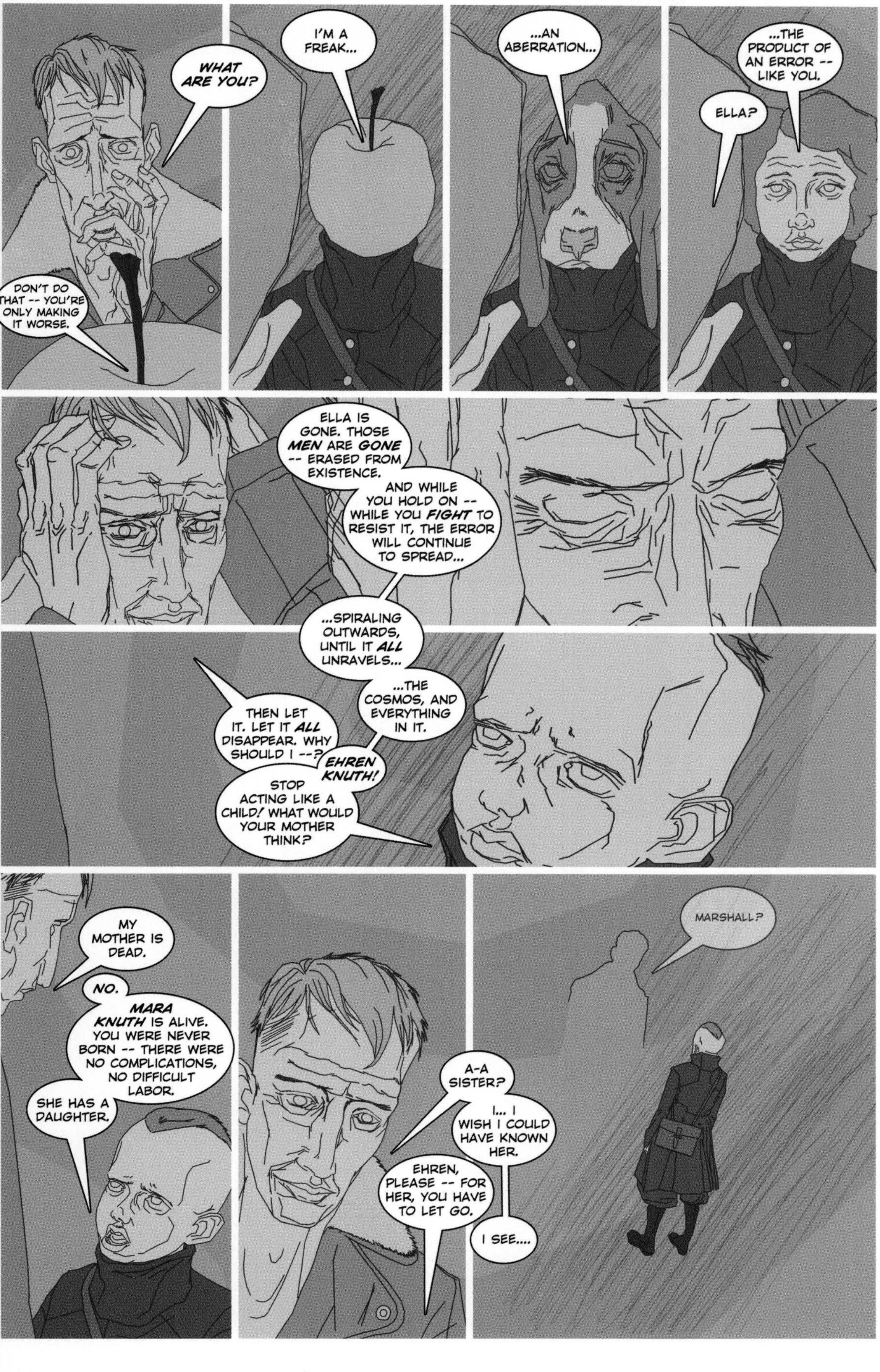
WHAT ARE YOU?
DON'T DO THAT -- YOU'RE ONLY MAKING IT WORSE.
I'M A FREAK...
...AN ABERRATION...
ELLA?
...THE PRODUCT OF AN ERROR -- LIKE YOU.
ELLA IS GONE. THOSE MEN ARE GONE -- ERASED FROM EXISTENCE.
AND WHILE YOU HOLD ON -- WHILE YOU FIGHT TO RESIST IT, THE ERROR WILL CONTINUE TO SPREAD...
...SPIRALING OUTWARDS, UNTIL IT ALL UNRAVELS...
THEN LET IT. LET IT ALL DISAPPEAR. WHY SHOULD I --?
...THE COSMOS, AND EVERYTHING IN IT.
EHREN KNUTH!
STOP ACTING LIKE A CHILD! WHAT WOULD YOUR MOTHER THINK?
MY MOTHER IS DEAD.
NO.
MARA KNUTH IS ALIVE. YOU WERE NEVER BORN -- THERE WERE NO COMPLICATIONS, NO DIFFICULT LABOR.
SHE HAS A DAUGHTER.
A-A SISTER?
I... I WISH I COULD HAVE KNOWN HER.
EHREN, PLEASE -- FOR HER, YOU HAVE TO LET GO.
I SEE....
MARSHALL?

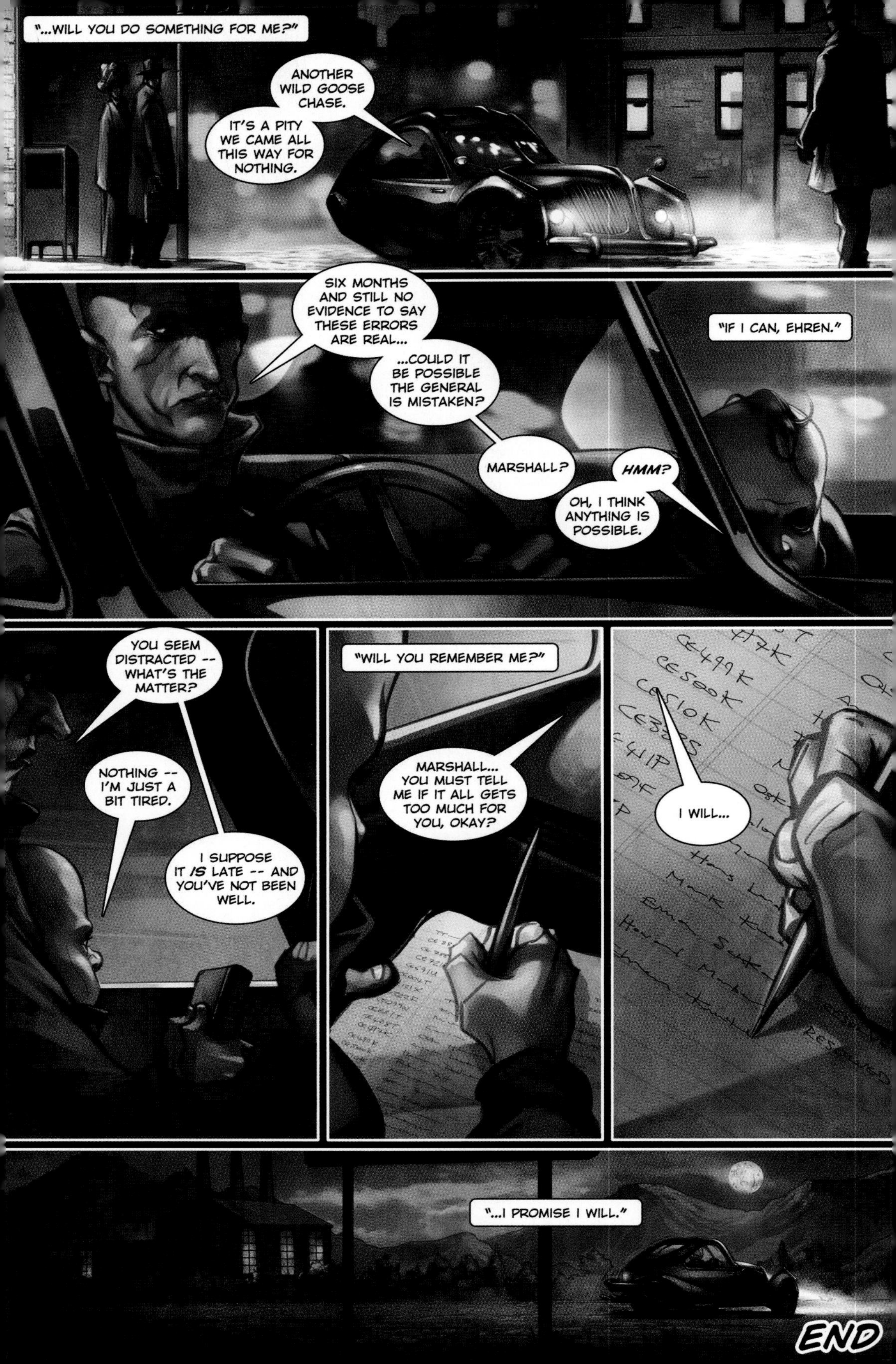
"...WILL YOU DO SOMETHING FOR ME?"
ANOTHER WILD GOOSE CHASE.
IT'S A PITY WE CAME ALL THIS WAY FOR NOTHING.
SIX MONTHS AND STILL NO EVIDENCE TO SAY THESE ERRORS ARE REAL...
"IF I CAN, EHREN."
...COULD IT BE POSSIBLE THE GENERAL IS MISTAKEN?
MARSHALL?
HMM?
OH, I THINK ANYTHING IS POSSIBLE.
YOU SEEM DISTRACTED -- WHAT'S THE MATTER?
NOTHING -- I'M JUST A BIT TIRED.
I SUPPOSE IT IS LATE -- AND YOU'VE NOT BEEN WELL.
"WILL YOU REMEMBER ME?"
MARSHALL... YOU MUST TELL ME IF IT ALL GETS TOO MUCH FOR YOU, OKAY?
I WILL...
"...I PROMISE I WILL."
END

IV

"I ENVY THEM THEIR FAITH.

THEIR KAISER IS DEAD...

"JUST CONFIRMED, SIR, THOUGH THE FUNERAL WAS HELD MONTHS AGO."

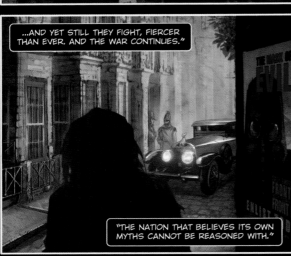

...AND YET STILL THEY FIGHT, FIERCER THAN EVER. AND THE WAR CONTINUES."

"THE NATION THAT BELIEVES ITS OWN MYTHS CANNOT BE REASONED WITH."

"WHERE NOW, THE LIONS OF CAUL?"

THOSE BLOODY LIGHTS....

Kernow Guardian

BUTCHERED COALITION ADVANCES

WITCHILL BEAST STRIKES AGAIN

FIFTH VICTIM FOUND

THEN WHAT ABOUT THIS NEW WOMAN -- THE KAISER'S WIDOW? ISN'T SHE A MODERATE?

IN PRINCIPLE, YES...

...BUT WITH THE HAWKS GATHERING SHE'LL DARE NOT RISK BEING PERCEIVED AS WEAK.

STILL, WE BELIEVE SHE WOULD BE RECEPTIVE, IF WE WERE TO MAKE THE FIRST MOVE.

IMPOSSIBLE! PARLIAMENT WOULD NOT STAND FOR IT, NOT AFTER THE EMBARRASSMENT OF BAAL.

WHICH IS WHY I'VE ASKED PAVEL KUDASHEV TO INTERVENE ON OUR BEHALF.*

AND HE'S AGREED? I'M ASTONISHED.

I THINK HE RECOGNIZES THE TIME FOR IDEALISM HAS PASSED.

URSA MUST EITHER HELP TO BROKER A LASTING PEACE, OR DECIDE WITH WHOM SHE STANDS.

PRIME MINISTER -- MA'AM...

...WE'RE ALL GLAD TO HEAR LADY FERMOY IS HOME SAFE.

GOD WILLING, SERGEANT, *ALL* OUR CHILDREN WILL BE HOME SOON.

"AND IF THEY REFUSE?"

*URSA'S FORMER AMBASSADOR TO MITTELEUROPA

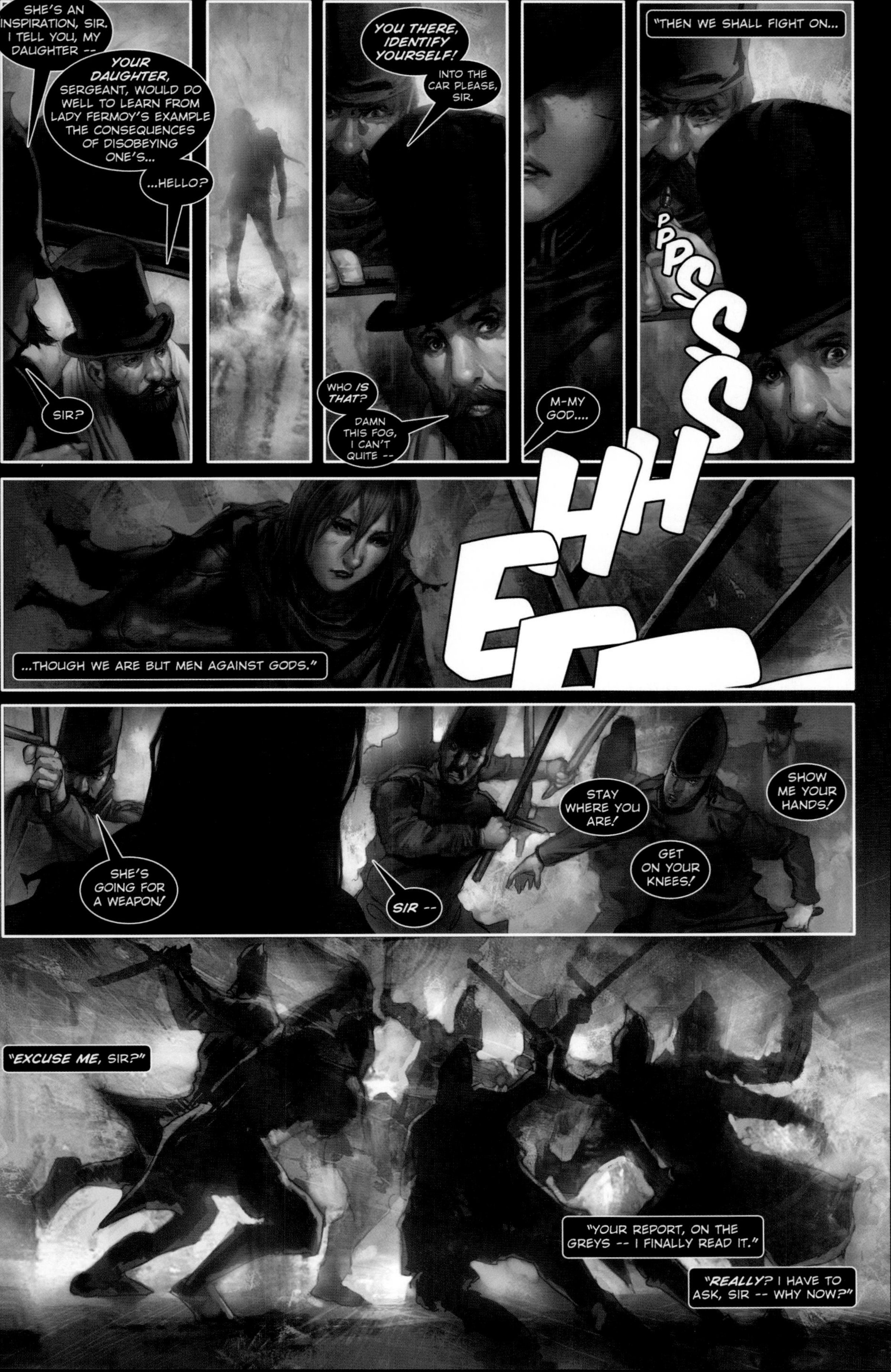
SHE'S AN INSPIRATION, SIR. I TELL YOU, MY DAUGHTER --
YOUR DAUGHTER, SERGEANT, WOULD DO WELL TO LEARN FROM LADY FERMOY'S EXAMPLE THE CONSEQUENCES OF DISOBEYING ONE'S...
...HELLO?
SIR?
YOU THERE, IDENTIFY YOURSELF!
INTO THE CAR PLEASE, SIR.
WHO IS THAT?
DAMN THIS FOG, I CAN'T QUITE --
M-MY GOD....
"THEN WE SHALL FIGHT ON...
PPPSSSHHEE
...THOUGH WE ARE BUT MEN AGAINST GODS."
SHE'S GOING FOR A WEAPON!
SIR --
STAY WHERE YOU ARE!
GET ON YOUR KNEES!
SHOW ME YOUR HANDS!
"EXCUSE ME, SIR?"
"YOUR REPORT, ON THE GREYS -- I FINALLY READ IT."
"REALLY? I HAVE TO ASK, SIR -- WHY NOW?"

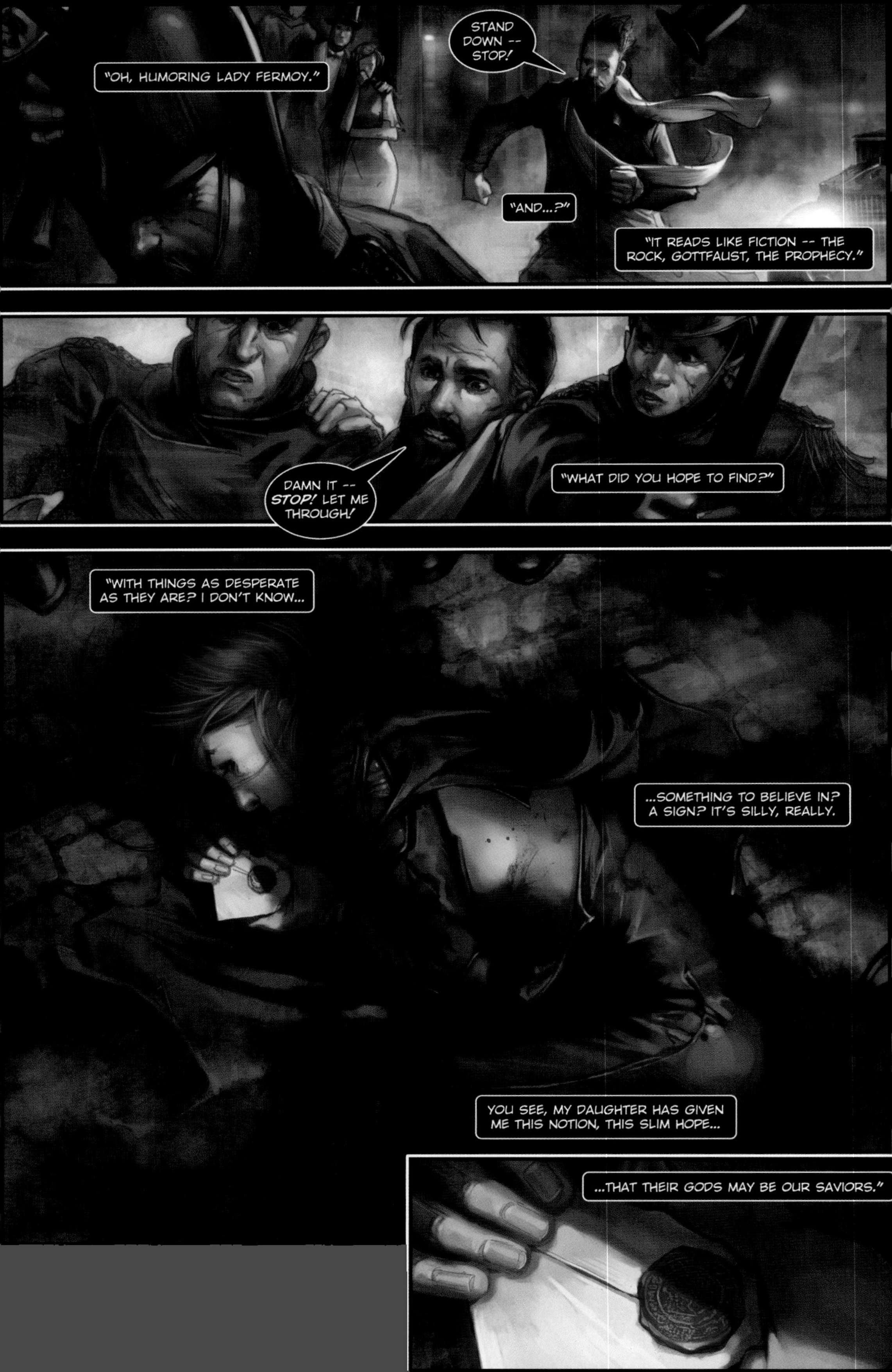
"OH, HUMORING LADY FERMOY."
STAND DOWN -- STOP!
"AND...?"
"IT READS LIKE FICTION -- THE ROCK, GOTTFAUST, THE PROPHECY."
DAMN IT -- STOP! LET ME THROUGH!
"WHAT DID YOU HOPE TO FIND?"
"WITH THINGS AS DESPERATE AS THEY ARE? I DON'T KNOW...
...SOMETHING TO BELIEVE IN? A SIGN? IT'S SILLY, REALLY.
YOU SEE, MY DAUGHTER HAS GIVEN ME THIS NOTION, THIS SLIM HOPE...
...THAT THEIR GODS MAY BE OUR SAVIORS."

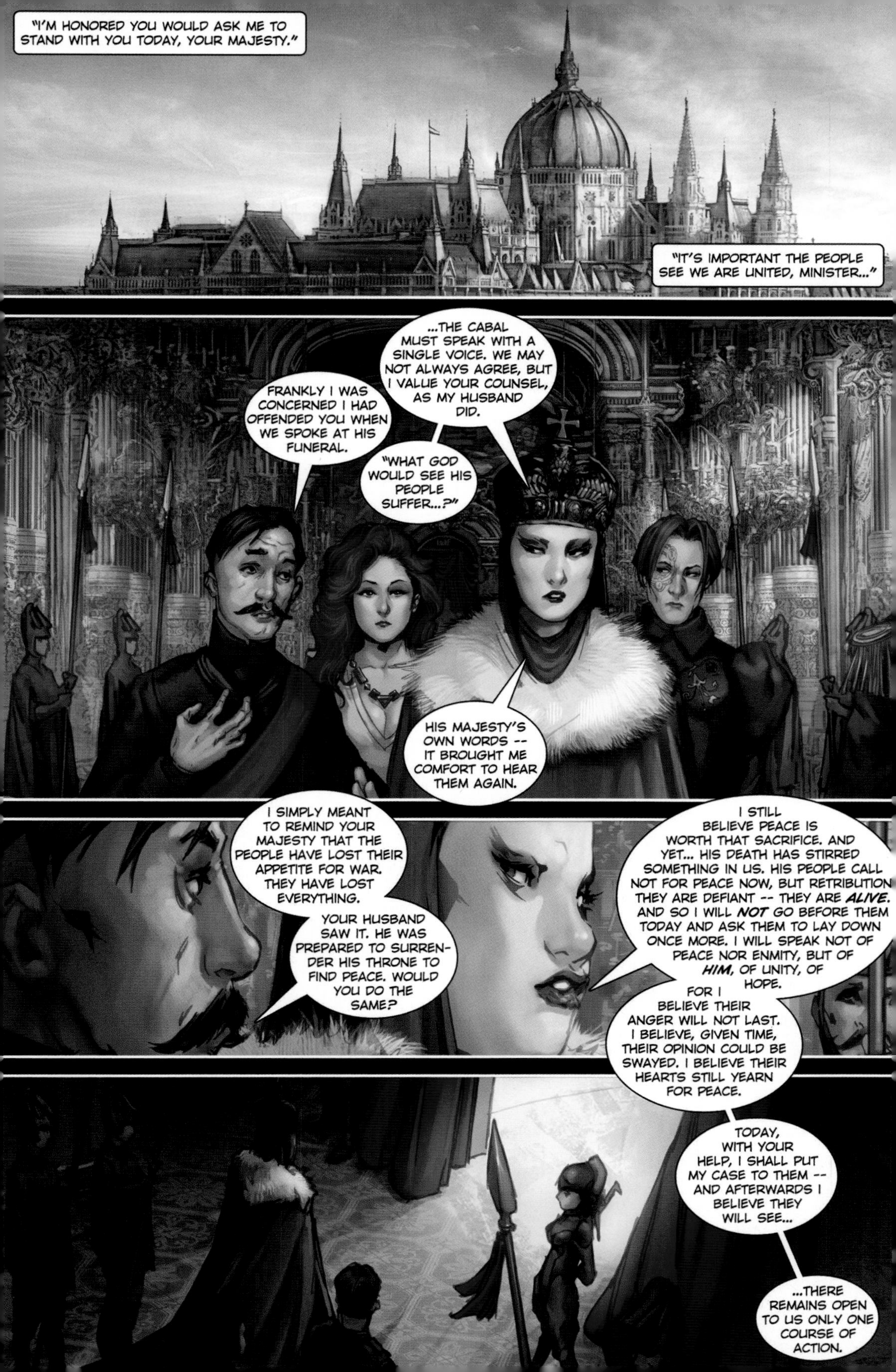
"I'M HONORED YOU WOULD ASK ME TO STAND WITH YOU TODAY, YOUR MAJESTY."
"IT'S IMPORTANT THE PEOPLE SEE WE ARE UNITED, MINISTER..."
...THE CABAL MUST SPEAK WITH A SINGLE VOICE. WE MAY NOT ALWAYS AGREE, BUT I VALUE YOUR COUNSEL, AS MY HUSBAND DID.
FRANKLY I WAS CONCERNED I HAD OFFENDED YOU WHEN WE SPOKE AT HIS FUNERAL.
"WHAT GOD WOULD SEE HIS PEOPLE SUFFER...?"
HIS MAJESTY'S OWN WORDS -- IT BROUGHT ME COMFORT TO HEAR THEM AGAIN.
I SIMPLY MEANT TO REMIND YOUR MAJESTY THAT THE PEOPLE HAVE LOST THEIR APPETITE FOR WAR. THEY HAVE LOST EVERYTHING.
YOUR HUSBAND SAW IT. HE WAS PREPARED TO SURRENDER HIS THRONE TO FIND PEACE. WOULD YOU DO THE SAME?
I STILL BELIEVE PEACE IS WORTH THAT SACRIFICE. AND YET... HIS DEATH HAS STIRRED SOMETHING IN US. HIS PEOPLE CALL NOT FOR PEACE NOW, BUT RETRIBUTION. THEY ARE DEFIANT -- THEY ARE ***ALIVE***. AND SO I WILL ***NOT*** GO BEFORE THEM TODAY AND ASK THEM TO LAY DOWN ONCE MORE. I WILL SPEAK NOT OF PEACE NOR ENMITY, BUT OF ***HIM***, OF UNITY, OF HOPE.
FOR I BELIEVE THEIR ANGER WILL NOT LAST. I BELIEVE, GIVEN TIME, THEIR OPINION COULD BE SWAYED. I BELIEVE THEIR HEARTS STILL YEARN FOR PEACE.
TODAY, WITH YOUR HELP, I SHALL PUT MY CASE TO THEM -- AND AFTERWARDS I BELIEVE THEY WILL SEE...
...THERE REMAINS OPEN TO US ONLY ONE COURSE OF ACTION.

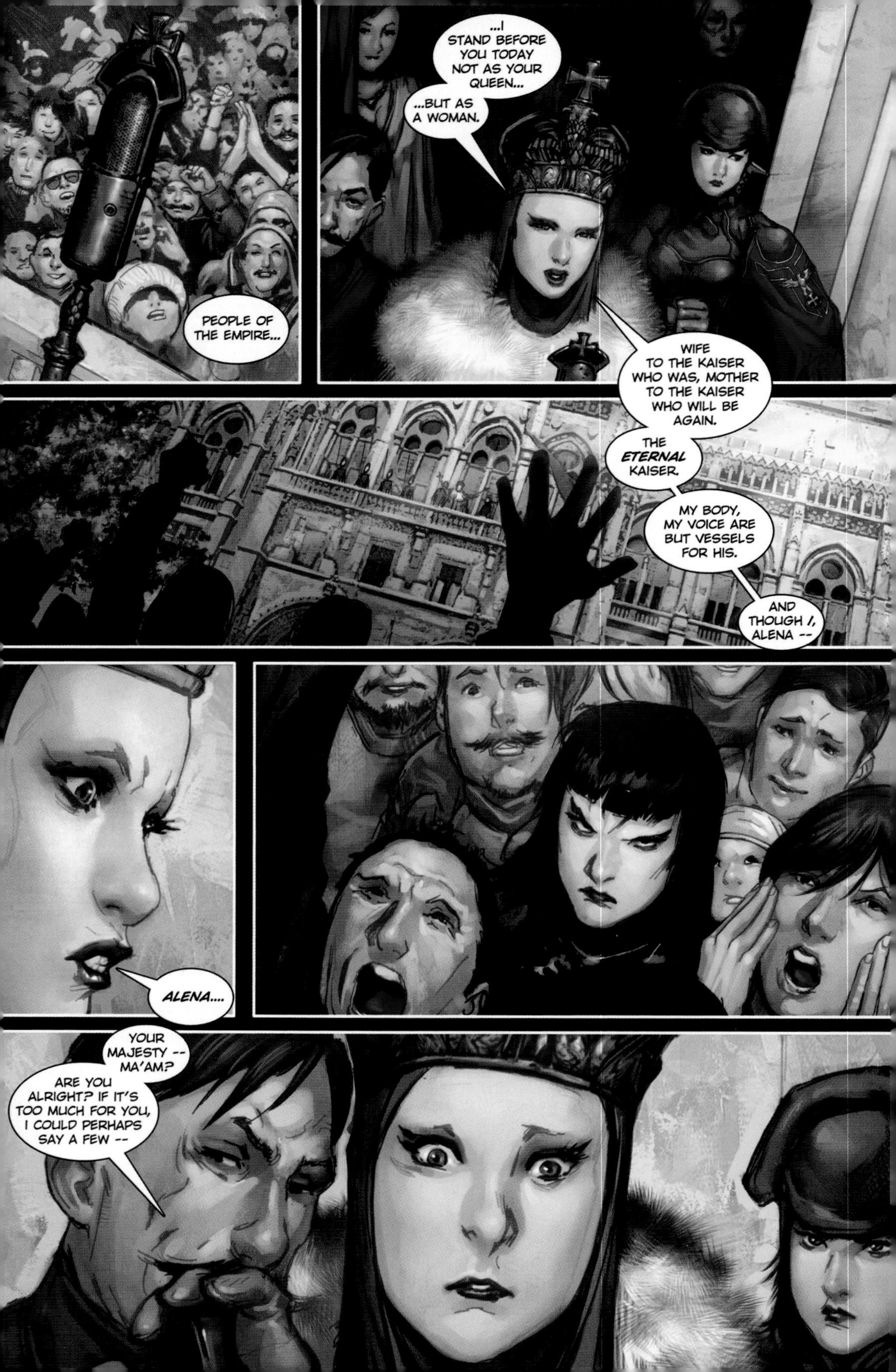
PEOPLE OF THE EMPIRE...
...I STAND BEFORE YOU TODAY NOT AS YOUR QUEEN...
...BUT AS A WOMAN.
WIFE TO THE KAISER WHO WAS, MOTHER TO THE KAISER WHO WILL BE AGAIN.
THE *ETERNAL* KAISER.
MY BODY, MY VOICE ARE BUT VESSELS FOR HIS.
AND THOUGH *I*, ALENA --
ALENA....
YOUR MAJESTY -- MA'AM?
ARE YOU ALRIGHT? IF IT'S TOO MUCH FOR YOU, I COULD PERHAPS SAY A FEW --

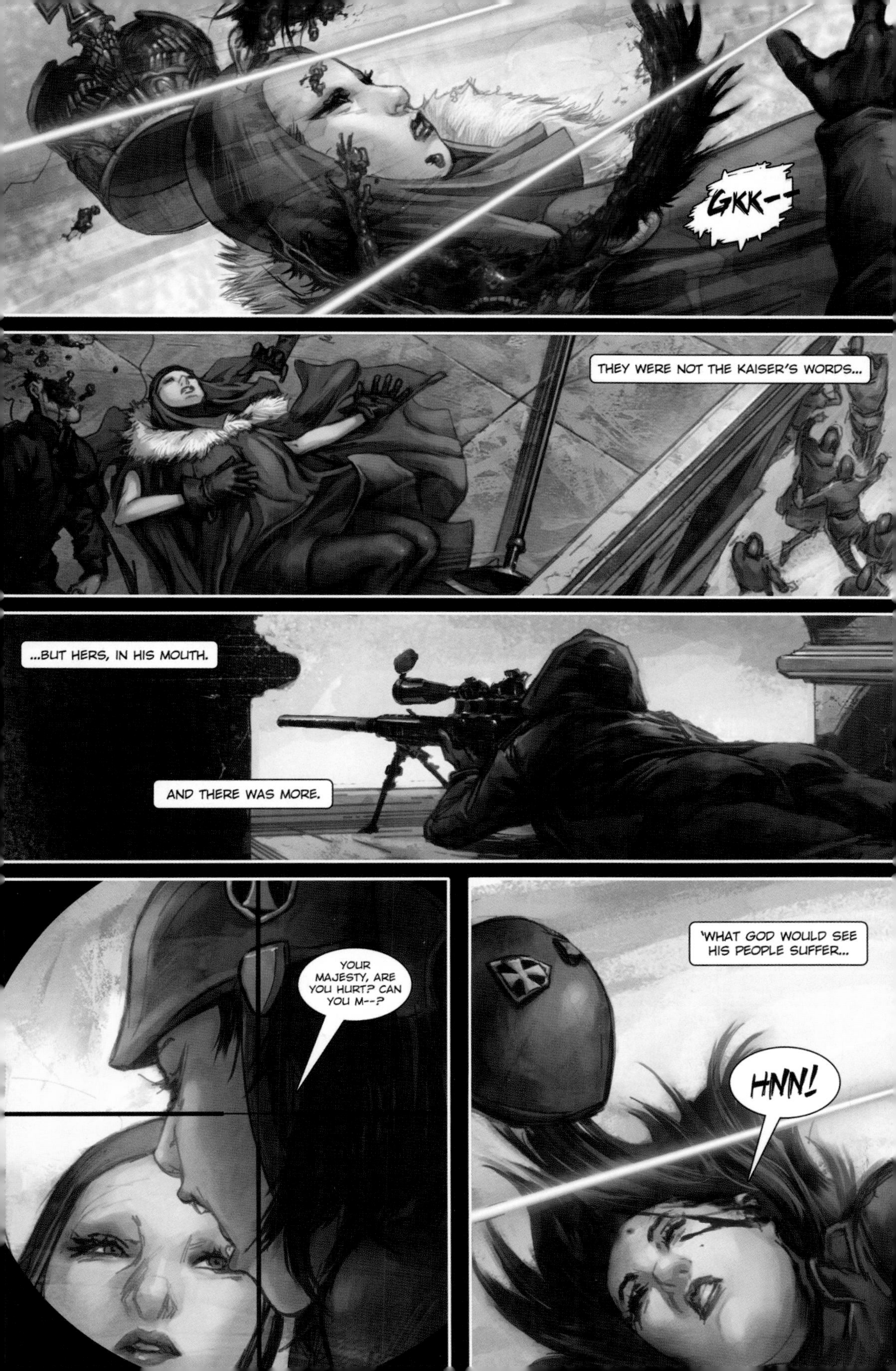
GKK--
THEY WERE NOT THE KAISER'S WORDS...
...BUT HERS, IN HIS MOUTH.
AND THERE WAS MORE.
YOUR MAJESTY, ARE YOU HURT? CAN YOU M--?
'WHAT GOD WOULD SEE HIS PEOPLE SUFFER...
HNN!

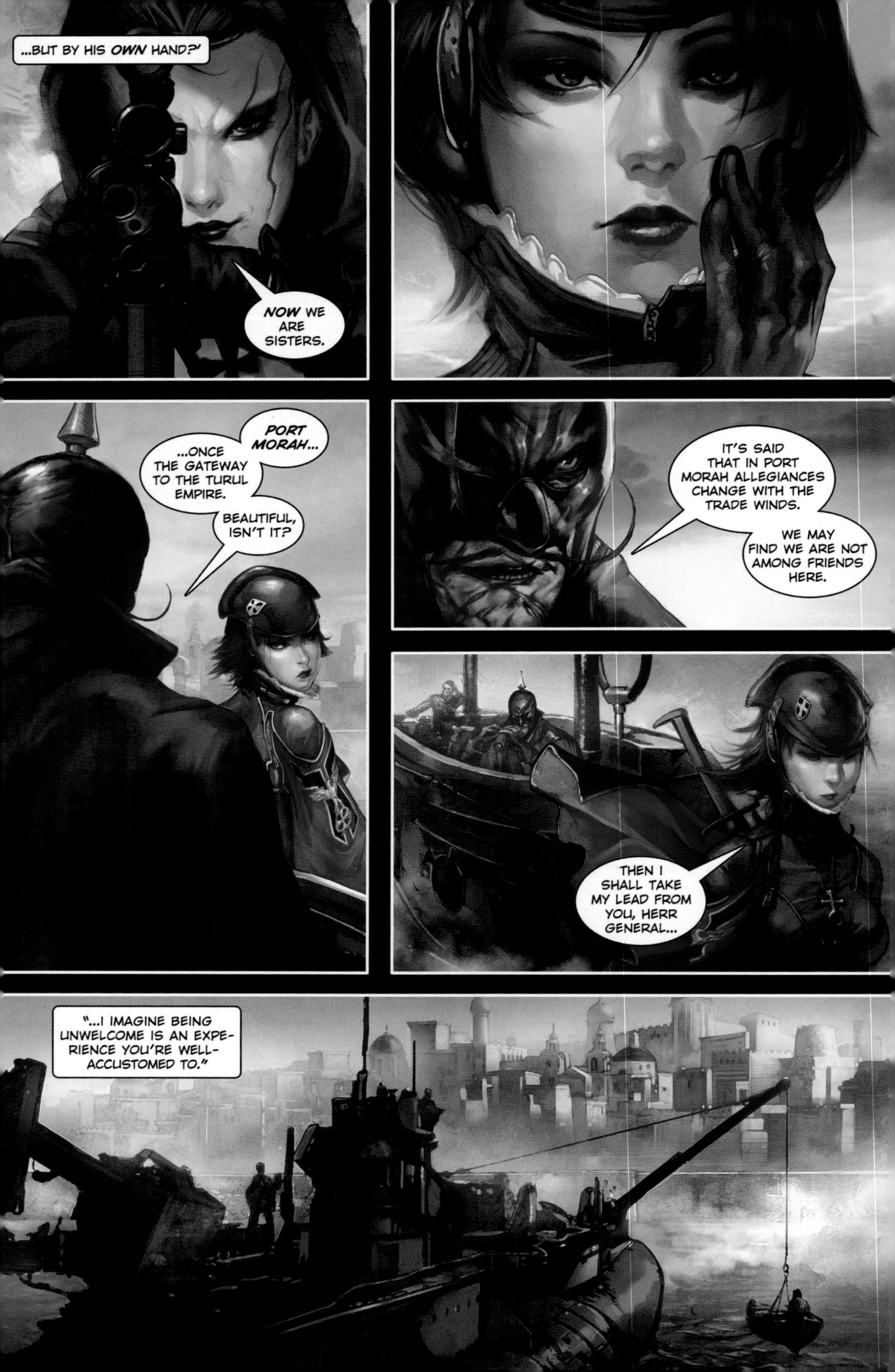

...BUT BY HIS *OWN* HAND?'
NOW WE ARE SISTERS.
PORT MORAH...
...ONCE THE GATEWAY TO THE TURUL EMPIRE.
BEAUTIFUL, ISN'T IT?
IT'S SAID THAT IN PORT MORAH ALLEGIANCES CHANGE WITH THE TRADE WINDS.
WE MAY FIND WE ARE NOT AMONG FRIENDS HERE.
THEN I SHALL TAKE MY LEAD FROM YOU, HERR GENERAL...
"...I IMAGINE BEING UNWELCOME IS AN EXPERIENCE YOU'RE WELL-ACCUSTOMED TO."

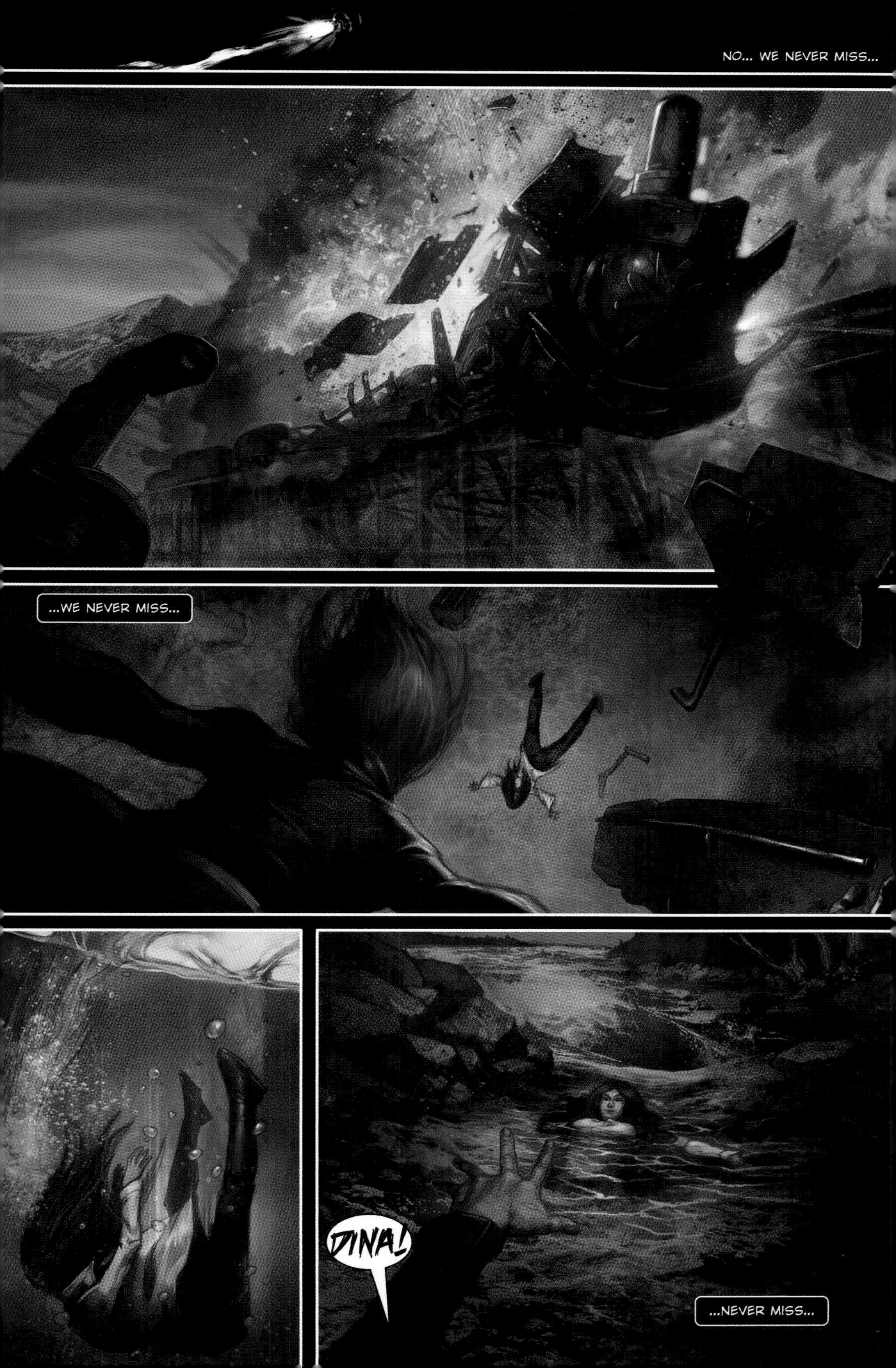
NO... WE NEVER MISS...
...WE NEVER MISS...
DINA!
...NEVER MISS...

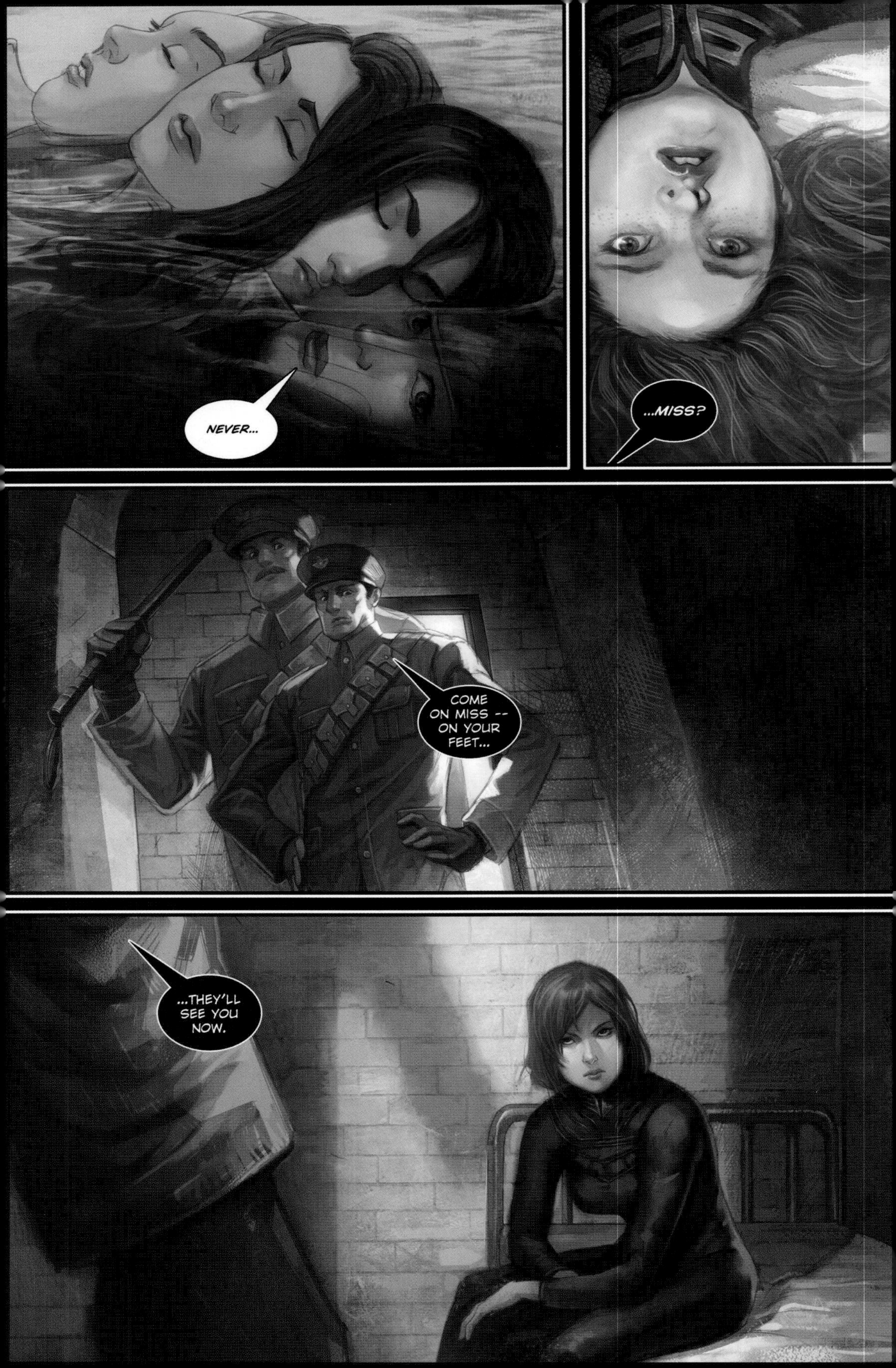
NEVER...
...MISS?
COME ON MISS -- ON YOUR FEET...
...THEY'LL SEE YOU NOW.

AT THE DAWN OF THE EMPIRE THE KAISER SENT HIS CHAMPION, GOTTFAUST, TO CLAIM THE SOUTHERN LANDS IN HIS NAME.

THE SOUTH THEN WAS RULED BY GIANTS AND SAVAGES, A PLACE ONLY THE BRAVEST OF MEN WOULD DARE TRESPASS.

MY LADY! HOW GOES IT?

GOTTFAUST SET OUT FROM THE OLD CAPITAL ALONE.

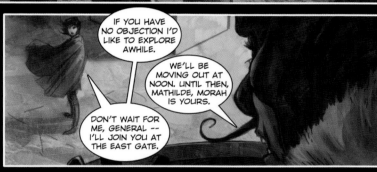

IF YOU HAVE NO OBJECTION I'D LIKE TO EXPLORE AWHILE.

WE'LL BE MOVING OUT AT NOON. UNTIL THEN, MATHILDE, MORAH IS YOURS.

DON'T WAIT FOR ME, GENERAL -- I'LL JOIN YOU AT THE EAST GATE.

SOON HE REACHED THE GREAT CAUSEWAY THAT ONCE SPANNED THE OCEAN FROM MITTELEUROPA TO THE LAND OF MORAH.

FROM A CLEAR BLUE SKY CAME A FEARSOME STORM.

WAVES TALLER THAN THE PALACE WALLS SWEPT ACROSS THE CAUSEWAY. BUT GOTT-FAUST PRESSED ON.

EXHAUSTED AND NEAR-DROWNED HE AT LAST FOUND REFUGE IN A RAMSHACKLE SHELTER MADE OF WHALE BONES.

?

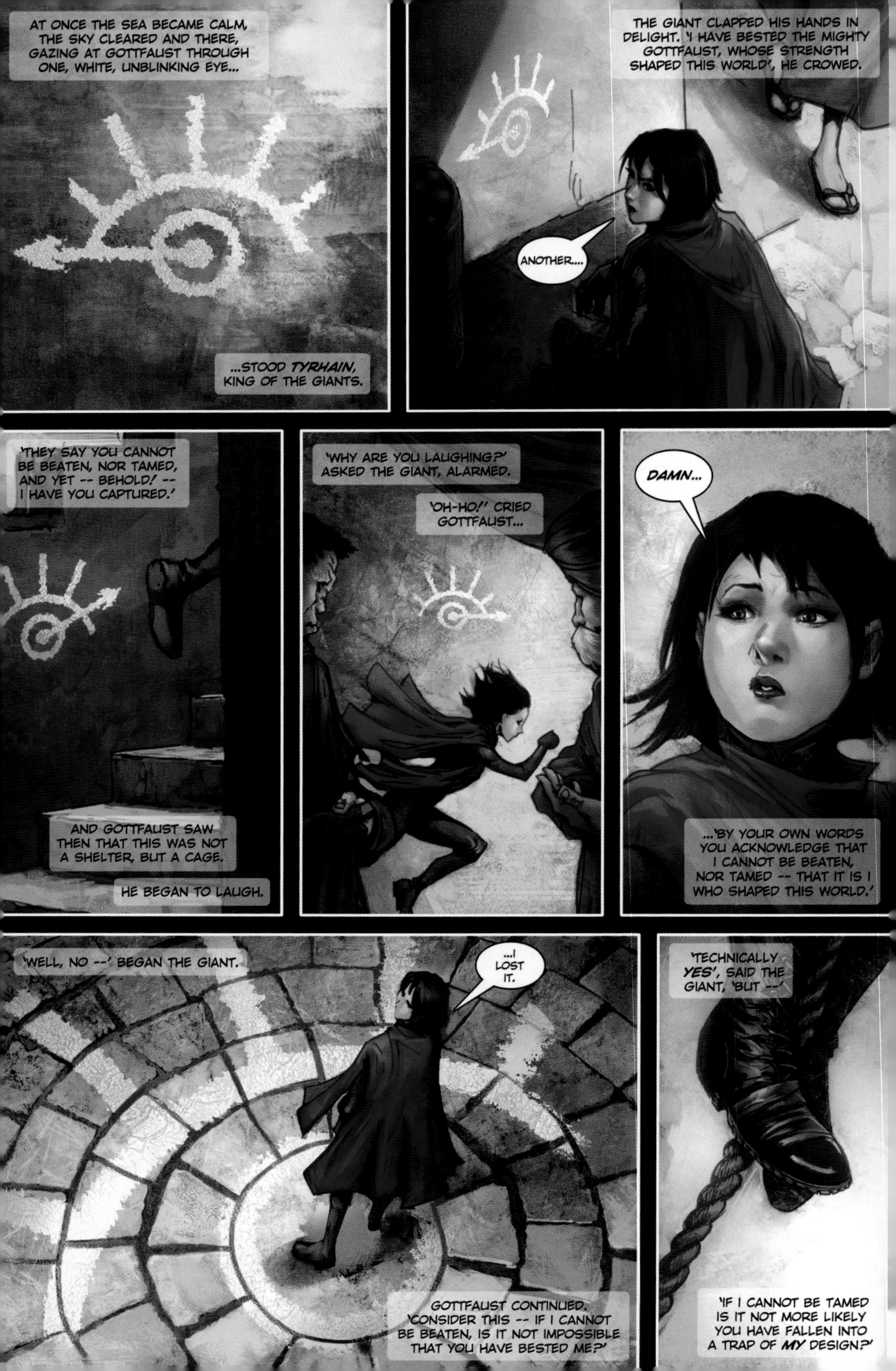

AT ONCE THE SEA BECAME CALM, THE SKY CLEARED AND THERE, GAZING AT GOTTFAUST THROUGH ONE, WHITE, UNBLINKING EYE...
...STOOD *TYRHAIN*, KING OF THE GIANTS.
THE GIANT CLAPPED HIS HANDS IN DELIGHT. 'I HAVE BESTED THE MIGHTY GOTTFAUST, WHOSE STRENGTH SHAPED THIS WORLD', HE CROWED.
ANOTHER....
'THEY SAY YOU CANNOT BE BEATEN, NOR TAMED, AND YET -- BEHOLD! -- I HAVE YOU CAPTURED.'
AND GOTTFAUST SAW THEN THAT THIS WAS NOT A SHELTER, BUT A CAGE.
HE BEGAN TO LAUGH.
'WHY ARE YOU LAUGHING?' ASKED THE GIANT, ALARMED.
'OH-HO!' CRIED GOTTFAUST...
DAMN...
...'BY YOUR OWN WORDS YOU ACKNOWLEDGE THAT I CANNOT BE BEATEN, NOR TAMED -- THAT IT IS I WHO SHAPED THIS WORLD.'
'WELL, NO --' BEGAN THE GIANT.
...I LOST IT.
GOTTFAUST CONTINUED. 'CONSIDER THIS -- IF I CANNOT BE BEATEN, IS IT NOT IMPOSSIBLE THAT YOU HAVE BESTED ME?'
'TECHNICALLY *YES*', SAID THE GIANT, 'BUT --'
'IF I CANNOT BE TAMED IS IT NOT MORE LIKELY YOU HAVE FALLEN INTO A TRAP OF *MY* DESIGN?'

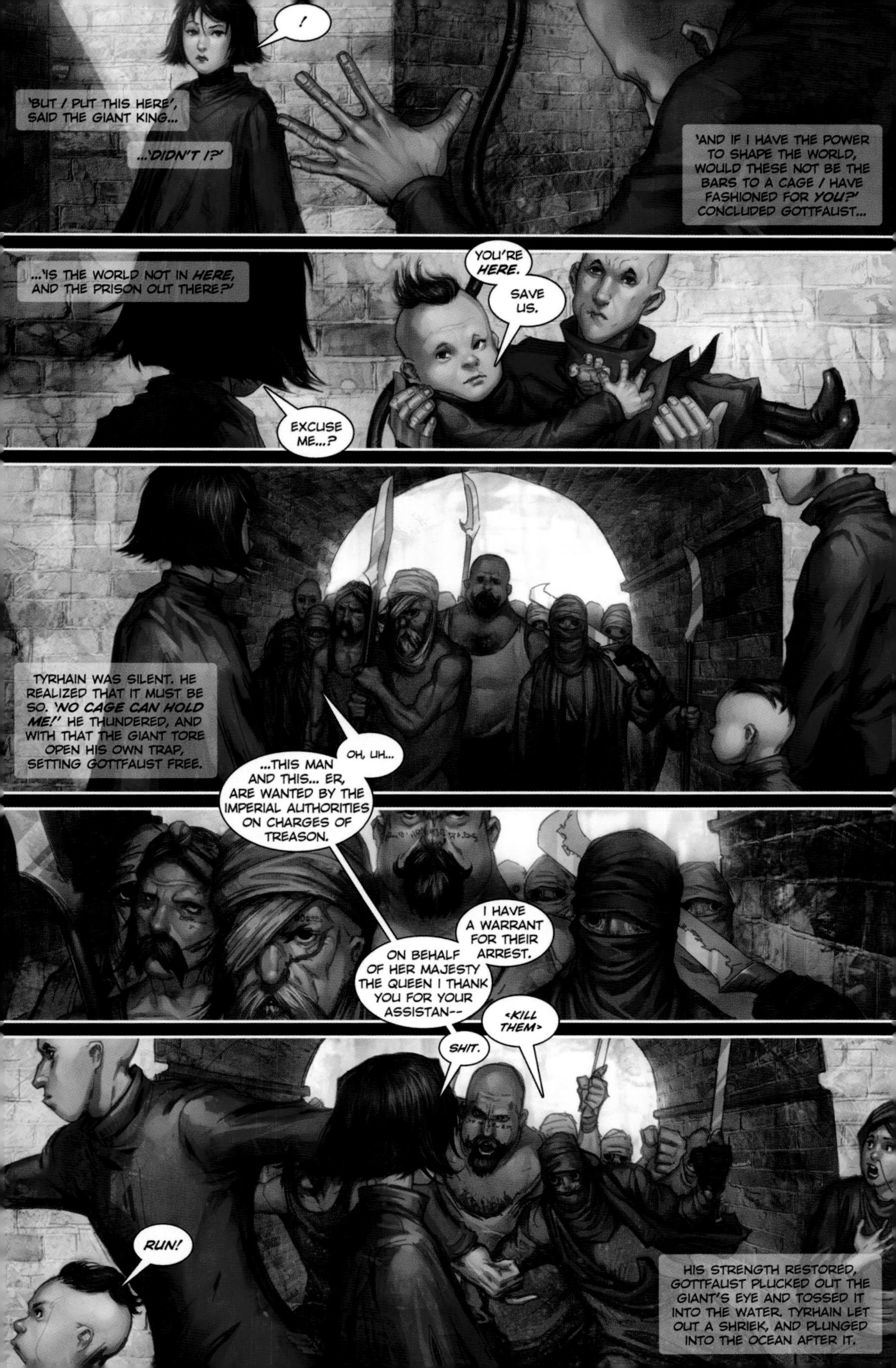
!
'BUT I PUT THIS HERE', SAID THE GIANT KING...
...'DIDN'T I?'
'AND IF I HAVE THE POWER TO SHAPE THE WORLD, WOULD THESE NOT BE THE BARS TO A CAGE I HAVE FASHIONED FOR YOU?' CONCLUDED GOTTFAUST...
...'IS THE WORLD NOT IN HERE, AND THE PRISON OUT THERE?'
YOU'RE HERE.
SAVE US.
EXCUSE ME...?
TYRHAIN WAS SILENT. HE REALIZED THAT IT MUST BE SO. 'NO CAGE CAN HOLD ME!' HE THUNDERED, AND WITH THAT THE GIANT TORE OPEN HIS OWN TRAP, SETTING GOTTFAUST FREE.
OH, UH...
...THIS MAN AND THIS... ER, ARE WANTED BY THE IMPERIAL AUTHORITIES ON CHARGES OF TREASON.
I HAVE A WARRANT FOR THEIR ARREST.
ON BEHALF OF HER MAJESTY THE QUEEN I THANK YOU FOR YOUR ASSISTAN--
<KILL THEM>
SHIT.
RUN!
HIS STRENGTH RESTORED, GOTTFAUST PLUCKED OUT THE GIANT'S EYE AND TOSSED IT INTO THE WATER. TYRHAIN LET OUT A SHRIEK, AND PLUNGED INTO THE OCEAN AFTER IT.

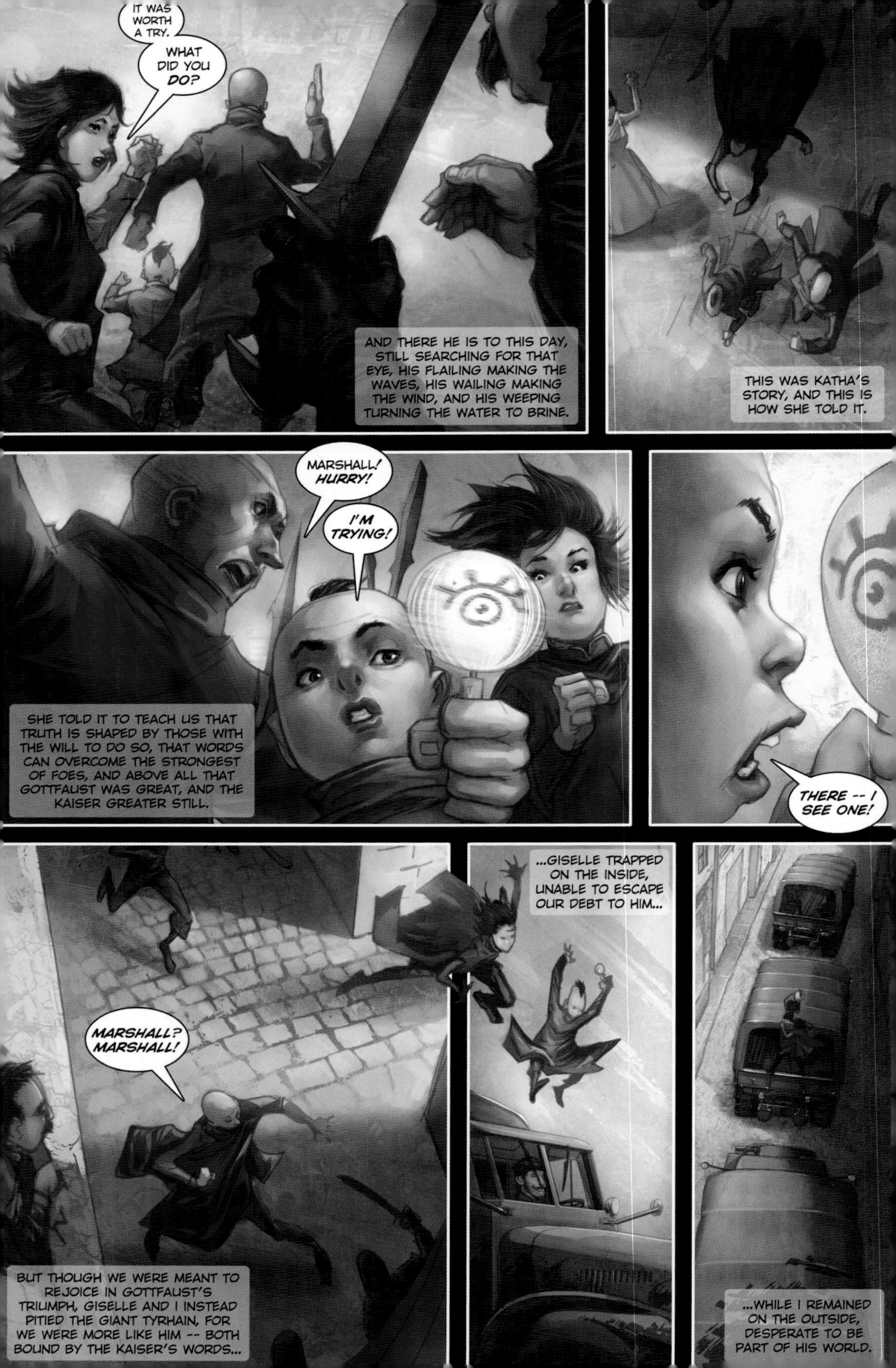
IT WAS WORTH A TRY.
WHAT DID YOU DO?
AND THERE HE IS TO THIS DAY, STILL SEARCHING FOR THAT EYE, HIS FLAILING MAKING THE WAVES, HIS WAILING MAKING THE WIND, AND HIS WEEPING TURNING THE WATER TO BRINE.
THIS WAS KATHA'S STORY, AND THIS IS HOW SHE TOLD IT.
MARSHALL! HURRY!
I'M TRYING!
SHE TOLD IT TO TEACH US THAT TRUTH IS SHAPED BY THOSE WITH THE WILL TO DO SO, THAT WORDS CAN OVERCOME THE STRONGEST OF FOES, AND ABOVE ALL THAT GOTTFAUST WAS GREAT, AND THE KAISER GREATER STILL.
THERE -- I SEE ONE!
MARSHALL? MARSHALL!
BUT THOUGH WE WERE MEANT TO REJOICE IN GOTTFAUST'S TRIUMPH, GISELLE AND I INSTEAD PITIED THE GIANT TYRHAIN, FOR WE WERE MORE LIKE HIM -- BOTH BOUND BY THE KAISER'S WORDS...
...GISELLE TRAPPED ON THE INSIDE, UNABLE TO ESCAPE OUR DEBT TO HIM...
...WHILE I REMAINED ON THE OUTSIDE, DESPERATE TO BE PART OF HIS WORLD.

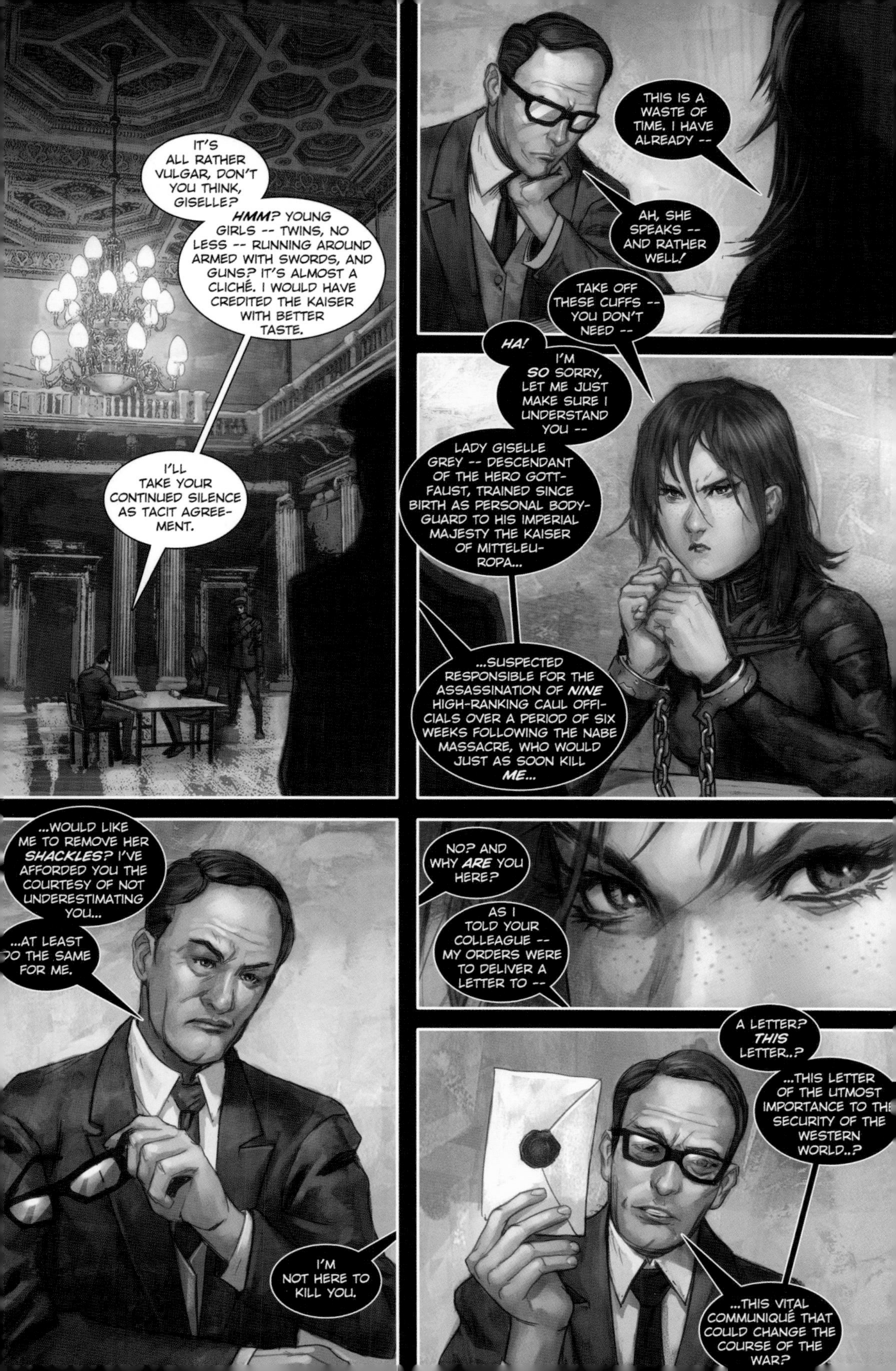
IT'S ALL RATHER VULGAR, DON'T YOU THINK, GISELLE?
HMM? YOUNG GIRLS -- TWINS, NO LESS -- RUNNING AROUND ARMED WITH SWORDS, AND GUNS? IT'S ALMOST A CLICHÉ. I WOULD HAVE CREDITED THE KAISER WITH BETTER TASTE.
I'LL TAKE YOUR CONTINUED SILENCE AS TACIT AGREEMENT.
THIS IS A WASTE OF TIME. I HAVE ALREADY --
AH, SHE SPEAKS -- AND RATHER WELL!
TAKE OFF THESE CUFFS -- YOU DON'T NEED --
HA!
I'M SO SORRY, LET ME JUST MAKE SURE I UNDERSTAND YOU --
LADY GISELLE GREY -- DESCENDANT OF THE HERO GOTTFAUST, TRAINED SINCE BIRTH AS PERSONAL BODYGUARD TO HIS IMPERIAL MAJESTY THE KAISER OF MITTELEUROPA...
...SUSPECTED RESPONSIBLE FOR THE ASSASSINATION OF NINE HIGH-RANKING CAUL OFFICIALS OVER A PERIOD OF SIX WEEKS FOLLOWING THE NABE MASSACRE, WHO WOULD JUST AS SOON KILL ME...
...WOULD LIKE ME TO REMOVE HER SHACKLES? I'VE AFFORDED YOU THE COURTESY OF NOT UNDERESTIMATING YOU...
...AT LEAST DO THE SAME FOR ME.
I'M NOT HERE TO KILL YOU.
NO? AND WHY ARE YOU HERE?
AS I TOLD YOUR COLLEAGUE -- MY ORDERS WERE TO DELIVER A LETTER TO --
A LETTER? THIS LETTER..?
...THIS LETTER OF THE UTMOST IMPORTANCE TO THE SECURITY OF THE WESTERN WORLD..?
...THIS VITAL COMMUNIQUÉ THAT COULD CHANGE THE COURSE OF THE WAR?

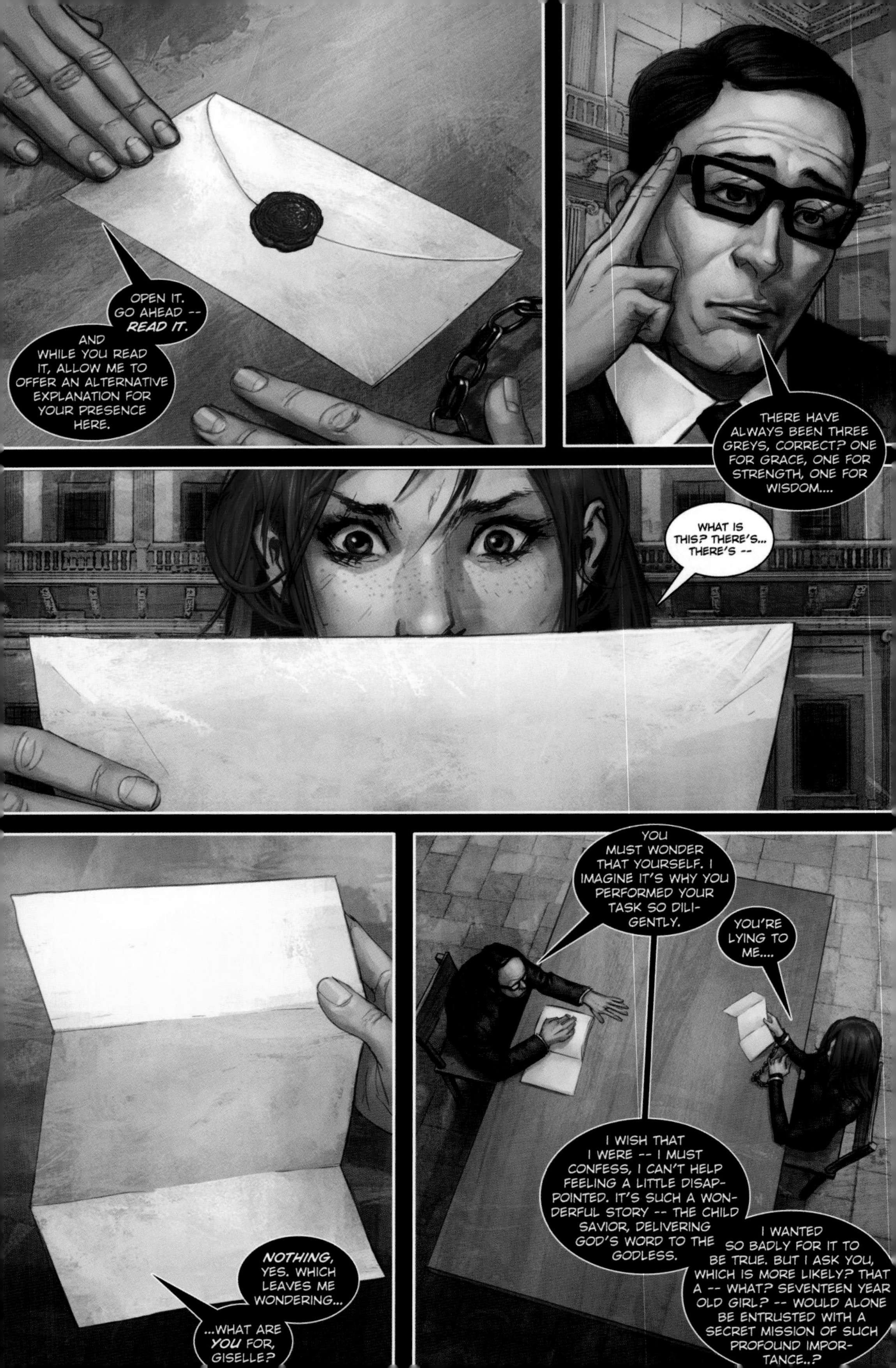
OPEN IT. GO AHEAD -- *READ IT*.
AND WHILE YOU READ IT, ALLOW ME TO OFFER AN ALTERNATIVE EXPLANATION FOR YOUR PRESENCE HERE.
THERE HAVE ALWAYS BEEN THREE GREYS, CORRECT? ONE FOR GRACE, ONE FOR STRENGTH, ONE FOR WISDOM....
WHAT IS THIS? THERE'S... THERE'S --
NOTHING, YES. WHICH LEAVES ME WONDERING...
...WHAT ARE *YOU* FOR, GISELLE?
YOU MUST WONDER THAT YOURSELF. I IMAGINE IT'S WHY YOU PERFORMED YOUR TASK SO DILI-GENTLY.
YOU'RE LYING TO ME....
I WISH THAT I WERE -- I MUST CONFESS, I CAN'T HELP FEELING A LITTLE DISAP-POINTED. IT'S SUCH A WON-DERFUL STORY -- THE CHILD SAVIOR, DELIVERING GOD'S WORD TO THE GODLESS.
I WANTED SO BADLY FOR IT TO BE TRUE. BUT I ASK YOU, WHICH IS MORE LIKELY? THAT A -- WHAT? SEVENTEEN YEAR OLD GIRL? -- WOULD ALONE BE ENTRUSTED WITH A SECRET MISSION OF SUCH PROFOUND IMPOR-TANCE..?

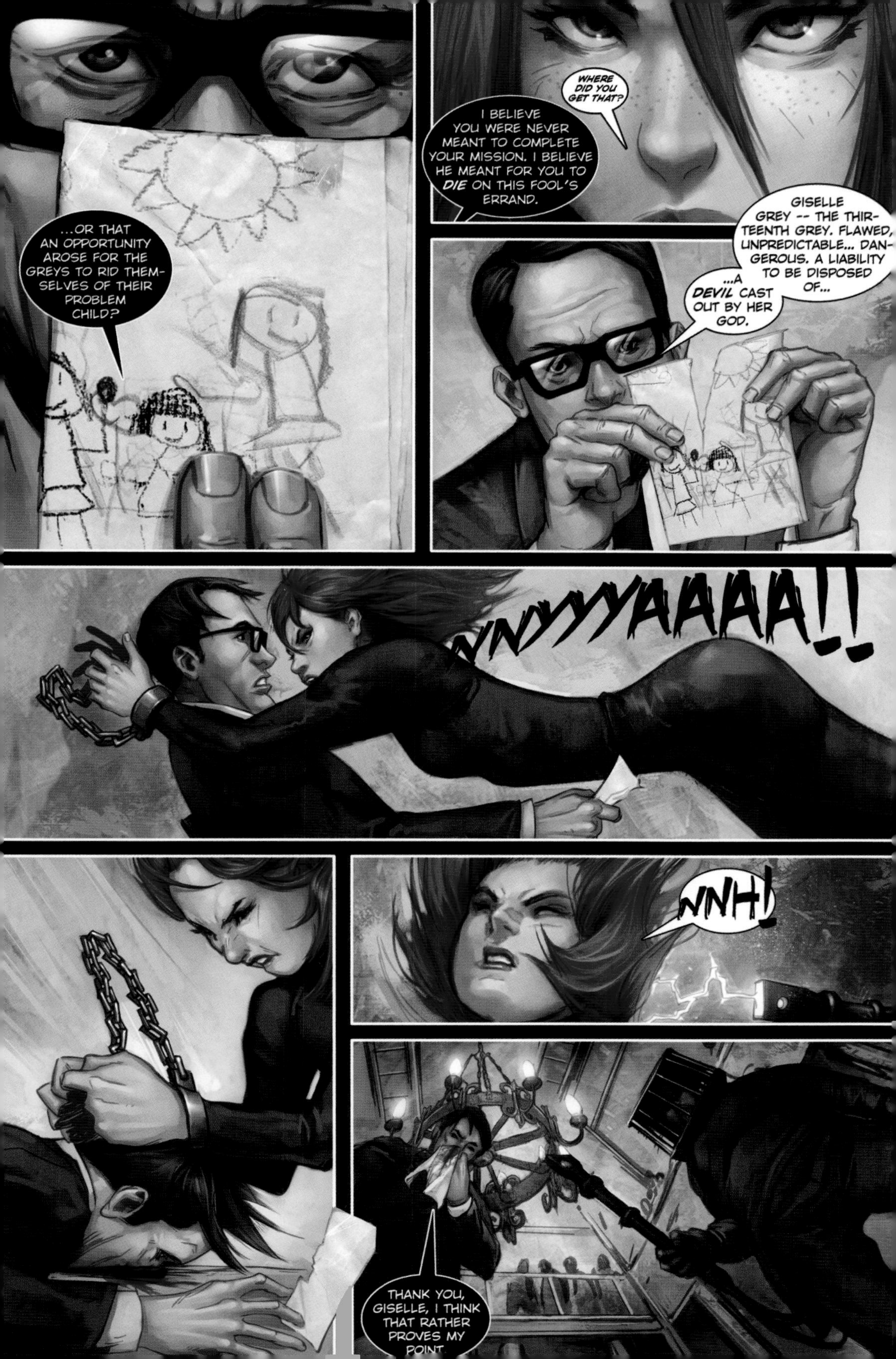
...OR THAT AN OPPORTUNITY AROSE FOR THE GREYS TO RID THEMSELVES OF THEIR PROBLEM CHILD?
WHERE DID YOU GET THAT?
I BELIEVE YOU WERE NEVER MEANT TO COMPLETE YOUR MISSION. I BELIEVE HE MEANT FOR YOU TO DIE ON THIS FOOL'S ERRAND.
GISELLE GREY -- THE THIRTEENTH GREY. FLAWED, UNPREDICTABLE... DANGEROUS. A LIABILITY TO BE DISPOSED OF...
...A DEVIL CAST OUT BY HER GOD.
NNYYYAAAA!!
WNH!
THANK YOU, GISELLE, I THINK THAT RATHER PROVES MY POINT.

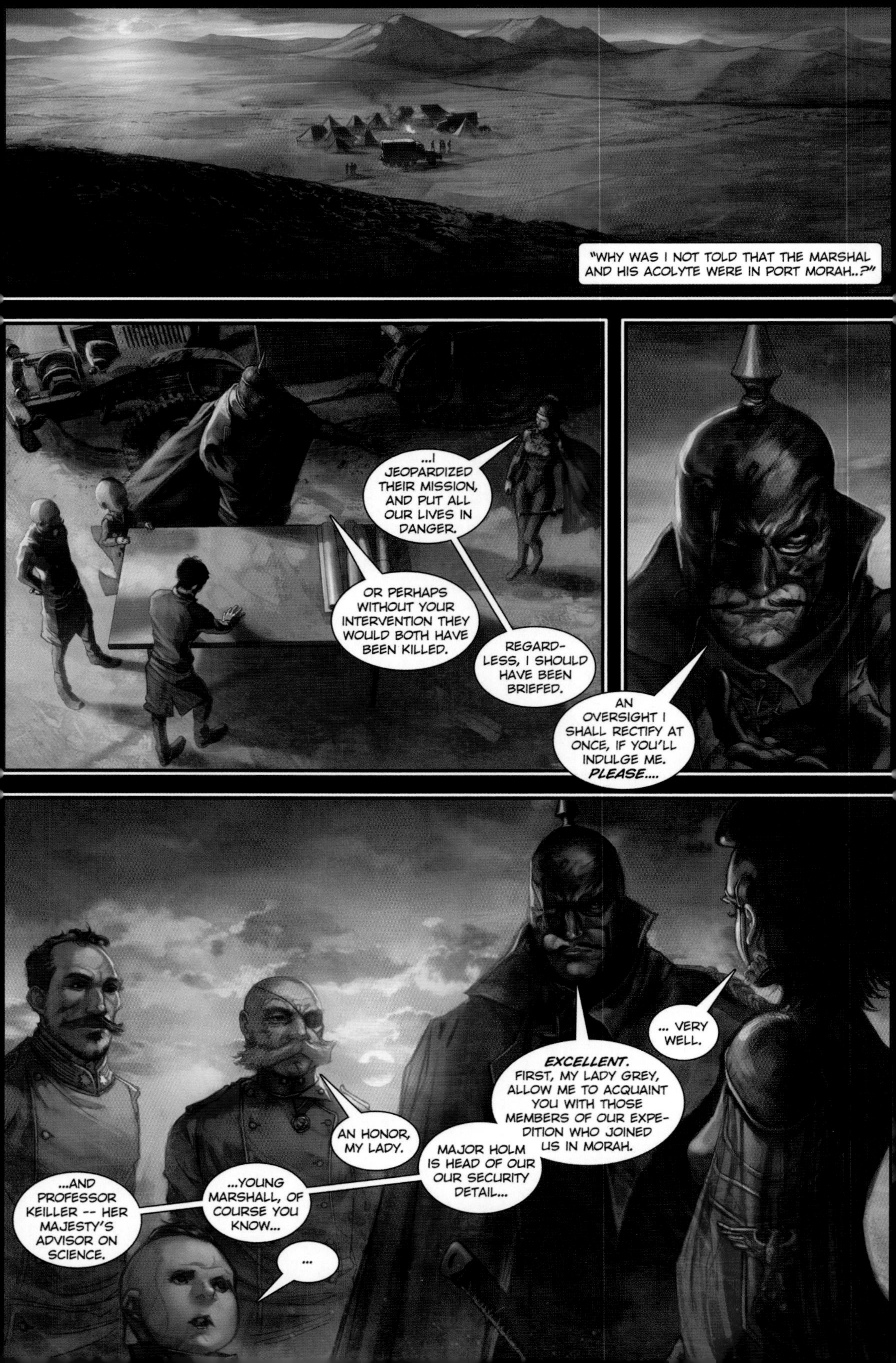
"WHY WAS I NOT TOLD THAT THE MARSHAL AND HIS ACOLYTE WERE IN PORT MORAH..?"
...I JEOPARDIZED THEIR MISSION, AND PUT ALL OUR LIVES IN DANGER.
OR PERHAPS WITHOUT YOUR INTERVENTION THEY WOULD BOTH HAVE BEEN KILLED.
REGARD- LESS, I SHOULD HAVE BEEN BRIEFED.
AN OVERSIGHT I SHALL RECTIFY AT ONCE, IF YOU'LL INDULGE ME. *PLEASE....*
... VERY WELL.
EXCELLENT. FIRST, MY LADY GREY, ALLOW ME TO ACQUAINT YOU WITH THOSE MEMBERS OF OUR EXPE- DITION WHO JOINED US IN MORAH.
MAJOR HOLM IS HEAD OF OUR OUR SECURITY DETAIL...
AN HONOR, MY LADY.
...YOUNG MARSHALL, OF COURSE YOU KNOW...
...
...AND PROFESSOR KEILLER -- HER MAJESTY'S ADVISOR ON SCIENCE.

THE QUEEN HAS ORDERED THE RETRIEVAL OF GOTTFAUST'S STONE, FOR SHE BELIEVES ITS POWER CAN BRING AN END TO THIS WAR.

THAT IS OUR MISSION'S OBJECTIVE.

WOULD YOU LIKE A *FRUIT DROP*, YOUNG MAN?

DON'T MISUNDERSTAND, MAJOR, I'M NOT A CHILD.

AFTER GOTTFAUST'S FALL THE STONE WAS BROKEN IN TWO, IN ORDER THAT NO ONE PERSON COULD WIELD IT. THE LARGEST PIECE WAS LOST IN THE CHAOS THAT FOLLOWED THE SIEGE OF *KEREC*.

IT HAS NOT BEEN SEEN IN OVER THREE-HUNDRED YEARS.

WHAT FLAVOR ARE THEY?

THE OTHER WAS RECOVERED IN *HEILIG*, AND TAKEN TO THE PALACE AT WALDSTATTEN. IT WAS NOT SAFE THERE, AND ONCE MORE WAS HIDDEN, AS YOU DISCOVERED, MATHILDE...

...I BELIEVE THAT SAME PIECE TO BE SOMEWHERE NEAR RAMISK, IN SOUTHERN TURUL --

SOMEWHERE? YOU DON'T KNOW WHERE THE *HEILIG* STONE IS HIDDEN? YOU LIED TO US!

YOU'LL COME TO UNDERSTAND, MY LADY, THERE ARE FEW ABSOLUTES WHERE THE ROCK IS CONCERNED.

THEN HOW DO YOU PROPOSE TO FIND IT?

WHEN THE STONE WAS BROKEN IT DID NOT SPLIT CLEANLY, BUT SHAT-TERED. THERE REMAINS A STRANGE FORCE OF ATTRACTION BETWEEN THE FRAGMENTS OF STONE -- WITH THE SMALLEST OF SHARDS ONE CAN LOCATE THE NEXT.

MARSHALL -- DO YOU HAVE IT?

I ALREADY TOLD YOU I DID.

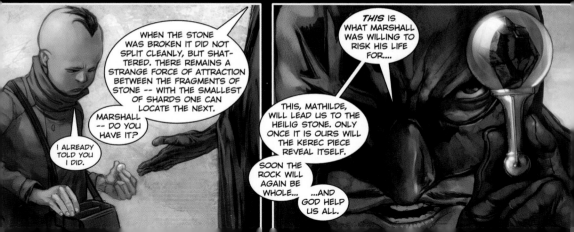

THIS IS WHAT MARSHALL WAS WILLING TO RISK HIS LIFE FOR....

THIS, MATHILDE, WILL LEAD US TO THE HEILIG STONE. ONLY ONCE IT IS OURS WILL THE KEREC PIECE REVEAL ITSELF.

SOON THE ROCK WILL AGAIN BE WHOLE...

...AND GOD HELP US ALL.

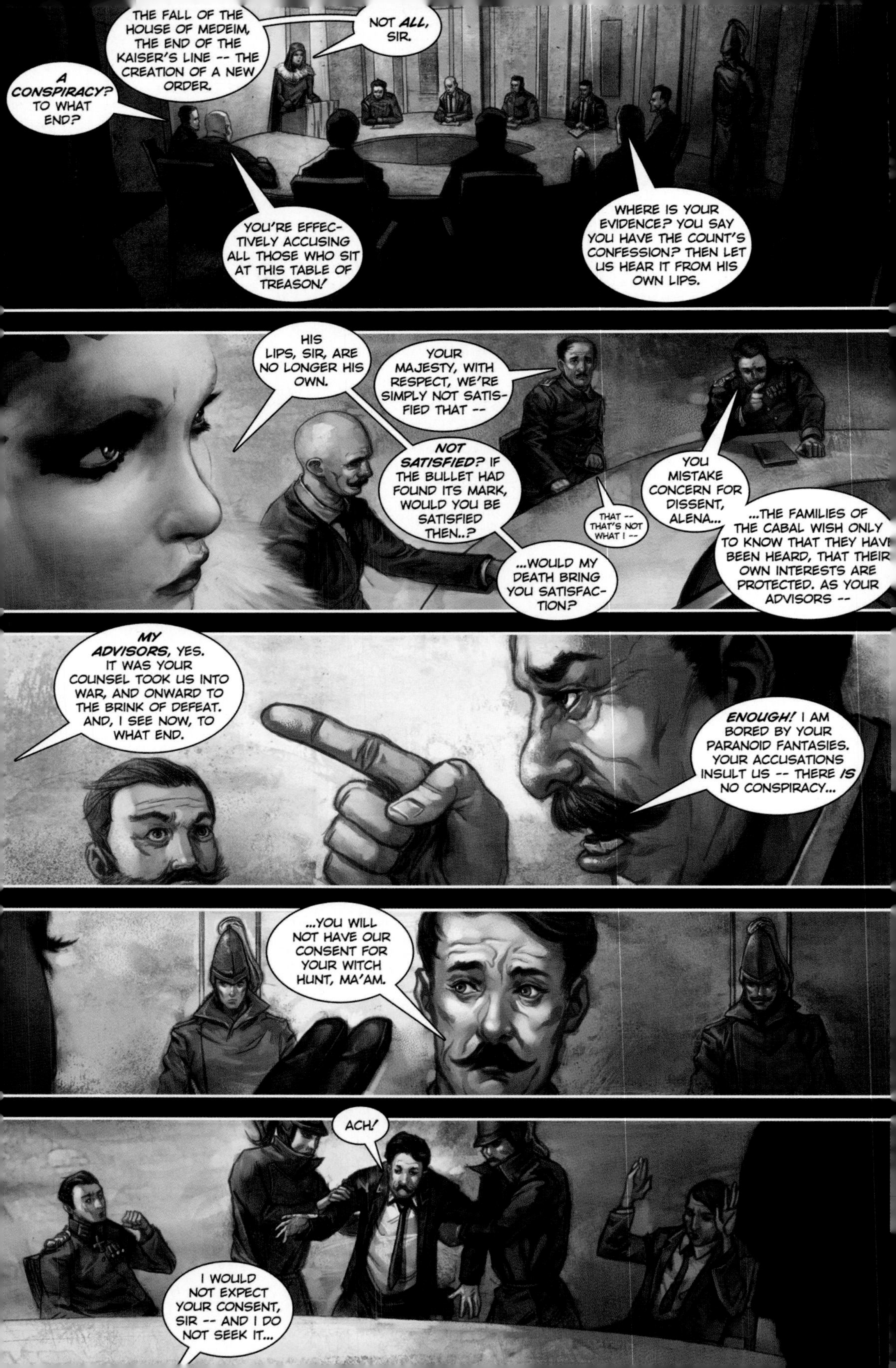
A CONSPIRACY? TO WHAT END?
THE FALL OF THE HOUSE OF MEDEIM, THE END OF THE KAISER'S LINE -- THE CREATION OF A NEW ORDER.
NOT ALL, SIR.
YOU'RE EFFECTIVELY ACCUSING ALL THOSE WHO SIT AT THIS TABLE OF TREASON!
WHERE IS YOUR EVIDENCE? YOU SAY YOU HAVE THE COUNT'S CONFESSION? THEN LET US HEAR IT FROM HIS OWN LIPS.
HIS LIPS, SIR, ARE NO LONGER HIS OWN.
YOUR MAJESTY, WITH RESPECT, WE'RE SIMPLY NOT SATISFIED THAT --
NOT SATISFIED? IF THE BULLET HAD FOUND ITS MARK, WOULD YOU BE SATISFIED THEN..?
...WOULD MY DEATH BRING YOU SATISFACTION?
THAT -- THAT'S NOT WHAT I --
YOU MISTAKE CONCERN FOR DISSENT, ALENA...
...THE FAMILIES OF THE CABAL WISH ONLY TO KNOW THAT THEY HAVE BEEN HEARD, THAT THEIR OWN INTERESTS ARE PROTECTED. AS YOUR ADVISORS --
MY ADVISORS, YES. IT WAS YOUR COUNSEL TOOK US INTO WAR, AND ONWARD TO THE BRINK OF DEFEAT. AND, I SEE NOW, TO WHAT END.
ENOUGH! I AM BORED BY YOUR PARANOID FANTASIES. YOUR ACCUSATIONS INSULT US -- THERE IS NO CONSPIRACY...
...YOU WILL NOT HAVE OUR CONSENT FOR YOUR WITCH HUNT, MA'AM.
ACH!
I WOULD NOT EXPECT YOUR CONSENT, SIR -- AND I DO NOT SEEK IT...

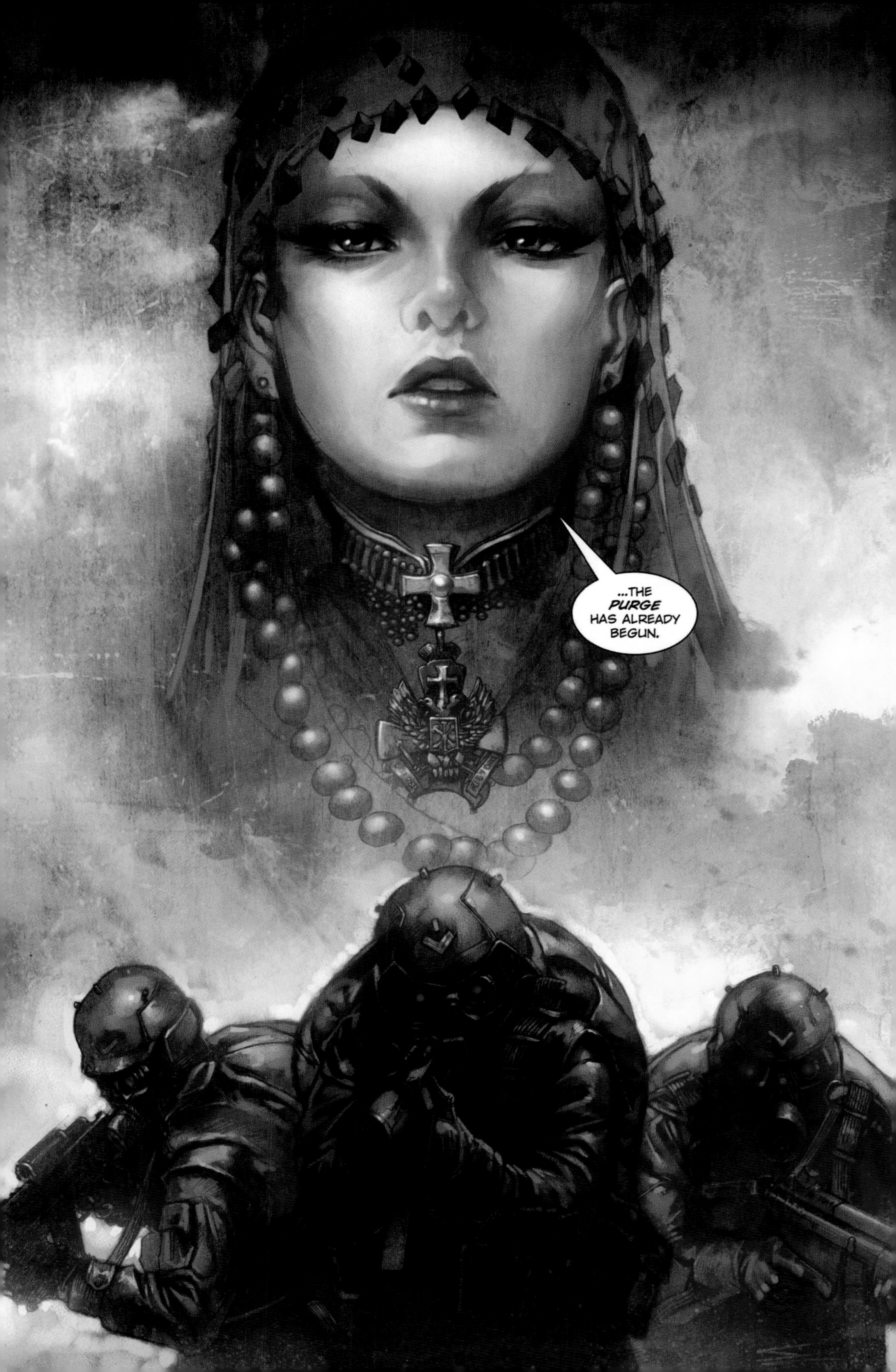
...THE *PURGE* HAS ALREADY BEGUN.

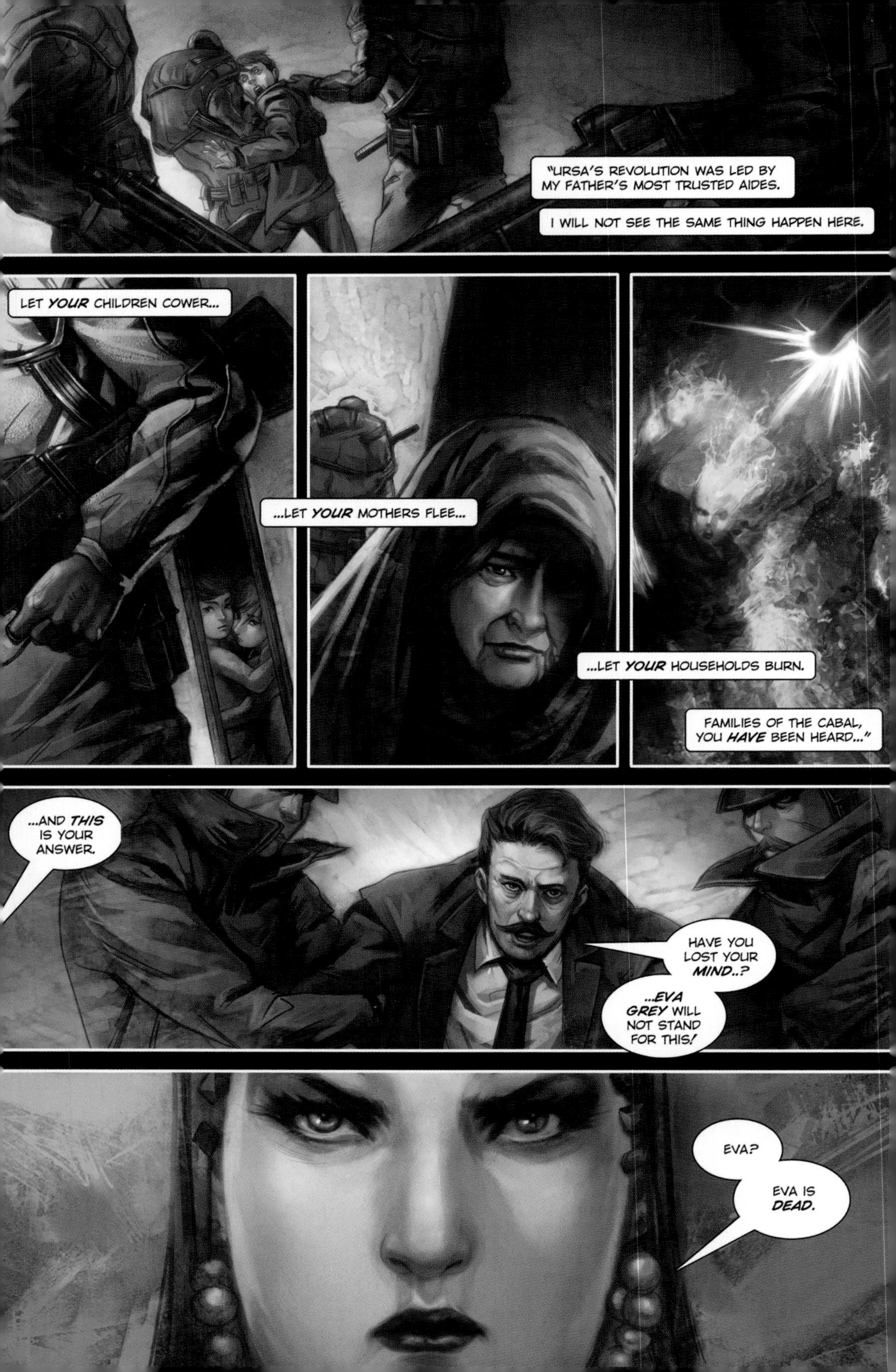
"URSA'S REVOLUTION WAS LED BY MY FATHER'S MOST TRUSTED AIDES.
I WILL NOT SEE THE SAME THING HAPPEN HERE.
LET *YOUR* CHILDREN COWER...
...LET *YOUR* MOTHERS FLEE...
...LET *YOUR* HOUSEHOLDS BURN.
FAMILIES OF THE CABAL, YOU *HAVE* BEEN HEARD..."
...AND *THIS* IS YOUR ANSWER.
HAVE YOU LOST YOUR *MIND*..?
...EVA GREY WILL NOT STAND FOR THIS!
EVA?
EVA IS *DEAD*.

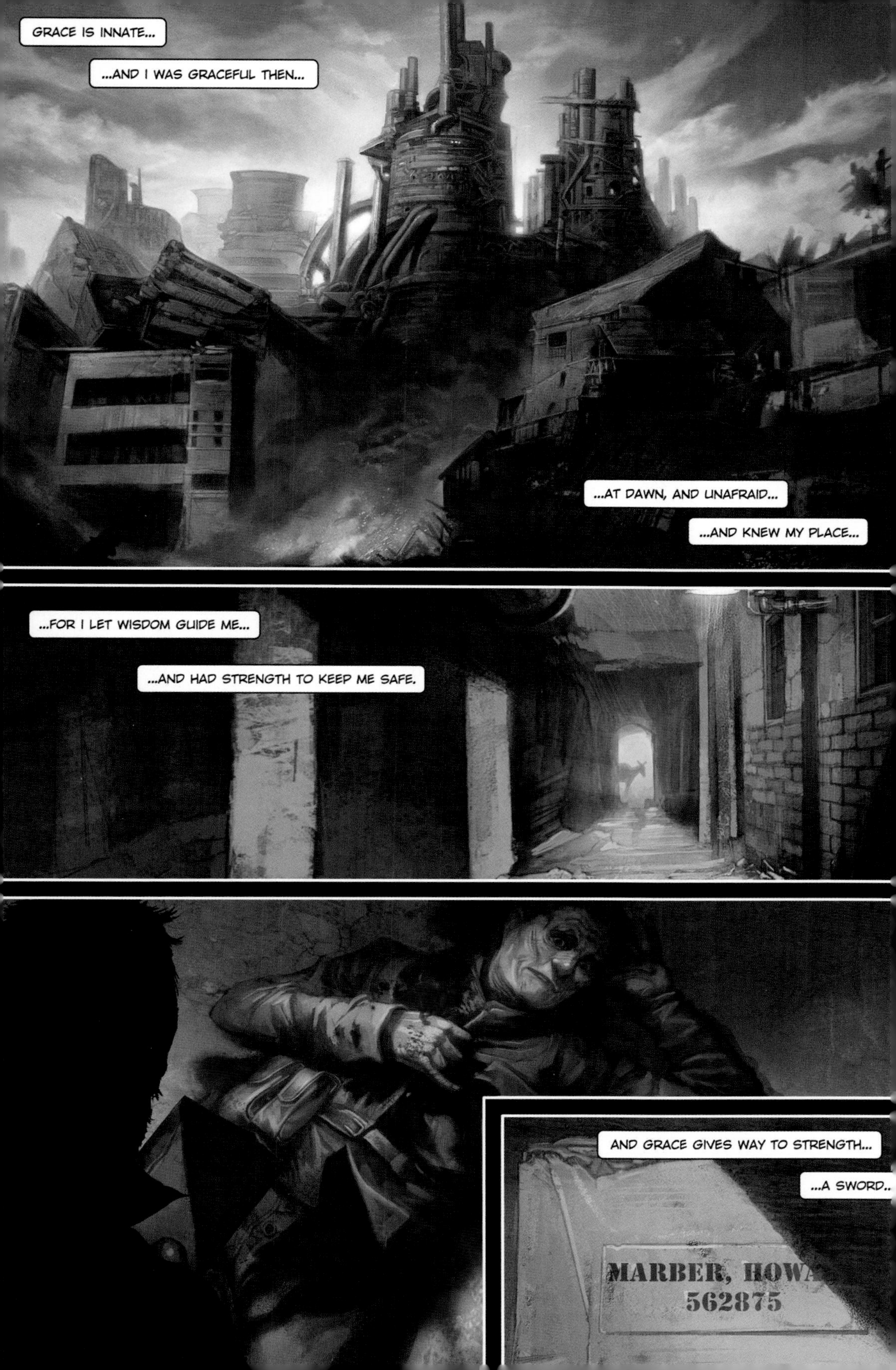
GRACE IS INNATE...
...AND I WAS GRACEFUL THEN...
...AT DAWN, AND UNAFRAID...
...AND KNEW MY PLACE...
...FOR I LET WISDOM GUIDE ME...
...AND HAD STRENGTH TO KEEP ME SAFE.
AND GRACE GIVES WAY TO STRENGTH...
...A SWORD...
MARBER, HOWA
562875

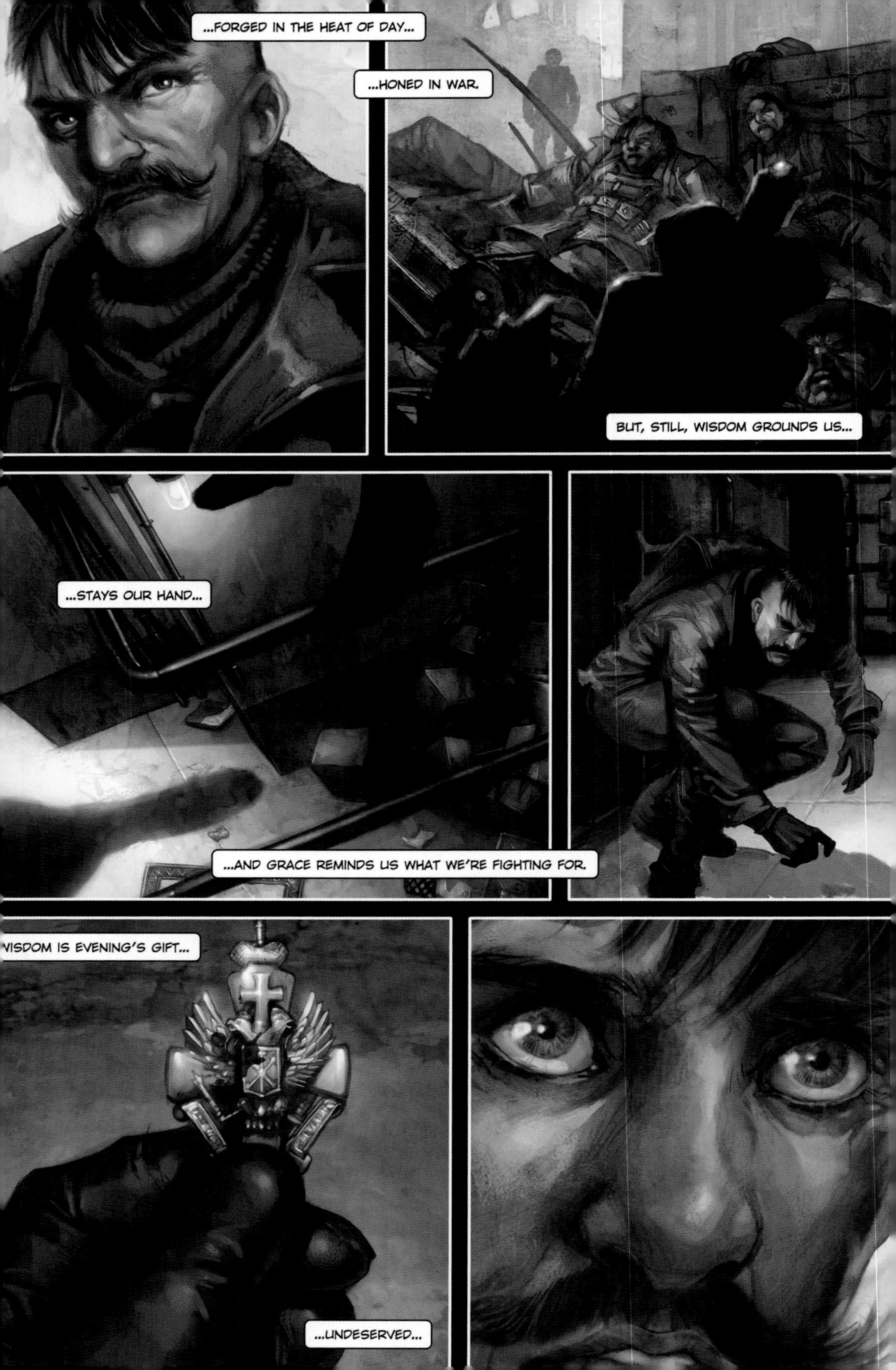

...FORGED IN THE HEAT OF DAY...
...HONED IN WAR.
BUT, STILL, WISDOM GROUNDS US...
...STAYS OUR HAND...
...AND GRACE REMINDS US WHAT WE'RE FIGHTING FOR.
WISDOM IS EVENING'S GIFT...
...UNDESERVED...

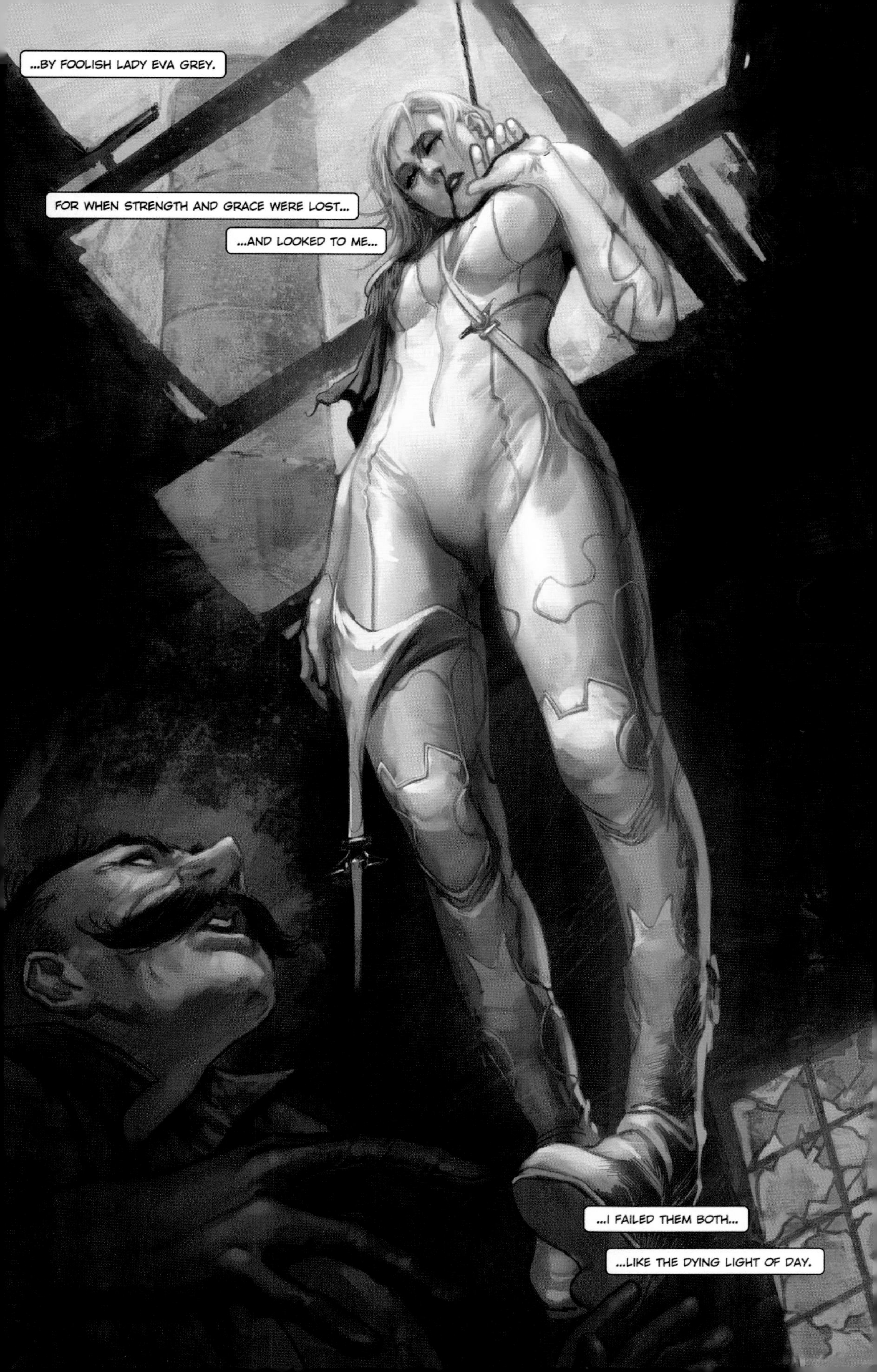
...BY FOOLISH LADY EVA GREY.
FOR WHEN STRENGTH AND GRACE WERE LOST...
...AND LOOKED TO ME...
...I FAILED THEM BOTH...
...LIKE THE DYING LIGHT OF DAY.

V

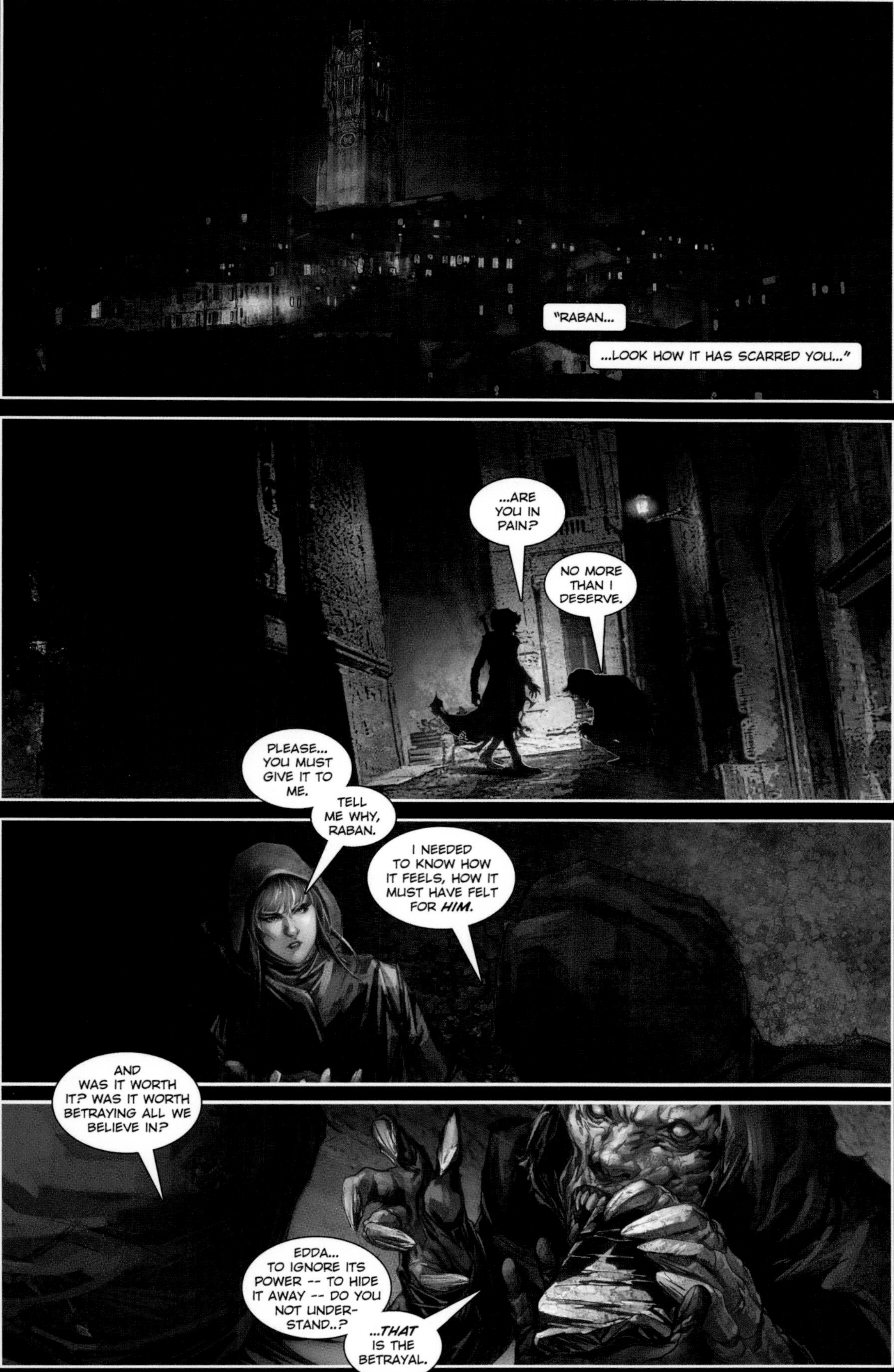
"RABAN...
...LOOK HOW IT HAS SCARRED YOU..."
...ARE YOU IN PAIN?
NO MORE THAN I DESERVE.
PLEASE... YOU MUST GIVE IT TO ME.
TELL ME WHY, RABAN.
I NEEDED TO KNOW HOW IT FEELS, HOW IT MUST HAVE FELT FOR *HIM*.
AND WAS IT WORTH IT? WAS IT WORTH BETRAYING ALL WE BELIEVE IN?
EDDA... TO IGNORE ITS POWER -- TO HIDE IT AWAY -- DO YOU NOT UNDER-STAND..?
...THAT IS THE BETRAYAL.

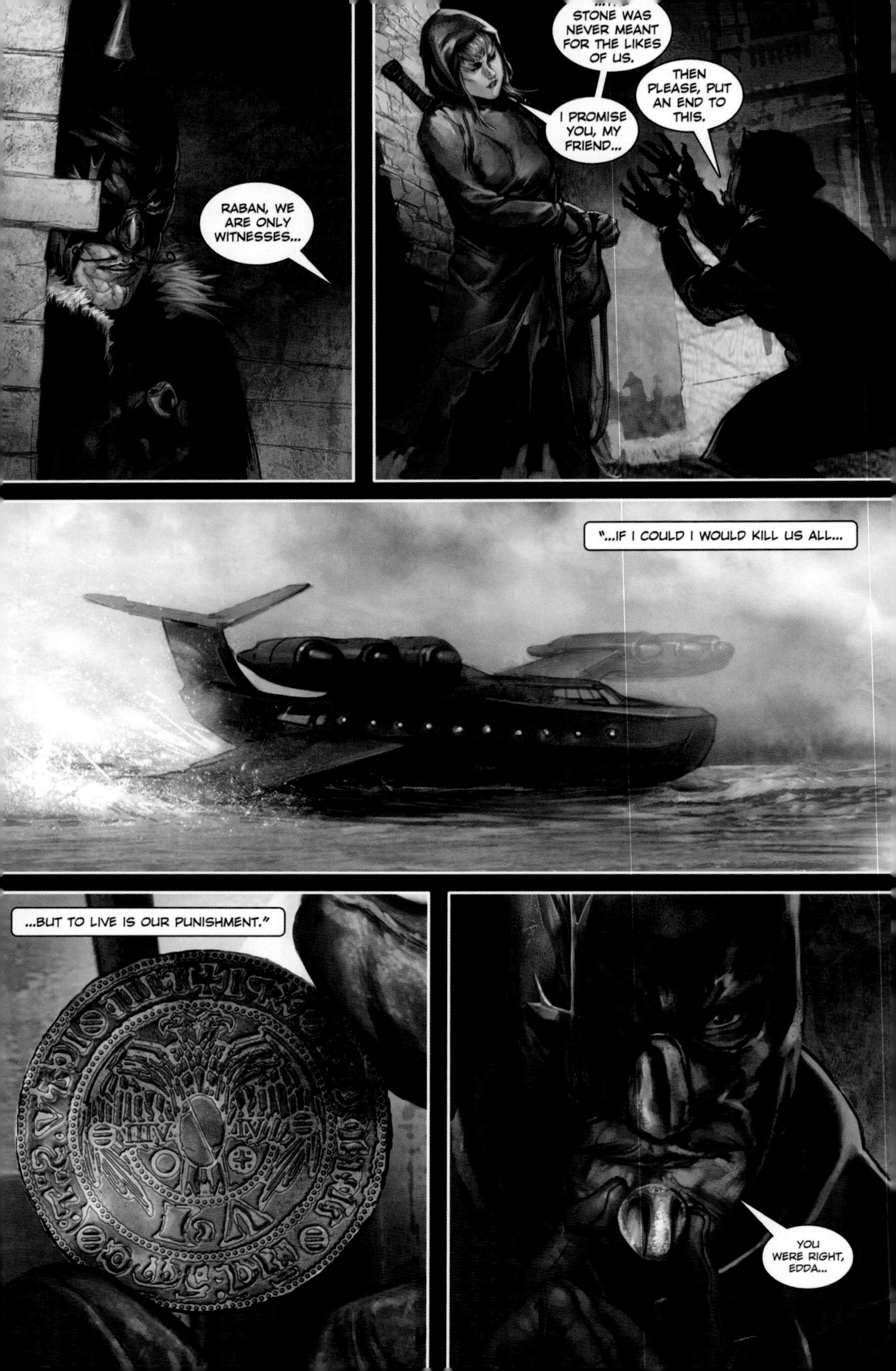
RABAN, WE ARE ONLY WITNESSES...
I PROMISE YOU, MY FRIEND...
STONE WAS NEVER MEANT FOR THE LIKES OF US.
THEN PLEASE, PUT AN END TO THIS.
"...IF I COULD I WOULD KILL US ALL...
...BUT TO LIVE IS OUR PUNISHMENT."
YOU WERE RIGHT, EDDA...

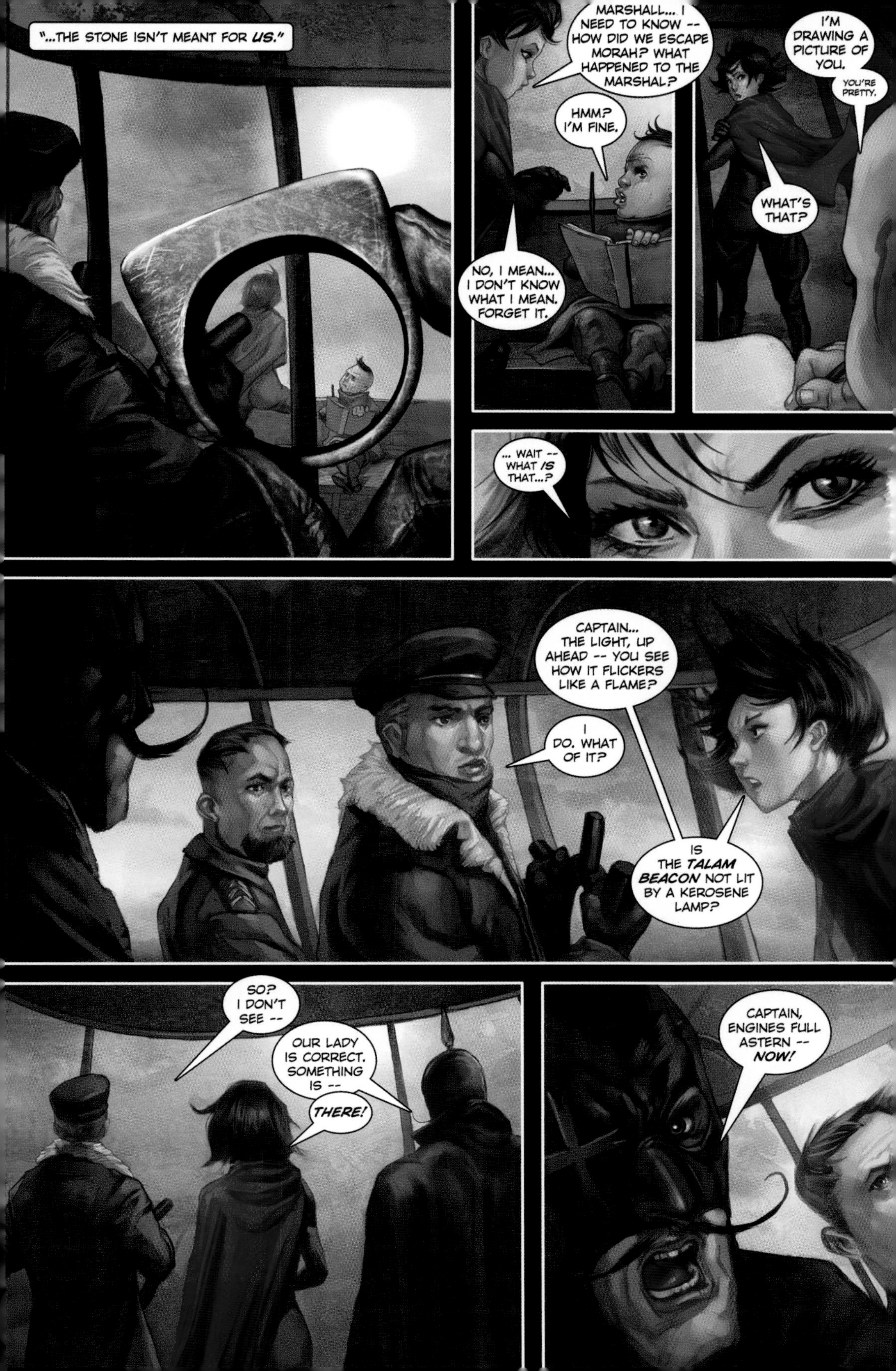
"...THE STONE ISN'T MEANT FOR *US.*"
MARSHALL... I NEED TO KNOW -- HOW DID WE ESCAPE MORAH? WHAT HAPPENED TO THE MARSHAL?
HMM? I'M FINE.
NO, I MEAN... I DON'T KNOW WHAT I MEAN. FORGET IT.
I'M DRAWING A PICTURE OF YOU.
YOU'RE PRETTY.
WHAT'S THAT?
... WAIT -- WHAT *IS* THAT...?
CAPTAIN... THE LIGHT, UP AHEAD -- YOU SEE HOW IT FLICKERS LIKE A FLAME?
I DO. WHAT OF IT?
IS THE ***TALAM BEACON*** NOT LIT BY A KEROSENE LAMP?
SO? I DON'T SEE --
OUR LADY IS CORRECT. SOMETHING IS --
THERE!
CAPTAIN, ENGINES FULL ASTERN -- ***NOW!***

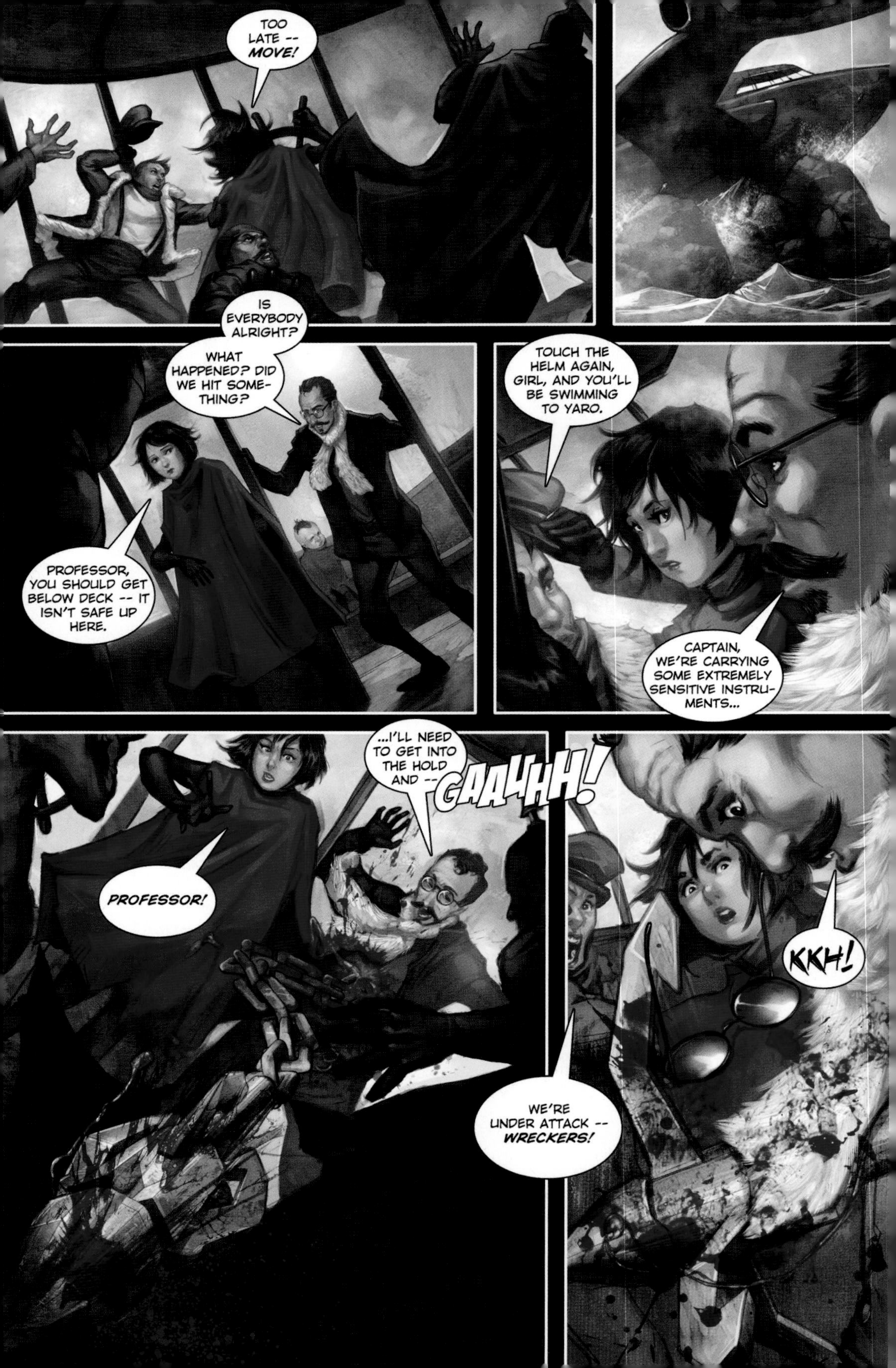
TOO LATE -- *MOVE!*
IS EVERYBODY ALRIGHT?
WHAT HAPPENED? DID WE HIT SOME-THING?
PROFESSOR, YOU SHOULD GET BELOW DECK -- IT ISN'T SAFE UP HERE.
TOUCH THE HELM AGAIN, GIRL, AND YOU'LL BE SWIMMING TO YARO.
CAPTAIN, WE'RE CARRYING SOME EXTREMELY SENSITIVE INSTRU-MENTS...
...I'LL NEED TO GET INTO THE HOLD AND --
GAAUHH!
PROFESSOR!
KKH!
WE'RE UNDER ATTACK -- *WRECKERS!*

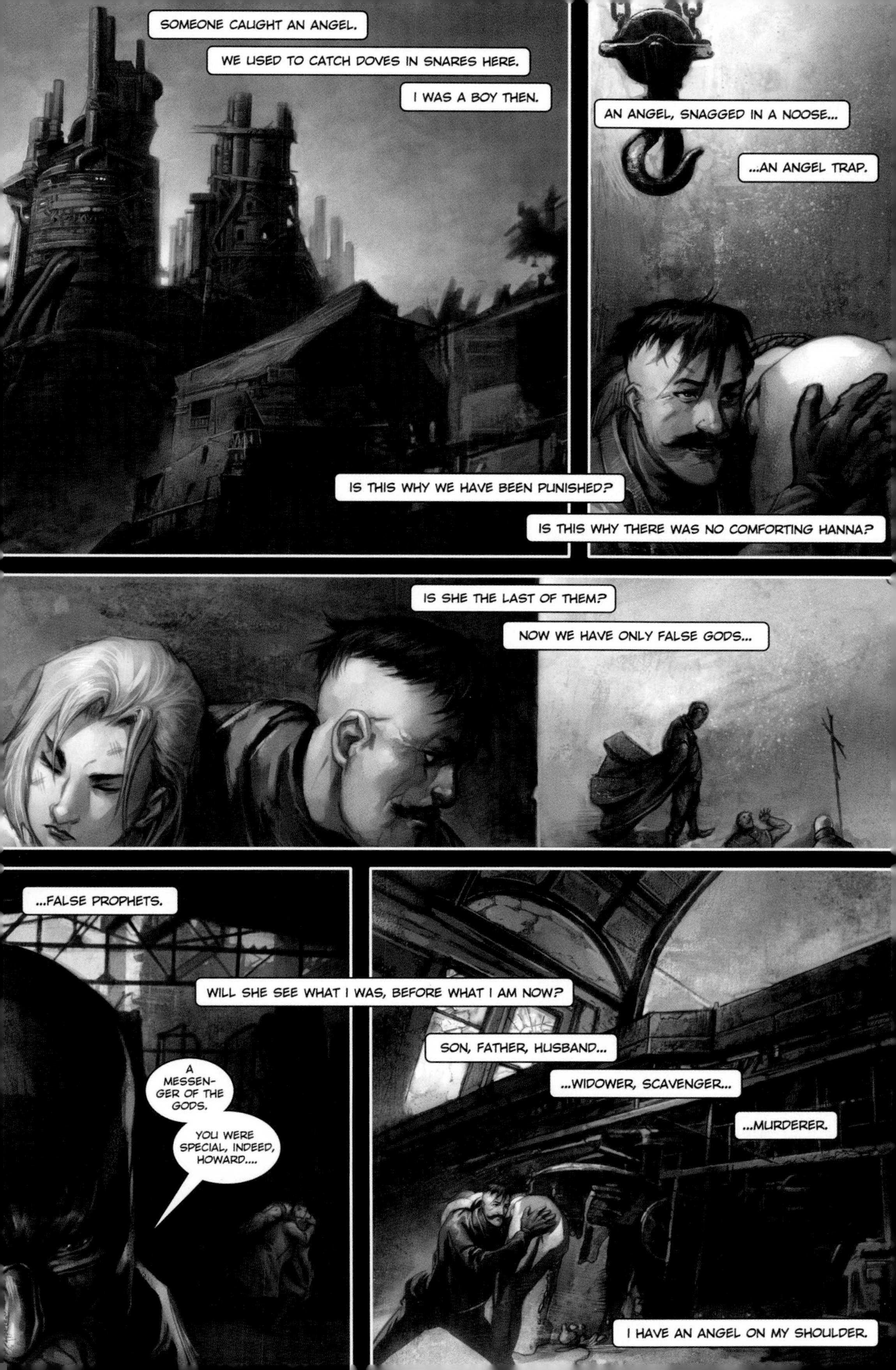
SOMEONE CAUGHT AN ANGEL.
WE USED TO CATCH DOVES IN SNARES HERE.
I WAS A BOY THEN.
AN ANGEL, SNAGGED IN A NOOSE...
...AN ANGEL TRAP.
IS THIS WHY WE HAVE BEEN PUNISHED?
IS THIS WHY THERE WAS NO COMFORTING HANNA?
IS SHE THE LAST OF THEM?
NOW WE HAVE ONLY FALSE GODS...
...FALSE PROPHETS.
WILL SHE SEE WHAT I WAS, BEFORE WHAT I AM NOW?
A MESSENGER OF THE GODS.
YOU WERE SPECIAL, INDEED, HOWARD....
SON, FATHER, HUSBAND...
...WIDOWER, SCAVENGER...
...MURDERER.
I HAVE AN ANGEL ON MY SHOULDER.

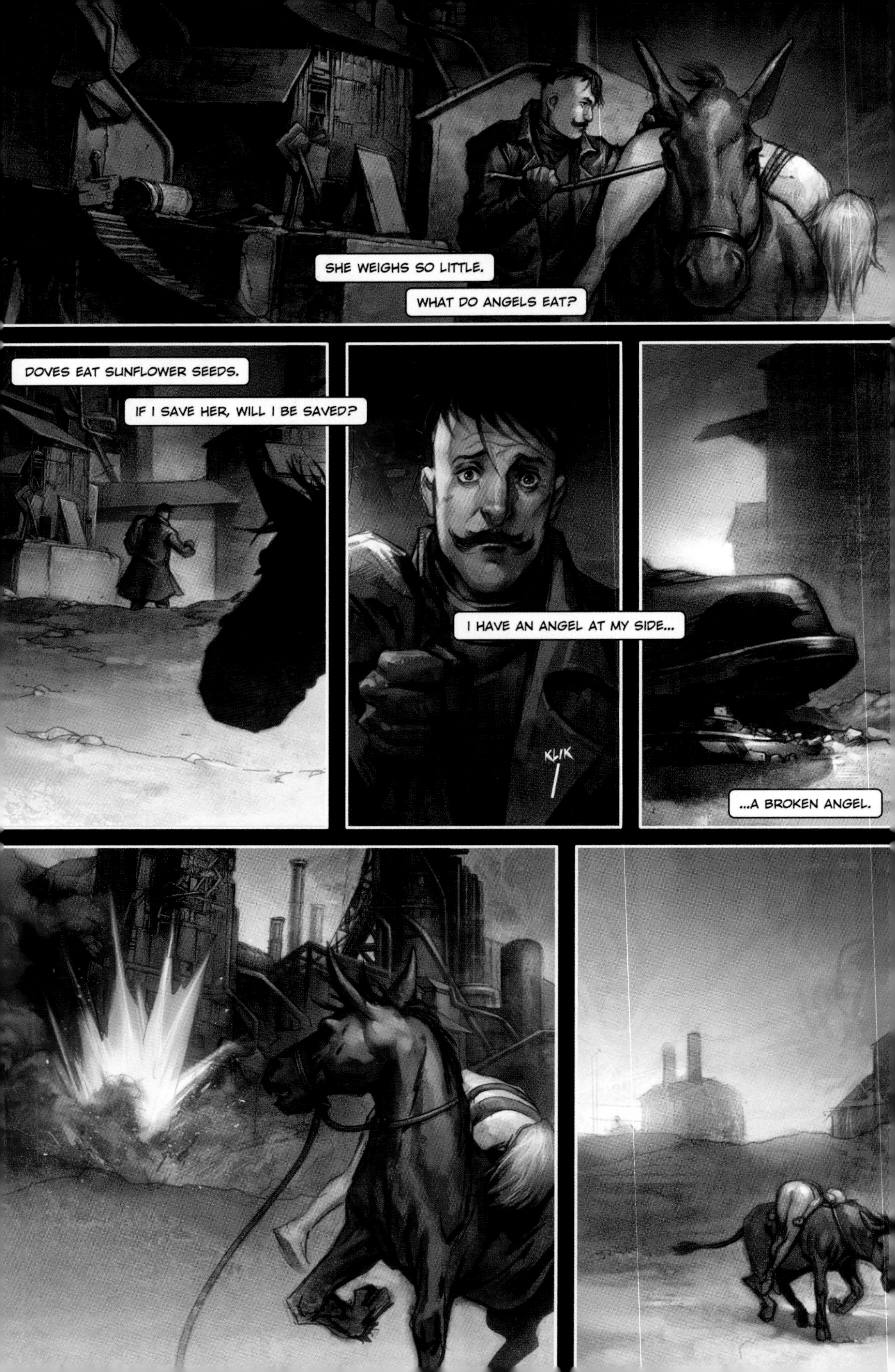
SHE WEIGHS SO LITTLE.
WHAT DO ANGELS EAT?
DOVES EAT SUNFLOWER SEEDS.
IF I SAVE HER, WILL I BE SAVED?
I HAVE AN ANGEL AT MY SIDE...
KLIK
...A BROKEN ANGEL.

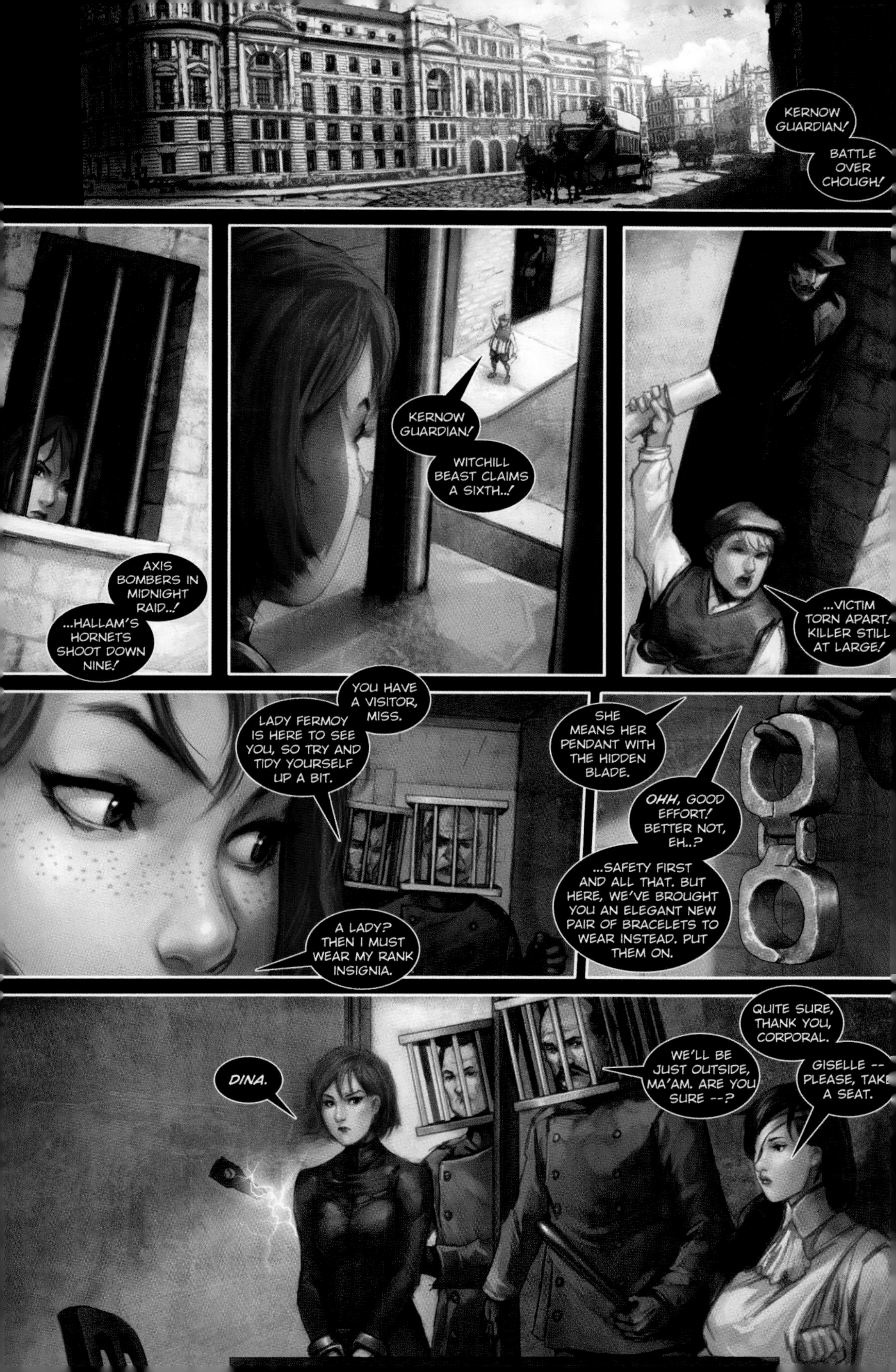
KERNOW GUARDIAN!
BATTLE OVER CHOUGH!
AXIS BOMBERS IN MIDNIGHT RAID..!
...HALLAM'S HORNETS SHOOT DOWN NINE!
KERNOW GUARDIAN!
WITCHILL BEAST CLAIMS A SIXTH..!
...VICTIM TORN APART. KILLER STILL AT LARGE!
YOU HAVE A VISITOR, MISS.
LADY FERMOY IS HERE TO SEE YOU, SO TRY AND TIDY YOURSELF UP A BIT.
A LADY? THEN I MUST WEAR MY RANK INSIGNIA.
SHE MEANS HER PENDANT WITH THE HIDDEN BLADE.
OHH, GOOD EFFORT! BETTER NOT, EH..?
...SAFETY FIRST AND ALL THAT. BUT HERE, WE'VE BROUGHT YOU AN ELEGANT NEW PAIR OF BRACELETS TO WEAR INSTEAD. PUT THEM ON.
DINA.
WE'LL BE JUST OUTSIDE, MA'AM. ARE YOU SURE --?
QUITE SURE, THANK YOU, CORPORAL.
GISELLE -- PLEASE, TAKE A SEAT.

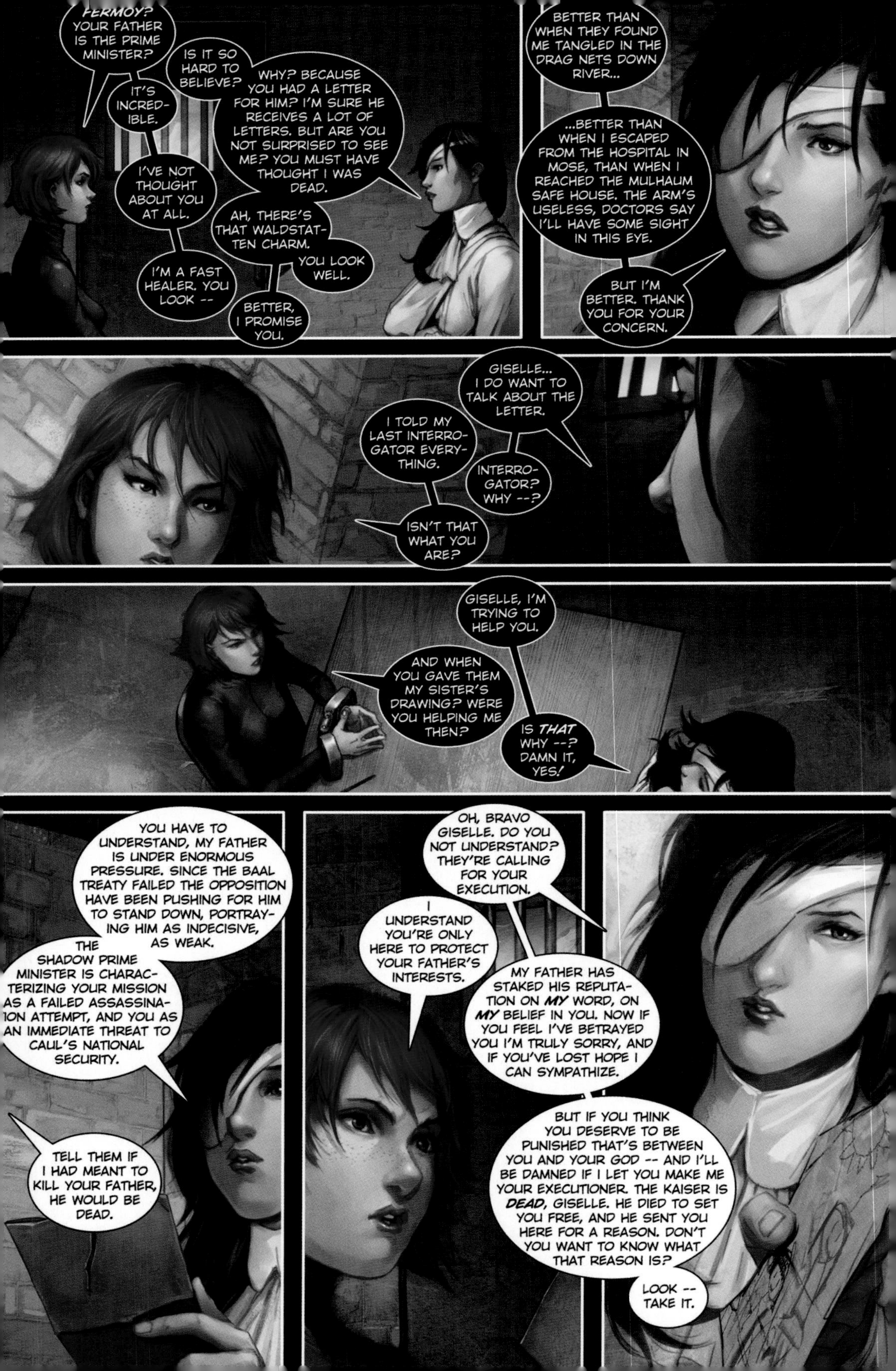

FERMOY? YOUR FATHER IS THE PRIME MINISTER?
IT'S INCREDIBLE.
IS IT SO HARD TO BELIEVE?
WHY? BECAUSE YOU HAD A LETTER FOR HIM? I'M SURE HE RECEIVES A LOT OF LETTERS. BUT ARE YOU NOT SURPRISED TO SEE ME? YOU MUST HAVE THOUGHT I WAS DEAD.
I'VE NOT THOUGHT ABOUT YOU AT ALL.
AH, THERE'S THAT WALDSTATTEN CHARM.
YOU LOOK WELL.
I'M A FAST HEALER. YOU LOOK --
BETTER, I PROMISE YOU.
BETTER THAN WHEN THEY FOUND ME TANGLED IN THE DRAG NETS DOWN RIVER...
...BETTER THAN WHEN I ESCAPED FROM THE HOSPITAL IN MOSE, THAN WHEN I REACHED THE MULHAUM SAFE HOUSE. THE ARM'S USELESS, DOCTORS SAY I'LL HAVE SOME SIGHT IN THIS EYE.
BUT I'M BETTER. THANK YOU FOR YOUR CONCERN.
GISELLE... I DO WANT TO TALK ABOUT THE LETTER.
I TOLD MY LAST INTERROGATOR EVERYTHING.
INTERROGATOR? WHY --?
ISN'T THAT WHAT YOU ARE?
GISELLE, I'M TRYING TO HELP YOU.
AND WHEN YOU GAVE THEM MY SISTER'S DRAWING? WERE YOU HELPING ME THEN?
IS *THAT* WHY --? DAMN IT, YES!
YOU HAVE TO UNDERSTAND, MY FATHER IS UNDER ENORMOUS PRESSURE. SINCE THE BAAL TREATY FAILED THE OPPOSITION HAVE BEEN PUSHING FOR HIM TO STAND DOWN, PORTRAYING HIM AS INDECISIVE, AS WEAK.
THE SHADOW PRIME MINISTER IS CHARACTERIZING YOUR MISSION AS A FAILED ASSASSINATION ATTEMPT, AND YOU AS AN IMMEDIATE THREAT TO CAUL'S NATIONAL SECURITY.
TELL THEM IF I HAD MEANT TO KILL YOUR FATHER, HE WOULD BE DEAD.
OH, BRAVO GISELLE. DO YOU NOT UNDERSTAND? THEY'RE CALLING FOR YOUR EXECUTION.
I UNDERSTAND YOU'RE ONLY HERE TO PROTECT YOUR FATHER'S INTERESTS.
MY FATHER HAS STAKED HIS REPUTATION ON *MY* WORD, ON *MY* BELIEF IN YOU. NOW IF YOU FEEL I'VE BETRAYED YOU I'M TRULY SORRY, AND IF YOU'VE LOST HOPE I CAN SYMPATHIZE.
BUT IF YOU THINK YOU DESERVE TO BE PUNISHED THAT'S BETWEEN YOU AND YOUR GOD -- AND I'LL BE DAMNED IF I LET YOU MAKE ME YOUR EXECUTIONER. THE KAISER IS *DEAD*, GISELLE. HE DIED TO SET YOU FREE, AND HE SENT YOU HERE FOR A REASON. DON'T YOU WANT TO KNOW WHAT THAT REASON IS?
LOOK -- TAKE IT.

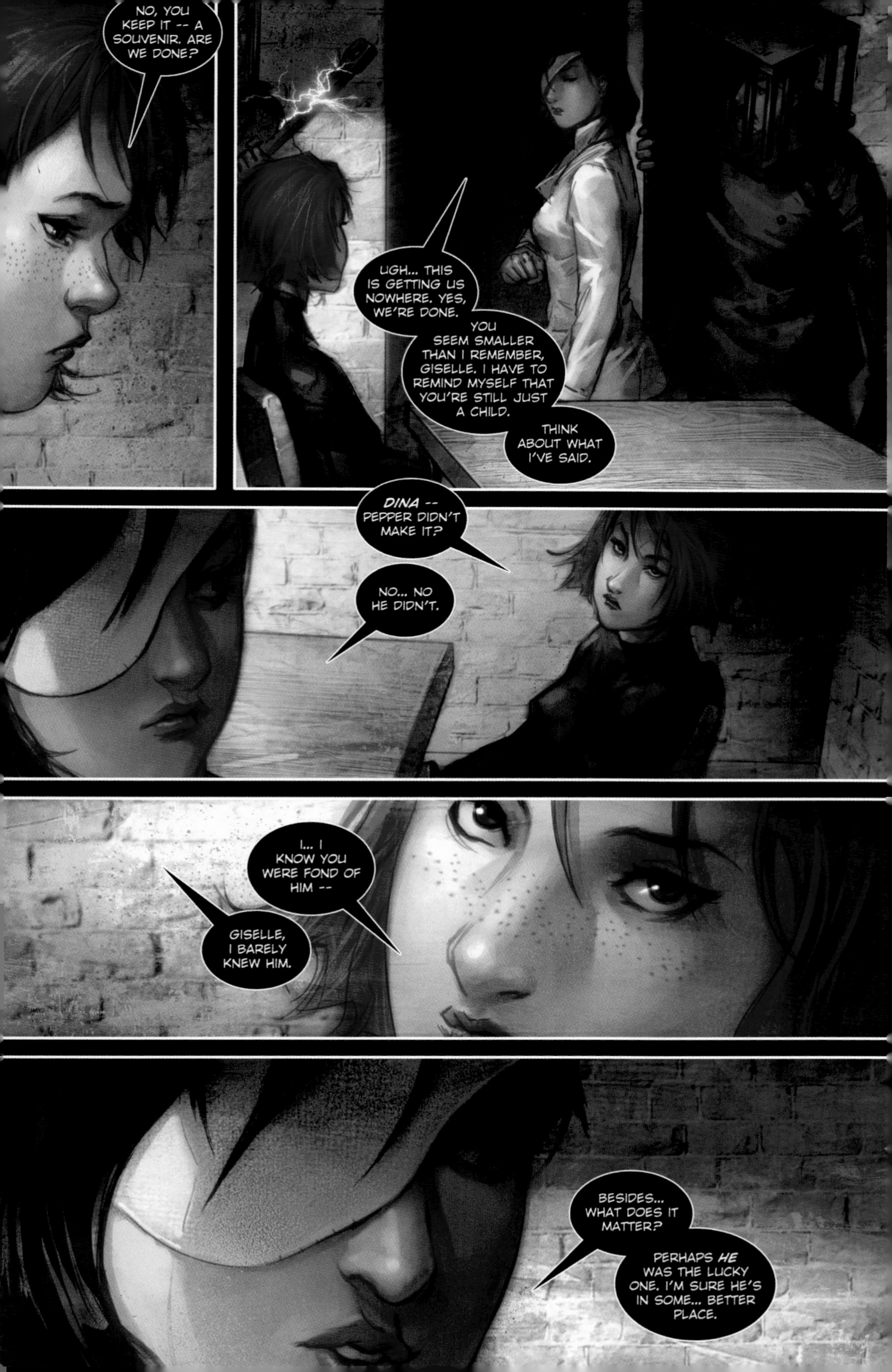
NO, YOU KEEP IT -- A SOUVENIR. ARE WE DONE?
UGH... THIS IS GETTING US NOWHERE. YES, WE'RE DONE.
YOU SEEM SMALLER THAN I REMEMBER, GISELLE. I HAVE TO REMIND MYSELF THAT YOU'RE STILL JUST A CHILD.
THINK ABOUT WHAT I'VE SAID.
DINA -- PEPPER DIDN'T MAKE IT?
NO... NO HE DIDN'T.
I... I KNOW YOU WERE FOND OF HIM --
GISELLE, I BARELY KNEW HIM.
BESIDES... WHAT DOES IT MATTER?
PERHAPS *HE* WAS THE LUCKY ONE. I'M SURE HE'S IN SOME... BETTER PLACE.

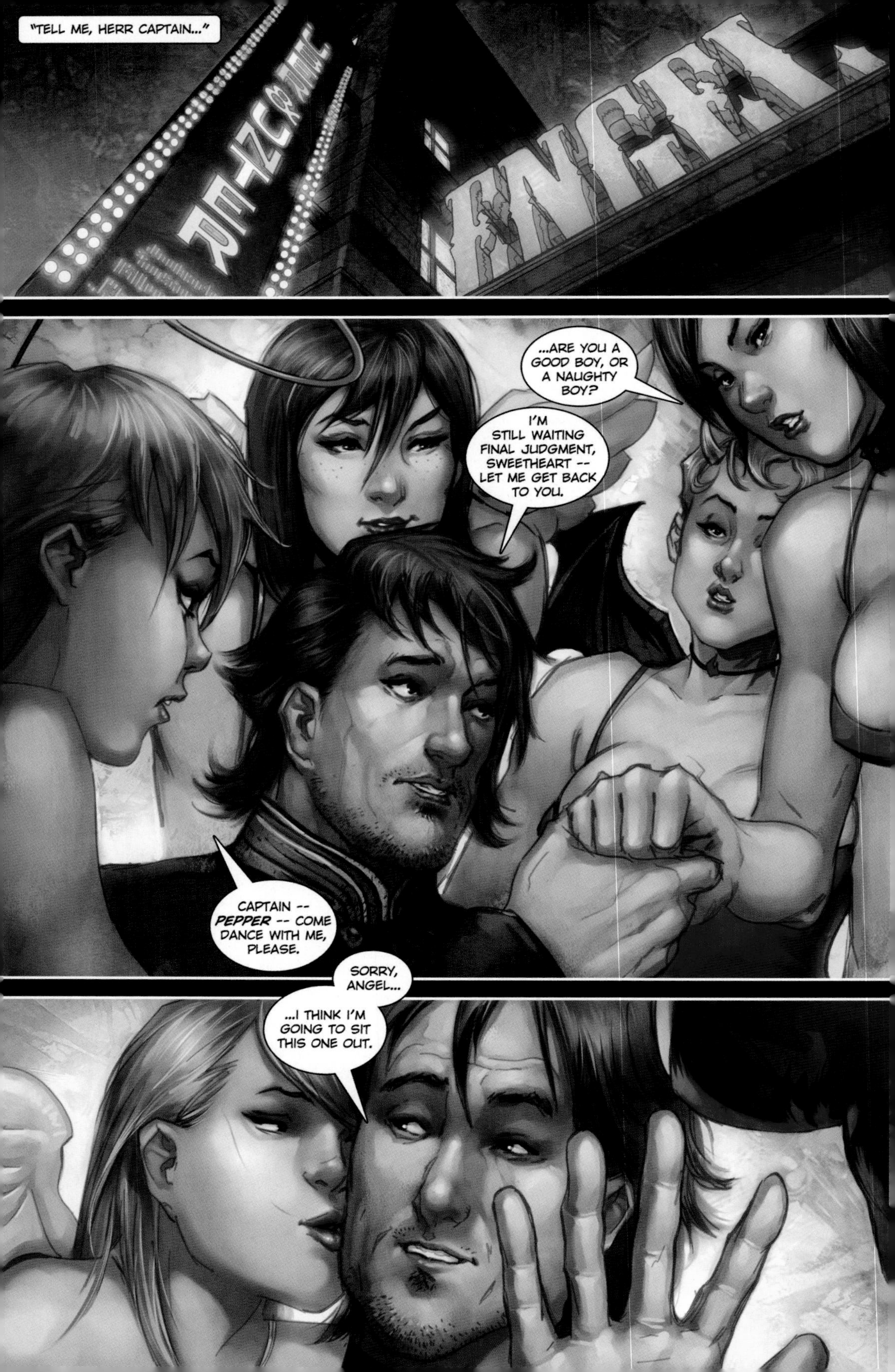
"TELL ME, HERR CAPTAIN..."
...ARE YOU A GOOD BOY, OR A NAUGHTY BOY?
I'M STILL WAITING FINAL JUDGMENT, SWEETHEART -- LET ME GET BACK TO YOU.
CAPTAIN -- *PEPPER* -- COME DANCE WITH ME, PLEASE.
SORRY, ANGEL...
...I THINK I'M GOING TO SIT THIS ONE OUT.

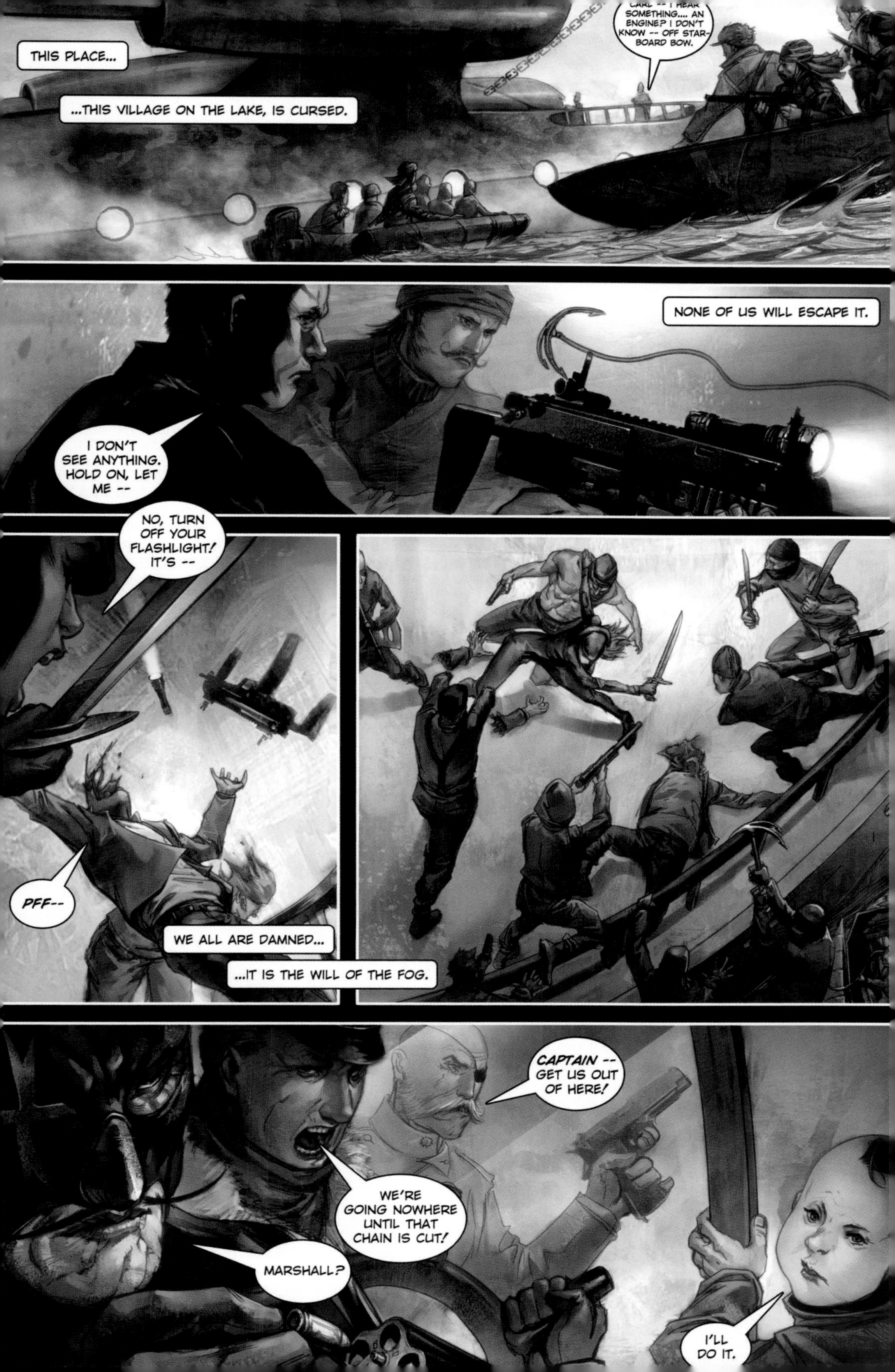
THIS PLACE...
...THIS VILLAGE ON THE LAKE, IS CURSED.
CARL -- I HEAR SOMETHING.... AN ENGINE? I DON'T KNOW -- OFF STARBOARD BOW.
NONE OF US WILL ESCAPE IT.
I DON'T SEE ANYTHING. HOLD ON, LET ME --
NO, TURN OFF YOUR FLASHLIGHT! IT'S --
PFF--
WE ALL ARE DAMNED...
...IT IS THE WILL OF THE FOG.
CAPTAIN -- GET US OUT OF HERE!
WE'RE GOING NOWHERE UNTIL THAT CHAIN IS CUT!
MARSHALL?
I'LL DO IT.

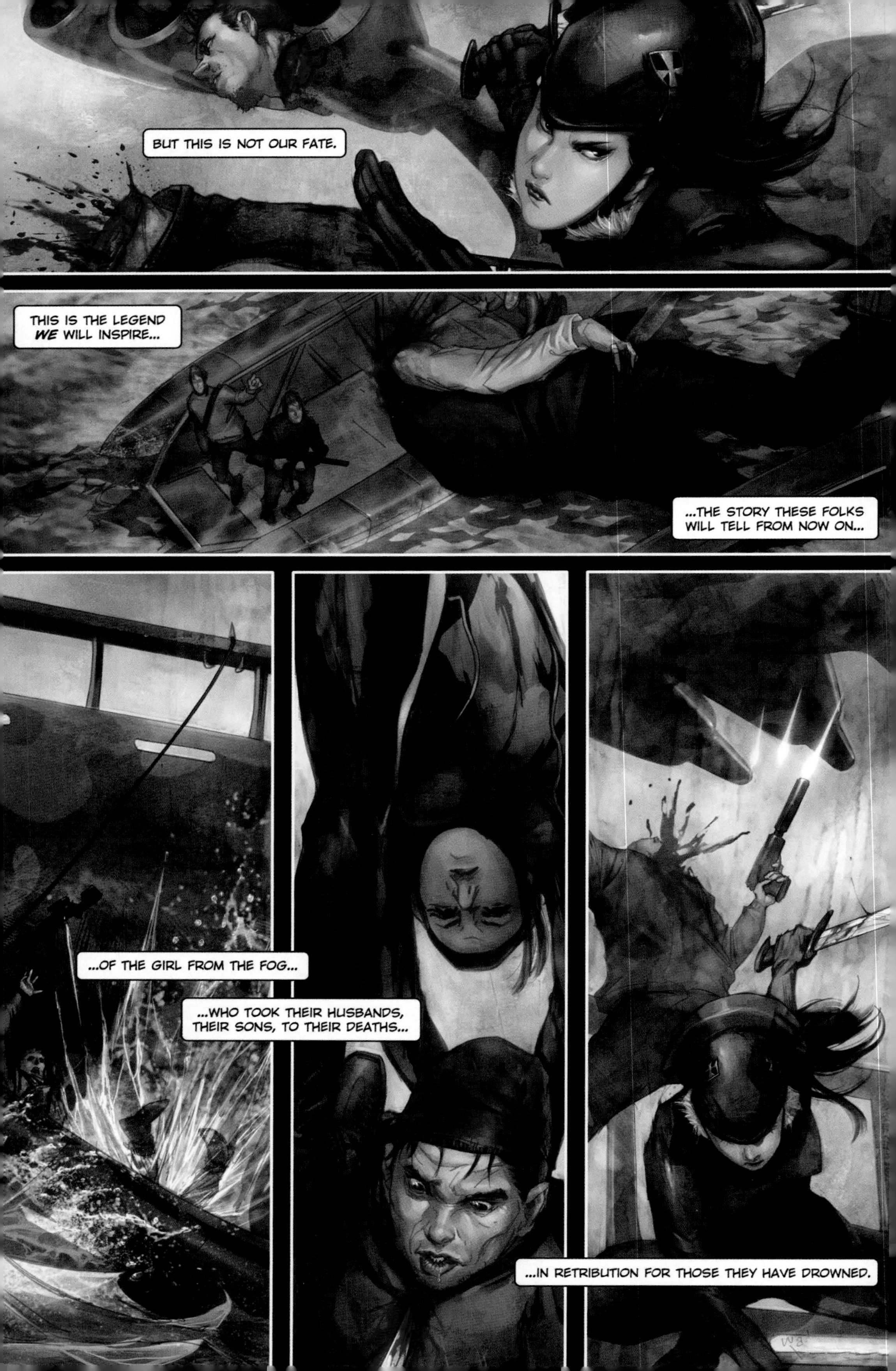
BUT THIS IS NOT OUR FATE.
THIS IS THE LEGEND *WE* WILL INSPIRE...
...THE STORY THESE FOLKS WILL TELL FROM NOW ON...
...OF THE GIRL FROM THE FOG...
...WHO TOOK THEIR HUSBANDS, THEIR SONS, TO THEIR DEATHS...
...IN RETRIBUTION FOR THOSE THEY HAVE DROWNED.

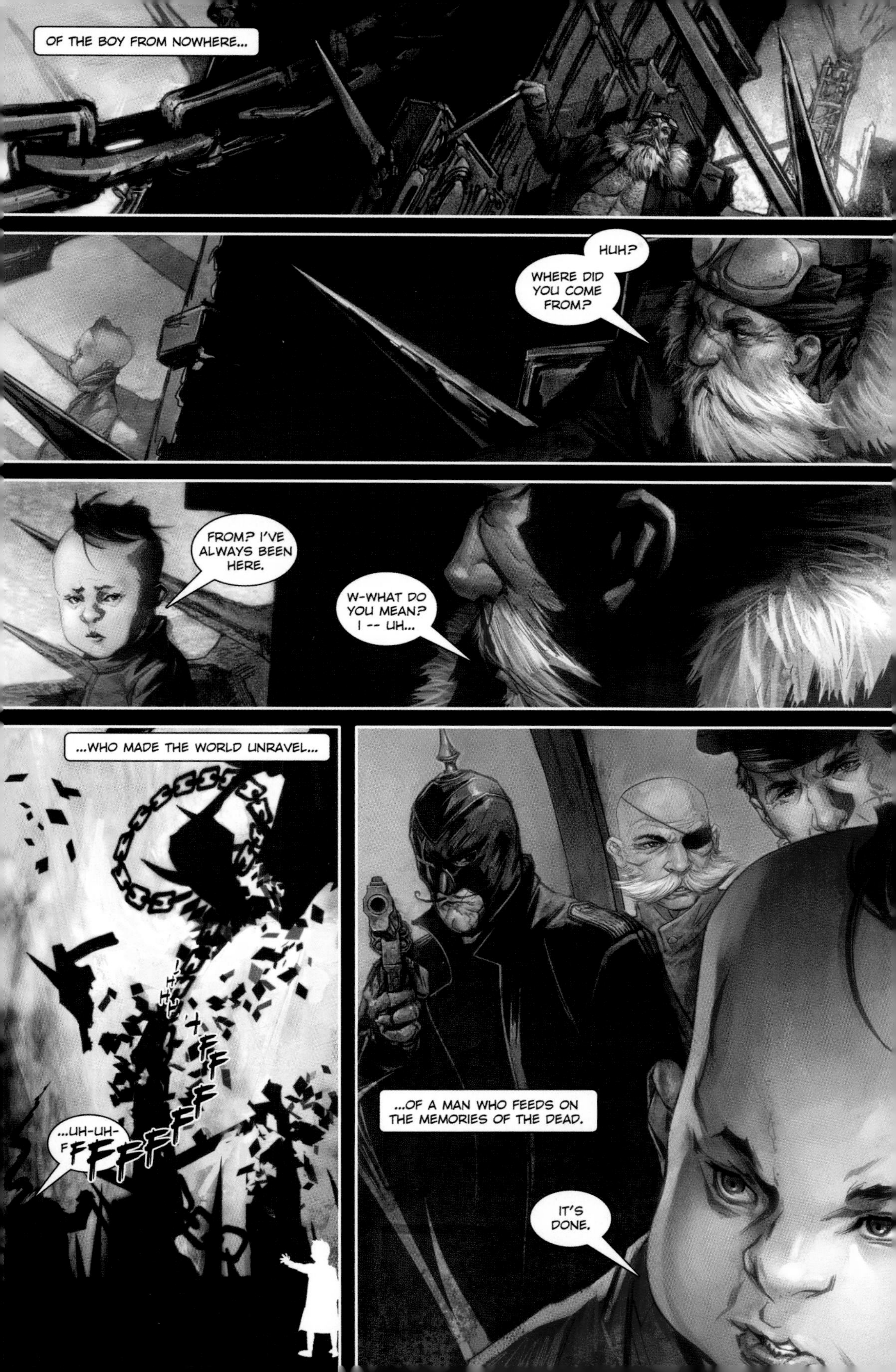
OF THE BOY FROM NOWHERE...
HUH?
WHERE DID YOU COME FROM?
FROM? I'VE ALWAYS BEEN HERE.
W-WHAT DO YOU MEAN? I -- UH...
...WHO MADE THE WORLD UNRAVEL...
...UH-UH-FFFFFFF
...OF A MAN WHO FEEDS ON THE MEMORIES OF THE DEAD.
IT'S DONE.

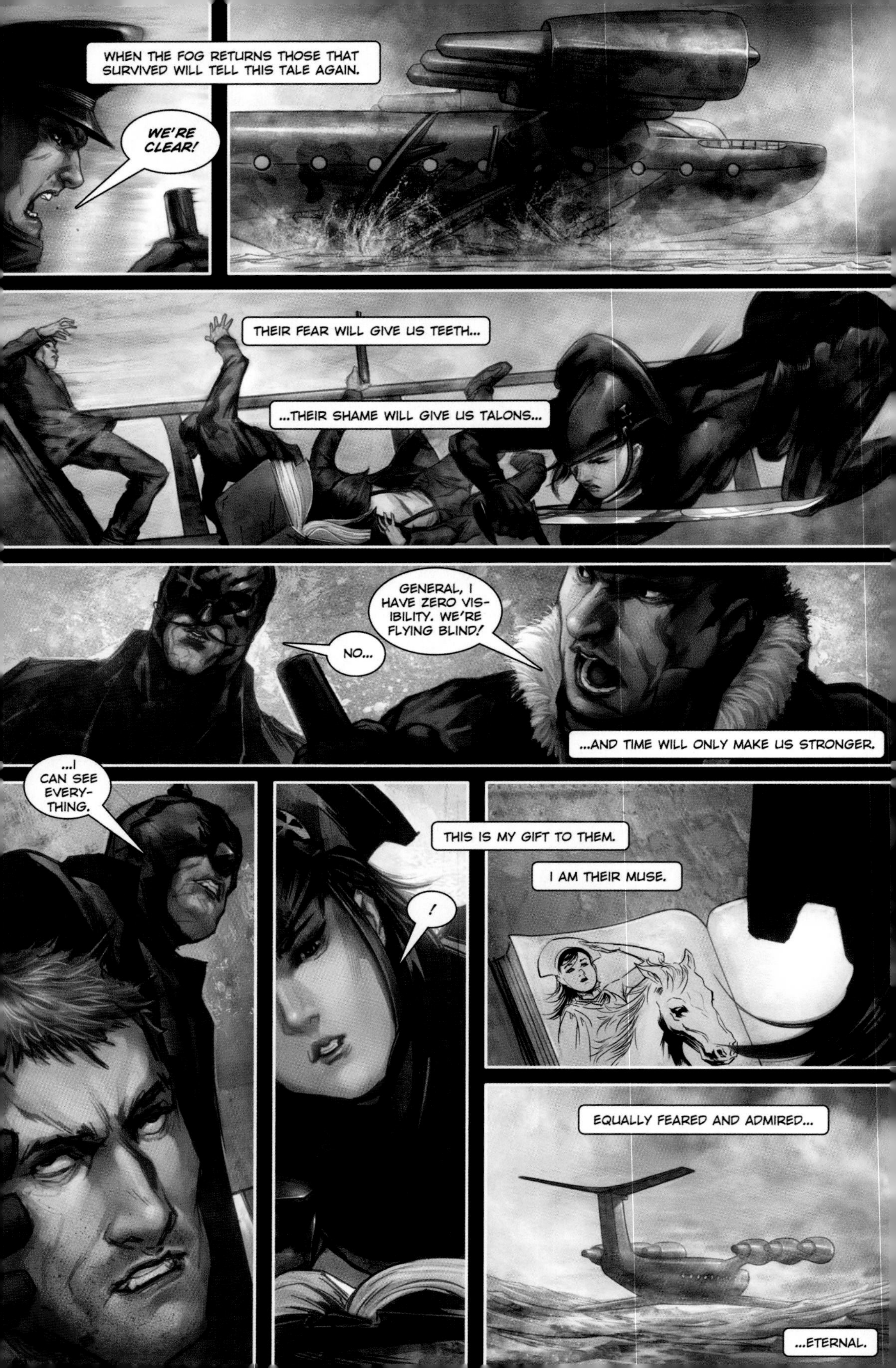

WHEN THE FOG RETURNS THOSE THAT SURVIVED WILL TELL THIS TALE AGAIN.
WE'RE CLEAR!
THEIR FEAR WILL GIVE US TEETH...
...THEIR SHAME WILL GIVE US TALONS...
NO...
GENERAL, I HAVE ZERO VIS-IBILITY. WE'RE FLYING BLIND!
...AND TIME WILL ONLY MAKE US STRONGER.
...I CAN SEE EVERY-THING.
!
THIS IS MY GIFT TO THEM.
I AM THEIR MUSE.
EQUALLY FEARED AND ADMIRED...
...ETERNAL.

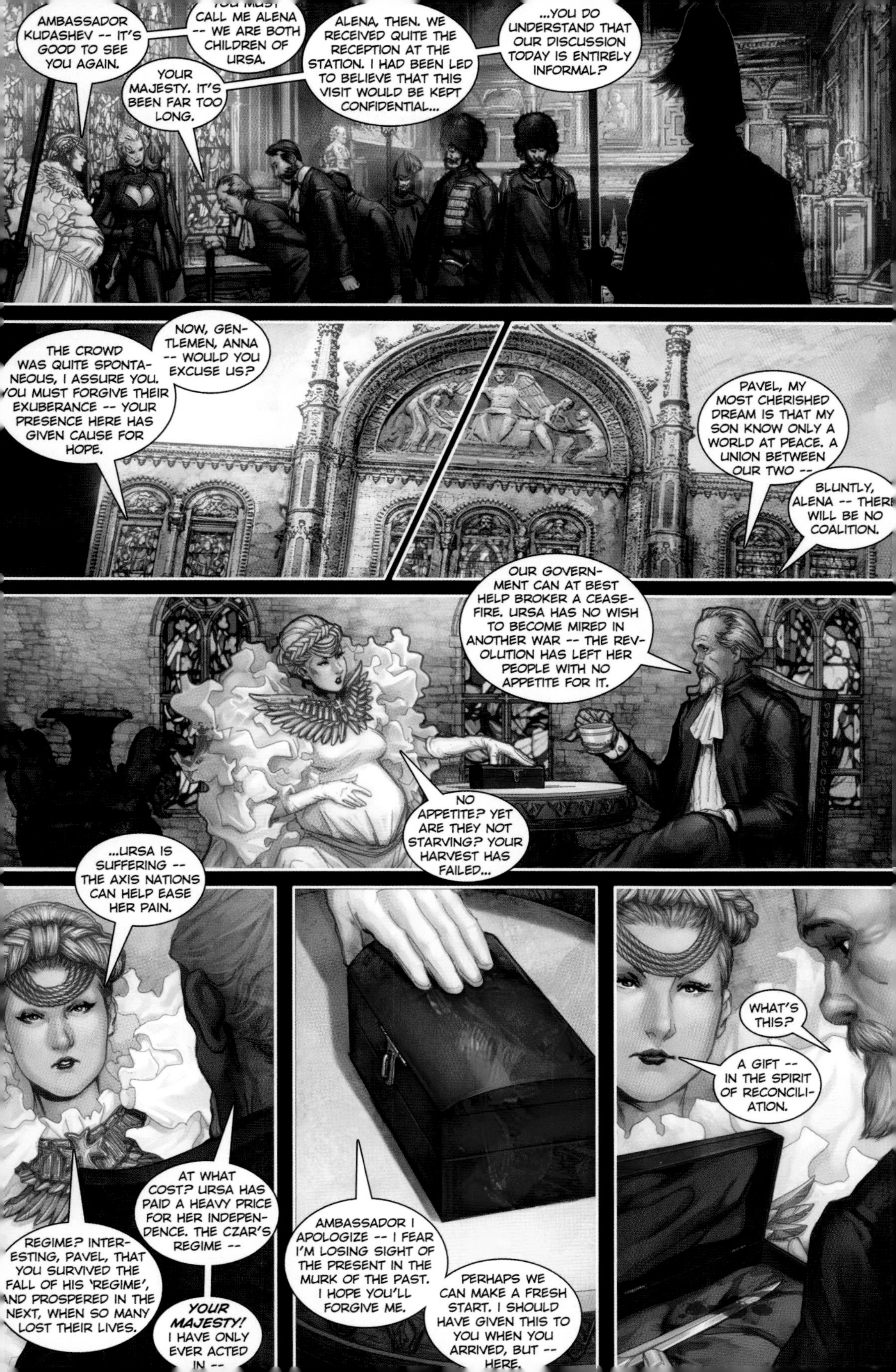

AMBASSADOR KUDASHEV -- IT'S GOOD TO SEE YOU AGAIN.
YOU MUST CALL ME ALENA -- WE ARE BOTH CHILDREN OF URSA.
YOUR MAJESTY. IT'S BEEN FAR TOO LONG.
ALENA, THEN. WE RECEIVED QUITE THE RECEPTION AT THE STATION. I HAD BEEN LED TO BELIEVE THAT THIS VISIT WOULD BE KEPT CONFIDENTIAL...
...YOU DO UNDERSTAND THAT OUR DISCUSSION TODAY IS ENTIRELY INFORMAL?
THE CROWD WAS QUITE SPONTANEOUS, I ASSURE YOU. YOU MUST FORGIVE THEIR EXUBERANCE -- YOUR PRESENCE HERE HAS GIVEN CAUSE FOR HOPE.
NOW, GENTLEMEN, ANNA -- WOULD YOU EXCUSE US?
PAVEL, MY MOST CHERISHED DREAM IS THAT MY SON KNOW ONLY A WORLD AT PEACE. A UNION BETWEEN OUR TWO --
BLUNTLY, ALENA -- THERE WILL BE NO COALITION.
OUR GOVERNMENT CAN AT BEST HELP BROKER A CEASE-FIRE. URSA HAS NO WISH TO BECOME MIRED IN ANOTHER WAR -- THE REVOLUTION HAS LEFT HER PEOPLE WITH NO APPETITE FOR IT.
NO APPETITE? YET ARE THEY NOT STARVING? YOUR HARVEST HAS FAILED...
...URSA IS SUFFERING -- THE AXIS NATIONS CAN HELP EASE HER PAIN.
AT WHAT COST? URSA HAS PAID A HEAVY PRICE FOR HER INDEPENDENCE. THE CZAR'S REGIME --
REGIME? INTERESTING, PAVEL, THAT YOU SURVIVED THE FALL OF HIS 'REGIME', AND PROSPERED IN THE NEXT, WHEN SO MANY LOST THEIR LIVES.
YOUR MAJESTY! I HAVE ONLY EVER ACTED IN --
AMBASSADOR I APOLOGIZE -- I FEAR I'M LOSING SIGHT OF THE PRESENT IN THE MURK OF THE PAST. I HOPE YOU'LL FORGIVE ME.
PERHAPS WE CAN MAKE A FRESH START. I SHOULD HAVE GIVEN THIS TO YOU WHEN YOU ARRIVED, BUT -- HERE.
WHAT'S THIS?
A GIFT -- IN THE SPIRIT OF RECONCILIATION.

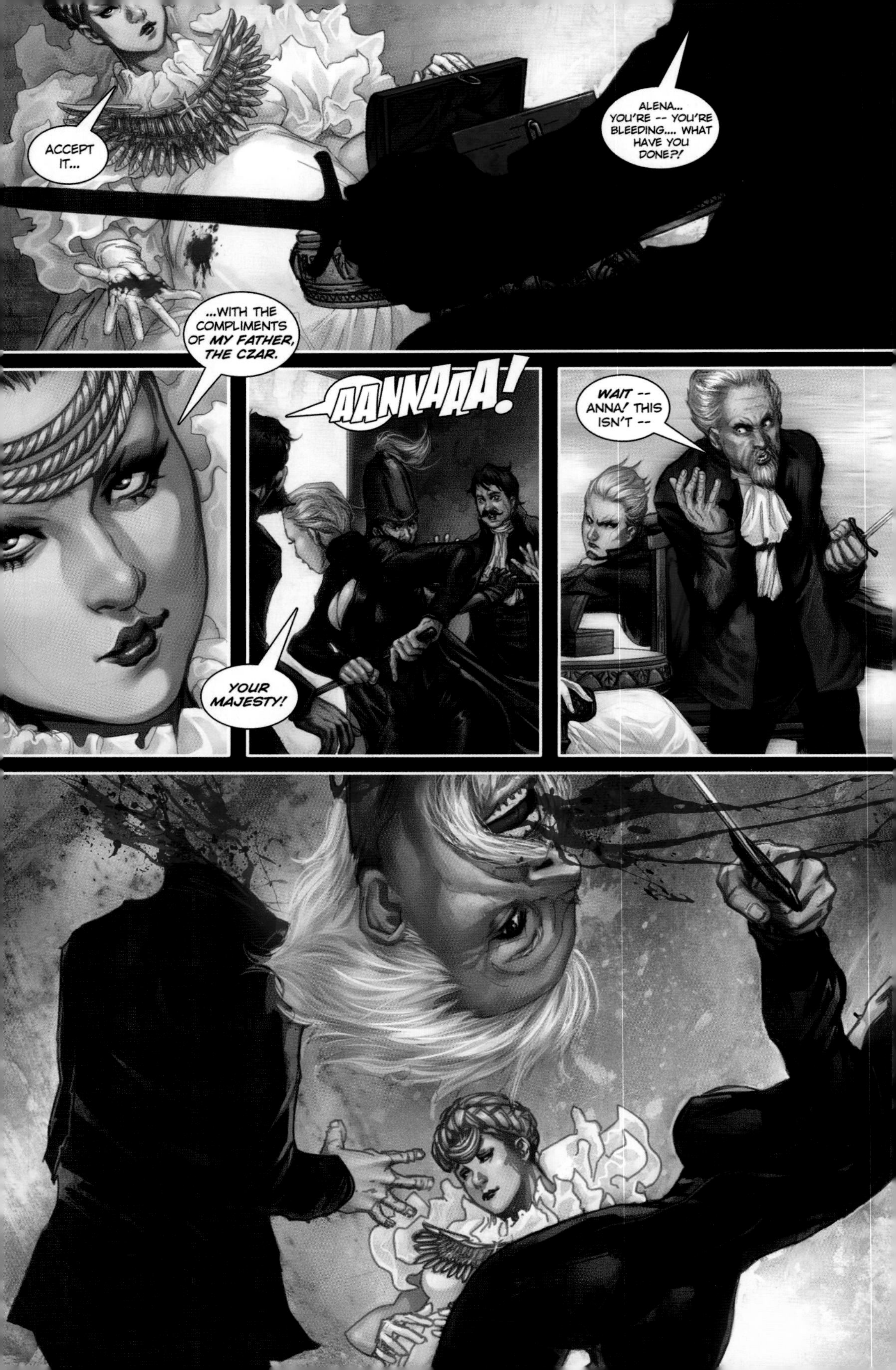
ACCEPT IT...
ALENA... YOU'RE -- YOU'RE BLEEDING.... WHAT HAVE YOU DONE?!
...WITH THE COMPLIMENTS OF *MY FATHER, THE CZAR.*
AANNAAA!
YOUR MAJESTY!
WAIT -- ANNA! THIS ISN'T --

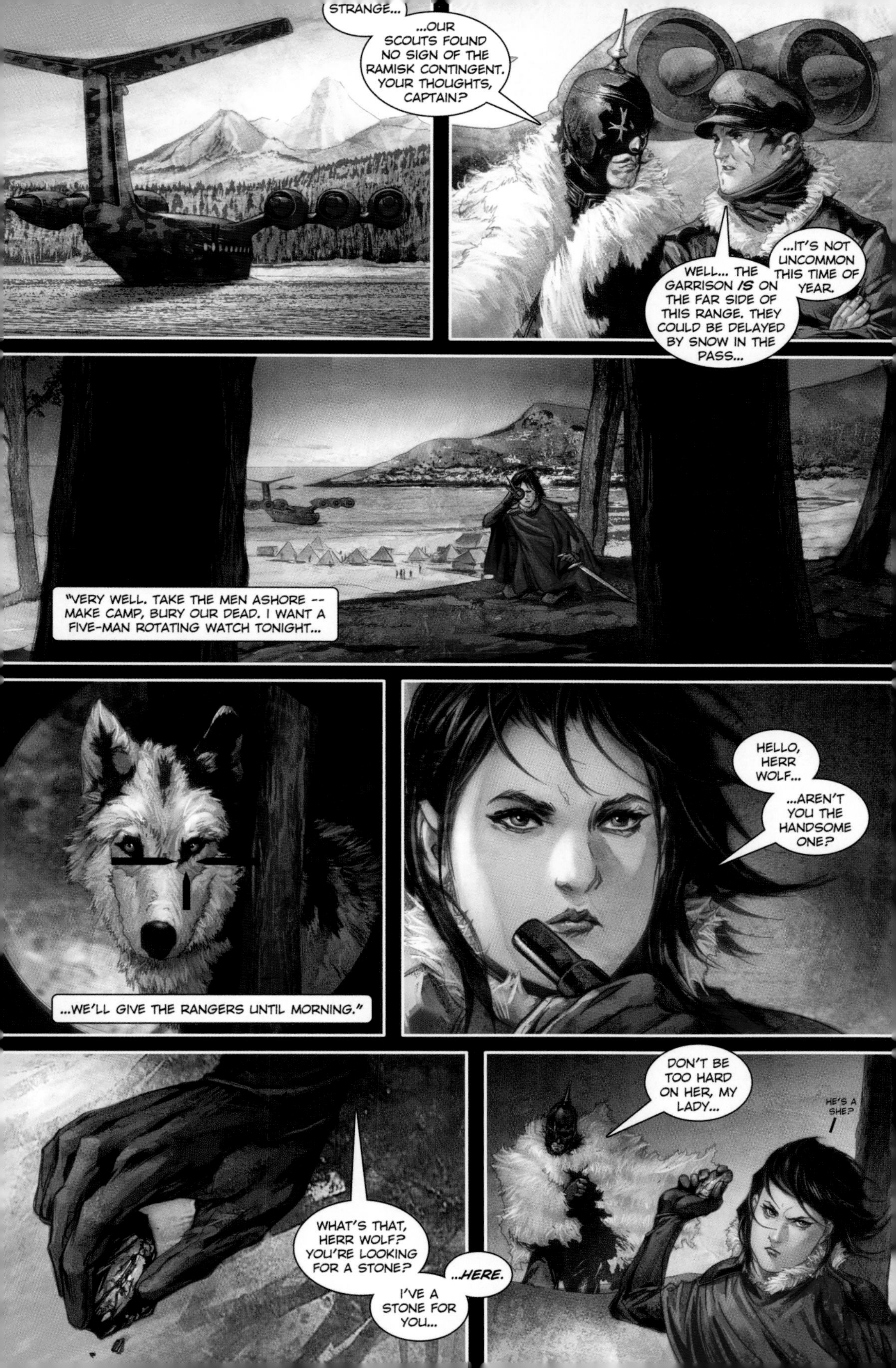
STRANGE...
...OUR SCOUTS FOUND NO SIGN OF THE RAMISK CONTINGENT. YOUR THOUGHTS, CAPTAIN?
WELL... THE GARRISON *IS* ON THE FAR SIDE OF THIS RANGE. THEY COULD BE DELAYED BY SNOW IN THE PASS...
...IT'S NOT UNCOMMON THIS TIME OF YEAR.
"VERY WELL. TAKE THE MEN ASHORE -- MAKE CAMP, BURY OUR DEAD. I WANT A FIVE-MAN ROTATING WATCH TONIGHT...
...WE'LL GIVE THE RANGERS UNTIL MORNING."
HELLO, HERR WOLF...
...AREN'T YOU THE HANDSOME ONE?
WHAT'S THAT, HERR WOLF? YOU'RE LOOKING FOR A STONE?
I'VE A STONE FOR YOU...
...*HERE.*
DON'T BE TOO HARD ON HER, MY LADY...
HE'S A SHE?

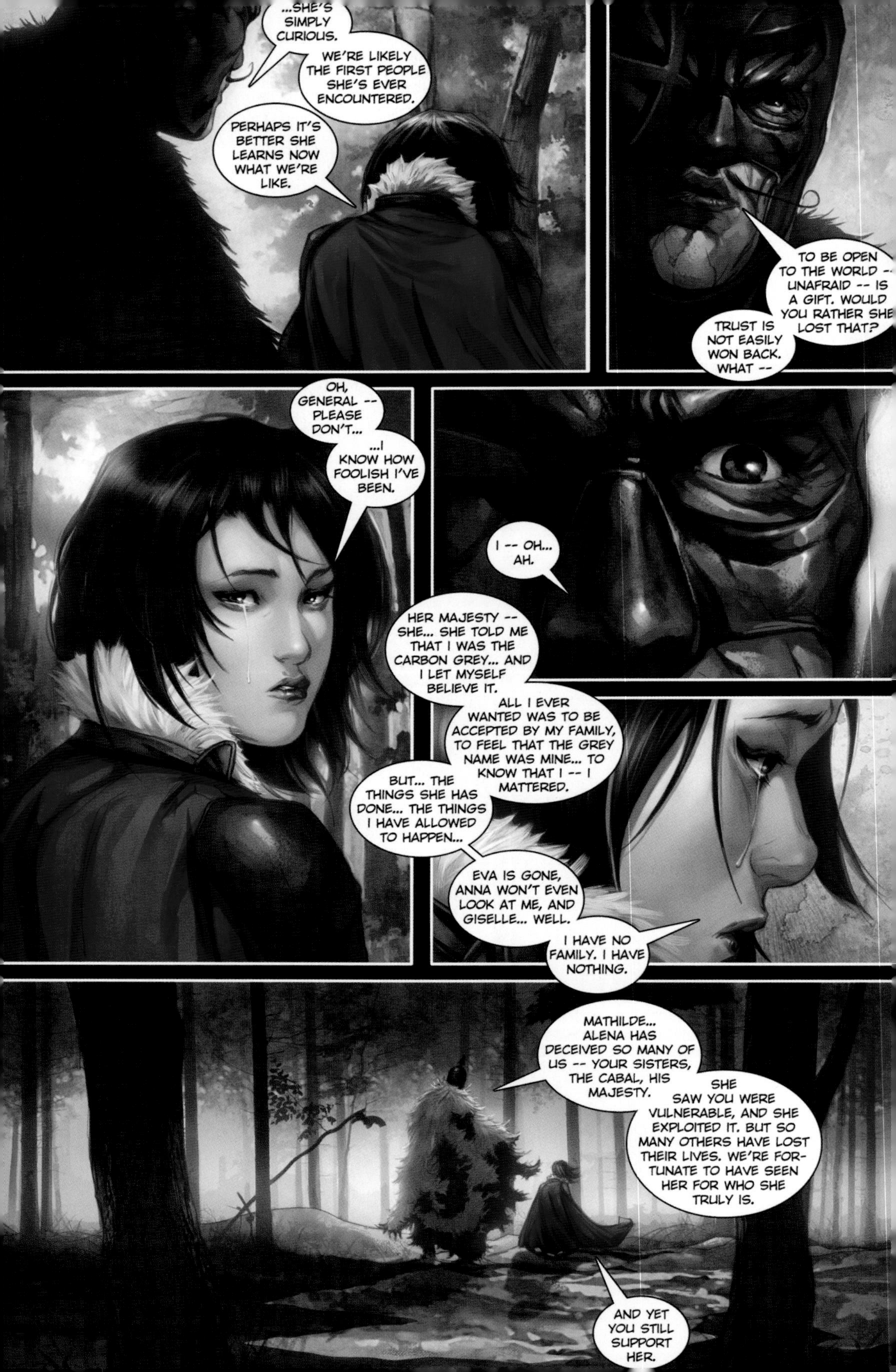
...SHE'S SIMPLY CURIOUS.
WE'RE LIKELY THE FIRST PEOPLE SHE'S EVER ENCOUNTERED.
PERHAPS IT'S BETTER SHE LEARNS NOW WHAT WE'RE LIKE.
TO BE OPEN TO THE WORLD -- UNAFRAID -- IS A GIFT. WOULD YOU RATHER SHE LOST THAT?
TRUST IS NOT EASILY WON BACK. WHAT --
OH, GENERAL -- PLEASE DON'T...
...I KNOW HOW FOOLISH I'VE BEEN.
I -- OH... AH.
HER MAJESTY -- SHE... SHE TOLD ME THAT I WAS THE CARBON GREY... AND I LET MYSELF BELIEVE IT.
ALL I EVER WANTED WAS TO BE ACCEPTED BY MY FAMILY, TO FEEL THAT THE GREY NAME WAS MINE... TO KNOW THAT I -- I MATTERED.
BUT... THE THINGS SHE HAS DONE... THE THINGS I HAVE ALLOWED TO HAPPEN...
EVA IS GONE, ANNA WON'T EVEN LOOK AT ME, AND GISELLE... WELL.
I HAVE NO FAMILY. I HAVE NOTHING.
MATHILDE... ALENA HAS DECEIVED SO MANY OF US -- YOUR SISTERS, THE CABAL, HIS MAJESTY.
SHE SAW YOU WERE VULNERABLE, AND SHE EXPLOITED IT. BUT SO MANY OTHERS HAVE LOST THEIR LIVES. WE'RE FOR-TUNATE TO HAVE SEEN HER FOR WHO SHE TRULY IS.
AND YET YOU STILL SUPPORT HER.

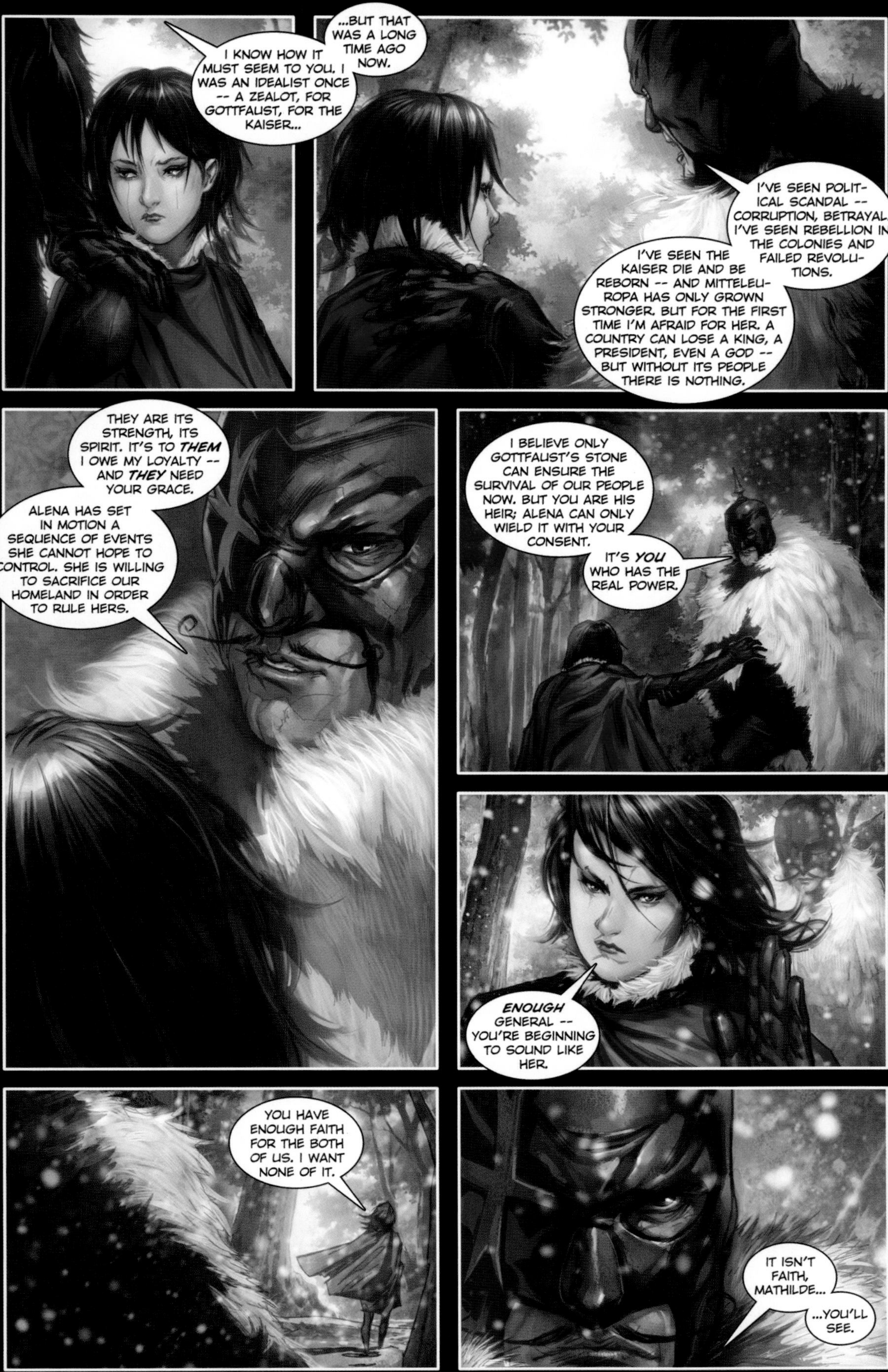
I KNOW HOW IT MUST SEEM TO YOU. I WAS AN IDEALIST ONCE -- A ZEALOT, FOR GOTTFAUST, FOR THE KAISER...
...BUT THAT WAS A LONG TIME AGO NOW.
I'VE SEEN POLITICAL SCANDAL -- CORRUPTION, BETRAYAL. I'VE SEEN REBELLION IN THE COLONIES AND FAILED REVOLUTIONS.
I'VE SEEN THE KAISER DIE AND BE REBORN -- AND MITTELEUROPA HAS ONLY GROWN STRONGER. BUT FOR THE FIRST TIME I'M AFRAID FOR HER. A COUNTRY CAN LOSE A KING, A PRESIDENT, EVEN A GOD -- BUT WITHOUT ITS PEOPLE THERE IS NOTHING.
THEY ARE ITS STRENGTH, ITS SPIRIT. IT'S TO *THEM* I OWE MY LOYALTY -- AND *THEY* NEED YOUR GRACE.
ALENA HAS SET IN MOTION A SEQUENCE OF EVENTS SHE CANNOT HOPE TO CONTROL. SHE IS WILLING TO SACRIFICE OUR HOMELAND IN ORDER TO RULE HERS.
I BELIEVE ONLY GOTTFAUST'S STONE CAN ENSURE THE SURVIVAL OF OUR PEOPLE NOW. BUT YOU ARE HIS HEIR; ALENA CAN ONLY WIELD IT WITH YOUR CONSENT.
IT'S *YOU* WHO HAS THE REAL POWER.
ENOUGH GENERAL -- YOU'RE BEGINNING TO SOUND LIKE HER.
YOU HAVE ENOUGH FAITH FOR THE BOTH OF US. I WANT NONE OF IT.
IT ISN'T FAITH, MATHILDE...
...YOU'LL SEE.

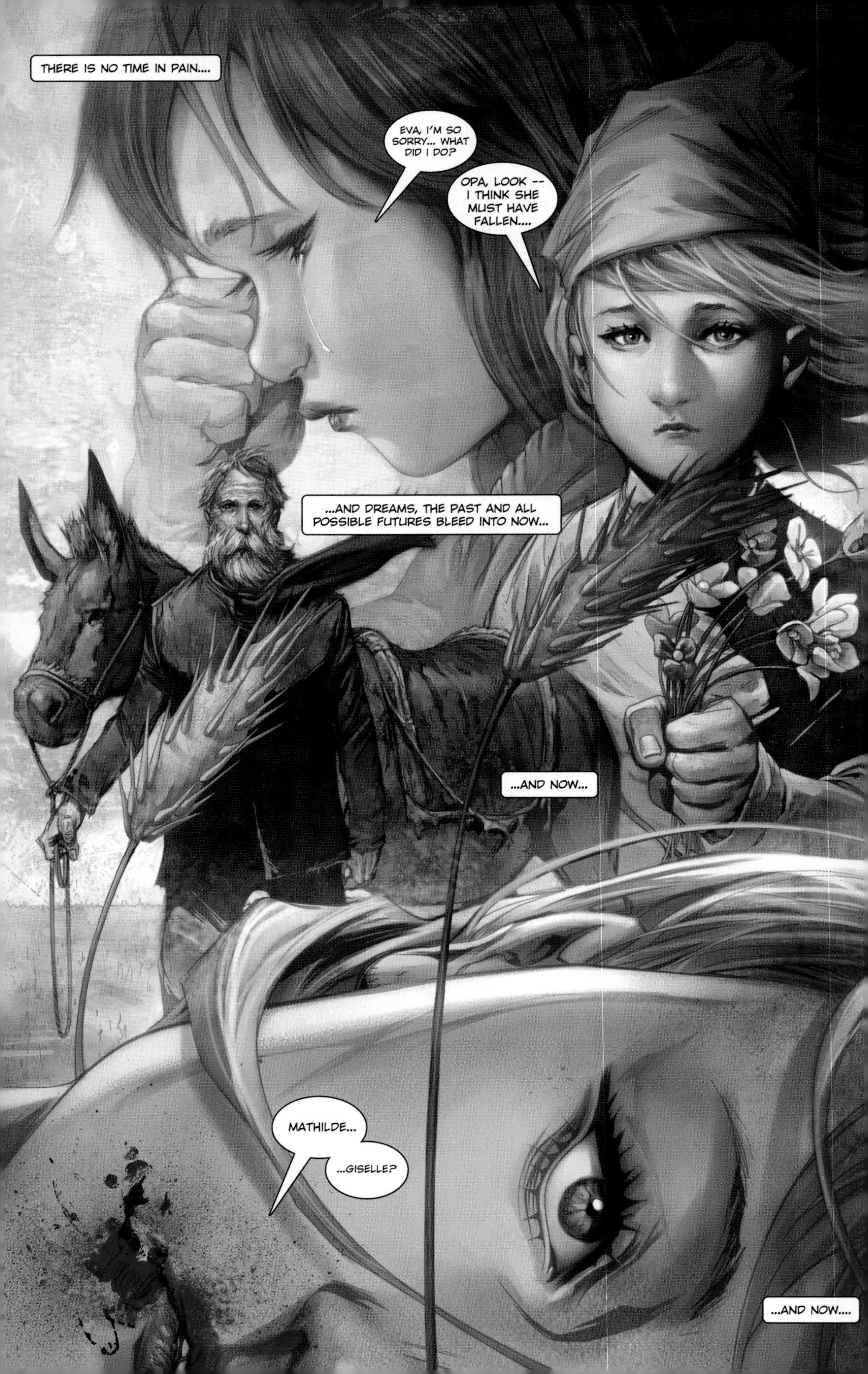
THERE IS NO TIME IN PAIN....
EVA, I'M SO SORRY... WHAT DID I DO?
OPA, LOOK -- I THINK SHE MUST HAVE FALLEN....
...AND DREAMS, THE PAST AND ALL POSSIBLE FUTURES BLEED INTO NOW...
...AND NOW...
MATHILDE...
...GISELLE?
...AND NOW....

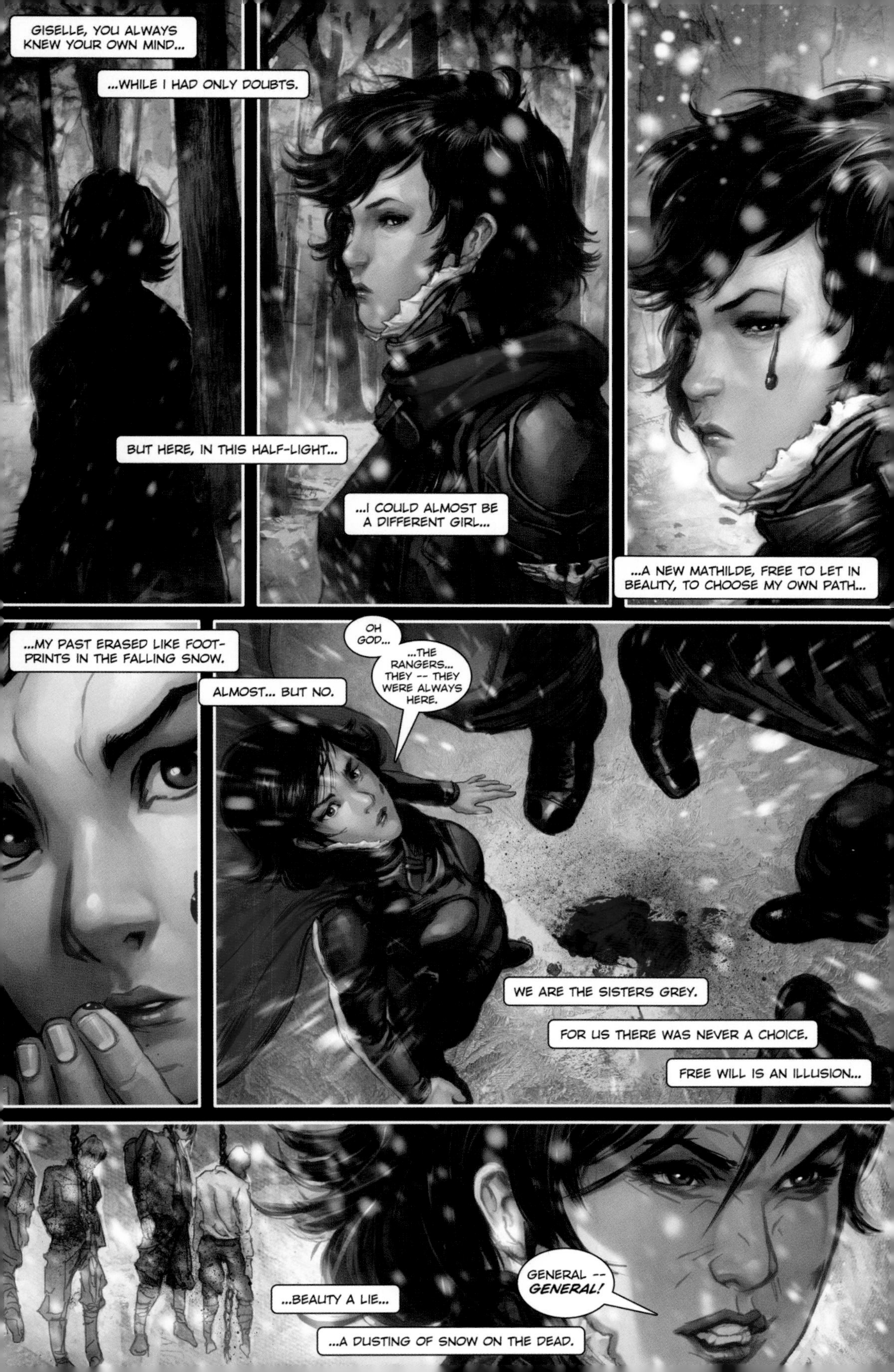
GISELLE, YOU ALWAYS KNEW YOUR OWN MIND...
...WHILE I HAD ONLY DOUBTS.
BUT HERE, IN THIS HALF-LIGHT...
...I COULD ALMOST BE A DIFFERENT GIRL...
...A NEW MATHILDE, FREE TO LET IN BEAUTY, TO CHOOSE MY OWN PATH...
...MY PAST ERASED LIKE FOOT-PRINTS IN THE FALLING SNOW.
ALMOST... BUT NO.
OH GOD...
...THE RANGERS... THEY -- THEY WERE ALWAYS HERE.
WE ARE THE SISTERS GREY.
FOR US THERE WAS NEVER A CHOICE.
FREE WILL IS AN ILLUSION...
...BEAUTY A LIE...
GENERAL -- *GENERAL!*
...A DUSTING OF SNOW ON THE DEAD.

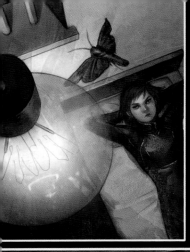

"ALWAYS SO SERIOUS, GISELLE."

I WONDER, HAVE I EVER SEEN YOU SMILE?

"ARE YOU NOT AFRAID, SIR?"

I'D BE LYING IF I TOLD YOU I WASN'T. MY FEARS ARE THOSE OF ANY MAN...

"...THIS IS A TEST OF FAITH FOR US BOTH."

THE SEAL...

"...THE SEAL IS THE MESSAGE!"

GUARD -- CORPORAL! I NEED TO SPEAK WITH LADY FERMOY... ...NOW!

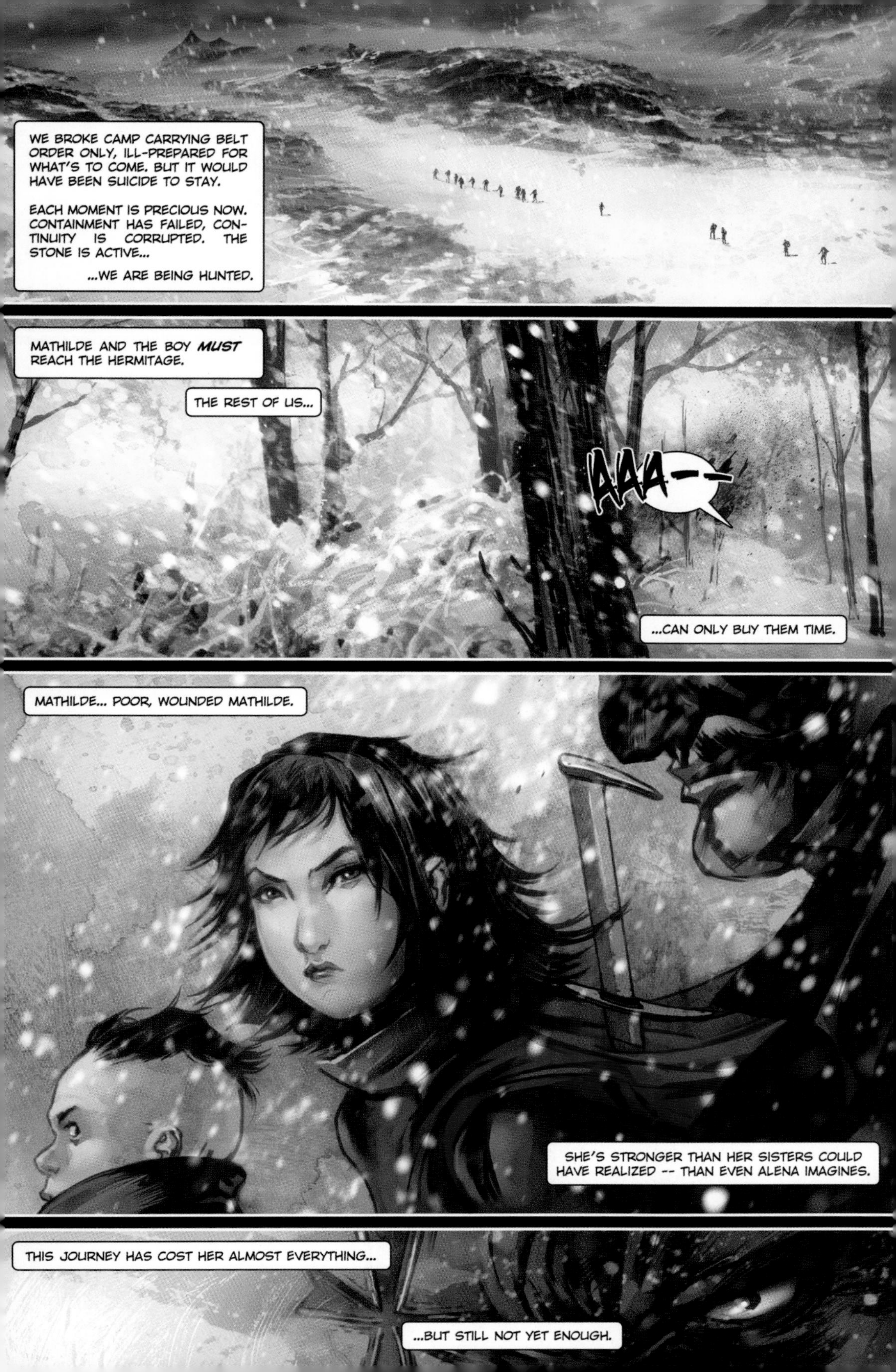
WE BROKE CAMP CARRYING BELT ORDER ONLY, ILL-PREPARED FOR WHAT'S TO COME. BUT IT WOULD HAVE BEEN SUICIDE TO STAY.
EACH MOMENT IS PRECIOUS NOW. CONTAINMENT HAS FAILED, CONTINUITY IS CORRUPTED. THE STONE IS ACTIVE...
...WE ARE BEING HUNTED.
MATHILDE AND THE BOY *MUST* REACH THE HERMITAGE.
THE REST OF US...
AAA--
...CAN ONLY BUY THEM TIME.
MATHILDE... POOR, WOUNDED MATHILDE.
SHE'S STRONGER THAN HER SISTERS COULD HAVE REALIZED -- THAN EVEN ALENA IMAGINES.
THIS JOURNEY HAS COST HER ALMOST EVERYTHING...
...BUT STILL NOT YET ENOUGH.

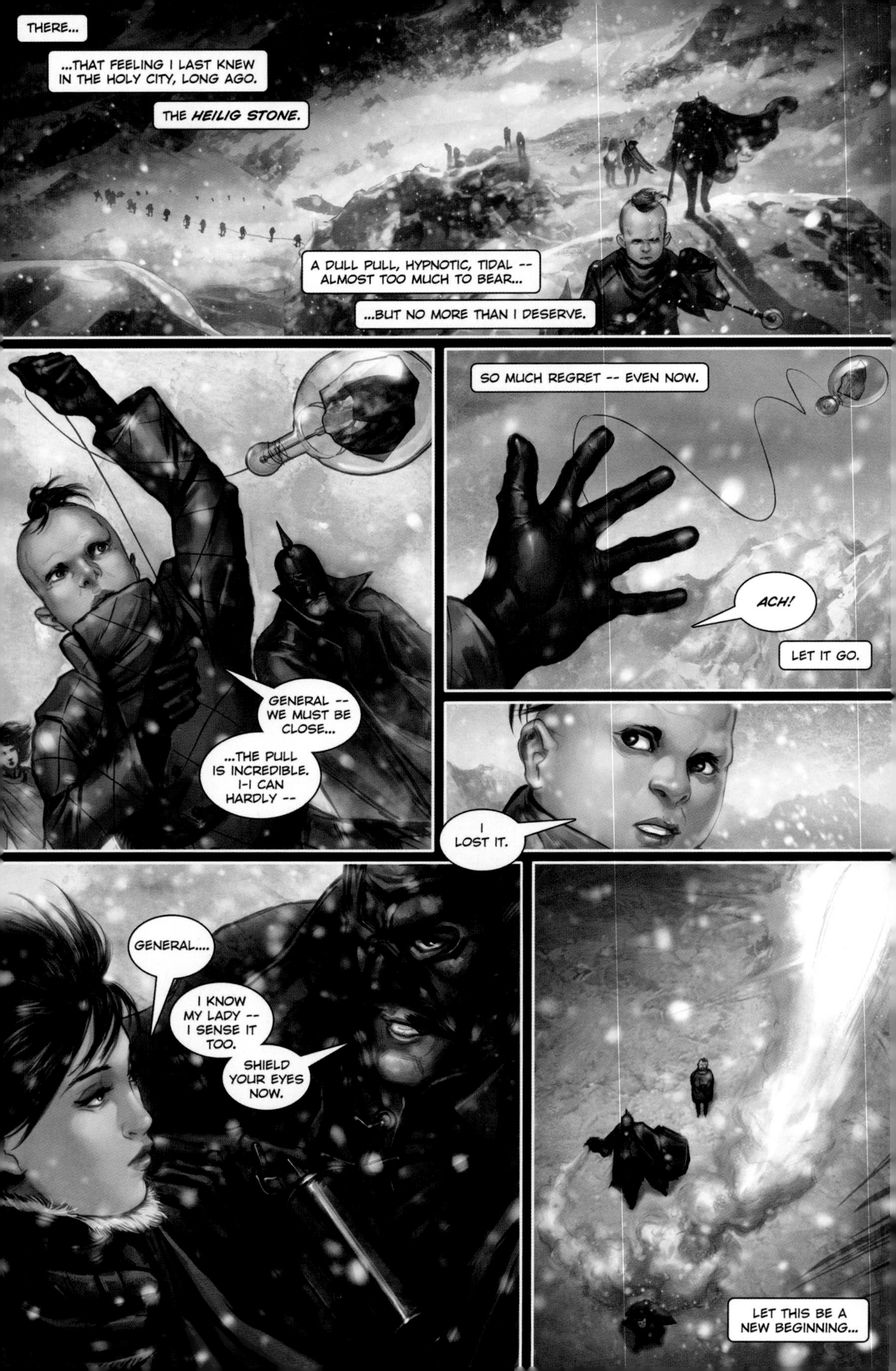
THERE...
...THAT FEELING I LAST KNEW IN THE HOLY CITY, LONG AGO.
THE *HEILIG STONE*.
A DULL PULL, HYPNOTIC, TIDAL -- ALMOST TOO MUCH TO BEAR...
...BUT NO MORE THAN I DESERVE.
GENERAL -- WE MUST BE CLOSE...
...THE PULL IS INCREDIBLE. I-I CAN HARDLY --
SO MUCH REGRET -- EVEN NOW.
ACH!
LET IT GO.
I LOST IT.
GENERAL....
I KNOW MY LADY -- I SENSE IT TOO.
SHIELD YOUR EYES NOW.
LET THIS BE A NEW BEGINNING...

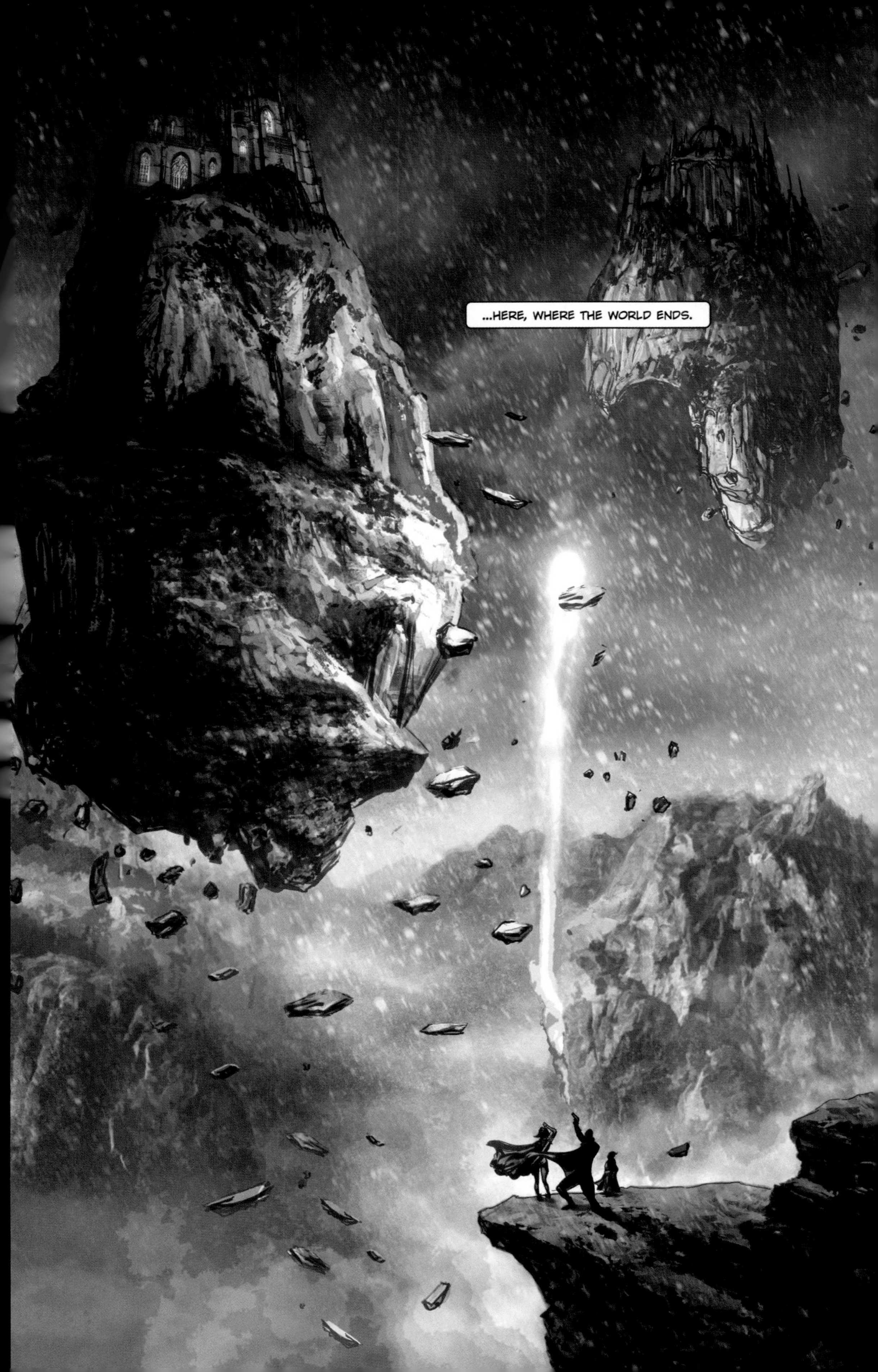
...HERE, WHERE THE WORLD ENDS.

VI

'HER IMPERIAL MAJESTY REMAINS GRAVELY ILL AT THIS HOUR...

ACH...

...IN THE WAKE OF TODAY'S ASSASSINATION ATTEMPT BY URSA'S AMBASSADOR, PAVEL KUDASHEV.

AS PALACE PHYSICIANS BATTLE TO SAVE THE LIFE OF THE KAISER CHILD...

...FOR WHAT HER FATHER DID IT'S NO SURPRISE.

STILL, A TERRIBLE BUSINESS.

...A CROWD OF THE DEVOTED HAS GATHERED AT SALISBURG, OFFERING SILENT PRAYER.

CONDEMNING THE ATTACK AS 'A COWARDLY ACT OF BETRAYAL', HER MAJESTY'S CHANCELLOR NEVERTHELESS CALLED FOR CALM...

...WARNING THAT REPRISALS AGAINST THOSE GOOD CITIZENS OF URSA LIVING HARMONIOUSLY AMONG US WILL NOT BE TOLERATED.

'HER MAJESTY'S WAY IS PEACE', HE TOLD THOSE AT THE VIGIL...

'...LET HER BENEVOLENCE ILLU-

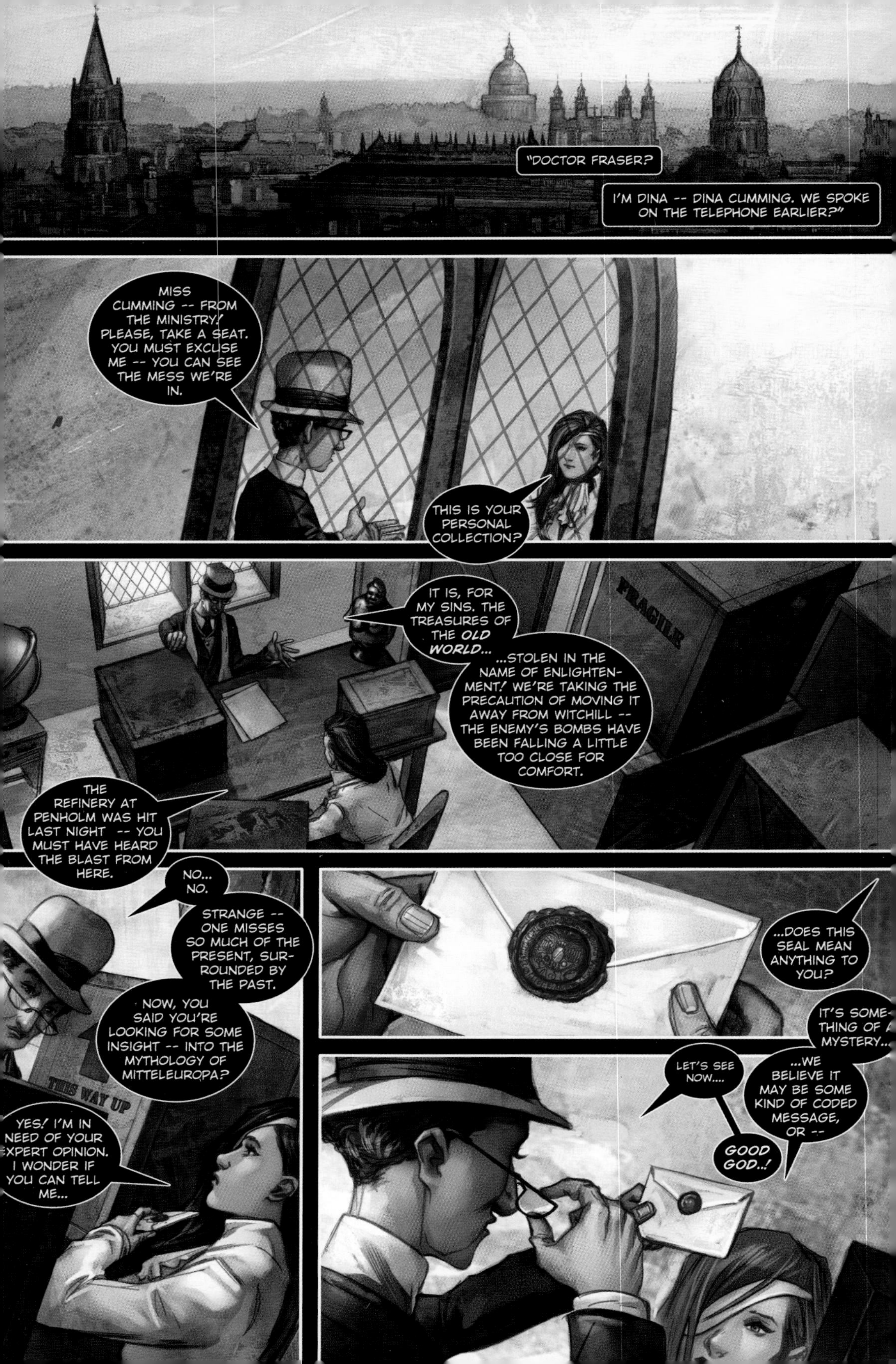
"DOCTOR FRASER?
I'M DINA -- DINA CUMMING. WE SPOKE ON THE TELEPHONE EARLIER?"
MISS CUMMING -- FROM THE MINISTRY! PLEASE, TAKE A SEAT. YOU MUST EXCUSE ME -- YOU CAN SEE THE MESS WE'RE IN.
THIS IS YOUR PERSONAL COLLECTION?
FRAGILE
IT IS, FOR MY SINS. THE TREASURES OF THE *OLD WORLD*...
...STOLEN IN THE NAME OF ENLIGHTENMENT! WE'RE TAKING THE PRECAUTION OF MOVING IT AWAY FROM WITCHILL -- THE ENEMY'S BOMBS HAVE BEEN FALLING A LITTLE TOO CLOSE FOR COMFORT.
THE REFINERY AT PENHOLM WAS HIT LAST NIGHT -- YOU MUST HAVE HEARD THE BLAST FROM HERE.
NO... NO.
STRANGE -- ONE MISSES SO MUCH OF THE PRESENT, SURROUNDED BY THE PAST.
NOW, YOU SAID YOU'RE LOOKING FOR SOME INSIGHT -- INTO THE MYTHOLOGY OF MITTELEUROPA?
THIS WAY UP
YES! I'M IN NEED OF YOUR EXPERT OPINION. I WONDER IF YOU CAN TELL ME...
...DOES THIS SEAL MEAN ANYTHING TO YOU?
IT'S SOMETHING OF A MYSTERY...
LET'S SEE NOW....
...WE BELIEVE IT MAY BE SOME KIND OF CODED MESSAGE, OR --
GOOD GOD..!

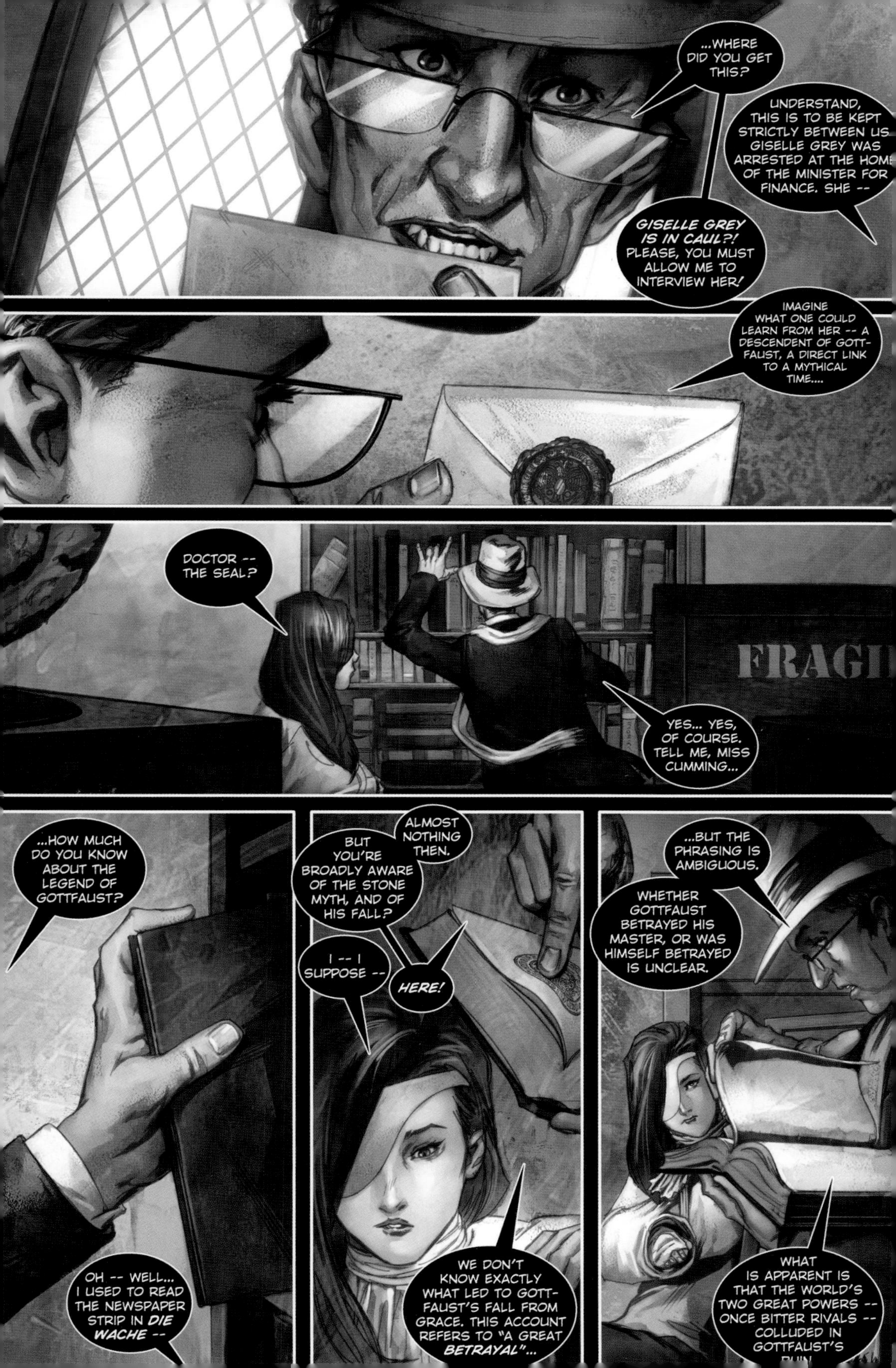
...WHERE DID YOU GET THIS?
UNDERSTAND, THIS IS TO BE KEPT STRICTLY BETWEEN US. GISELLE GREY WAS ARRESTED AT THE HOM OF THE MINISTER FOR FINANCE. SHE --
GISELLE GREY IS IN CAUL?! PLEASE, YOU MUST ALLOW ME TO INTERVIEW HER!
IMAGINE WHAT ONE COULD LEARN FROM HER -- A DESCENDENT OF GOTT-FAUST, A DIRECT LINK TO A MYTHICAL TIME....
DOCTOR -- THE SEAL?
FRAGI
YES... YES, OF COURSE. TELL ME, MISS CUMMING...
...HOW MUCH DO YOU KNOW ABOUT THE LEGEND OF GOTTFAUST?
OH -- WELL... I USED TO READ THE NEWSPAPER STRIP IN *DIE WACHE* --
ALMOST NOTHING THEN.
BUT YOU'RE BROADLY AWARE OF THE STONE MYTH, AND OF HIS FALL?
I -- I SUPPOSE --
HERE!
WE DON'T KNOW EXACTLY WHAT LED TO GOTT-FAUST'S FALL FROM GRACE. THIS ACCOUNT REFERS TO "A GREAT *BETRAYAL*"...
...BUT THE PHRASING IS AMBIGUOUS.
WHETHER GOTTFAUST BETRAYED HIS MASTER, OR WAS HIMSELF BETRAYED IS UNCLEAR.
WHAT IS APPARENT IS THAT THE WORLD'S TWO GREAT POWERS -- ONCE BITTER RIVALS -- COLLUDED IN GOTTFAUST'S

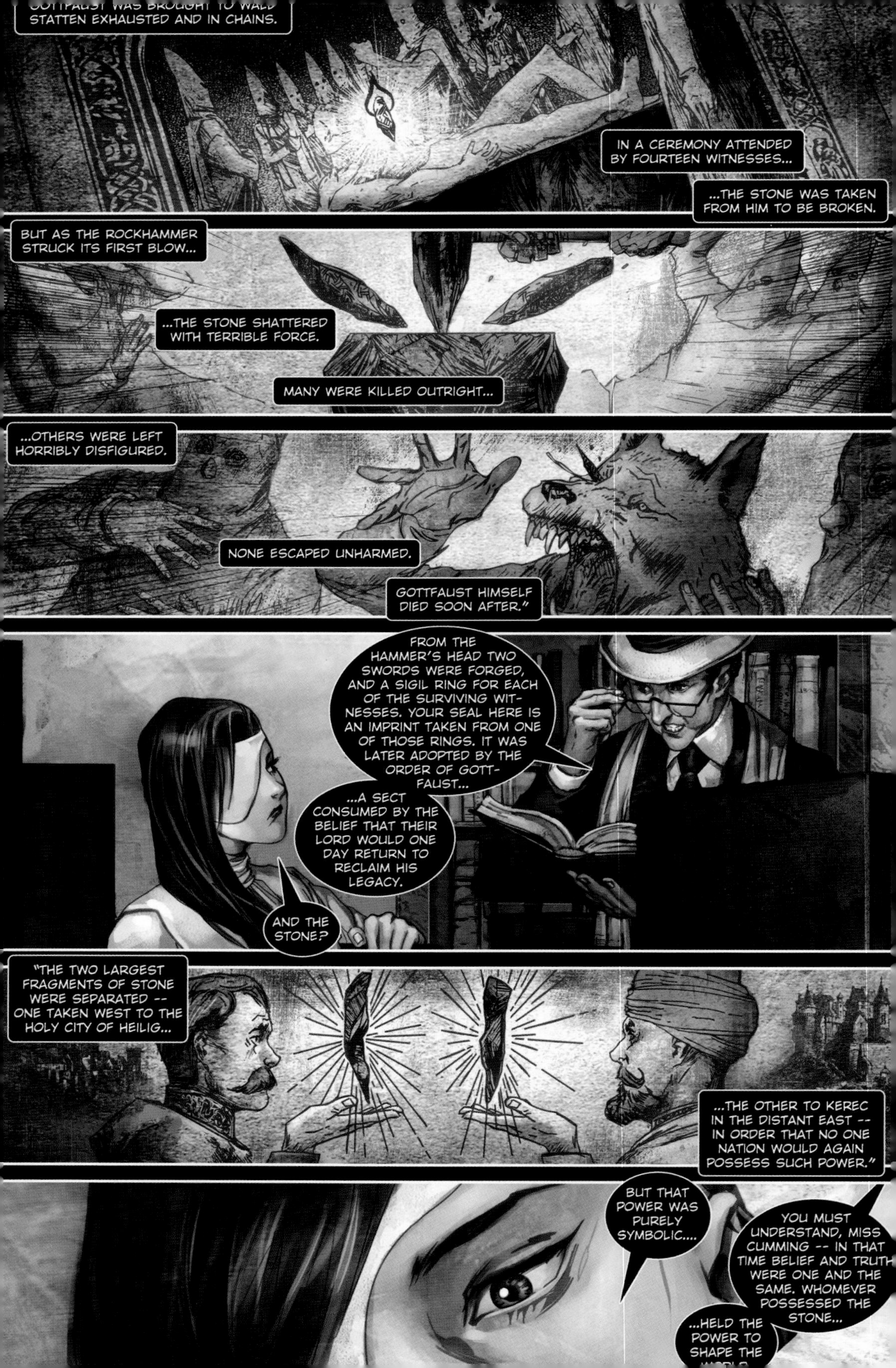
GOTTFAUST WAS BROUGHT TO WALD STATTEN EXHAUSTED AND IN CHAINS.
IN A CEREMONY ATTENDED BY FOURTEEN WITNESSES...
...THE STONE WAS TAKEN FROM HIM TO BE BROKEN.
BUT AS THE ROCKHAMMER STRUCK ITS FIRST BLOW...
...THE STONE SHATTERED WITH TERRIBLE FORCE.
MANY WERE KILLED OUTRIGHT...
...OTHERS WERE LEFT HORRIBLY DISFIGURED.
NONE ESCAPED UNHARMED.
GOTTFAUST HIMSELF DIED SOON AFTER."
FROM THE HAMMER'S HEAD TWO SWORDS WERE FORGED, AND A SIGIL RING FOR EACH OF THE SURVIVING WITNESSES. YOUR SEAL HERE IS AN IMPRINT TAKEN FROM ONE OF THOSE RINGS. IT WAS LATER ADOPTED BY THE ORDER OF GOTTFAUST...
...A SECT CONSUMED BY THE BELIEF THAT THEIR LORD WOULD ONE DAY RETURN TO RECLAIM HIS LEGACY.
AND THE STONE?
"THE TWO LARGEST FRAGMENTS OF STONE WERE SEPARATED -- ONE TAKEN WEST TO THE HOLY CITY OF HEILIG...
...THE OTHER TO KEREC IN THE DISTANT EAST -- IN ORDER THAT NO ONE NATION WOULD AGAIN POSSESS SUCH POWER."
BUT THAT POWER WAS PURELY SYMBOLIC....
YOU MUST UNDERSTAND, MISS CUMMING -- IN THAT TIME BELIEF AND TRUTH WERE ONE AND THE SAME. WHOMEVER POSSESSED THE STONE...
...HELD THE POWER TO SHAPE THE

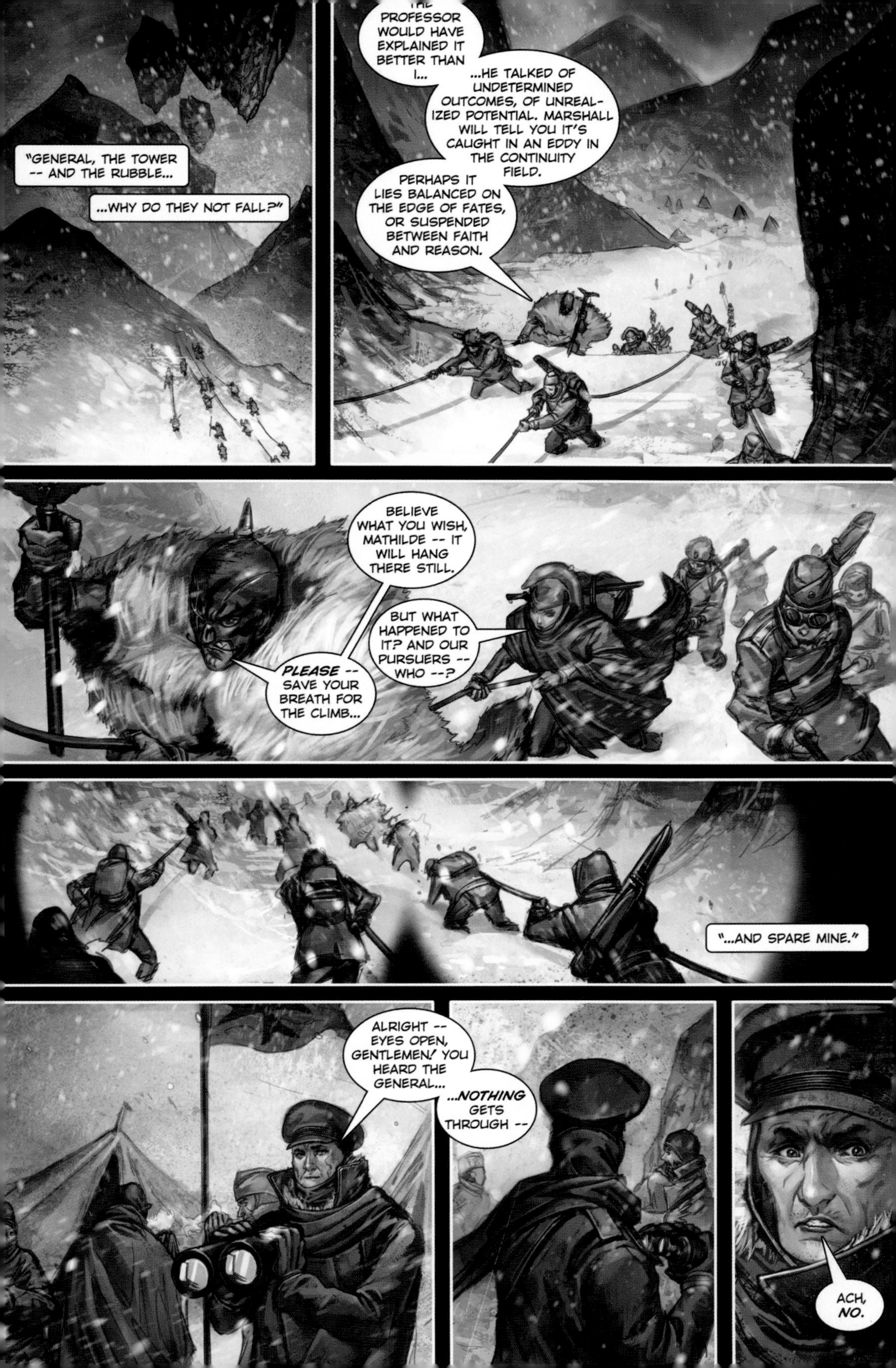
"GENERAL, THE TOWER -- AND THE RUBBLE...
...WHY DO THEY NOT FALL?"
THE PROFESSOR WOULD HAVE EXPLAINED IT BETTER THAN I...
...HE TALKED OF UNDETERMINED OUTCOMES, OF UNREALIZED POTENTIAL. MARSHALL WILL TELL YOU IT'S CAUGHT IN AN EDDY IN THE CONTINUITY FIELD.
PERHAPS IT LIES BALANCED ON THE EDGE OF FATES, OR SUSPENDED BETWEEN FAITH AND REASON.
BELIEVE WHAT YOU WISH, MATHILDE -- IT WILL HANG THERE STILL.
BUT WHAT HAPPENED TO IT? AND OUR PURSUERS -- WHO --?
PLEASE -- SAVE YOUR BREATH FOR THE CLIMB...
"...AND SPARE MINE."
ALRIGHT -- EYES OPEN, GENTLEMEN! YOU HEARD THE GENERAL...
...***NOTHING*** GETS THROUGH --
ACH, ***NO.***

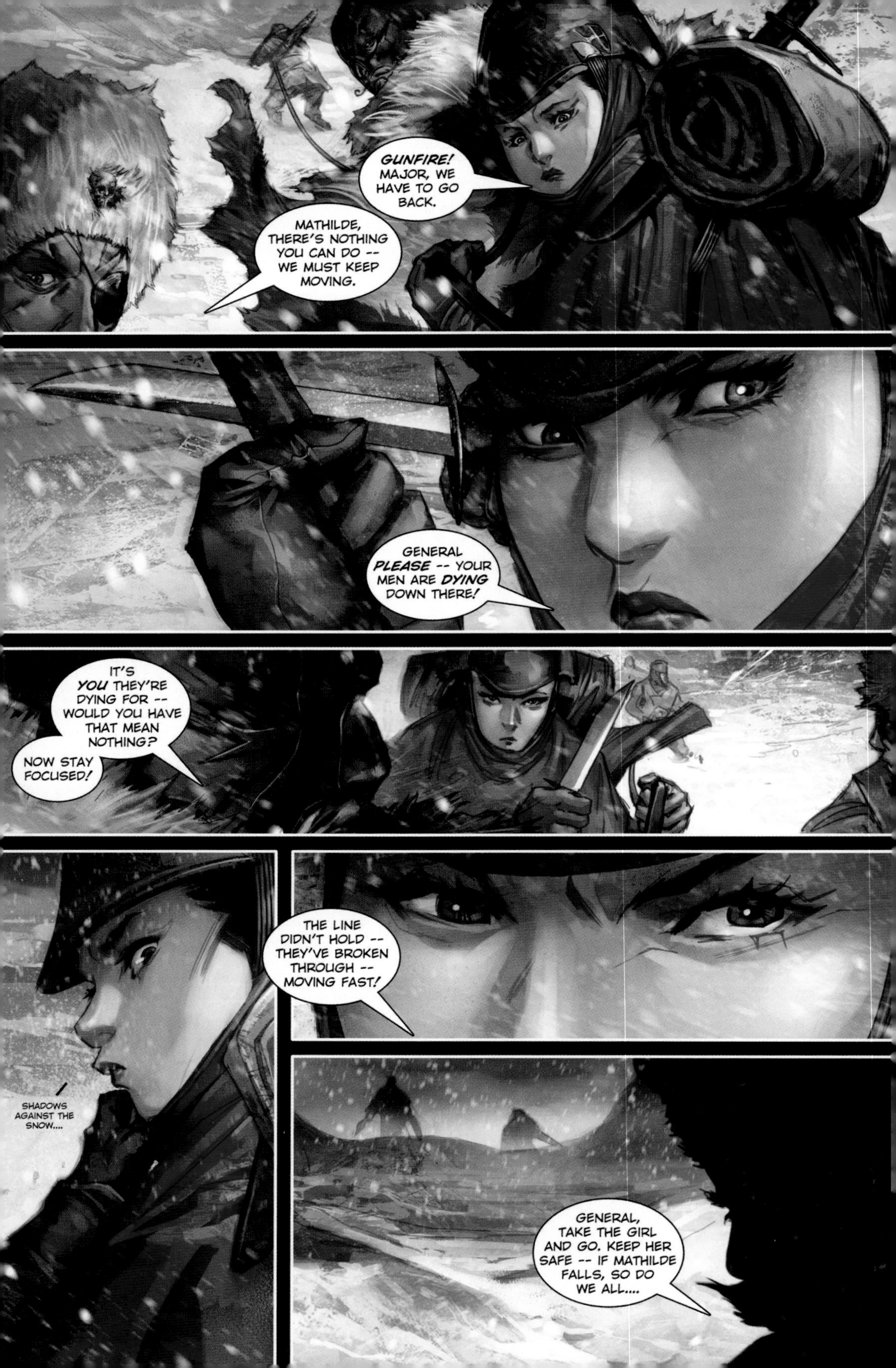
GUNFIRE! MAJOR, WE HAVE TO GO BACK.
MATHILDE, THERE'S NOTHING YOU CAN DO -- WE MUST KEEP MOVING.
GENERAL PLEASE -- YOUR MEN ARE DYING DOWN THERE!
IT'S YOU THEY'RE DYING FOR -- WOULD YOU HAVE THAT MEAN NOTHING?
NOW STAY FOCUSED!
THE LINE DIDN'T HOLD -- THEY'VE BROKEN THROUGH -- MOVING FAST!
SHADOWS AGAINST THE SNOW....
GENERAL, TAKE THE GIRL AND GO. KEEP HER SAFE -- IF MATHILDE FALLS, SO DO WE ALL....

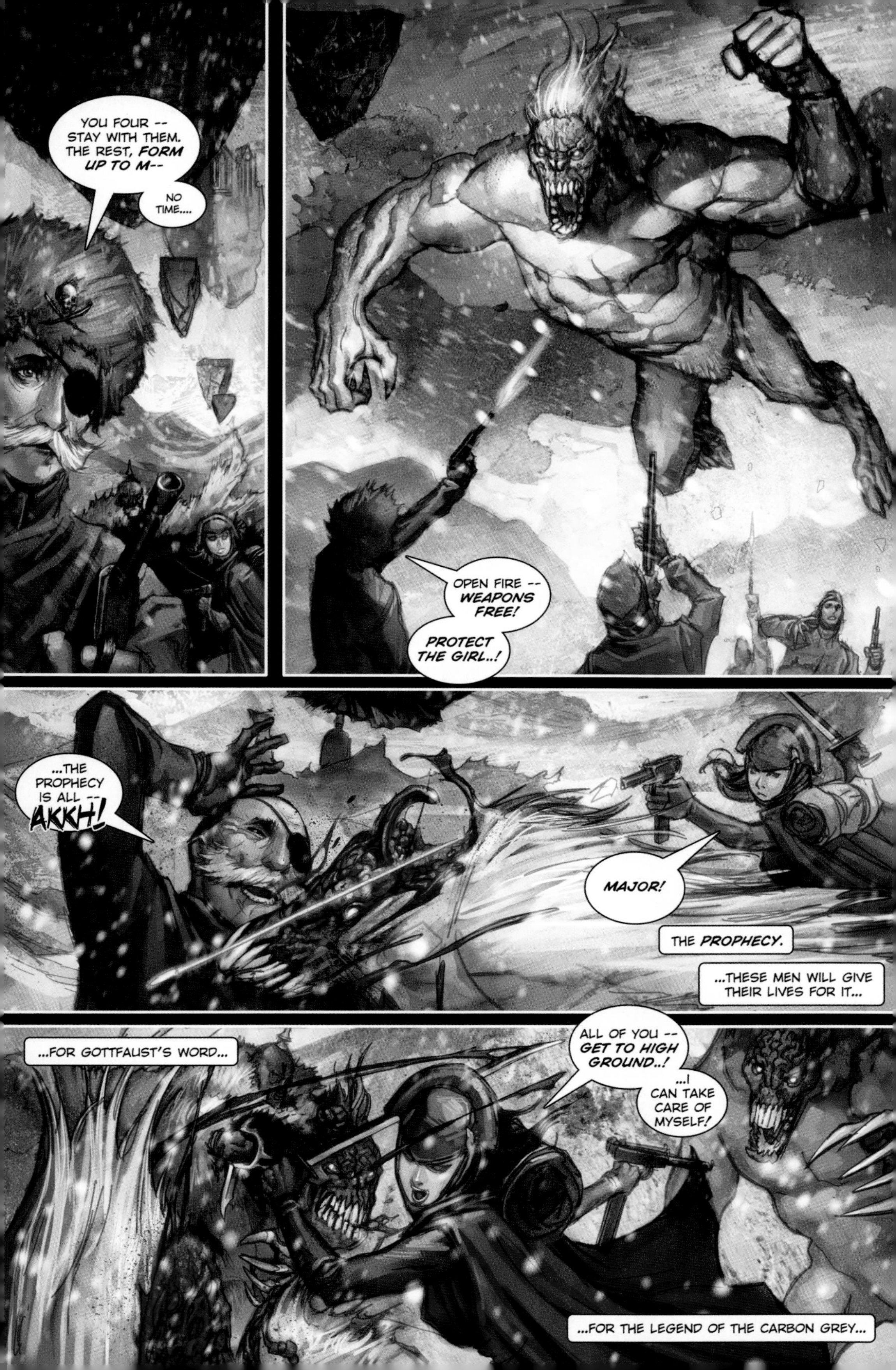
YOU FOUR -- STAY WITH THEM. THE REST, FORM UP TO M--
NO TIME....
OPEN FIRE -- WEAPONS FREE!
PROTECT THE GIRL..!
...THE PROPHECY IS ALL -- AKKH!
MAJOR!
THE PROPHECY.
...THESE MEN WILL GIVE THEIR LIVES FOR IT...
...FOR GOTTFAUST'S WORD...
ALL OF YOU -- GET TO HIGH GROUND..!
...I CAN TAKE CARE OF MYSELF!
...FOR THE LEGEND OF THE CARBON GREY...

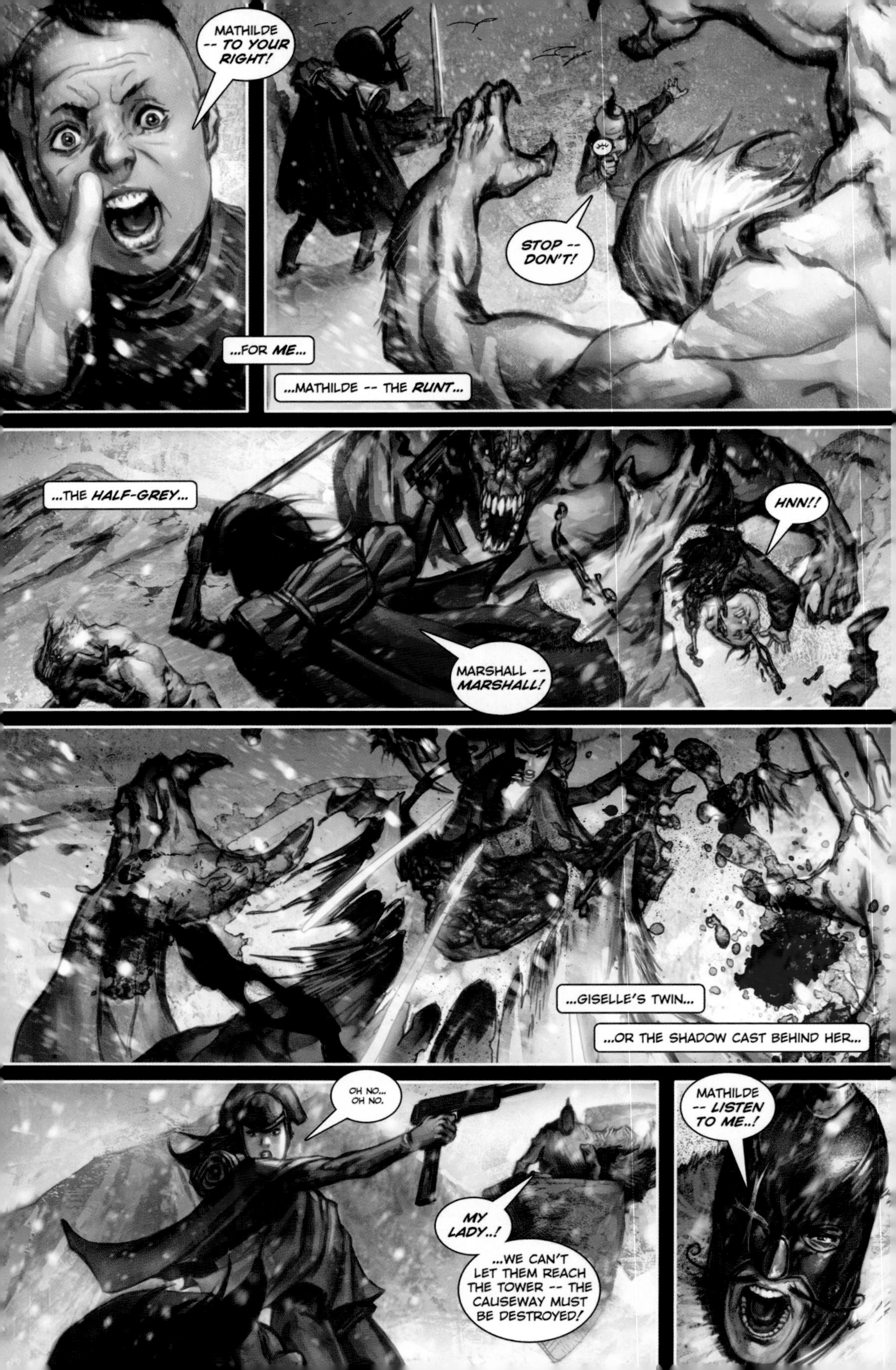
MATHILDE -- TO YOUR RIGHT!
...FOR ME...
STOP -- DON'T!
...MATHILDE -- THE RUNT...
...THE HALF-GREY...
HNN!!
MARSHALL -- MARSHALL!
...GISELLE'S TWIN...
...OR THE SHADOW CAST BEHIND HER...
OH NO... OH NO.
MY LADY..!
...WE CAN'T LET THEM REACH THE TOWER -- THE CAUSEWAY MUST BE DESTROYED!
MATHILDE -- LISTEN TO ME..!

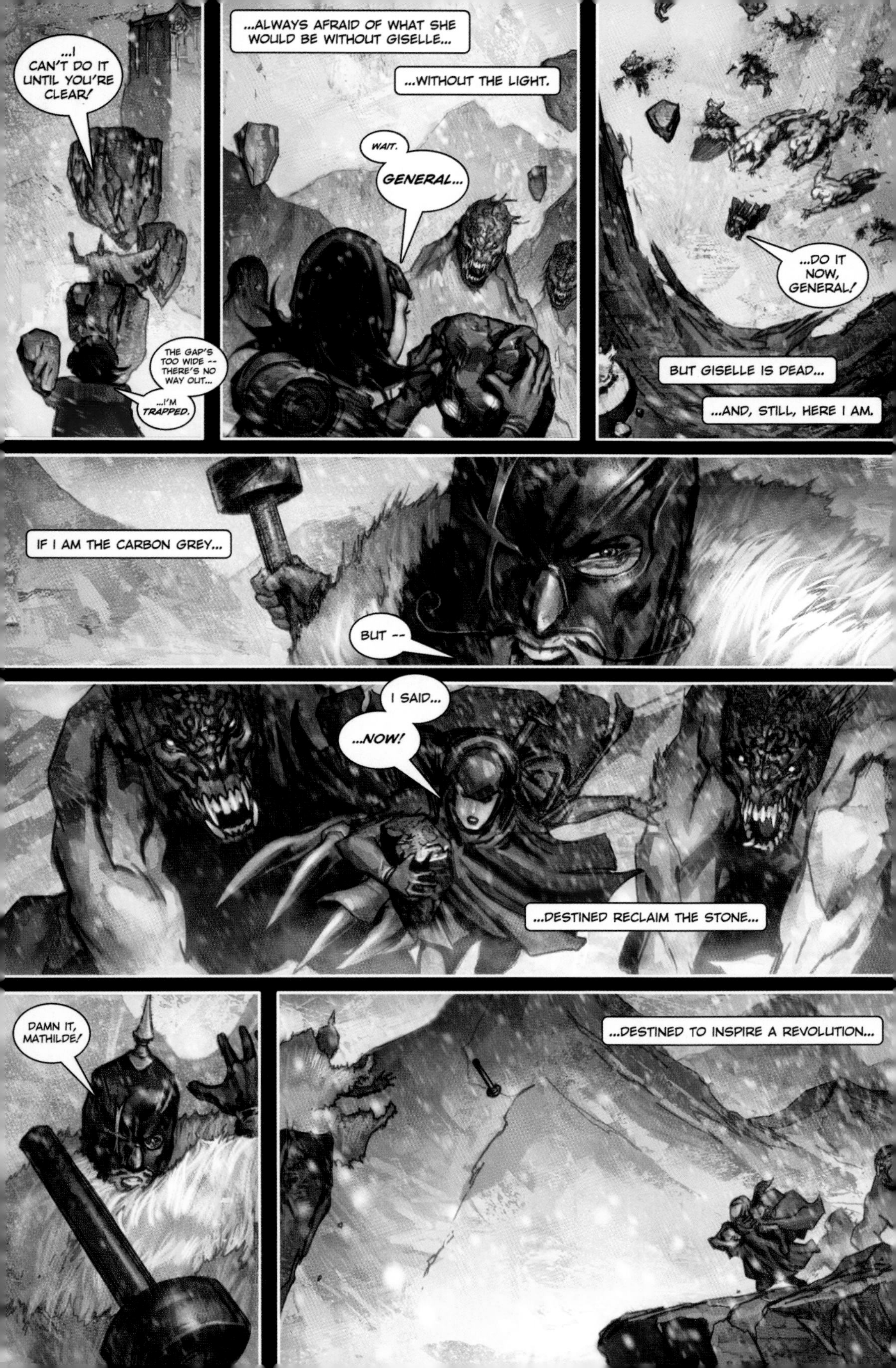
...I CAN'T DO IT UNTIL YOU'RE CLEAR!
THE GAP'S TOO WIDE -- THERE'S NO WAY OUT...
...I'M *TRAPPED.*
...ALWAYS AFRAID OF WHAT SHE WOULD BE WITHOUT GISELLE...
...WITHOUT THE LIGHT.
WAIT.
GENERAL...
...DO IT NOW, GENERAL!
BUT GISELLE IS DEAD...
...AND, STILL, HERE I AM.
IF I AM THE CARBON GREY...
BUT --
I SAID...
...NOW!
...DESTINED RECLAIM THE STONE...
DAMN IT, MATHILDE!
...DESTINED TO INSPIRE A REVOLUTION...

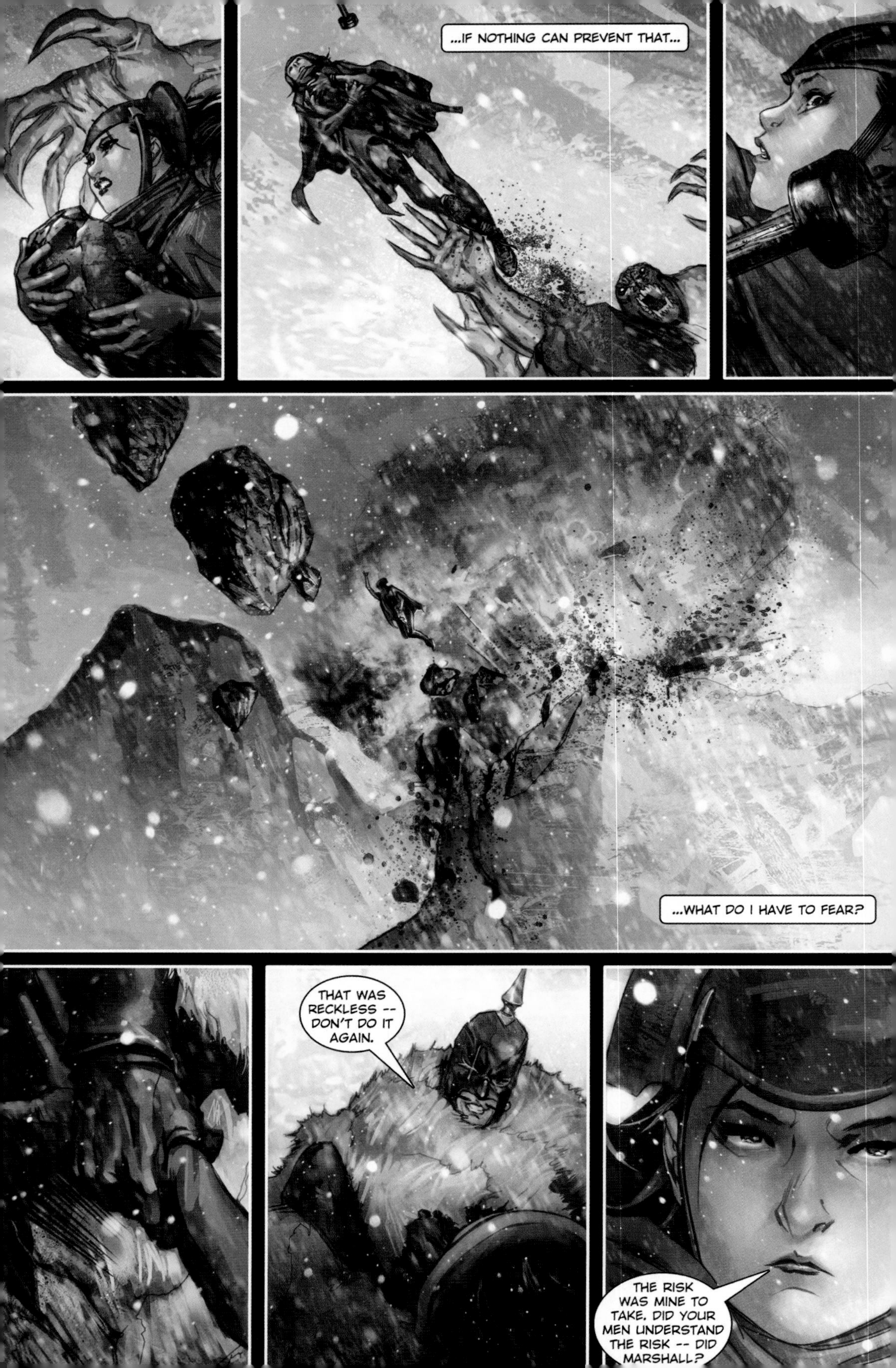

...IF NOTHING CAN PREVENT THAT...
...WHAT DO I HAVE TO FEAR?
THAT WAS RECKLESS -- DON'T DO IT AGAIN.
THE RISK WAS MINE TO TAKE. DID YOUR MEN UNDERSTAND THE RISK -- DID MARSHALL?

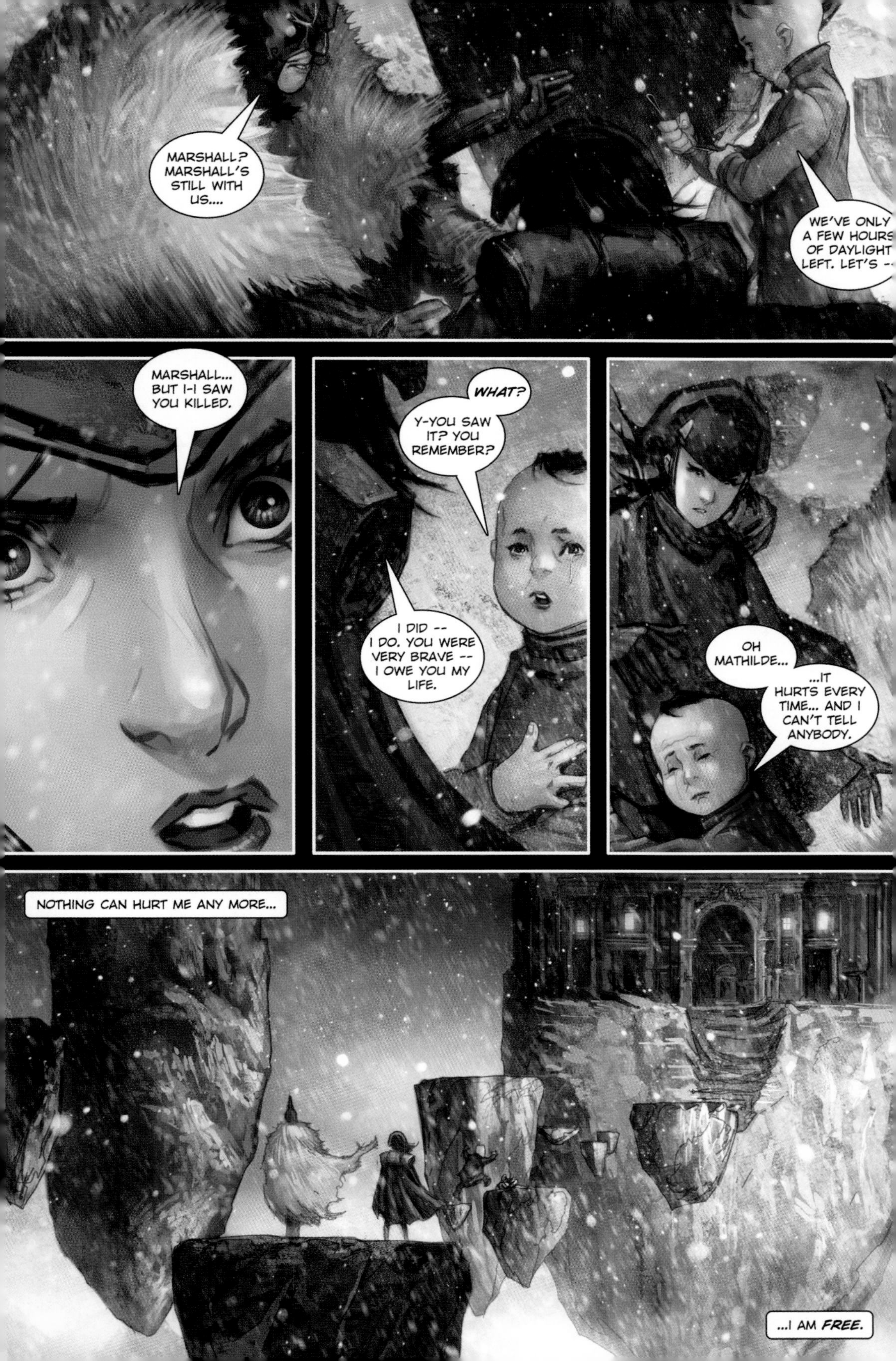
MARSHALL? MARSHALL'S STILL WITH US....
WE'VE ONLY A FEW HOURS OF DAYLIGHT LEFT. LET'S --
MARSHALL... BUT I-I SAW YOU KILLED.
WHAT?
Y-YOU SAW IT? YOU REMEMBER?
I DID -- I DO. YOU WERE VERY BRAVE -- I OWE YOU MY LIFE.
OH MATHILDE...
...IT HURTS EVERY TIME... AND I CAN'T TELL ANYBODY.
NOTHING CAN HURT ME ANY MORE...
...I AM FREE.

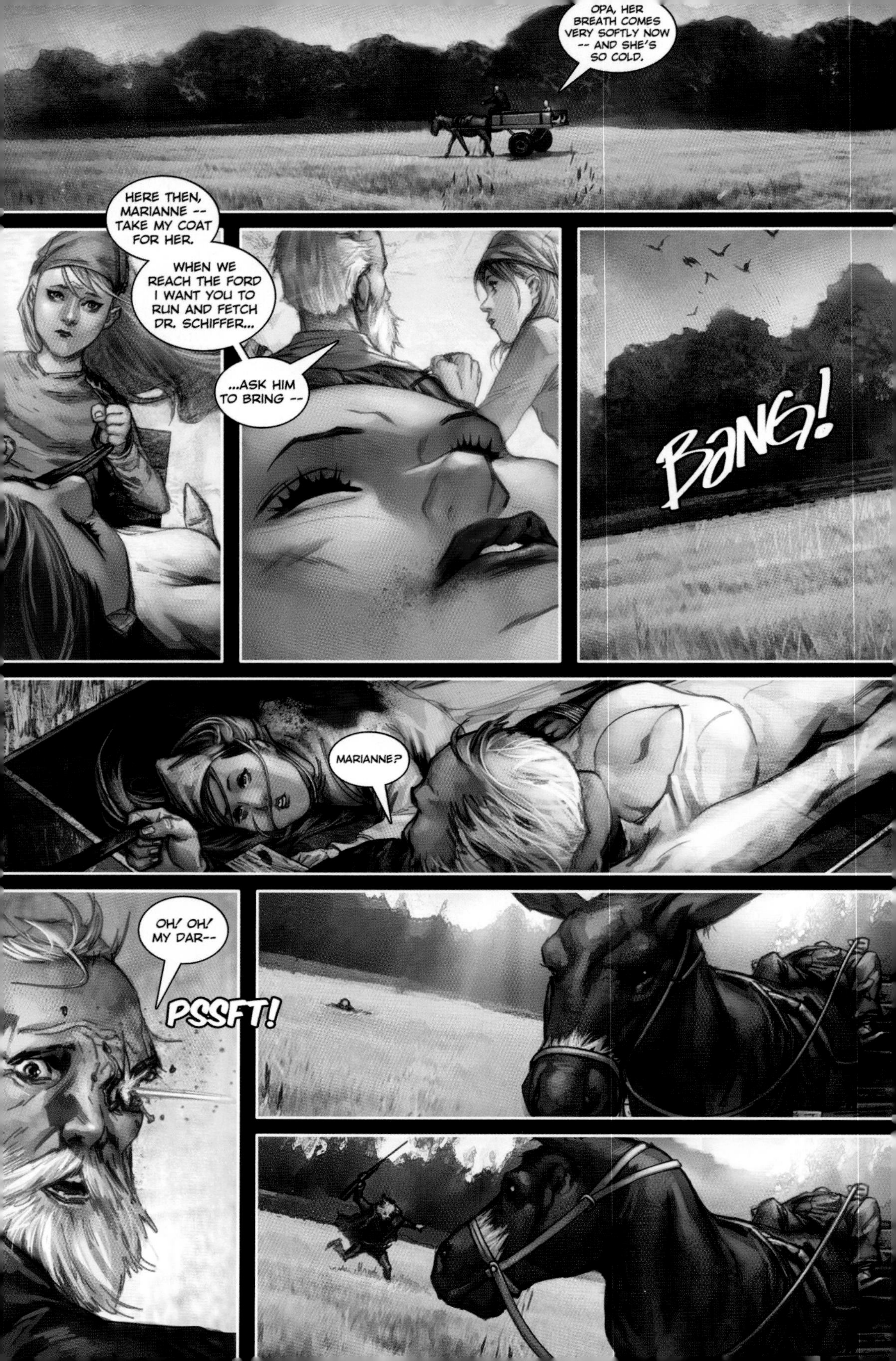
OPA, HER BREATH COMES VERY SOFTLY NOW -- AND SHE'S SO COLD.
HERE THEN, MARIANNE -- TAKE MY COAT FOR HER.
WHEN WE REACH THE FORD I WANT YOU TO RUN AND FETCH DR. SCHIFFER...
...ASK HIM TO BRING --
BANG!
MARIANNE?
OH! OH! MY DAR--
PSSFT!

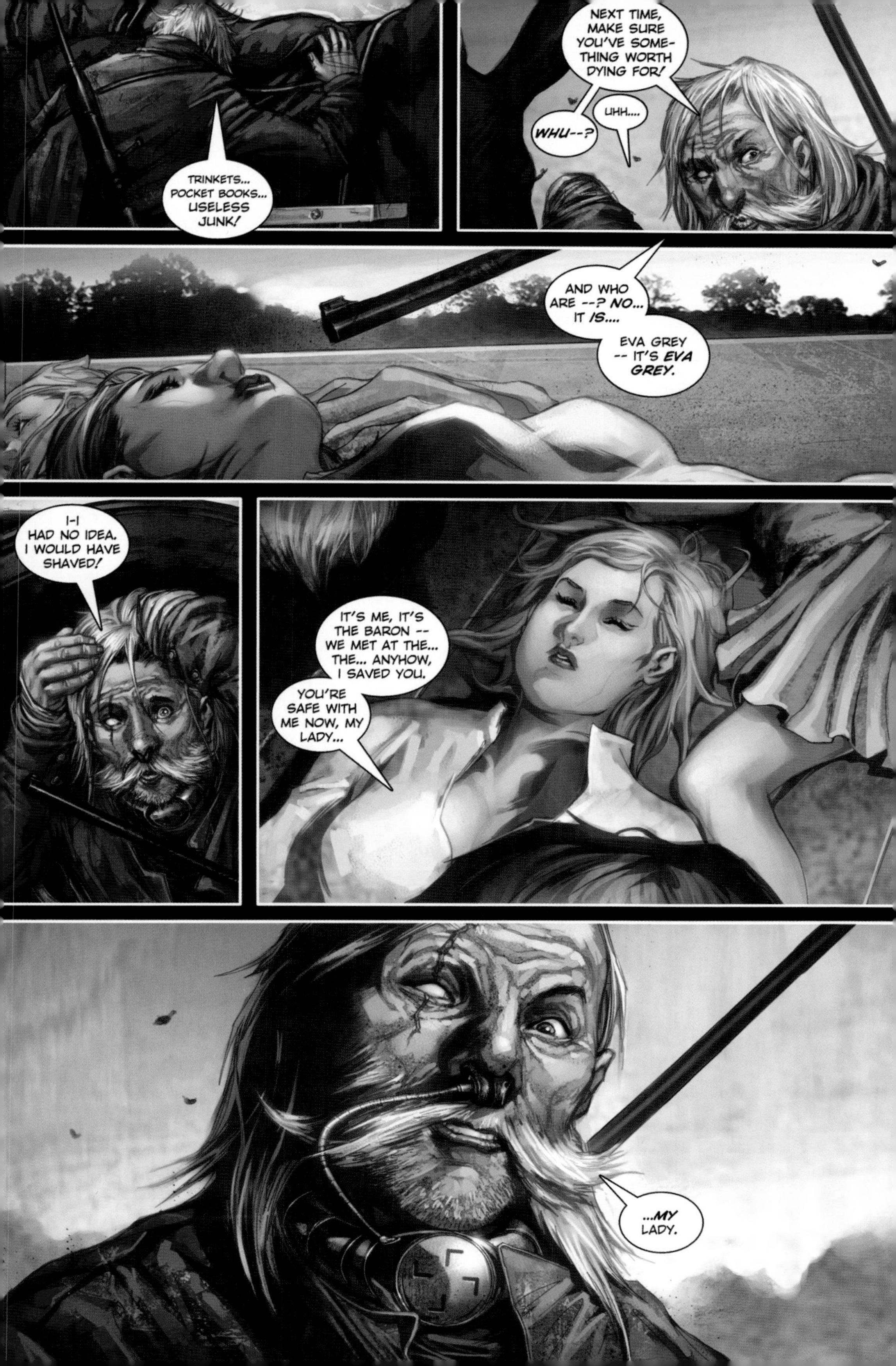
TRINKETS... POCKET BOOKS... USELESS JUNK!
NEXT TIME, MAKE SURE YOU'VE SOME-THING WORTH DYING FOR!
WHU--?
UHH....
AND WHO ARE --? NO... IT IS....
EVA GREY -- IT'S EVA GREY.
I-I HAD NO IDEA. I WOULD HAVE SHAVED!
IT'S ME, IT'S THE BARON -- WE MET AT THE... THE... ANYHOW, I SAVED YOU.
YOU'RE SAFE WITH ME NOW, MY LADY...
...MY LADY.

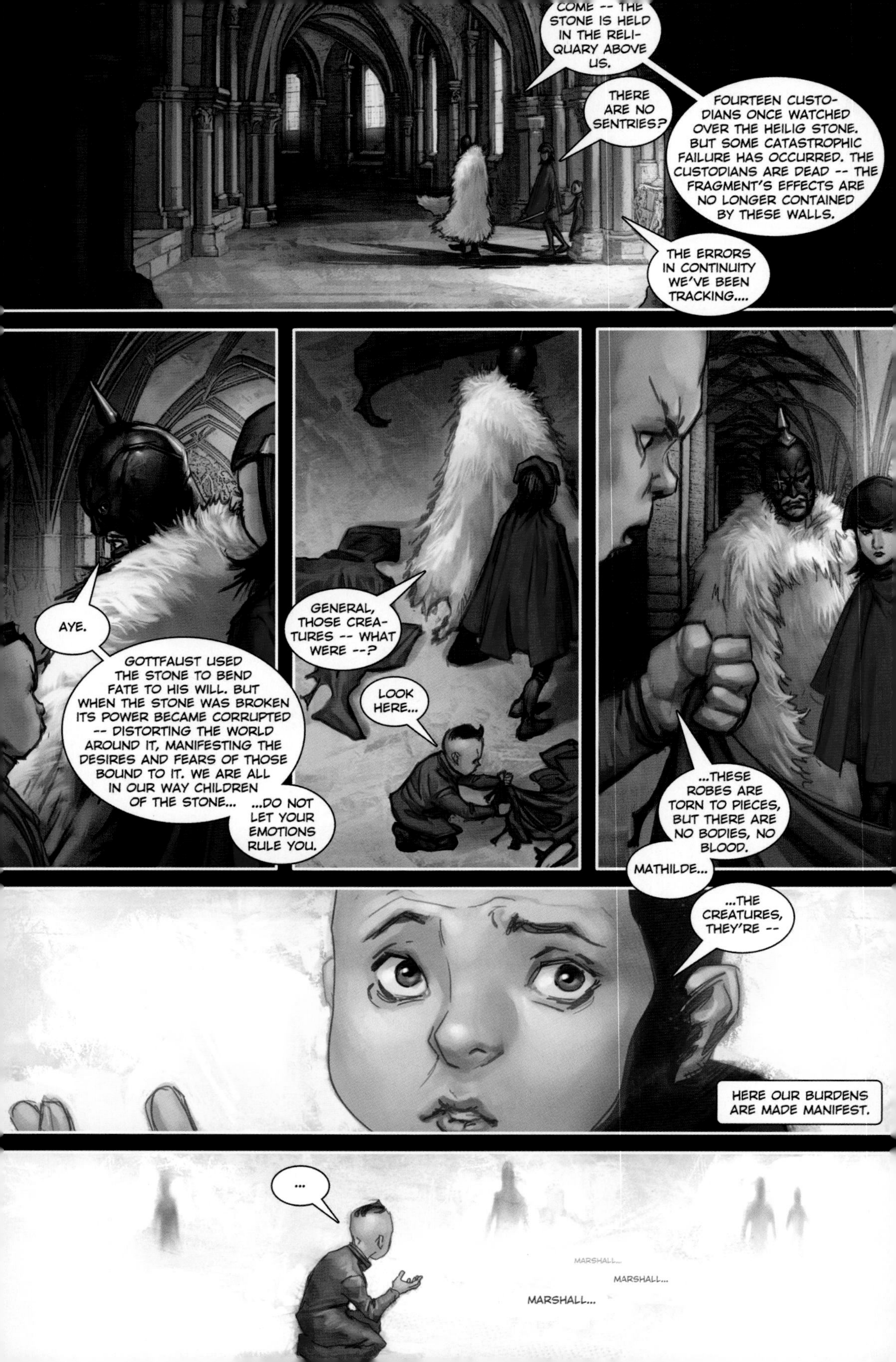
COME -- THE STONE IS HELD IN THE RELI-QUARY ABOVE US.
THERE ARE NO SENTRIES?
FOURTEEN CUSTO-DIANS ONCE WATCHED OVER THE HEILIG STONE. BUT SOME CATASTROPHIC FAILURE HAS OCCURRED. THE CUSTODIANS ARE DEAD -- THE FRAGMENT'S EFFECTS ARE NO LONGER CONTAINED BY THESE WALLS.
THE ERRORS IN CONTINUITY WE'VE BEEN TRACKING....
AYE.
GOTTFAUST USED THE STONE TO BEND FATE TO HIS WILL. BUT WHEN THE STONE WAS BROKEN ITS POWER BECAME CORRUPTED -- DISTORTING THE WORLD AROUND IT, MANIFESTING THE DESIRES AND FEARS OF THOSE BOUND TO IT. WE ARE ALL IN OUR WAY CHILDREN OF THE STONE...
...DO NOT LET YOUR EMOTIONS RULE YOU.
GENERAL, THOSE CREA-TURES -- WHAT WERE --?
LOOK HERE...
...THESE ROBES ARE TORN TO PIECES, BUT THERE ARE NO BODIES, NO BLOOD.
MATHILDE...
...THE CREATURES, THEY'RE --
HERE OUR BURDENS ARE MADE MANIFEST.
...
MARSHALL...
MARSHALL...
MARSHALL...

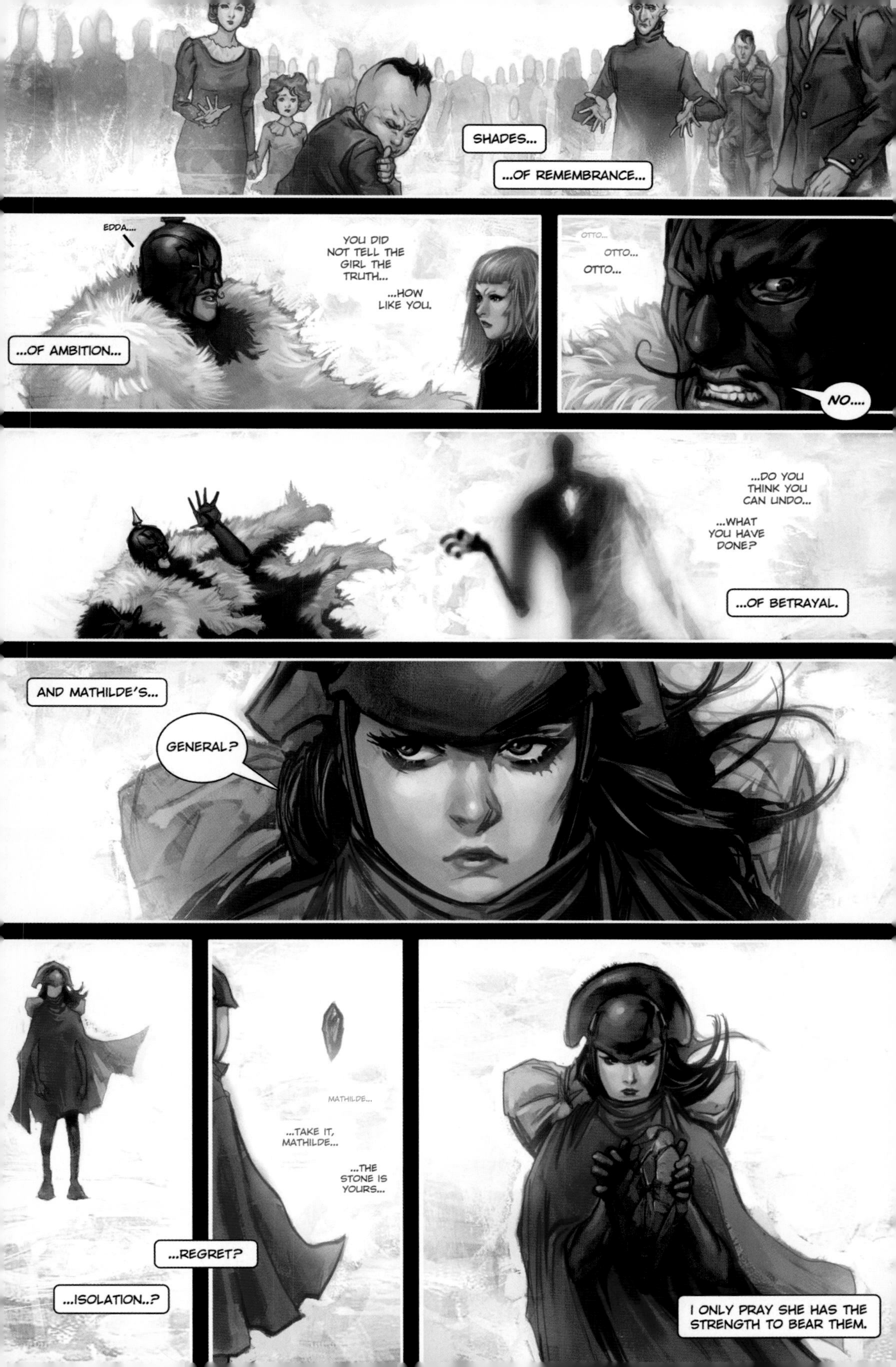

SHADES...
...OF REMEMBRANCE...
EDDA....
...OF AMBITION...
YOU DID NOT TELL THE GIRL THE TRUTH...
...HOW LIKE YOU.
OTTO...
OTTO...
OTTO...
NO....
...DO YOU THINK YOU CAN UNDO...
...WHAT YOU HAVE DONE?
...OF BETRAYAL.
AND MATHILDE'S...
GENERAL?
...ISOLATION..?
...REGRET?
MATHILDE...
...TAKE IT, MATHILDE...
...THE STONE IS YOURS...
I ONLY PRAY SHE HAS THE STRENGTH TO BEAR THEM.

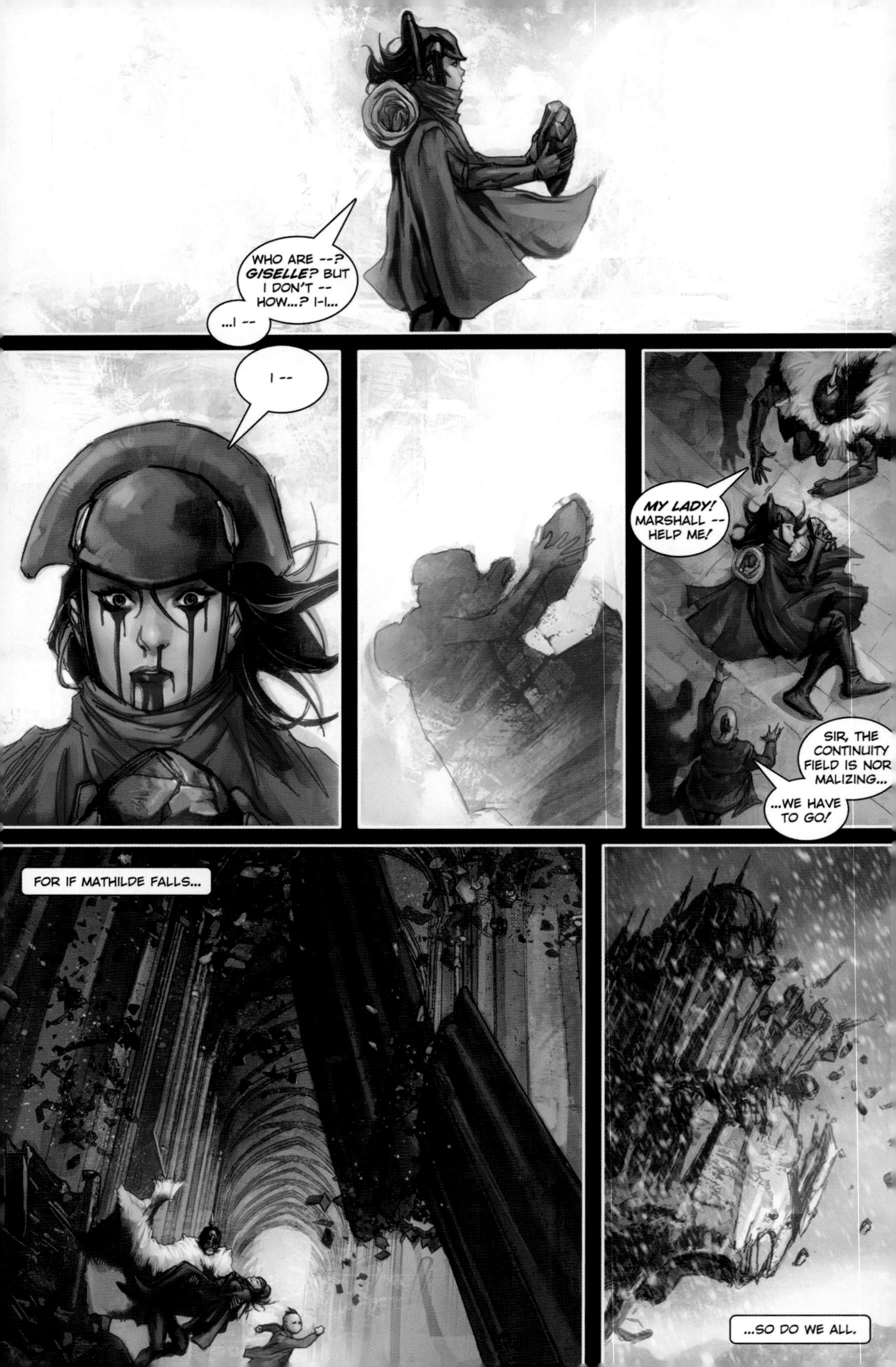

WHO ARE --? GISELLE? BUT I DON'T -- HOW...? I-I...
...I --
I --
MY LADY! MARSHALL -- HELP ME!
SIR, THE CONTINUITY FIELD IS NOR MALIZING...
...WE HAVE TO GO!
FOR IF MATHILDE FALLS...
...SO DO WE ALL.

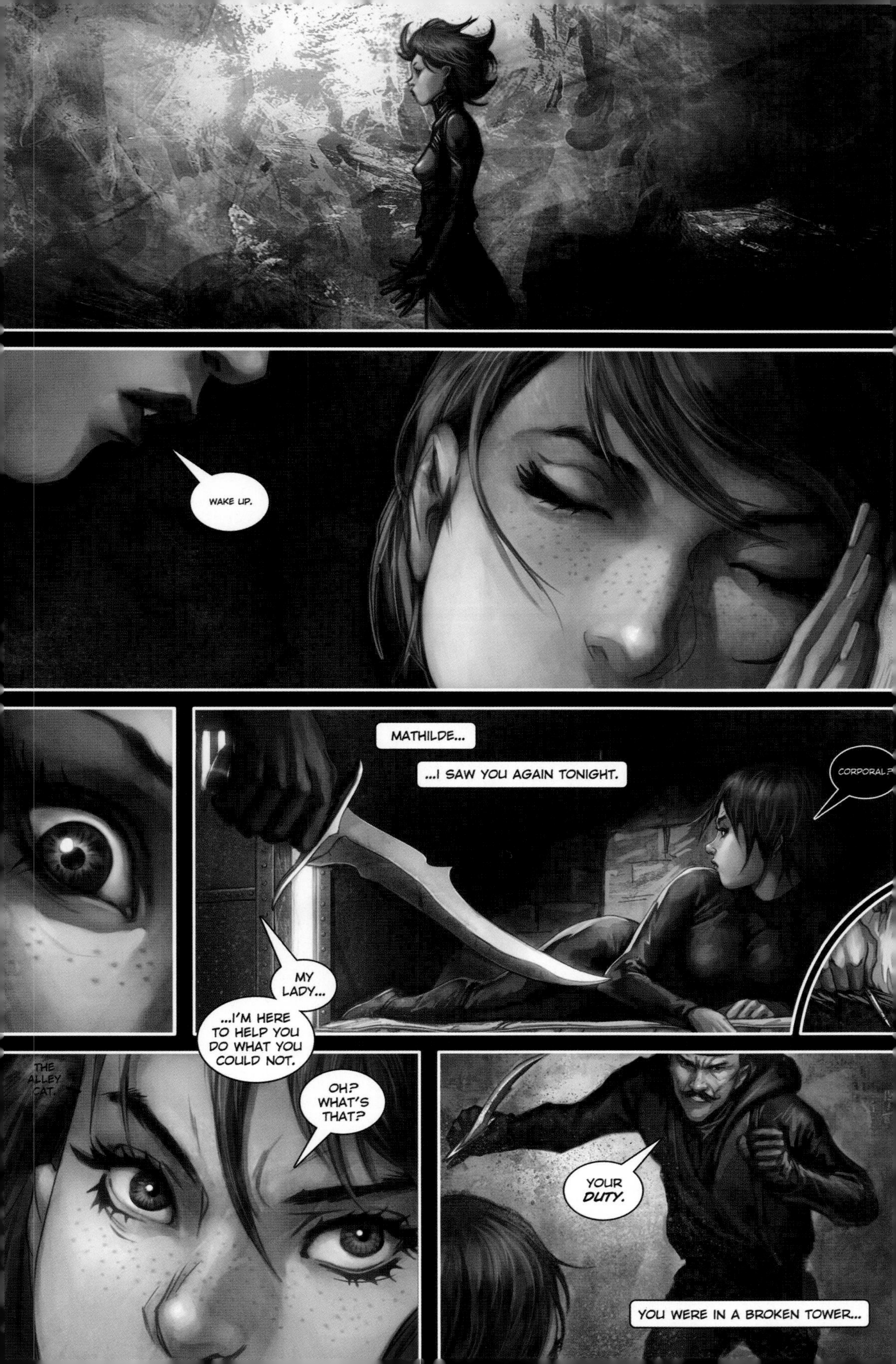
WAKE UP.
MATHILDE...
...I SAW YOU AGAIN TONIGHT.
MY LADY...
...I'M HERE TO HELP YOU DO WHAT YOU COULD NOT.
CORPORAL?
THE ALLEY CAT.
OH? WHAT'S THAT?
YOUR *DUTY*.
YOU WERE IN A BROKEN TOWER...

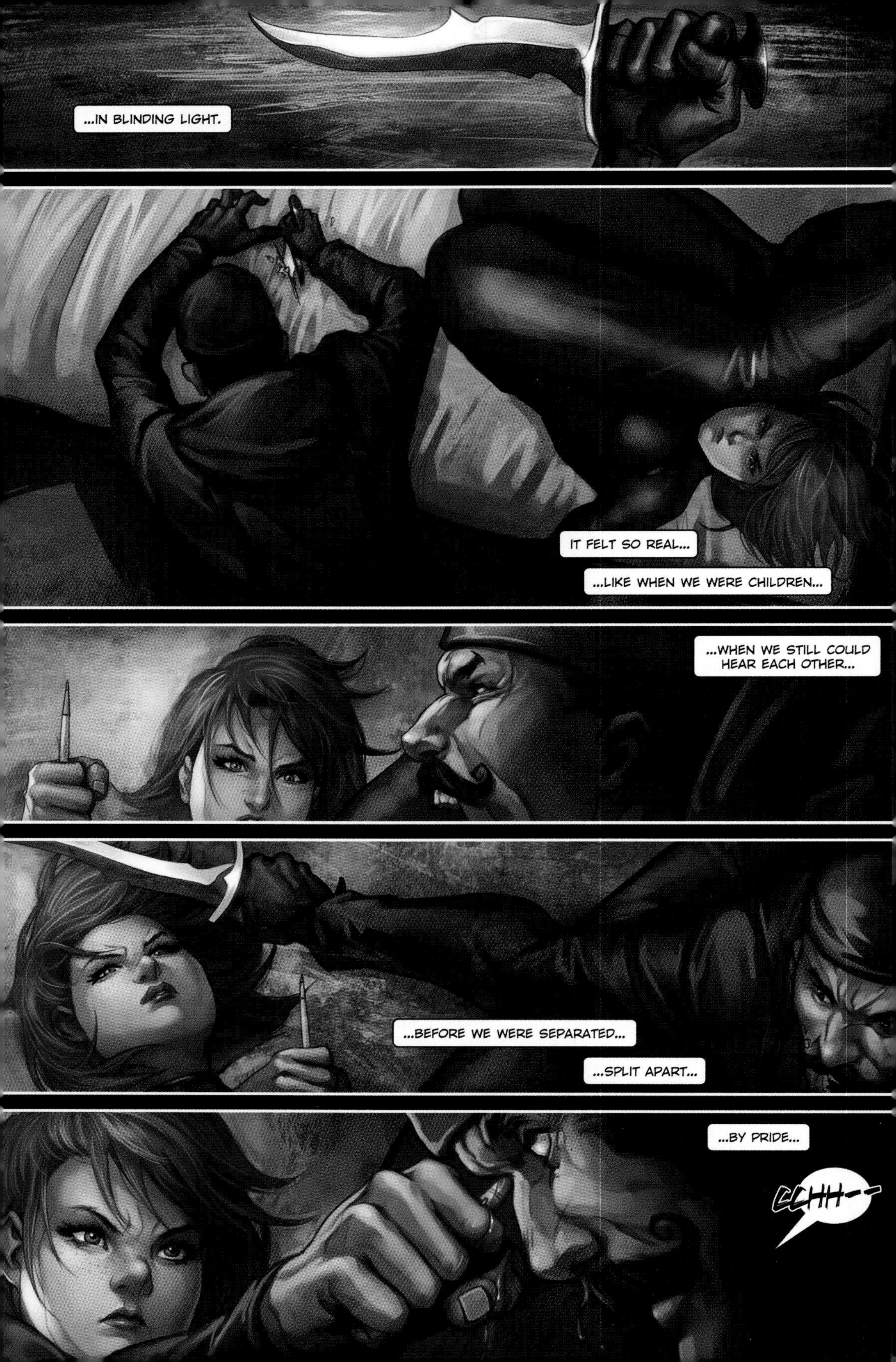
...IN BLINDING LIGHT.
IT FELT SO REAL...
...LIKE WHEN WE WERE CHILDREN...
...WHEN WE STILL COULD HEAR EACH OTHER...
...BEFORE WE WERE SEPARATED...
...SPLIT APART...
...BY PRIDE...
CCHH--

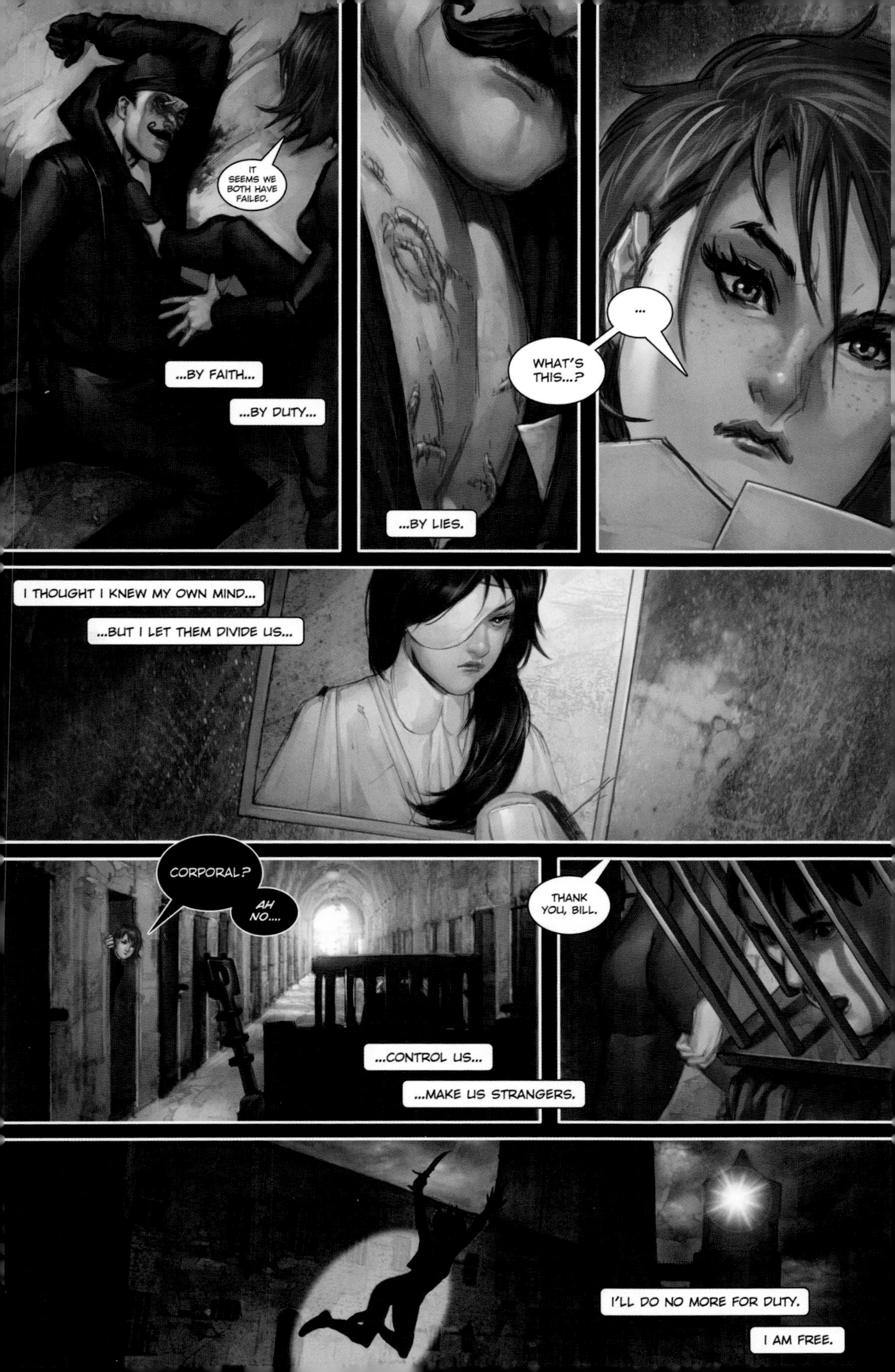
IT SEEMS WE BOTH HAVE FAILED.
...BY FAITH...
...BY DUTY...
...BY LIES.
...
WHAT'S THIS...?
I THOUGHT I KNEW MY OWN MIND...
...BUT I LET THEM DIVIDE US...
CORPORAL?
AH NO....
...CONTROL US...
...MAKE US STRANGERS.
THANK YOU, BILL.
I'LL DO NO MORE FOR DUTY.
I AM FREE.

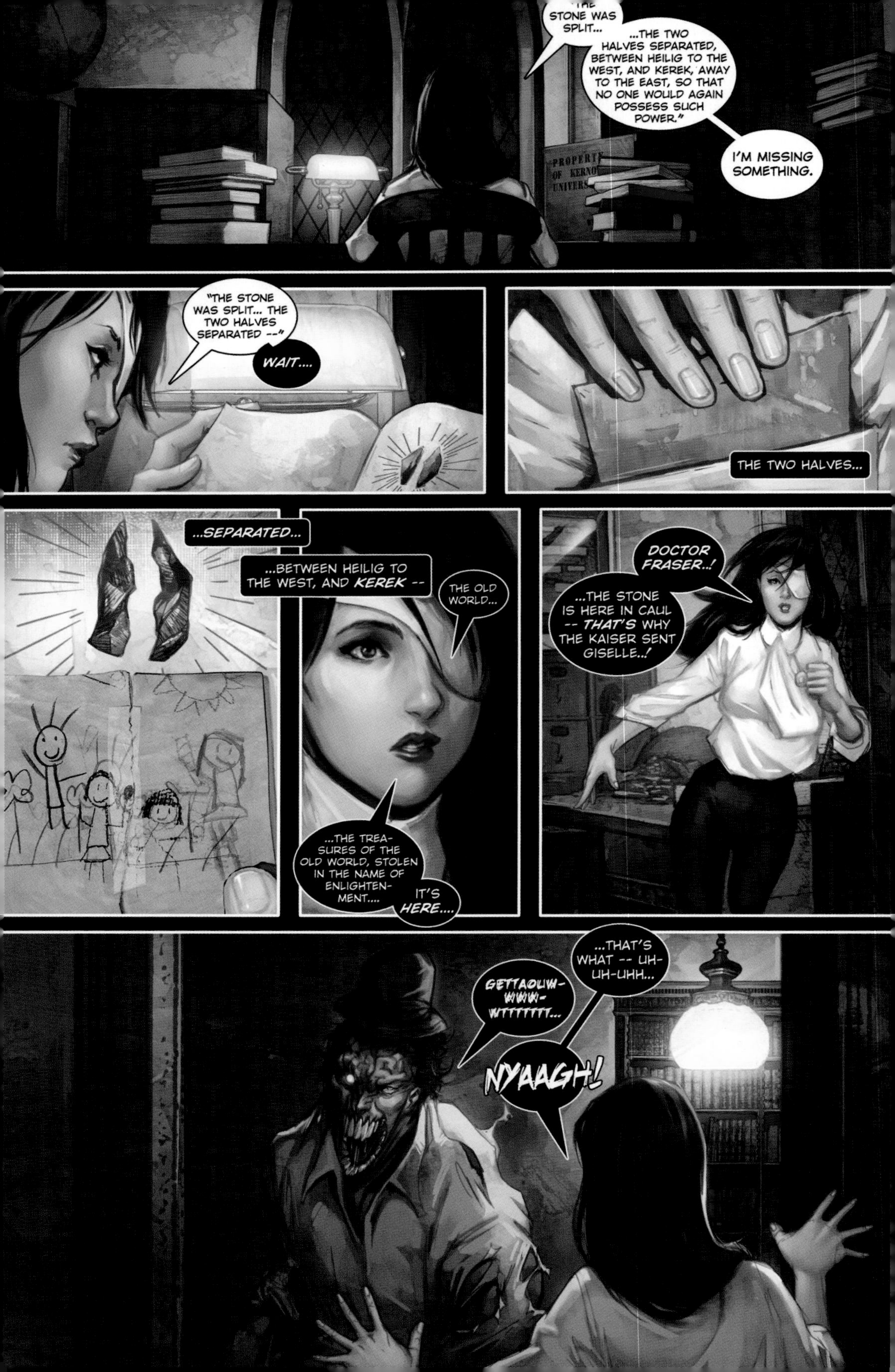
"THE STONE WAS SPLIT...
...THE TWO HALVES SEPARATED, BETWEEN HEILIG TO THE WEST, AND KEREK, AWAY TO THE EAST, SO THAT NO ONE WOULD AGAIN POSSESS SUCH POWER."
I'M MISSING SOMETHING.
"THE STONE WAS SPLIT... THE TWO HALVES SEPARATED --"
WAIT....
THE TWO HALVES...
...SEPARATED...
...BETWEEN HEILIG TO THE WEST, AND KEREK --
THE OLD WORLD...
...THE TREASURES OF THE OLD WORLD, STOLEN IN THE NAME OF ENLIGHTENMENT....
IT'S HERE....
DOCTOR FRASER..!
...THE STONE IS HERE IN CAUL -- THAT'S WHY THE KAISER SENT GISELLE..!
GETTAOUW-WWW-WTTTTTTT...
...THAT'S WHAT -- UH-UH-UHH...
NYAAGH!

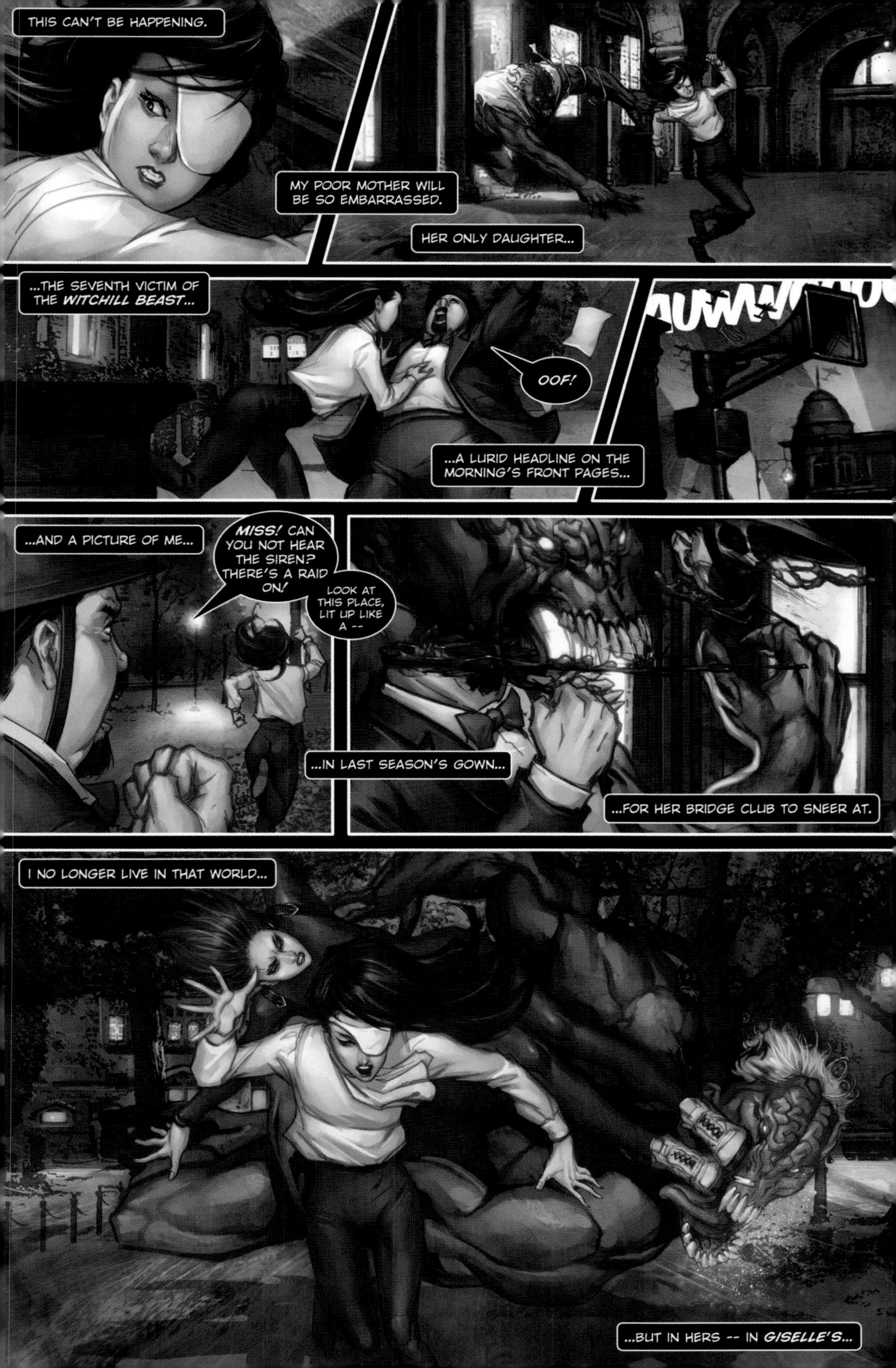
THIS CAN'T BE HAPPENING.
MY POOR MOTHER WILL BE SO EMBARRASSED.
HER ONLY DAUGHTER...
...THE SEVENTH VICTIM OF THE *WITCHILL BEAST*...
OOF!
...A LURID HEADLINE ON THE MORNING'S FRONT PAGES...
...AND A PICTURE OF ME...
MISS! CAN YOU NOT HEAR THE SIREN? THERE'S A RAID ON!
LOOK AT THIS PLACE, LIT UP LIKE A --
...IN LAST SEASON'S GOWN...
...FOR HER BRIDGE CLUB TO SNEER AT.
I NO LONGER LIVE IN THAT WORLD...
...BUT IN HERS -- IN *GISELLE'S*...

...WHERE MEN CAN BECOME MONSTERS...

DOCTOR -- CAMERON!

...WHERE BELIEF AND TRUTH ARE ONE AND THE SAME...

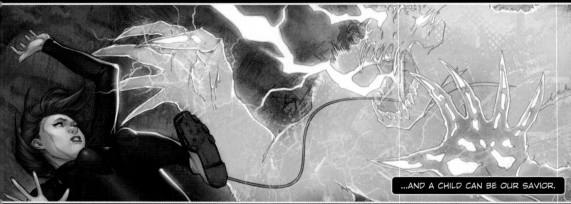

...AND A CHILD CAN BE OUR SAVIOR.

COME ON, TROUBLE -- UP!

I'M AFRAID TO ASK WHAT YOU'RE DOING HERE -- BUT I'M GLAD THAT YOU ARE.

DINA -- YOUR ARM....

... WHAT ABOUT MY ARM?

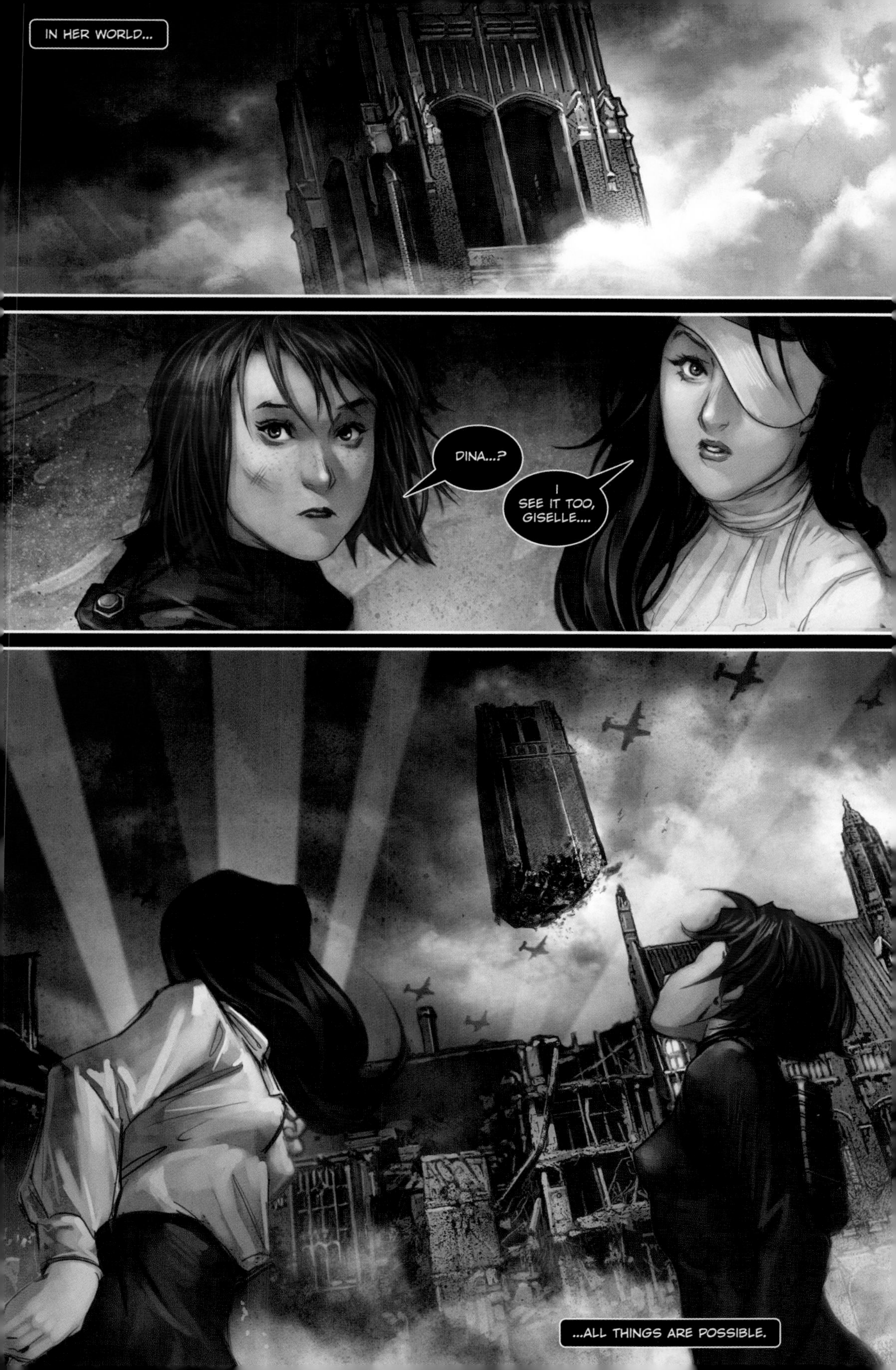
IN HER WORLD...
DINA...?
I SEE IT TOO, GISELLE....
...ALL THINGS ARE POSSIBLE.

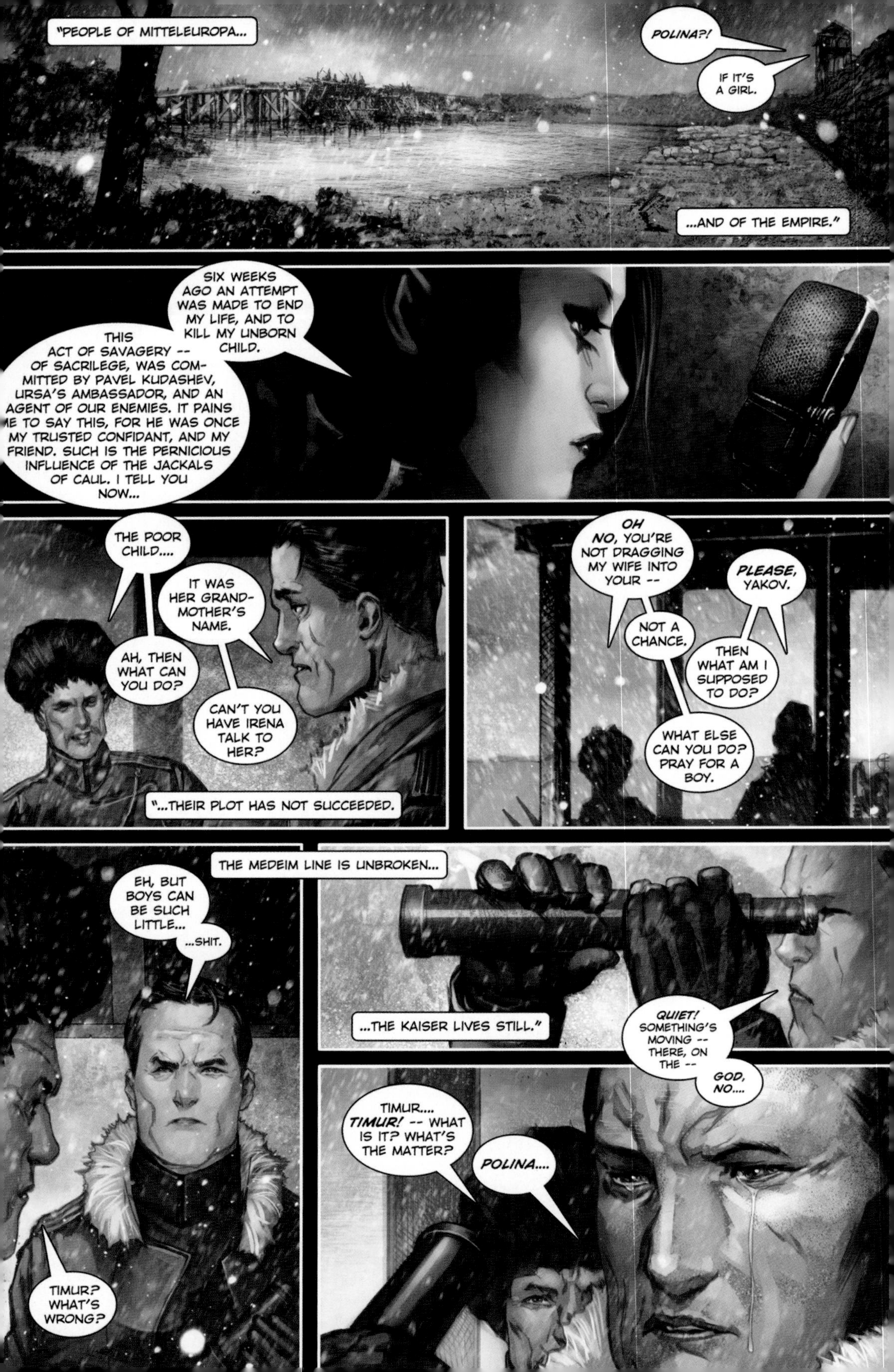
"PEOPLE OF MITTELEUROPA...
POLINA?!
IF IT'S A GIRL.
...AND OF THE EMPIRE."
SIX WEEKS AGO AN ATTEMPT WAS MADE TO END MY LIFE, AND TO KILL MY UNBORN CHILD.
THIS ACT OF SAVAGERY -- OF SACRILEGE, WAS COMMITTED BY PAVEL KUDASHEV, URSA'S AMBASSADOR, AND AN AGENT OF OUR ENEMIES. IT PAINS ME TO SAY THIS, FOR HE WAS ONCE MY TRUSTED CONFIDANT, AND MY FRIEND. SUCH IS THE PERNICIOUS INFLUENCE OF THE JACKALS OF CAUL. I TELL YOU NOW...
THE POOR CHILD....
IT WAS HER GRANDMOTHER'S NAME.
AH, THEN WHAT CAN YOU DO?
CAN'T YOU HAVE IRENA TALK TO HER?
"...THEIR PLOT HAS NOT SUCCEEDED.
OH NO, YOU'RE NOT DRAGGING MY WIFE INTO YOUR --
PLEASE, YAKOV.
NOT A CHANCE.
THEN WHAT AM I SUPPOSED TO DO?
WHAT ELSE CAN YOU DO? PRAY FOR A BOY.
THE MEDEIM LINE IS UNBROKEN...
EH, BUT BOYS CAN BE SUCH LITTLE...
...SHIT.
TIMUR? WHAT'S WRONG?
...THE KAISER LIVES STILL."
QUIET! SOMETHING'S MOVING -- THERE, ON THE --
GOD, NO....
TIMUR.... TIMUR! -- WHAT IS IT? WHAT'S THE MATTER?
POLINA....

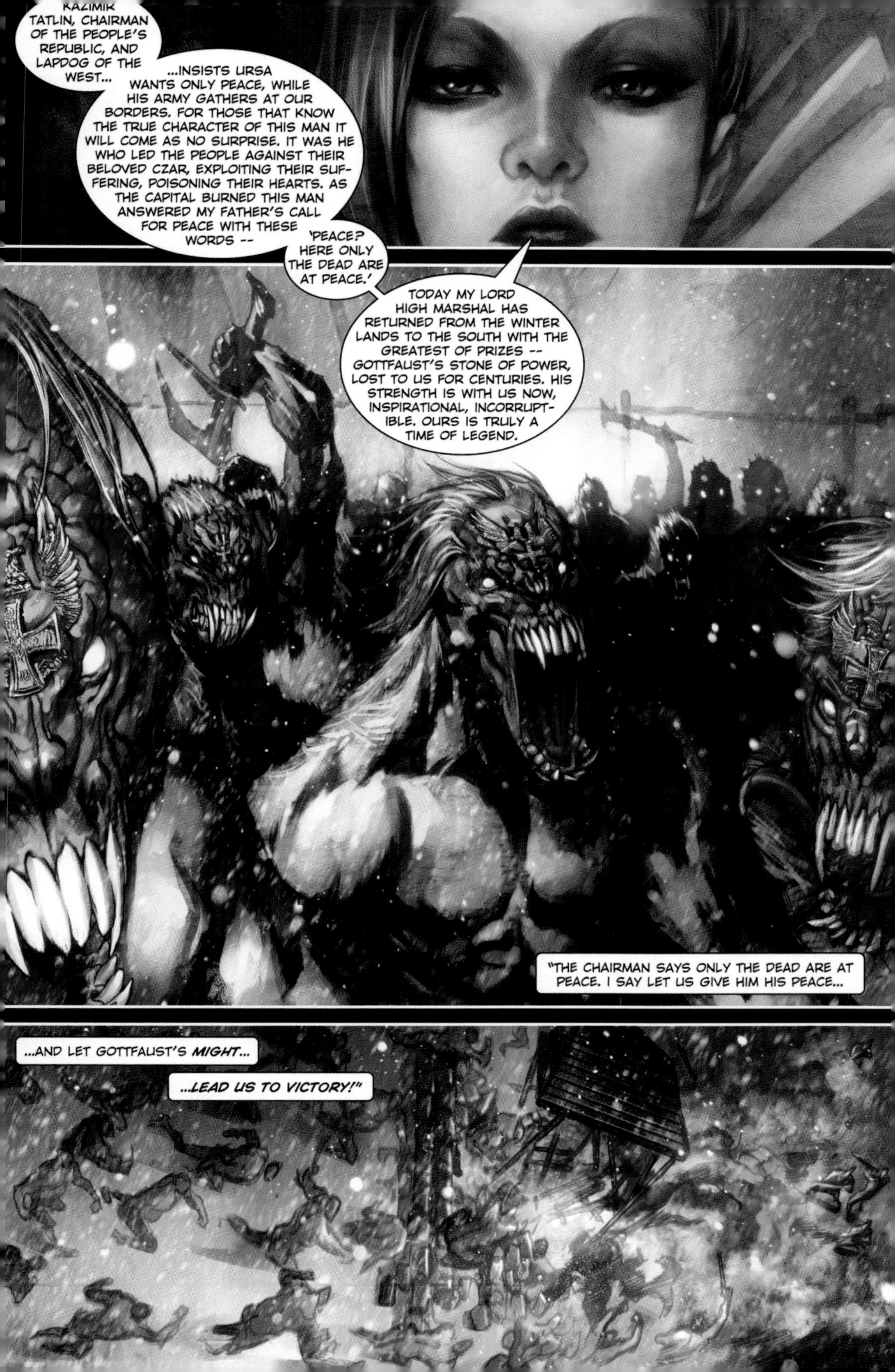
KAZIMIR TATLIN, CHAIRMAN OF THE PEOPLE'S REPUBLIC, AND LAPDOG OF THE WEST...
...INSISTS URSA WANTS ONLY PEACE, WHILE HIS ARMY GATHERS AT OUR BORDERS. FOR THOSE THAT KNOW THE TRUE CHARACTER OF THIS MAN IT WILL COME AS NO SURPRISE. IT WAS HE WHO LED THE PEOPLE AGAINST THEIR BELOVED CZAR, EXPLOITING THEIR SUFFERING, POISONING THEIR HEARTS. AS THE CAPITAL BURNED THIS MAN ANSWERED MY FATHER'S CALL FOR PEACE WITH THESE WORDS --
'PEACE? HERE ONLY THE DEAD ARE AT PEACE.'
TODAY MY LORD HIGH MARSHAL HAS RETURNED FROM THE WINTER LANDS TO THE SOUTH WITH THE GREATEST OF PRIZES -- GOTTFAUST'S STONE OF POWER, LOST TO US FOR CENTURIES. HIS STRENGTH IS WITH US NOW, INSPIRATIONAL, INCORRUPTIBLE. OURS IS TRULY A TIME OF LEGEND.
"THE CHAIRMAN SAYS ONLY THE DEAD ARE AT PEACE. I SAY LET US GIVE HIM HIS PEACE...
...AND LET GOTTFAUST'S *MIGHT*...
...LEAD US TO VICTORY!"

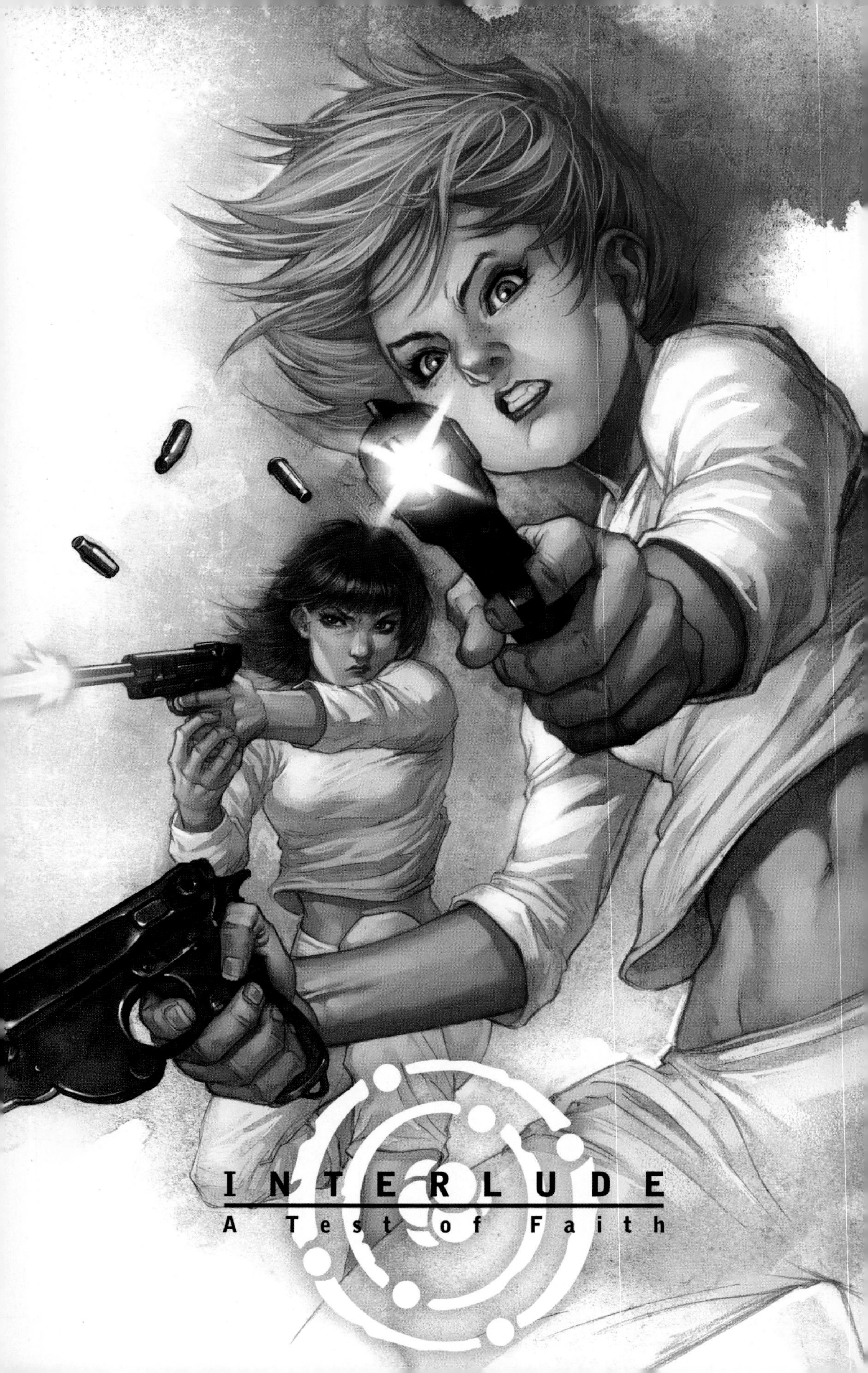

INTERLUDE
A Test of Faith

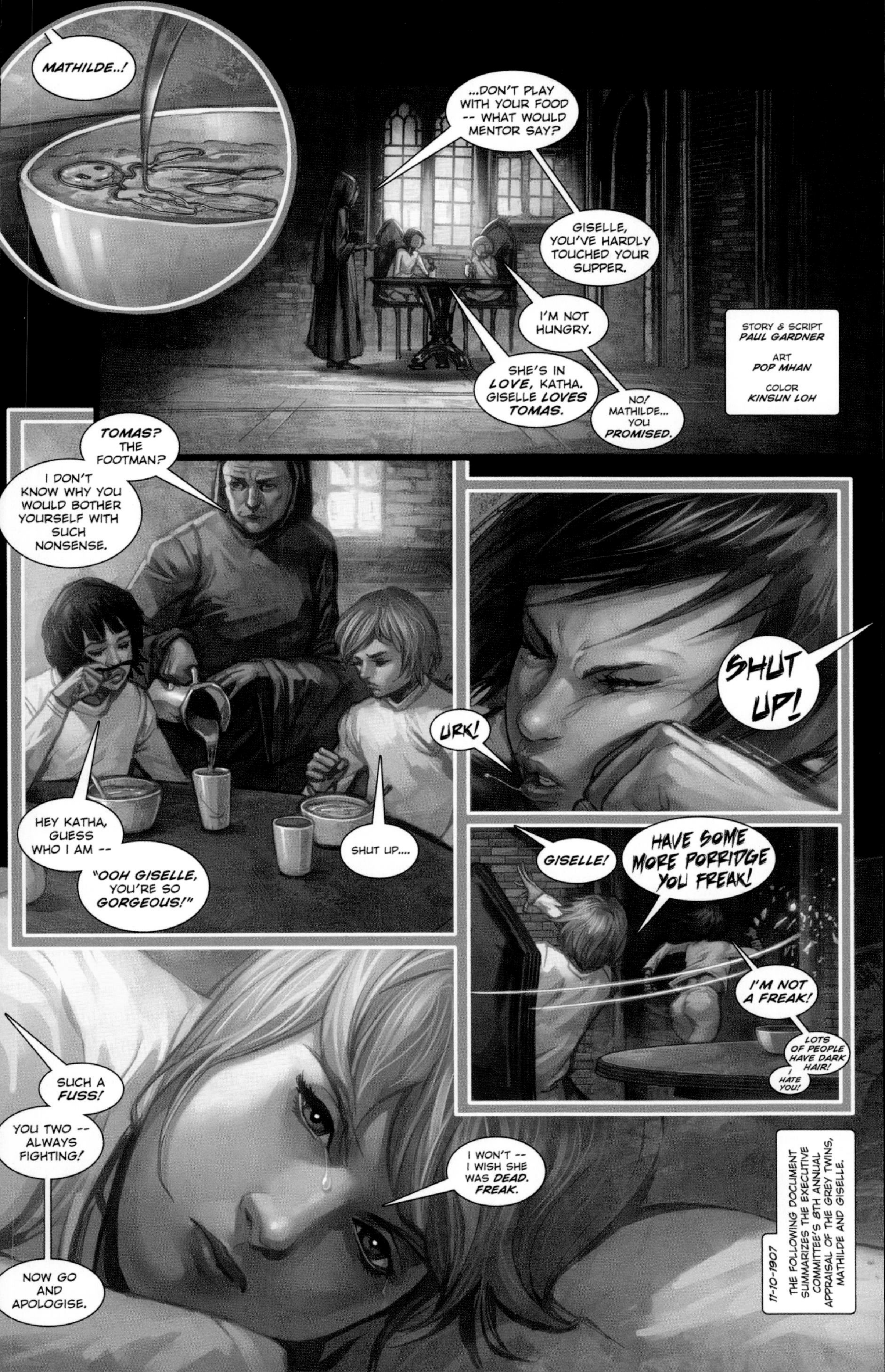
MATHILDE..!
...DON'T PLAY WITH YOUR FOOD -- WHAT WOULD MENTOR SAY?
GISELLE, YOU'VE HARDLY TOUCHED YOUR SUPPER.
I'M NOT HUNGRY.
SHE'S IN LOVE, KATHA. GISELLE LOVES TOMAS.
NO! MATHILDE... YOU PROMISED.
STORY & SCRIPT PAUL GARDNER
ART POP MHAN
COLOR KINSUN LOH
TOMAS? THE FOOTMAN?
I DON'T KNOW WHY YOU WOULD BOTHER YOURSELF WITH SUCH NONSENSE.
HEY KATHA, GUESS WHO I AM --
"OOH GISELLE, YOU'RE SO GORGEOUS!"
SHUT UP....
URK!
SHUT UP!
GISELLE!
HAVE SOME MORE PORRIDGE YOU FREAK!
I'M NOT A FREAK!
LOTS OF PEOPLE HAVE DARK HAIR!
I HATE YOU!
SUCH A FUSS!
YOU TWO -- ALWAYS FIGHTING!
NOW GO AND APOLOGISE.
I WON'T -- I WISH SHE WAS DEAD. FREAK.
11-10-1907
THE FOLLOWING DOCUMENT SUMMARIZES THE EXECUTIVE COMMITTEE'S 8TH ANNUAL APPRAISAL OF THE GREY TWINS, MATHILDE AND GISELLE.

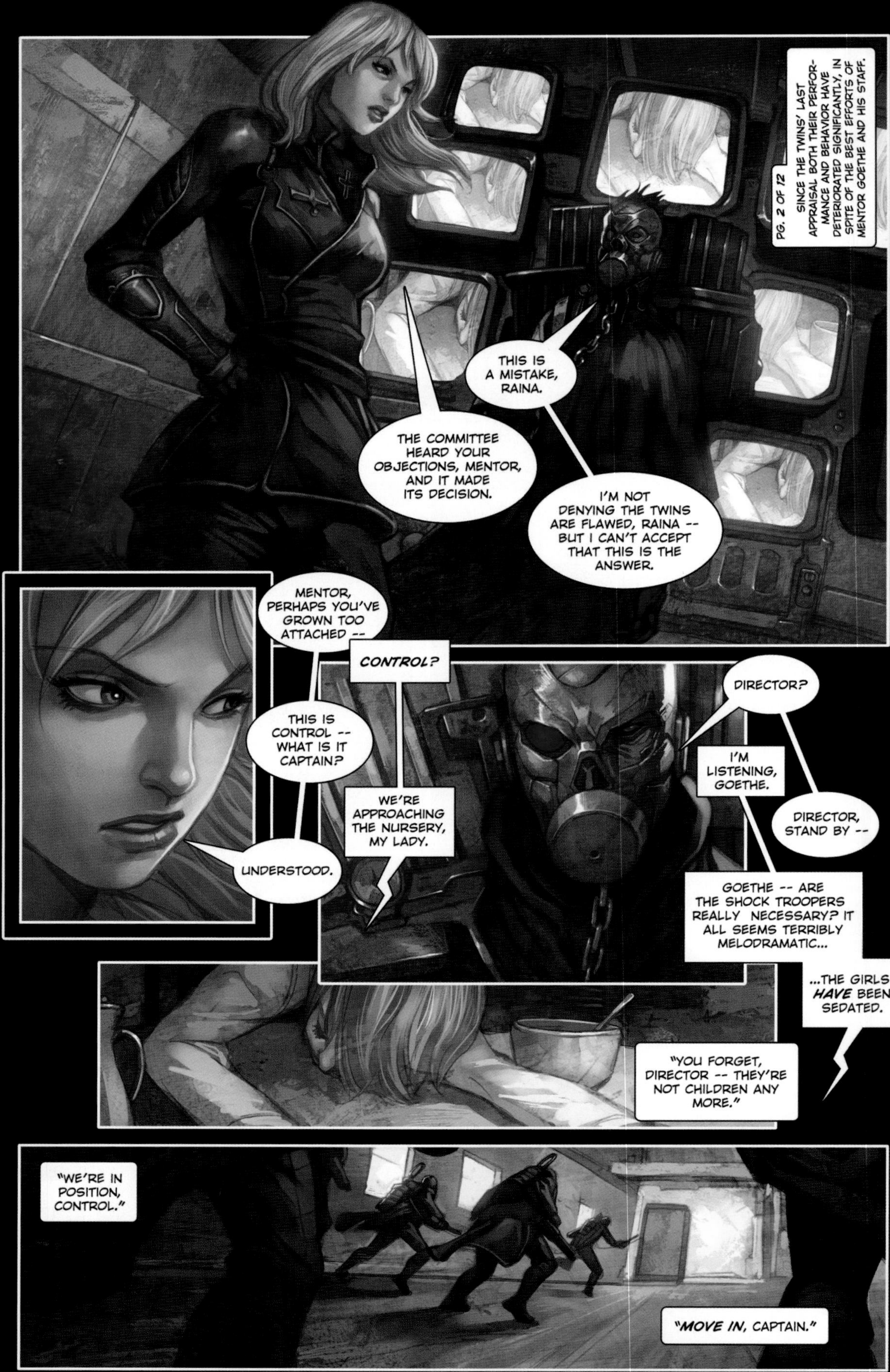
PG. 2 OF 12
SINCE THE TWINS' LAST APPRAISAL BOTH THEIR PERFORMANCE AND BEHAVIOR HAVE DETERIORATED SIGNIFICANTLY, IN SPITE OF THE BEST EFFORTS OF MENTOR GOETHE AND HIS STAFF.
THIS IS A MISTAKE, RAINA.
THE COMMITTEE HEARD YOUR OBJECTIONS, MENTOR, AND IT MADE ITS DECISION.
I'M NOT DENYING THE TWINS ARE FLAWED, RAINA -- BUT I CAN'T ACCEPT THAT THIS IS THE ANSWER.
MENTOR, PERHAPS YOU'VE GROWN TOO ATTACHED --
CONTROL?
THIS IS CONTROL -- WHAT IS IT CAPTAIN?
WE'RE APPROACHING THE NURSERY, MY LADY.
UNDERSTOOD.
DIRECTOR?
I'M LISTENING, GOETHE.
DIRECTOR, STAND BY --
GOETHE -- ARE THE SHOCK TROOPERS REALLY NECESSARY? IT ALL SEEMS TERRIBLY MELODRAMATIC...
...THE GIRLS *HAVE* BEEN SEDATED.
"YOU FORGET, DIRECTOR -- THEY'RE NOT CHILDREN ANY MORE."
"WE'RE IN POSITION, CONTROL."
"*MOVE IN*, CAPTAIN."

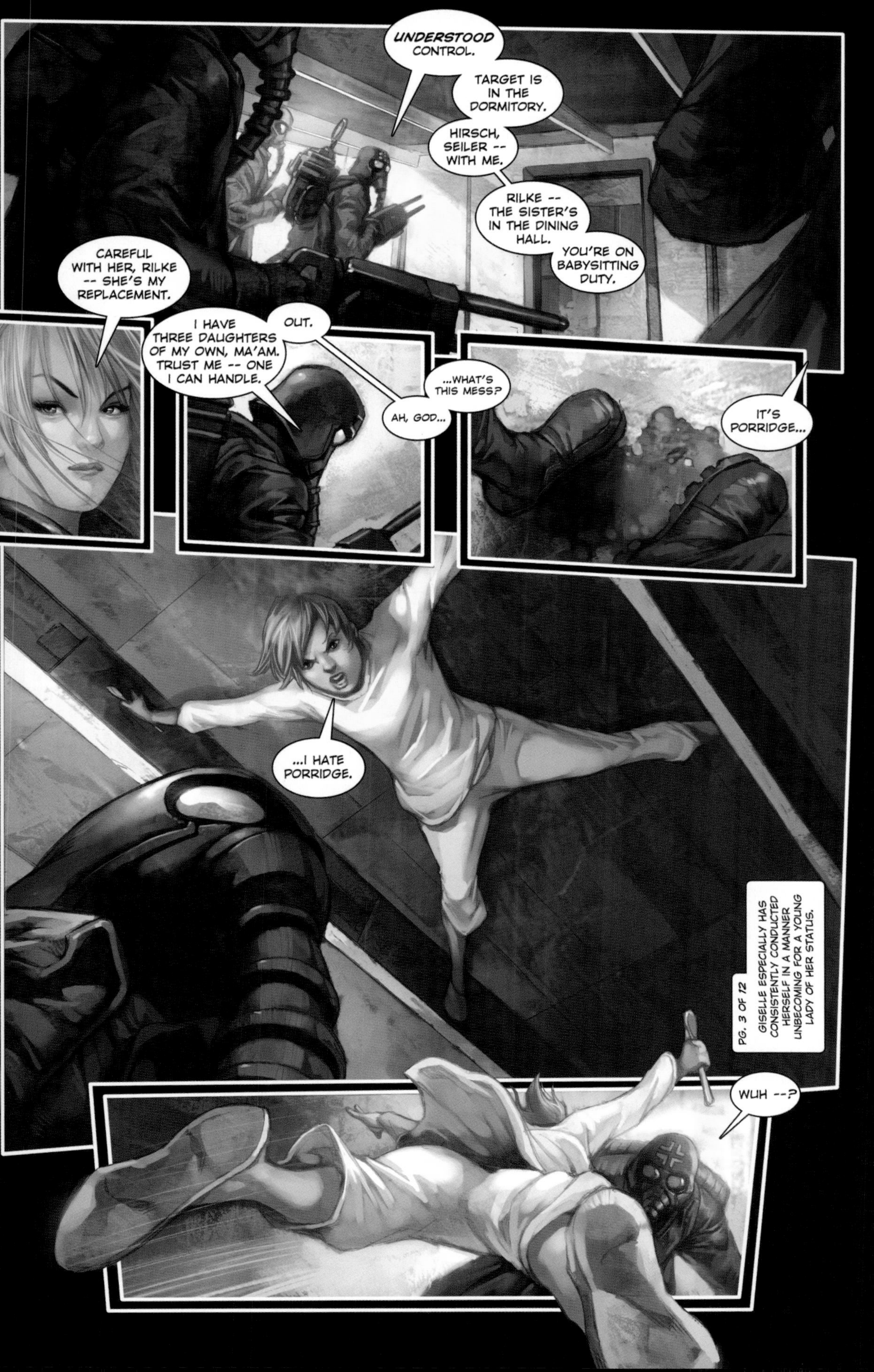
UNDERSTOOD CONTROL.
TARGET IS IN THE DORMITORY.
HIRSCH, SEILER -- WITH ME.
RILKE -- THE SISTER'S IN THE DINING HALL.
YOU'RE ON BABYSITTING DUTY.
CAREFUL WITH HER, RILKE -- SHE'S MY REPLACEMENT.
I HAVE THREE DAUGHTERS OF MY OWN, MA'AM. TRUST ME -- ONE I CAN HANDLE.
OUT.
AH, GOD...
...WHAT'S THIS MESS?
IT'S PORRIDGE...
...I HATE PORRIDGE.
PG. 3 OF 12
GISELLE ESPECIALLY HAS CONSISTENTLY CONDUCTED HERSELF IN A MANNER UNBECOMING FOR A YOUNG LADY OF HER STATUS.
WUH --?

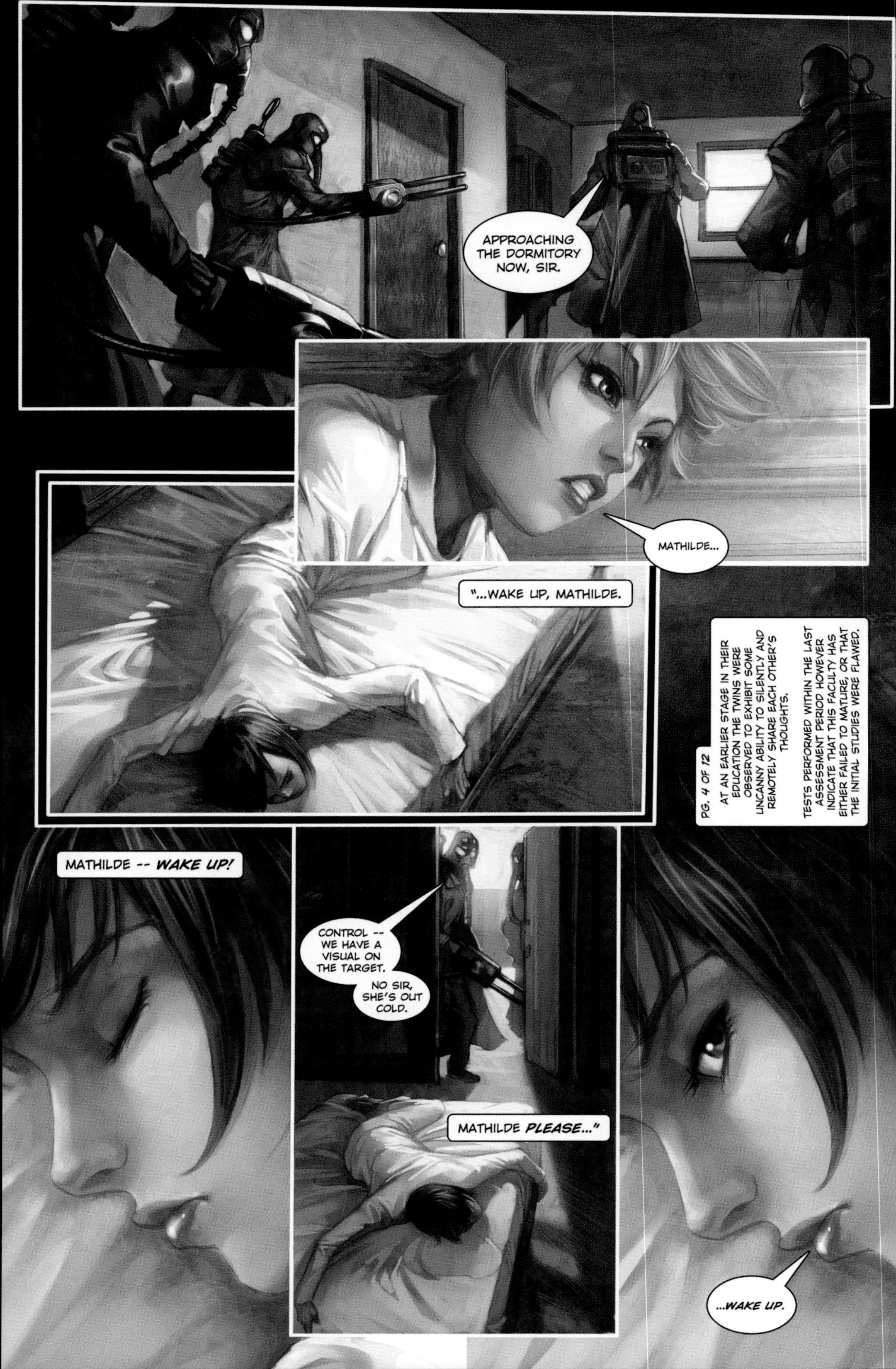
APPROACHING THE DORMITORY NOW, SIR.
MATHILDE...
"...WAKE UP, MATHILDE.
PG. 4 OF 12
AT AN EARLIER STAGE IN THEIR EDUCATION THE TWINS WERE OBSERVED TO EXHIBIT SOME UNCANNY ABILITY TO SILENTLY AND REMOTELY SHARE EACH OTHER'S THOUGHTS.
TESTS PERFORMED WITHIN THE LAST ASSESSMENT PERIOD HOWEVER INDICATE THAT THIS FACULTY HAS EITHER FAILED TO MATURE, OR THAT THE INITIAL STUDIES WERE FLAWED.
MATHILDE -- *WAKE UP!*
CONTROL -- WE HAVE A VISUAL ON THE TARGET.
NO SIR, SHE'S OUT COLD.
MATHILDE *PLEASE...*"
...WAKE UP.

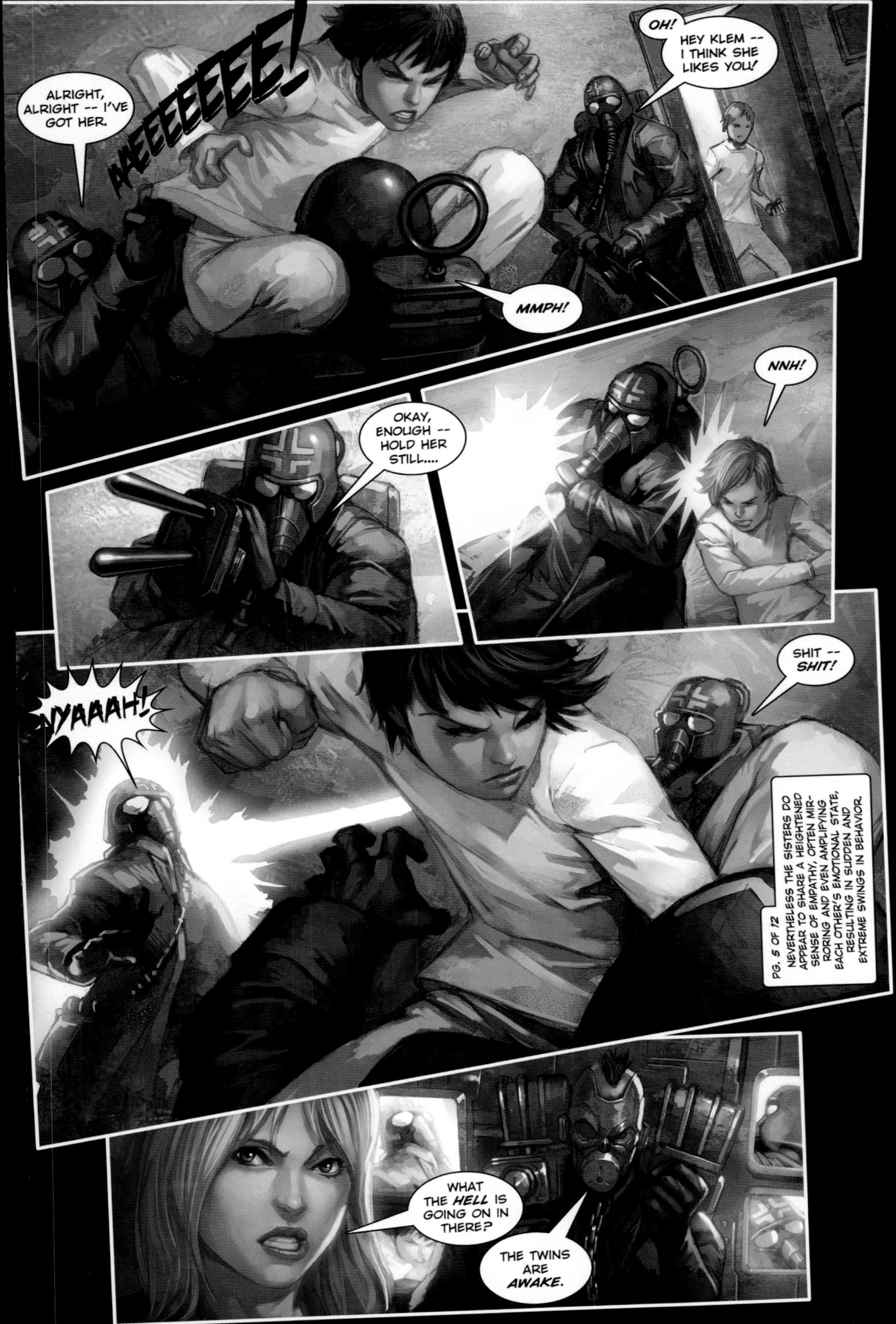
ALRIGHT, ALRIGHT -- I'VE GOT HER.
AAEEEEEEE!
OH!
HEY KLEM -- I THINK SHE LIKES YOU!
MMPH!
OKAY, ENOUGH -- HOLD HER STILL....
NNH!
NYAAAH!
SHIT -- SHIT!
PG. 5 OF 12
NEVERTHELESS THE SISTERS DO APPEAR TO SHARE A HEIGHTENED SENSE OF EMPATHY, OFTEN MIRRORING AND EVEN AMPLIFYING EACH OTHER'S EMOTIONAL STATE, RESULTING IN SUDDEN AND EXTREME SWINGS IN BEHAVIOR.
WHAT THE HELL IS GOING ON IN THERE?
THE TWINS ARE AWAKE.

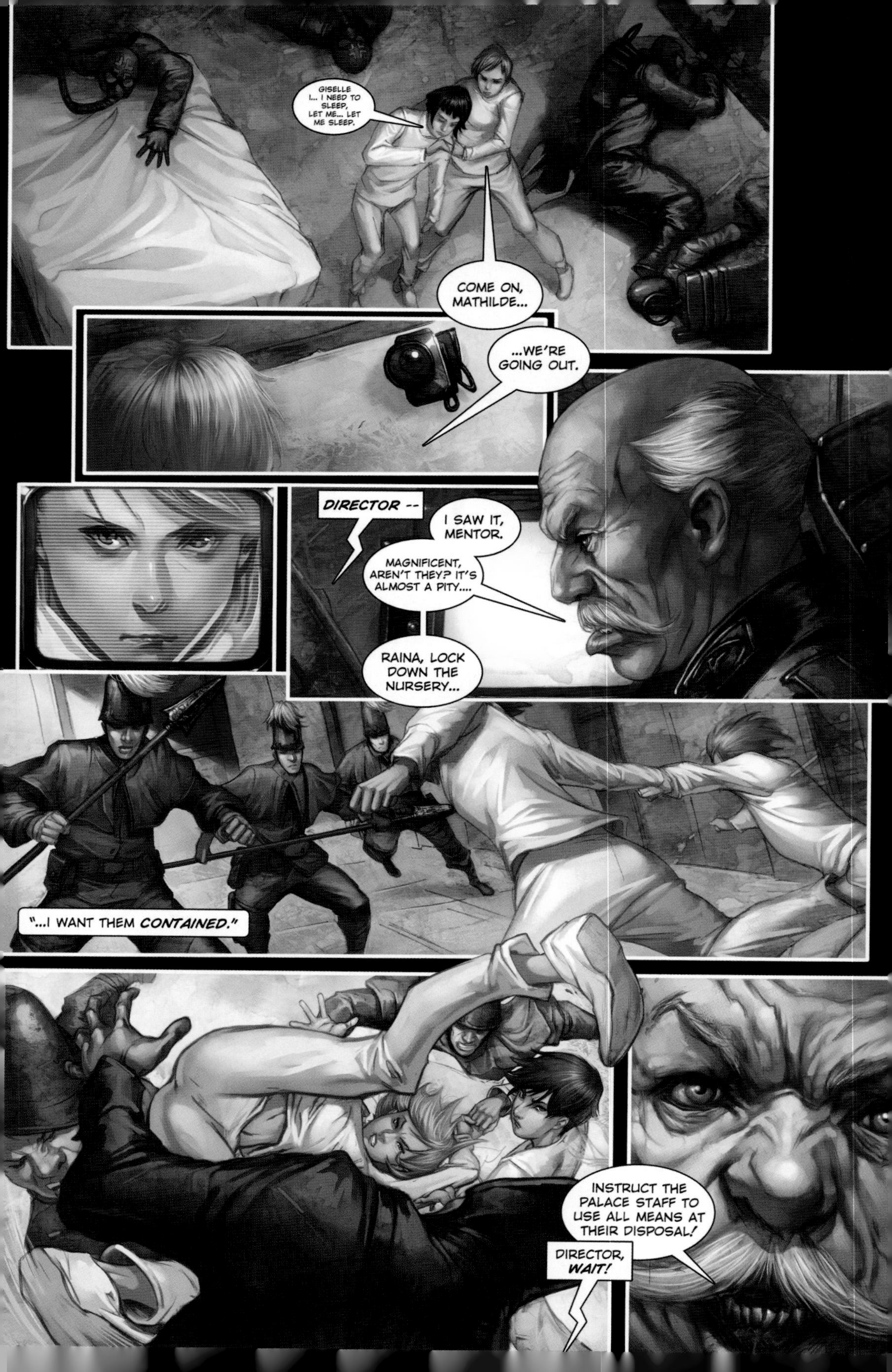
GISELLE I... I NEED TO SLEEP, LET ME... LET ME SLEEP.
COME ON, MATHILDE...
...WE'RE GOING OUT.
DIRECTOR --
I SAW IT, MENTOR.
MAGNIFICENT, AREN'T THEY? IT'S ALMOST A PITY....
RAINA, LOCK DOWN THE NURSERY...
"...I WANT THEM CONTAINED."
INSTRUCT THE PALACE STAFF TO USE ALL MEANS AT THEIR DISPOSAL!
DIRECTOR, WAIT!

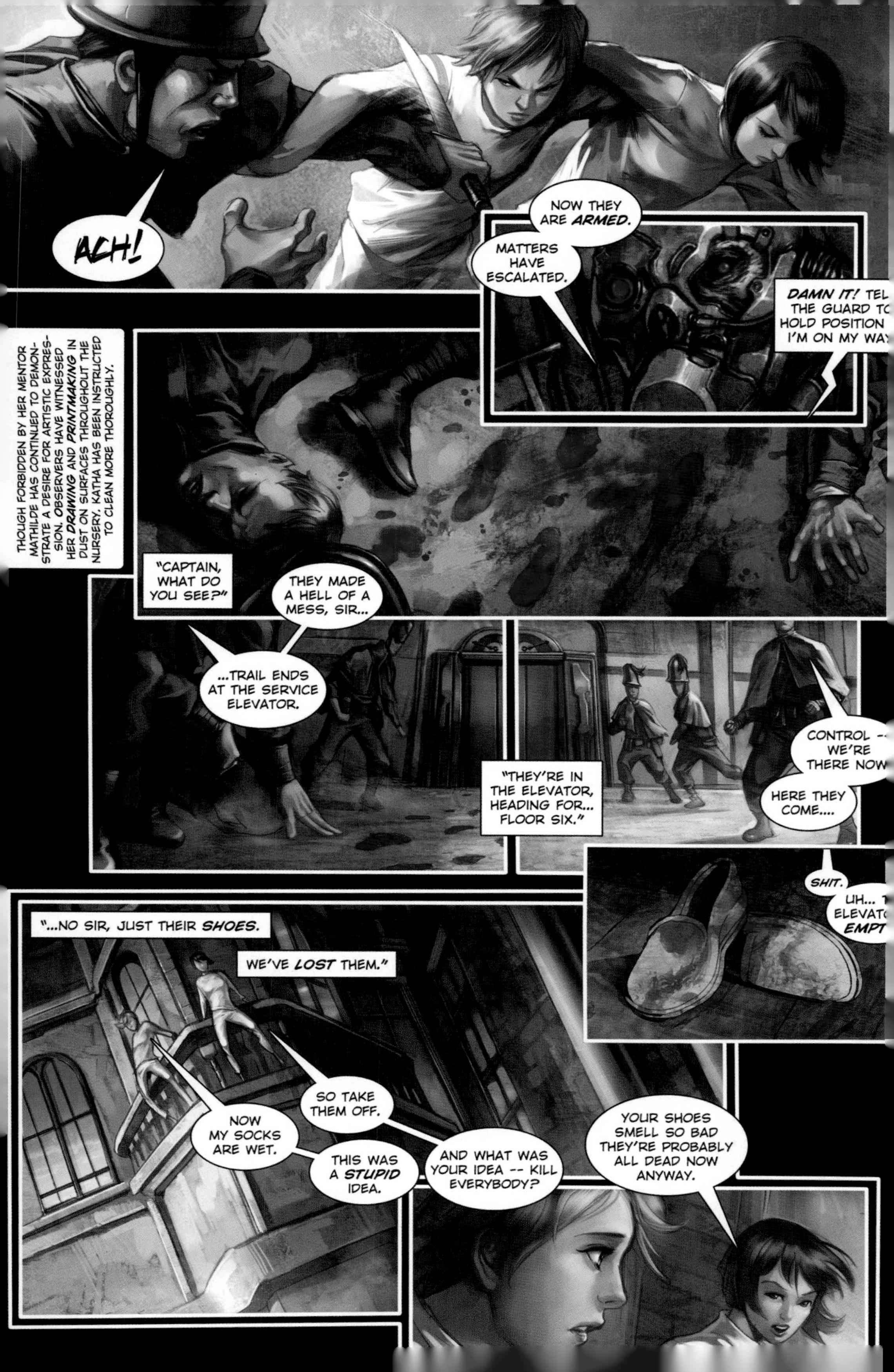
ACH!
NOW THEY ARE *ARMED.*
MATTERS HAVE ESCALATED.
DAMN IT! TEL THE GUARD TO HOLD POSITION I'M ON MY WA
THOUGH FORBIDDEN BY HER MENTOR MATHILDE HAS CONTINUED TO DEMONSTRATE A DESIRE FOR ARTISTIC EXPRESSION. OBSERVERS HAVE WITNESSED HER *DRAWING* AND *PRINTMAKING* IN DUST ON SURFACES THROUGHOUT THE NURSERY. KATHA HAS BEEN INSTRUCTED TO CLEAN MORE THOROUGHLY.
"CAPTAIN, WHAT DO YOU SEE?"
THEY MADE A HELL OF A MESS, SIR...
...TRAIL ENDS AT THE SERVICE ELEVATOR.
"THEY'RE IN THE ELEVATOR, HEADING FOR... FLOOR SIX."
CONTROL -- WE'RE THERE NOW
HERE THEY COME....
SHIT.
UH... T ELEVATO *EMPT*
"...NO SIR, JUST THEIR *SHOES.*
WE'VE *LOST* THEM."
NOW MY SOCKS ARE WET.
SO TAKE THEM OFF.
THIS WAS A *STUPID* IDEA.
AND WHAT WAS YOUR IDEA -- KILL EVERYBODY?
YOUR SHOES SMELL SO BAD THEY'RE PROBABLY ALL DEAD NOW ANYWAY.

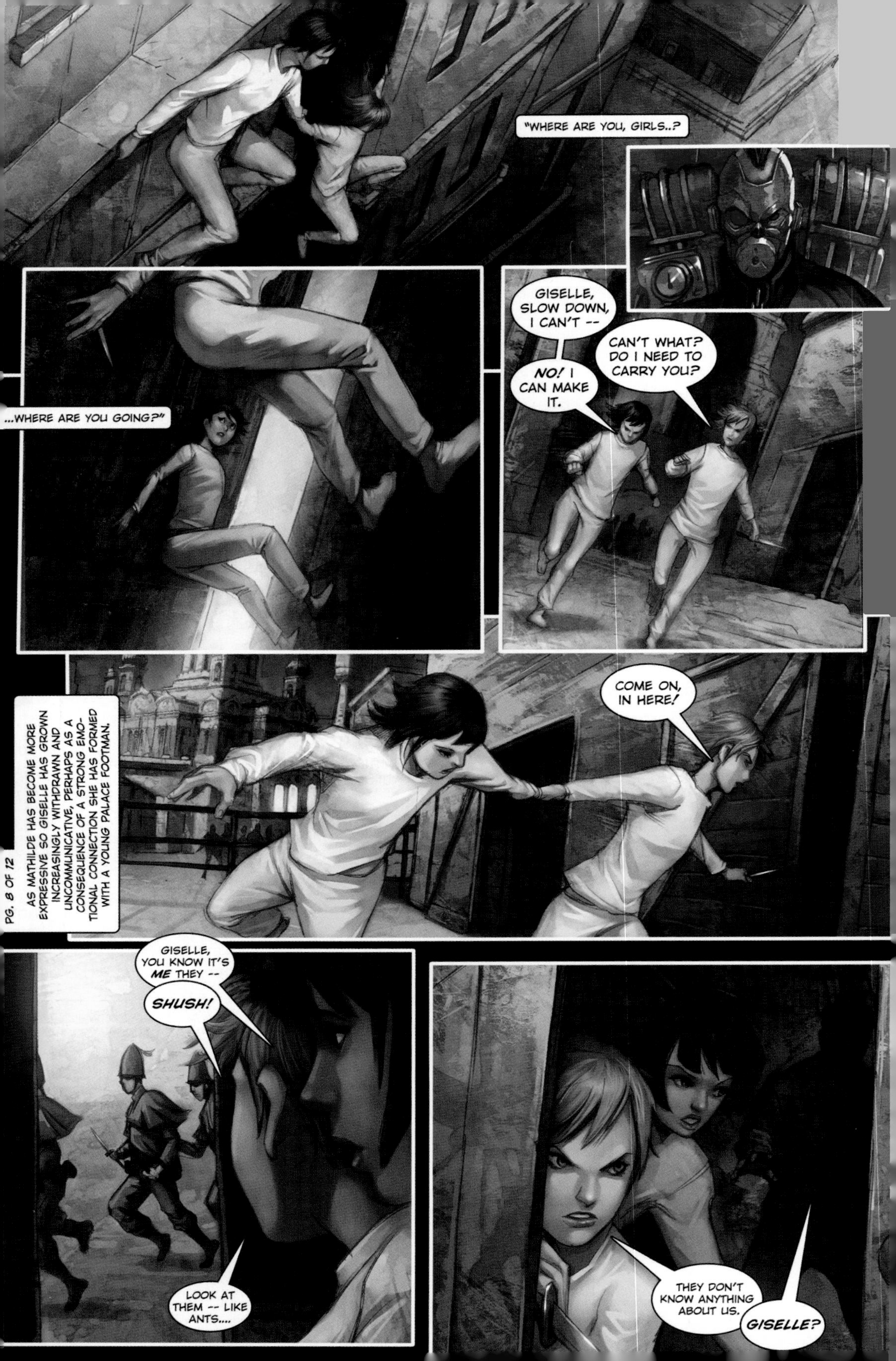
"WHERE ARE YOU, GIRLS..?
...WHERE ARE YOU GOING?"
GISELLE, SLOW DOWN, I CAN'T --
CAN'T WHAT? DO I NEED TO CARRY YOU?
NO! I CAN MAKE IT.
PG. 8 OF 12
AS MATHILDE HAS BECOME MORE EXPRESSIVE SO GISELLE HAS GROWN INCREASINGLY WITHDRAWN AND UNCOMMUNICATIVE, PERHAPS AS A CONSEQUENCE OF A STRONG EMOTIONAL CONNECTION SHE HAS FORMED WITH A YOUNG PALACE FOOTMAN.
COME ON, IN HERE!
GISELLE, YOU KNOW IT'S ME THEY --
SHUSH!
LOOK AT THEM -- LIKE ANTS....
THEY DON'T KNOW ANYTHING ABOUT US.
GISELLE?

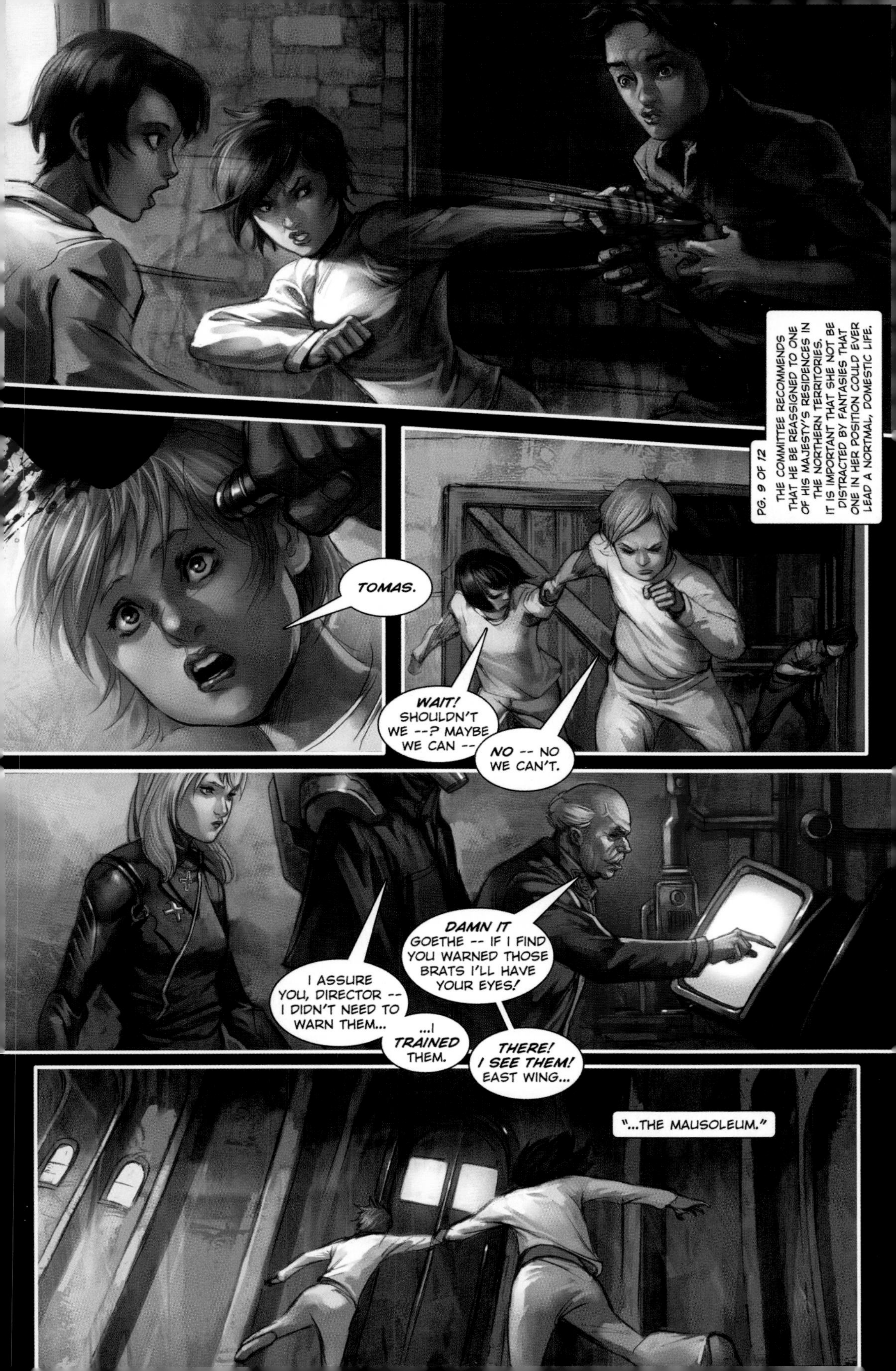
PG. 9 OF 12
THE COMMITTEE RECOMMENDS THAT HE BE REASSIGNED TO ONE OF HIS MAJESTY'S RESIDENCES IN THE NORTHERN TERRITORIES. IT IS IMPORTANT THAT SHE NOT BE DISTRACTED BY FANTASIES THAT ONE IN HER POSITION COULD EVER LEAD A NORMAL, DOMESTIC LIFE.
TOMAS.
WAIT! SHOULDN'T WE --? MAYBE WE CAN --
NO -- NO WE CAN'T.
I ASSURE YOU, DIRECTOR -- I DIDN'T NEED TO WARN THEM...
DAMN IT GOETHE -- IF I FIND YOU WARNED THOSE BRATS I'LL HAVE YOUR EYES!
...I TRAINED THEM.
THERE! I SEE THEM! EAST WING...
"...THE MAUSOLEUM."

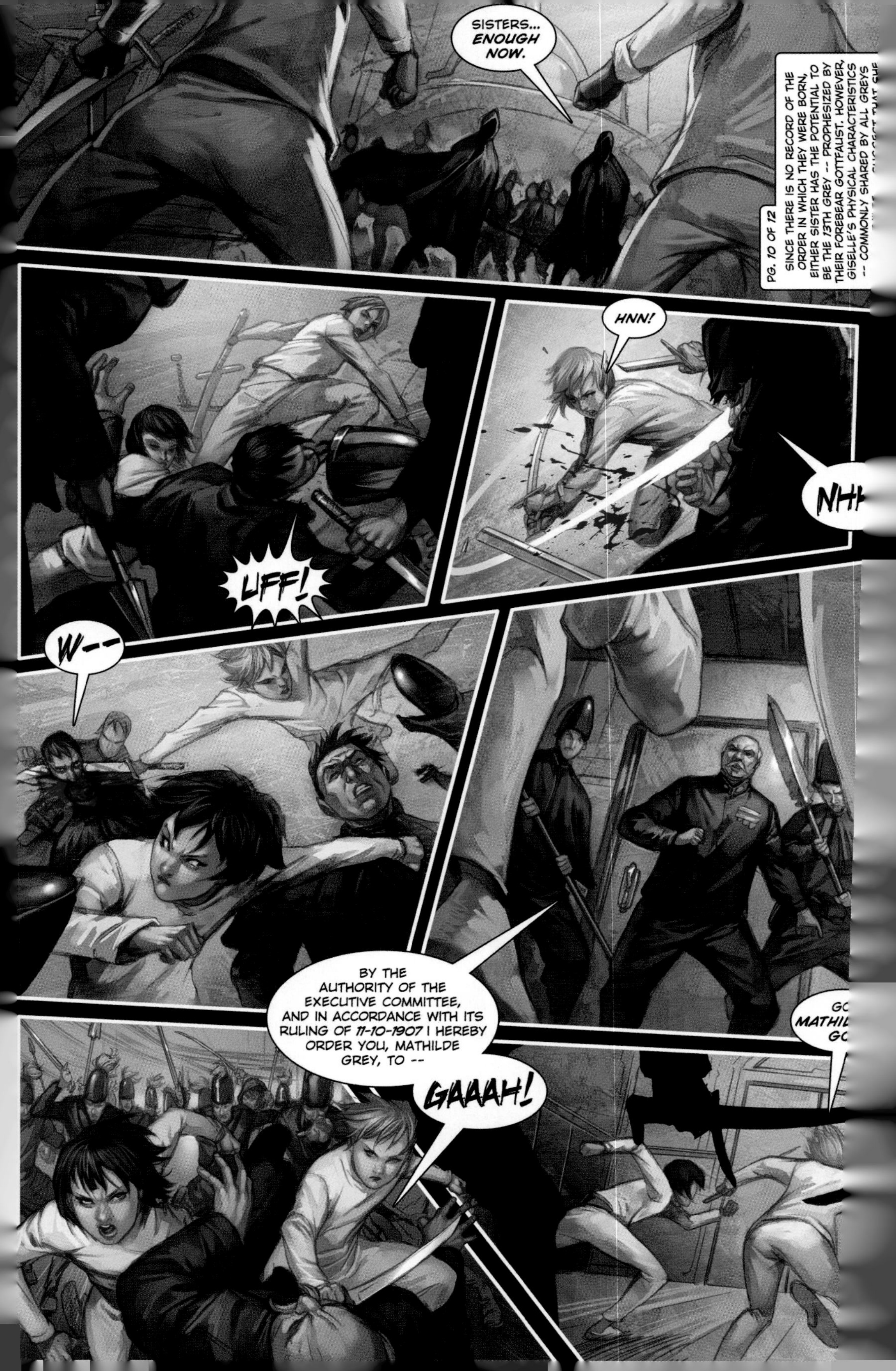
SISTERS... *ENOUGH NOW.*
PG. 10 OF 12
SINCE THERE IS NO RECORD OF THE ORDER IN WHICH THEY WERE BORN, EITHER SISTER HAS THE POTENTIAL TO BE THE *13TH GREY* -- PROPHESIZED BY THEIR FOREBEAR GOTTFAUST. HOWEVER, GISELLE'S PHYSICAL CHARACTERISTICS -- COMMONLY SHARED BY ALL GREYS
UFF!
HNN!
NH
W--
BY THE AUTHORITY OF THE EXECUTIVE COMMITTEE, AND IN ACCORDANCE WITH ITS RULING OF *11-10-1907* I HEREBY ORDER YOU, MATHILDE GREY, TO --
GAAAH!

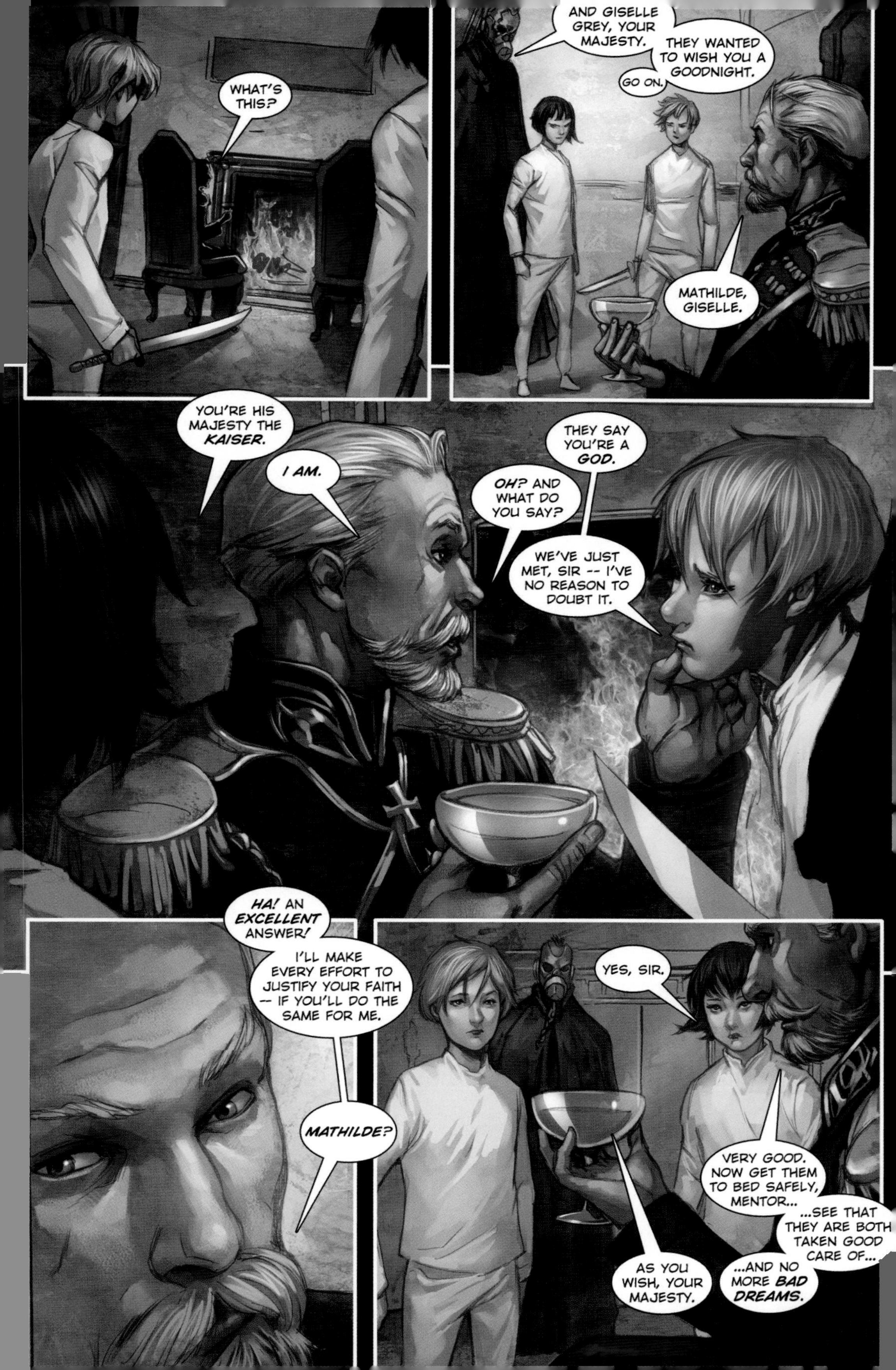
WHAT'S THIS?
AND GISELLE GREY, YOUR MAJESTY.
THEY WANTED TO WISH YOU A GOODNIGHT.
GO ON.
MATHILDE, GISELLE.
YOU'RE HIS MAJESTY THE *KAISER*.
I AM.
THEY SAY YOU'RE A *GOD*.
OH? AND WHAT DO YOU SAY?
WE'VE JUST MET, SIR -- I'VE NO REASON TO DOUBT IT.
HA! AN *EXCELLENT* ANSWER*!*
I'LL MAKE EVERY EFFORT TO JUSTIFY YOUR FAITH -- IF YOU'LL DO THE SAME FOR ME.
MATHILDE?
YES, SIR.
VERY GOOD. NOW GET THEM TO BED SAFELY, MENTOR...
...SEE THAT THEY ARE BOTH TAKEN GOOD CARE OF...
...AND NO MORE *BAD DREAMS*.
AS YOU WISH, YOUR MAJESTY.

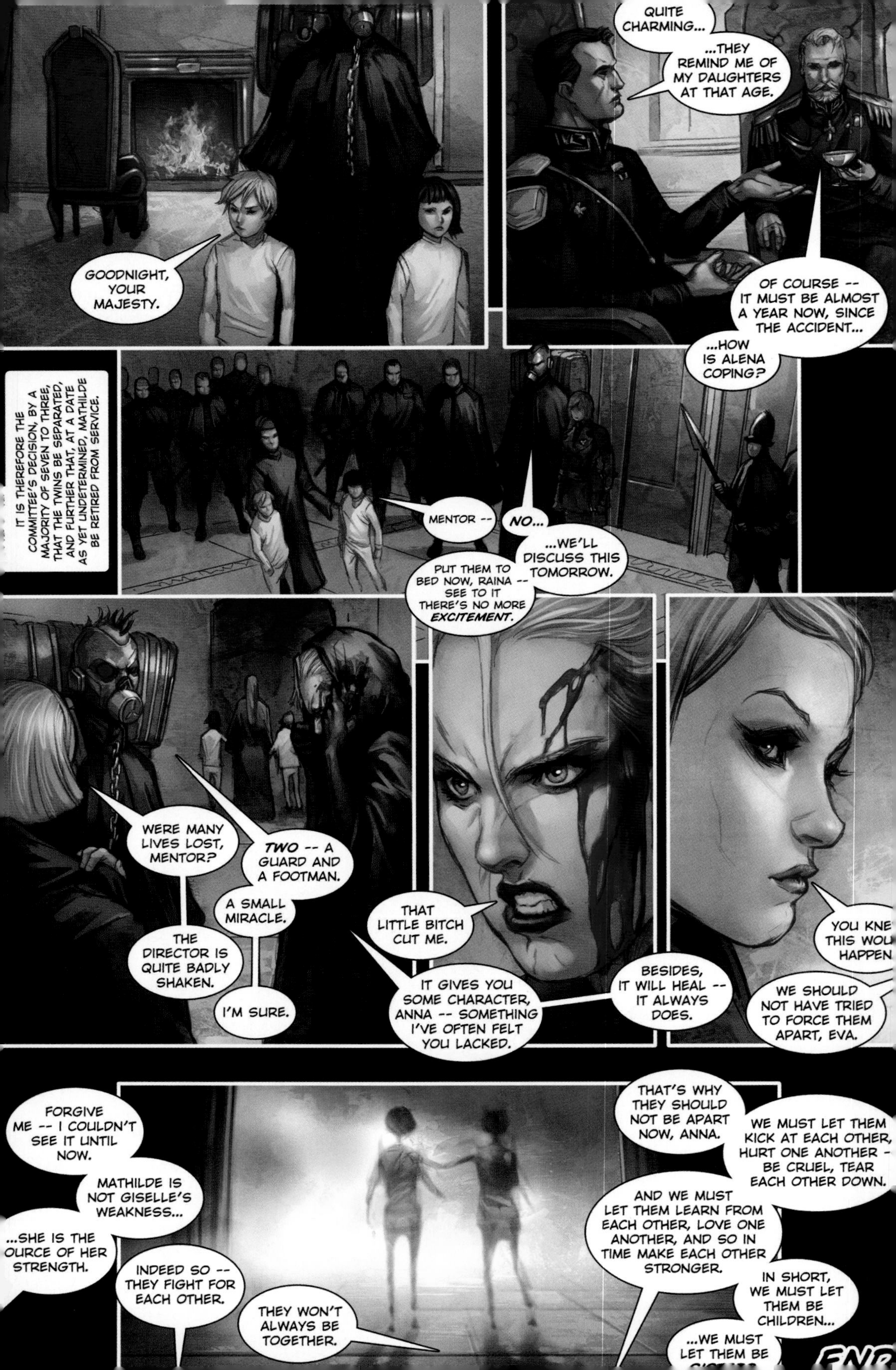
GOODNIGHT, YOUR MAJESTY.
QUITE CHARMING...
...THEY REMIND ME OF MY DAUGHTERS AT THAT AGE.
OF COURSE -- IT MUST BE ALMOST A YEAR NOW, SINCE THE ACCIDENT...
...HOW IS ALENA COPING?
IT IS THEREFORE THE COMMITTEE'S DECISION, BY A MAJORITY OF SEVEN TO THREE, THAT THE TWINS BE SEPARATED, AND FURTHER THAT, AT A DATE AS YET UNDETERMINED, MATHILDE BE RETIRED FROM SERVICE.
MENTOR --
NO...
...WE'LL DISCUSS THIS TOMORROW.
PUT THEM TO BED NOW, RAINA -- SEE TO IT THERE'S NO MORE *EXCITEMENT*.
WERE MANY LIVES LOST, MENTOR?
TWO -- A GUARD AND A FOOTMAN.
A SMALL MIRACLE.
THE DIRECTOR IS QUITE BADLY SHAKEN.
I'M SURE.
THAT LITTLE BITCH CUT ME.
IT GIVES YOU SOME CHARACTER, ANNA -- SOMETHING I'VE OFTEN FELT YOU LACKED.
BESIDES, IT WILL HEAL -- IT ALWAYS DOES.
YOU KNE THIS WOU HAPPEN
WE SHOULD NOT HAVE TRIED TO FORCE THEM APART, EVA.
FORGIVE ME -- I COULDN'T SEE IT UNTIL NOW.
MATHILDE IS NOT GISELLE'S WEAKNESS...
...SHE IS THE OURCE OF HER STRENGTH.
INDEED SO -- THEY FIGHT FOR EACH OTHER.
THEY WON'T ALWAYS BE TOGETHER.
THAT'S WHY THEY SHOULD NOT BE APART NOW, ANNA.
WE MUST LET THEM KICK AT EACH OTHER, HURT ONE ANOTHER - BE CRUEL, TEAR EACH OTHER DOWN.
AND WE MUST LET THEM LEARN FROM EACH OTHER, LOVE ONE ANOTHER, AND SO IN TIME MAKE EACH OTHER STRONGER.
IN SHORT, WE MUST LET THEM BE CHILDREN...
...WE MUST LET THEM BE

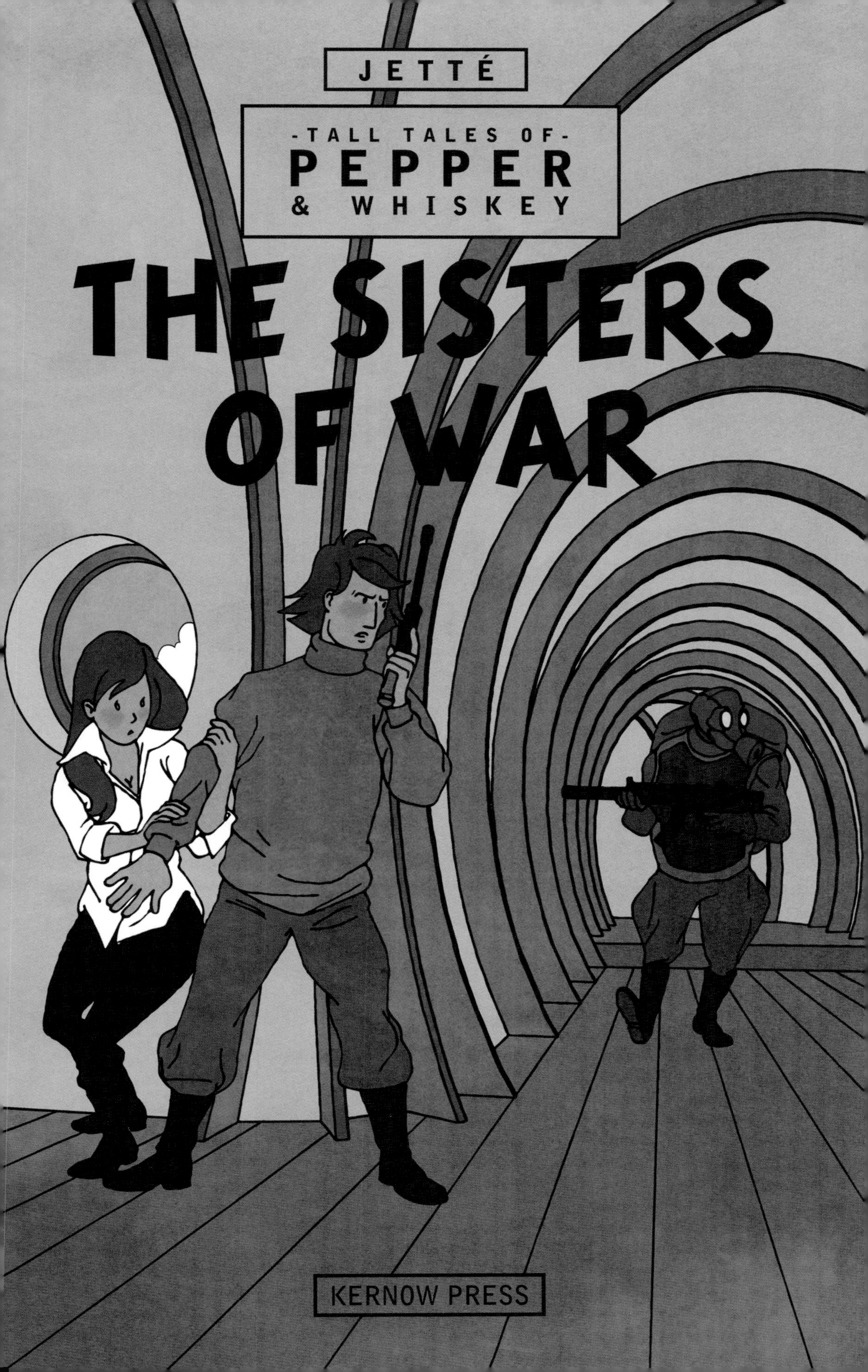
JETTÉ
-TALL TALES OF-
PEPPER
& WHISKEY
THE SISTERS
OF WAR
KERNOW PRESS

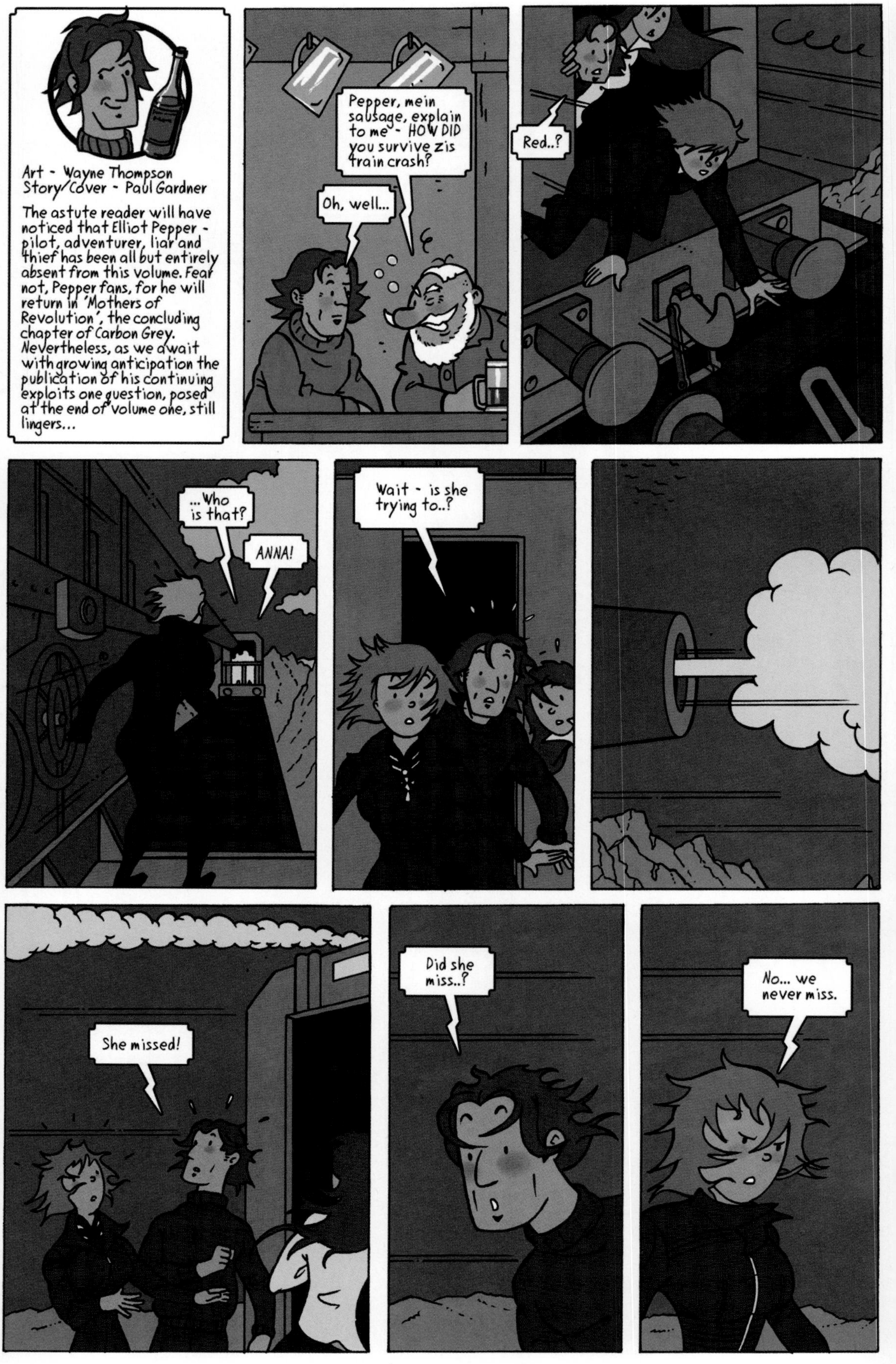
Art - Wayne Thompson
Story/Cover - Paul Gardner
The astute reader will have noticed that Elliot Pepper - pilot, adventurer, liar and thief has been all but entirely absent from this volume. Fear not, Pepper fans, for he will return in 'Mothers of Revolution', the concluding chapter of Carbon Grey. Nevertheless, as we await with growing anticipation the publication of his continuing exploits one question, posed at the end of volume one, still lingers...
Pepper, mein sausage, explain to me - HOW DID you survive zis train crash?
Oh, well...
Red..?
...Who is that?
ANNA!
Wait - is she trying to..?
She missed!
Did she miss..?
No... we never miss.

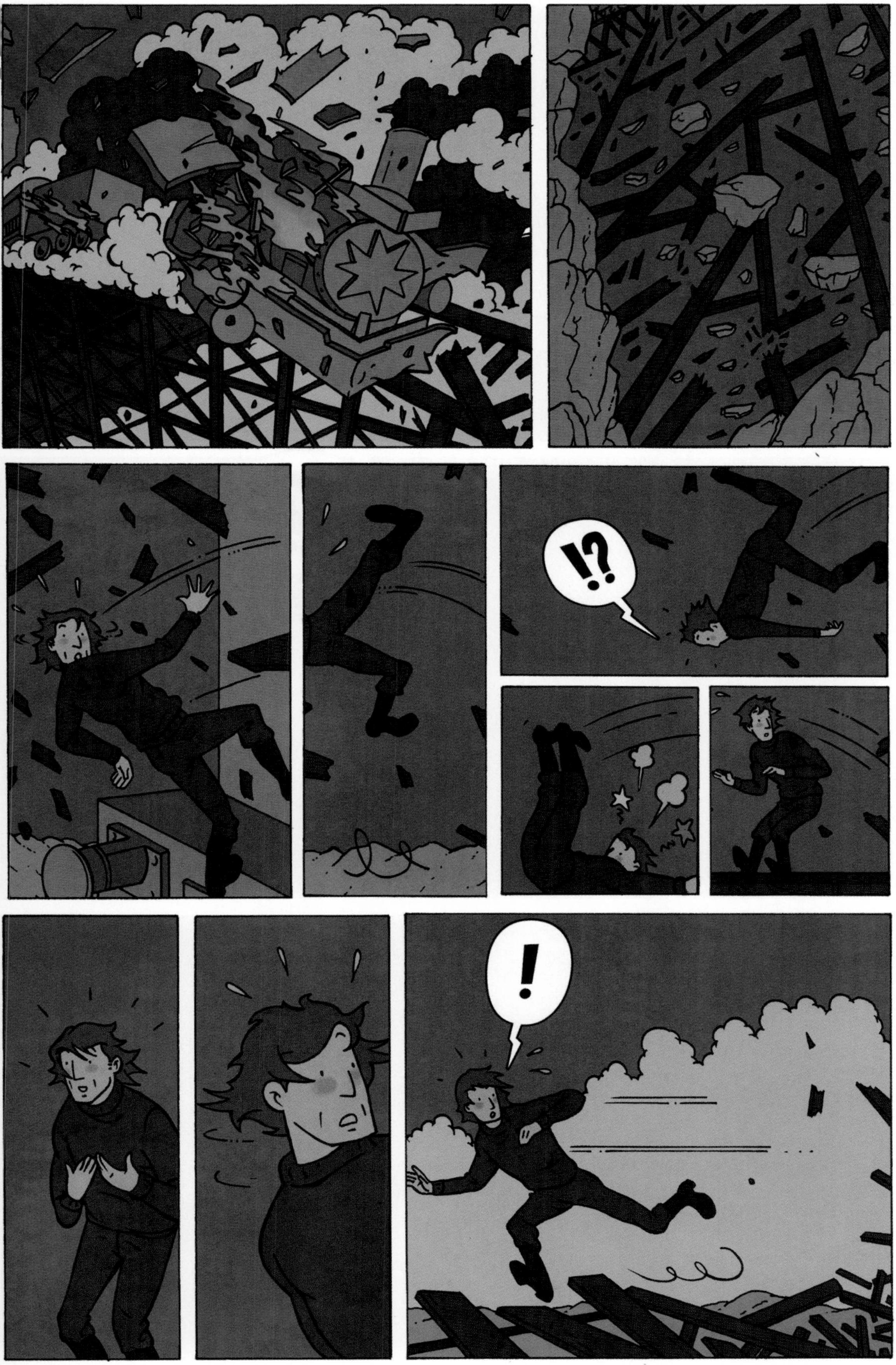

!?
!

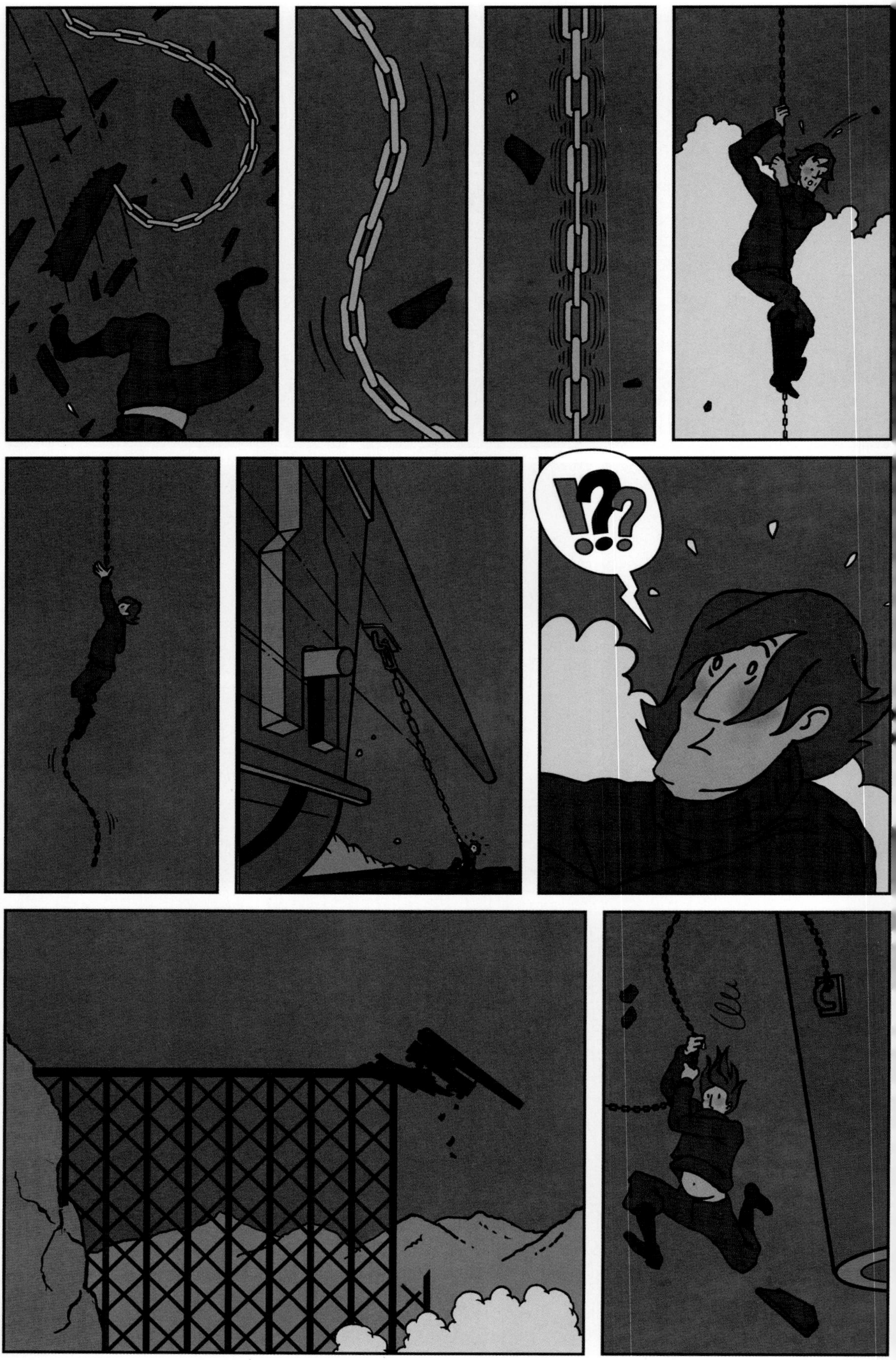
!??

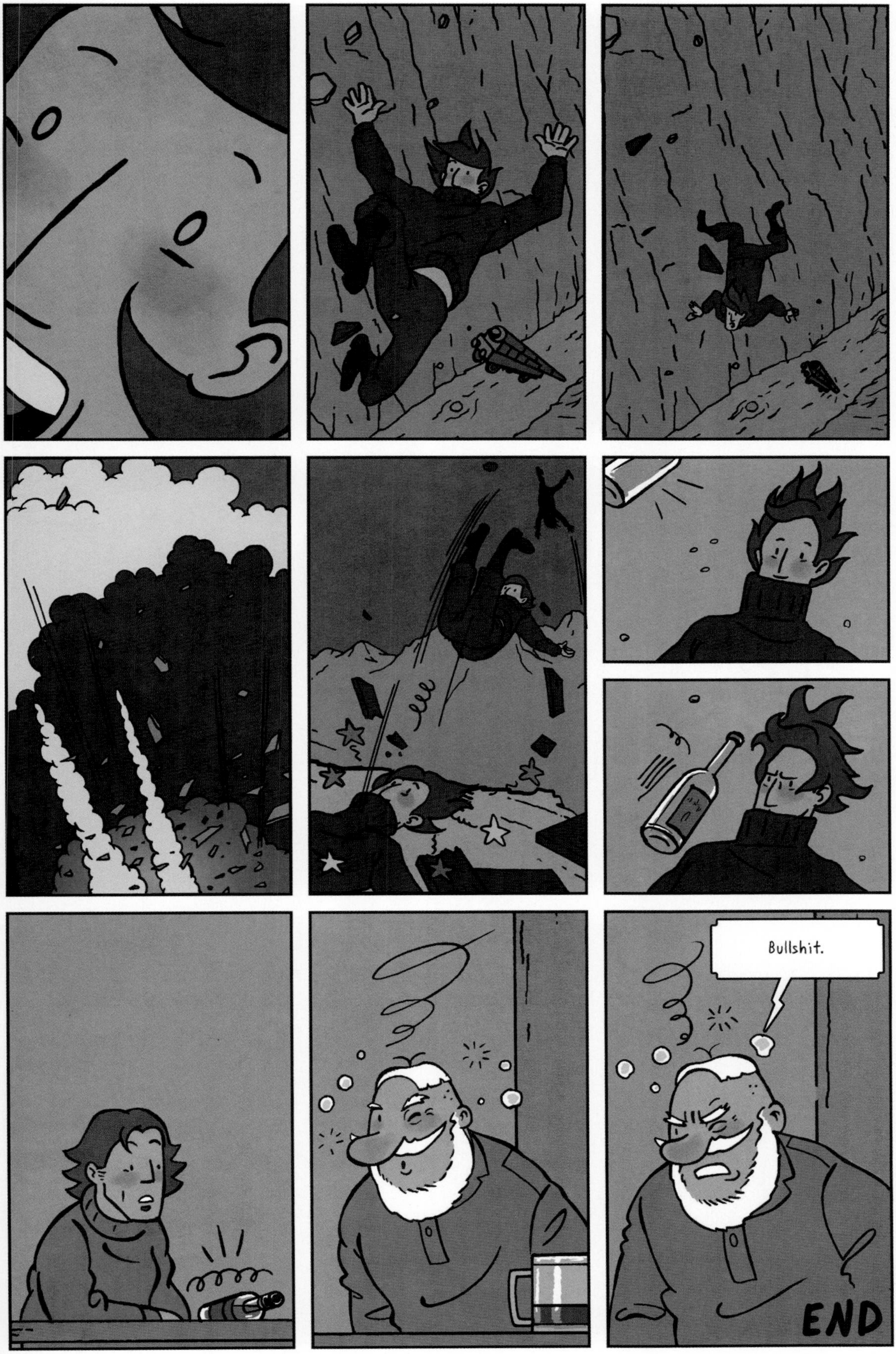
Bullshit.
END

VII

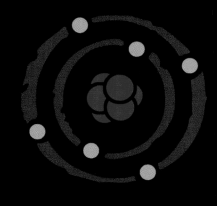

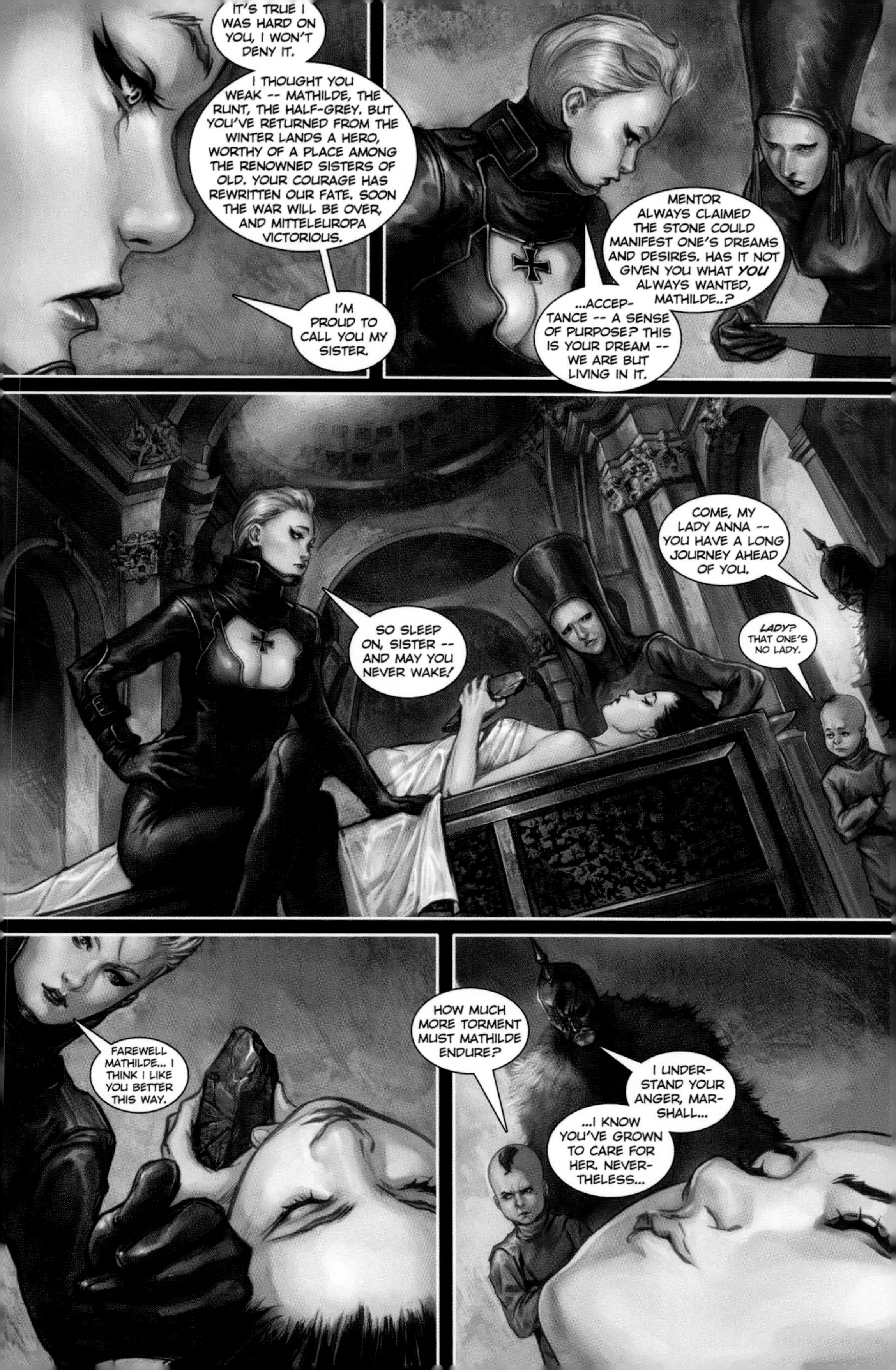
IT'S TRUE I WAS HARD ON YOU, I WON'T DENY IT.
I THOUGHT YOU WEAK -- MATHILDE, THE RUNT, THE HALF-GREY. BUT YOU'VE RETURNED FROM THE WINTER LANDS A HERO, WORTHY OF A PLACE AMONG THE RENOWNED SISTERS OF OLD. YOUR COURAGE HAS REWRITTEN OUR FATE. SOON THE WAR WILL BE OVER, AND MITTELEUROPA VICTORIOUS.
I'M PROUD TO CALL YOU MY SISTER.
MENTOR ALWAYS CLAIMED THE STONE COULD MANIFEST ONE'S DREAMS AND DESIRES. HAS IT NOT GIVEN YOU WHAT *YOU* ALWAYS WANTED, MATHILDE..?
...ACCEPTANCE -- A SENSE OF PURPOSE? THIS IS YOUR DREAM -- WE ARE BUT LIVING IN IT.
SO SLEEP ON, SISTER -- AND MAY YOU NEVER WAKE!
COME, MY LADY ANNA -- YOU HAVE A LONG JOURNEY AHEAD OF YOU.
LADY? THAT ONE'S NO LADY.
FAREWELL MATHILDE... I THINK I LIKE YOU BETTER THIS WAY.
HOW MUCH MORE TORMENT MUST MATHILDE ENDURE?
I UNDERSTAND YOUR ANGER, MARSHALL...
...I KNOW YOU'VE GROWN TO CARE FOR HER. NEVERTHELESS...

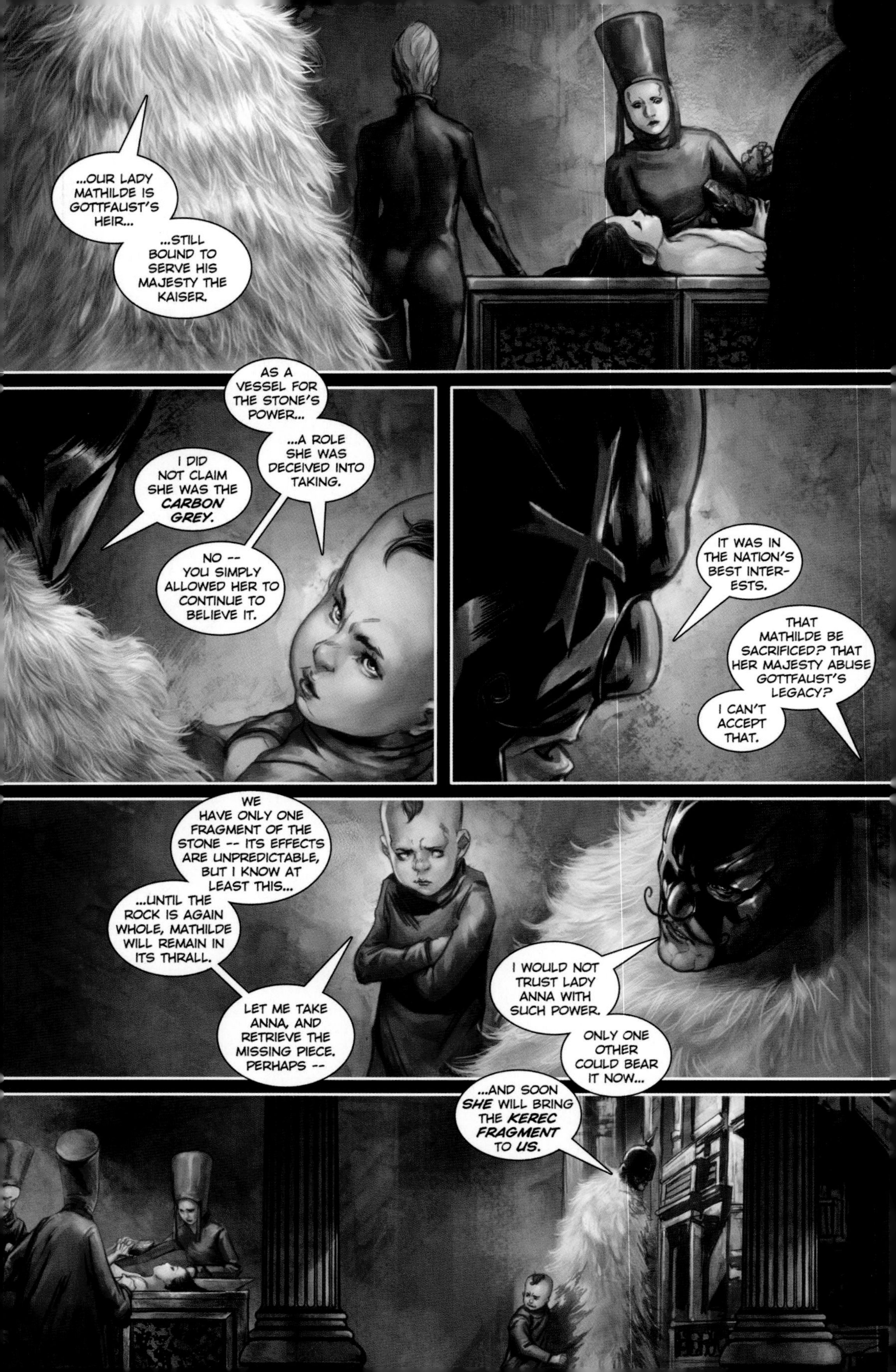
...OUR LADY MATHILDE IS GOTTFAUST'S HEIR...
...STILL BOUND TO SERVE HIS MAJESTY THE KAISER.
I DID NOT CLAIM SHE WAS THE CARBON GREY.
AS A VESSEL FOR THE STONE'S POWER...
...A ROLE SHE WAS DECEIVED INTO TAKING.
NO -- YOU SIMPLY ALLOWED HER TO CONTINUE TO BELIEVE IT.
IT WAS IN THE NATION'S BEST INTER-ESTS.
THAT MATHILDE BE SACRIFICED? THAT HER MAJESTY ABUSE GOTTFAUST'S LEGACY?
I CAN'T ACCEPT THAT.
WE HAVE ONLY ONE FRAGMENT OF THE STONE -- ITS EFFECTS ARE UNPREDICTABLE, BUT I KNOW AT LEAST THIS...
...UNTIL THE ROCK IS AGAIN WHOLE, MATHILDE WILL REMAIN IN ITS THRALL.
LET ME TAKE ANNA, AND RETRIEVE THE MISSING PIECE. PERHAPS --
I WOULD NOT TRUST LADY ANNA WITH SUCH POWER.
ONLY ONE OTHER COULD BEAR IT NOW...
...AND SOON SHE WILL BRING THE KEREC FRAGMENT TO US.

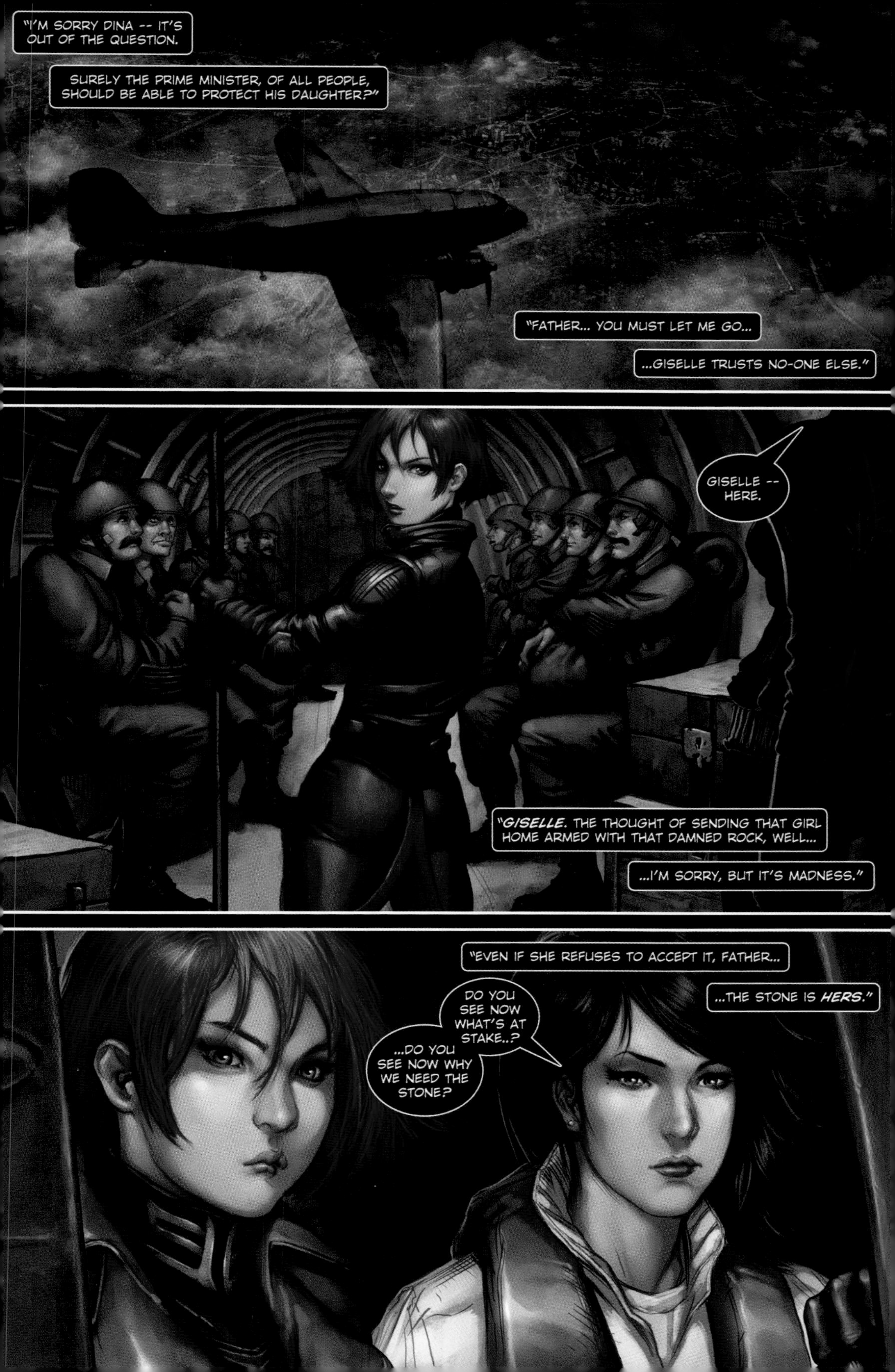
"I'M SORRY DINA -- IT'S OUT OF THE QUESTION.
SURELY THE PRIME MINISTER, OF ALL PEOPLE, SHOULD BE ABLE TO PROTECT HIS DAUGHTER?"
"FATHER... YOU MUST LET ME GO...
...GISELLE TRUSTS NO-ONE ELSE."
GISELLE -- HERE.
"*GISELLE.* THE THOUGHT OF SENDING THAT GIRL HOME ARMED WITH THAT DAMNED ROCK, WELL...
...I'M SORRY, BUT IT'S MADNESS."
"EVEN IF SHE REFUSES TO ACCEPT IT, FATHER...
...THE STONE IS *HERS.*"
DO YOU SEE NOW WHAT'S AT STAKE..?
...DO YOU SEE NOW WHY WE NEED THE STONE?

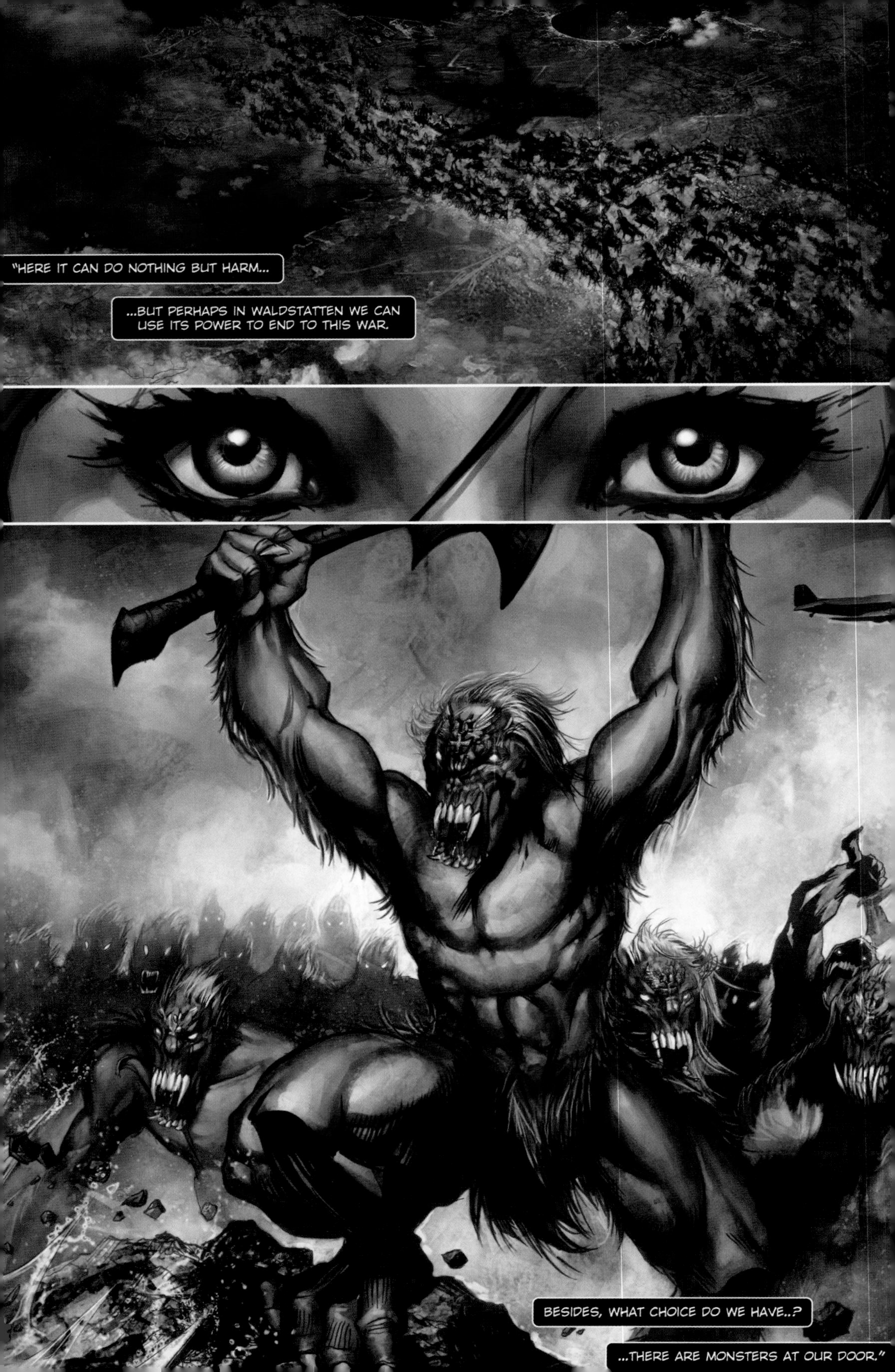
"HERE IT CAN DO NOTHING BUT HARM...
...BUT PERHAPS IN WALDSTATTEN WE CAN USE ITS POWER TO END TO THIS WAR.
BESIDES, WHAT CHOICE DO WE HAVE..?
...THERE ARE MONSTERS AT OUR DOOR."

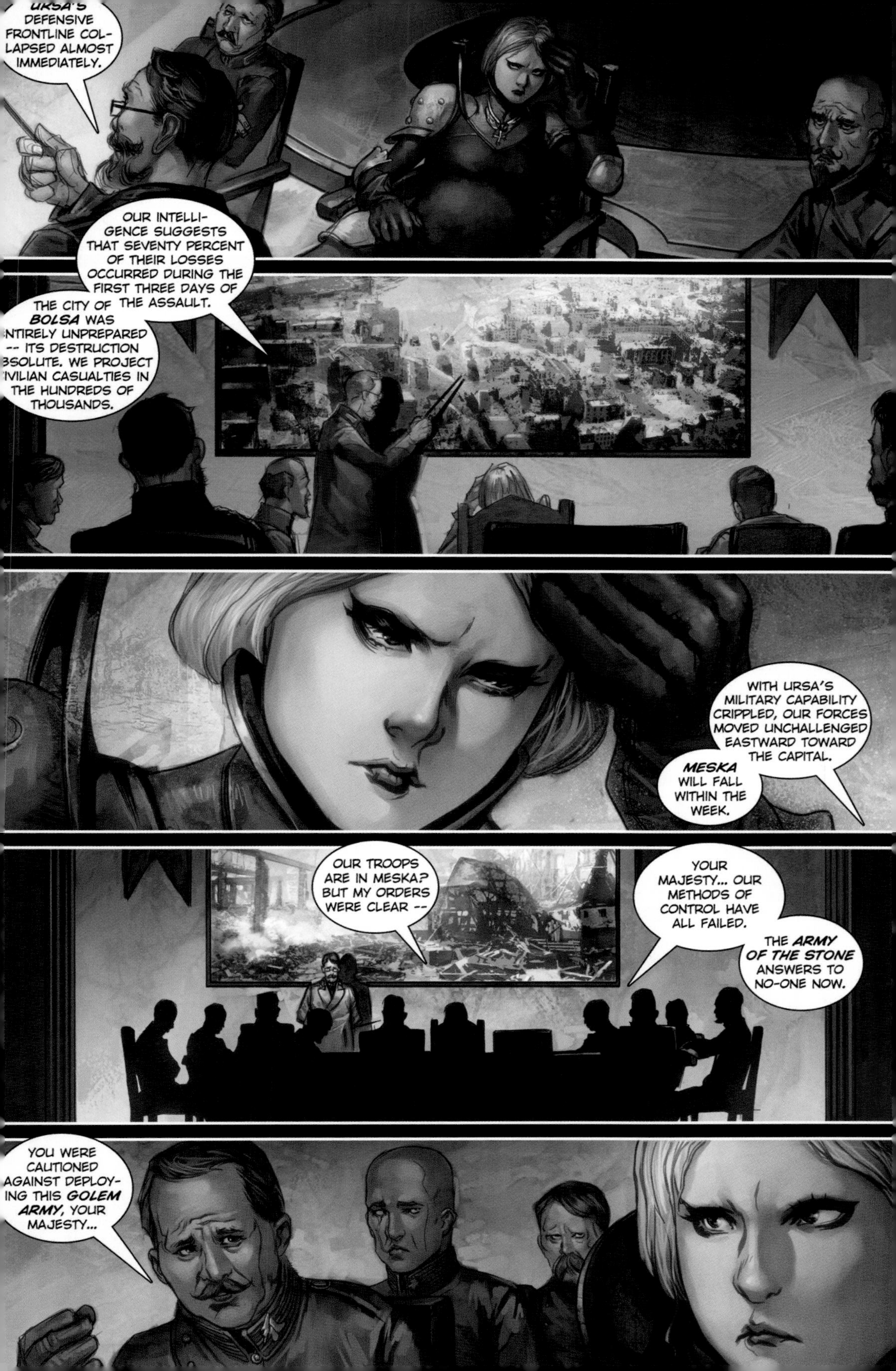
URSA'S DEFENSIVE FRONTLINE COL-LAPSED ALMOST IMMEDIATELY.
OUR INTELLI-GENCE SUGGESTS THAT SEVENTY PERCENT OF THEIR LOSSES OCCURRED DURING THE FIRST THREE DAYS OF THE ASSAULT.
THE CITY OF BOLSA WAS NTIRELY UNPREPARED -- ITS DESTRUCTION BSOLUTE. WE PROJECT IVILIAN CASUALTIES IN THE HUNDREDS OF THOUSANDS.
WITH URSA'S MILITARY CAPABILITY CRIPPLED, OUR FORCES MOVED UNCHALLENGED EASTWARD TOWARD THE CAPITAL.
MESKA WILL FALL WITHIN THE WEEK.
OUR TROOPS ARE IN MESKA? BUT MY ORDERS WERE CLEAR --
YOUR MAJESTY... OUR METHODS OF CONTROL HAVE ALL FAILED.
THE ARMY OF THE STONE ANSWERS TO NO-ONE NOW.
YOU WERE CAUTIONED AGAINST DEPLOY-ING THIS GOLEM ARMY, YOUR MAJESTY...

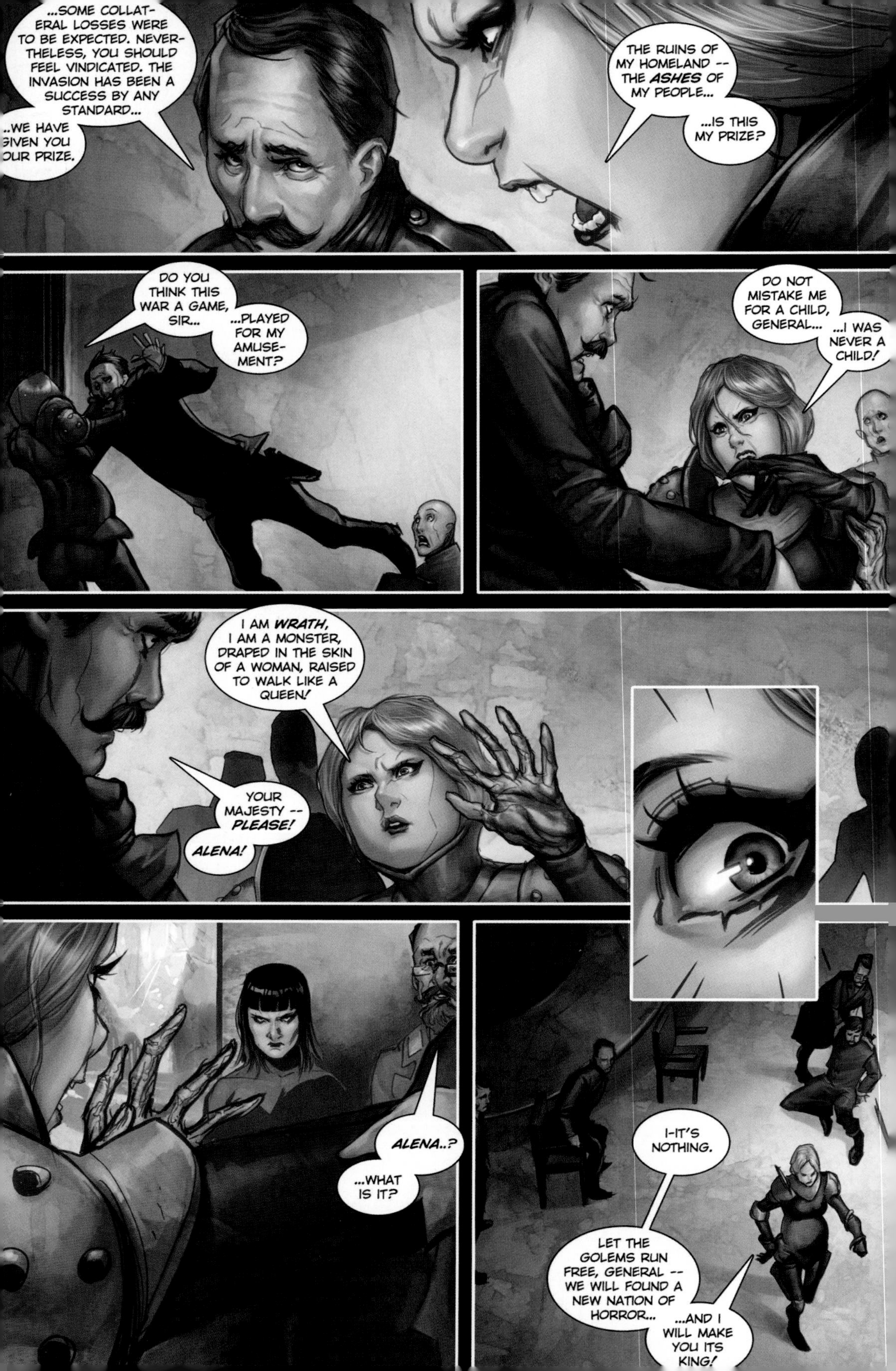
...SOME COLLATERAL LOSSES WERE TO BE EXPECTED. NEVERTHELESS, YOU SHOULD FEEL VINDICATED. THE INVASION HAS BEEN A SUCCESS BY ANY STANDARD...
..WE HAVE GIVEN YOU OUR PRIZE.
THE RUINS OF MY HOMELAND -- THE *ASHES* OF MY PEOPLE...
...IS THIS MY PRIZE?
DO YOU THINK THIS WAR A GAME, SIR...
...PLAYED FOR MY AMUSEMENT?
DO NOT MISTAKE ME FOR A CHILD, GENERAL...
...I WAS NEVER A CHILD!
I AM *WRATH*, I AM A MONSTER, DRAPED IN THE SKIN OF A WOMAN, RAISED TO WALK LIKE A QUEEN!
YOUR MAJESTY -- *PLEASE!*
ALENA!
ALENA..?
...WHAT IS IT?
I-IT'S NOTHING.
LET THE GOLEMS RUN FREE, GENERAL -- WE WILL FOUND A NEW NATION OF HORROR...
...AND I WILL MAKE YOU ITS KING!

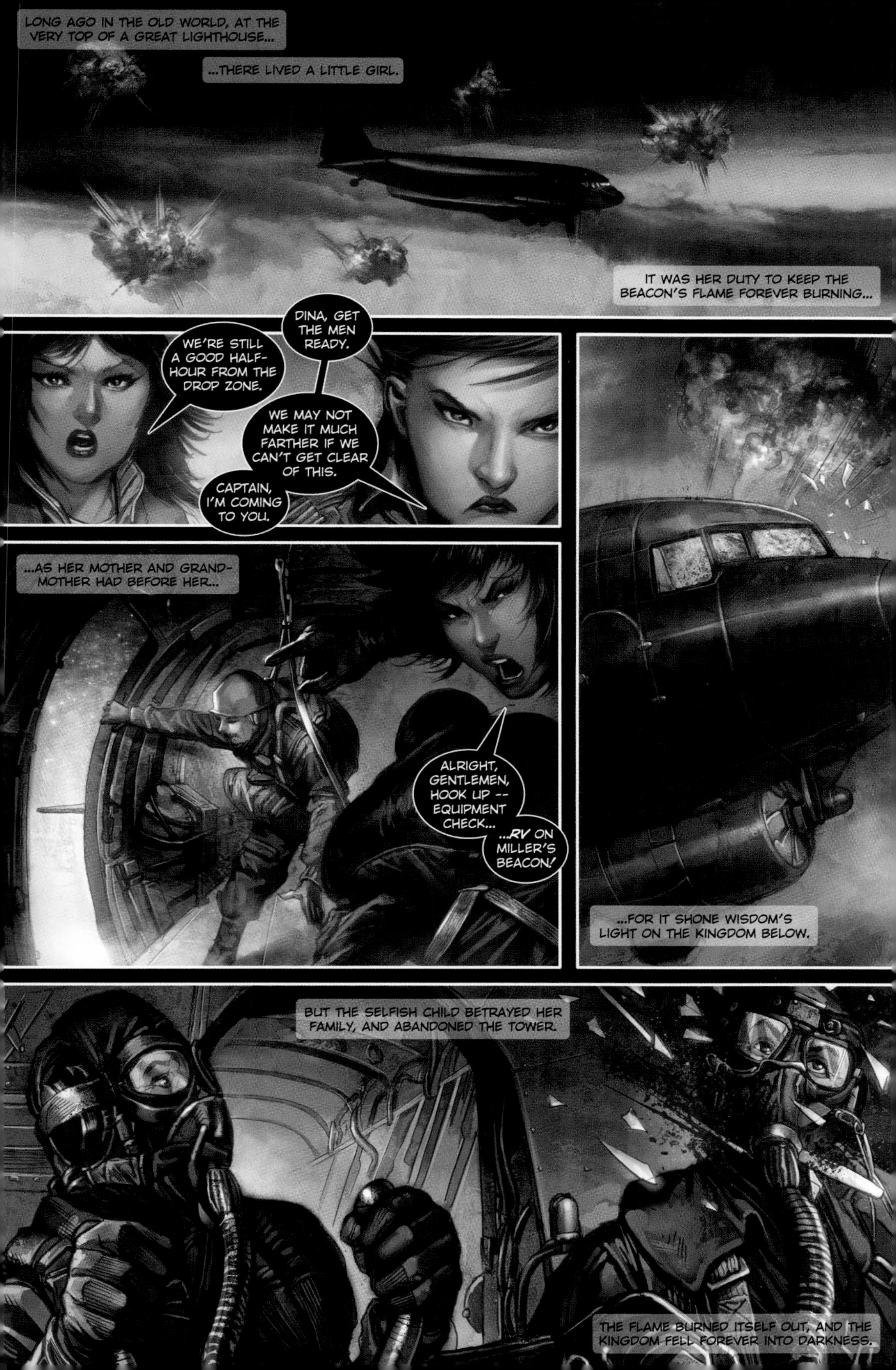
LONG AGO IN THE OLD WORLD, AT THE VERY TOP OF A GREAT LIGHTHOUSE...
...THERE LIVED A LITTLE GIRL.
IT WAS HER DUTY TO KEEP THE BEACON'S FLAME FOREVER BURNING...
WE'RE STILL A GOOD HALF-HOUR FROM THE DROP ZONE.
DINA, GET THE MEN READY.
WE MAY NOT MAKE IT MUCH FARTHER IF WE CAN'T GET CLEAR OF THIS.
CAPTAIN, I'M COMING TO YOU.
...AS HER MOTHER AND GRAND-MOTHER HAD BEFORE HER...
ALRIGHT, GENTLEMEN, HOOK UP -- EQUIPMENT CHECK...
...RV ON MILLER'S BEACON!
...FOR IT SHONE WISDOM'S LIGHT ON THE KINGDOM BELOW.
BUT THE SELFISH CHILD BETRAYED HER FAMILY, AND ABANDONED THE TOWER.
THE FLAME BURNED ITSELF OUT, AND THE KINGDOM FELL FOREVER INTO DARKNESS.

AS CHILDREN WE WERE TOLD MANY STORIES.

DINA, THE CREW'S DEAD...

...THE CONTROLS ARE SHOT -- GET OUT OF THERE.

YOU'LL HAVE IT.

OUR AIRSPEED'S TOO HIGH -- I NEED THIRTY SECONDS AT EIGHTY-FIVE KNOTS OR LESS!

GO -- GO!

MATHILDE FOUND IN THEM A REFUGE FROM HER OWN LIFE...

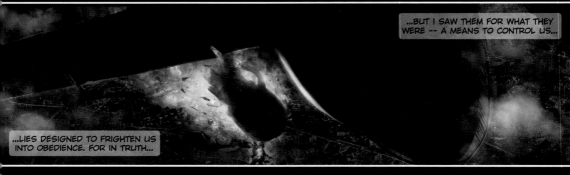

...BUT I SAW THEM FOR WHAT THEY WERE -- A MEANS TO CONTROL US...

...LIES DESIGNED TO FRIGHTEN US INTO OBEDIENCE. FOR IN TRUTH...

...WE HAVE ALWAYS LIVED IN DARKNESS, WHILE THOSE IN POWER DESCRIBED THE WORLD TO US...

...AND TOLD US WE COULD SEE.

GISELLE -- WE NEED TO MOVE!

BELIEVE ME, I'LL BE RIGHT BEHIND YOU.

I'M RETURNING THE FLAME TO WALDSTATTEN -- NOT TO BRING LIGHT TO THE CITY...

...BUT TO BURN IT DOWN.

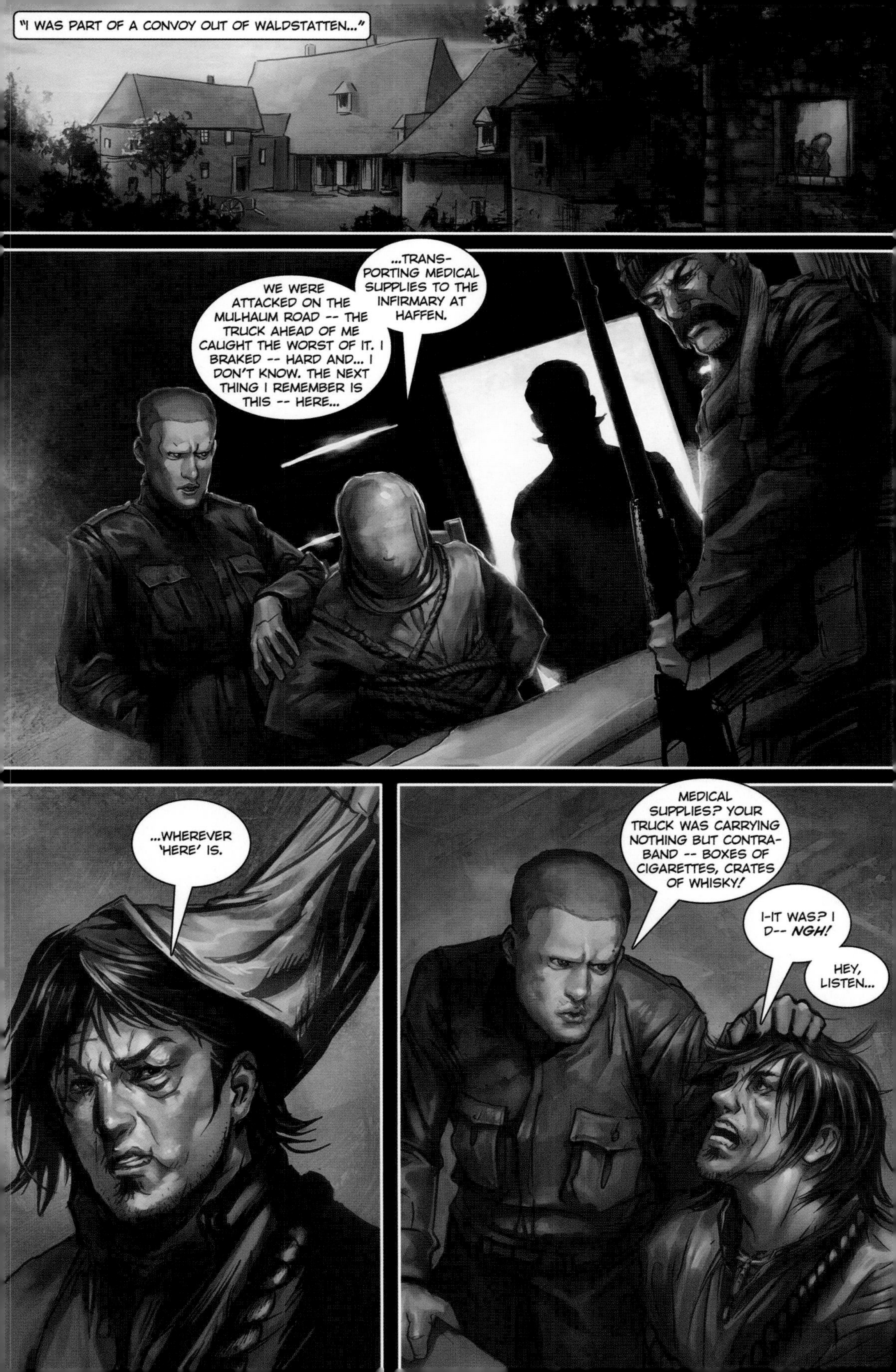
"I WAS PART OF A CONVOY OUT OF WALDSTATTEN..."
WE WERE ATTACKED ON THE MULHAUM ROAD -- THE TRUCK AHEAD OF ME CAUGHT THE WORST OF IT. I BRAKED -- HARD AND... I DON'T KNOW. THE NEXT THING I REMEMBER IS THIS -- HERE...
...TRANS-PORTING MEDICAL SUPPLIES TO THE INFIRMARY AT HAFFEN.
...WHEREVER 'HERE' IS.
MEDICAL SUPPLIES? YOUR TRUCK WAS CARRYING NOTHING BUT CONTRA-BAND -- BOXES OF CIGARETTES, CRATES OF WHISKY!
I-IT WAS? I D-- NGH!
HEY, LISTEN...

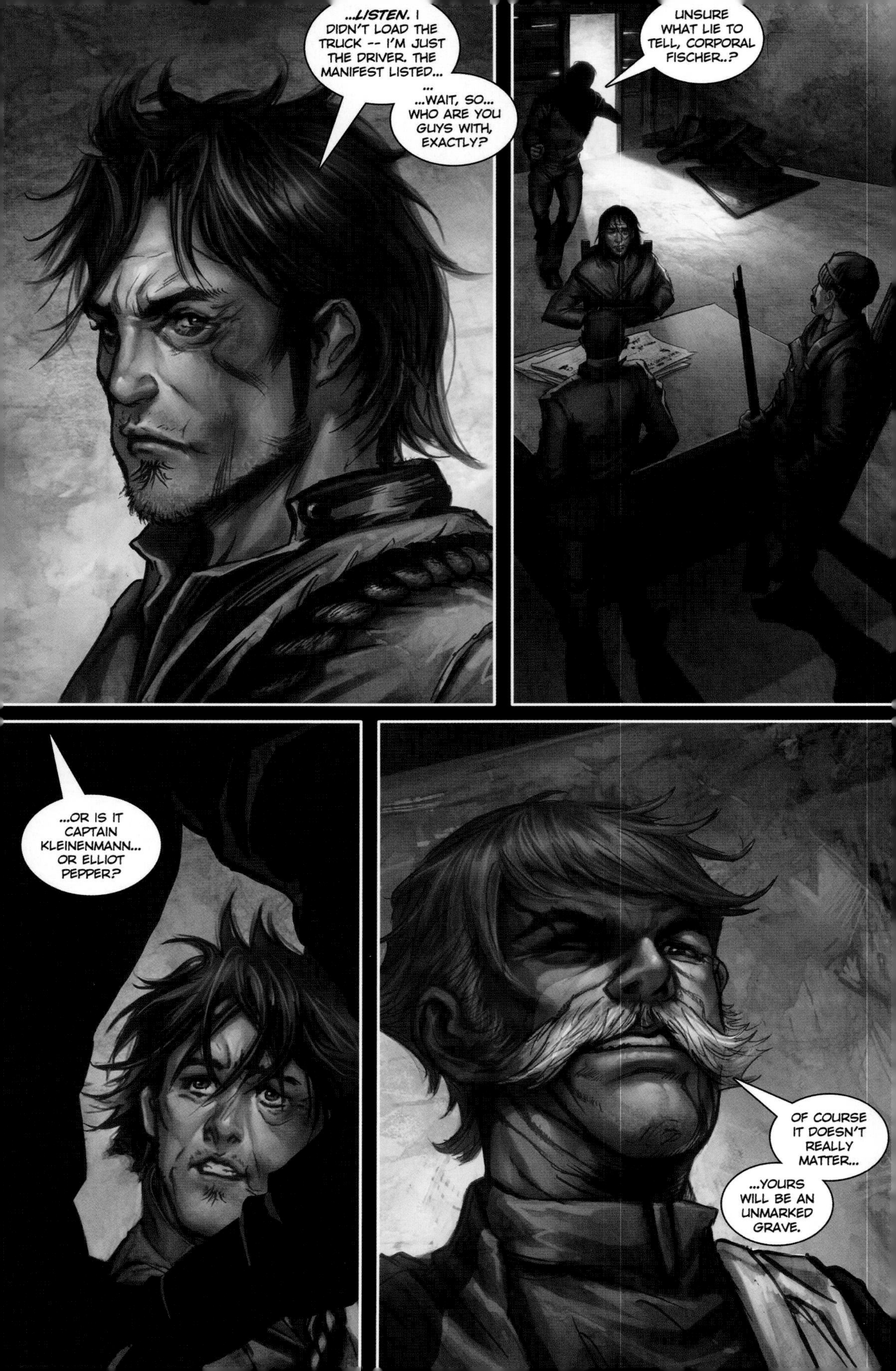
...LISTEN. I DIDN'T LOAD THE TRUCK -- I'M JUST THE DRIVER. THE MANIFEST LISTED...
...
...WAIT, SO... WHO ARE YOU GUYS WITH, EXACTLY?
UNSURE WHAT LIE TO TELL, CORPORAL FISCHER..?
...OR IS IT CAPTAIN KLEINENMANN... OR ELLIOT PEPPER?
OF COURSE IT DOESN'T REALLY MATTER...
...YOURS WILL BE AN UNMARKED GRAVE.

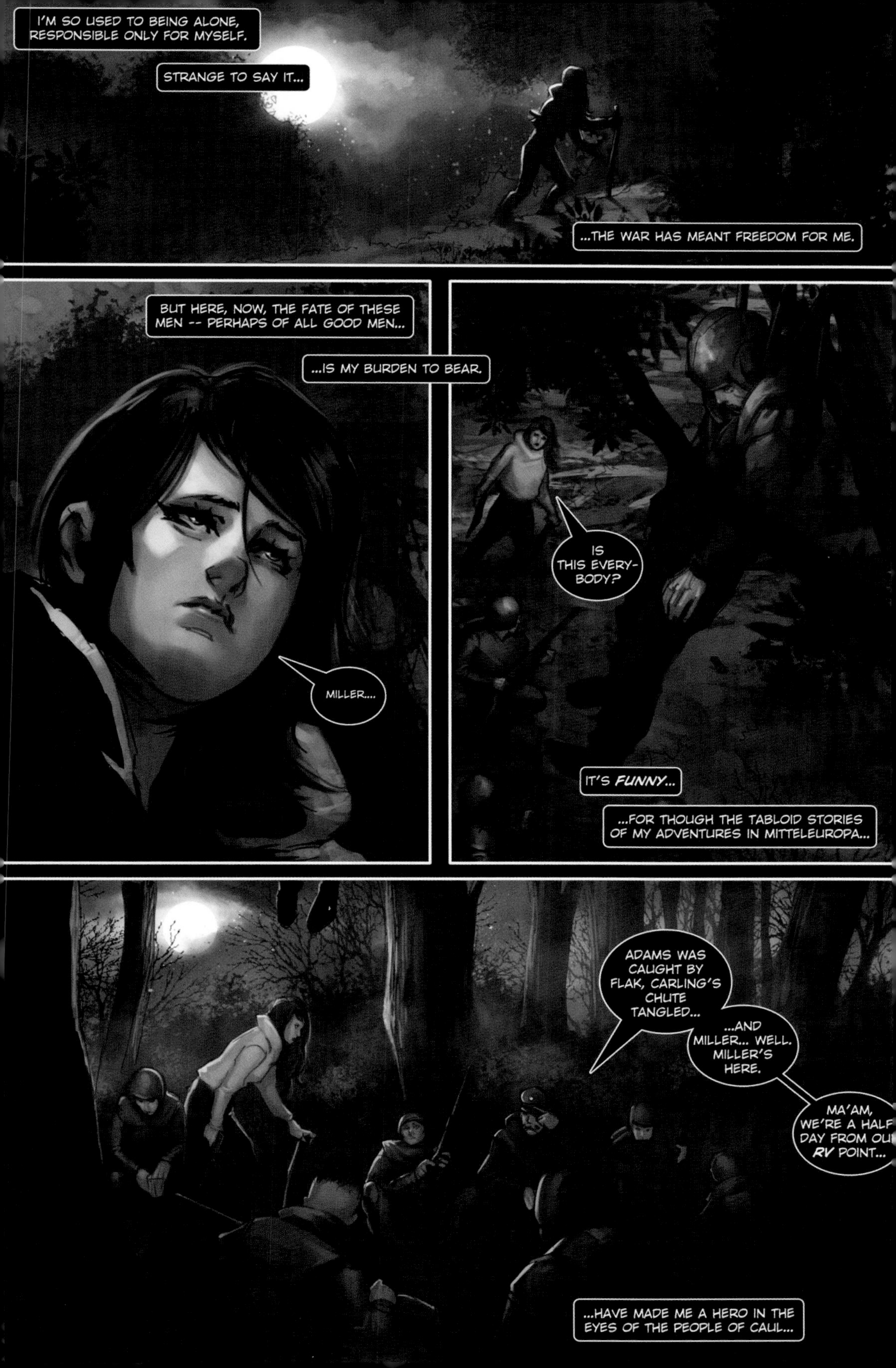

I'M SO USED TO BEING ALONE, RESPONSIBLE ONLY FOR MYSELF.
STRANGE TO SAY IT...
...THE WAR HAS MEANT FREEDOM FOR ME.
BUT HERE, NOW, THE FATE OF THESE MEN -- PERHAPS OF ALL GOOD MEN...
...IS MY BURDEN TO BEAR.
MILLER....
IS THIS EVERY-BODY?
IT'S *FUNNY*...
...FOR THOUGH THE TABLOID STORIES OF MY ADVENTURES IN MITTELEUROPA...
ADAMS WAS CAUGHT BY FLAK, CARLING'S CHUTE TANGLED...
...AND MILLER... WELL. MILLER'S HERE.
MA'AM, WE'RE A HALF DAY FROM OU *RV* POINT...
...HAVE MADE ME A HERO IN THE EYES OF THE PEOPLE OF CAUL...

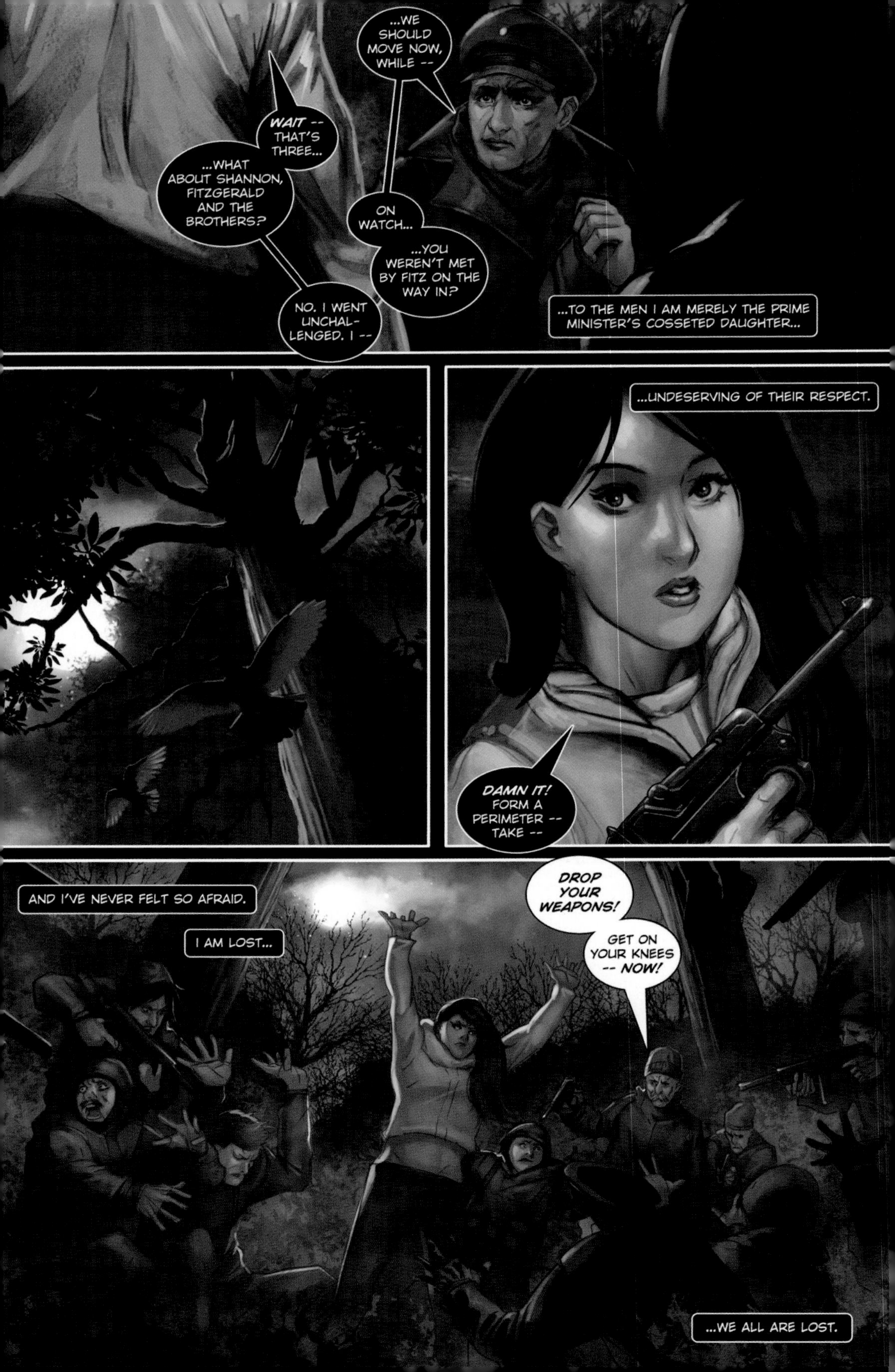
...WE SHOULD MOVE NOW, WHILE --
WAIT -- THAT'S THREE...
...WHAT ABOUT SHANNON, FITZGERALD AND THE BROTHERS?
ON WATCH...
...YOU WEREN'T MET BY FITZ ON THE WAY IN?
NO. I WENT UNCHAL-LENGED. I --
...TO THE MEN I AM MERELY THE PRIME MINISTER'S COSSETED DAUGHTER...
...UNDESERVING OF THEIR RESPECT.
DAMN IT! FORM A PERIMETER -- TAKE --
AND I'VE NEVER FELT SO AFRAID.
I AM LOST...
DROP YOUR WEAPONS!
GET ON YOUR KNEES -- NOW!
...WE ALL ARE LOST.

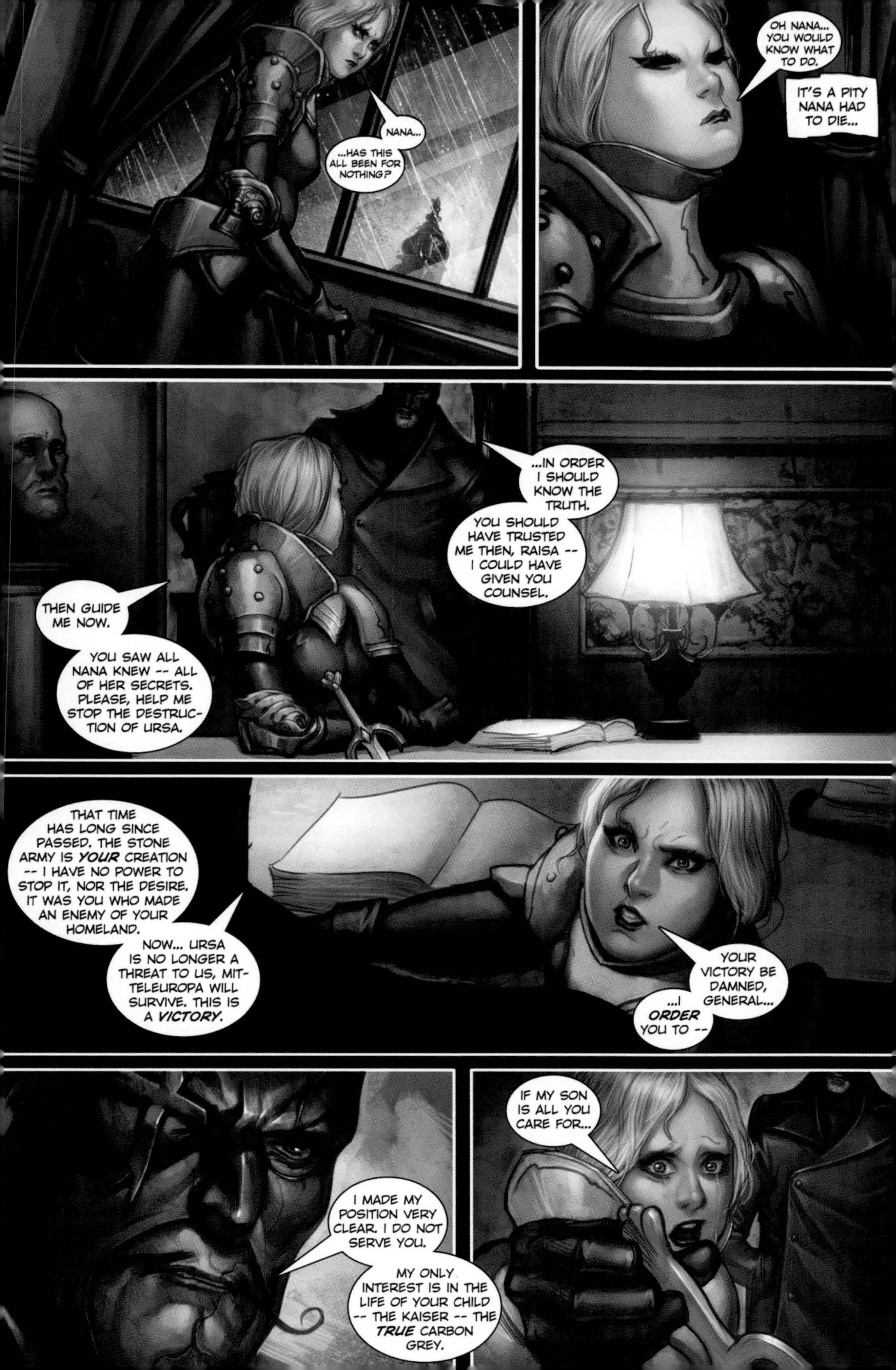

NANA...
...HAS THIS ALL BEEN FOR NOTHING?
OH NANA... YOU WOULD KNOW WHAT TO DO.
IT'S A PITY NANA HAD TO DIE...
...IN ORDER I SHOULD KNOW THE TRUTH.
YOU SHOULD HAVE TRUSTED ME THEN, RAISA -- I COULD HAVE GIVEN YOU COUNSEL.
THEN GUIDE ME NOW.
YOU SAW ALL NANA KNEW -- ALL OF HER SECRETS. PLEASE, HELP ME STOP THE DESTRUCTION OF URSA.
THAT TIME HAS LONG SINCE PASSED. THE STONE ARMY IS *YOUR* CREATION -- I HAVE NO POWER TO STOP IT, NOR THE DESIRE. IT WAS YOU WHO MADE AN ENEMY OF YOUR HOMELAND.
NOW... URSA IS NO LONGER A THREAT TO US, MITTELEUROPA WILL SURVIVE. THIS IS A *VICTORY*.
YOUR VICTORY BE DAMNED, GENERAL...
...I *ORDER* YOU TO --
I MADE MY POSITION VERY CLEAR. I DO NOT SERVE YOU.
MY ONLY INTEREST IS IN THE LIFE OF YOUR CHILD -- THE KAISER -- THE *TRUE* CARBON GREY.
IF MY SON IS ALL YOU CARE FOR...

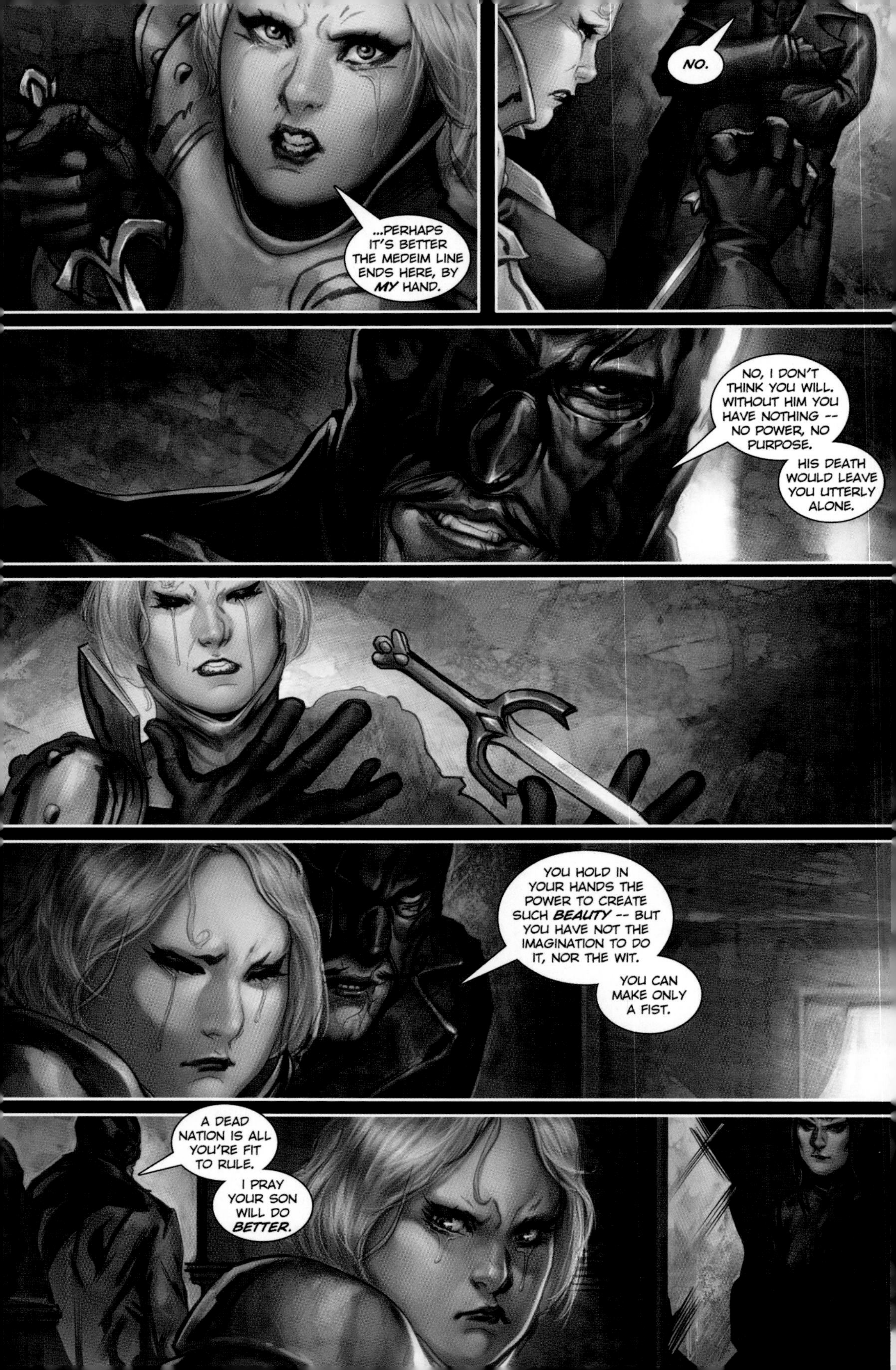
...PERHAPS IT'S BETTER THE MEDEIM LINE ENDS HERE, BY MY HAND.
NO.
NO, I DON'T THINK YOU WILL. WITHOUT HIM YOU HAVE NOTHING -- NO POWER, NO PURPOSE.
HIS DEATH WOULD LEAVE YOU UTTERLY ALONE.
YOU HOLD IN YOUR HANDS THE POWER TO CREATE SUCH BEAUTY -- BUT YOU HAVE NOT THE IMAGINATION TO DO IT, NOR THE WIT.
YOU CAN MAKE ONLY A FIST.
A DEAD NATION IS ALL YOU'RE FIT TO RULE.
I PRAY YOUR SON WILL DO BETTER.

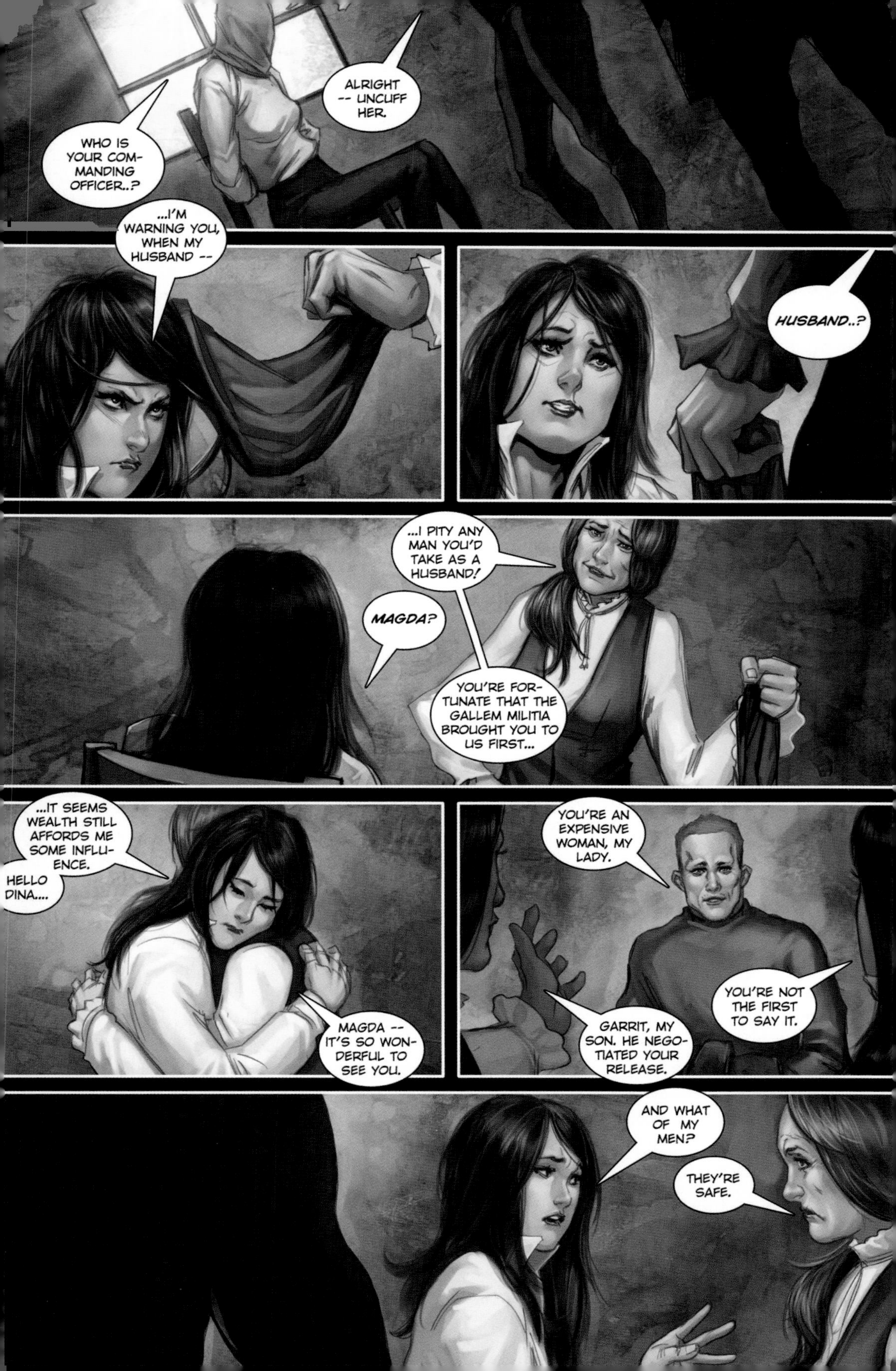
WHO IS YOUR COM-MANDING OFFICER..?
ALRIGHT -- UNCUFF HER.
...I'M WARNING YOU, WHEN MY HUSBAND --
HUSBAND..?
...I PITY ANY MAN YOU'D TAKE AS A HUSBAND!
MAGDA?
YOU'RE FOR-TUNATE THAT THE GALLEM MILITIA BROUGHT YOU TO US FIRST...
...IT SEEMS WEALTH STILL AFFORDS ME SOME INFLU-ENCE.
HELLO DINA....
MAGDA -- IT'S SO WON-DERFUL TO SEE YOU.
YOU'RE AN EXPENSIVE WOMAN, MY LADY.
GARRIT, MY SON. HE NEGO-TIATED YOUR RELEASE.
YOU'RE NOT THE FIRST TO SAY IT.
AND WHAT OF MY MEN?
THEY'RE SAFE.

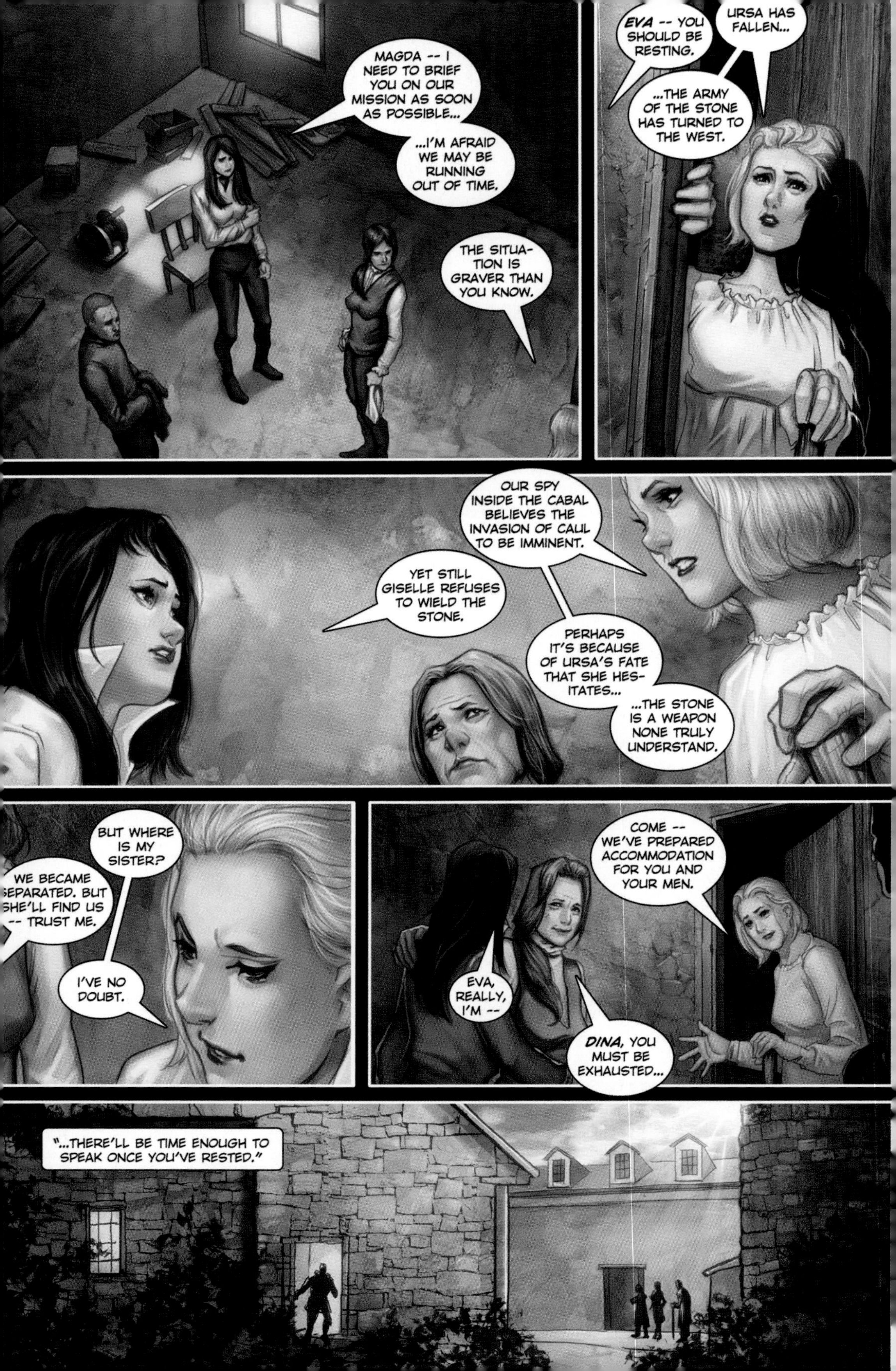
MAGDA -- I NEED TO BRIEF YOU ON OUR MISSION AS SOON AS POSSIBLE...
...I'M AFRAID WE MAY BE RUNNING OUT OF TIME.
THE SITUATION IS GRAVER THAN YOU KNOW.
EVA -- YOU SHOULD BE RESTING.
URSA HAS FALLEN...
...THE ARMY OF THE STONE HAS TURNED TO THE WEST.
OUR SPY INSIDE THE CABAL BELIEVES THE INVASION OF CAUL TO BE IMMINENT.
YET STILL GISELLE REFUSES TO WIELD THE STONE.
PERHAPS IT'S BECAUSE OF URSA'S FATE THAT SHE HESITATES...
...THE STONE IS A WEAPON NONE TRULY UNDERSTAND.
BUT WHERE IS MY SISTER?
WE BECAME SEPARATED. BUT SHE'LL FIND US -- TRUST ME.
I'VE NO DOUBT.
COME -- WE'VE PREPARED ACCOMMODATION FOR YOU AND YOUR MEN.
EVA, REALLY, I'M --
DINA, YOU MUST BE EXHAUSTED...
"...THERE'LL BE TIME ENOUGH TO SPEAK ONCE YOU'VE RESTED."

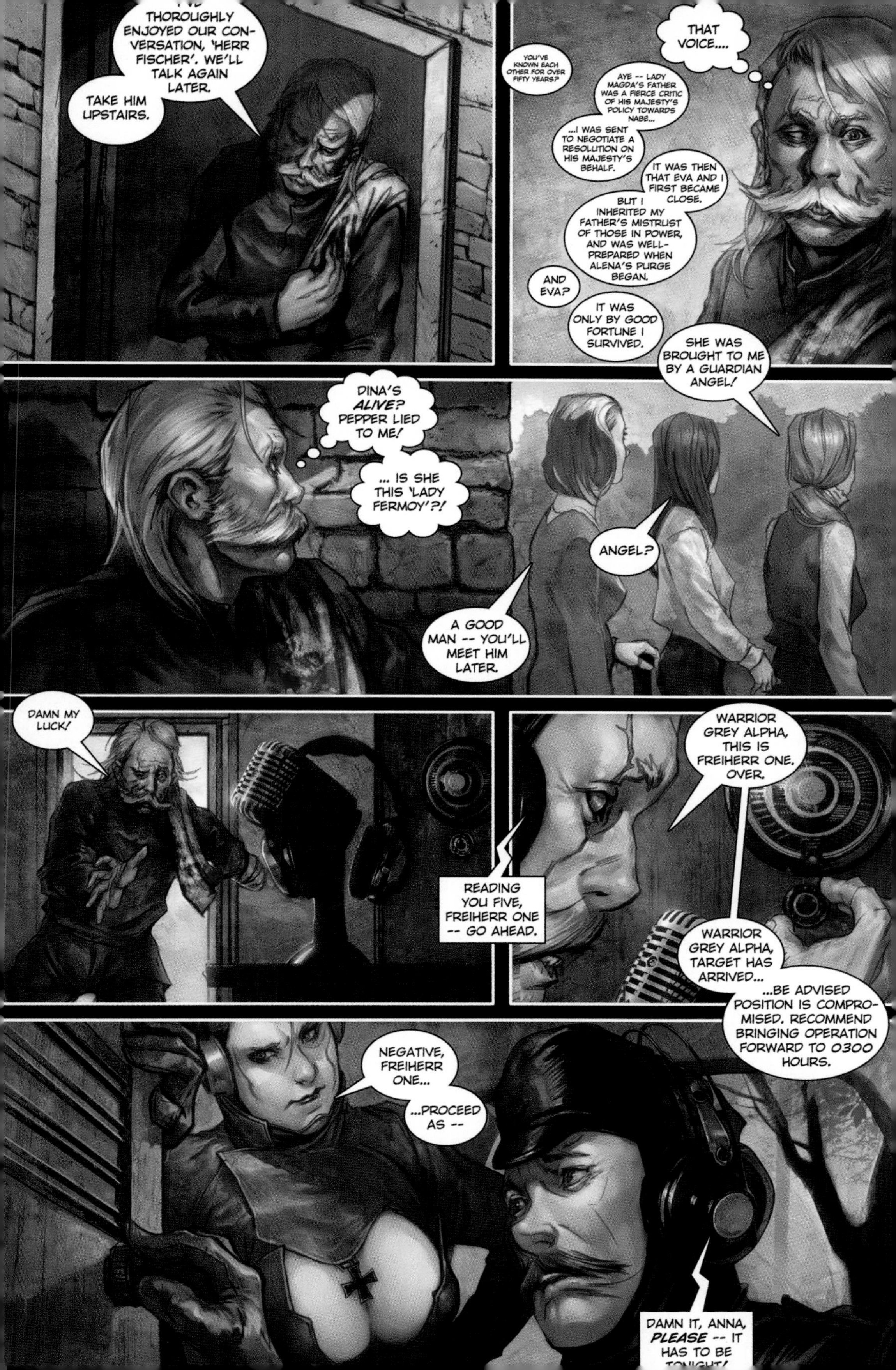
THOROUGHLY ENJOYED OUR CON-VERSATION, 'HERR FISCHER'. WE'LL TALK AGAIN LATER.
TAKE HIM UPSTAIRS.
THAT VOICE....
YOU'VE KNOWN EACH OTHER FOR OVER FIFTY YEARS?
AYE -- LADY MAGDA'S FATHER WAS A FIERCE CRITIC OF HIS MAJESTY'S POLICY TOWARDS NABE...
...I WAS SENT TO NEGOTIATE A RESOLUTION ON HIS MAJESTY'S BEHALF.
IT WAS THEN THAT EVA AND I FIRST BECAME CLOSE.
BUT I INHERITED MY FATHER'S MISTRUST OF THOSE IN POWER, AND WAS WELL-PREPARED WHEN ALENA'S PURGE BEGAN.
AND EVA?
IT WAS ONLY BY GOOD FORTUNE I SURVIVED.
SHE WAS BROUGHT TO ME BY A GUARDIAN ANGEL!
DINA'S *ALIVE*? PEPPER LIED TO ME!
... IS SHE THIS 'LADY FERMOY'?!
ANGEL?
A GOOD MAN -- YOU'LL MEET HIM LATER.
DAMN MY LUCK!
WARRIOR GREY ALPHA, THIS IS FREIHERR ONE. OVER.
READING YOU FIVE, FREIHERR ONE -- GO AHEAD.
WARRIOR GREY ALPHA, TARGET HAS ARRIVED...
...BE ADVISED POSITION IS COMPRO-MISED. RECOMMEND BRINGING OPERATION FORWARD TO 0300 HOURS.
NEGATIVE, FREIHERR ONE...
...PROCEED AS --
DAMN IT, ANNA, *PLEASE* -- IT HAS TO BE

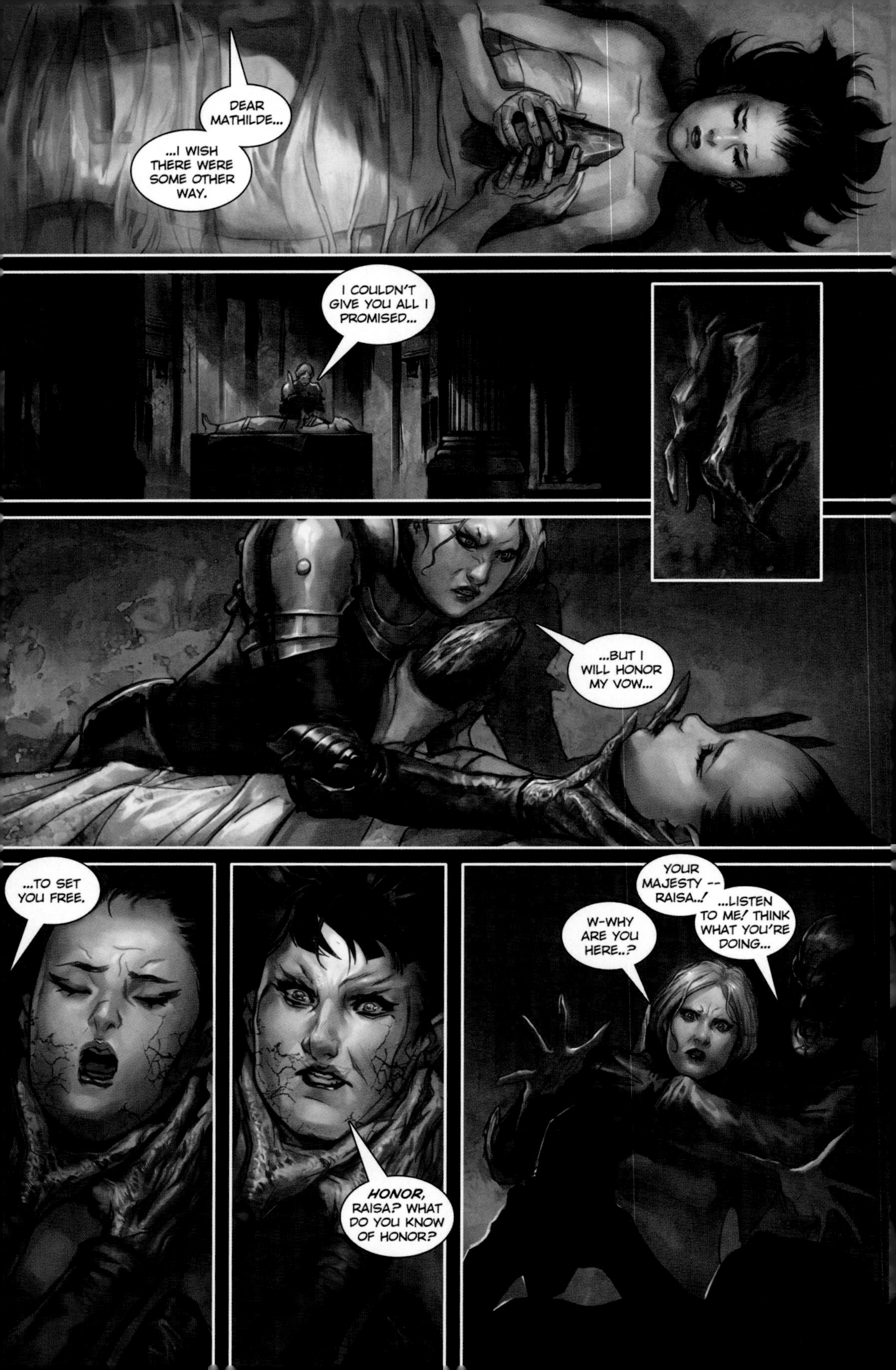
DEAR MATHILDE...
...I WISH THERE WERE SOME OTHER WAY.
I COULDN'T GIVE YOU ALL I PROMISED...
...BUT I WILL HONOR MY VOW...
...TO SET YOU FREE.
HONOR, RAISA? WHAT DO YOU KNOW OF HONOR?
YOUR MAJESTY -- RAISA..!
W-WHY ARE YOU HERE..?
...LISTEN TO ME! THINK WHAT YOU'RE DOING...

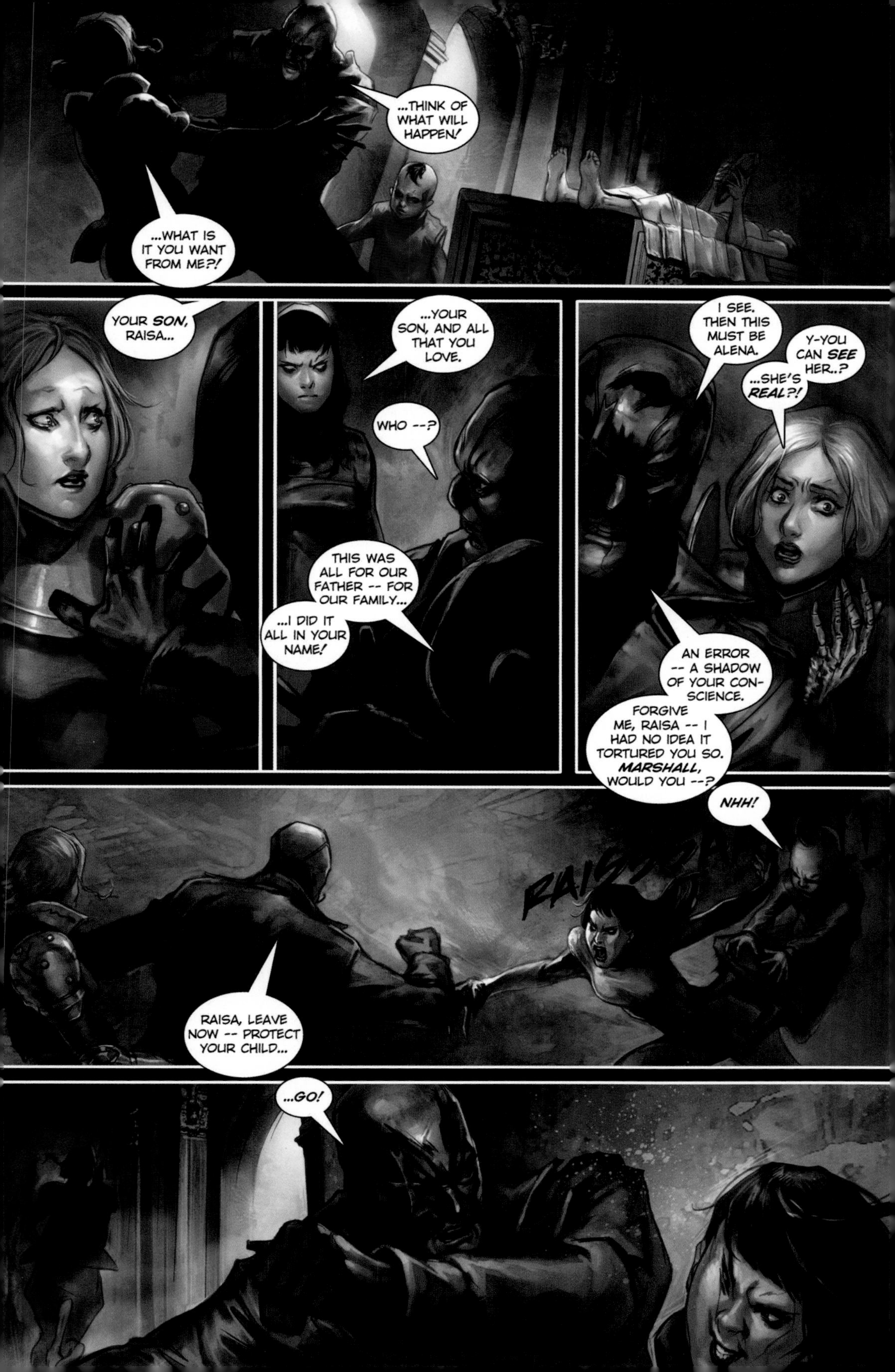
...THINK OF WHAT WILL HAPPEN!
...WHAT IS IT YOU WANT FROM ME?!
YOUR **SON,** RAISA...
...YOUR SON, AND ALL THAT YOU LOVE.
WHO --?
THIS WAS ALL FOR OUR FATHER -- FOR OUR FAMILY...
...I DID IT ALL IN YOUR NAME!
I SEE. THEN THIS MUST BE ALENA.
Y-YOU CAN **SEE** HER..?
...SHE'S **REAL?!**
AN ERROR -- A SHADOW OF YOUR CONSCIENCE.
FORGIVE ME, RAISA -- I HAD NO IDEA IT TORTURED YOU SO. **MARSHALL,** WOULD YOU --?
NHH!
RAISA, LEAVE NOW -- PROTECT YOUR CHILD...
...GO!

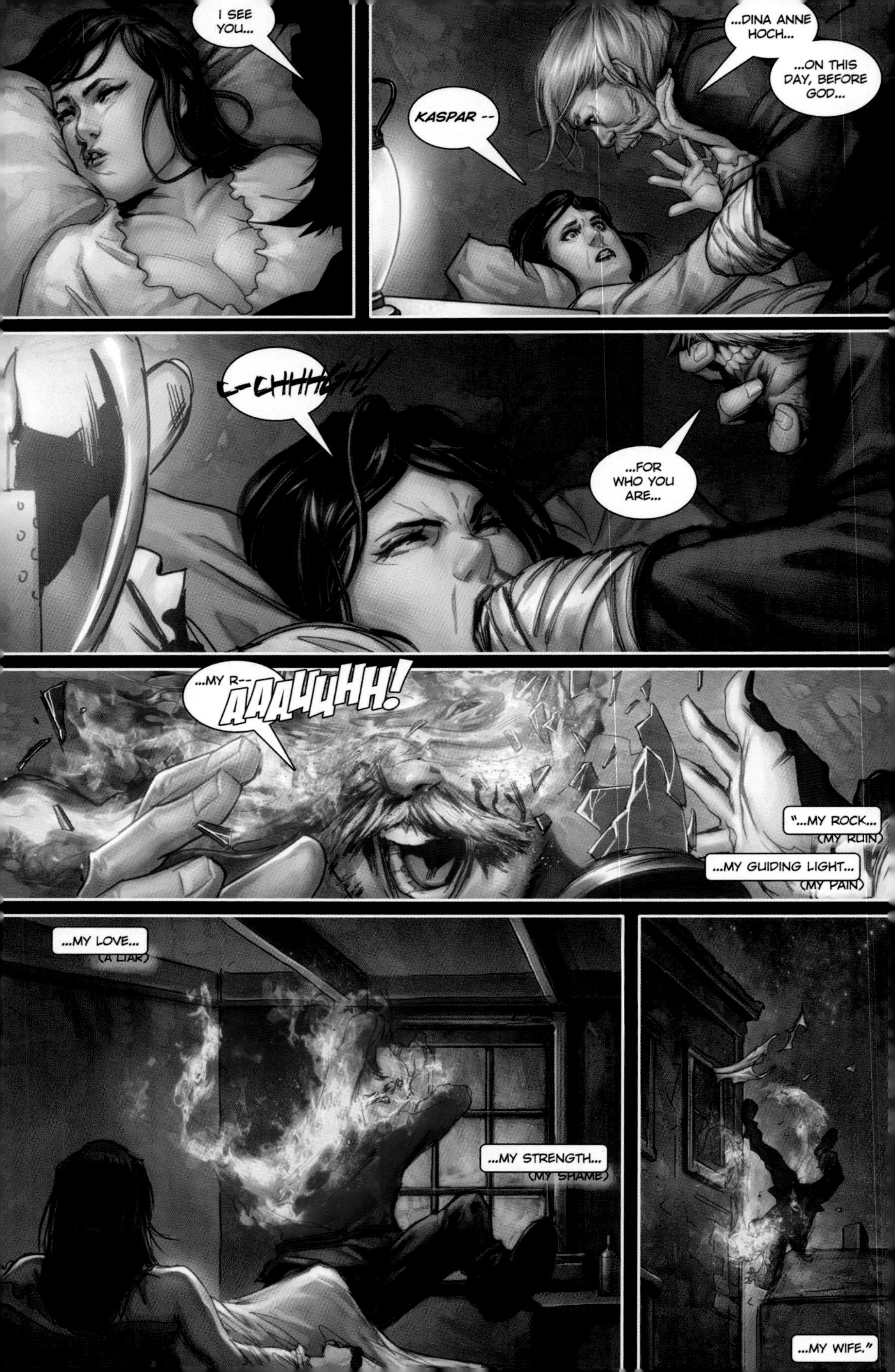
I SEE YOU...
KASPAR --
...DINA ANNE HOCH...
...ON THIS DAY, BEFORE GOD...
...FOR WHO YOU ARE...
...MY R-- AAAUUHH!
"...MY ROCK...
(MY RUIN)
...MY GUIDING LIGHT...
(MY PAIN)
...MY LOVE...
(A LIAR)
...MY STRENGTH...
(MY SHAME)
...MY WIFE."

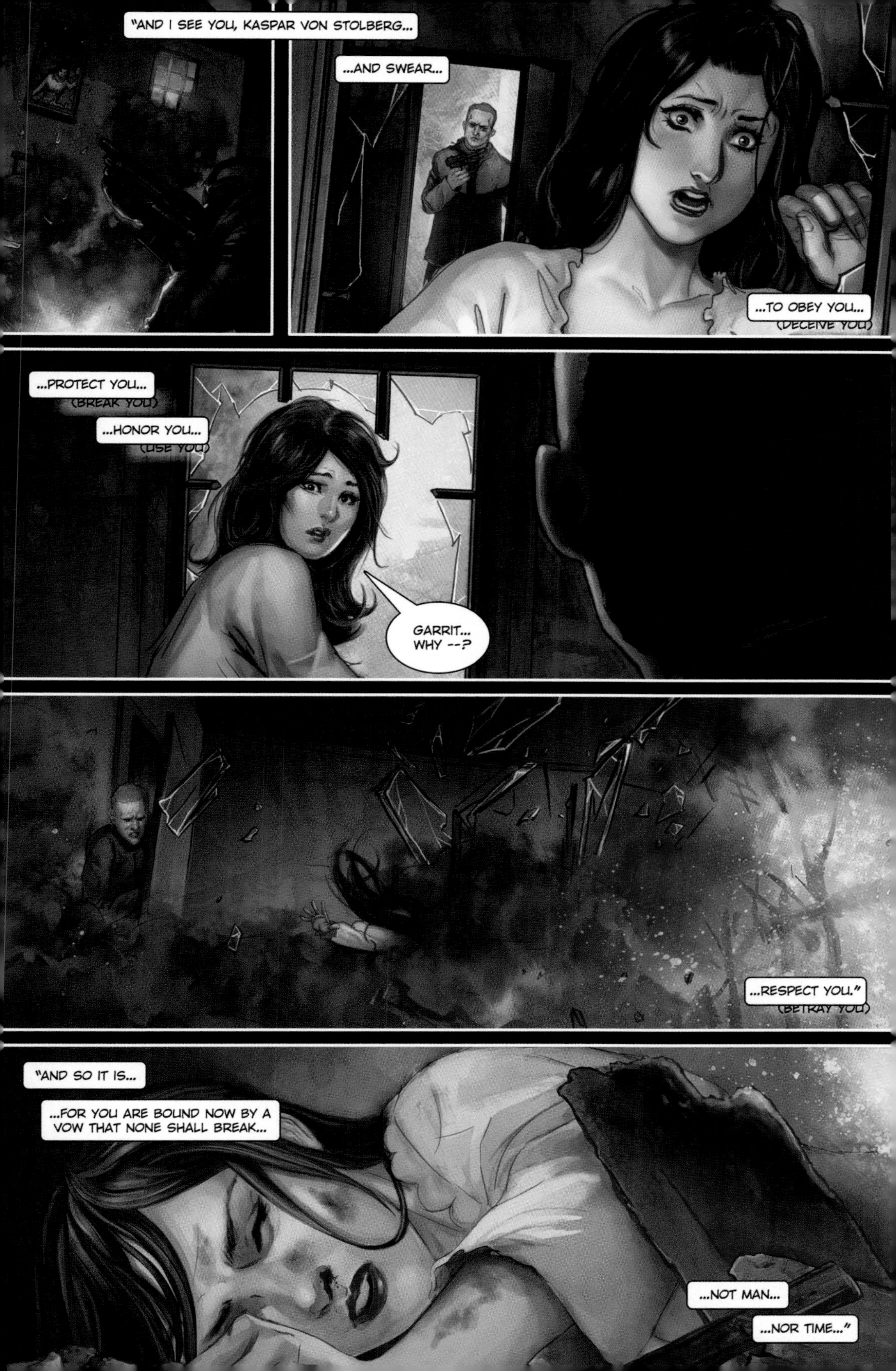
"AND I SEE YOU, KASPAR VON STOLBERG...
...AND SWEAR...
...TO OBEY YOU...
(DECEIVE YOU)
...PROTECT YOU...
(BREAK YOU)
...HONOR YOU...
(USE YOU)
GARRIT... WHY --?
...RESPECT YOU."
(BETRAY YOU)
"AND SO IT IS...
...FOR YOU ARE BOUND NOW BY A VOW THAT NONE SHALL BREAK...
...NOT MAN...
...NOR TIME..."

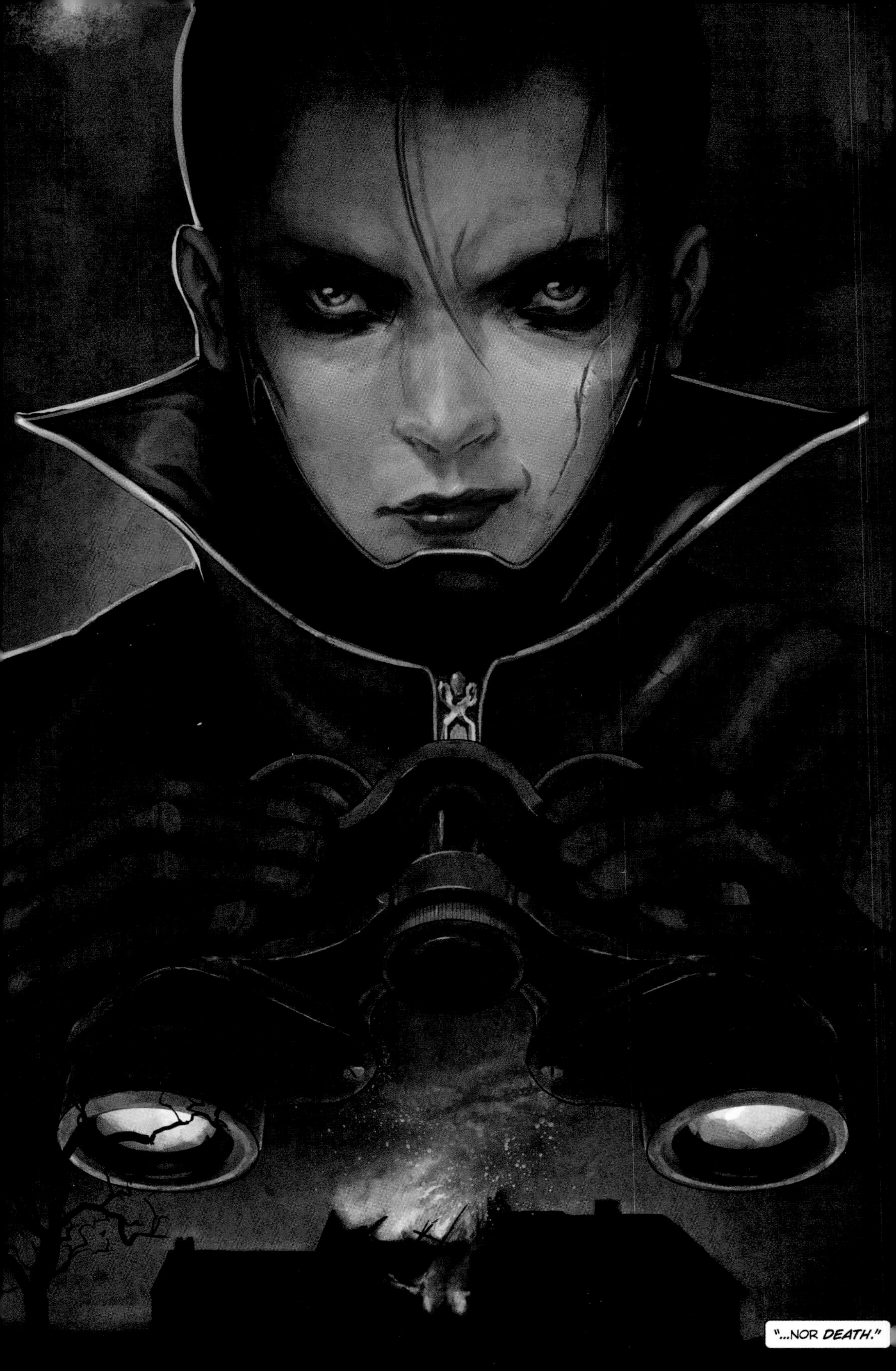
"...NOR *DEATH*."

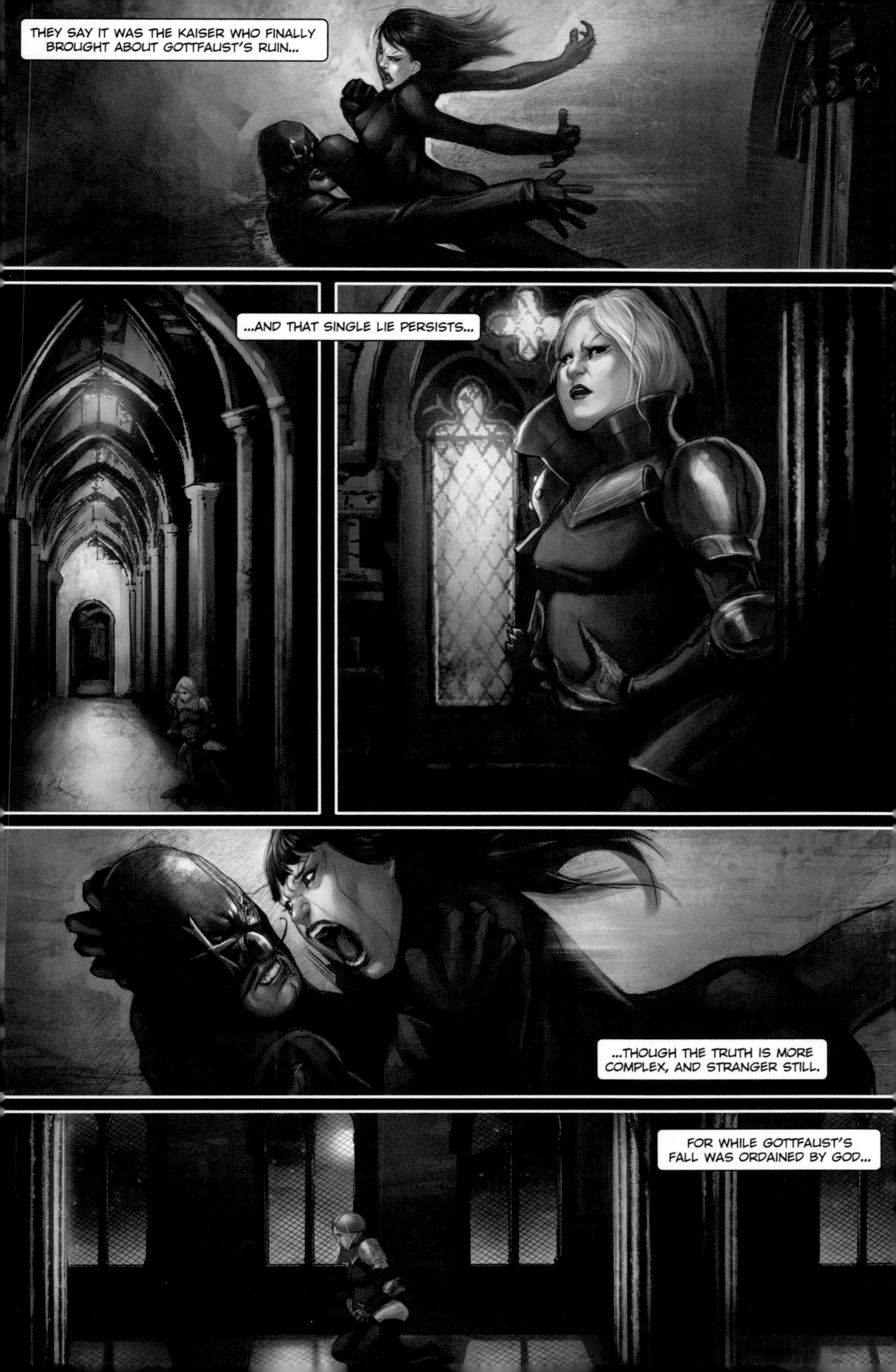
THEY SAY IT WAS THE KAISER WHO FINALLY BROUGHT ABOUT GOTTFAUST'S RUIN...
...AND THAT SINGLE LIE PERSISTS...
...THOUGH THE TRUTH IS MORE COMPLEX, AND STRANGER STILL.
FOR WHILE GOTTFAUST'S FALL WAS ORDAINED BY GOD...

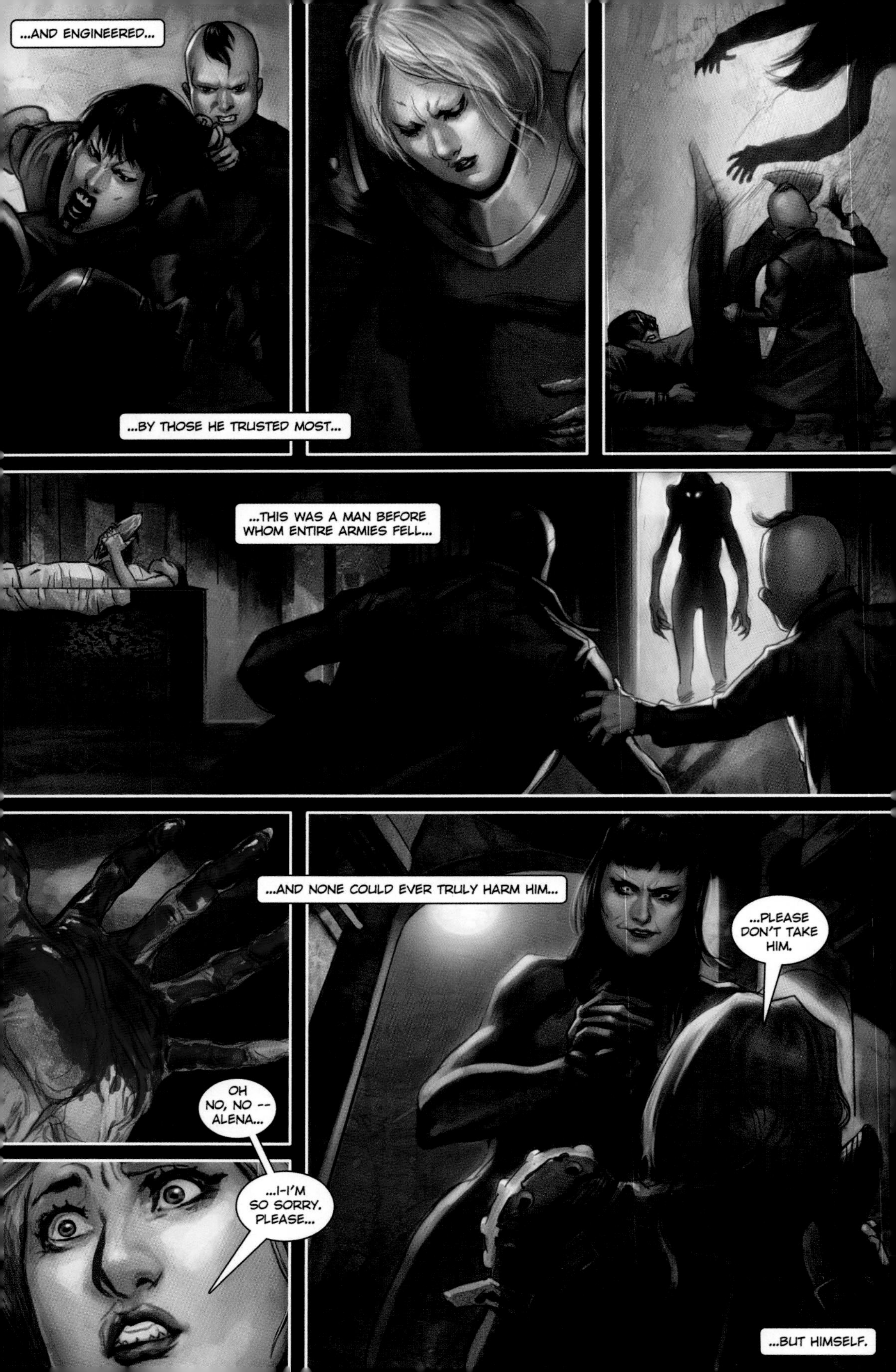
...AND ENGINEERED...
...BY THOSE HE TRUSTED MOST...
...THIS WAS A MAN BEFORE WHOM ENTIRE ARMIES FELL...
OH NO, NO -- ALENA...
...AND NONE COULD EVER TRULY HARM HIM...
...PLEASE DON'T TAKE HIM.
...I-I'M SO SORRY. PLEASE...
...BUT HIMSELF.

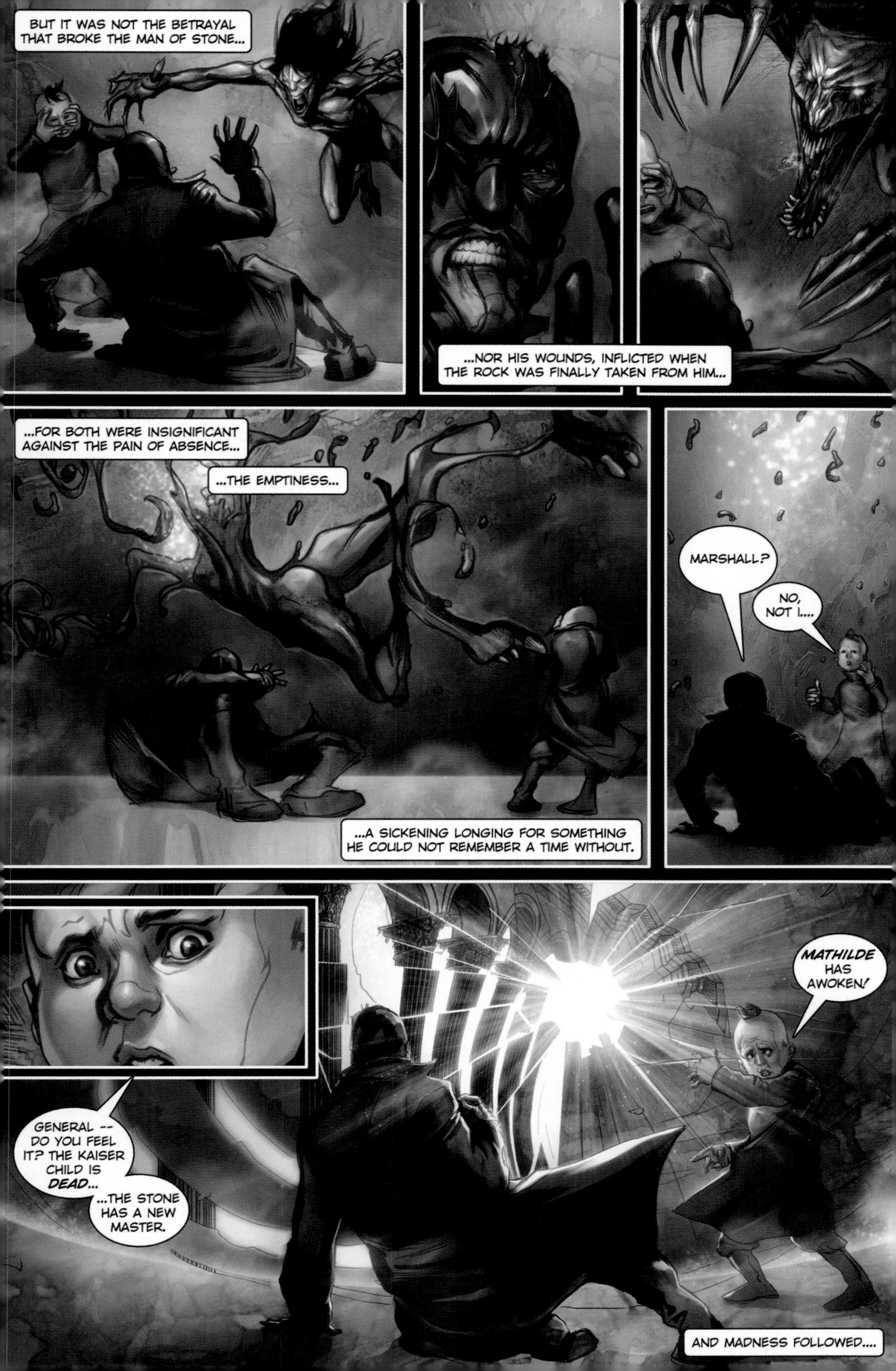
BUT IT WAS NOT THE BETRAYAL THAT BROKE THE MAN OF STONE...
...NOR HIS WOUNDS, INFLICTED WHEN THE ROCK WAS FINALLY TAKEN FROM HIM...
...FOR BOTH WERE INSIGNIFICANT AGAINST THE PAIN OF ABSENCE...
...THE EMPTINESS...
...A SICKENING LONGING FOR SOMETHING HE COULD NOT REMEMBER A TIME WITHOUT.
MARSHALL?
NO, NOT I....
GENERAL -- DO YOU FEEL IT? THE KAISER CHILD IS *DEAD*...
...THE STONE HAS A NEW MASTER.
MATHILDE HAS AWOKEN!
AND MADNESS FOLLOWED....

VIII

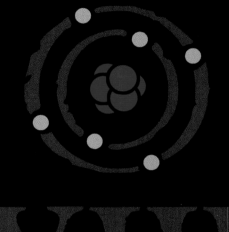

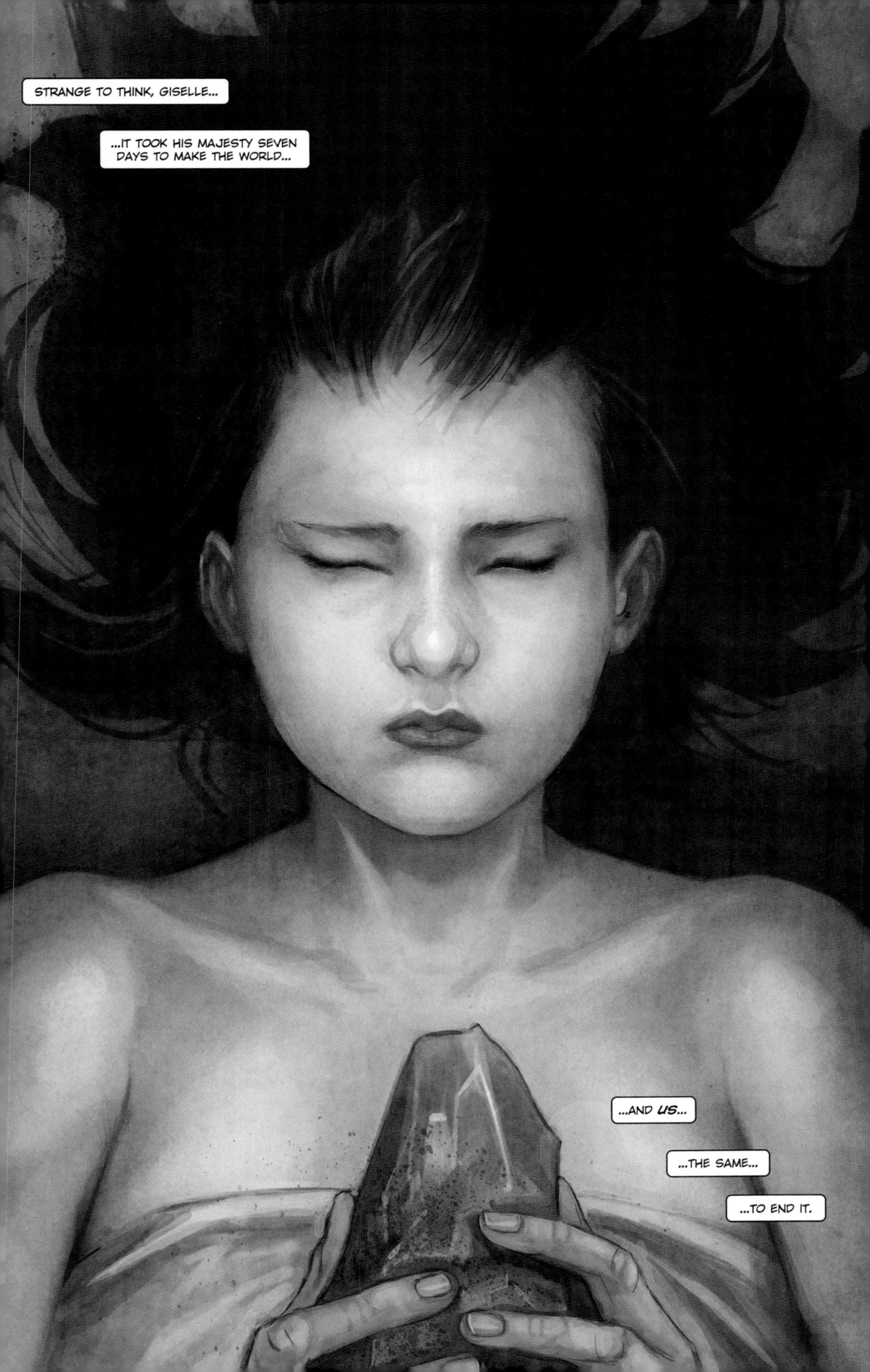
STRANGE TO THINK, GISELLE...
...IT TOOK HIS MAJESTY SEVEN DAYS TO MAKE THE WORLD...
...AND *US*...
...THE SAME...
...TO END IT.

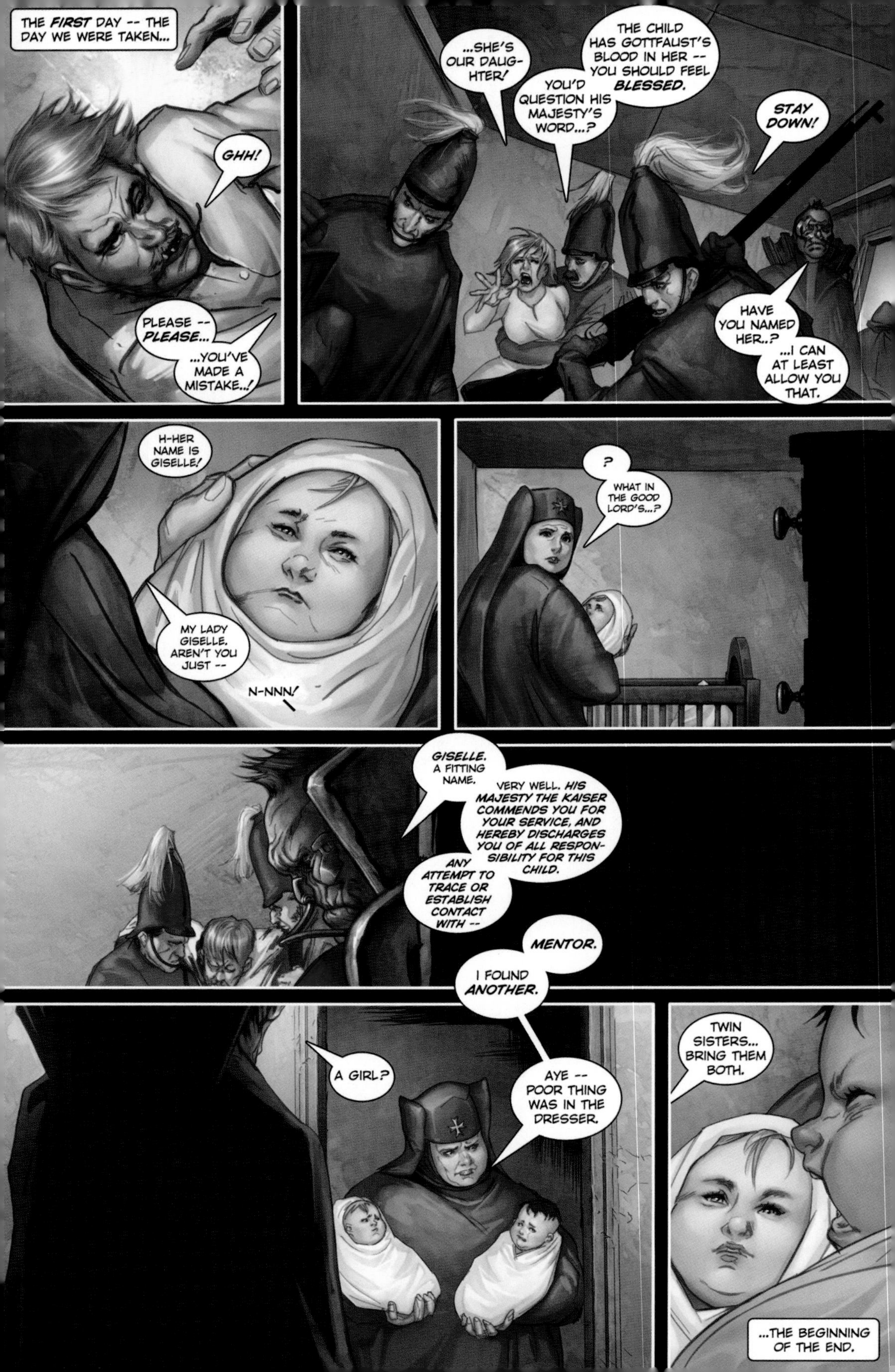
THE *FIRST* DAY -- THE DAY WE WERE TAKEN...
GHH!
PLEASE -- *PLEASE*...
...YOU'VE MADE A MISTAKE..!
...SHE'S OUR DAUGHTER!
THE CHILD HAS GOTTFAUST'S BLOOD IN HER -- YOU SHOULD FEEL *BLESSED.*
YOU'D QUESTION HIS MAJESTY'S WORD...?
STAY DOWN!
HAVE YOU NAMED HER..?
...I CAN AT LEAST ALLOW YOU THAT.
H-HER NAME IS GISELLE!
MY LADY GISELLE. AREN'T YOU JUST --
N-NNN!
?
WHAT IN THE GOOD LORD'S...?
GISELLE. A FITTING NAME.
VERY WELL. *HIS MAJESTY THE KAISER COMMENDS YOU FOR YOUR SERVICE, AND HEREBY DISCHARGES YOU OF ALL RESPONSIBILITY FOR THIS CHILD.*
ANY ATTEMPT TO TRACE OR ESTABLISH CONTACT WITH --
MENTOR.
I FOUND *ANOTHER.*
A GIRL?
AYE -- POOR THING WAS IN THE DRESSER.
TWIN SISTERS... BRING THEM BOTH.
...THE BEGINNING OF THE END.

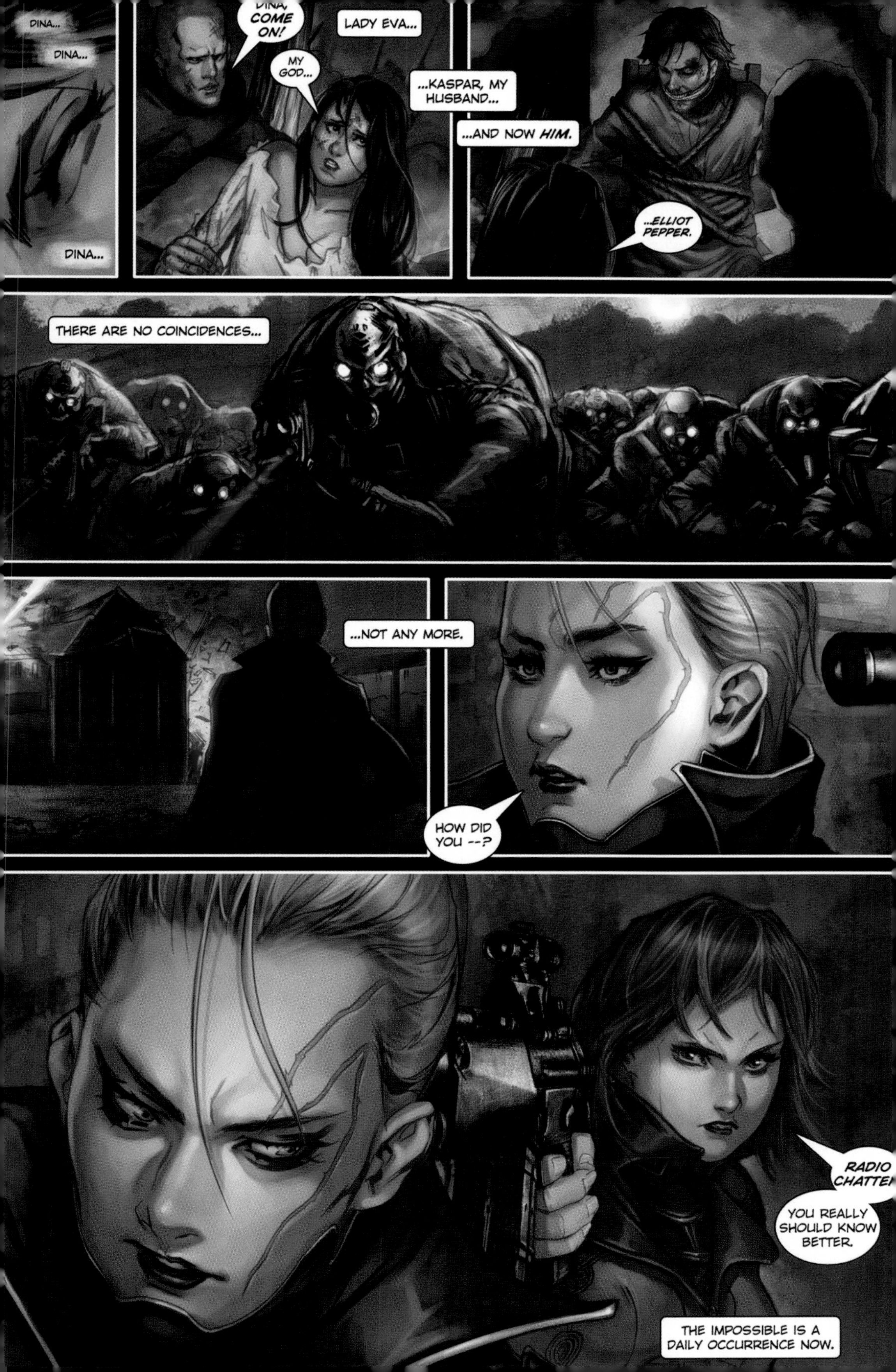
DINA...
DINA...
DINA...
DINA, COME ON!
LADY EVA...
MY GOD...
...KASPAR, MY HUSBAND...
...AND NOW HIM.
...ELLIOT PEPPER.
THERE ARE NO COINCIDENCES...
...NOT ANY MORE.
HOW DID YOU --?
RADIO CHATTE
YOU REALLY SHOULD KNOW BETTER.
THE IMPOSSIBLE IS A DAILY OCCURRENCE NOW.

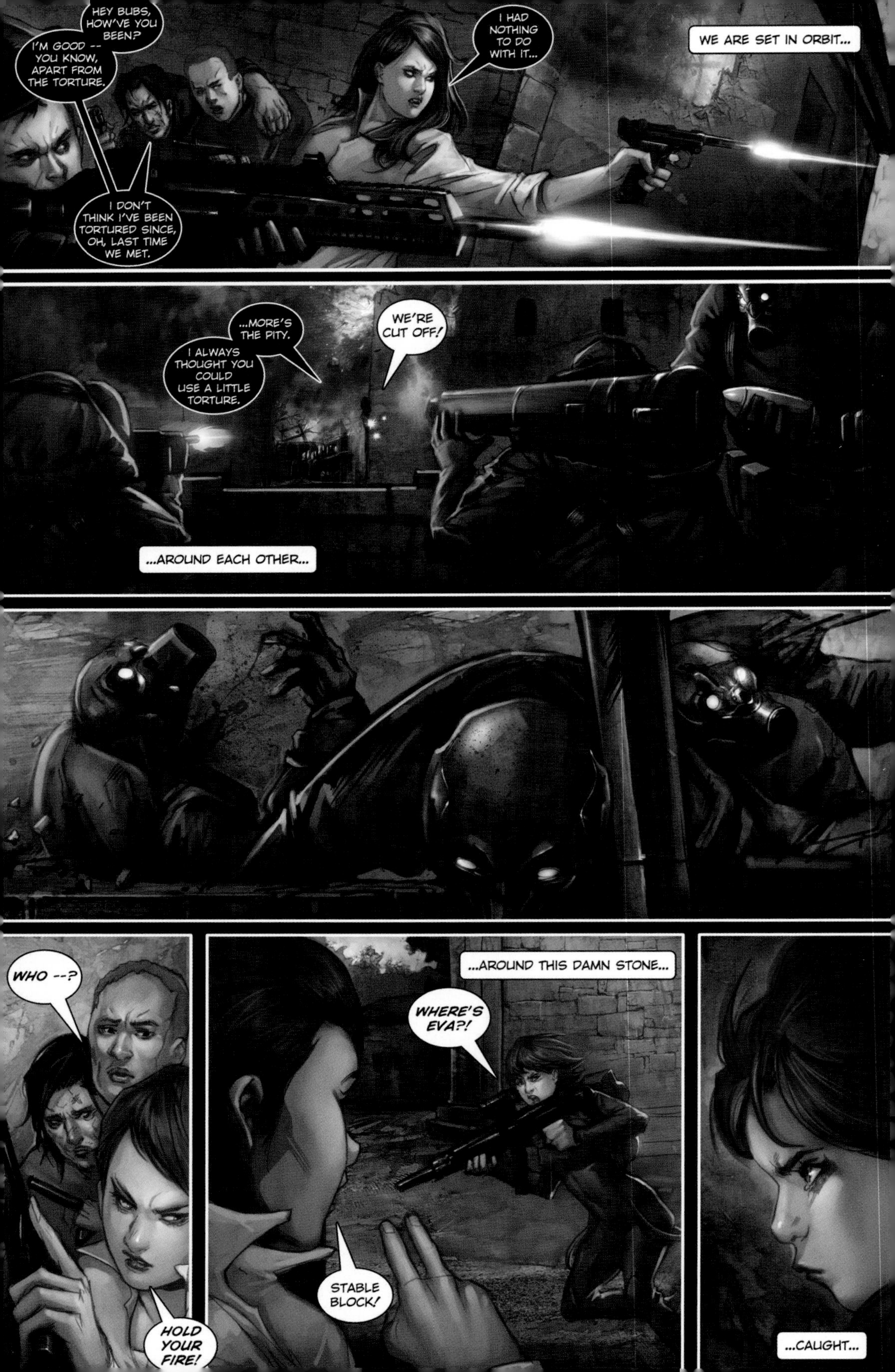
HEY BUBS, HOW'VE YOU BEEN?
I'M GOOD -- YOU KNOW, APART FROM THE TORTURE.
I DON'T THINK I'VE BEEN TORTURED SINCE, OH, LAST TIME WE MET.
I HAD NOTHING TO DO WITH IT...
WE ARE SET IN ORBIT...
I ALWAYS THOUGHT YOU COULD USE A LITTLE TORTURE.
...MORE'S THE PITY.
WE'RE CUT OFF!
...AROUND EACH OTHER...
WHO --?
HOLD YOUR FIRE!
...AROUND THIS DAMN STONE...
WHERE'S EVA?!
STABLE BLOCK!
...CAUGHT...

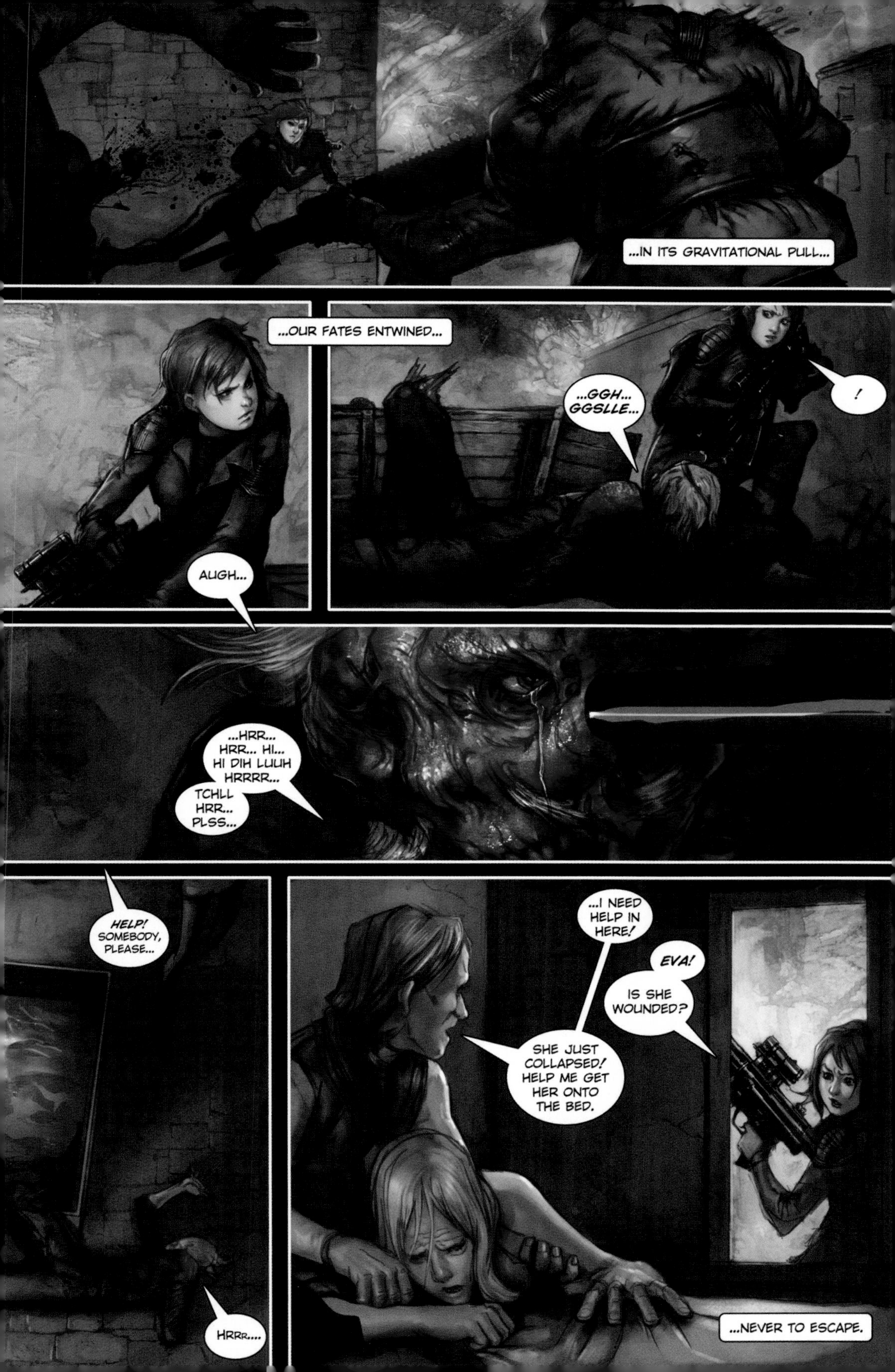

...IN ITS GRAVITATIONAL PULL...
...OUR FATES ENTWINED...
AUGH...
...GGH... GGSLLE...
!
...HRR... HRR... HI... HI DIH LUUH HRRRR...
TCHLL HRR... PLSS...
HELP! SOMEBODY, PLEASE...
HRRR....
...I NEED HELP IN HERE!
EVA!
IS SHE WOUNDED?
SHE JUST COLLAPSED! HELP ME GET HER ONTO THE BED.
...NEVER TO ESCAPE.

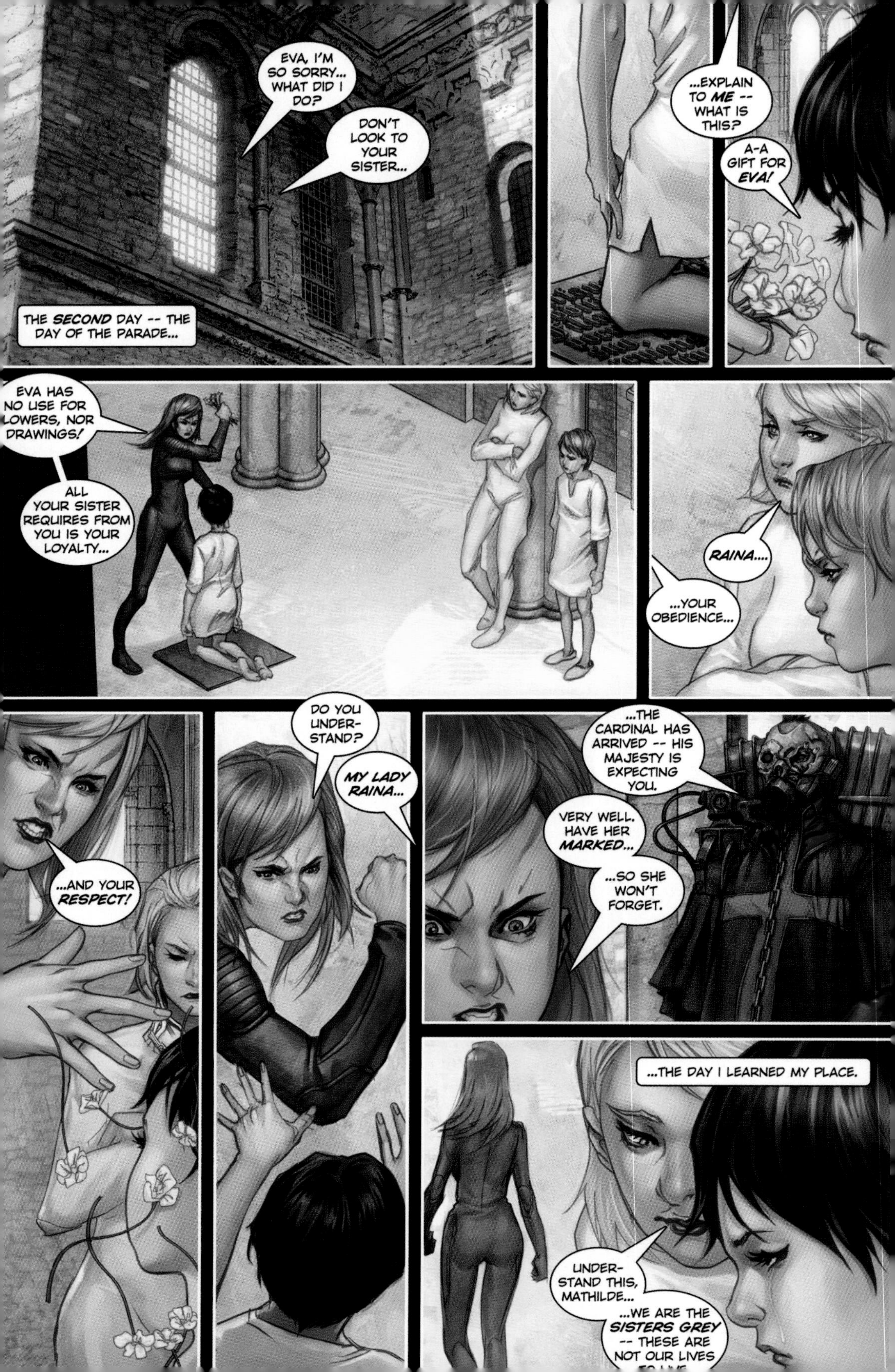

EVA, I'M SO SORRY... WHAT DID I DO?
DON'T LOOK TO YOUR SISTER...
THE *SECOND* DAY -- THE DAY OF THE PARADE...
...EXPLAIN TO *ME* -- WHAT IS THIS?
A-A GIFT FOR *EVA!*
EVA HAS NO USE FOR LOWERS, NOR DRAWINGS!
ALL YOUR SISTER REQUIRES FROM YOU IS YOUR LOYALTY...
RAINA....
...YOUR OBEDIENCE...
...AND YOUR *RESPECT!*
DO YOU UNDER-STAND?
MY LADY RAINA...
...THE CARDINAL HAS ARRIVED -- HIS MAJESTY IS EXPECTING YOU.
VERY WELL. HAVE HER *MARKED*...
...SO SHE WON'T FORGET.
...THE DAY I LEARNED MY PLACE.
UNDER-STAND THIS, MATHILDE...
...WE ARE THE *SISTERS GREY* -- THESE ARE NOT OUR LIVES

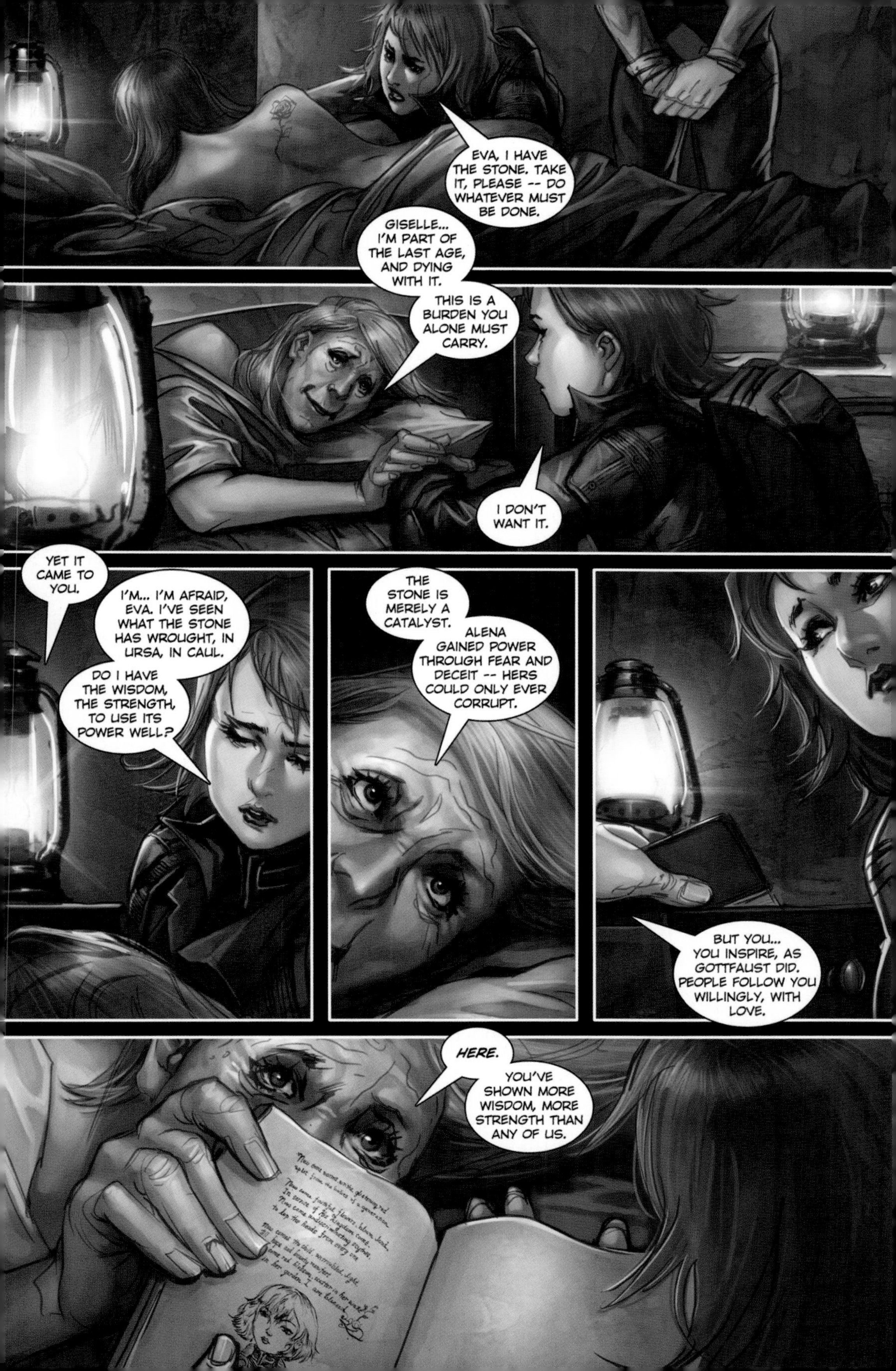
EVA, I HAVE THE STONE. TAKE IT, PLEASE -- DO WHATEVER MUST BE DONE.
GISELLE... I'M PART OF THE LAST AGE, AND DYING WITH IT.
THIS IS A BURDEN YOU ALONE MUST CARRY.
I DON'T WANT IT.
YET IT CAME TO YOU.
I'M... I'M AFRAID, EVA. I'VE SEEN WHAT THE STONE HAS WROUGHT, IN URSA, IN CAUL.
DO I HAVE THE WISDOM, THE STRENGTH, TO USE ITS POWER WELL?
THE STONE IS MERELY A CATALYST.
ALENA GAINED POWER THROUGH FEAR AND DECEIT -- HERS COULD ONLY EVER CORRUPT.
BUT YOU... YOU INSPIRE, AS GOTTFAUST DID. PEOPLE FOLLOW YOU WILLINGLY, WITH LOVE.
HERE.
YOU'VE SHOWN MORE WISDOM, MORE STRENGTH THAN ANY OF US.

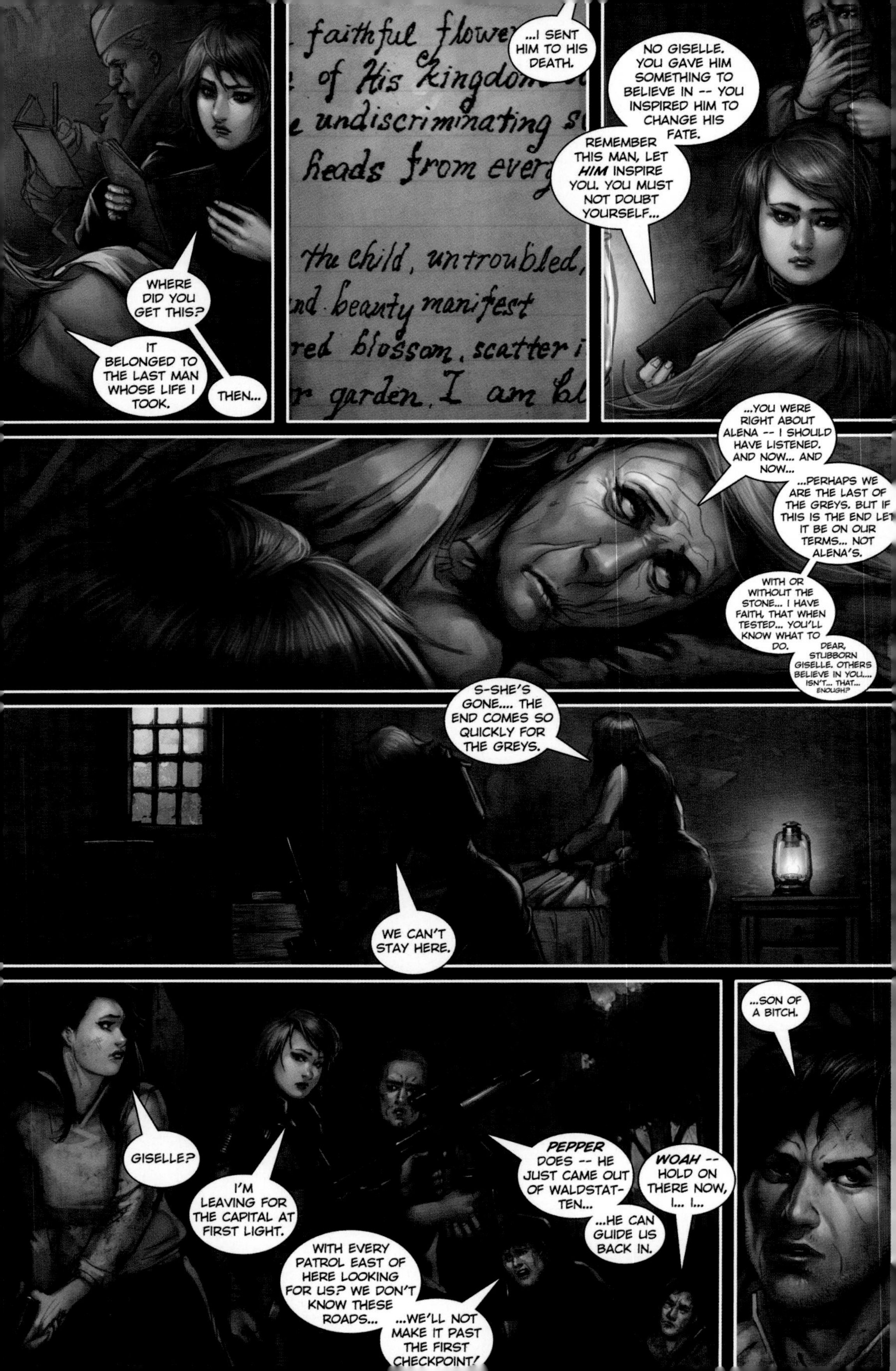

WHERE DID YOU GET THIS?
IT BELONGED TO THE LAST MAN WHOSE LIFE I TOOK.
THEN...
faithful flower
of His kingdom
undiscriminating s
heads from every
the child, untroubled,
nd beauty manifest
red blossom, scatter i
r garden. I am bl
...I SENT HIM TO HIS DEATH.
NO GISELLE. YOU GAVE HIM SOMETHING TO BELIEVE IN -- YOU INSPIRED HIM TO CHANGE HIS FATE.
REMEMBER THIS MAN, LET ***HIM*** INSPIRE YOU. YOU MUST NOT DOUBT YOURSELF...
...YOU WERE RIGHT ABOUT ALENA -- I SHOULD HAVE LISTENED. AND NOW... AND NOW...
...PERHAPS WE ARE THE LAST OF THE GREYS. BUT IF THIS IS THE END LET IT BE ON OUR TERMS... NOT ALENA'S.
WITH OR WITHOUT THE STONE... I HAVE FAITH, THAT WHEN TESTED... YOU'LL KNOW WHAT TO DO.
DEAR, STUBBORN GISELLE. OTHERS BELIEVE IN YOU... ISN'T... THAT... ENOUGH?
S-SHE'S GONE.... THE END COMES SO QUICKLY FOR THE GREYS.
WE CAN'T STAY HERE.
GISELLE?
I'M LEAVING FOR THE CAPITAL AT FIRST LIGHT.
WITH EVERY PATROL EAST OF HERE LOOKING FOR US? WE DON'T KNOW THESE ROADS...
...WE'LL NOT MAKE IT PAST THE FIRST CHECKPOINT!
PEPPER DOES -- HE JUST CAME OUT OF WALDSTAT-TEN...
...HE CAN GUIDE US BACK IN.
WOAH -- HOLD ON THERE NOW, I... I...
...SON OF A BITCH.

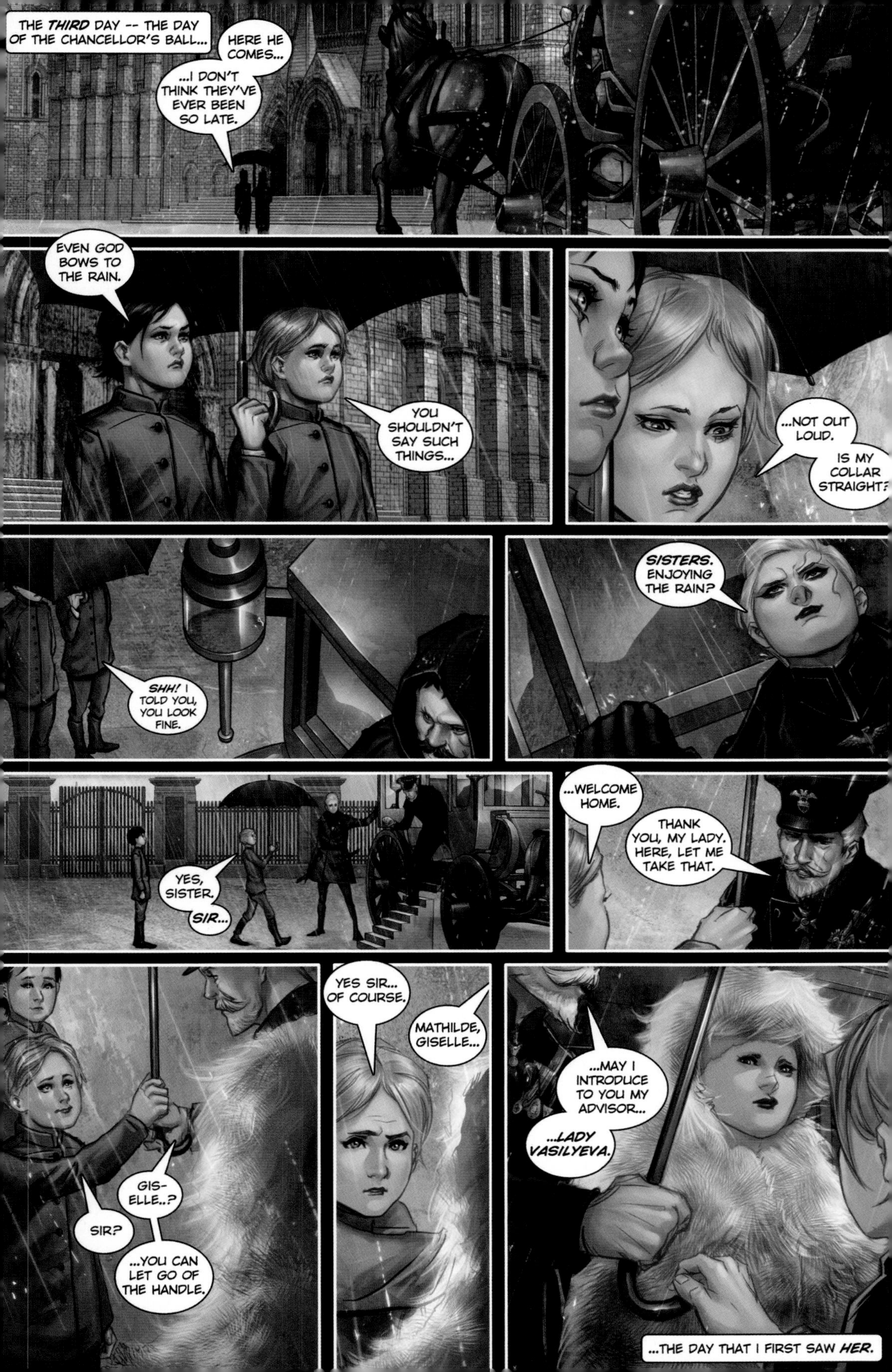
THE THIRD DAY -- THE DAY OF THE CHANCELLOR'S BALL...
HERE HE COMES...
...I DON'T THINK THEY'VE EVER BEEN SO LATE.
EVEN GOD BOWS TO THE RAIN.
YOU SHOULDN'T SAY SUCH THINGS...
...NOT OUT LOUD.
IS MY COLLAR STRAIGHT?
SHH! I TOLD YOU, YOU LOOK FINE.
SISTERS. ENJOYING THE RAIN?
YES, SISTER.
SIR...
...WELCOME HOME.
THANK YOU, MY LADY. HERE, LET ME TAKE THAT.
GIS-ELLE..?
SIR?
...YOU CAN LET GO OF THE HANDLE.
YES SIR... OF COURSE.
MATHILDE, GISELLE...
...MAY I INTRODUCE TO YOU MY ADVISOR...
...LADY VASILYEVA.
...THE DAY THAT I FIRST SAW HER.

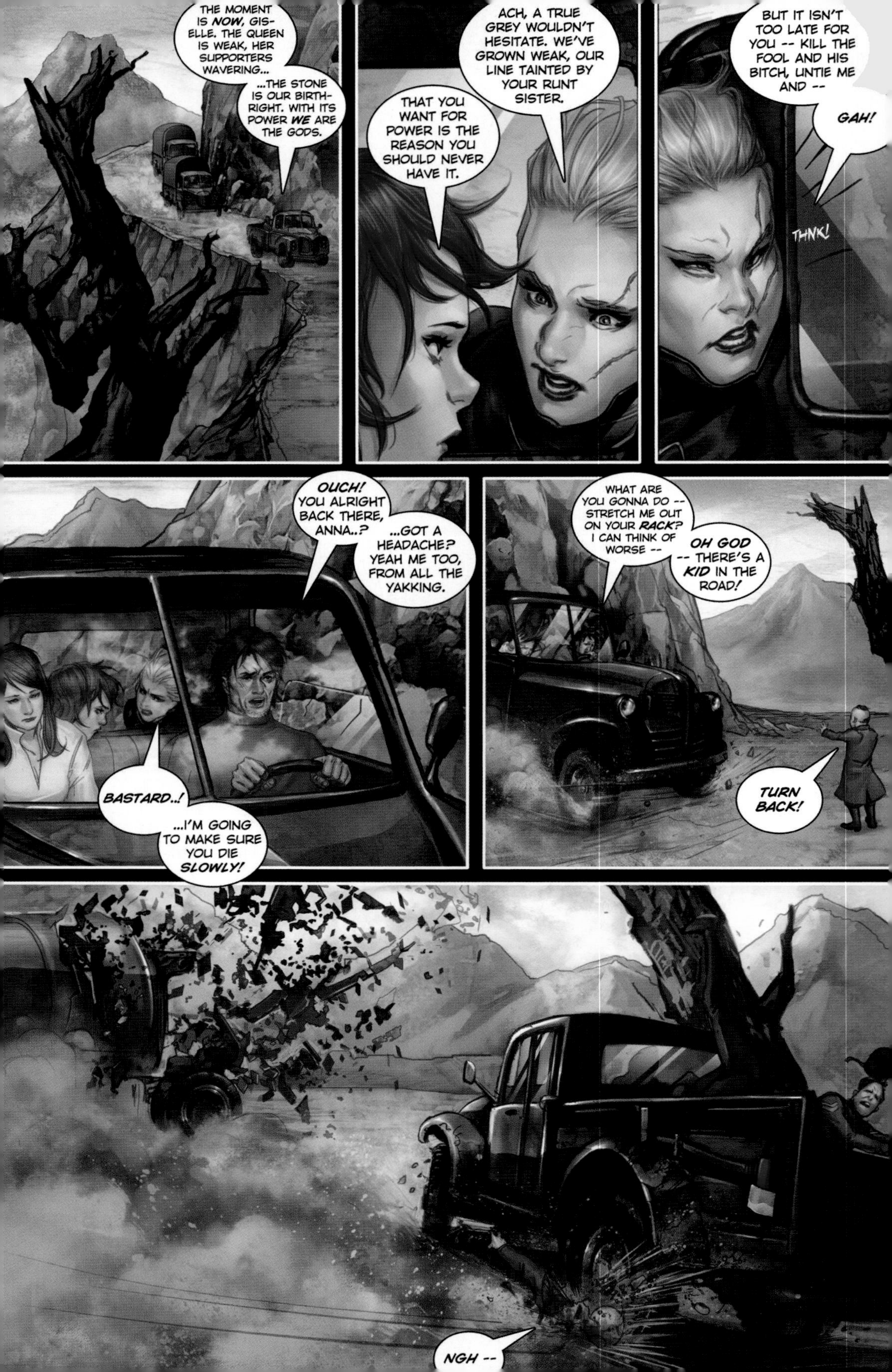
THE MOMENT IS NOW, GISELLE. THE QUEEN IS WEAK, HER SUPPORTERS WAVERING...
...THE STONE IS OUR BIRTHRIGHT. WITH ITS POWER WE ARE THE GODS.
THAT YOU WANT FOR POWER IS THE REASON YOU SHOULD NEVER HAVE IT.
ACH, A TRUE GREY WOULDN'T HESITATE. WE'VE GROWN WEAK, OUR LINE TAINTED BY YOUR RUNT SISTER.
BUT IT ISN'T TOO LATE FOR YOU -- KILL THE FOOL AND HIS BITCH, UNTIE ME AND --
GAH!
THNK!
OUCH! YOU ALRIGHT BACK THERE, ANNA..?
...GOT A HEADACHE? YEAH ME TOO, FROM ALL THE YAKKING.
BASTARD..!
...I'M GOING TO MAKE SURE YOU DIE SLOWLY!
WHAT ARE YOU GONNA DO -- STRETCH ME OUT ON YOUR RACK? I CAN THINK OF WORSE --
OH GOD -- THERE'S A KID IN THE ROAD!
TURN BACK!
NGH --

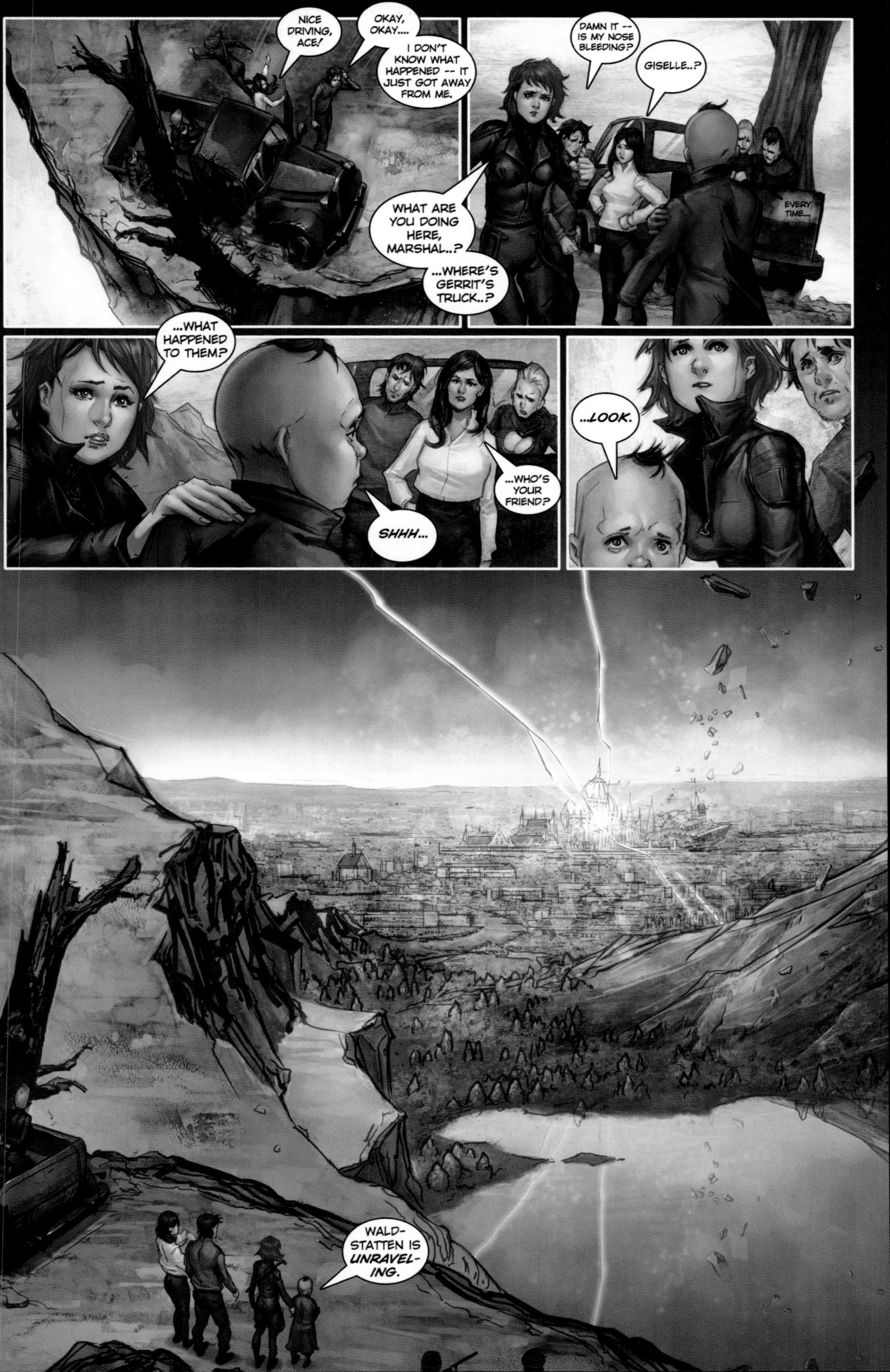
NICE DRIVING, ACE!
OKAY, OKAY.... I DON'T KNOW WHAT HAPPENED -- IT JUST GOT AWAY FROM ME.
DAMN IT -- IS MY NOSE BLEEDING?
GISELLE..?
WHAT ARE YOU DOING HERE, MARSHAL..?
EVERY TIME...
...WHERE'S GERRIT'S TRUCK..?
...WHAT HAPPENED TO THEM?
...WHO'S YOUR FRIEND?
SHHH...
...LOOK.
WALD-STATTEN IS UNRAVEL-ING.

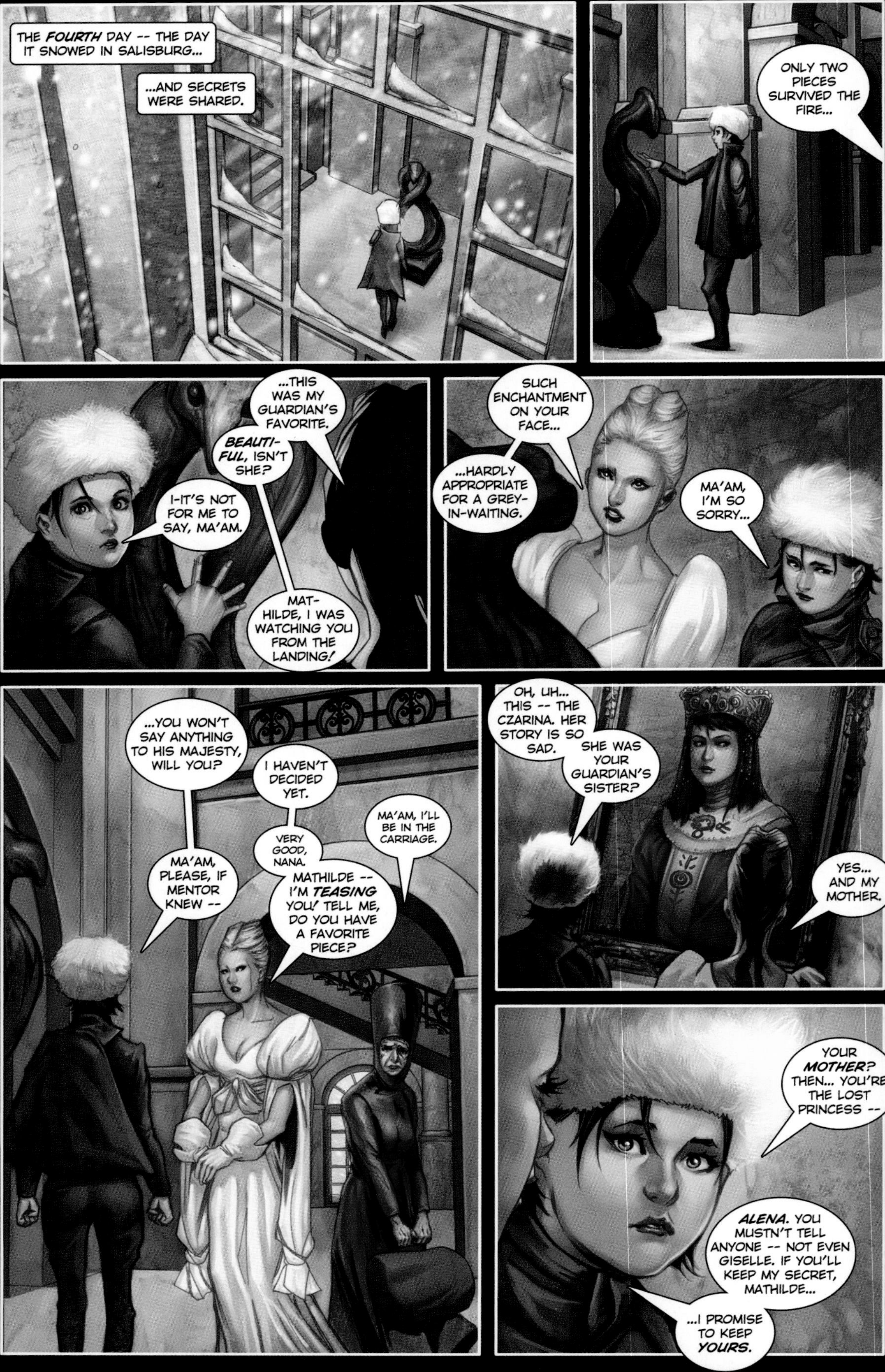
THE FOURTH DAY -- THE DAY IT SNOWED IN SALISBURG...
...AND SECRETS WERE SHARED.
ONLY TWO PIECES SURVIVED THE FIRE...
...THIS WAS MY GUARDIAN'S FAVORITE.
BEAUTIFUL, ISN'T SHE?
I-IT'S NOT FOR ME TO SAY, MA'AM.
MATHILDE, I WAS WATCHING YOU FROM THE LANDING!
SUCH ENCHANTMENT ON YOUR FACE...
...HARDLY APPROPRIATE FOR A GREY-IN-WAITING.
MA'AM, I'M SO SORRY...
...YOU WON'T SAY ANYTHING TO HIS MAJESTY, WILL YOU?
I HAVEN'T DECIDED YET.
MA'AM, I'LL BE IN THE CARRIAGE.
VERY GOOD, NANA.
MA'AM, PLEASE, IF MENTOR KNEW --
MATHILDE -- I'M TEASING YOU! TELL ME, DO YOU HAVE A FAVORITE PIECE?
OH, UH... THIS -- THE CZARINA. HER STORY IS SO SAD.
SHE WAS YOUR GUARDIAN'S SISTER?
YES... AND MY MOTHER.
YOUR MOTHER? THEN... YOU'RE THE LOST PRINCESS --
ALENA. YOU MUSTN'T TELL ANYONE -- NOT EVEN GISELLE. IF YOU'LL KEEP MY SECRET, MATHILDE...
...I PROMISE TO KEEP YOURS.

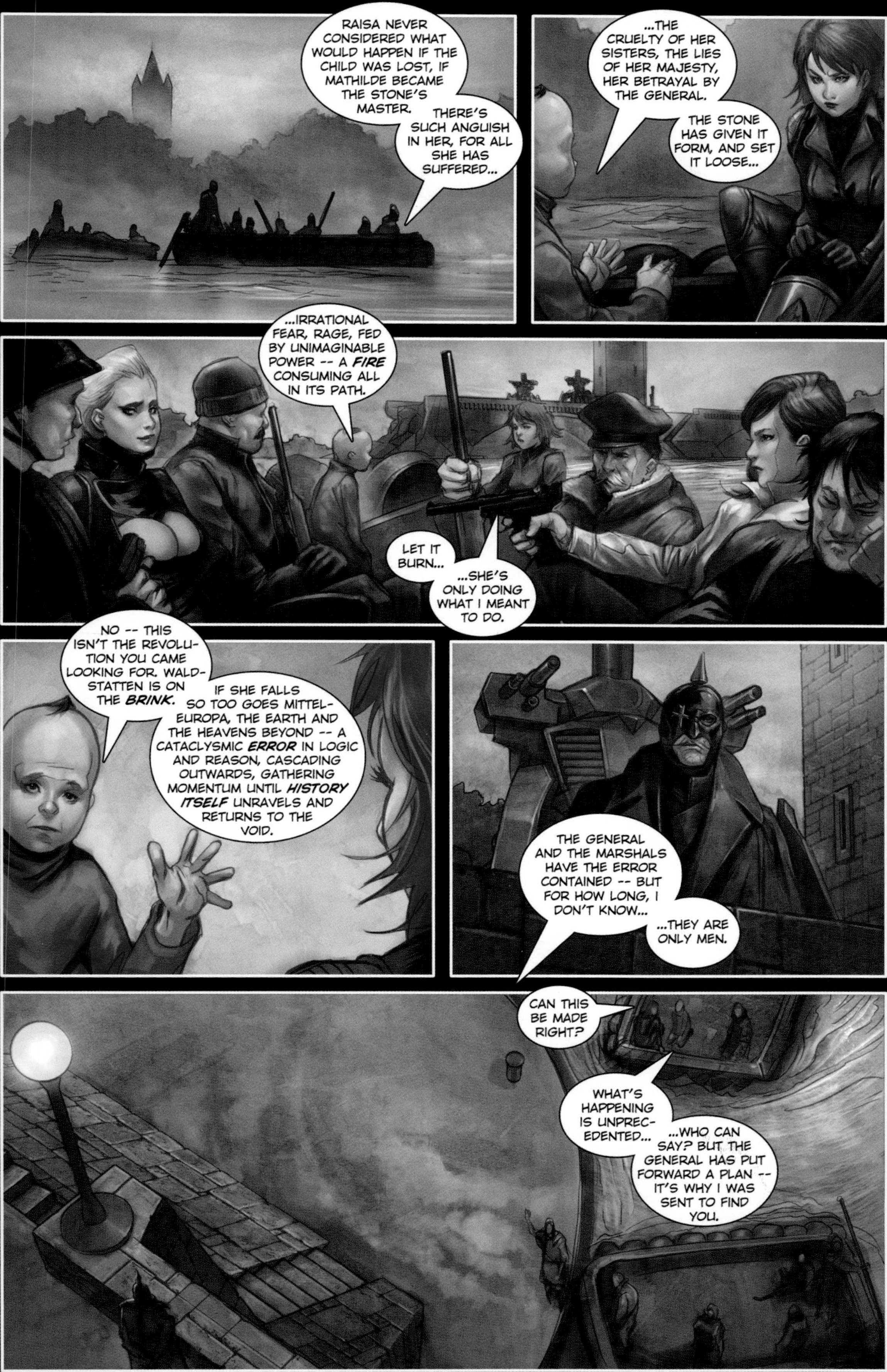
RAISA NEVER CONSIDERED WHAT WOULD HAPPEN IF THE CHILD WAS LOST, IF MATHILDE BECAME THE STONE'S MASTER.
THERE'S SUCH ANGUISH IN HER, FOR ALL SHE HAS SUFFERED...
...THE CRUELTY OF HER SISTERS, THE LIES OF HER MAJESTY, HER BETRAYAL BY THE GENERAL.
THE STONE HAS GIVEN IT FORM, AND SET IT LOOSE...
...IRRATIONAL FEAR, RAGE, FED BY UNIMAGINABLE POWER -- A *FIRE* CONSUMING ALL IN ITS PATH.
LET IT BURN...
...SHE'S ONLY DOING WHAT I MEANT TO DO.
NO -- THIS ISN'T THE REVOLUTION YOU CAME LOOKING FOR. WALDSTATTEN IS ON THE *BRINK*.
IF SHE FALLS SO TOO GOES MITTELEUROPA, THE EARTH AND THE HEAVENS BEYOND -- A CATACLYSMIC *ERROR* IN LOGIC AND REASON, CASCADING OUTWARDS, GATHERING MOMENTUM UNTIL *HISTORY ITSELF* UNRAVELS AND RETURNS TO THE VOID.
THE GENERAL AND THE MARSHALS HAVE THE ERROR CONTAINED -- BUT FOR HOW LONG, I DON'T KNOW...
...THEY ARE ONLY MEN.
CAN THIS BE MADE RIGHT?
WHAT'S HAPPENING IS UNPRECEDENTED...
...WHO CAN SAY? BUT THE GENERAL HAS PUT FORWARD A PLAN -- IT'S WHY I WAS SENT TO FIND YOU.

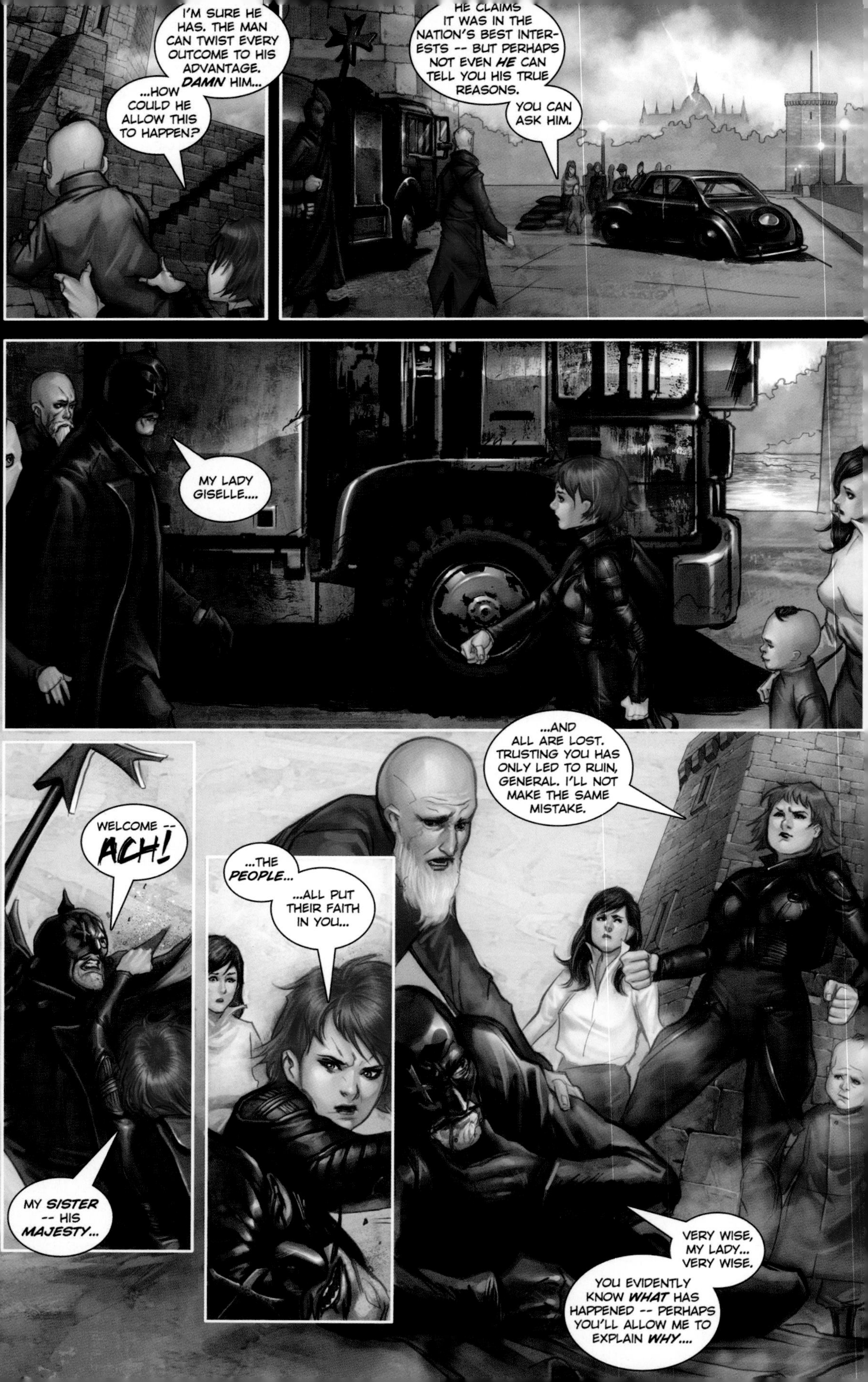
I'M SURE HE HAS. THE MAN CAN TWIST EVERY OUTCOME TO HIS ADVANTAGE. *DAMN* HIM...
...HOW COULD HE ALLOW THIS TO HAPPEN?
HE CLAIMS IT WAS IN THE NATION'S BEST INTER-ESTS -- BUT PERHAPS NOT EVEN *HE* CAN TELL YOU HIS TRUE REASONS.
YOU CAN ASK HIM.
MY LADY GISELLE....
WELCOME --
ACH!
MY *SISTER* -- HIS *MAJESTY*...
...THE *PEOPLE*...
...ALL PUT THEIR FAITH IN YOU...
...AND ALL ARE LOST. TRUSTING YOU HAS ONLY LED TO RUIN, GENERAL. I'LL NOT MAKE THE SAME MISTAKE.
VERY WISE, MY LADY... VERY WISE.
YOU EVIDENTLY KNOW *WHAT* HAS HAPPENED -- PERHAPS YOU'LL ALLOW ME TO EXPLAIN *WHY*....

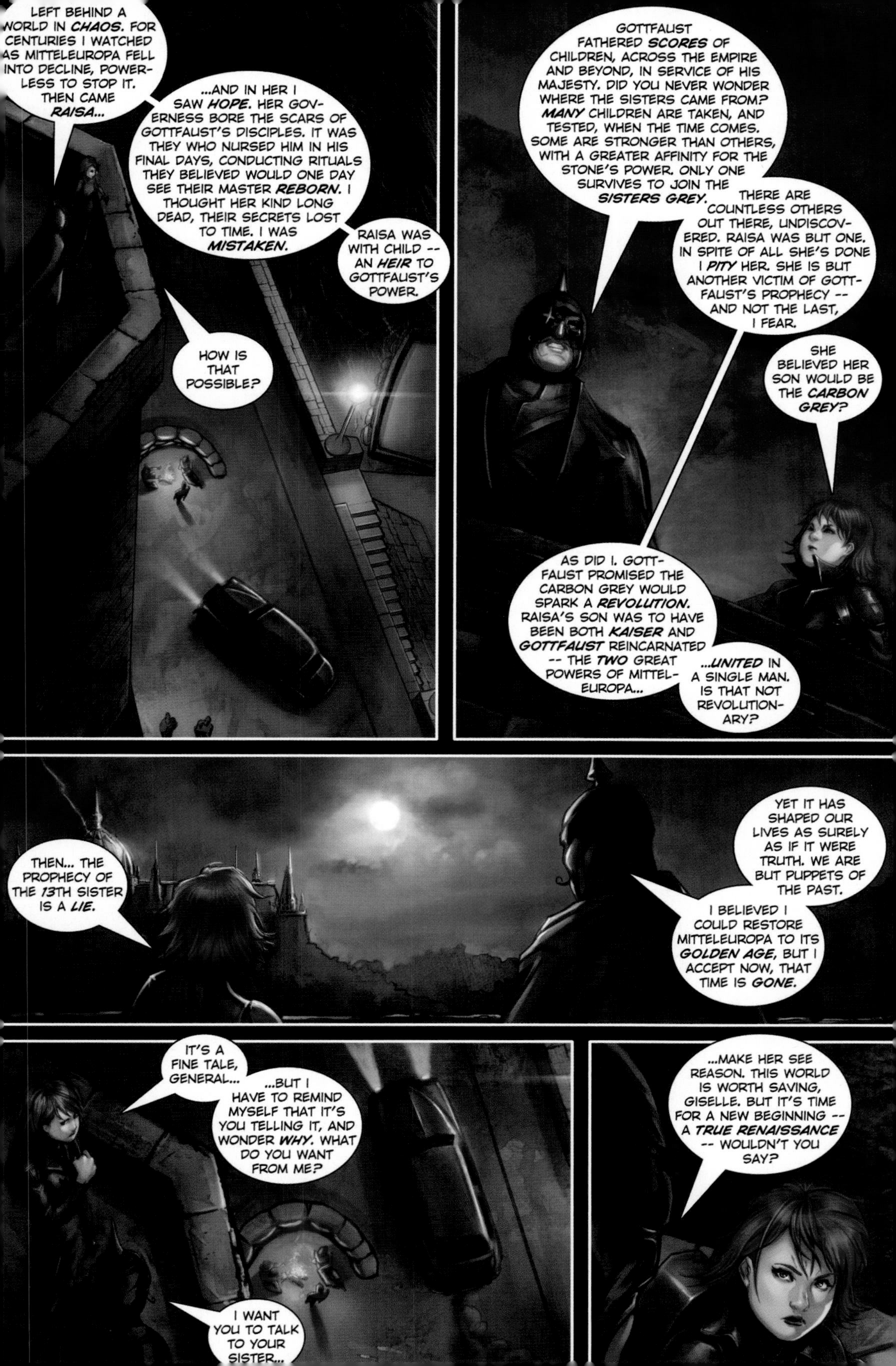
LEFT BEHIND A WORLD IN CHAOS. FOR CENTURIES I WATCHED AS MITTELEUROPA FELL INTO DECLINE, POWERLESS TO STOP IT. THEN CAME RAISA...
...AND IN HER I SAW HOPE. HER GOVERNESS BORE THE SCARS OF GOTTFAUST'S DISCIPLES. IT WAS THEY WHO NURSED HIM IN HIS FINAL DAYS, CONDUCTING RITUALS THEY BELIEVED WOULD ONE DAY SEE THEIR MASTER REBORN. I THOUGHT HER KIND LONG DEAD, THEIR SECRETS LOST TO TIME. I WAS MISTAKEN.
RAISA WAS WITH CHILD -- AN HEIR TO GOTTFAUST'S POWER.
HOW IS THAT POSSIBLE?
GOTTFAUST FATHERED SCORES OF CHILDREN, ACROSS THE EMPIRE AND BEYOND, IN SERVICE OF HIS MAJESTY. DID YOU NEVER WONDER WHERE THE SISTERS CAME FROM? MANY CHILDREN ARE TAKEN, AND TESTED, WHEN THE TIME COMES. SOME ARE STRONGER THAN OTHERS, WITH A GREATER AFFINITY FOR THE STONE'S POWER. ONLY ONE SURVIVES TO JOIN THE SISTERS GREY.
THERE ARE COUNTLESS OTHERS OUT THERE, UNDISCOVERED. RAISA WAS BUT ONE. IN SPITE OF ALL SHE'S DONE I PITY HER. SHE IS BUT ANOTHER VICTIM OF GOTTFAUST'S PROPHECY -- AND NOT THE LAST, I FEAR.
SHE BELIEVED HER SON WOULD BE THE CARBON GREY?
AS DID I. GOTTFAUST PROMISED THE CARBON GREY WOULD SPARK A REVOLUTION. RAISA'S SON WAS TO HAVE BEEN BOTH KAISER AND GOTTFAUST REINCARNATED -- THE TWO GREAT POWERS OF MITTELEUROPA...
...UNITED IN A SINGLE MAN. IS THAT NOT REVOLUTIONARY?
THEN... THE PROPHECY OF THE 13TH SISTER IS A LIE.
YET IT HAS SHAPED OUR LIVES AS SURELY AS IF IT WERE TRUTH. WE ARE BUT PUPPETS OF THE PAST.
I BELIEVED I COULD RESTORE MITTELEUROPA TO ITS GOLDEN AGE, BUT I ACCEPT NOW, THAT TIME IS GONE.
IT'S A FINE TALE, GENERAL...
...BUT I HAVE TO REMIND MYSELF THAT IT'S YOU TELLING IT, AND WONDER WHY. WHAT DO YOU WANT FROM ME?
I WANT YOU TO TALK TO YOUR SISTER...
...MAKE HER SEE REASON. THIS WORLD IS WORTH SAVING, GISELLE. BUT IT'S TIME FOR A NEW BEGINNING -- A TRUE RENAISSANCE -- WOULDN'T YOU SAY?

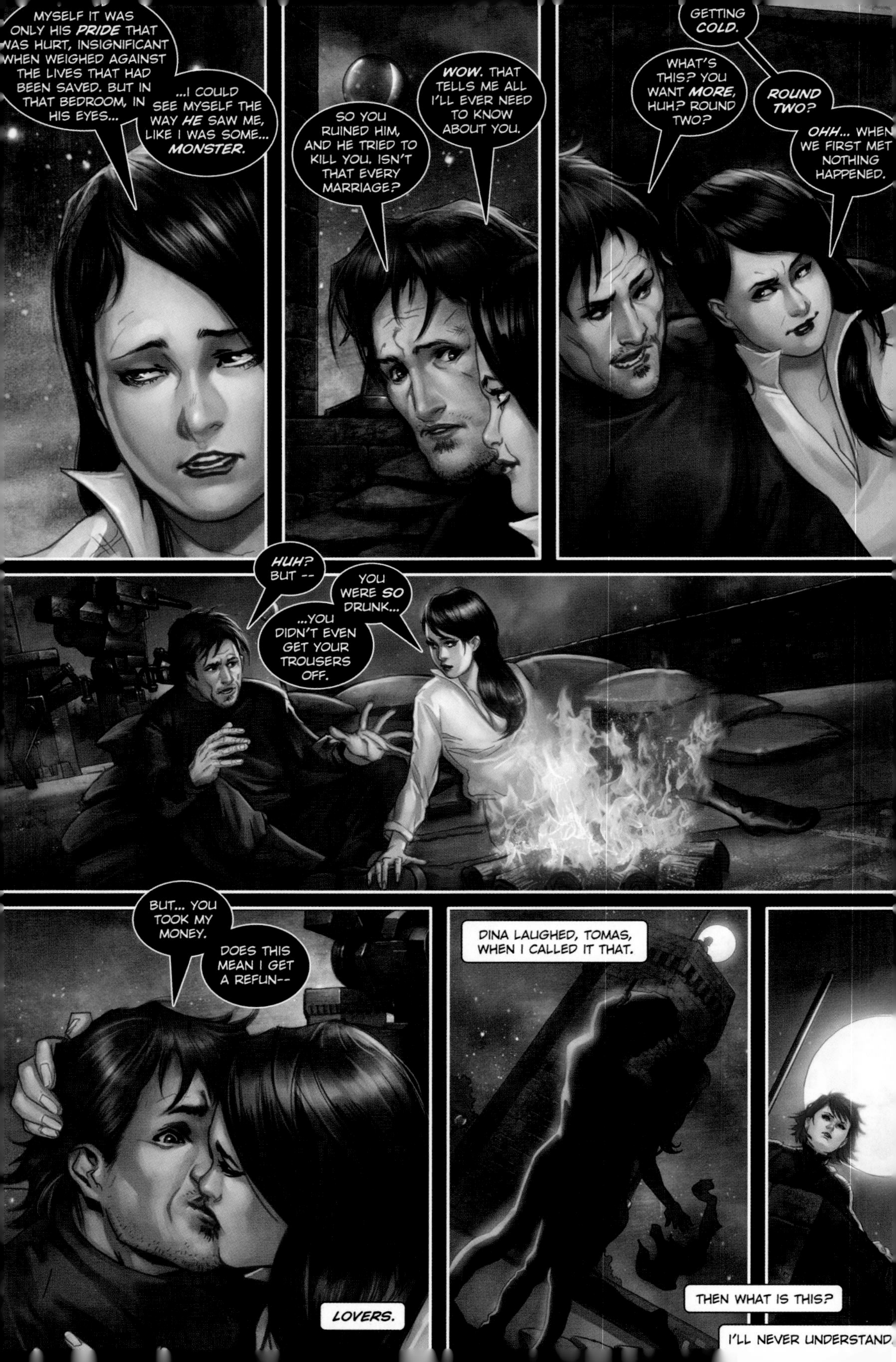
MYSELF IT WAS ONLY HIS PRIDE THAT WAS HURT, INSIGNIFICANT WHEN WEIGHED AGAINST THE LIVES THAT HAD BEEN SAVED. BUT IN THAT BEDROOM, IN HIS EYES...
...I COULD SEE MYSELF THE WAY HE SAW ME, LIKE I WAS SOME... MONSTER.
SO YOU RUINED HIM, AND HE TRIED TO KILL YOU. ISN'T THAT EVERY MARRIAGE?
WOW. THAT TELLS ME ALL I'LL EVER NEED TO KNOW ABOUT YOU.
GETTING COLD.
WHAT'S THIS? YOU WANT MORE, HUH? ROUND TWO?
ROUND TWO?
OHH... WHEN WE FIRST MET NOTHING HAPPENED.
HUH? BUT --
YOU WERE SO DRUNK...
...YOU DIDN'T EVEN GET YOUR TROUSERS OFF.
BUT... YOU TOOK MY MONEY.
DOES THIS MEAN I GET A REFUN--
LOVERS.
DINA LAUGHED, TOMAS, WHEN I CALLED IT THAT.
THEN WHAT IS THIS?
I'LL NEVER UNDERSTAND.

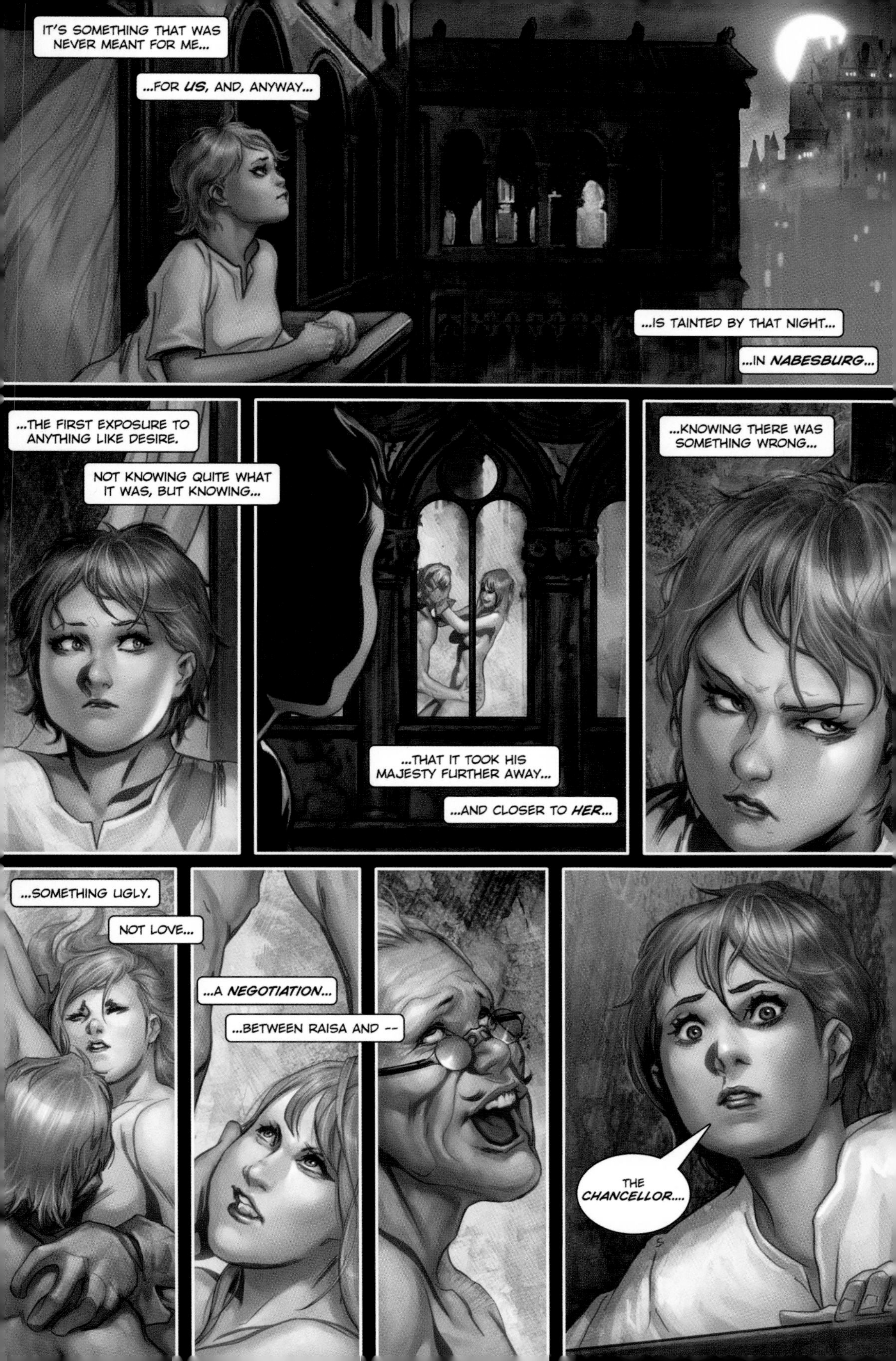
IT'S SOMETHING THAT WAS NEVER MEANT FOR ME...
...FOR US, AND, ANYWAY...
...IS TAINTED BY THAT NIGHT...
...IN NABESBURG...
...THE FIRST EXPOSURE TO ANYTHING LIKE DESIRE.
NOT KNOWING QUITE WHAT IT WAS, BUT KNOWING...
...THAT IT TOOK HIS MAJESTY FURTHER AWAY...
...AND CLOSER TO HER...
...KNOWING THERE WAS SOMETHING WRONG...
...SOMETHING UGLY.
NOT LOVE...
...A NEGOTIATION...
...BETWEEN RAISA AND --
THE CHANCELLOR....

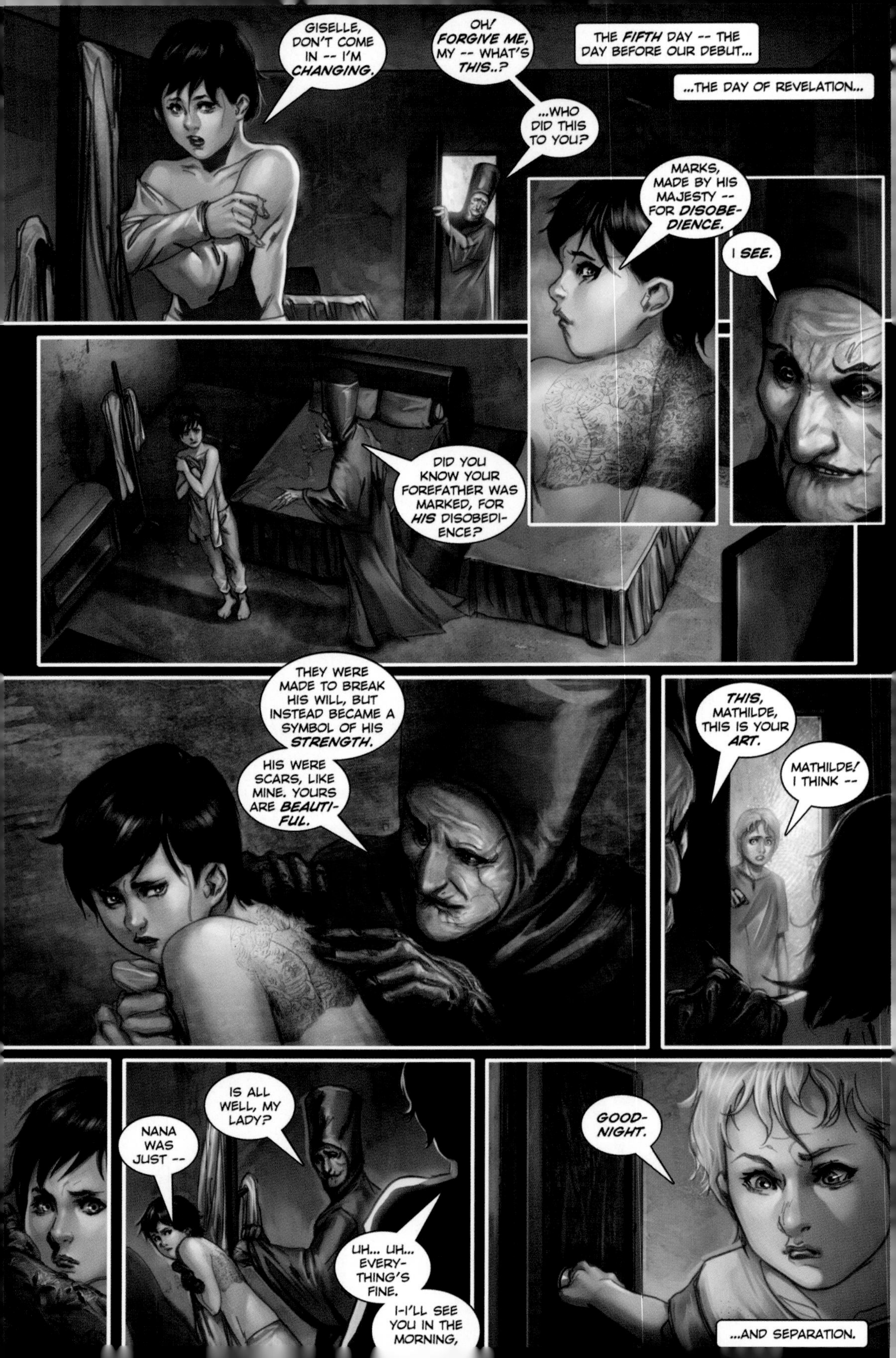
GISELLE, DON'T COME IN -- I'M CHANGING.
OH! FORGIVE ME, MY -- WHAT'S THIS..?
...WHO DID THIS TO YOU?
THE FIFTH DAY -- THE DAY BEFORE OUR DEBUT...
...THE DAY OF REVELATION...
MARKS, MADE BY HIS MAJESTY -- FOR DISOBEDIENCE.
I SEE.
DID YOU KNOW YOUR FOREFATHER WAS MARKED, FOR HIS DISOBEDIENCE?
THEY WERE MADE TO BREAK HIS WILL, BUT INSTEAD BECAME A SYMBOL OF HIS STRENGTH.
HIS WERE SCARS, LIKE MINE. YOURS ARE BEAUTIFUL.
THIS, MATHILDE, THIS IS YOUR ART.
MATHILDE! I THINK --
IS ALL WELL, MY LADY?
NANA WAS JUST --
UH... UH... EVERYTHING'S FINE.
I-I'LL SEE YOU IN THE MORNING,
GOOD-NIGHT.
...AND SEPARATION.

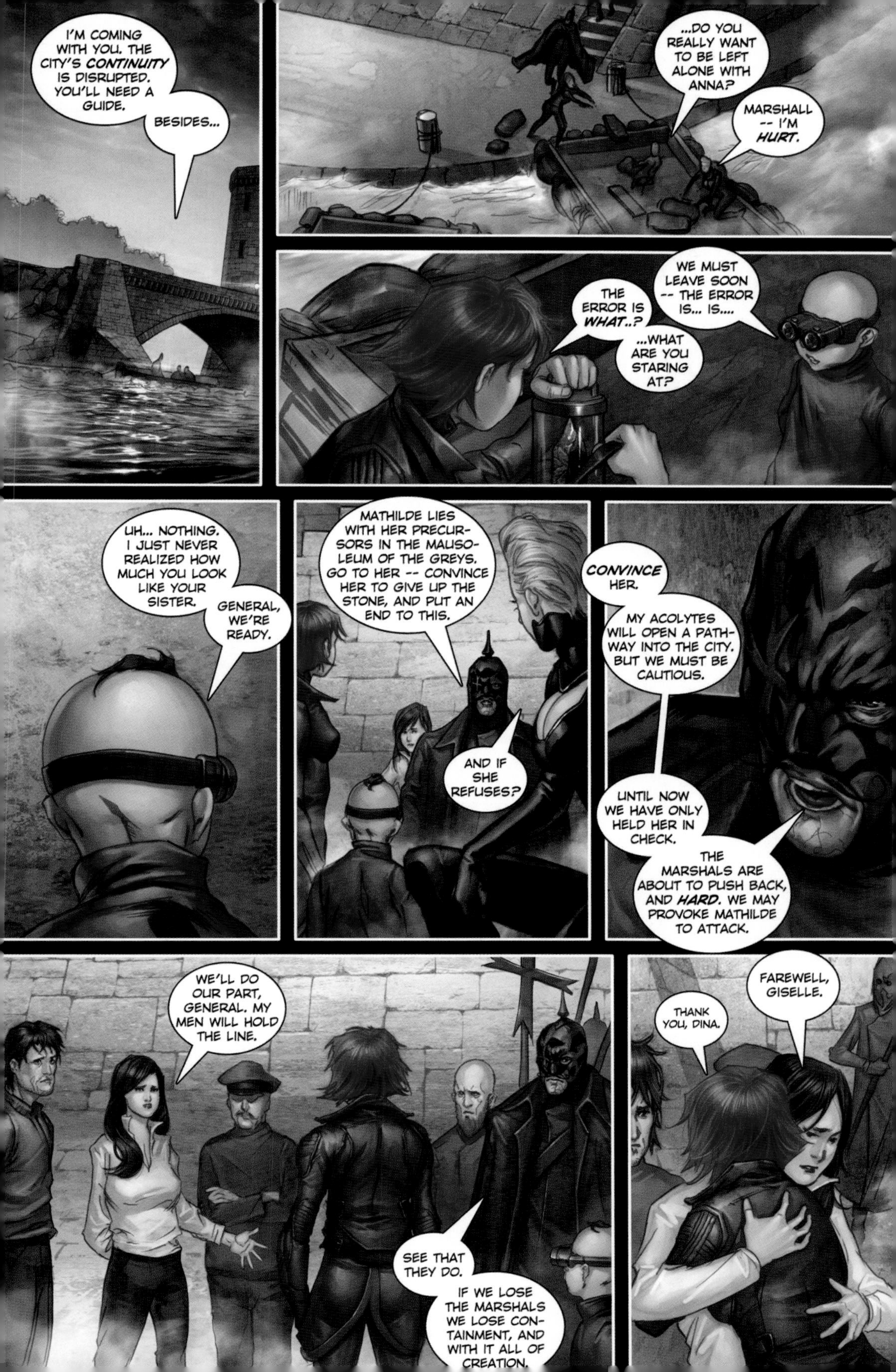
I'M COMING WITH YOU. THE CITY'S *CONTINUITY* IS DISRUPTED. YOU'LL NEED A GUIDE.
BESIDES...
...DO YOU REALLY WANT TO BE LEFT ALONE WITH ANNA?
MARSHALL -- I'M *HURT*.
WE MUST LEAVE SOON -- THE ERROR IS... IS....
THE ERROR IS *WHAT*..?
...WHAT ARE YOU STARING AT?
UH... NOTHING. I JUST NEVER REALIZED HOW MUCH YOU LOOK LIKE YOUR SISTER.
GENERAL, WE'RE READY.
MATHILDE LIES WITH HER PRECUR-SORS IN THE MAUSO-LEUM OF THE GREYS. GO TO HER -- CONVINCE HER TO GIVE UP THE STONE, AND PUT AN END TO THIS.
AND IF SHE REFUSES?
CONVINCE HER.
MY ACOLYTES WILL OPEN A PATH-WAY INTO THE CITY. BUT WE MUST BE CAUTIOUS.
UNTIL NOW WE HAVE ONLY HELD HER IN CHECK.
THE MARSHALS ARE ABOUT TO PUSH BACK, AND *HARD*. WE MAY PROVOKE MATHILDE TO ATTACK.
WE'LL DO OUR PART, GENERAL. MY MEN WILL HOLD THE LINE.
SEE THAT THEY DO.
IF WE LOSE THE MARSHALS WE LOSE CON-TAINMENT, AND WITH IT ALL OF CREATION.
THANK YOU, DINA.
FAREWELL, GISELLE.

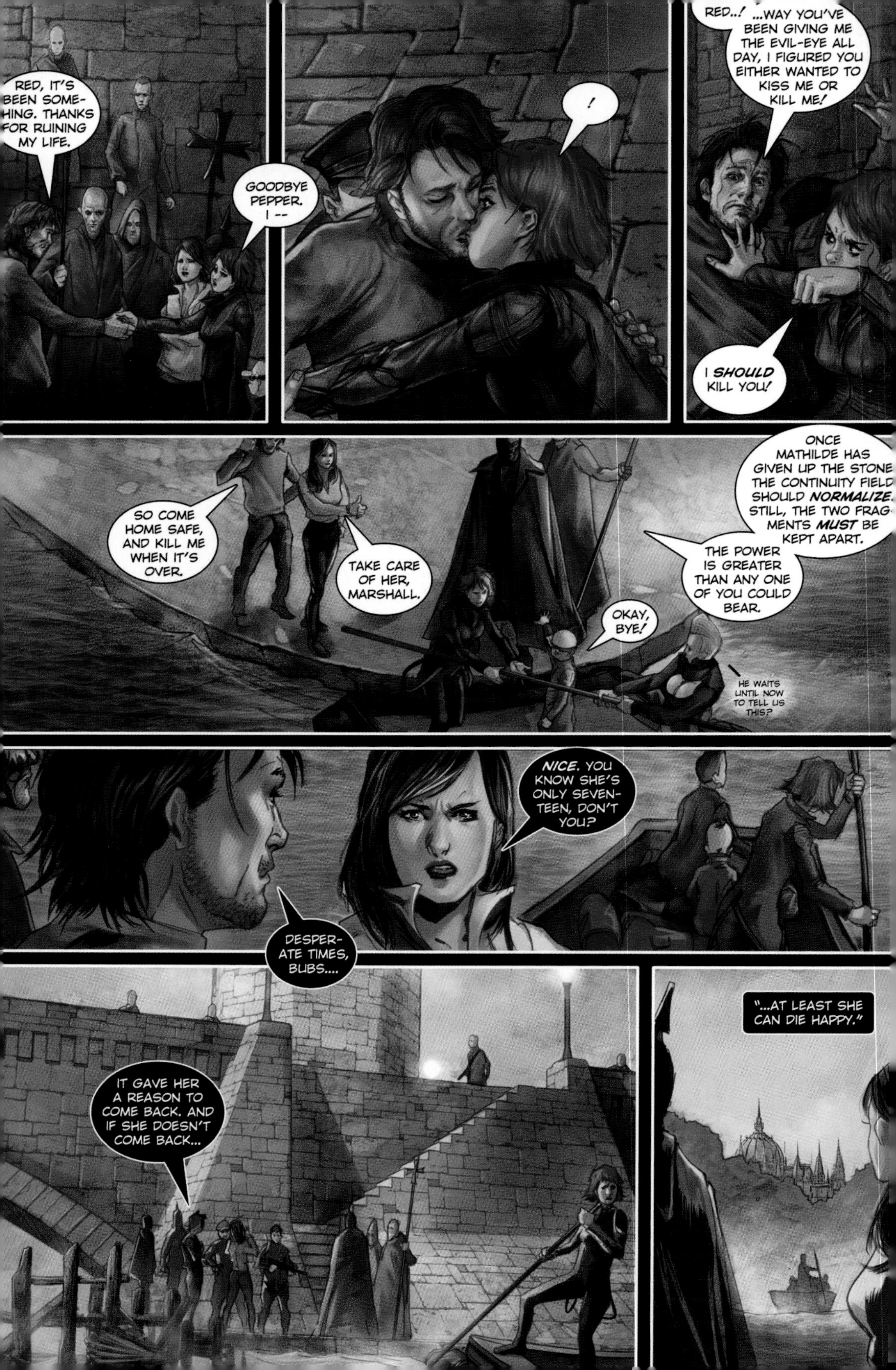
RED, IT'S BEEN SOME-THING. THANKS FOR RUINING MY LIFE.
GOODBYE PEPPER. I --
!
RED..! ...WAY YOU'VE BEEN GIVING ME THE EVIL-EYE ALL DAY, I FIGURED YOU EITHER WANTED TO KISS ME OR KILL ME!
I *SHOULD* KILL YOU!
SO COME HOME SAFE, AND KILL ME WHEN IT'S OVER.
TAKE CARE OF HER, MARSHALL.
ONCE MATHILDE HAS GIVEN UP THE STONE THE CONTINUITY FIELD SHOULD *NORMALIZE*. STILL, THE TWO FRAG-MENTS *MUST* BE KEPT APART.
THE POWER IS GREATER THAN ANY ONE OF YOU COULD BEAR.
OKAY, BYE!
HE WAITS UNTIL NOW TO TELL US THIS?
NICE. YOU KNOW SHE'S ONLY SEVEN-TEEN, DON'T YOU?
DESPER-ATE TIMES, BUBS....
IT GAVE HER A REASON TO COME BACK. AND IF SHE DOESN'T COME BACK...
"...AT LEAST SHE CAN DIE HAPPY."

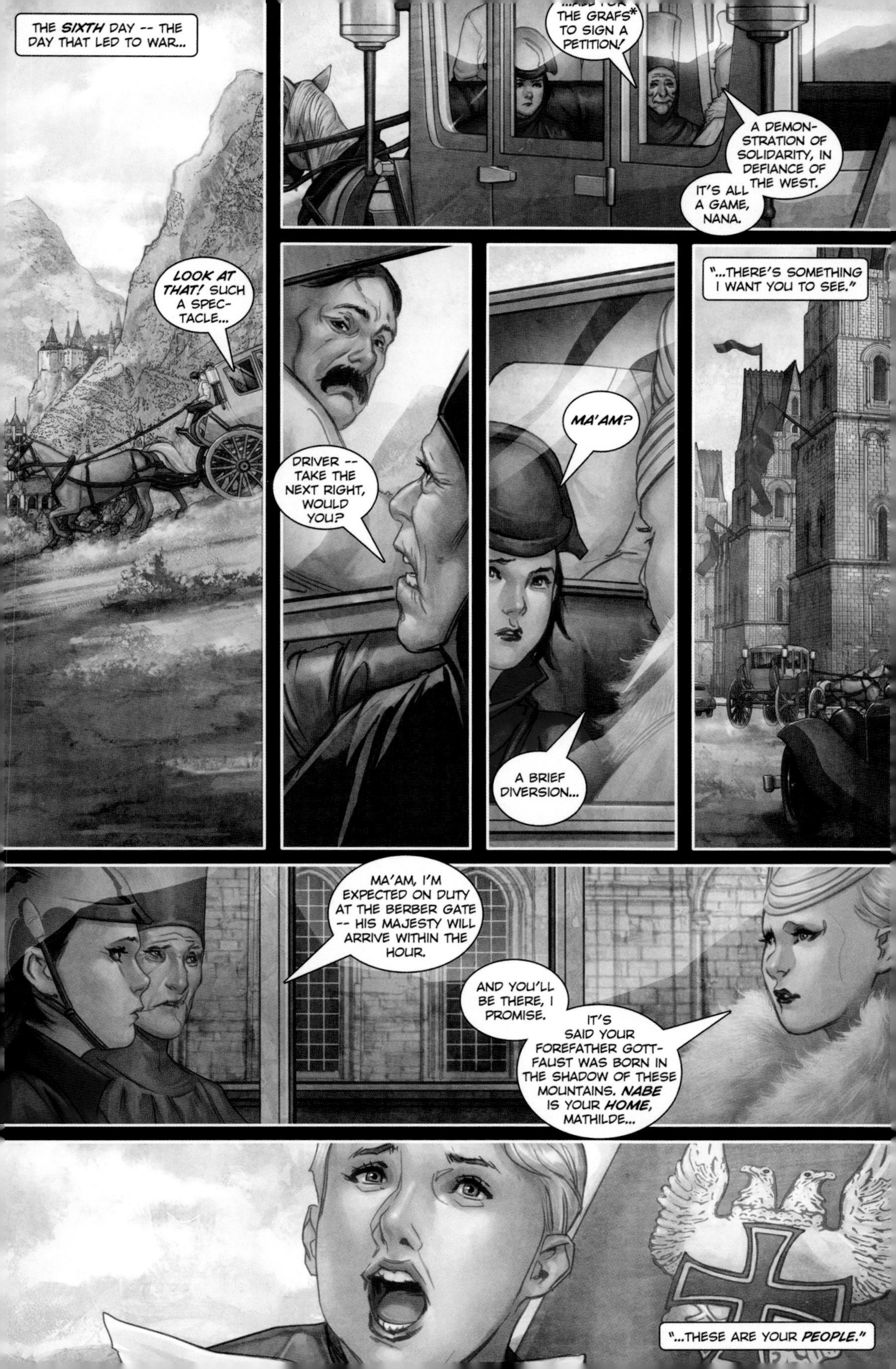

THE *SIXTH* DAY -- THE DAY THAT LED TO WAR...
LOOK AT THAT! SUCH A SPECTACLE...
THE GRAFS* TO SIGN A PETITION!
A DEMONSTRATION OF SOLIDARITY, IN DEFIANCE OF THE WEST.
IT'S ALL A GAME, NANA.
DRIVER -- TAKE THE NEXT RIGHT, WOULD YOU?
MA'AM?
A BRIEF DIVERSION...
"...THERE'S SOMETHING I WANT YOU TO SEE."
MA'AM, I'M EXPECTED ON DUTY AT THE BERBER GATE -- HIS MAJESTY WILL ARRIVE WITHIN THE HOUR.
AND YOU'LL BE THERE, I PROMISE.
IT'S SAID YOUR FOREFATHER GOTTFAUST WAS BORN IN THE SHADOW OF THESE MOUNTAINS. *NABE* IS YOUR *HOME*, MATHILDE...
"...THESE ARE YOUR *PEOPLE*."

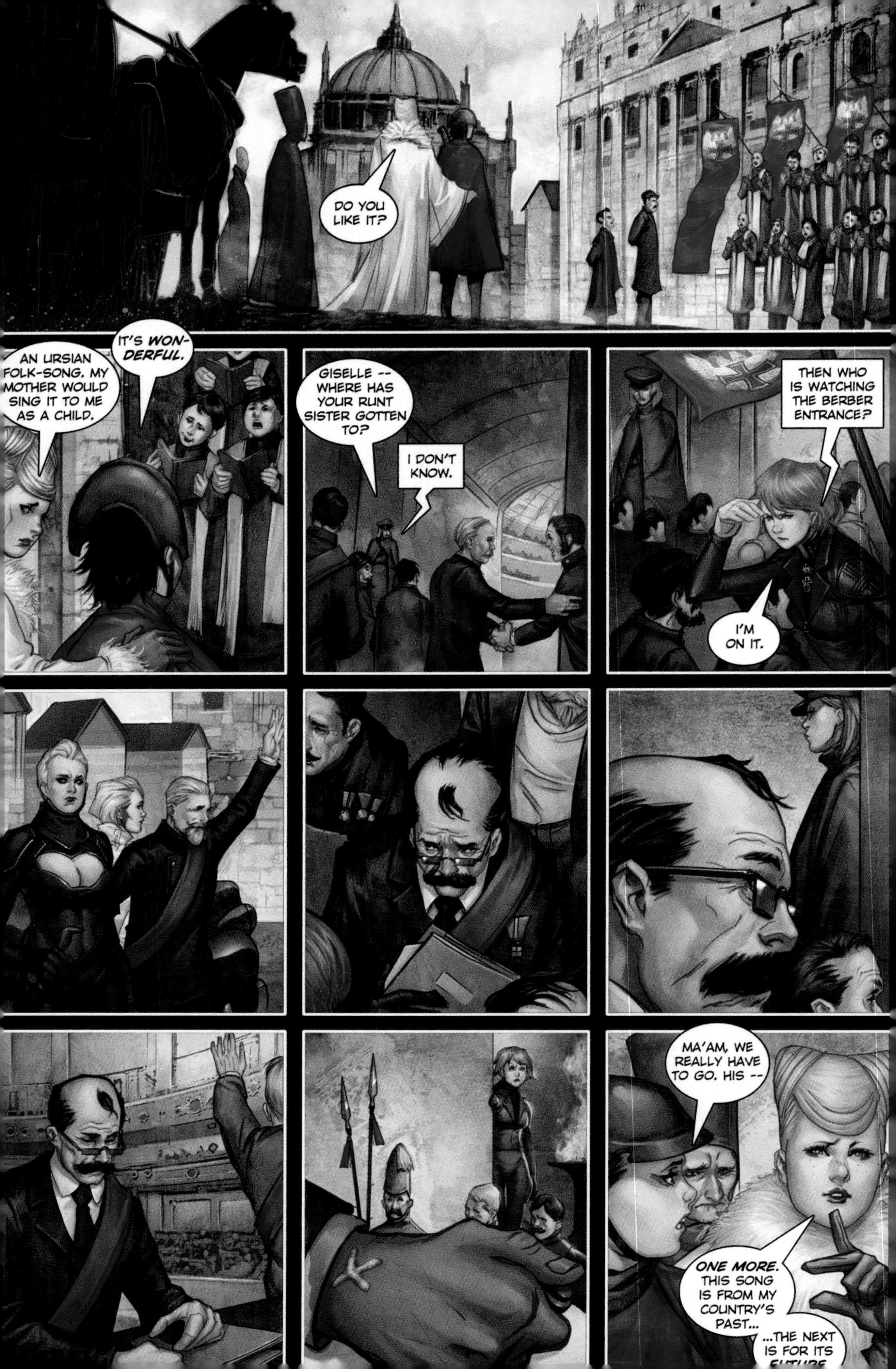
DO YOU LIKE IT?
AN URSIAN FOLK-SONG. MY MOTHER WOULD SING IT TO ME AS A CHILD.
IT'S ***WON-DERFUL.***
GISELLE -- WHERE HAS YOUR RUNT SISTER GOTTEN TO?
I DON'T KNOW.
THEN WHO IS WATCHING THE BERBER ENTRANCE?
I'M ON IT.
MA'AM, WE REALLY HAVE TO GO. HIS --
ONE MORE. THIS SONG IS FROM MY COUNTRY'S PAST...
...THE NEXT IS FOR ITS

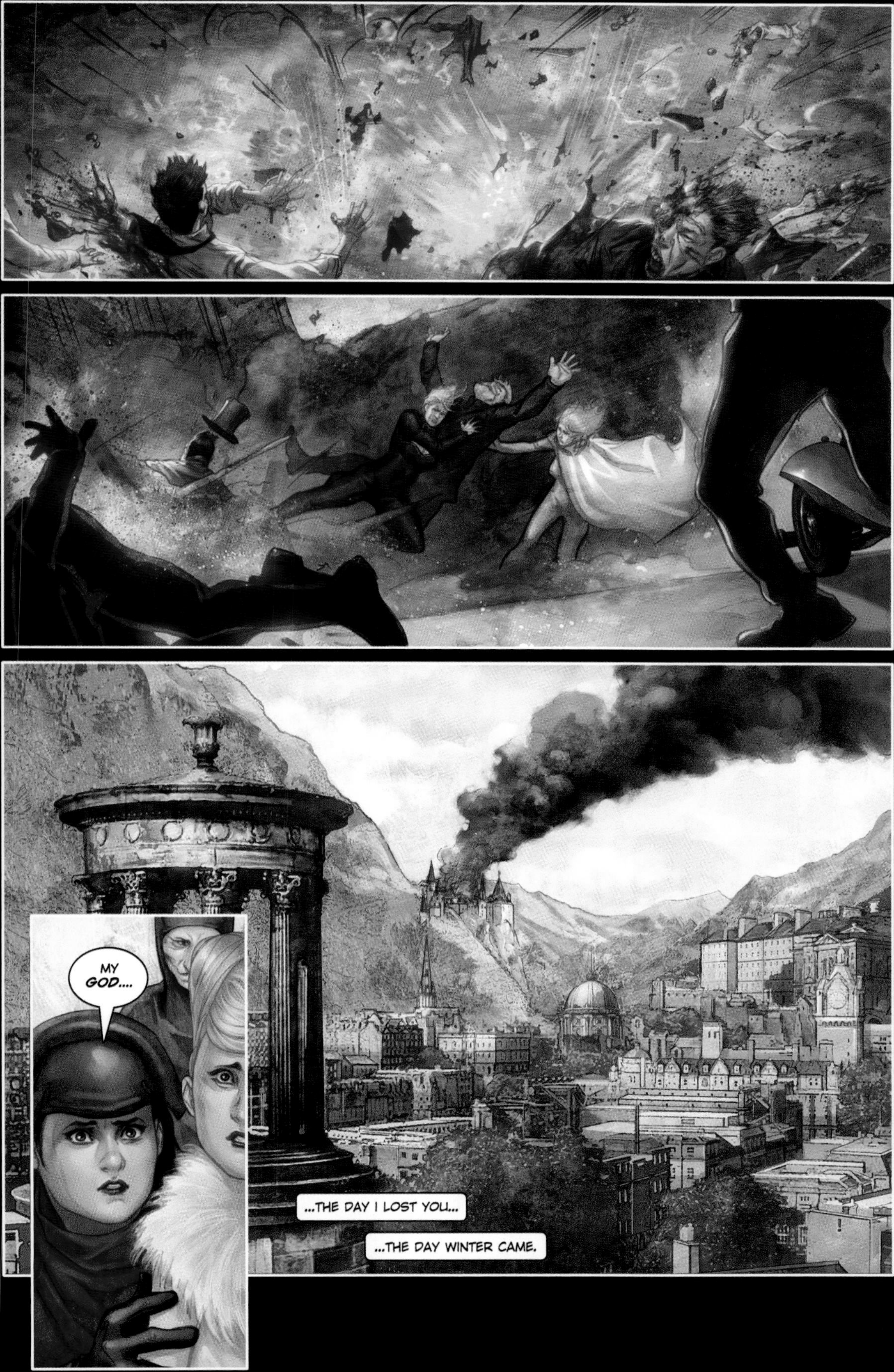
MY GOD....
...THE DAY I LOST YOU...
...THE DAY WINTER CAME.

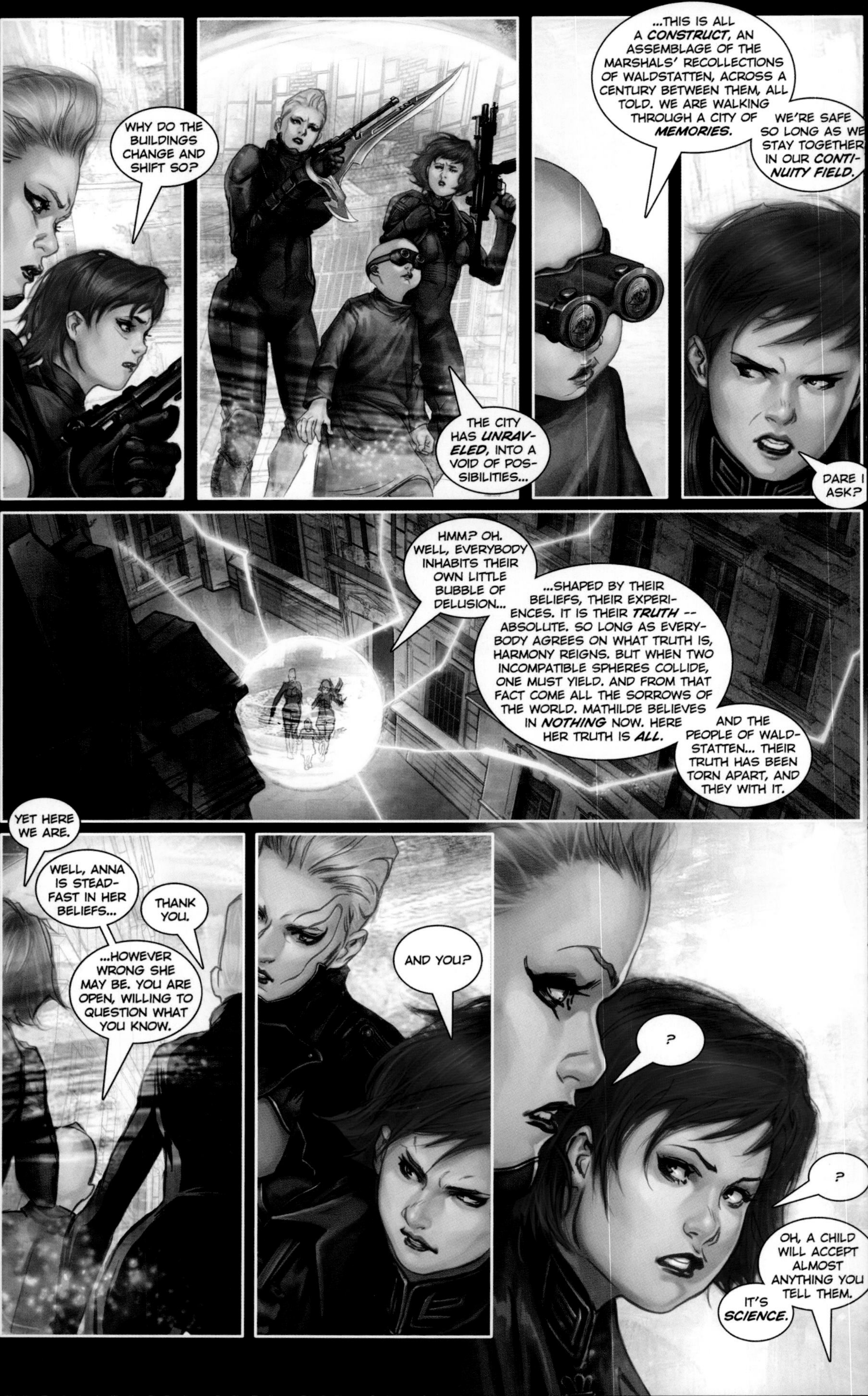
WHY DO THE BUILDINGS CHANGE AND SHIFT SO?
THE CITY HAS *UNRAVELED*, INTO A VOID OF POSSIBILITIES...
...THIS IS ALL A *CONSTRUCT*, AN ASSEMBLAGE OF THE MARSHALS' RECOLLECTIONS OF WALDSTATTEN, ACROSS A CENTURY BETWEEN THEM, ALL TOLD. WE ARE WALKING THROUGH A CITY OF *MEMORIES*.
WE'RE SAFE SO LONG AS WE STAY TOGETHER IN OUR *CONTINUITY FIELD*.
DARE I ASK?
HMM? OH. WELL, EVERYBODY INHABITS THEIR OWN LITTLE BUBBLE OF DELUSION...
...SHAPED BY THEIR BELIEFS, THEIR EXPERIENCES. IT IS THEIR *TRUTH* -- ABSOLUTE. SO LONG AS EVERYBODY AGREES ON WHAT TRUTH IS, HARMONY REIGNS. BUT WHEN TWO INCOMPATIBLE SPHERES COLLIDE, ONE MUST YIELD. AND FROM THAT FACT COME ALL THE SORROWS OF THE WORLD. MATHILDE BELIEVES IN *NOTHING* NOW. HERE HER TRUTH IS *ALL*.
AND THE PEOPLE OF WALDSTATTEN... THEIR TRUTH HAS BEEN TORN APART, AND THEY WITH IT.
YET HERE WE ARE.
WELL, ANNA IS STEADFAST IN HER BELIEFS...
THANK YOU.
...HOWEVER WRONG SHE MAY BE. YOU ARE OPEN, WILLING TO QUESTION WHAT YOU KNOW.
AND YOU?
?
?
OH, A CHILD WILL ACCEPT ALMOST ANYTHING YOU TELL THEM.
IT'S *SCIENCE*.

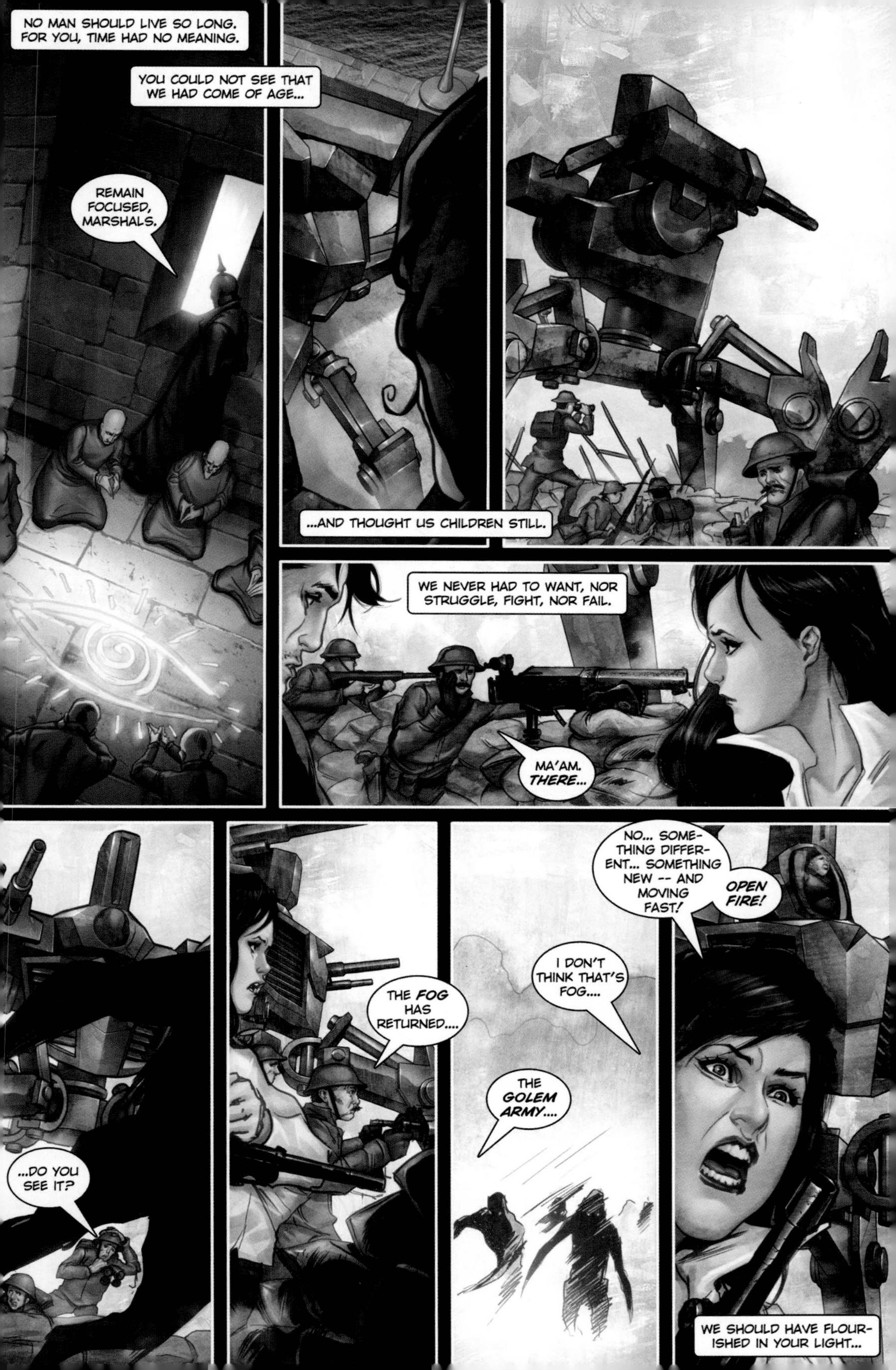
NO MAN SHOULD LIVE SO LONG. FOR YOU, TIME HAD NO MEANING.
REMAIN FOCUSED, MARSHALS.
YOU COULD NOT SEE THAT WE HAD COME OF AGE...
...AND THOUGHT US CHILDREN STILL.
WE NEVER HAD TO WANT, NOR STRUGGLE, FIGHT, NOR FAIL.
MA'AM. *THERE*...
...DO YOU SEE IT?
THE *FOG* HAS RETURNED....
I DON'T THINK THAT'S FOG....
THE *GOLEM ARMY*....
NO... SOME-THING DIFFER-ENT... SOMETHING NEW -- AND MOVING FAST!
OPEN FIRE!
WE SHOULD HAVE FLOUR-ISHED IN YOUR LIGHT...

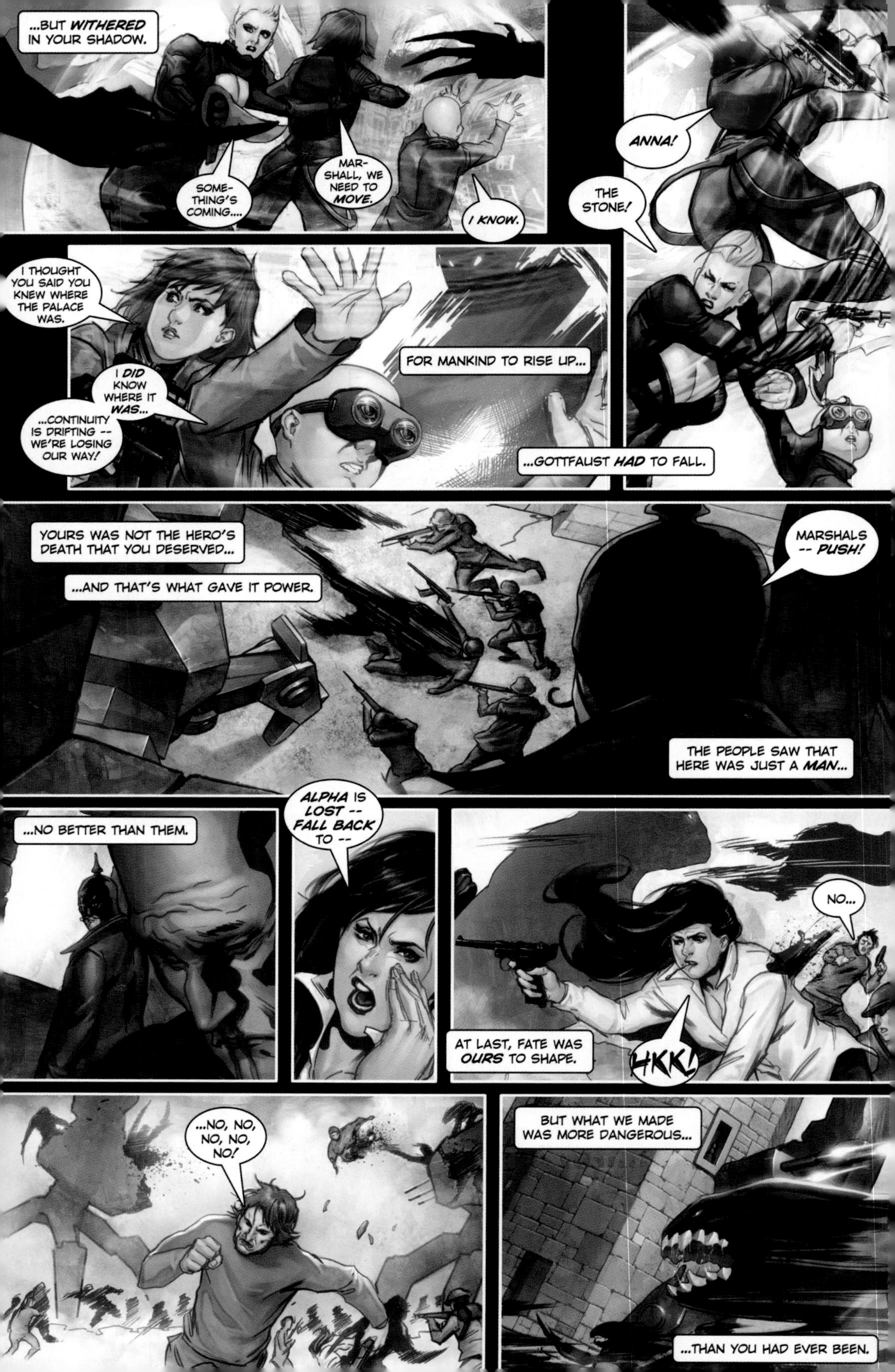
...BUT WITHERED IN YOUR SHADOW.
SOMETHING'S COMING....
MARSHALL, WE NEED TO MOVE.
I KNOW.
I THOUGHT YOU SAID YOU KNEW WHERE THE PALACE WAS.
I DID KNOW WHERE IT WAS...
...CONTINUITY IS DRIFTING -- WE'RE LOSING OUR WAY!
FOR MANKIND TO RISE UP...
...GOTTFAUST HAD TO FALL.
ANNA!
THE STONE!
YOURS WAS NOT THE HERO'S DEATH THAT YOU DESERVED...
...AND THAT'S WHAT GAVE IT POWER.
MARSHALS -- PUSH!
THE PEOPLE SAW THAT HERE WAS JUST A MAN...
...NO BETTER THAN THEM.
ALPHA IS LOST -- FALL BACK TO --
NO...
AT LAST, FATE WAS OURS TO SHAPE.
HKK!
...NO, NO, NO, NO, NO!
BUT WHAT WE MADE WAS MORE DANGEROUS...
...THAN YOU HAD EVER BEEN.

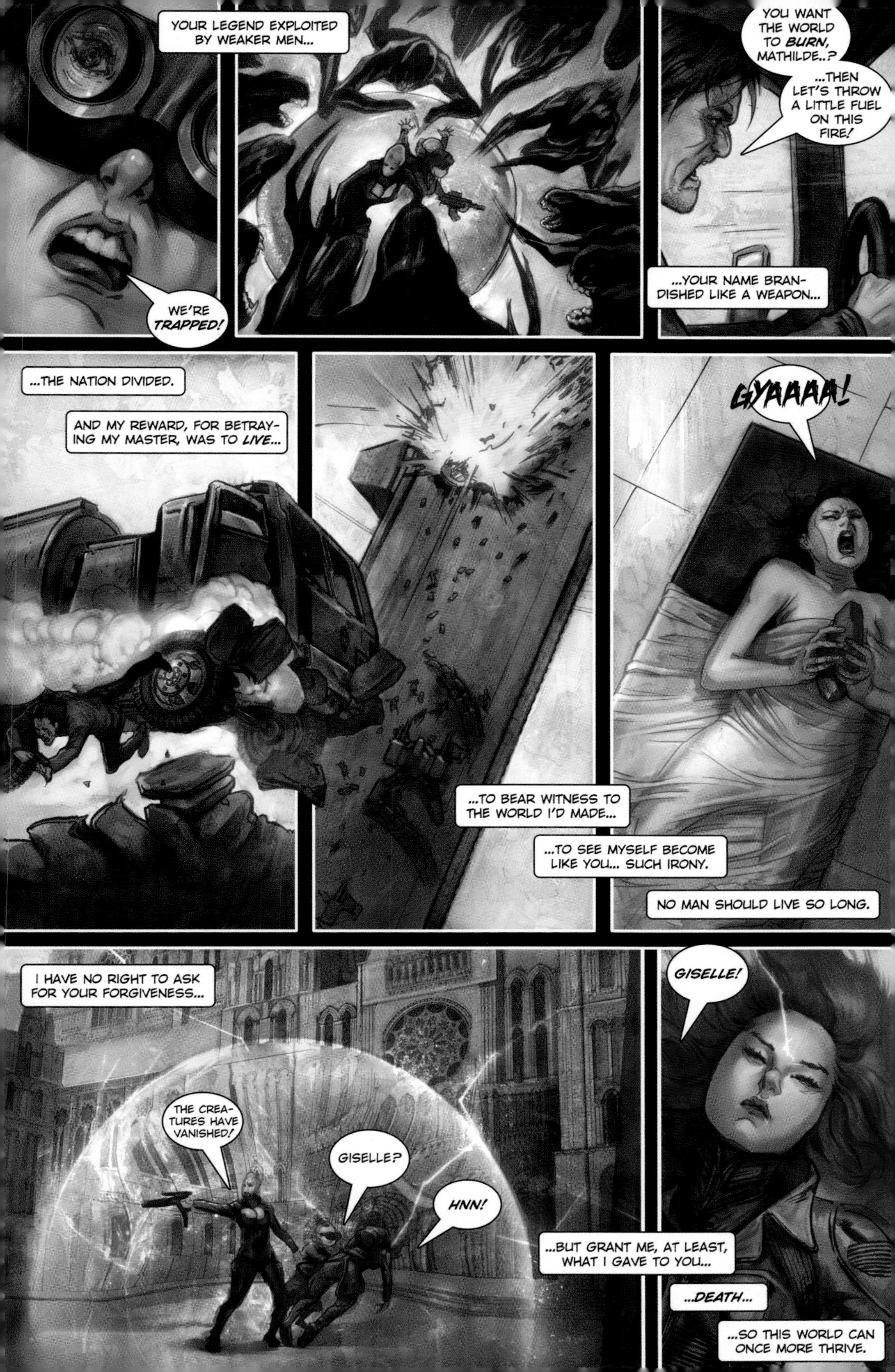
YOUR LEGEND EXPLOITED BY WEAKER MEN...
WE'RE TRAPPED!
YOU WANT THE WORLD TO BURN, MATHILDE..?
...THEN LET'S THROW A LITTLE FUEL ON THIS FIRE!
...YOUR NAME BRANDISHED LIKE A WEAPON...
...THE NATION DIVIDED.
AND MY REWARD, FOR BETRAYING MY MASTER, WAS TO LIVE...
...TO BEAR WITNESS TO THE WORLD I'D MADE...
GYAAAA!
...TO SEE MYSELF BECOME LIKE YOU... SUCH IRONY.
NO MAN SHOULD LIVE SO LONG.
I HAVE NO RIGHT TO ASK FOR YOUR FORGIVENESS...
THE CREATURES HAVE VANISHED!
GISELLE?
HNN!
GISELLE!
...BUT GRANT ME, AT LEAST, WHAT I GAVE TO YOU...
...DEATH...
...SO THIS WORLD CAN ONCE MORE THRIVE.

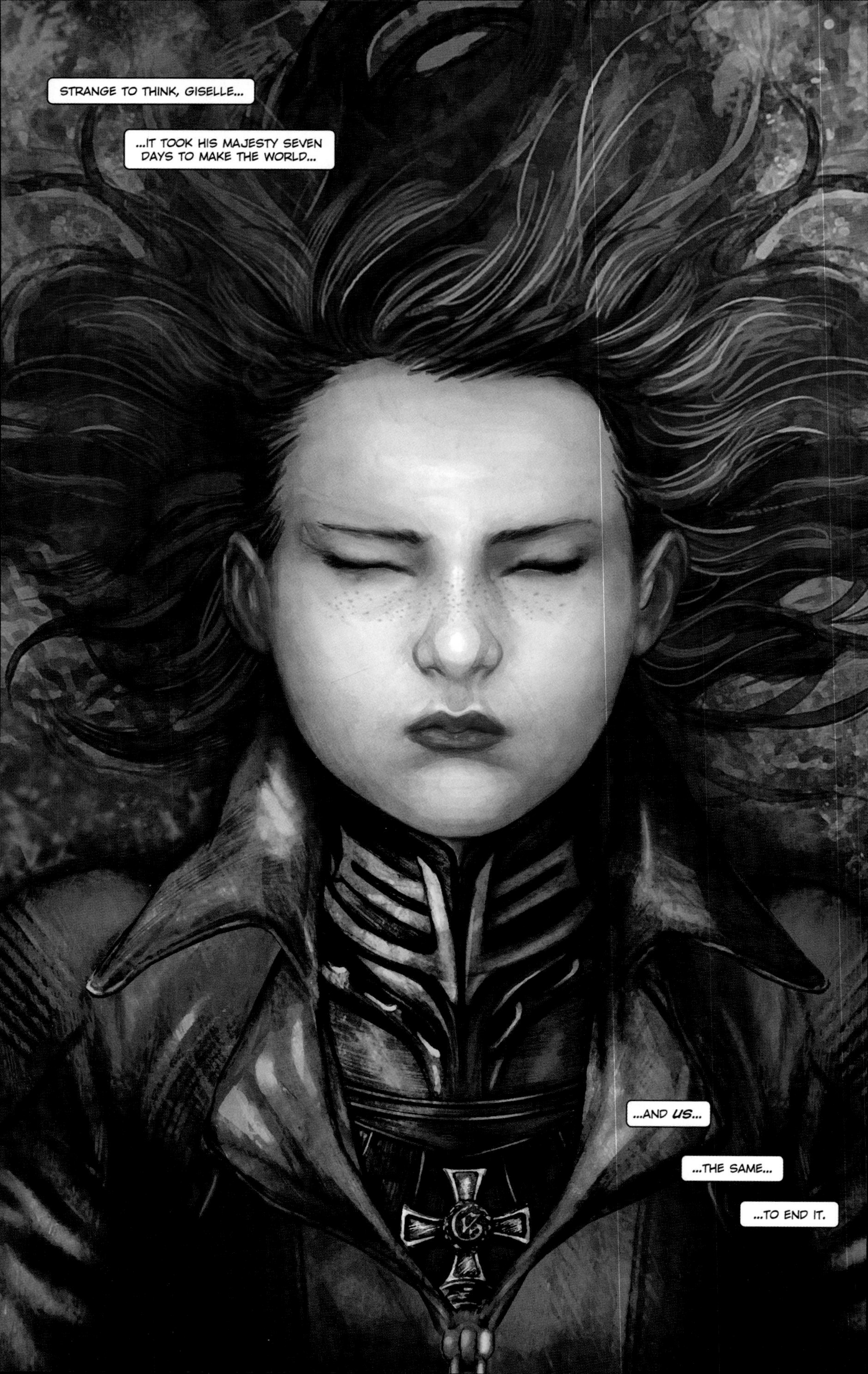
STRANGE TO THINK, GISELLE...
...IT TOOK HIS MAJESTY SEVEN DAYS TO MAKE THE WORLD...
...AND US...
...THE SAME...
...TO END IT.

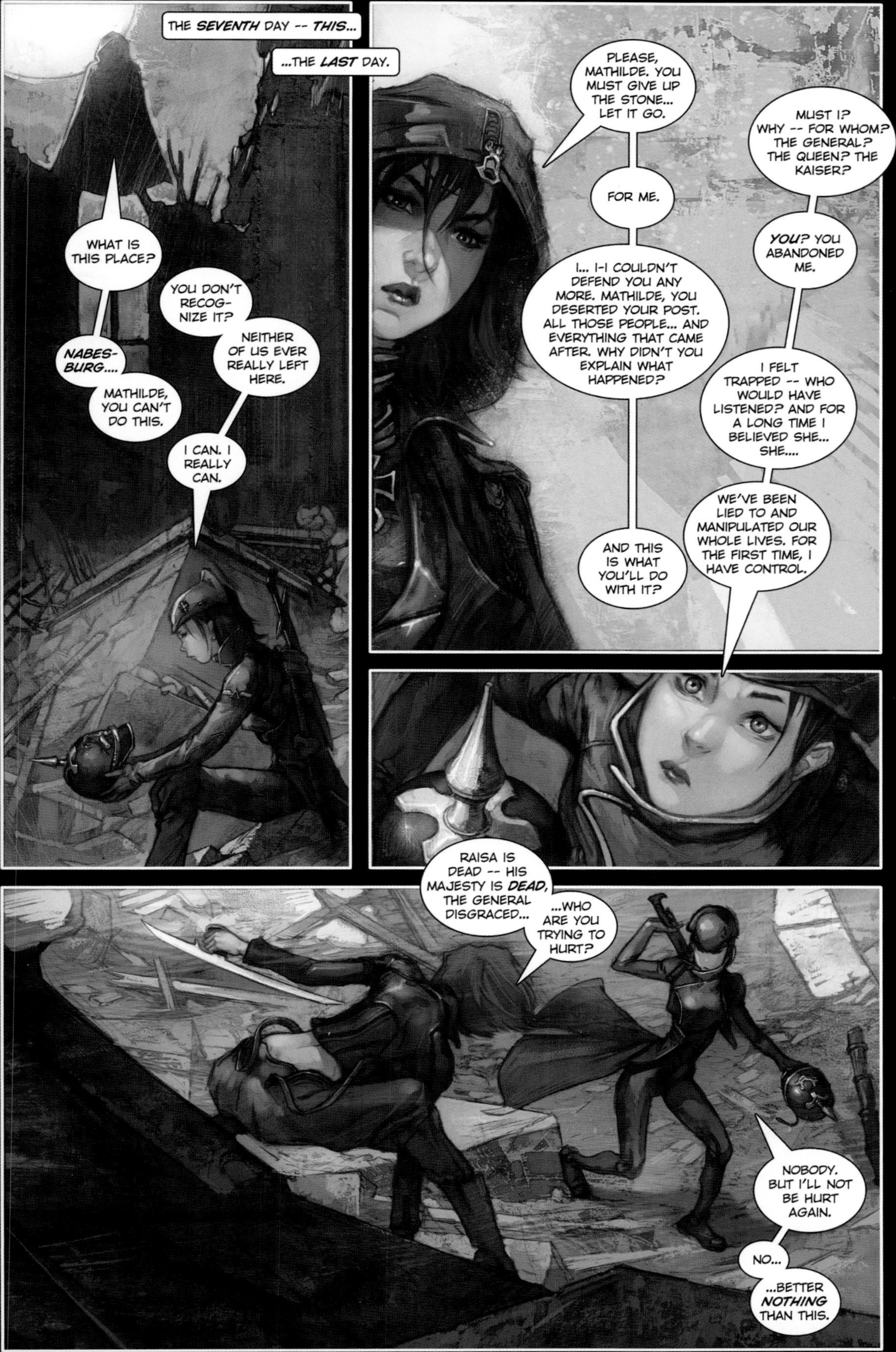
THE ***SEVENTH*** DAY -- ***THIS...***
...THE ***LAST*** DAY.
WHAT IS THIS PLACE?
YOU DON'T RECOG-NIZE IT?
NABES-BURG....
NEITHER OF US EVER REALLY LEFT HERE.
MATHILDE, YOU CAN'T DO THIS.
I CAN. I REALLY CAN.
PLEASE, MATHILDE. YOU MUST GIVE UP THE STONE... LET IT GO.
MUST I? WHY -- FOR WHOM? THE GENERAL? THE QUEEN? THE KAISER?
FOR ME.
YOU? YOU ABANDONED ME.
I... I-I COULDN'T DEFEND YOU ANY MORE. MATHILDE, YOU DESERTED YOUR POST. ALL THOSE PEOPLE... AND EVERYTHING THAT CAME AFTER. WHY DIDN'T YOU EXPLAIN WHAT HAPPENED?
I FELT TRAPPED -- WHO WOULD HAVE LISTENED? AND FOR A LONG TIME I BELIEVED SHE... SHE....
WE'VE BEEN LIED TO AND MANIPULATED OUR WHOLE LIVES. FOR THE FIRST TIME, I HAVE CONTROL.
AND THIS IS WHAT YOU'LL DO WITH IT?
RAISA IS DEAD -- HIS MAJESTY IS ***DEAD,*** THE GENERAL DISGRACED...
...WHO ARE YOU TRYING TO HURT?
NOBODY. BUT I'LL NOT BE HURT AGAIN.
NO...
...BETTER ***NOTHING*** THAN THIS.

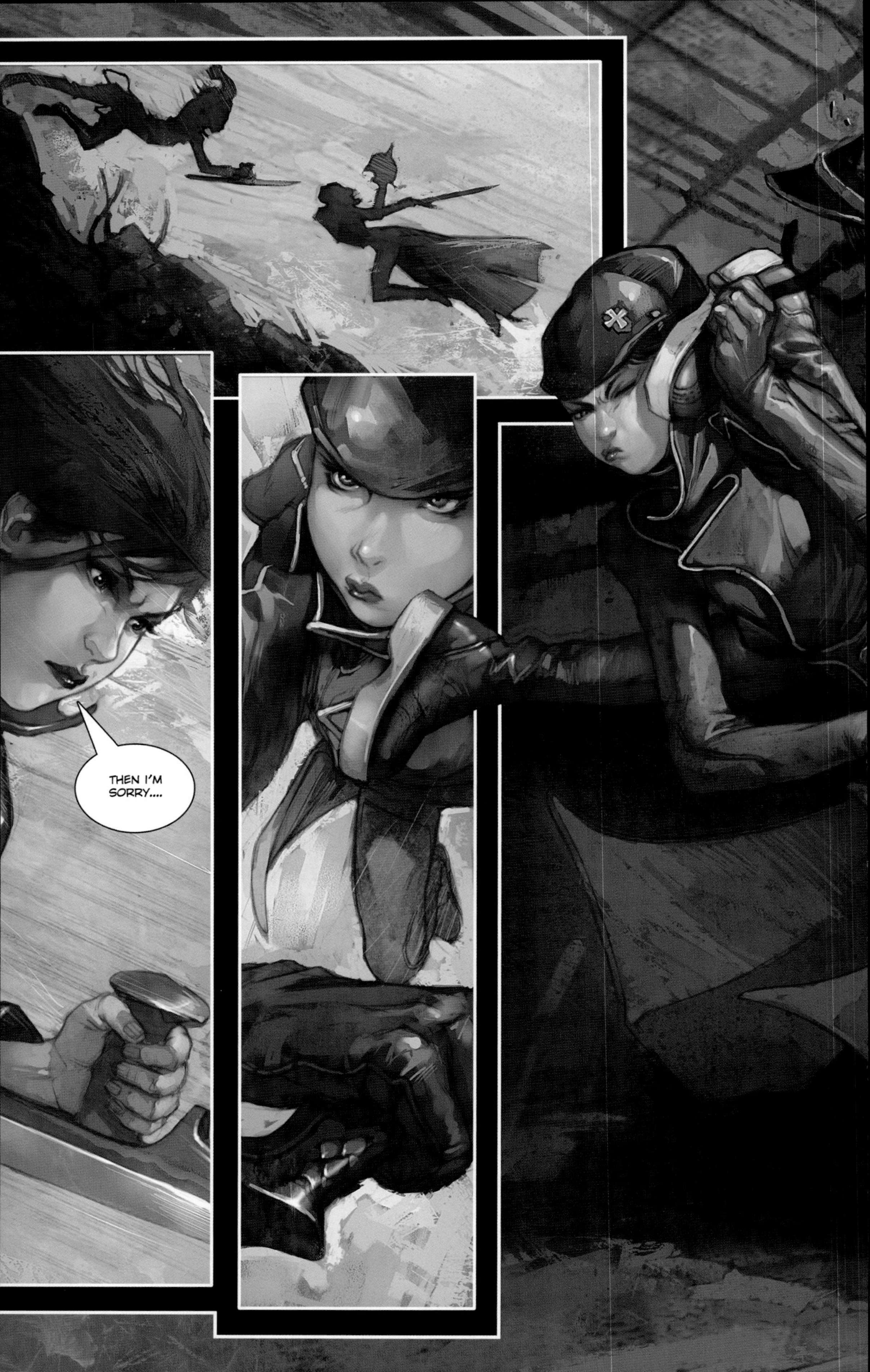
THEN I'M SORRY....

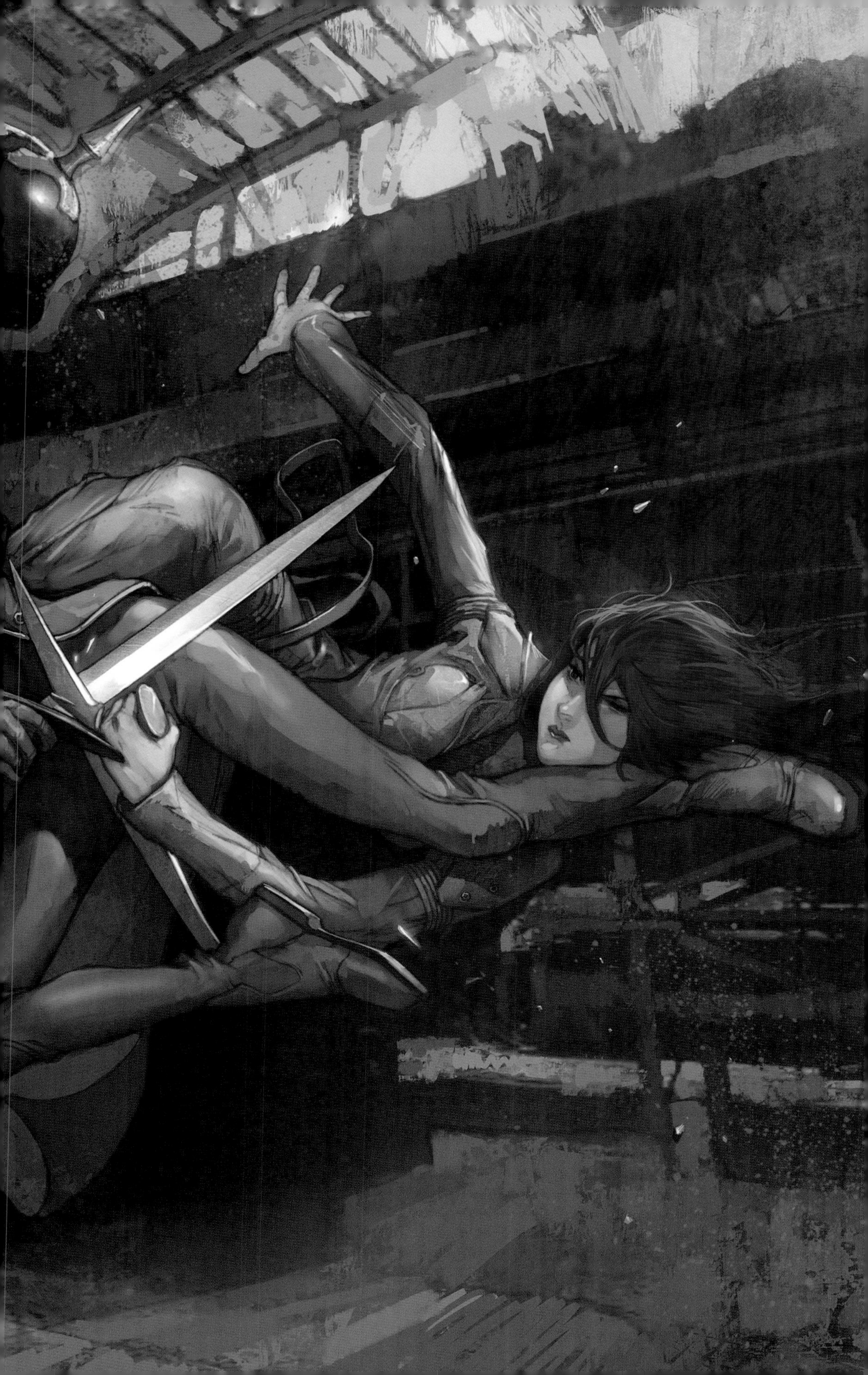

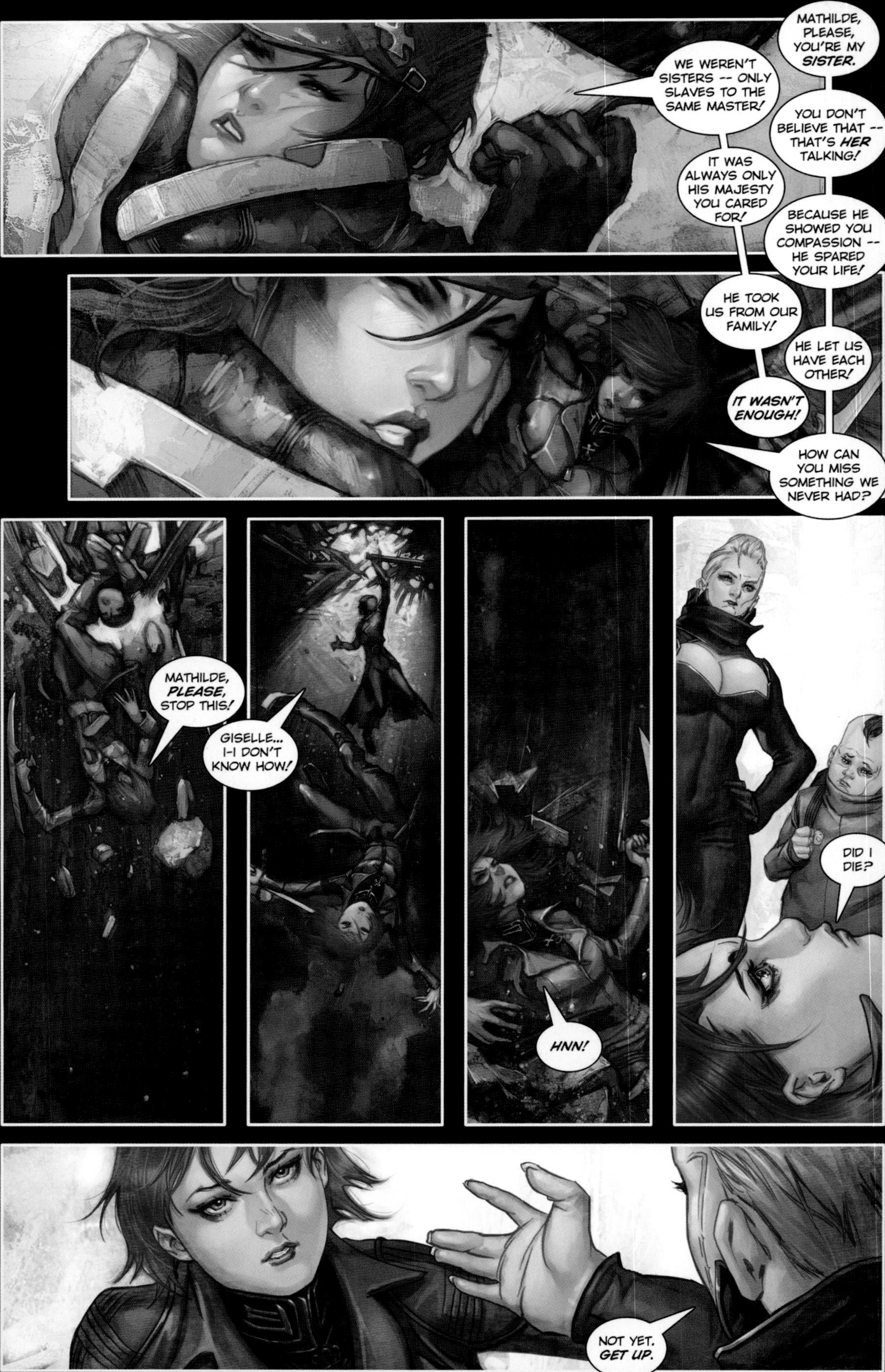
MATHILDE, PLEASE, YOU'RE MY *SISTER.*
WE WEREN'T SISTERS -- ONLY SLAVES TO THE SAME MASTER!
YOU DON'T BELIEVE THAT -- THAT'S *HER* TALKING!
IT WAS ALWAYS ONLY HIS MAJESTY YOU CARED FOR!
BECAUSE HE SHOWED YOU COMPASSION -- HE SPARED YOUR LIFE!
HE TOOK US FROM OUR FAMILY!
HE LET US HAVE EACH OTHER!
IT WASN'T ENOUGH!
HOW CAN YOU MISS SOMETHING WE NEVER HAD?
MATHILDE, *PLEASE,* STOP THIS!
GISELLE... I-I DON'T KNOW HOW!
HNN!
DID I DIE?
NOT YET. *GET UP.*

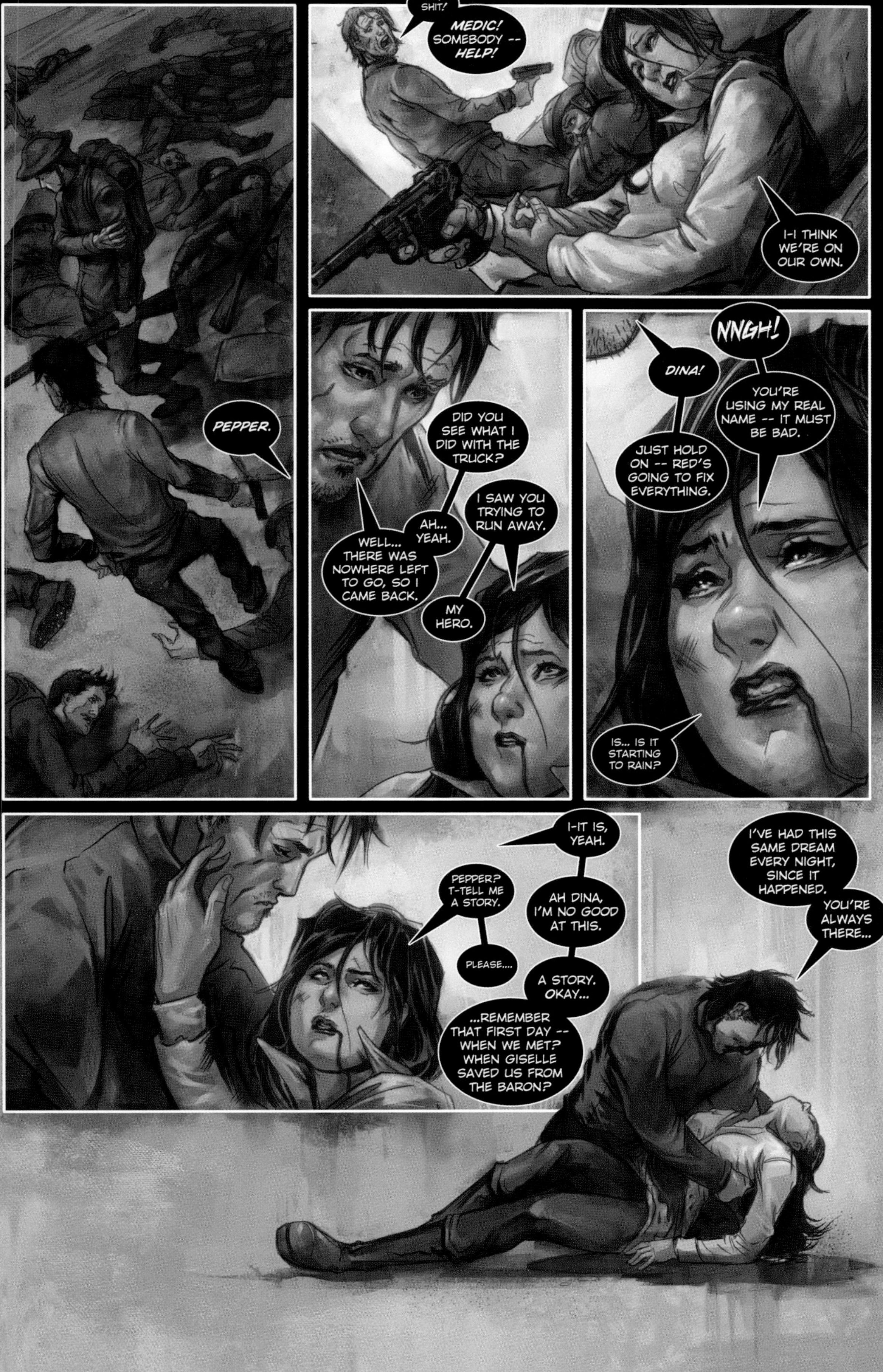
PEPPER.
AH, SHIT!
MEDIC! SOMEBODY -- HELP!
I-I THINK WE'RE ON OUR OWN.
DID YOU SEE WHAT I DID WITH THE TRUCK?
AH... YEAH.
WELL... THERE WAS NOWHERE LEFT TO GO, SO I CAME BACK.
I SAW YOU TRYING TO RUN AWAY.
MY HERO.
DINA!
NNGH!
YOU'RE USING MY REAL NAME -- IT MUST BE BAD.
JUST HOLD ON -- RED'S GOING TO FIX EVERYTHING.
IS... IS IT STARTING TO RAIN?
PEPPER? T-TELL ME A STORY.
PLEASE....
I-IT IS, YEAH.
AH DINA, I'M NO GOOD AT THIS.
A STORY. OKAY...
...REMEMBER THAT FIRST DAY -- WHEN WE MET? WHEN GISELLE SAVED US FROM THE BARON?
I'VE HAD THIS SAME DREAM EVERY NIGHT, SINCE IT HAPPENED.
YOU'RE ALWAYS THERE...

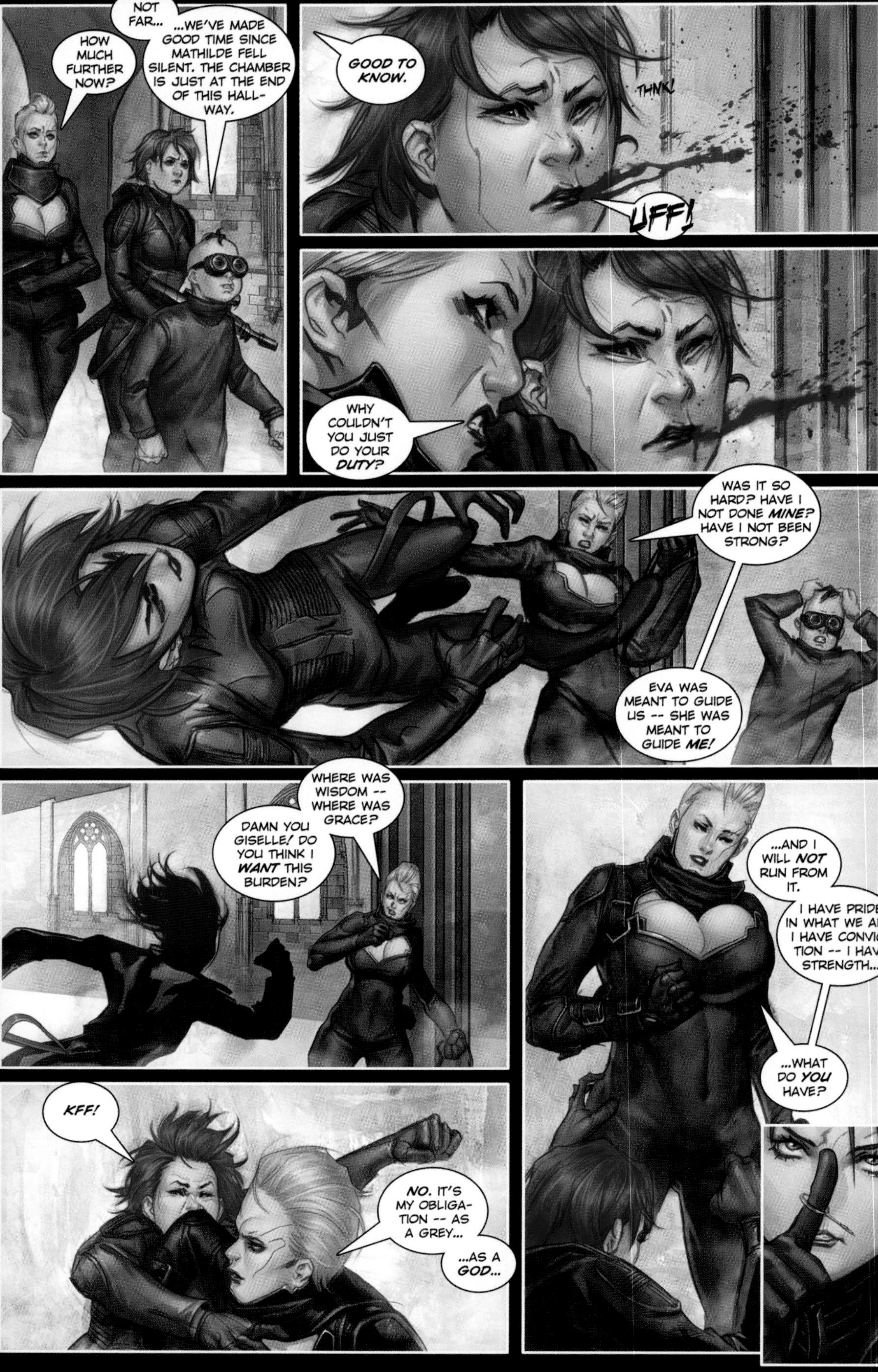
HOW MUCH FURTHER NOW?
NOT FAR...
...WE'VE MADE GOOD TIME SINCE MATHILDE FELL SILENT. THE CHAMBER IS JUST AT THE END OF THIS HALL-WAY.
GOOD TO KNOW.
THNK!
UFF!
WHY COULDN'T YOU JUST DO YOUR DUTY?
WAS IT SO HARD? HAVE I NOT DONE MINE? HAVE I NOT BEEN STRONG?
EVA WAS MEANT TO GUIDE US -- SHE WAS MEANT TO GUIDE ME!
WHERE WAS WISDOM -- WHERE WAS GRACE?
DAMN YOU GISELLE! DO YOU THINK I WANT THIS BURDEN?
KFF!
NO. IT'S MY OBLIGA-TION -- AS A GREY...
...AS A GOD...
...AND I WILL NOT RUN FROM IT.
I HAVE PRIDE IN WHAT WE A
I HAVE CONVIC TION -- I HAV STRENGTH...
...WHAT DO YOU HAVE?

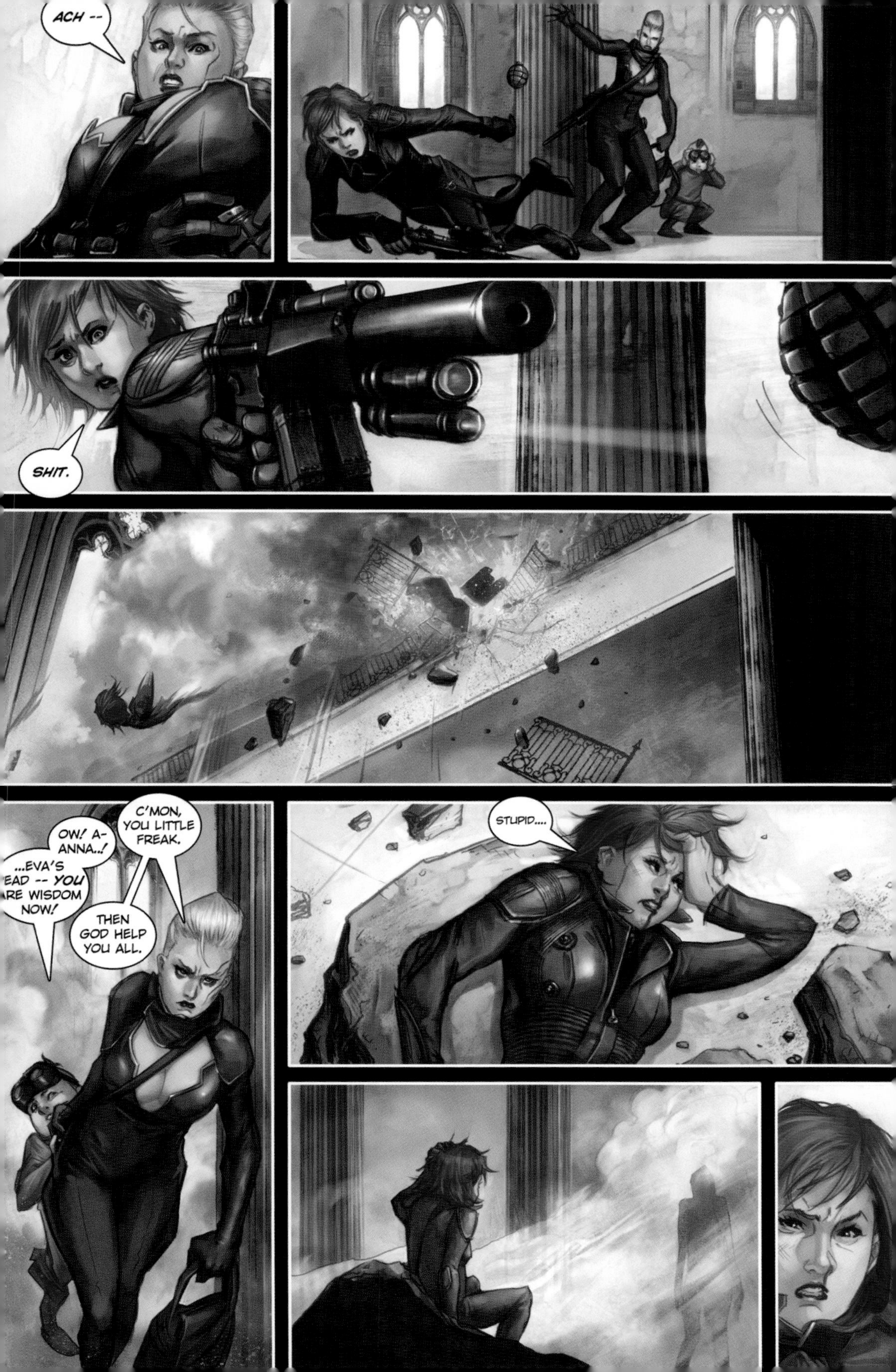
ACH --
SHIT.
OW! A-ANNA..!
...EVA'S EAD -- YOU RE WISDOM NOW!
C'MON, YOU LITTLE FREAK.
THEN GOD HELP YOU ALL.
STUPID....

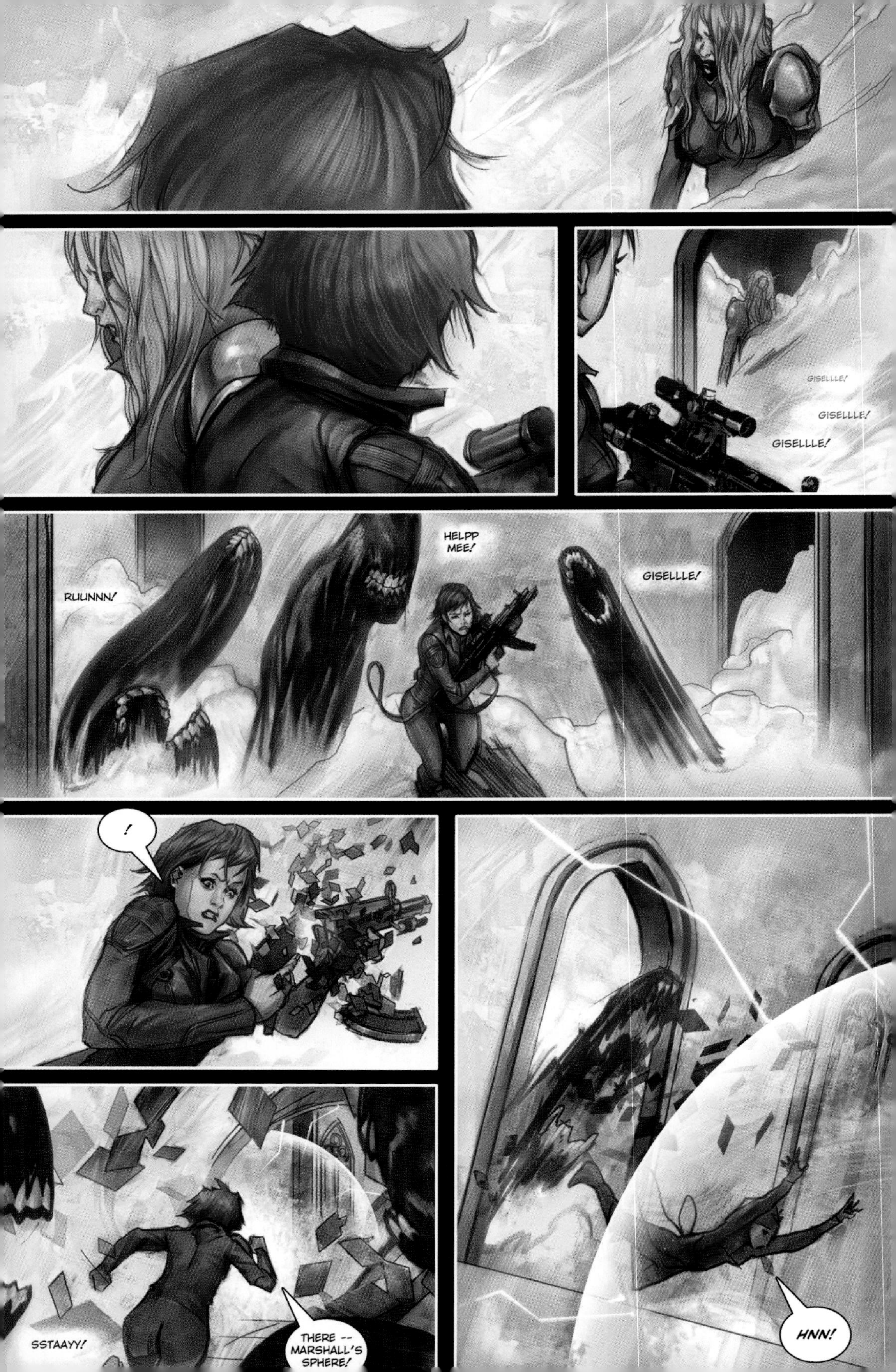
GISELLLE!
GISELLLE!
GISELLLE!
RUUNNN!
HELPP MEE!
GISELLLE!
!
HNN!
SSTAAYY!
THERE -- MARSHALL'S SPHERE!

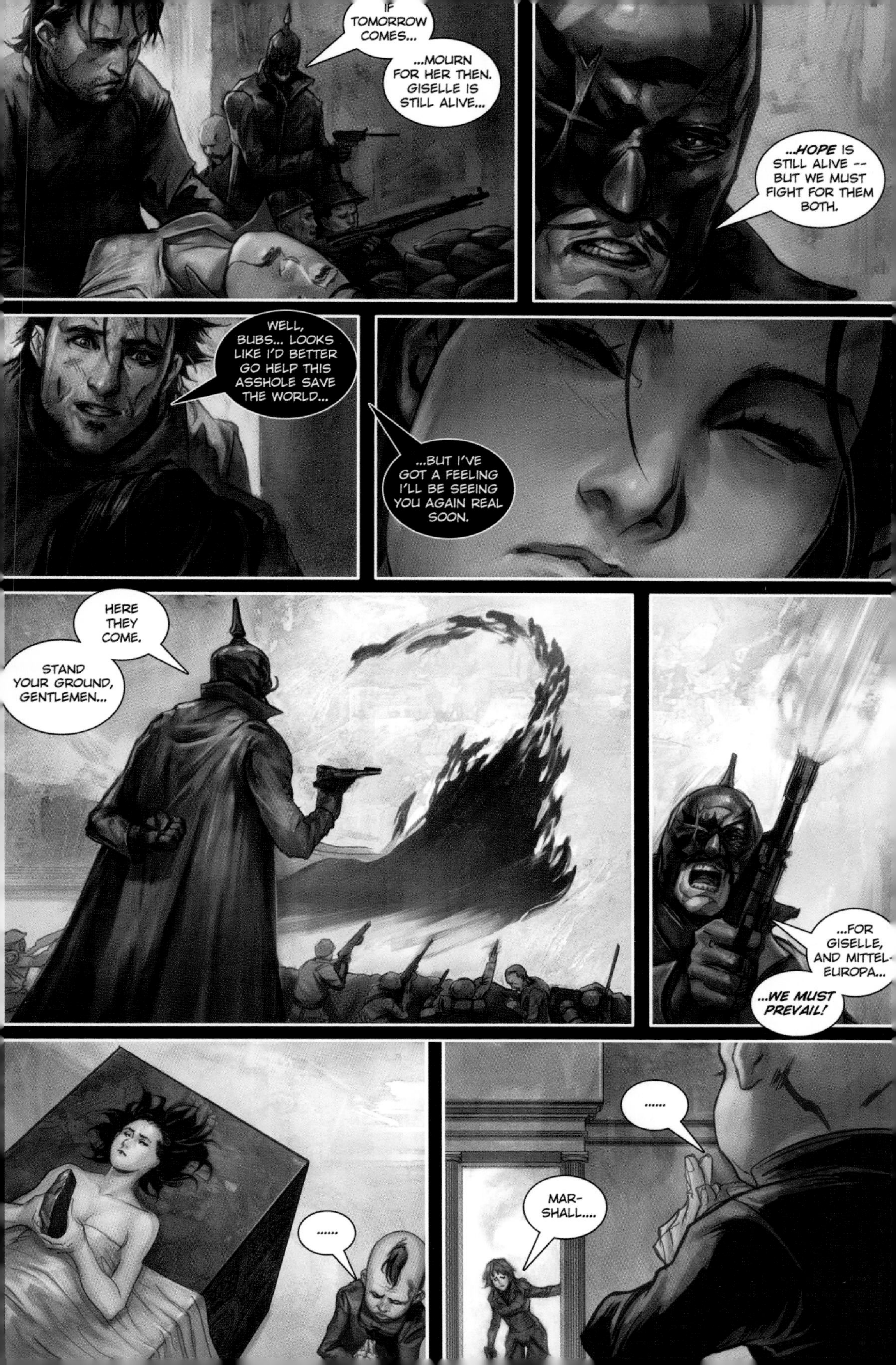
IF TOMORROW COMES...
...MOURN FOR HER THEN. GISELLE IS STILL ALIVE...
...*HOPE* IS STILL ALIVE -- BUT WE MUST FIGHT FOR THEM BOTH.
WELL, BUBS... LOOKS LIKE I'D BETTER GO HELP THIS ASSHOLE SAVE THE WORLD...
...BUT I'VE GOT A FEELING I'LL BE SEEING YOU AGAIN REAL SOON.
HERE THEY COME.
STAND YOUR GROUND, GENTLEMEN...
...FOR GISELLE, AND MITTEL-EUROPA...
...WE MUST PREVAIL!
......
MAR-SHALL....
......

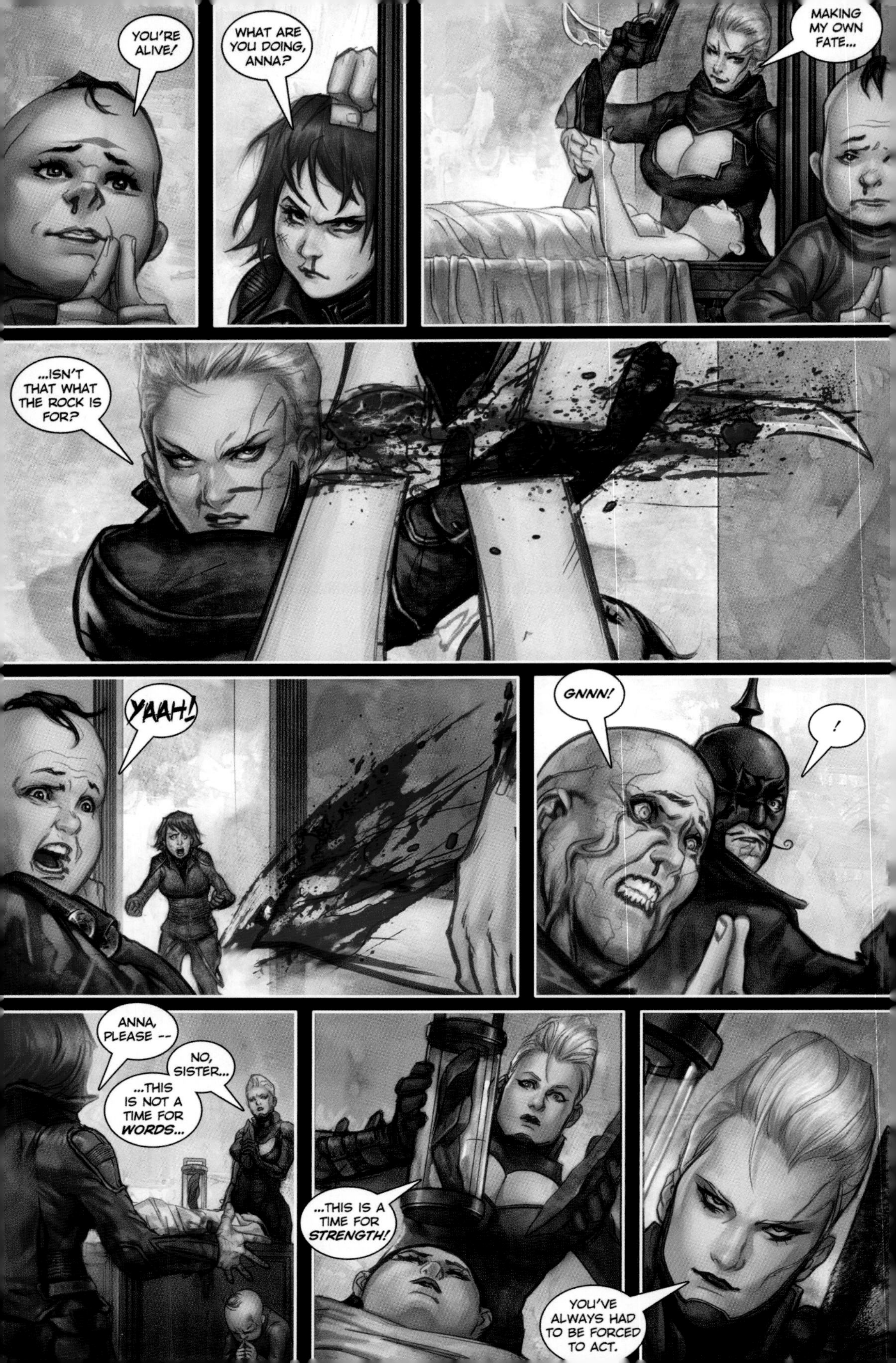
YOU'RE ALIVE!
WHAT ARE YOU DOING, ANNA?
MAKING MY OWN FATE...
...ISN'T THAT WHAT THE ROCK IS FOR?
YAAH!
GNNN!
!
ANNA, PLEASE --
NO, SISTER...
...THIS IS NOT A TIME FOR WORDS...
...THIS IS A TIME FOR STRENGTH!
YOU'VE ALWAYS HAD TO BE FORCED TO ACT.

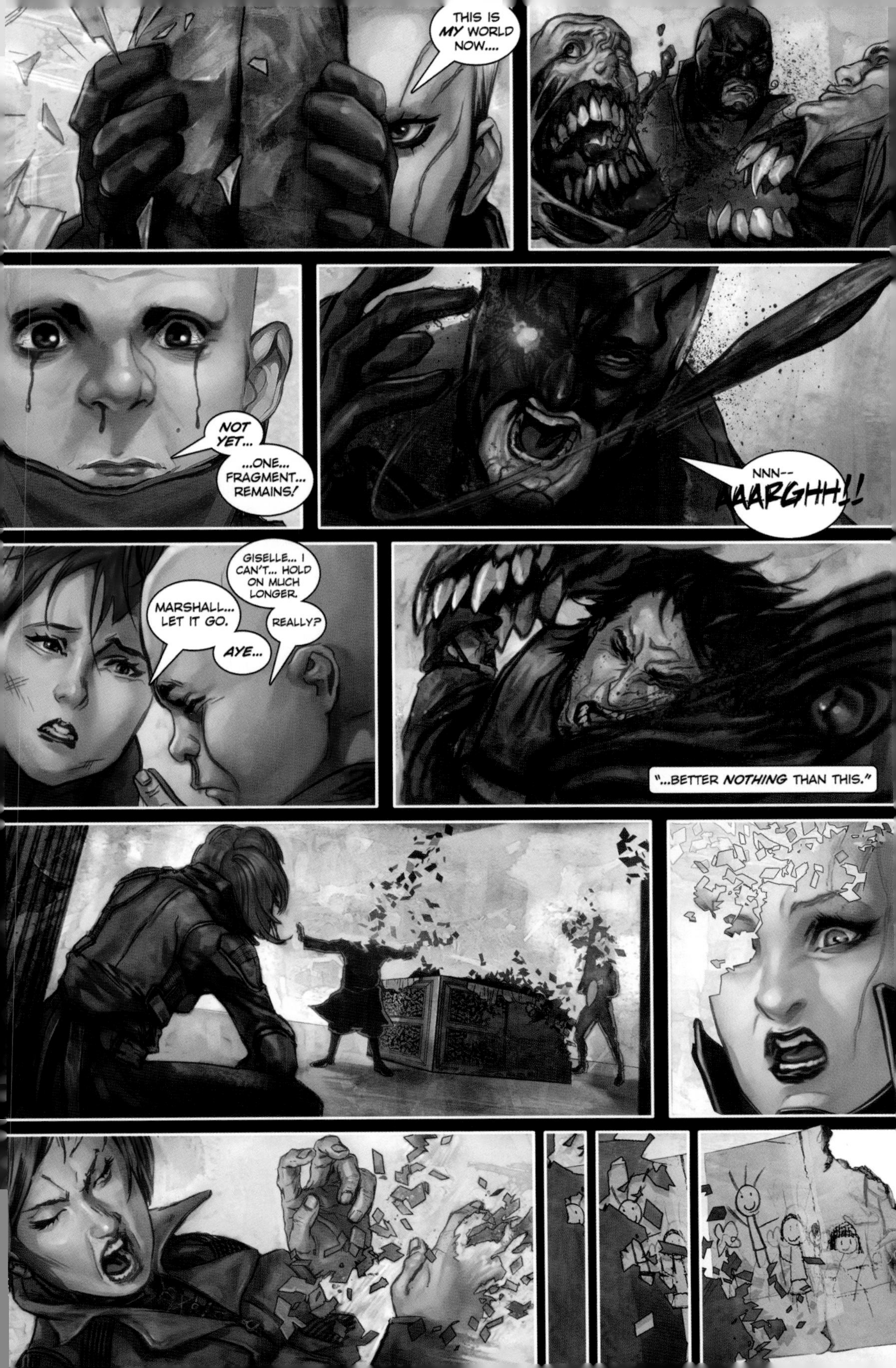
THIS IS *MY* WORLD NOW....
NOT YET...
...ONE... FRAGMENT... REMAINS!
NNN-- AAARGHH!!
GISELLE... I CAN'T... HOLD ON MUCH LONGER.
MARSHALL... LET IT GO.
REALLY?
AYE...
"...BETTER *NOTHING* THAN THIS."

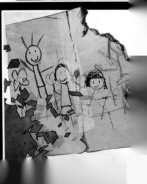

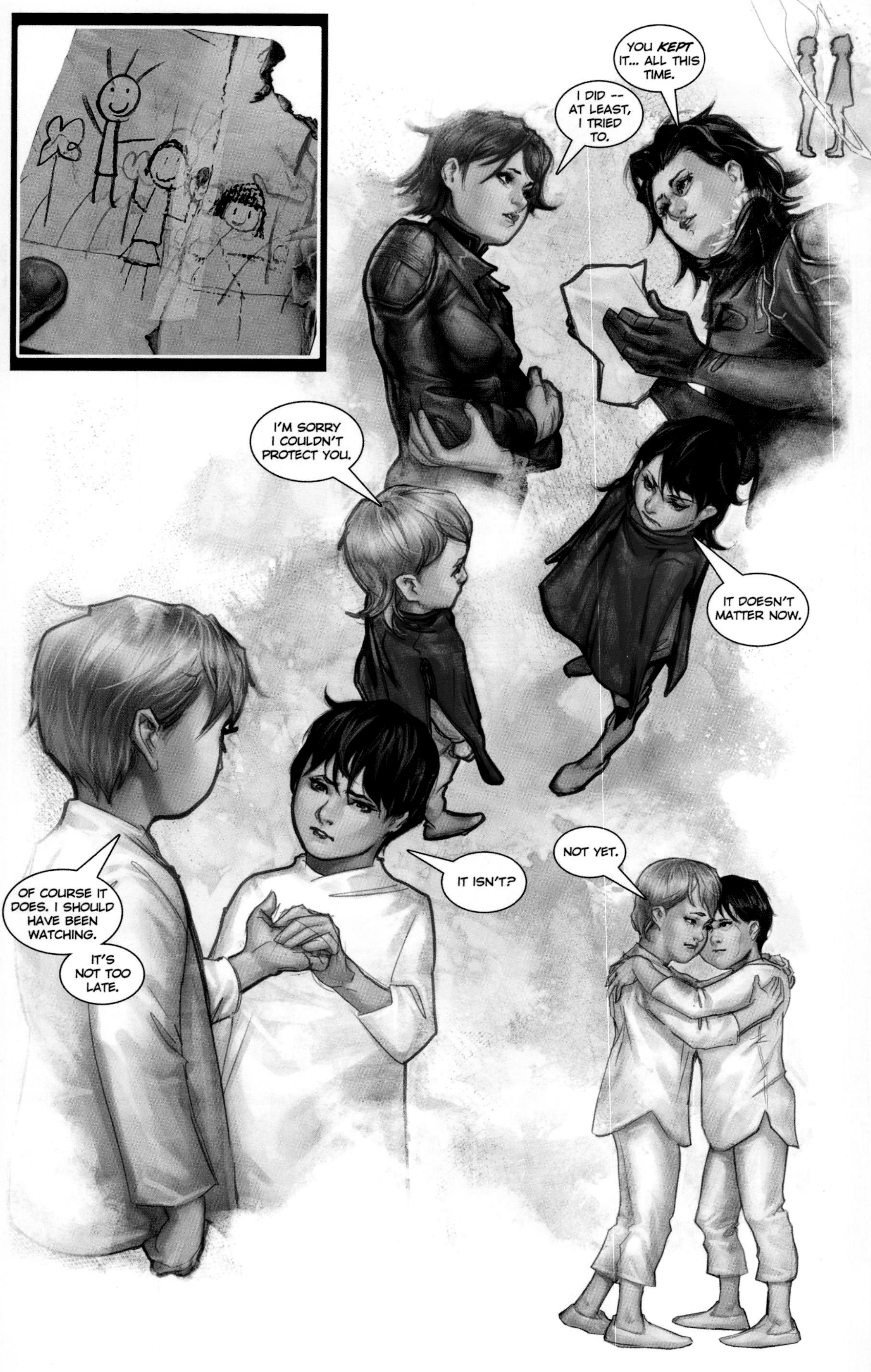

I DID -- AT LEAST, I TRIED TO.
YOU KEPT IT... ALL THIS TIME.
I'M SORRY I COULDN'T PROTECT YOU.
IT DOESN'T MATTER NOW.
OF COURSE IT DOES. I SHOULD HAVE BEEN WATCHING.
IT'S NOT TOO LATE.
IT ISN'T?
NOT YET.

LET'S MAKE SOMETHING TOGETHER....

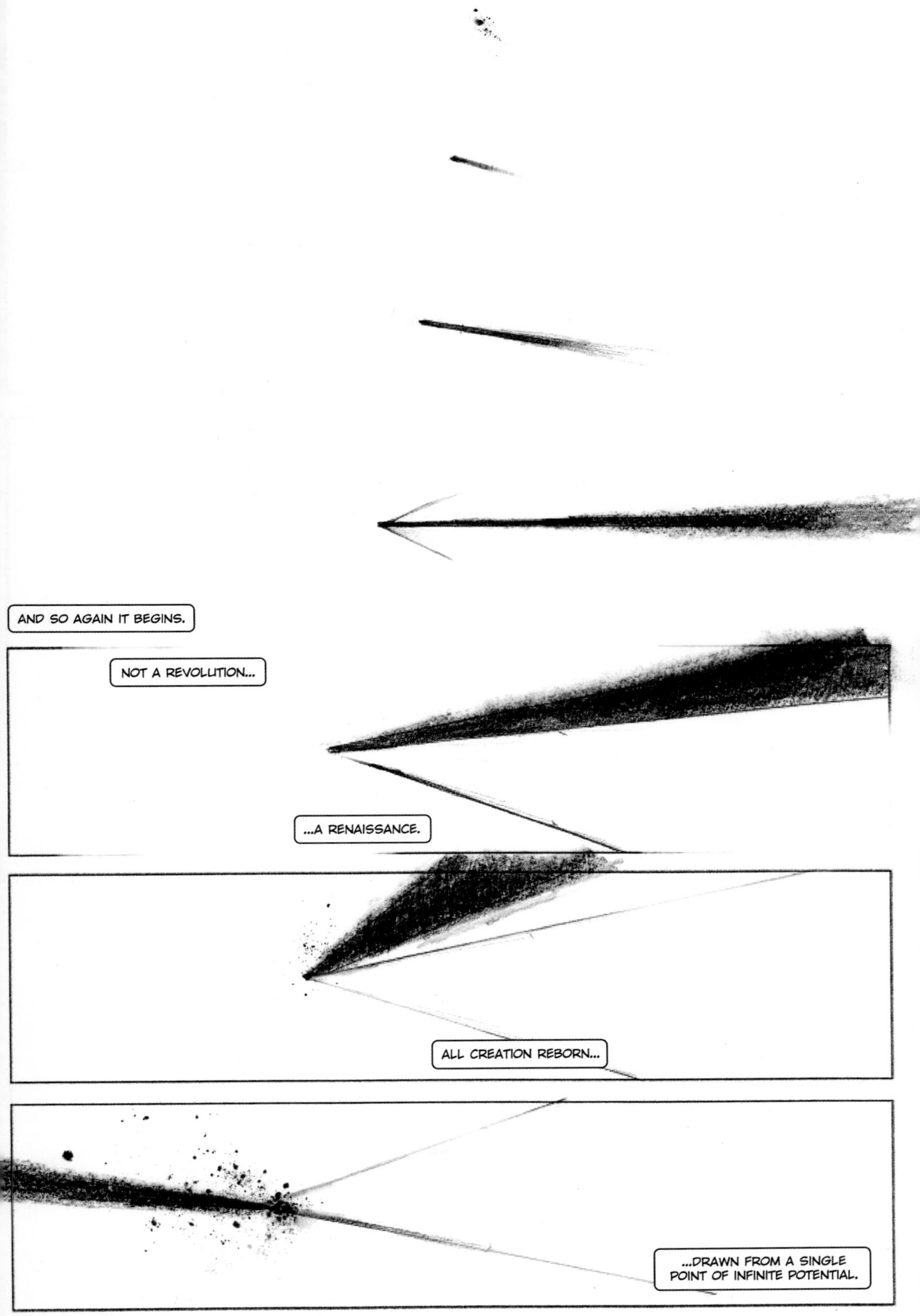
AND SO AGAIN IT BEGINS.
NOT A REVOLUTION...
...A RENAISSANCE.
ALL CREATION REBORN...
...DRAWN FROM A SINGLE POINT OF INFINITE POTENTIAL.

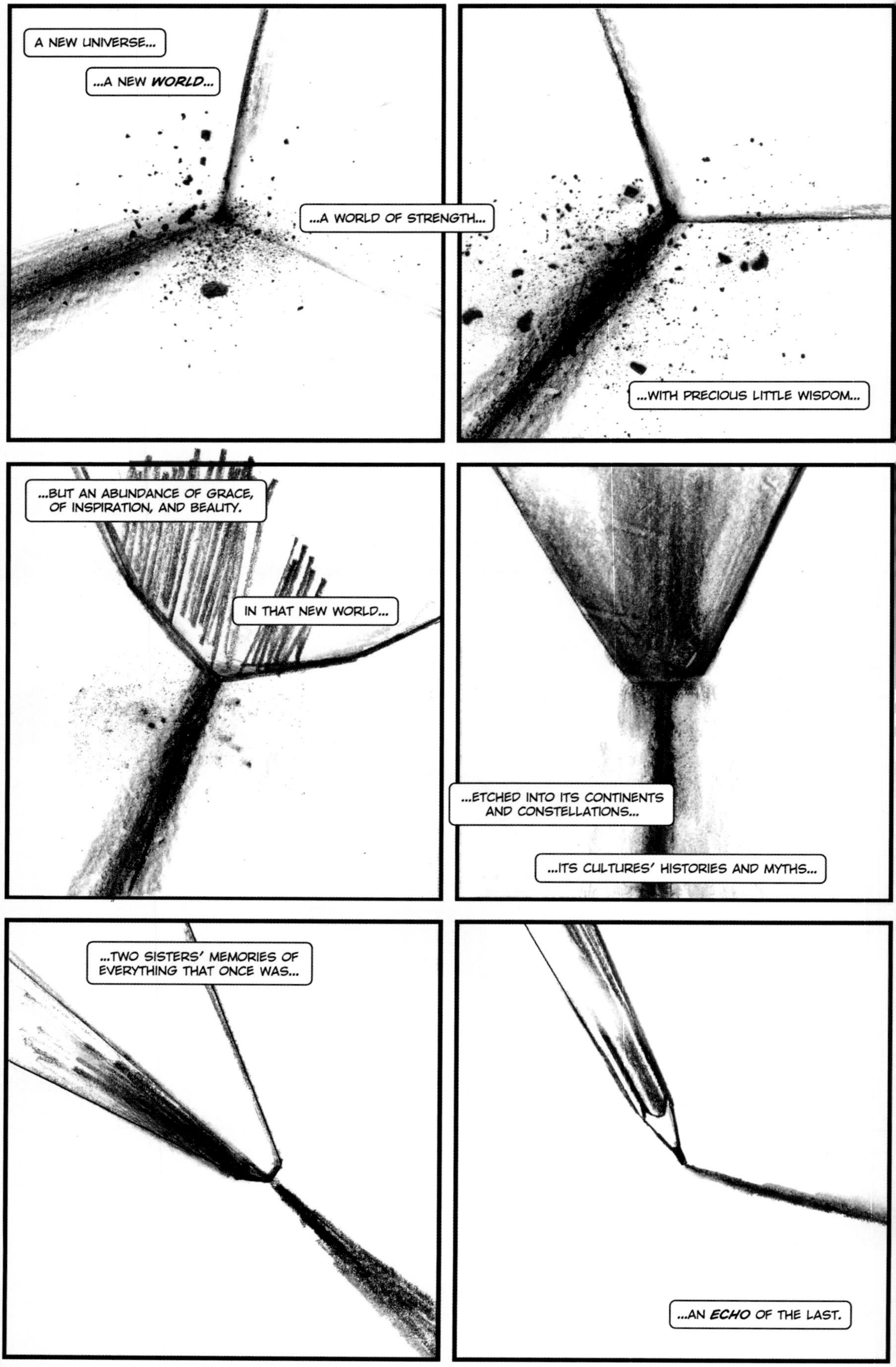
A NEW UNIVERSE...
...A NEW *WORLD*...
...A WORLD OF STRENGTH...
...WITH PRECIOUS LITTLE WISDOM...
...BUT AN ABUNDANCE OF GRACE, OF INSPIRATION, AND BEAUTY.
IN THAT NEW WORLD...
...ETCHED INTO ITS CONTINENTS AND CONSTELLATIONS...
...ITS CULTURES' HISTORIES AND MYTHS...
...TWO SISTERS' MEMORIES OF EVERYTHING THAT ONCE WAS...
...AN *ECHO* OF THE LAST.

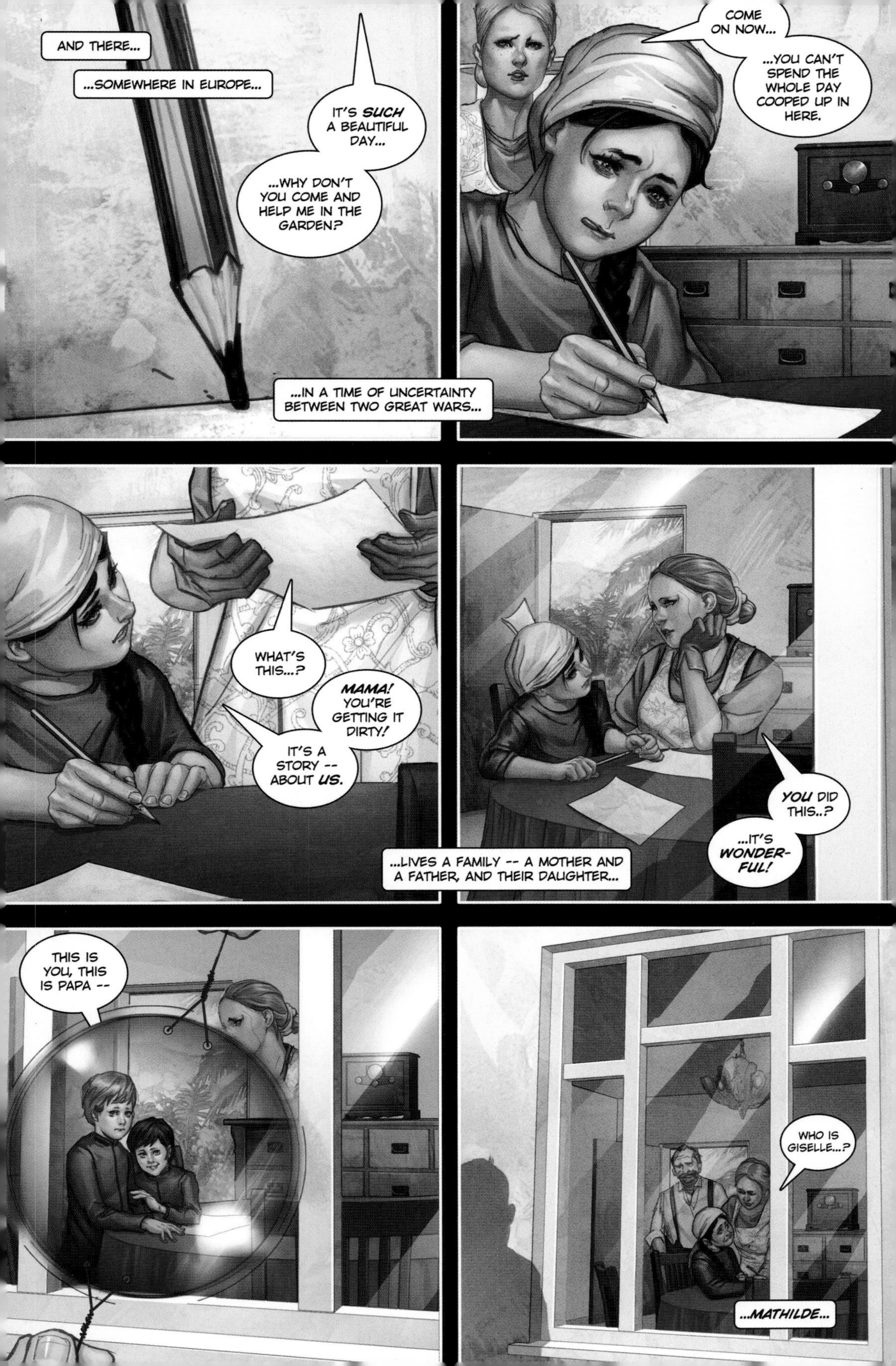
AND THERE...
...SOMEWHERE IN EUROPE...
IT'S SUCH A BEAUTIFUL DAY...
...WHY DON'T YOU COME AND HELP ME IN THE GARDEN?
...IN A TIME OF UNCERTAINTY BETWEEN TWO GREAT WARS...
COME ON NOW...
...YOU CAN'T SPEND THE WHOLE DAY COOPED UP IN HERE.
WHAT'S THIS...?
MAMA! YOU'RE GETTING IT DIRTY!
IT'S A STORY -- ABOUT US.
...LIVES A FAMILY -- A MOTHER AND A FATHER, AND THEIR DAUGHTER...
YOU DID THIS..?
...IT'S WONDER-FUL!
THIS IS YOU, THIS IS PAPA --
WHO IS GISELLE...?
...MATHILDE...

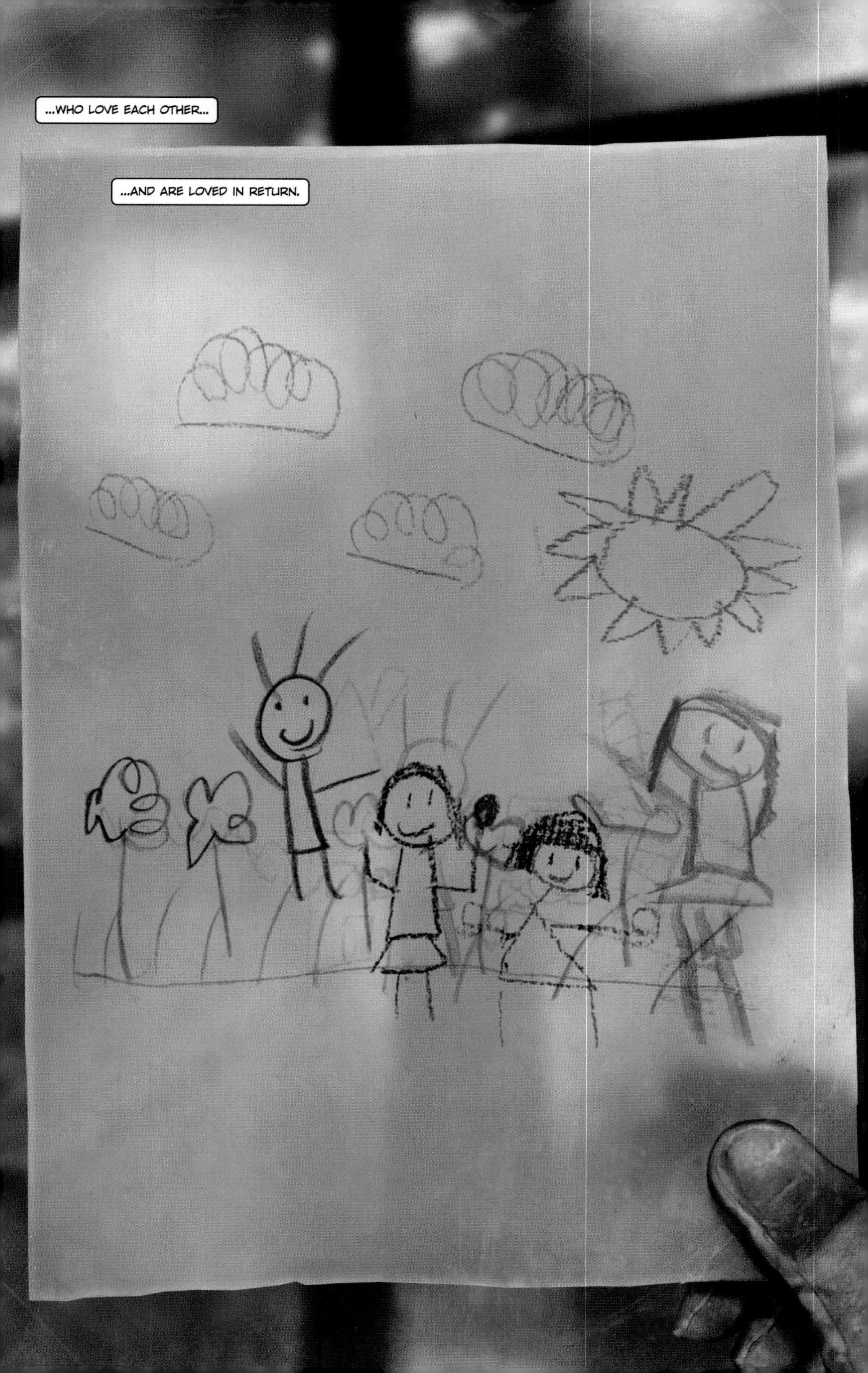
...WHO LOVE EACH OTHER...
...AND ARE LOVED IN RETURN.

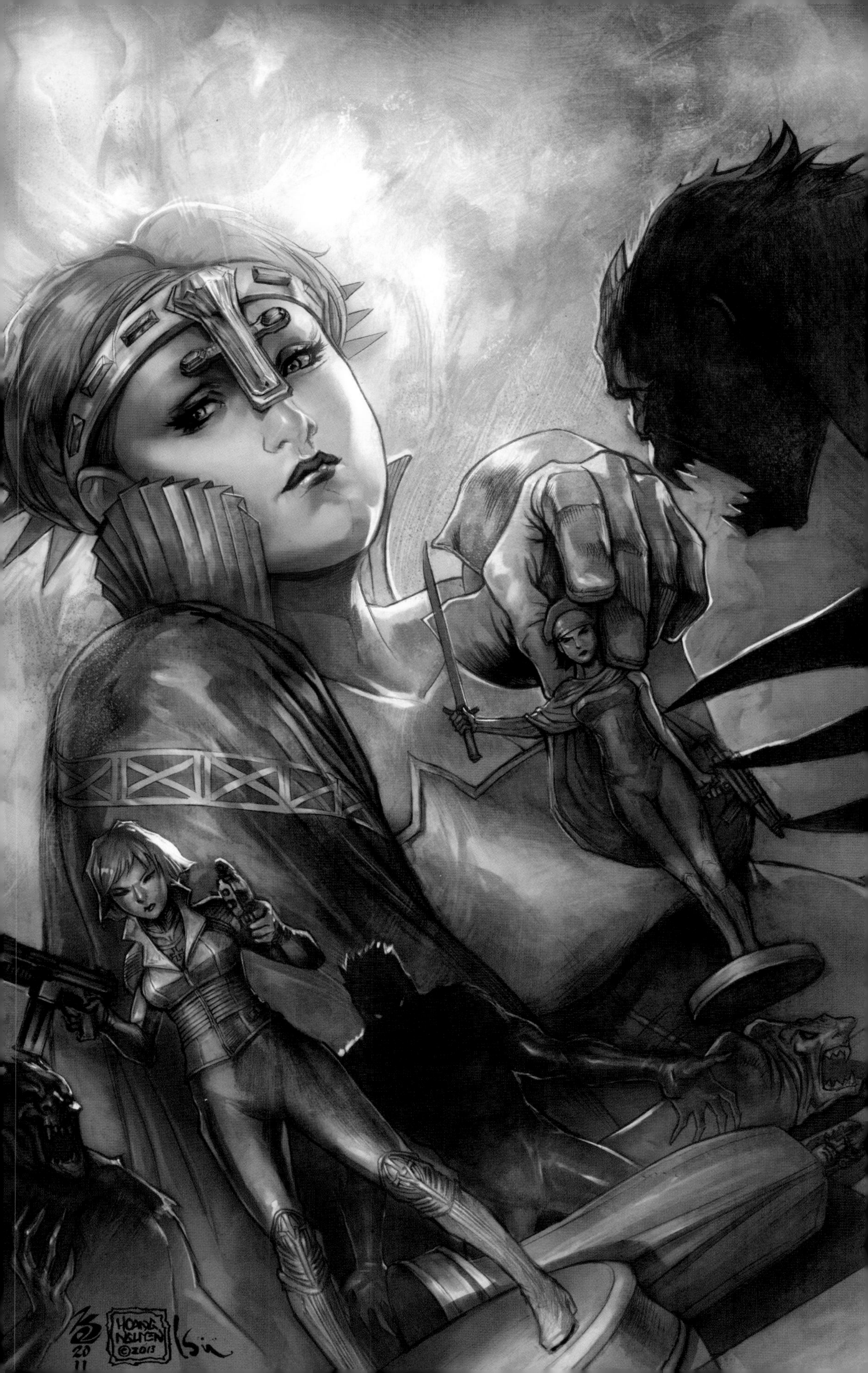
2011
HOANG NGUYEN ©2013

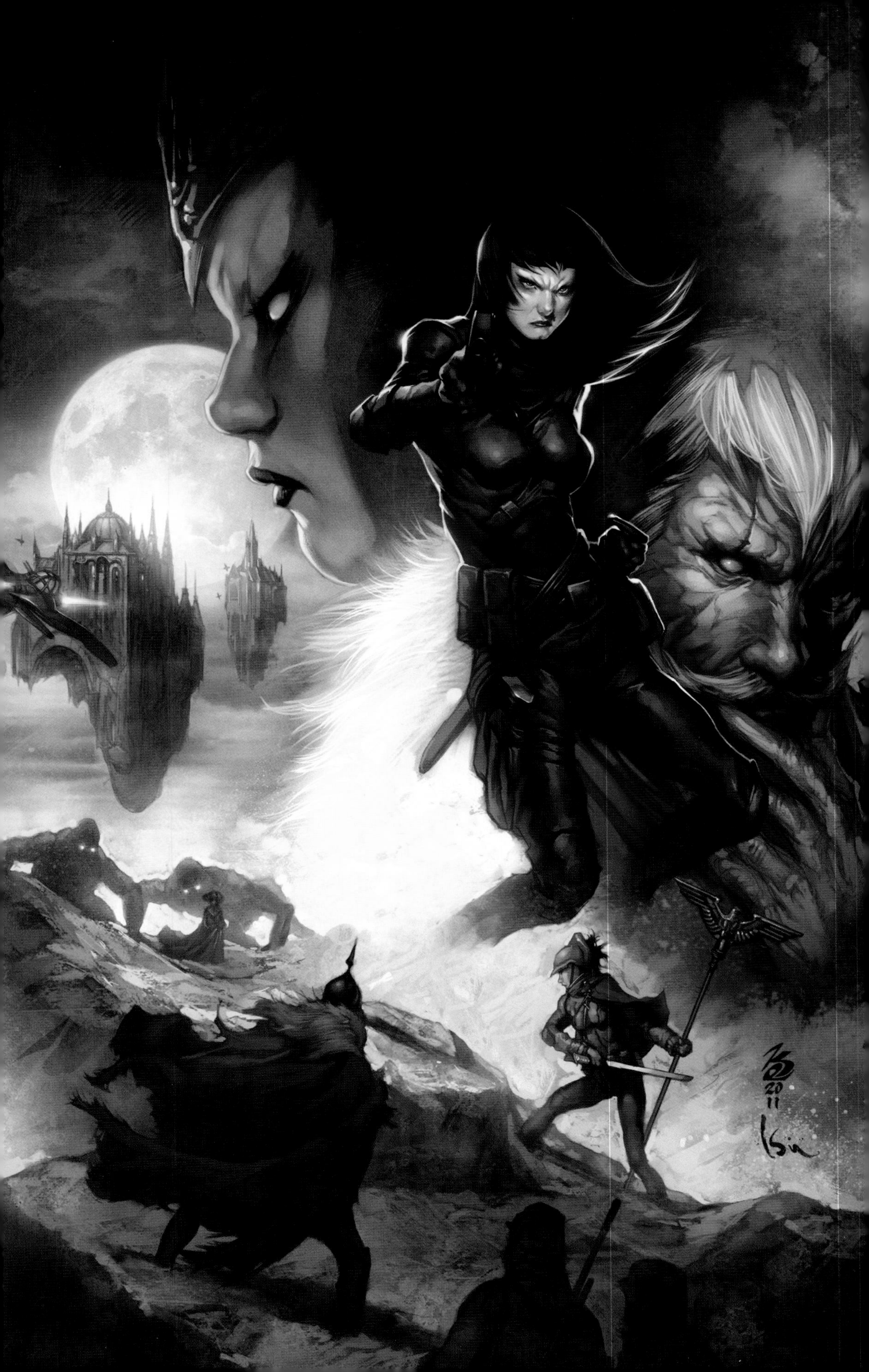

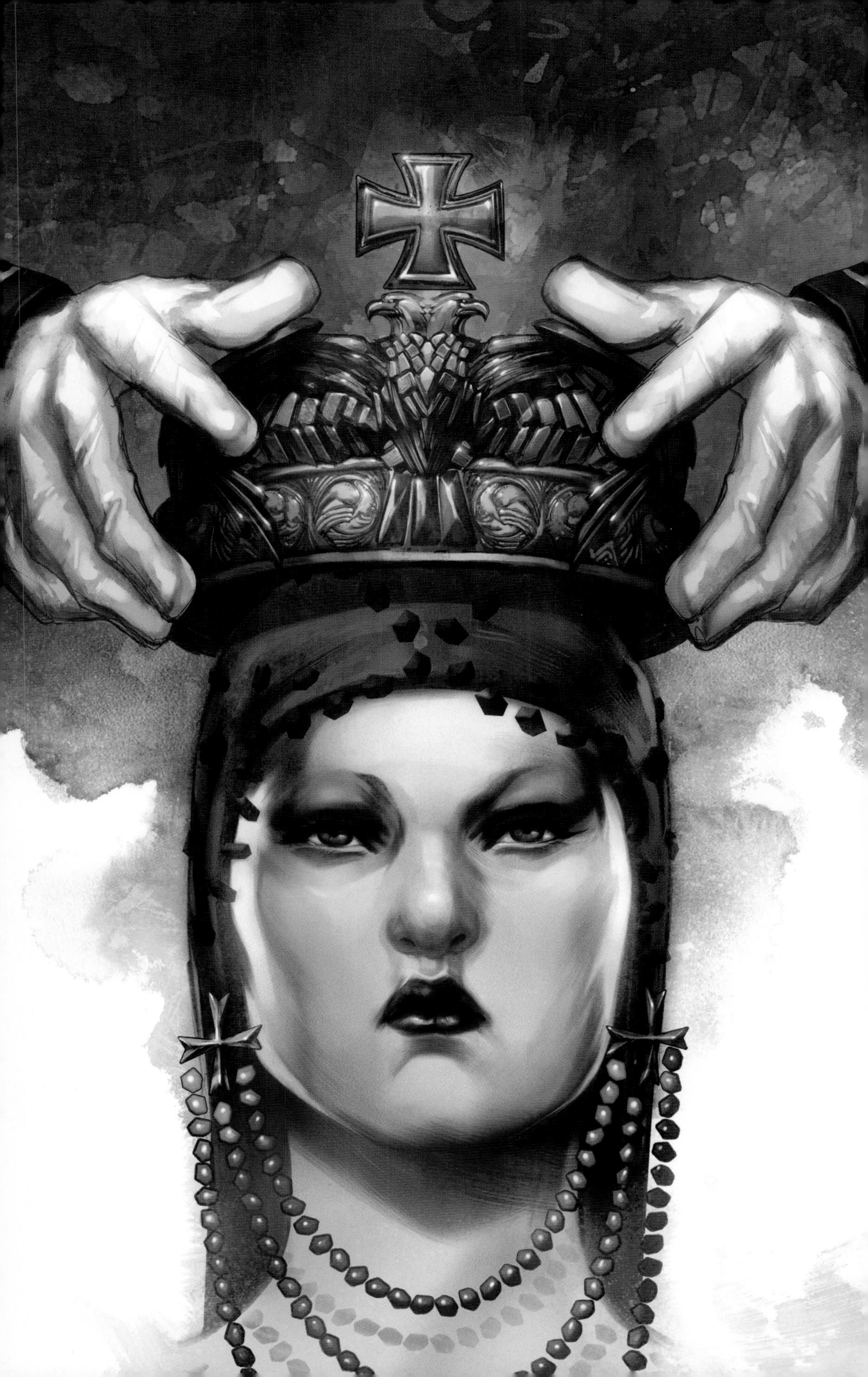

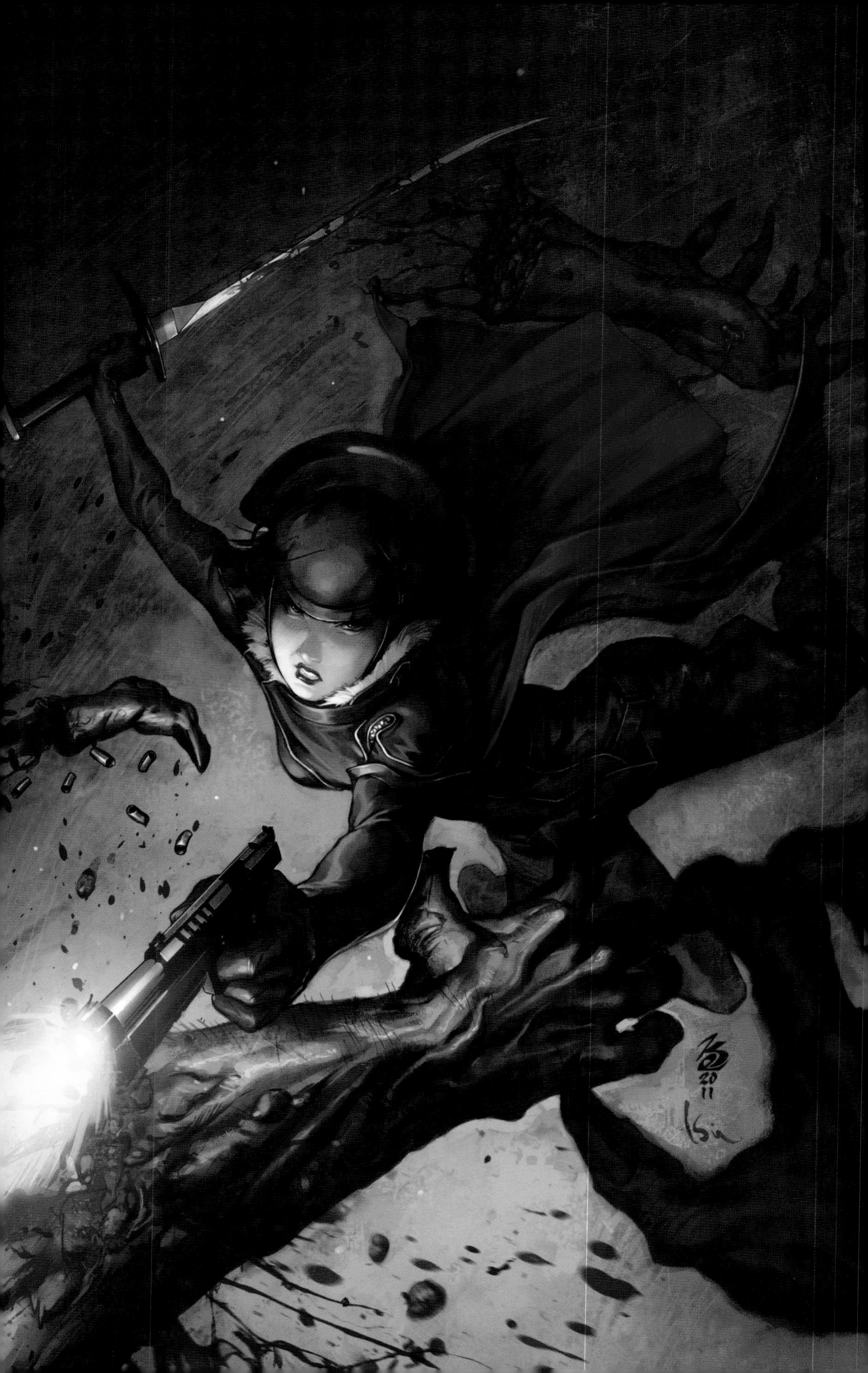

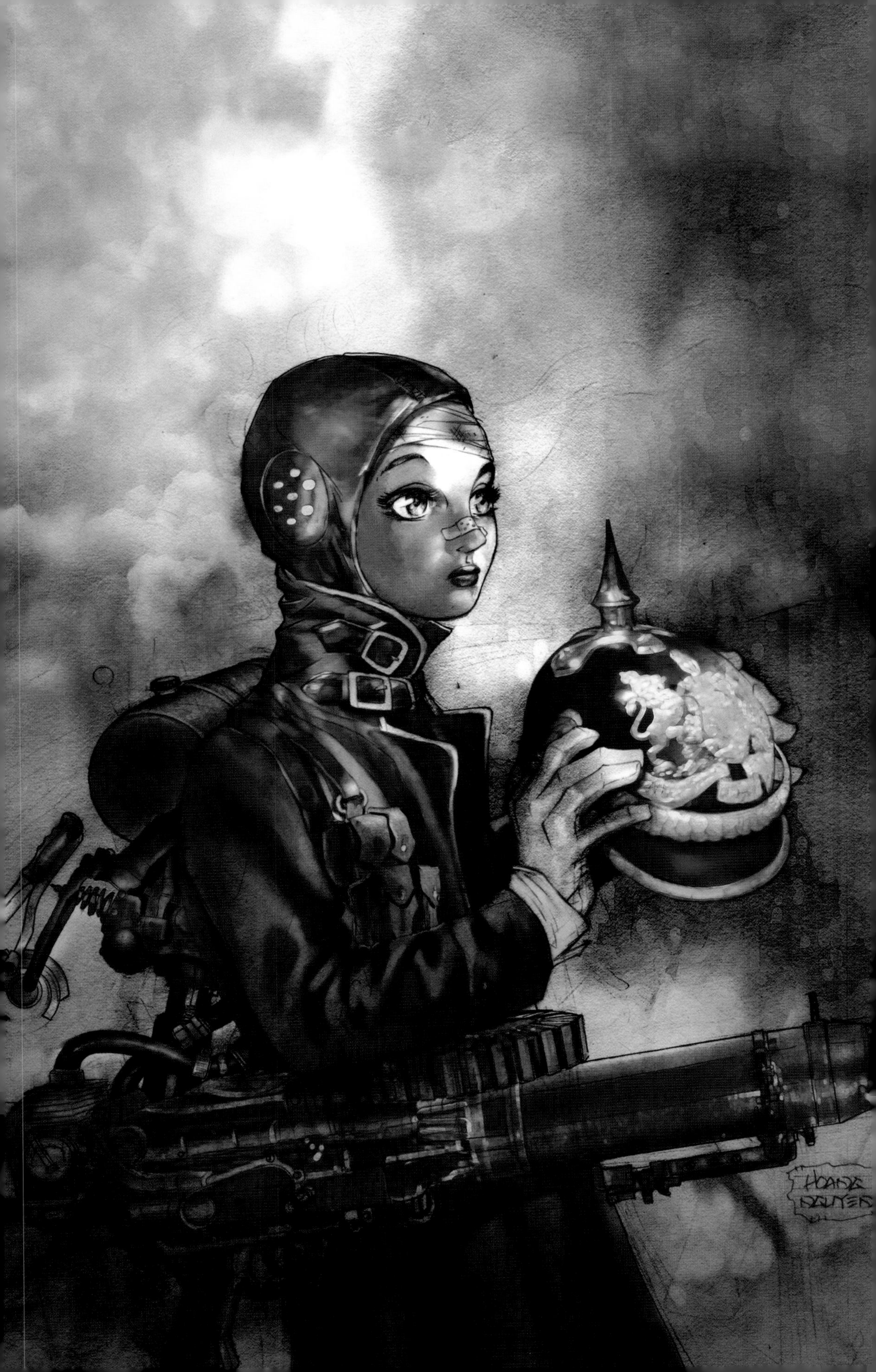
HOANG NGUYEN

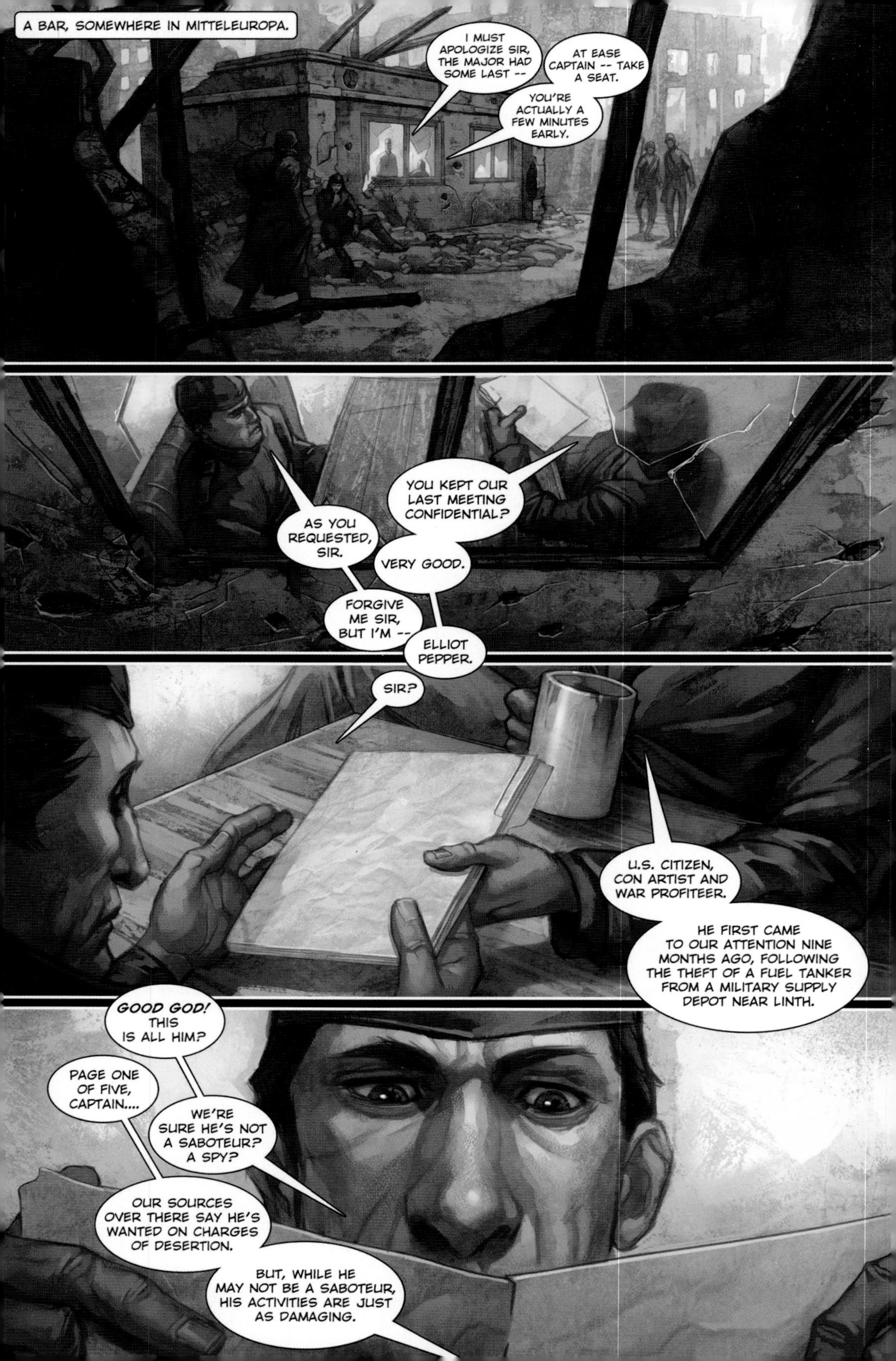
A BAR, SOMEWHERE IN MITTELEUROPA.
I MUST APOLOGIZE SIR, THE MAJOR HAD SOME LAST --
AT EASE CAPTAIN -- TAKE A SEAT.
YOU'RE ACTUALLY A FEW MINUTES EARLY.
YOU KEPT OUR LAST MEETING CONFIDENTIAL?
AS YOU REQUESTED, SIR.
VERY GOOD.
FORGIVE ME SIR, BUT I'M --
ELLIOT PEPPER.
SIR?
U.S. CITIZEN, CON ARTIST AND WAR PROFITEER.
HE FIRST CAME TO OUR ATTENTION NINE MONTHS AGO, FOLLOWING THE THEFT OF A FUEL TANKER FROM A MILITARY SUPPLY DEPOT NEAR LINTH.
GOOD GOD! THIS IS ALL HIM?
PAGE ONE OF FIVE, CAPTAIN....
WE'RE SURE HE'S NOT A SABOTEUR? A SPY?
OUR SOURCES OVER THERE SAY HE'S WANTED ON CHARGES OF DESERTION.
BUT, WHILE HE MAY NOT BE A SABOTEUR, HIS ACTIVITIES ARE JUST AS DAMAGING.